W9-AFK-369

THE OTTOMAN EMPIRE
AND ITS SUCCESSORS 1801-1927

THE
OTTOMAN EMPIRE
AND ITS SUCCESSORS
1801–1927

WILLIAM MILLER

being a revised and enlarged edition of
THE OTTOMAN EMPIRE
1801–1913

"Who doubts but the *Grecian* Christians, Descendants of
the ancient Possessors of that Country, may justly cast
off the *Turkish* yoke which they have so long groaned
under whenever they have an opportunity to do it?"

LOCKE, *Of Civil Government.*

1966
OCTAGON BOOKS, INC.
New York

WINGATE COLLEGE LIBRARY
WINGATE, N. C.

Published by Frank Cass & Co. Ltd.,
10 Woburn Walk, London W.C.1
by arrangement with Cambridge University Press.

Published in the United States of America
1966 by Octagon Books, Inc.

First Edition	1913
Second Edition	1923
Third Edition	1927
New Impression	1966

Library of Congress Catalog Card No. 66–26861

Printed in Great Britain

GENERAL PREFACE

The aim of this series is to sketch the history of Modern Europe, with that of its chief colonies and conquests, from about the end of the fifteenth century down to the present time. In one or two cases the story commences at an earlier date: in the case of the colonies it generally begins later. The histories of the different countries are described, as a rule, separately; for it is believed that, except in epochs like that of the French Revolution and Napoleon I, the connection of events will thus be better understood and the continuity of historical development more clearly displayed.

The series is intended for the use of all persons anxious to understand the nature of existing political conditions. "The roots of the present lie deep in the past"; and the real significance of contemporary events cannot be grasped unless the historical causes which have led to them are known. The plan adopted makes it possible to treat the history of the last four centuries in considerable detail, and to embody the most important results of modern research. It is hoped therefore that the series will be useful not only to beginners but to students who have already acquired some general knowledge of European History. For those who wish to carry their studies further, the bibliography appended to each volume will act as a guide to original sources of information and works of a more special character.

Considerable attention is paid to political geography; and each volume is furnished with such maps and plans as may be requisite for the illustration of the text.

G. W. PROTHERO.

37231

PREFACE TO THE SECOND EDITION

THE present work has been based, wherever possible, upon the original documents, and is the result of many years' study of the Eastern Question. I am indebted to the editors of *The English Historical* and *The Westminster Reviews* for permission to reprint with considerable additions two articles contributed to those periodicals; and I desire to thank H. E. M. J. Gennádios, former Greek Minister in London, for access to his unrivalled collection of pamphlets, and Cav. Pasqualucci, librarian of the Consulta, for his courtesy in allowing me to use the library of the Italian Foreign Office.

With regard to the spelling of Greek names, while common words have been written in their popular, unaccented form, rarer words have been reproduced in Greek dress with their accents. Slav names have been transliterated.

W. M.

ROME,
July 22, 1922.

PREFACE TO THE THIRD EDITION

THE additional pages of the third edition, so far as Greece is concerned, are largely the work of an eye-witness; for, resident in Athens since November, 1923, I have been a spectator of all the political movements connected with the creation of the Hellenic Republic.

W. M.

ATHENS,
July, 1927.

EDITORIAL NOTE

The later relations of Turkey and other Powers with Egypt are not included in this work, having been discussed in another volume of this series, *The Colonization of Africa*.

TABLE OF CONTENTS

CHAPTER I

THE OTTOMAN EMPIRE AT THE DAWN OF THE XIXth CENTURY

Relations of Turkey with the four great Powers, France, Russia, Austria, and Great Britain—Eastern policy of Prussia—Extent of the Ottoman empire in Europe—In Asia, and Africa—Organisation and races of European Turkey—Local tyrants—Division between Mussulmans and Christians—Bosnian feudalism—Condition of the Serbs—The Albanians—The Greeks—The Greek Church—The Phanariotes—State of Greece: privileged communities I

CHAPTER II

NAPOLEON IN THE NEAR EAST (1801-15)

The French in Dalmatia—Destruction of the Republics of Poljitza and Ragusa—France and Montenegro—First Russo-Turkish war of the century—Duckworth before Constantinople—Paper partition of Turkey at Tilsit—Second French occupation of the Ionian Islands—Capture of the Islands by the British—Treaty of Bucharest—Congresses of Vienna and Paris: British protectorate over the Ionian Islands . 31

CHAPTER III

THE SERVIAN RISINGS (1804-17)

Tyranny of the Janissaries—Mild rule and murder of Hajji Mustapha—Servian loyal rising of 1804: Kara George—Servian overtures to Austria and Russia—Servian victories—Palace revolutions in Constantinople—Russian protectorate over Servia—Treaty of Bucharest abandons the Serbs—Second Servian rising of 1815: Milosh Obrenovich—Murder of Kara George—Milosh recognised as chief . 46

Contents

CHAPTER IV

THE PREFACE OF GREEK INDEPENDENCE (1815–21)

The British in the Ionian Islands : Sir Thomas Maitland, first Lord High Commissioner—Constitution of 1817—The cession of Párga—Ali Pasha declared a rebel, appeals to the Greeks—The *Philikè Hetairía*—Alexander Hypselántes, leader of the Greek movement, crosses the Pruth—Rival Roumanian rising of Tudor Vladimirescu—Battles of Dragashani and Skuleni—Native princes in the Danubian Principalities 58

CHAPTER V

THE WAR OF GREEK INDEPENDENCE (1821–9)

Outbreak of the Revolution—Heroic death of Diákos—Spread of the insurrection to the islands—Murder of the Patriarch Gregory V—Three stages in the war—The " Peloponnesian Senate "—Arrival of Demétrios Hypselántes and Alexander Mavrokordátos—Sack of Tripolitsá—Constitution of Epídauros—End of Ali Pasha—Massacre of Chios—Foundation of Hermoúpolis—Capitulation of the Akropolis —Greek victory at Dervenáki—Defeat at Péta—First " Commissioner " of Crete—Second National Assembly at Astros—Canning's Philhellenism—Russian proposal for three Greek principalities—Death of Márko Bótzares—Byron in Greece—The first Greek loan—Byron's death at Mesolónghi—" War of the Primates "—Destruction of Kássos and Psará—Ibrahim lands in the Morea—Santa Rosa at Navarino—Second siege of Mesolónghi—Death of Odysseús—The sortie from Mesolónghi—Protocol of April 4, 1826—Turkish siege of the Akropolis —Death of Karaïskákes—Second surrender of the Akropolis—Third National Assembly at Troizén : Capo d'Istria elected President of Greece—Treaty of London of 1827—Battle of Navarino—Death of Hastings—The Cretans at Graboûsa—Arrival of Capo d'Istria—The " Panhellénion "—Policy of the President—France compels the Egyptians to evacuate the Morea—Destruction of Tripolitsá—Protocol of March 22, 1829—Fourth National Assembly at Argos—Battle of Pétra : end of the war 71

CHAPTER VI

THE CREATION OF THE GREEK KINGDOM (1829–33)

Protocols of February 3, 1830: Leopold of Saxe-Coburg "Sovereign Prince of Greece"—Leopold refuses—Conflict between Capo d'Istria and the Hydriotes—Catastrophe of Póros—Assassination of Capo d'Istria—Provisional Commission of three—Fifth National Assembly at Argos—Agostino chosen President: civil war—Otho "King of Greece"—Limits of the kingdom—Samian autonomy—Crete united with Egypt—Triumph of Koléttes and the "Constitutionalists"— Anarchy—National Assembly at Prónoia—Flight of the Senate from Nauplia—Fight with the French at Argos—Arrival of Otho—Prosperity of the Ionian Islands—Napier in Cephalonia—Adam Lord High Commissioner—The "Ionian Academy"—Parties in the Islands . 106

CHAPTER VII

THE BALKAN AND SYRIAN DIFFICULTIES OF TURKEY (1822–45)

Roumanian Nationalist movement: Asaki and Eliade—Convention of Akkerman—Russo-Turkish war of 1828–9: Russian occupation of the Principalities—Treaty of Adrianople—The *règlement organique*— Servia at Akkerman and Adrianople—Grant of Servian autonomy: Milosh hereditary Prince of an enlarged Servia—Turkish garrisons of the Servian fortresses—Despotism of Milosh: "Constitution of Sretenje"—British support of Milosh—Creation of a Servian Senate— Milosh abdicates—Milan Obrenovich II—Michael Obrenovich III's first reign—Alexander Karageorgevich elected Prince—"The Dragon of Bosnia"—Ali Pasha Rizvanbegovich—Union of the Piperi with Montenegro—Peter II reorganises Montenegro: abolition of the civil "governorship"—His conflicts with the Turks—Revolt of Mehemet Ali: invasion of Syria—The Russians "protect" the Sultan: treaty of Hunkiar Iskelesi—Battle of Nezib—Death of Mahmûd II—Quadrilateral convention of 1840—Settlement of Egypt and Thasos— "Convention of the Straits"—Charter of Gül-khâneh—The Lebanon 125

CHAPTER VIII

GREECE UNDER THE BAVARIAN AUTOCRACY (1833–43)

The Regency—Disbanding of the irregulars—Bureaucratic system—Ecclesiastical policy—Conspiracy of Kolokotrónes—Revolt of the Mainates— Recall of Maurer and Abel—Insurrection in Arkadía and Messenía—

The capital removed from Nauplia to Athens—Otho's majority—
Insurrection in Akarnanía—Rudhart Prime Minister—Founding of the
University—" British," " French," and "Russian" parties—Crete
under the Egyptians—The Cretan insurrection of 1841—The revolution
of September 3/15 at Athens—Progress of Greece during the decade
1833–43   156

CHAPTER IX

The Greek and Ionian Constitutions (1843–53)

The Greek Constitution of 1844—Administration of Koléttes—The Mousoûros incident—Local disturbances—The Pacifico case : Cervi and
Sapienza—The "Synodal Tome" of 1850: independence of the Church
in Greece—Nugent, Douglas and Mackenzie in the Ionian Islands—
Seaton's reforms in the Constitution: introduction of a free press—
Risings in Cephalonia—The first reformed Ionian Parliament—
Bibescu and Michael Sturdza in the Principalities—Roumanian revolution of 1848—Convention of Balta Liman—Reigns of Barbe Stirbeiu
and Gregory V Ghika—Austrophil policy of Servia—Montenegro :
succession of Danilo—Abolition of the theocratic system—Count
Leiningen's mission   174

CHAPTER X

The Crimean War (1853–6)

The Holy Places—Mentschikoff's mission—Motives of Napoleon III—
Overtures of the Tsar—Stratford de Redcliffe—Settlement of the
original dispute—Fresh Russian demands—The Russians cross the
Pruth—"The Vienna Note"—Destruction of the Turkish fleet at
Sinope—British ultimatum—The Allies at Varna—British officers'
defence of Silistria—Russia evacuates the Principalities—Effects of the
war upon the Balkan races: Servia and Montenegro—Excitement in
Greece : insurrections in Thessaly and Epirus—The Allies occupy the
Piraeus—The cholera at Athens—The landing in the Crimea—Battle
of the Alma—Siege of Sebastopol—Battles of Balaclava and Inkerman—The Crimean winter—"The four points"—Battle of the
Tchernaya—Fall of Sebastopol—Congress and treaty of Paris—Small
results of the treaty—The Montenegrin and Greek protocols .   199

CHAPTER XI

THE UNION OF THE DANUBIAN PRINCIPALITIES (1856–62)

Growth of the Unionist idea—Convention of Paris—Election of Couza as Prince—First united Roumanian Assembly—Deposition of Alexander Karageorgevich—Restoration of Milosh—Second reign of Michael Obrenovich III—Bombardment of Belgrade—Partial evacuation of the Servian fortresses—Turco-Montenegrin war of 1858 : battle of Grahovo —Assassination of Danilo—Accession of Nicholas I—Herzegovinian rising of 1861—Turco-Montenegrin war of 1862—Convention of Scutari—Greek finance—Question of the Greek succession—Effect of the Austro-Italian war of 1859 on Greece—Combination of circumstances against Otho—Revolt at Nauplia—Greek revolution of 1862 : abdication of Otho **243**

CHAPTER XII

THE CESSION OF THE IONIAN ISLANDS (1862–4)

Meeting of the National Assembly—Election of Prince Alfred as King— The search for a sovereign—Prince George of Denmark chosen "King of the Hellenes"—Fighting at Athens between "the Plain" and "the Mountain"—Arrival of King George—The Ionian question : scheme for the colonisation of Corfù and Paxo—The two stolen despatches— Gladstone's mission—Storks Lord High Commissioner—Union of the Ionian Islands with Greece—Neutralisation of Corfù and Paxo— Destruction of the Corfiote fortresses—The Greek Constitution of 1864 . . . . **270**

CHAPTER XIII

REFORMS AND THEIR RESULTS : THE LEBANON AND CRETE (1856–69)

Hatti-Humayûn of 1856—Murder of the consuls at Jedda—The Massacres in the Lebanon—French expedition to Syria—Organisation of the Lebanon in 1861–4—The Cretan Insurrections of 1858 and 1866–9— Defence of Arkádion—"Organic Statute of 1868"—Turkish ultimatum to Greece—Hobart Pasha at Syra—Conference of Paris . . **298**

CHAPTER XIV

THE ROUMANIAN AND SERVIAN QUESTIONS (1862-75)

Murder of Barbe Catargi—Secularisation of the monasteries—Couza's *coup d'état*—Agrarian law—Free education—Deposition of Couza—Prince Charles of Hohenzollern—Sigmaringen Prince of Roumania—Constitution of 1866 : the Jewish question—The Prince's recognition by the Sultan—His difficult position during the Franco-German war—The railway question—Servia : suggested Serbo-Greek alliance—Complete Turkish evacuation of Servia—Assassination of Michael—Milan Obrenovich IV Prince of Servia—The Regency : constitution of 1869—Milan's situation 319

CHAPTER XV

THE BULGARIAN EXARCHATE (1870-5)

Early Bulgarian risings—Bulgarian schools and books—The demand for national bishops—Relations with the Papacy—Tartar and Circassian immigration—Midhat's administration—The Bulgarian emigrants at Bucharest—Creation of the Bulgarian Exarchate—The "Apostles"—Liberation of the Black Sea—The "Marathon massacres"—The Lávrion mines—Constitutional questions at Athens . . 338

CHAPTER XVI

THE BALKAN CRISIS OF 1875-8

State of Bosnia and the Herzegovina—The rising at Nevesinje—Grievances of the insurgents—Revolt in Bosnia—The Andrássy note—The Berlin Memorandum—Servia and Montenegro declare war on Turkey—"Benkovski" in the Sredna Gora—The massacre of Batak : the "Bulgarian Atrocities"—Murder of the consuls at Salonika—Deposition and death of Abdul Aziz—Murad V's brief reign : accession of Abdul Hamid II—The Servian war of 1876—Successful Montenegrin campaign—The Constantinople conference—"Midhat's Parliament"—The London protocol—The Russo-Turkish war of 1877-8—Russo-Roumanian convention—Siege of Plevna—Second Montenegrin campaign—Second Servian war—Feeling in Great Britain—The "Œcumenical government" at Athens—Insurrections in. Epirus, Thessaly, and Crete—The treaty of San Stefano—The treaty of Berlin—The Cyprus convention—Present state of the Berlin treaty 358

CHAPTER XVII

THE UNION OF THE TWO BULGARIAS (1878-87)

The Arab Tabia question—The regulation of the Danube—Roumania proclaimed a kingdom—Her relations with the Triple Alliance—The Austrians occupy Bosnia—The *sanjak* of Novibazar : Austro-Turkish convention of 1879—The "Albanian League": Gusinje and Plava— The "Corti compromise"—The cession of Dulcigno—Kidnapping of the Mirdite Prince—Rectification of the Greek frontier—The Berlin conference of 1880—Greece receives Thessaly and Arta—Crete : the Pact of Halépa—Alexander of Battenberg first Prince of Bulgaria— *Coup d'état* of 1881—Constitution of Eastern Roumelia—The "Pomak Republic"—The Philippopolis revolution—Serbo-Bulgarian war: battle of Slivnitza—Blockade of Greece—Kidnapping of Alexander— His return and abdication—Kaulbars in Bulgaria—Election of Prince Ferdinand 399

CHAPTER XVIII

ARMENIA, CRETE, AND MACEDONIA (1887-1908)

The Armenian massacres—The Cretan insurrection and firman of 1889— The insurrection of 1896—Col. Vássos in Crete—Bombardment of Akrotéri—The Greco-Turkish war of 1897—The International Commission of Control—Prince George of Greece High Commissioner in Crete—The Opposition at Thérisso—M. Zaïmes High Commissioner— Rival races and Churches in Macedonia—The Macedonian Committee —Austro-Russian schemes of reform : the Mürzsteg programme—The bands in Macedonia—The occupation of Mitylene—Stambulov's rule in Bulgaria—His fall and assassination—Reconciliation with Russia : conversion of Prince Boris—Social condition of Bulgaria—Servia : the royal divorce—Servian constitution of 1889—Milan's abdication— Alexander's *coups d'état*—His marriage—Constitution of 1901 : third *coup d'état*—Murder of Alexander and Draga—Election of Prince Peter Karageorgevich as King : constitution of June 1903—Rule of the regicides—Progress of Montenegro : the Italian marriage—Montenegrin constitution of 1905—Results of emigration—Italian influence —Roumanian social problems : (1) the land, (2) the Jews—Roumanian foreign policy—Greek internal politics since 1898—Cyprus—The "Twelve Islands"—Thasos—Samos 427

CHAPTER XIX

THE TURKISH REVOLUTION (1908-12)

The " Committee of Union and Progress "—The revival of the Turkish constitution—Fraternisation of the Ottomans—Declaration of Bulgarian Independence—Annexation of Bosnia and the Herzegovina—Crete proclaims union with Greece—The counter-revolution in Turkey —The massacre at Adana—Deposition of Abdul Hamid II—Mohammed V—Settlement of the Bosnian and Bulgarian questions—Crete : attitude of the Powers—Increasing Turkish demands—Withdrawal of the international troops from Crete—The flag incident : Turkish notes to Greece—The Greek Military League—The two National Assemblies: M. Venizélos Premier—The revised Greek Constitution—The policy of "Turkification"—Albanian insurrection of 1911—The Libyan war: loss of Tripoli and the Cyrenaica—Italian occupation of 13 islands 474

CHAPTER XX

THE BALKAN LEAGUE AND ITS RESULTS (1912-14)

Symptoms of unrest—Montenegro declares war: capture of Tuzi—Balkan ultimatum—The four states against Turkey—Victories of the Allies: fall of Üsküb and Salonika and battle of Lüle Burgas—Armistice of Chatalja—Balkan Conference in St James' Palace—Revolution at Constantinople—Denunciation of the armistice—Surrender of Joánnina—Assassination of King George: accession of King Constantine—Surrender of Adrianople—Armistice of Bulair—Naval demonstration against Montenegro—Surrender of Scutari and its cession by Montenegro—Treaty of London—Italian opposition to Greece—Second Balkan war—Victories of the Greeks and Servians over the Bulgarians: battles of Kilkich, the Bregalnitza, Demir Hissar, and Djumaia—Armed intervention of Roumania—The Turks recover Adrianople—Peace of Bucharest—Turco-Bulgarian treaty—Prince William of Wied becomes Prince of Albania—" Autonomous Epirus "—Civil war in Albania—Assassination of the Austrian Heir-Apparent—Austrian note to Servia—Outbreak of the European war . . . 498

CHAPTER XXI

THE NEAR EAST IN THE EUROPEAN WAR (1914-23)

Double Servian victory over the Austrians—Great Britain declares war on Turkey: annexation of Cyprus—Policy of· M. Venizélos—Diplomatic effects of Italian intervention—Bulgaria enters the war—Annihilation of Servia and Montenegro—Evacuation of the Dardanelles—Surrender of Roûpel—Roumania enters the war: Allied offensive in Macedonia— The Venizelist Government at Salonika—The "First of December" at Athens—King Constantine's deposition—The Pact of Corfù: the Jugoslav state—The Italians in Albania—The liberation of Jerusalem— The· Armenian massacres—The Roumanian collapse: fourth treaty of Bucharest—The Bulgarian and Turkish armistices—The treaties of Neuilly and Sèvres—The Kemalist movement—Fall of M. Venizélos— Revision of the Sèvres treaty—Albanian independence—The "Adriatic question"·--The end of Montenegro—The Asia Minor disaster—King Constantine's second deposition—Execution of "the Six"—The treaty of Lausanne—Italian bombardment of Corfù 523

CHAPTER XXII

THE GREEK, TURKISH AND ALBANIAN REPUBLICS (1923-27)

The Counter-revolution—Departure of King George II—Return and failure of M. Venizélos—Proclamation of the Hellenic Republi c—The *plébiscite*—Successive Republican Cabinets—General Pángalos' *coup d'état* and dictatorship—The Presidential election of 1926—General Pángalos' deposition—The street-fighting of September 9—The "Œcumenical Government"—The Turkish Republic—The Agrarian revolution in Roumania—Death of King Ferdinand—Jugoslav foreign policy—Bulgaria's position—The Italo-Albanian Pact—Summary of the whole period 550

TABLE OF RULERS 564

BIBLIOGRAPHY 568

INDEX 595

MAPS

The Ottoman Empire in Europe 1856 . . . *To face* p. 242
Diagram to illustrate the Treaty of San Stefano . *To face* p. 386
The Ottoman Empire in Europe after the Treaty of Berlin, 1878 . . . . *To face* p. 398
The Ottoman Empire in Europe after the treaty of Lausanne, 1923 . . . . *To face* p. 547
The Ottoman Empire in 1801 . . . . *At end*

CHAPTER I

THE OTTOMAN EMPIRE AT THE DAWN OF THE NINETEENTH CENTURY

THE near eastern question may be defined as the problem of filling up the vacuum created by the gradual disappearance of the Turkish empire from Europe. Its history, therefore, may be said to begin at the moment when that empire, having attained its zenith, commenced to decline. The European dominions of Turkey reached their greatest extent in the latter half of the seventeenth century, when "the great Greek island" of Crete, as the modern Hellenes love to call it, at last surrendered to the Turkish forces, and the king of Poland ceded Podolia to the Sultan. But the close of that same century witnessed the shrinkage of the Turkish frontiers. The peace of Karlovitz in 1699 has been justly called "the first dismemberment of the Ottoman empire." It was the initial step in the historical process which has slowly but surely gone on ever since. The eighteenth century saw the continuation of the work begun at Karlovitz, though now and again the Turkish dominions gained some temporary advantage, and European statesmen anticipated the dismemberment of the Sultan's European possessions and formed schemes for the partition of the spoil.

At the beginning of the nineteenth century there were only four great European Powers, instead of six, directly interested in the eastern question, for Italy was not yet made and Prussia was only of the second rank, while Venice had ceased to exist.

Of these four—France, Russia, Austria, and Great Britain—the first had been for centuries the traditional ally of the Sultans. Francis I, who had begun his reign by proposing, as so many sovereigns have done since, the partition of Turkey, was the founder of this alliance, which, with occasional intervals of anti-Turkish feeling, was the fixed policy of his successors. In spite of the scandal caused to devout Catholics by this union of France, "the eldest daughter of the Church," with the head of the infidel Turks, Francis found it politic to use Suleyman the Magnificent as an ally in his struggle with the house of Austria, the historic rival of the French monarchy. The power and geographical position of Turkey at that period, its naval forces and the requirements of French trade in the Levant, were all strong arguments, which outweighed any crusading instincts of the astute French king, just as in our own day we have seen the German Emperor champion the Turkish cause in the interests of German commerce. Together the French and Ottoman fleets bombarded Nice, while Toulon served as the Turkish base of operations. By the capitulations of 1535, which were the most practical result of the Franco-Turkish alliance, the French received permission to trade in all the Ottoman ports—a privilege conceded to the vessels of other nations only on condition of flying the French flag. French subjects, residing in Turkey, were permitted the free exercise of their religion, and the custody of the Holy Places was entrusted to French Catholics. Henry II carried on the friendly policy of his father, and concluded a treaty with Suleyman, the object of which was to secure the co-operation of the Turkish fleet against the house of Austria. For a time the alliance ceased to be aggressive, but at the beginning of the seventeenth century French influence was predominant at Constantinople. The capitulations were renewed in 1604; and all nations except the English and the Venetians were compelled to seek the protection, and trade under the flag, of France in the Levant. But the capitulations of 1604 mark in this respect a change from those of 1535. France now had powerful rivals in the east; England, Venice, and Holland exercised a competing influence on the Bosphorus; and in 1634 the Greeks assumed the custody of the Holy Places, thus foreshadowing the conflict which two centuries later led to the Crimean war. The French began to turn against the Turks; the plan of a new crusade was drawn up by a French priest; a "sure means of destroying" the Ottoman empire was published by a French diplomatist. At the battle of St Gothard in 1664, French troops assisted the Austrians to beat the Turks; during the siege of Candia French men-of-war brought aid to the Venetians, and the memory of the French commander, the duc de Beaufort, has still lingered outside the walls of that town. In fact, Louis XIV, though he tried to prevent Sobieski from saving Vienna, was hostile to the Turkish empire. His fleets entered the Dardanelles, and he obtained in 1673 new capitulations, recognising him as the sole protector of the eastern Catholics.

In the eighteenth century, the old friendly relations were resumed; and Turkey, menaced by Austria and Russia and already declining in force, was glad to avail herself of the good offices of France. The French ambassador at the time of the peace of Belgrade, by checkmating Austria, saved Servia to Turkey for three generations, and his influence was such that he became a sort of "Grand Vizier of the Christians." The capitulations of 1740, completing those of 1673, were the reward of French assistance, and remain at the present day a memorial of the Marquis de Villeneuve's diplomatic success. Numbers of French officers endeavoured, like the Germans in our day, to reform the Turkish army; and Bonneval and Baron de Tott worked hard in the Turkish cause. But the treaty of Kutchuk-Kaïnardji ("the little fountain") in 1774 ruined French influence, and substituted for it that of Russia; and the French revolution prevented France from taking an active part in eastern affairs, though indirectly by means of French

émigrés, who found their way to the Orient, it spread a
knowledge of the French language and French customs. Soon
the Ottoman dominions felt the weight of Bonaparte's influence.
"It is of no use for us," he wrote to the Directory, "to try to
maintain the Turkish empire; we shall witness its fall in our
time." The treaty of Campo-Formio in 1797 made France the
near neighbour of the Sultan by ceding to her the Ionian
Islands—"more interesting to us than all Italy put together,"
as Bonaparte said—with Butrinto, Arta, Vónitza, and all the
former Venetian establishments in Albania south of the gulf
of the Drin. The great French conqueror paid special
attention to the Greeks; and two emissaries of the French
government in Greece, the brothers Stefanopoli, members of
the Greek colony at Cargèse in Corsica, were sent on one of
those semi-scientific, semi-political missions, dear to modern
foreign offices, to spread his fame in the Peloponnese. A
legend grew up around the victorious general. Greek philologists discovered that his name was merely an Italian translation of two Greek words (κάλο μέρος) and that he must
therefore be descended from the Imperial family of the
Kaloméroi Porphyrogénnetoi, whose glories he was destined to
renew; Greek historians, remembering the emigration of the
Mainates to Corsica more than a century earlier, boldly
proclaimed him as the offspring of one of those Spartan
families; and the women of Maina kept a lamp lighted before
his portrait, "as before that of the Virgin." The idea of a
restoration of the Byzantine empire with his aid became
general among the Greeks; and Bonaparte was regarded as a
deliverer of the Hellenic race. Not content with organising
the Ionian Islands as "the departments of Corcyra (comprising the islands of Corfù, Paxo, Antipaxo, and Fano, with
their continental dependencies, Butrinto and Párga), Ithaca
(including the islands of Santa Mavra, Cephalonia, and Ithaca,
with Préveza and Vónitza on the gulf of Arta), and the Aegean
Sea" (a vague term, which embraced—for the moment—Zante,

the Strophádes, Cerigo, and Dragoméstre in Akarnanía), the
French government founded in the two Danubian Principalities,
where the Greek element was predominant, two consulates,
one at Bucharest, the other at Jassy, thus reviving an idea of
Catherine de Médicis, who had once meditated colonising the
Principalities with Huguenots, in order to create French
industries and influence in the east. The Egyptian expedition
of Bonaparte at last caused the Sultan to declare war against
France, his traditional ally, and to ally himself with Russia, his
traditional enemy. Russia was alarmed at the success of the
French propaganda among the Greeks, and desirous that a
strong French protectorate over the Christians of Turkey
should not rise up as a barrier to her own schemes. Britain,
engaged in a life-and-death struggle with France, joined the
Russo-Turkish alliance, and the natural result was the loss of
French possessions and the destruction of French trade in the
east. The Ionian Islands were occupied by the Russians and
Turks; the French commercial houses in the Levant were
ruined. France, therefore, at the beginning of the nineteenth
century, was no longer the upholder of the Ottoman empire.
Bonaparte had, by his erratic genius, reversed her secular
policy, and forced Russia, in self-defence, to defend the Turk.

But Ottoman statesmen could have no illusions as to the
ultimate aims of the northern Power. For generations Russia
and Turkey had been rivals, and a series of Russo-Turkish
wars had been chronicled even before the nineteenth century
added four more to their number. By a curious anticipation
of modern history, it was in the Crimea that the two nations
first came into contact. A quarter of a century after the
capture of Constantinople, Mohammed II claimed the suzerainty of the Crim Tartars, whose prince was the ally of the
ruler of Moscow. The Russian merchants at Kaffa and Azov
were now brought into relations with the Turkish authorities,
and their grievances occasioned the despatch of the first
Russian embassy to Constantinople in 1495. Other Russian

embassies followed, and for a long time pacific relations were maintained between the two governments. But the raids of the Tartars into Russian territory and the vengeance exacted by Russian hordes caused considerable friction; and at last, in 1569, the first armed conflict took place between troops of the two states. It is curious to find western Powers urging on the Russians at that period to drive the Turks out of Europe, and already recognising Russia as the natural protectress of the eastern Christians, while the fear of Russia's growing strength was felt in Turkey alone. No western statesman seems to have suspected at that moment that Russia on the Bosphorus would be a menace to Europe; but even the Sultans, at that time at the height of their glory, hesitated to retaliate on a Power which might, they thought, prove too strong for them even then. It was not for another century that a formal war broke out between the rivals, in consequence of the Turkish acquisition of Podolia, which seemed to threaten Russian interests. The result was an increase of Russian territory at Kiev and the desire for further gains. Even so early as this, too, the Tsar posed as the guardian of religious interests by obtaining a safe-conduct for Russian pilgrims on their way to Jerusalem. The political and theological aims of Russia thus became inextricably mixed, just as the missionary has been to other nations the pioneer of the soldier.

Peter the Great gave a great impetus to the anti-Turkish policy of Russia. His capture of Azov was not permanent any more than the free use of the Black Sea for his new navy; but it was he who sent the first Russian man-of-war to the Bosphorus; though its mission was pacific, it was a sign of the future. Equally significant were the beginnings of Russian intrigues in the two Danubian Principalities, whose princes corresponded with the Tsar, and his proclamation to the Greeks, to whom he foretold the approaching restoration of the Byzantine empire. The holy war, which broke out between Russia and Turkey and was concluded by the treaty

of the Pruth in 1711, was a proof, like so many of its
successors, of the military strength of even a politically feeble
empire.   The humiliating terms of that treaty, which imposed
the retrocession of Azov to Turkey and the suppression of the
Russian embassy at Constantinople, were, however, modified
a few years later; and a permanent embassy was re-established
in the Turkish capital.   It is worth noticing that on this
occasion the influence of England was, for the first time, used
against Russia.   Since the formation of the Russian navy, the
English Levant Company, which, in the beginning of the
eighteenth century, had all the trade of the near east in its
hands, had become alarmed at the rivalry of Russian merchants; and the English ambassador at Constantinople, in
opposing for this reason the return of his Russian colleague,
drew the attention of the Porte to the dangers of a political
and religious propaganda by Russian agents among the
Sultan's Christian subjects.   Having gained her point in regard
to her embassy, Russia went on with characteristic tenacity of
purpose to recover her lost foothold at Azov; and despite the
efforts of England and Holland, united in their opposition to
further development of Russian trade in the east, again declared
war against the Sultan in 1736, and again occupied Moldavia.
By the peace of Belgrade she regained Azov, but only on
condition that its fortifications were destroyed, that no Russian
man-of-war should enter the sea of that name or the Euxine,
and that all the Russian Black Sea trade should be carried in
Turkish bottoms.   A lull in the eastern question followed, for
the great Powers were busy elsewhere.

The accession of Catherine II revived the plans of Peter
the Great.   Russian agents were sent to stir up the Greeks
and Montenegrins; war broke out in 1768; and a Russian fleet,
largely officered by Englishmen, was despatched to the
Peloponnese, received the submission of 18 islands in the
Archipelago, and at one moment threatened Constantinople
itself.   But the greatest triumph of this war was the memorable

treaty which concluded it. The obscure Bulgarian[1] village of
Kutchuk-Kaïnardji, where this instrument was signed, has
given its name to one of the most stupendous acts of Turkish
folly. It was not so much the territorial losses of Turkey that
mattered, though Russia's retention of Azov, Kinburn, Kertch,
and Yeni Kaleh gave her the means of dominating the Black
Sea, which her ships were now allowed to navigate, while her
guardianship of the Crimean Mussulmans naturally foreshadowed their absorption in her empire nine years later.
The really fatal clauses of the treaty were those which gave
her the right of making representations on behalf of the Greek
Church in Turkey and of "speaking in favour of the Roumanian
Principalities," which furnished pretexts for constant interference in the internal affairs of the Ottoman dominions. The
convention of Ainali-Kavak in 1779 confirmed the provisions
of that treaty, and stipulated that the tribute which the two
Danubian Principalities had to pay to the Porte "should be
imposed with moderation and humanity "—an arrangement
which did not prevent the Russian ambassador at Constantinople
from demanding, no less than the Turkish government, ample
pecuniary proof of the fitness for office of the candidates for
the two Danubian thrones. Against the wishes of the Turks,
a Russian consulate was now established at Bucharest, as
a centre of intrigue ; and we find the Prussian consul at Jassy
soon complaining that these agents were "put everywhere,
without any necessity, perhaps to win over the inhabitants."
Russia had, indeed, supplanted France as the oracle of the
Porte, and had taught the eastern Christians to look to
her for protection against their sovereign. The Grand-duke
Constantine was educated to be the emperor of a new Greek
empire ; and Catherine II received a memorial from a Greek
deputation. By the peace of Jassy in 1792, which closed the
next war between the Russians and the Turks, the former, in
spite of the threatened opposition of England and Prussia,
moved their frontier up to the Dniester. This was the last

---

[1] Ceded to Roumania in 1913.

dispute between the two rivals in the eighteenth century; and, as we have seen, the close of that period witnessed their temporary alliance in order to defeat the ambitious schemes of Bonaparte in the east.

Austria, lately the chief competitor of Russia in the Balkan peninsula, was early brought into hostile contact with the advancing Turkish armies. In the fifteenth century the Turks began their attacks on the Hungarians, who were at that period the vanguard of Christendom against the Moslem. A century later Budapest was captured and remained, together with the greater part of Hungary, under Turkish rule for about 150 years. But the close of the seventeenth century marked the retreat of the Ottoman armies from Hungarian soil. After the defeat of the Turks before Vienna and the emancipation of Budapest frequent Austrian expeditions invaded Bosnia, over which the Hungarian crown possessed old historic rights ; while an Austrian force captured Vidin in Bulgaria and Nish in Servia, and penetrated into Macedonia as far as Üsküb, where Stephen Dushan had fixed the capital of the medieval Servian empire. Prince Eugene made in 1697 his memorable march to Sarajevo along the same route that was afterwards followed by the army of occupation in 1878. "Yet another campaign," said a Turkish statesman, on hearing that Macedonia was invaded, "and the Austrians will be under the walls of Stambûl." But these feats of arms were without permanent results, and Üsküb is the furthest point on the road to Salonika that an Austrian army has ever reached. The peace of Karlovitz, however, finally excluded the Turks from Hungary (except the *Banat* of Temesvár, which they abandoned nineteen years later), gave Transylvania to Austria, and effected a complete change in the relations between that Power and the Turks. Austria had hitherto regarded the Turk as an aggressive enemy to be repulsed ; she henceforth looked upon him either as a weak foe to be attacked or as a bulwark, to be strengthened at need, against the advance of Russia, in whom

she saw a rival in the east all the more dangerous because
there were many Slav subjects of Austria, who might be
attracted by the Russian national and religious propaganda.

The eighteenth century furnishes examples of all these
three points of view.　Sometimes, Austria was mainly actuated
by the desire for Turkish territory; and then she was willing
to avail herself of Russian aid, even at the risk of Russian
aggrandisement.　This was the case in the war of 1736–39,
when the Austrian and Russian armies were united against
the Turks; in the projected partition of Turkey between
Catherine II and Joseph II, which awarded the Crimea to
the former and Bosnia and the Herzegovina to the latter; and
in the war of 1787–91, when once again the two states were
allies, and the Turks their common foes.　But it is a curious
fact that, whenever this policy has been pursued by Austria,
her successes have been much less than when she attacked
Turkey single-handed.　Whereas the result of the Austro-
Turkish war, which was ended by the peace of Passarovitz,
was to give part of Servia, North Bosnia, and Little Wallachia,
as well as the *Banat*, to Austria, her co-operation with Russia
in 1736 cost her all her gains south of the Danube and Little
Wallachia, while the alliance of 1787 brought her nothing
more than the town of Orsova and two small places on the
Croatian frontier.　On the other hand, during the Russo-
Turkish war which was ended by the treaty of Kutchuk-
Kaïnardji, Austria proposed a secret treaty with Turkey, as
soon as she saw that the Russians were becoming too
successful.　As the reward of her services, she was to receive
once more Little Wallachia; and when Russia, in alarm,
concluded peace, another Roumanian province, the Bukovina,
became, and has till lately remained, Austrian.　At this
period the Austrian diplomatist, Thugut, believed the fall of
Turkey to be at hand, and designated the two Danubian
principalities as his country's share of the spoil.　An Austrian
consul was accordingly placed there to counteract the schemes

of his Russian colleague. But the French revolution and the death of Joseph II saved by an accident, as has so often been the case since, the life of the "sick man," and diverted the attention of Austrian statesmen from the east to the west.

But the eighteenth century had done much to shape the course of Austrian policy in the regions of the Balkans. The twenty-one years' Austrian occupation of Little Wallachia, a large portion of what is now Servia, and a slice of North Bosnia, between 1718 and 1739, was the beginning of that movement which has been resumed in so striking a manner in our own time. Austria then became an important factor in the eastern question, and undertook, though only temporarily, that duty for which destiny seemed to mark her out. The effects of those twenty-one years of European civilisation were not wholly lost on the peoples who were put back under Turkish sway by the treaty of Belgrade. While the Austrian rule was unpopular among the Roumanians of Little Wallachia owing to its insistence upon the regular payment of taxes, the Serbs of Turkey henceforth regarded Austria as the only power which, under existing conditions, could set them free. Numbers of their ancestors had settled in Hungary after the downfall of Servian independence in the fifteenth century; and two Serb patriarchs of Ipek, accompanied by thousands of their flock, had more recently followed that example by migrating thither. The Hungarian Serbs were among the most brilliant soldiers of Prince Eugene; and at the outbreak of every fresh Austro-Turkish war their brethren in Servia took up arms on the Austrian side. A Serb poet hailed Joseph II as "the protector of the Serb race," and the Serb leaders bitterly reproached his successor for making peace with Turkey in 1791. Nor can we be surprised at their regrets. For the first time since the Turkish conquest, Servia had shown signs of material progress during the two brief decades of the previous Austrian occupation; and they naturally hoped that this time Austria would not retire beyond the Danube

and the Save. Knowing little of western politics, they could
not understand why the Power which had taken Belgrade and
entered Bosnia should make peace on the most modest terms.
But the last decade of the century gave Austria a further
foothold in the near east. Just as the same year that had
witnessed the disappearance of Venice from the Peloponnese
witnessed also the first appearance of Austria as a Balkan
state, so the same year that saw the death of the Republic of
St Mark saw too the assumption of her heritage on the
Adriatic by the Hapsburgs. The treaty of Campo-Formio
in 1797, which handed over the Dalmatian possessions of
Venice to Austria, substituted a strong Power for a declining
one as the neighbour of Turkey and Montenegro, and indicated
to the anxious Sultan that the state which had thus annexed
the Illyrian coastline would probably one day occupy the
Bosnian territory behind it.

England was not, like Russia and Austria, the territorial
neighbour of Turkey; but, even before the foundation of
her Indian empire, she had interests in the east, owing to her
large Levant trade. So early as the beginning of the sixteenth
century a Levantine was named English consul at Chios; in
1520 the first English consul was appointed to Crete.
Elizabeth gained free trading facilities in the Turkish dominions for her subjects, who had previously carried on their
commerce with the near east in the "argosies" of the
Ragusan republic, then the greatest mercantile community
of the Balkan peninsula. It is said that the origin of our
trade in the Levant in ships of our own was a petty quarrel
concerning the duty on currants; but, whatever the cause, the
interest of England in the affairs of Turkey was primarily
commercial, and down to the beginning of the nineteenth
century English influence in that part of the world was almost
entirely due to "the Company of Merchants of the Levant,"
who received letters patent from Elizabeth in 1581. It was in
the following year, on the first of the company's ships that

sailed to Constantinople, that William Harebone went out as the first English ambassador to the Sultan. Like all his successors in that post down to 1803, he was appointed and paid, not by the English government, but by the company; and his chief duty was to develop English trade. At the same time, he was instructed to obtain the Sultan's support against the "idolatrous" Spaniards, for the Spanish Armada was soon to descend upon our shores. This admixture of commerce, politics, and religion was eminently characteristic of English statecraft; and the ambassador did not neglect any part of his instructions. He began at once to appoint more consuls, and both he and his successor, Sir Edward Barton, used ingenious theological arguments to prejudice the Sultan's advisers against Spain. The Turks admitted that there could not be much difference between their own religious views and those of Giaours who excluded images and pictures from their churches. But Spain had the riches of the New World at her back; and no help was sent by the Turks, though Barton was so popular with the Sultan that he accompanied him to the war in Hungary.

James I confirmed the company in its monopoly; and in spite of the insolence with which Christians were treated by the Turks in the middle of the seventeenth century, English ships visited Greece; and a Mussulman once observed that Englishmen "always persisted in what they said, even at the peril of their lives." The English ambassador was entrusted by the Austrians with the money to bribe the chief Ottoman representative at the peace of Karlovitz; and it was our representative who, at the peace of Passarovitz, obtained for the Turkish province of the Herzegovina the two small outlets on the sea, the enclave of Klek and the Sutorina, which were so important during the insurrection of 1875–6, and were till 1908 among the curiosities of political geography. During the eighteenth century, when Russia had come to the front as the possible successor of the Turk in Europe, British statesmen were, as a

WINGATE COLLEGE LIBRARY
WINGATE, N. C.

rule, without fear of Muscovite aggrandisement. At one moment, as we have seen, Britain tried to make peace between Russia and Turkey in the interests of her own trade, and in 1719 Stanhope had desired "to drive the Muscovite as far as possible"; but in the middle of the century France was our great commercial rival in the Levant, where the English company had lost much ground in consequence of Villeneuve's vigorous support of Turkey. It was France, too, and not Russia, which then threatened India; and the opening of the Black Sea to Russian ships was even regarded as an advantage for English merchants, who would thus find a new market. We saw that the Russian fleet, which nearly took Constantinople and destroyed the Turkish navy at Tchesmé in 1770, was largely under the direction of English officers; and Turkish officials asked England to explain what her policy really was. On the eve of the fatal treaty of Kutchuk-Kaïnardji we find Lord Chatham writing that he is "quite a Russ," but our ambassador at Constantinople was not of that opinion. So early as 1786 Mirabeau contemplated a Russian advance on India. In 1791 it was the intention of Pitt, had he had the support of the country, to declare war on Russia, in order to maintain the balance of power; and, while Fox was enthusiastically on the side of Russia, Pitt pointed out the uses of Turkey as our ally. But, by a combination of the two policies, the century closed with a triple alliance of England, Russia, and Turkey against the French invaders of Egypt.

In view of the great influence of Germany in Turkish affairs at a recent time, a few words may be said about the eastern policy of Prussia during the period of which we have just given a sketch. The Great Elector sought to use the Danubian Principalities in his schemes against Poland; and one of their Princes, after his deposition by the Turks, endeavoured to obtain aid in Brandenburg. Frederick the Great saw that the expansion of Russia in the east could not injure him—for he had few interests there—but would neutralise

the rival power of Austria. His representative at Constantinople occasionally interceded on behalf of a Moldavian ruler;
and a Prussian consul was appointed in that country, partly on
the characteristic ground that he asked no salary. Frederick
regarded Turkey as a useful means of keeping Austria busy,
and so of assisting his own plans of conquest; and Frederick
William II formed a triple alliance with England and Holland,
to check the Austro-Russian combination against Turkey
between 1787–91. But in their time the German trade in the
east was in Austrian, rather than Prussian, hands, and Prussia's
territorial aspirations were not in the direction of the Ottoman
empire; at most she demanded compensation elsewhere for
the gains of other nations in the east.

We thus find four great Powers at the beginning of the
nineteenth century directly or indirectly affected by the
eastern question: France, in the main the protectress of
the Sultan, and also the protectress of the Catholics of the
Levant; Russia, with her grand scheme of a new Byzantine
empire already sketched out, and her efforts to attract her
Orthodox co-religionists in the Turkish dominions already
begun; Austria, oscillating between the fear of Russia and the
desire of Turkish territory; and Great Britain, commonly
favouring a policy of friendship with Russia. Above all, we
have seen that there was a general conviction that sooner or
later the rest of the Turkish empire in Europe would go.

Still the opening of the nineteenth century found the Sultan
the possessor of a vast European domain. He held the
whole island of Crete, from its then capital of Candia; for even
the warlike Sphakiotes, long independent, had been forced to
pay the *haratch*, or capitation tax, in 1770. The rest of the
modern kingdom of Greece was his, except the Ionian Islands;
and even they for the moment constituted a republic under
the joint protection of the Tsar and himself. All the former
dependencies of the islands on the mainland, except Párga,
were Turkish, having been captured by Ali Pasha of Joánnina

and then formally handed over to Turkey by the convention with Russia in 1800. All that is now known as European Turkey was then part of the Ottoman empire; and modern Bulgaria, modern Servia, Albania, Bosnia and the Herzegovina, and more than half of the former kingdom of Montenegro were direct possessions of the Sultan. Beyond the Danube, the two Principalities of Moldavia and Wallachia, including at that time Bessarabia and stretching as far as the Dniester, formed tributary states, governed by Greek Princes, selected by the Porte from the wealthy families of the Phanar at Constantinople. It may be estimated that the Turkish dominions in Europe in 1801 measured 238,000 square miles, and contained 8,000,000 inhabitants. Their present area is calculated at 10,655 square miles, with a population of 2,000,000 souls, mostly residents of the capital. Such is the result in figures of a little over a century's "consolidation," as Lord Beaconsfield called it.

Asia had always been the stronghold of the Turks; thence they came and thither one day they will return. Their losses there have been accordingly far smaller than in Europe. The dawn of the last century found the Asian frontiers of the empire slightly more extended along the Black Sea coast than they are now; and to-day Asiatic Turkey, also after the treaty of Lausanne, is estimated to contain 400,000 square miles with 6,000,000 inhabitants. In Africa, where, since Tripoli and the Cyrenaica have been "placed under Italian sovereignty,"[1] and Egypt under an independent sovereign, Turkey no longer possesses dominion, she was then about to recover Egypt by British arms from the French; Tripoli, where Ahmed Karamanli had achieved virtual independence in 1714, was nominally a tributary province, but really a "Regency" of pirates, whose chief was then the notorious Yusuf Pasha; while Tunisia, under a Bey, and Algeria, ruled by a Dey, were theoretically subject to

[1] "Poste sotto la sovranità piena ed intera del Regno d' Italia," is the phrase used in the decree of Nov. 5, 1911. The above figures are those of the treaty of Lausanne, with Col. Cornwall's estimate of population.

the Sultan—a subjection seldom pleaded by the local rulers except when some powerful naval power threatened to punish the piracies of the Barbary States.

The European empire of Turkey was at that period divided into five governorships, which were subdivided into provinces and again into districts. In addition to these governorships there were the two Danubian Principalities, which had the misfortune to enjoy a quasi-independence, worse even than the lot of the Sultan's direct possessions. The five European governments were known as Roumelia, Bosnia (including Vidin in Bulgaria), Silistria (including Belgrade), Djezair (including the Peloponnese and many of the Greek islands), and Crete; and the governor of Roumelia, who was styled in Turkish *beylerbey*, or "prince of princes," was the commander-in-chief of all the European contingents in time of war. These five European governments comprised nine pashaliks : Roumelia, Belgrade, Bosnia, Scutari, Joánnina, Negropont, the Morea, Candia, and the Archipelago. The Sultan's subjects in our continent were of various races—Turks, Greeks, Bulgarians, Serbs, Albanians, and Roumanians; but there were some common misfortunes which they all had to bear, though these were much lighter in the case of the Mussulmans than in that of the Christians. The former found it easier to bring their complaints to the ear of the Sultan, while their interests were protected in the provinces by the little bodies of local worthies, who assisted the governor in the discharge of his duties. But, even a century ago, the fate of the provincials was so hard as to attract the sympathy of even avowed partisans of the Turks. In reading of their sufferings, one is reminded of the grim descriptions which the Roman satirists give of the exactions of their own provincial authorities. It was not that the fixed and recognised taxation of the empire was heavy, but that the whole administrative system, excellent though it might be in theory, was utterly rotten in practice. Corruption had entered into the Sublime Porte, and everything was to be bought. A pasha, appointed to a provincial governorship for a year, had to pay a heavy price for his appointment, and recouped himself at the cost of his province. As the end of his year approached, he found it necessary to renew his bribes at Constantinople, if he wished to remain at his post ; and for that too the unhappy province had to pay. Bad as this system was if the pasha were a rich man and had capital at his disposal to invest in a governorship, it was much worse when, as usually happened, he was poor, and therefore compelled to borrow at heavy interest from some Greek or Armenian banker, who thus had a sort of lien on the revenues of the province. The judges, appointed in Constantinople in the same way as the governors, sold justice without scruple ; and the officers who executed their sentences were even more odious to the people. The authorities were also fond of imposing taxes, merely as temporary expedients, which tended to become permanent institutions. It was calculated at this time that about one half of the product of each man's industry was paid to the government in one way or another throughout the provinces ; and, when we consider the need which the governors had of money, we cannot wonder at this high proportion of taxation to income. The frequent journeys of the pashas, the presents inseparable from Oriental administration, the necessity of sending a messenger on the smallest business, as there was no postal service, and the luxury and vast establishments kept up by the great officials, all involved a heavy expenditure. The general insecurity of the country, owing to bands of brigands, repressed all industry ; there were few means of investing money safely ; and the deterioration of the roads, which had once struck English travellers as superior to those of their own country, increased the difficulties of commercial intercourse.

Selim III, who at this time sat on the throne, was, it is true, a reforming Sultan, anxious to raise his empire from its declining state, and willing to take western nations as his model. He made, for a moment, a clean sweep of the

Bulgarian and Macedonian brigands and the Aegean pirates, repaired the ruinous fortresses on his frontiers, and employed French shipbuilders to construct men-of-war. But, like most autocrats, he was powerless to change a whole system of misgovernment with a stroke of his pen. Albania and Epirus, always the most dangerous part of European Turkey, were in such a state that a Turk could not venture to show his face there, while all travellers were liable to be murdered with impunity by the natives of that mountainous region. In many parts of the empire hereditary tyrants, known as *dereh beys*, or "lords of the valleys," terrorised their humble neighbours. Here and there great pashas, like Ali of Joánnina and Pasvanoglu of Vidin, fought for their own hands and acted like semi-independent sovereigns. The "lion of Joánnina" has been made familiar to the reader by the poetry of Lord Byron and the prose of Jókai, while, as a forerunner of the Greek revolution, he has gained a place in the best-known chapter of modern Oriental history. Ali belonged to an Albanian Mussulman family of Tepelen, which had once been Christian ; but his grandfather had fallen for the Crescent in 1716 at the siege of Corfù. Pasha of Joánnina since 1788, he had distinguished himself by his cruelty, ability, and ambition ; poets sang in Greek how he had thrown a beautiful lady into the lake and avenged the injuries done to his family by the impartial destruction of both a Christian and a Mohammedan community ; a British traveller summed up his character as a "mixture of magnificence and meanness." Osman Pasvanoglu, though almost forgotten now, was in his day scarcely inferior to Ali in influence. With the true fanaticism of a Bosnian Mussulman he declared against the reforms of his sovereign, whose real and only friend he pretended to be. Master of the "virgin-fortress" of Vidin, he showed his loyalty by defeating the Sultan's armies and despoiling his fellow-subjects. He raised a private force of his own, levied his own taxes, coined his own money, and sent his representative to Paris to

negotiate on his own account with the French government.   A
British consul visited his court ; and such was the terror of his
name that there was a general stampede from Bucharest on
the approach of his men.   Severe as were the sufferings of the
Roumanians and Bulgarians from his depredations, the cost of
maintaining an army to oppose him was an even greater burden
to the Wallachian peasants.   It was on this occasion that
Hangerli, their Prince, confiscated practically all the cattle of
his people, and thus left them without sustenance in a winter
which has become proverbial as one of the four plagues of that
sorely oppressed principality.   The Bulgarians experienced in
their turn the usual fate which at that time befell a country
through which a Turkish army marched.   Southern Bulgaria
was reported to be almost destitute of inhabitants, and its now
flourishing capital was left a heap of corpses and charred
timber.   The fearful ravages of the plague in most Turkish
cities completed the devastation of the empire, though in this
respect the European provinces suffered less than the Asiatic.

The division of the Sultan's subjects into two sharply defined
classes, those who were Mohammedans and those who were not,
was the cause of much evil.   It has been justly said that the
Turkish government has shown itself far more tolerant of
religious opinions than many so-called Christian nations.   The
welcome extended by Turkey in the fifteenth century to the
Spanish, and in the nineteenth to the Russian Jews, contrasts
most favourably with the Jewish persecutions in Catholic Spain
and Orthodox Russia.   Such was the hatred which one sect of
Christians felt for another, that the Bogomiles of Bosnia
preferred to be conquered by the Sultan rather than converted by the Pope, and the Orthodox Greeks chose to be
the subjects of infidel Turks rather than of Catholic Venetians.
Mohammed II, like the great statesman that he was, saw at
once that the Greek church might become in his hands a
powerful support of the Ottoman rule.   He accordingly restored the Œcumenical Patriarchate of Constantinople and

made the Patriarch his tool. But, with all his tolerance for
freedom of thought, the Mussulman regarded the Christians
as an inferior caste. The *râyahs* had to put up with a hundred
slights, and were made to feel that they were outside the pale
of the dominant religion. They were liable to all sorts of
aggravating rules, which regulated the colour of their clothes,
the style of their houses, and the professions which they might
enter. Their women were exposed to the *droit de seigneur* at
the pleasure of the young bloods of Islâm; if their children
were no longer taken as a tribute for the Sultan's armies, and
they were exempt from compulsory military service, they had
to victual and do all the dirty work of the Ottoman forces,
build military roads and fortresses, transport artillery, and carry
munitions of war. It was no wonder, then, that those of little
faith abandoned Christianity for a religion which would assure
them the respect of the Turks, and the right, equally dear to
them as perverts, of despising and maltreating their former
co-religionists. Numbers of Serbs in Bosnia, numbers of
Greeks in Crete, many Bogomiles in Bulgaria, embraced Islâm
after the Turkish conquest; and the Bosnian, Cretan, Bulgarian,
and Albanian Mussulmans became the most conservative of all
the Sultan's subjects in their opposition to reforms, the most
fanatical of all Mohammedans in their devotion to the law of
the prophet. Popular phraseology, which calls these people
" Turks," obscures the fact that some of the worst oppressors of
the Christians in Turkey were not Turks at all, but perverts
from Christianity, of the same race as the persecuted. The
high road to honours was to profess Islâm; and it became
proverbial that " one must be the son of a Christian renegade
to attain to the highest dignities of the Turkish empire."
Thus, in Bosnia, although a Turkish governor was sent from
Constantinople, he was a mere figure-head; and all real power
was centred in the great Bosnian nobles, who gradually became
hereditary headmen of the divisions of that country. So strong
was the influence of these Mussulman Serbs that they permitted

the pasha to remain at Sarajevo for no more than forty-eight hours, and resisted all attempts to move the official capital from Travnik thither. So the Bosnian *begs* administered that province on feudal lines, and were quite content with a system which allowed them to do as they pleased at home and provided them with the occasional luxury of a foray abroad. It was only when the Turkish military power began to decline and Bosnia was invaded by Austrian armies, that the Bosnian Mussulmans began to doubt the wisdom of the Sultan's government.

In Servia, where there was no native aristocracy as in Bosnia, a number of these Bosnian *begs* were settled as landowners, forming the majority of the *spahi*, or cavalry, who were the sole possessors of the soil, to the complete exclusion of the *râyah* from all rights of ownership. There were at this period some 132,000 of these military landowners in all Turkey, some 900 in the pashalik of Belgrade. In return for their lands they owed military service to the Sultan; but even in time of peace they were mostly absentees, idling away their days in the towns and letting the despised Christians manage their farms. In addition to these *spahi*, another military force, the Janissaries, were to be found in detachments through the provinces. Their leaders, or *dahi*, were often more powerful than the Sultan's representative, and not only maltreated the Christian peasants, but even seized the lands of the Mohammedan *spahi* with impunity. The natives had, indeed, some small share in the administration; and when, as was the case in Servia at this period, the pasha was a just man, their chosen representatives could temper the wind to their shorn flock. The head-man of the village, the village magistrate, and, in many cases, the district official or (in Serb) *oborknes*, who was responsible for the collection of the Turkish taxes, and acted as a medium between the pasha and the taxpayers, were elected by the people. The *oborknes*, whether so elected or nominated by the pasha, usually held office for life—it had formerly been an hereditary post—and acquired considerable influence both with the Turkish officials and the Serb peasants. Not a few of these local worthies became leaders of the Servian revolution. One branch of the Serbs formed the only independent state of the peninsula—the principality of Montenegro, governed since 1696 by Prince-Bishops, or *Vladikas* of the family of Petrovich, a dignity which descended, as the theocratic ruler could not marry, from uncle to nephew[1]. A *firman* of 1799 had recognised that the Montenegrins had never been subjects of the Porte.

The Albanians had offered, under their hero Skanderbeg, the most determined resistance to the Turkish conquest; and even at the beginning of the nineteenth century, as indeed later, their land was hardly under the control of its nominal sovereign. Divided by three religions—the Catholic, the Orthodox, and the Mohammedan—and split up into two main branches—the Ghegs and the Tosks—and into numerous tribes, the Albanians were alike in their love of fighting. The best regiments in the Turkish army, the crack regiment in the kingdom of Naples, were composed of these warriors, who in our own time formed the bodyguard of the timorous Sultan. Even before the Turks had conquered Greece, Albanian colonies had settled there; and in southern Italy there is a large Albanian element. In northern Albania one tribe, the Catholic Mirdites, enjoyed practical independence under an hereditary ruler of the family of Gion (John) Marcu, called "captain" by his men, but "prince" by Europeans from a mistranslation of the name of Prenk (Peter), borne by each successive chief. In Epirus, the Orthodox Souliotes, an admirable blend of Greeks and Hellenised Albanians, who won the admiration of Byron, formed a sort of military commonwealth, composed first of four, then of eleven villages, paying in time of peace the tithe and the capitation-tax to the Porte, but in wartime maintaining practical independence by their swords. At

---

[1] Arsenije Plamenatz (1779–81) was an exception.

once rulers and ruled, they levied the same imposts from the Parasouliotes, or inhabitants of some 60 conquered hamlets, who depended upon them, till, after a three years' struggle, Soûli was betrayed to Ali Pasha in 1803, the women hurled themselves and their babes in the dance of death from the rock of Zálongo, and the survivors fled to Corfù.

Of all the Christian races beneath the rule of the Turk, the Greeks were at that time the most important and the most prosperous. They had had, like the Serbs, the advantage early in the eighteenth century of being, though for a very short period, under the administration of a western Power; and the Venetian government of the Morea, though not by any means popular while it lasted, nor remembered with any gratitude, was a great advance upon Turkish rule. Although Russia, when she invaded the Morea in 1770, clearly demonstrated that her aim was not to make the Greeks free but to make them her subjects, and abandoned them so soon as it suited her purpose, the treaty of Kaïnardji placed them more or less under her influence; and later arrangements entitled the Greek islanders to trade under her flag. The French revolution not only provided the Greeks, and especially those who inhabited the Ionian Islands during the first French occupation, with majestic phrases about the liberty of nations and the equality of men, but indirectly favoured Greek commerce, owing to the fact that the Turkish government was generally neutral and its flag could therefore go anywhere. The Greeks combine two usually irreconcilable qualities—great aptitude for business and great love of book-learning. Both these qualities, already developed at the beginning of the nineteenth century, tended to prepare them for national independence, though neither of them implied the possession of that political training which nations only acquire, as a rule, after centuries of experience. Commerce led them to visit other and better-governed countries, and so to draw inferences as to their own future prospects; literature,

as created by Eugénios Boúlgaris the Corfiote, and Koraês
the Chiote, formed a bond of national union; and Rhégas
of Velestino gave to the impending Greek revolution its
Marseillaise, while "to Joánnina," in the phrase of a Greek
writer, "Greece owes the regeneration of her education."

Travellers noticed that the Greeks bore "the Turkish yoke
with greater impatience than other Christians," although,
except in Crete, they had perhaps less to complain of than
their fellows. They occupied, indeed, a position of superiority
towards the Sultan's other Christian subjects. For the Greek
Patriarch was the ecclesiastical head of all the Christian
population, irrespective of race, throughout the Balkan
peninsula. The services of the Greek Church and clergy
in the struggle for Greek independence were very great; but
by Bulgarians and Serbs, and still more in Moldavia and
Wallachia, the Greek bishop was regarded as a foreign agent.
With the suppression of the two ancient autocephalous Serb
and Bulgarian Churches of Ipek and Ochrida in 1766–7, the
last ecclesiastical bulwarks of those Slav races fell before the
influence of the Greek clergy, who had long been as supreme
in the spiritual life of the peninsula as the Turkish officials
were in its political affairs. The Greek bishop, chosen from
the Phanariotes of Constantinople, usually had to buy his see,
just as the Turkish pasha bought his post, and made the
people pay him back what he had expended. He was
generally a valuable ally of the pasha, because he wanted the
latter's aid to compel the peasants to comply with his requests,
while he could render various diplomatic services to the pasha
in return. Under the influence of these spiritual pastors, who
rarely spoke any language but Greek, and, of course, con
ducted the service in that tongue, Slavs and Roumanians
alike became outwardly hellenised. Their own languages
were despised as barbarous jargons; to speak Greek came to
be considered as the mark of a gentleman; the two Roumanian codes were published, and even Bulgarian business

correspondence conducted in Greek, as the most useful and widest spoken idiom of the near east. Foreigners therefore might be excused for considering the Greek Church as co-extensive with the Greek race and for reckoning up the Christian population of the Balkan peninsula at this period as collectively " Greeks." Rhégas poetically assumed that "all the Macedonians " would " rise together," that " Bulgarians and Albanians, Serbs and Roumanians " would " draw the sword" for the cause of Greece and liberty. Until our own day, enthusiasts alone imagined the beautiful picture of the Christian races of the east united against the Turk. For the cardinal difficulty of the eastern question always had been, before the Balkan League of 1912, the mutual animosities of these very same Christian races. For the Bulgarians sought to free themselves not only from the political domination of the Turks, but from the ecclesiastical authority of the Greeks; and in our time the quarrels of the Patriarchists and Exarchists have been quite as serious as those of Mussulmans and Christians.

Apart altogether from their ecclesiastical influence, the Greeks found many profitable careers open to them in the Turkish service. Their superior intelligence and linguistic skill enabled them to attain distinction as dragomans and envoys of the Porte. Their happy hunting-ground was beyond the Danube in the Principalities of Moldavia and Wallachia, where thrones could be bought by the great Phanariote families of Constantinople and fortunes could be made out of the administration. It was noticed by travellers that the Greeks of the Turkish capital were less moral than those of the islands; and the descriptions which contemporaries have left us of the Phanar, the quarter of that city where the Patriarchate was situated, represent it at this period as an academy of intrigue—the only weapon by which the weak can circumvent the strong. Greek historians accuse the Phanariotes of pride towards their own fellow-countrymen, and of forgetting that their own position depended upon the uncertain favour of a tyrant. Indeed, few portions of oriental history are so unedifying as that which records the reigns of the Phanariote Hospodars at Bucharest and Jassy during a large part of the eighteenth and the nineteenth centuries. The luxury of the two alien princes contrasted as strongly with the poverty of their subjects as did their proud demeanour to the Roumanians with their enforced humility to the Turks. "The two Hospodars," said a Turkish proverb, "are the eyes of the Ottoman empire, turned towards Europe." They were, in fact, the real foreign secretaries of the Sultan; but they betrayed their master, whenever it suited their own purpose to play the game of Austria or Russia at his expense. The chief aim of the Hospodar of Wallachia, the richer principality, was to keep his place and make money out of it; the chief object of the Hospodar of Moldavia was to obtain promotion to Bucharest. Thus, the two became bitter rivals, while all the time there were hungry place-hunters at Constantinople, eager to dispossess them both. Under this system, these two provinces, justly called "the granary of the capital," became perhaps the most miserable part of the whole empire. Nature had done much for the great plains of the Danube, the fine slopes of the Carpathians; but the government had ruined the country for the poor Roumanian peasant. His songs are full of lamentations over his woes and of denunciations of the oppressors who caused them—the Turk, who was his over-lord, the Russian, who came to "deliver" him in the name of religion, the Jew, who plundered him, the Phanariote, who misgoverned him under the authority of the Sultan. But it is only fair to recognise the diplomatic ability, the superior culture, the greater refinement, and the political experience of the Phanariotes, who furnished to the Greek revolution its leading statesman, in the person of Alexander Mavrokordátos, and contributed a valuable element to the society of the young Greek kingdom.

In Greece itself, though there were no such brilliant openings for talent as in Moldavia and Wallachia, scope was found for the administrative abilities of the natives. The primates, or *kodjabashis*, formed a kind of official aristocracy, whose business it was to assess the share of the taxes that each person had to pay. They were agents of the Turkish dignitaries, who farmed the taxes, and, in some respects, imitated their Turkish patrons. In the Peloponnese, where local administration was better organised than elsewhere, there was, even under the Turks, some attempt at self-government. Every village elected a head-man; and these head-men collectively with the townsfolk elected representatives, who chose the primate of the province. All the primates resided at Tripolitsá, the capital; and their interests were represented by a delegate at Constantinople. Here and there Greek communities enjoyed even greater privileges. The island of Chios was the most favoured of them all. Before the Turkish conquest, it had been governed by a Genoese mercantile company—the first instance of one of those chartered companies so common in our own day. The Turks continued the enlightened Genoese system of government; and the Chiotes were better off than any other Greeks at the beginning of the nineteenth century. The three "Nautical Islands" of Hýdra, Spétsai, and Psará, the nurseries of the future Greek fleet, almost unknown before the eighteenth century, had suddenly risen to be flourishing communities, where the sailors had a share in the ships and their cargoes. At this time Hýdra was governed by George Boúlgares, a capable administrator, Spétsai by a similar local official, known as a *zampítes* (or "policeman"), and Psará by a council of "elders." Tênos, after five centuries of Venetian rule, was another example of a Greek island, in the affairs of which the Turks interfered but little; while Naxos, once the capital of a Catholic duchy, retained, together with some vestiges of Latin civilisation, the right to govern itself according to its own customs. The 12 southern Sporádes had enjoyed special privileges, ratified by successive Sultans since the conquest of Rhodes. In the mountainous districts of Pindus and Olympus, the Christians had another and more dangerous privilege, that of bearing arms, and so forming, under the name of *armatoloí*, a local militia. In their "free villages," or *eleutherochória* (the name may still be found in that region), they formed military communities, which in the eighteenth century had excited the apprehensions of the government. Repeated attempts were made to weaken them, but it was not till the time of Ali of Joánnina that these efforts were successful.

The "24 hamlets of Volo," each with its school-house, aroused the admiration of travellers; while the flourishing community of Ambelákia on the slopes of Ossa, thanks to its dye-works, vied with the prosperity of the villages on Pélion, till local jealousies and British competition ruined Ambelákia and the sword of Ali destroyed the autonomy of all the "24 hamlets" save Zagorá. On the peninsula of Chalkidiké a confederation of villages, the so-called *Mademochória*, elected the local authorities; while "the Holy Mountain" of Athos enjoyed the privilege of self-government, and the Turkish official, who resided at Karýes, the capital of this theocratic republic, interfered in its affairs as little as the *Madem-aga* in those of the Chalkidic confederacy. At the extreme south of Greece, Maina, after the rising of 1770, was governed by a local chief, appointed for life by the Sultan and dignified with the title of *bey*; and in practice the tribute consisted of as much money as would lie on the flat blade of a sabre. Levádeia, then the chief town in eastern Greece, was governed by the local magnates, whose president represented the town in all negotiations with the Turkish civil and military authorities. Finally, Athens was the private property of the Sultan, who let it out for life to the highest bidder. The Turkish authorities consisted of the *voïvode* (or "governor"), appointed by the Imperial Mint, the *cadi* (or "judge"), the *mufti* (or "bishop"), and the *disdar-aga* (or "commander of the garrison"), who lived with his harem in the Eréchtheion. But the Athenians annually elected their "elders"; and their own "agents" (ἐπίτροποι) conducted the business of the community with the Turkish officials. The tyranny of Hajji Ali the Haseki, who repeatedly held the office of *voïvode* in the latter part of the eighteenth century, had combined with two recent plagues to diminish the prosperity and population of the city, which contained about 10,000 inhabitants. Even then Athens could boast an historian in the person of John Benizélos, the Athenian schoolmaster.

Thus, at the dawn of the nineteenth century, we find religion, rather than race, the dividing line between the subjects of the Sultan. The Mussulmans, whether Turks or the descendants of Bulgarian, Bosnian, Albanian, or Cretan converts from Christianity, formed a dominant caste; the Christians, except the comparatively few Catholics in Bosnia, Albania, Servia, Bulgaria, and in one or two of the Greek islands, were classed together as Greeks, because they belonged to the Greek Church and owned the spiritual authority of the Œcumenical Patriarch. European statesmen, except perhaps in the case of the Serbs, had scarcely become conscious of the fact that the eastern question would have to consider the claims of other Christian races of Turkey than the Greeks as heirs to some part of the Turkish empire. The principle of nationalities was not yet a powerful force in politics; and the career of Napoleon in the near east, as elsewhere, was its negation.

CHAPTER II

NAPOLEON IN THE NEAR EAST (1801–15)

THE relations between the four great Powers and the Sultan changed considerably during the early years of the nineteenth century, for the selfish inconsistencies of Napoleon's policy caused them to support or oppose the Turks according to the requirements of the moment, without much regard for any general principle. Turkey, like other countries, was simply a pawn in the great game, which the Corsican played for his own hand.

Both Great Britain and Russia reaped some reward for their assistance to the Sultan against the invaders of Egypt. The grateful Turks presented the Levant Company with the site of the present British Embassy at Constantinople; the Russians obtained a more important concession, the so-called *hatti-sherîf*, or Imperial ordinance, of 1802, which provided that the Hospodars of Moldavia and Wallachia should not be deposed without the consent of the Tsar, and that the term of their office should be seven years. This provision was a further increase of Russia's influence in the Danubian Principalities, a step beyond the advantage gained by her at Ainali-Kavak (see p. 8). The two Princes were now Russian agents, and showed an independence of the Sultan which was as marked as their servility towards the Tsar.

France was reconciled to Turkey in 1802; and Colonel Sébastiani was sent on a special mission to the Levant, ostensibly for the promotion of French trade, really to report on the strategic importance of various places in the east. In 1805 the treaty of Pressburg, by which Austria ceded to Napoleon her lately acquired possessions in Dalmatia, gave France the only footing she has ever had in the Balkan peninsula. It was on this occasion that Talleyrand drew up a famous memoir on the eastern question, in which he advised the French Emperor to give Austria as compensation Moldavia and Wallachia, and so bar the road to Constantinople against the Russians. Had the idea been carried out, the history of the near east would have been changed, and the war of 1877 might have never taken place.

The nine years' French occupation of Dalmatia has not been adequately described by any English historian; but it deserves attention as an example of the mistakes which even so great a genius as Napoleon I could make in the government of a country placed on the confines of west and east. The long Venetian rule over Dalmatia has left a permanent mark on the coast towns; but it was the policy of the Republic of St Mark to repress Dalmatian trade and prevent the spread of enlightened ideas. The Austrians during their first brief ownership, from 1797 to 1805, had no time to effect much; but they began to make roads, which were wholly wanting in the Venetian times, though even in this respect they had not accomplished much when the French succeeded them in the administration of the province. Napoleon's emissaries had, therefore, practically everything to create, and at first they set about their work with considerable common-sense. But there are two distinct periods in the French government of Dalmatia, each of which has a separate character of its own and represents a different aspect of Napoleonic policy. So long as Dalmatia formed part of the Kingdom of Italy, from 1805 to 1809, the French Emperor, still dreaming of Balkan conquests, and even of an advance on India, regarded the Illyrian coast-line as an excellent base from which to start. He realised the value of the harbour of Gravosa and the

Bocche di Cattaro as future naval stations, and impressed upon
the distinguished men whom he sent to govern the Dalmatians
in those early years the necessity of adapting their methods
to the local requirements.   Marmont and Dandolo, who
succeeded his first representative, Molitor, were, as an Austrian
historian has said, " the two most eminent administrators that
Dalmatia has ever had," but they were quite unable to
agree together ; the civilian thought the soldier an interfering
ignoramus, and the soldier treated the civilian as an unpractical
pedant.   Yet both, in their way, did something for the benefit
of the province committed to their charge.   Molitor had not
greatly altered the Austrian system, but Dandolo lost no time
in founding a newspaper, the first in Dalmatia, in starting a
high school, and in making a bid for the support of the
Orthodox clergy, who had hitherto been under the Catholics,
by giving them a bishop of their own persuasion.   This
measure, which the Austrians had already meditated in order
to break the influence of Montenegro in Dalmatia, had, however, the effect of estranging the Catholics without securing
the gratitude of the Orthodox.   When the Russians invaded
Dalmatia, the latter were their strongest supporters ; and
throughout the French occupation the Dalmatian clergy of
all denominations depicted the agents of Napoleon as atheists
and regicides, and used their vast influence with the ignorant
people against their rulers.   Marmont, on the other hand, has
left a permanent reputation in the country as a road-maker ;
and the peasants still tell the marvellous tale how the French
general " mounted his horse and bade his soldiers make roads,"
and how "when he dismounted, lo ! the roads were made.'
A Frenchman, too, drew up an accurate chart of the difficult
Dalmatian coast, with its countless islands and dangerous
currents ; while another of his compatriots induced even the
conservative natives to recognise the advantages of vaccina-
tion, and so diminished the terrible scourge of most oriental
lands.

After 1809 Napoleon's schemes changed, and he looked upon Dalmatia merely as a nursery for tall soldiers and its inhabitants as food for powder.   Now, it is a curious fact that the same people who had willingly furnished aid to Venice in her last days resolutely refused to follow the standards of the French Emperor.   From first to last the conscription was most unpopular in the country; and, when war broke out between France and Austria in 1809, the Dalmatians rose almost as one man against the French.   From this time, too, the country was treated without the smallest regard to its special conditions.   No longer a part of the Kingdom of Italy, but forming, together with Ragusa, two of the seven "Illyrian Provinces," it ceased to have a separate history from that of the other dominions of Napoleon.   The Illyrian kingdom, composed as it was of five nationalities —Germans, Italians, Croats, Serbs, and Slovenes—had no unity, while there was nothing in common between the Norman or Breton peasant and the Dalmatian fisherman.   Yet the Dalmatian, no less than the Norman and Breton, was now subjected to the rigid and unbending *Code Napoléon* ; what was good for France was declared to be good for Dalmatia ; and, in the room of men like Dandolo and Marmont, inexperienced *doctrinaires* or mechanical clerks were sent to govern the people on hard-and-fast rules, laid down in Paris, without the least regard for the past history or present needs of the governed.   The elaborate organisation of the "Illyrian Provinces" in 1811 was a complete failure, as the French candidly admitted ; everything was sacrificed to the desire for centralisation ; and when, in 1814, the Austrians re-entered Dalmatia they were hailed as liberators.   Moreover, the trade of the country suffered greatly from the British cruisers during the struggle against Napoleon, though there was some compensating benefit to those Dalmatian islands—Lissa, Curzola, Lesina, and the Ragusan archipelago—which were regularly occupied by our forces between 1812 and 1815.   The important naval station of Lissa, in particular, where the British fleet defeated the French in 1811, became a centre of trade during our brief occupation. In two years its population was nearly trebled; all the nationalities hostile to Napoleon found shelter there; and at no period of its history, before or since, has the island known such prosperity. Curzola was provided by the British governor with local institutions; and an inscription still preserves his memory there and expresses the gratitude of the inhabitants. In the five Ragusan islands the old Ragusan laws were restored by our representatives, and native nobles placed at the head of their respective administrations. Britain has no cause to be ashamed of the part she played at a critical time in a country whose manly sailors are scarcely inferior to her own.

But, if the French occupation of Dalmatia has left little constructive work, except Marmont's roads, behind it, it destroyed for ever two interesting survivals of the middle ages —the Republics of Poljitza and Ragusa. It is curious that Napoleon, who spared the tiny Italian commonwealth of San Marino, should have swept away its Illyrian counterpart. The mountain-republic of Poljitza, with a population of between 6000 and 7000, had maintained its independence under Hungarian and Venetian protection for centuries. Governed by a highly aristocratic constitution, and tempering its constitutional theories with frequent appeals to violence, as befitted a Balkan state, it was unwise enough to take sides with the Russians, who hounded it on against the French in 1807. The result was the destruction of the Republic and its incorporation with the rest of Dalmatia—an arrangement never since disturbed, although, on St George's day 1911, by order of the Emperor, the three communes, which occupied the territory of the Republic, were formed into one, having its exact historic boundaries. More tragic still was the end of Ragusa, a Republic which had existed in one form or another for over eleven centuries, and won the proud title of "The South Slavonic Athens." At this time the Republic numbered

35,000 inhabitants, and consisted of the city of the same name, the town of Ragusa Vecchia, the district of Canali between that place and the Bocche di Cattaro, the beautiful valley of the Ombla, the long peninsula of Sabbioncello, and the five islands of Lagosta, Meleda, Giupana, Mezzo, and Calamotta. The Austrians had not touched its liberties and had refused to aid the refractory Canalesi, who were discontented with the republican government. But, at the news of the treaty of Pressburg, the Russians had occupied the Bocche di Cattaro ; and Ragusa was thus placed between them and the French. The latter declared their intention of occupying its territory, but of evacuating it as soon as the Russians should have withdrawn. This promise was wilfully broken by Napoleon, whose officers, Lauriston and Marmont, seem both to have been ashamed of the transaction. The siege of Ragusa by the Russians and their allies, the Montenegrins and the Canalesi, did much harm to the suburbs, but was raised by the French under Molitor. Once, however, in possession of the city, the French showed no sign of going. The lower orders of Ragusa were in favour of French annexation as an alternative to the aristocratic rule of their fellow countrymen. The nobles made a final effort to save the commonwealth, and in vain appealed to Austria and Turkey. The standard of San Biagio, patron of Ragusa, ceased to float above the famous statue of Orlando ; and on the last day of January 1808, a French colonel informed the assembled Senate that "the Republic of Ragusa has ceased to exist." Marmont was created Duc de Raguse ; and the Republican territory became, first, a part of the Kingdom of Italy, and then one of the "Illyrian Provinces." Six years later Ragusa was freed from the French by the combined Austrian and British forces ; but, though the nobles hoped for a revival of the Republic, the people welcomed Austrian, as they had welcomed French, rule, and Ragusa till 1919 remained, like the rest of Dalmatia, under the sway of the Hapsburgs.

One other result of the French occupation of Dalmatia was to bring Montenegro for the first time within the circle of European politics. At the beginning of the nineteenth century the warriors of the Black Mountain were quite outside the pale of civilisation, and passed their time in almost incessant struggles against the Turks. But their traditional friendship· with Russia made them willing to assist the latter power in its seizure of the Bocche di Cattaro in 1806; and, as we have seen, they took part in the siege of Ragusa. The French found the Prince-Bishop of Montenegro, Peter I, so tiresome an opponent that they in vain endeavoured to appease him by offering to make him Patriarch of Dalmatia; and, after the treaty of Tilsit had given them undisturbed possession of the Bocche, they thought it well to be on good terms with so awkward a neighbour. But the wary Peter, though he granted Marmont an interview, declined to receive a French consul at Cetinje; and, when Vialla de Sommières was instructed by Napoleon to draw up a report on Montenegro, he had to obtain his political information under the pretext of botanising. The Prince-Bishop would not hear of the French Emperor's offer of his protection; and, as soon as the news of the retreat from Moscow reached him, he prepared to attack the garrisons of Napoleon, who had planned the wholesale deportation of Montenegrins to the Low Countries. Peter gladly co-operated with the British fleet in the siege of Cattaro in 1813, but his tenure of that coveted place was of short duration. Next year, on the advice of the Tsar, he restored it to Austria, which for 105 years held it.

Meanwhile, on the other side of the Balkan peninsula, the diplomacy of Napoleon had not been idle. In 1806, in consequence of the deposition of the Hospodars of Moldavia and Wallachia, without the consent of Russia, at Sébastiani's suggestion, the Russian troops entered the Principalities, and the first Russo-Turkish war of the century began. The Tsar had legal right on his side, for the deposition of the Hospodars

was a direct violation of the ordinance of 1802 ; and in Great
Britain he found a willing ally.   A British ultimatum in 1807
demanded the expulsion of Sébastiani, and a declaration of
war against France, the alliance of Turkey with Russia and
Great Britain, the cession of the Danubian Principalities to the
Tsar, and the surrender of the Turkish fleet, together with the
forts at the Dardanelles, to the British admiral. As the Sultan,
encouraged by the French, rejected this ultimatum, the British
fleet entered the Dardanelles, as Elphinston had advised in
1770, and appeared before Constantinople.   But the admiral
allowed himself to be entangled in those negotiations which
Turkish statesmen know so well how to spin out.   Had he
shown the decision of another British admiral in Crete ninety-
one years later, the world might have witnessed the spectacle
of a British occupation of Constantinople.   But he wasted
precious time in despatch-writing ; and, while he wrote, the
Turks, urged on by the French and encouraged by the Sultan
in person, worked at the fortifications.   Admiral Duckworth
had to retreat beyond the Dardanelles ; Constantinople was
saved.   Occupied with Napoleon, neither Russia nor Great
Britain could prosecute a war against Turkey with vigour ; and
the preoccupations of the Powers seemed, as usual, to be the
best safeguard of the Sultan.   But suddenly the world learnt
that Napoleon and the Tsar had become reconciled by the
peace of Tilsit, and that, in order to prosecute his plans
against England, the French Emperor had changed his eastern
policy, and was ready to sacrifice Turkey to the requirements
of his ambition.   Only a few months earlier he had declared
it to be his " mission to save her."

    The scheme for the partition of the Turkish empire in
Europe, which was sketched out by Napoleon in his interview
with the Tsar Alexander I at Tilsit, was not more practical
than such plans have been in later days.   But, rough as it
was, it still contained one or two pregnant suggestions, which
even now are not without value in the discussion of the

eastern question. Napoleon was willing to cede Bessarabia, Moldavia, Wallachia, and North Bulgaria to Russia, taking as his own share Albania, Thessaly as far as the gulf of Salonika, the Morea and Crete, while Austria was to be appeased with a part of Bosnia and Servia. The heir of Peter the Great and Catherine II was not, however, content with his portion of the spoils. He was willing to allow Napoleon to take, in addition to the already large French claims, the islands of the Archipelago, Syria, and Egypt, if Russia could have Roumelia and Constantinople. We have it on the authority of an eye-witness, the French Emperor's private secretary, that Napoleon replied by indignantly placing his finger on the spot on the map, which represented the Turkish capital, and exclaiming : " Constantinople ! Constantinople ! never ! for it is the empire of the world." Subsequent events have perhaps diminished the strategic value of that marvellous site ; but few will deny that it was long the goal of Russian ambition, though of all the Turkish provinces assigned to Russia at Tilsit, Bessarabia is the only one that she till very lately incorporated in her empire. France, at that time in occupation of Dalmatia, and about to re-enter into possession of the Ionian Islands, might not unnaturally aspire to further acquisitions in the near east —an aspiration now abandoned ; while Napoleon's concession of part of Bosnia to Austria was an anticipation of the Berlin Treaty of 1878. By a secret article the two Emperors pledged themselves, in the event of the failure of French diplomacy to make its influence felt with the new Sultan, to "free all European Turkey, except Roumelia and the capital, from the yoke and vexations of the Turks." No time was lost in preparing for this philanthropic partition. Marmont was ordered to procure information about Bosnia, Macedonia, Thrace, Greece, and Albania, their resources and their military situation, and to be less friendly with the pasha of Bosnia, at whose residence the French had a consul-general. As another consequence of the Franco-Russian treaty, the French were reinstated in the Ionian Islands. The possession of the Bocche di Cattaro and Corfù seemed, indeed, to be a prelude to a grand campaign against Turkey, which might, as a British diplomatist wrote, be a prelude to a still grander campaign against the rest of Europe.

The Ionians, who had welcomed the democratic French with enthusiasm in 1797, as an agreeable relief from the pride of the Venetians, showed themselves completely indifferent to the second French occupation ten years later. In the interval, under the unpopular protectorate of Russia and Turkey, the islands on March 21, 1800, had been erected into a "Septinsular Republic," which, though shorn of their former continental dependencies, formed the first autonomous Greek state of modern times. Unfortunately, this Ionian common-wealth had been indulging in the luxury of constant changes of administration. Three constitutions had been proclaimed in two years; and a small revolution had demonstrated that Corfù had not greatly altered since the days when it furnished Thucydides with moral maxims on the wickedness of civic strife. At first a beautiful scheme of federation was tried. A federal Senate, whose president was styled *árchon*, met at Corfù, and a local council of nobles sat in each island. But the democrats found this arrangement too aristocratic, and the federalists found that it tended to separation. Cephalonia and Ithaca proclaimed their independence, and Zante hoisted the British flag. A National Assembly was held at Corfù, and the other islands were left to look after themselves. Then Russia intervened and granted one of those constitutions which she is fond of bestowing on her "spheres of influence" outside her direct dominions. But the returning French made short work with Ionian self-government. Napoleon was more than ever convinced of the strategic importance of Corfù; "the greatest misfortune that could happen to me," he said, "would be its loss." So he now organised the Ionian Islands on a purely military footing; the native Senate had no power, and the

French governed absolutely, to the great disgust of the inhabitants. But this second French occupation was not much longer than the first. The British took Zante, Cephalonia, Ithaca, and Cerigo in October 1809, with the object of protecting Sicily, then occupied by our troops, and Santa Mavra in April 1810. Brigadier Oswald organised these islands, and military governors were appointed. But, as the frequent changes of those officials caused inconvenience, Lieut.-General James Campbell was appointed Civil and Military Governor. Two out of the seven islands—Corfù and Paxo—alone remained to the French. Paxo was taken in February 1814, but the blockade of Corfù proved futile. Napoleon wrote that " Corfù acquires more importance every day ; for the English, if they were its masters, would be masters of the Adriatic too." But, if he prized it as " the key of the Adriatic," if an Ionian Academy was founded under his auspices, he did nothing for its economic interests. The Corfiote trade was ruined by the blockade ; the superb olive-trees of the island were cut down by the French troops ; and when the French government ordered its surrender to the British upon the first fall of Napoleon in pursuance of the convention of Paris of April 23, 1814, an order executed on June 24, the French administration, though the French governor Donzelot personally left behind him pleasant memories, had contented the islanders as little as that of Venice or that of Russia.

Napoleon's designs for the partition of Turkey at Tilsit were modified in 1808, when he again met the Tsar at Erfurt. He had learned to see the hopelessness of any large plan of operations in the east, while he had the west upon his hands. He now conceded Moldavia and Wallachia alone to Russia, took nothing for himself from Turkey, and joined with the Tsar in guaranteeing the other Turkish provinces. The result of these negotiations was to induce Britain and Turkey to end their mutual hostilities, and in 1809 to sign the peace of the

Dardanelles. But in spite of a brief armistice, the Russo-Turkish war continued. The Russians once more found that it was not an easy matter to conquer their hereditary enemies; but the victory rested with them. They crossed the Danube, and, more fortunate than in 1854, took the strong fortress of Silistria. The Danubian towns of Nikopolis, Svishtov, and Rustchuk passed into their hands, when the changing policy of Napoleon caused them to pause. The Tsar, foreseeing the French Emperor's impending attack upon him, had to withdraw troops for the defence of his own dominions. As in 1829, so in 1812, Russia played what the "new diplomacy" would call "a game of bluff." She pretended to have in her hands cards which she did not possess. She pretended that her differences with Napoleon would be arranged peacefully, and, having gained a considerable success over the Turks, expressed a willingness to negotiate. The Turkish government, mindful of the way in which Napoleon had thrown over his good friend, the Sultan, at Tilsit, paid no heed to the arguments of the French agents in favour of continuing the war. The Russian demands were moderate, and they were accepted. There was no question now of a Russian annexation of the Danubian Principalities as a whole. But by the treaty of Bucharest in 1812 the Tsar received the territory between the Dniester and the Pruth, which is known by the generic name of Bessarabia. For the Roumanians the cession of Bessarabia was a terrible blow. Austria had taken from them the Bukovina; now Russia took another piece of their land. During the six years of the war they had learned to dread their "liberators," who were quartered upon them, who made them labour at the fortifications and provide waggons and oxen for the transport service, who extorted large sums from the nobles, sold titles to the highest bidder, flooded the country with a debased currency, and favoured the Greek monks at the expense of the natives. The full information which we possess on the state of Moldavia and Wallachia at this period proves the utter misery of the poor, the utter corruption of the rich, the utter demoralisation of all classes under the Russian occupation. Wherever the Russian armies passed "the earth groaned," says a chronicler; and, to crown all, in spite of the protests of the native aristocracy and its efforts to convince the Porte of its folly in yielding so rich a prize, Bessarabia was to go to swell the dominions of the Tsar, and the Pruth was to become the frontier of his empire.

The treaty of Bucharest was a fatal blunder on the part of Turkey; less than a month after its signature Napoleon formally declared war against Russia; and the Sultan, regretting his undue haste in making peace, disgraced his Grand Vizier and cut off the heads of his plenipotentiaries. But the influence of Great Britain, once more in the ascendant at Constantinople and once more directed to the great object of breaking the power of the French colossus, restrained the ardour of the war party. Moreover, the internal state of Turkey was such as to demand the undivided attention of the government. Servia was in arms against the Sultan; Ali of Joánnina was practically independent in Epirus; Pasvanoglu had found a successor at Vidin; great chieftains kept armies of their own in Thrace and Macedonia. Still, it is probable that, as at the treaty of Falksen a century earlier, so at Bucharest in 1812, the Turks, without much risk, might have obtained better terms. On both occasions they were sold by their agents; on both occasions Russia got better terms than she could have expected. The Sultan, it is true, endeavoured to recover Bessarabia through the good offices of Austria at the congress of Vienna after the fall of Napoleon. But he only received the reply that such a retrocession was out of the question. Russia, on her part, did all she could to prevent the inhabitants of her new province from emigrating to join their brothers in Moldavia; and so closely did she guard the frontier that the Moldaves, accustomed to draw their supplies of food from Bessarabia, suffered great privations.

The career of Napoleon was over, and but little of his great plans of conquest in the east had been accomplished; even of that little practically nothing remained. His seven "Illyrian Provinces" were restored to Austria; the Ionian Islands were, after a long discussion, erected into an independent state under the protection of Great Britain. At the congress of Vienna the British plenipotentiary had proposed that the islands should be placed under an Austrian protectorate —a proposal which had much to commend it. As the heir of Venice, the Austrian Emperor could claim to have inherited the former Venetian possessions, while the master of Corfù commanded the approach to the Adriatic and would protect the Austrian seaboard in Dalmatia. This was, however, opposed by the Tsar, who urged that the wishes of the islanders for a British protectorate should be respected. For this argument there was much to be said. Great Britain had conquered six of the seven islands from the French; and her troops were occupying the seventh by virtue of its surrender by the new French government. At the congress of Paris the British representatives accordingly proposed that the seven islands and their former dependencies on the mainland and elsewhere should pass under the complete sovereignty of King George III. The Russian plenipotentiary, Count Capo d'Istria, himself a Corfiote and destined to be the future President of Greece, insisted, however, on the freedom and independence of the islands, and was willing to cede no more than a protectorate over them and their former dependencies to Great Britain. The final arrangement, signed at Paris in 1815, was that the Seven Islands and the small islets depending on them should form an independent state, under the denomination of "the United States of the Ionian Islands," and under a British protectorate. As Lord Bathurst, the Colonial Secretary of that date, under whose department the islands were placed, saw clearly enough, this arrangement was unsatisfactory and incomplete. It placed the British government in an invidious position, because it enabled the Ionians, who were not easily contented, to represent Great Britain as a tyrannical power whose main object was to repress their liberties. Moreover, the settlement was incomplete in another way. For the former dependencies of the islands on the mainland, which had been awarded to Turkey, as we have seen, by the Russo-Turkish convention of 1800, were allowed to remain a part of the Ottoman empire. Párga alone of them was still unconquered; and the subsequent fate of that place showed what an error had been committed by the British diplomatists in this affair. Count Capo d'Istria, while unwilling to grant Great Britain the absolute sovereignty over the Ionian Islands and their dependencies on the continent, was nevertheless most anxious that the latter should not be severed from the former under his scheme for a British protectorate. The British, however, contended that if they could not have the absolute sovereignty they would have nothing to do with the continental dependencies of the islands. They were undesirous of mixing themselves up in Turkish affairs and of disturbing the Turkish occupation. Unlike the Venetians, who had styled those places in Epirus " the eyes and ears of the Republic" on the mainland, the British showed in 1815, as at much later periods, that they cared very little for, perhaps understood very little about, that Balkan peninsula which Napoleon had tried to partition, but which even his genius had found an insoluble problem.

CHAPTER III

THE SERVIAN RISINGS (1804-17)

WHILE Napoleon was sketching the dismemberment of the Turkish empire in Europe, that empire was being shaken by a revolution from within. Servia, which since its final absorption in Turkey in 1459 had given the government comparatively little trouble, was convulsed by a movement which, from small beginnings, led to the complete independence of that country and heralded the struggles of other Balkan races for freedom.

In its first stage the Servian rising was not directed against the Turkish government, but against the Janissaries; and the Serbs long protested that they were loyal to the Sultan, and only wished to live in peace under his paternal rule. Their land had suffered more than any other part of Europe from the presence of the terrible band of men which was at this time the scourge of the Turkish empire and the dread of neighbouring realms. As the Belgrade pashalik, like that of Bagdad, was far removed from the capital, it was the custom to send thither the most turbulent members of the Janissaries' corps. They had constantly outraged the Hungarian frontier; and at the treaty of Svishtov it had been stipulated that they should be withdrawn from Servia. Many of them entered the service of Pasvanoglu; but, when that rebel was induced to make peace with his sovereign and appointed pasha of Vidin in 1799, he stipulated that the Porte should fulfil the promise which he had made to the Janissaries and restore them to the pashalik of 'Belgrade. The Porte, anxious to weaken

Pasvanoglu's forces or else desirous to pacify him at the cost of the Serbs, consented in an evil hour; and the Janissaries came back to their old hunting-ground. Austria was too much occupied with western affairs to protest against the infraction of the treaty; and it seemed as if the former bad state of things had returned with the returning Janissaries. But a great deal had happened since they had left Servia. The Serbs had been governed for the last five years by a pasha, Hajji Mustapha, so mild and just, that they called him their "mother," and the Turks branded him as a "renegade." No Turkish ruler was ever more beloved by his Christian subjects. With an enlightenment rare in the east, he did all he could to encourage trade, put down violence with a firm hand, and allowed the Serbs to rebuild their ruinous churches and monasteries. He had armed them against Pasvanoglu and his Janissaries for the defence of Servia during one of that rebel's invasions; and their national spirit, already kindled by the late Austro-Turkish war, was thus further aroused. It was in this state of public feeling that the Janissaries arrived.

Those masterful pretorians at once saw that, so long as Hajji Mustapha lived, they could not do as they pleased, and they lost little time in plotting his destruction. Another invasion of Pasvanoglu gave them the desired opportunity; and, in 1801, at a moment when Belgrade was denuded of troops, they murdered the pasha in the fortress, and their four chiefs divided his pashalik among themselves. The Sultan, occupied with the war against France, was unable to send an army against them; and, at their request, replaced the dead pasha by a successor, who, as an ex-captain of Janissaries, was their willing tool. The leaders now reassumed the title of *dahi*, and governed the people, Mohammedan as well as Christian, in the most arbitrary manner. The administration of justice was in their hands; and, in order further to secure their position, they invited kindred spirits from Bosnia and Albania to plunder the province, which they treated as their private property. No wonder that brigandage, which had almost ceased under Hajji Mustapha, began to reappear; and it was calculated that a tenth of the population took to the mountains. The Mohammedan *spahi*, seeing their privileges as landowners threatened, now joined hands with the Christians against the common oppressors. Through their instrumentality a petition was sent to the Sultan setting forth the grievances of the Serbs; and the Sultan replied by threatening the Janissaries, that, if they continued in their evil practices, he would send against them an army, "not of Turks, but of men of another faith and another race." By a process of exhaustion the Janissaries arrived at the conclusion that these words could only refer to the Serbs; and they at once resolved to anticipate an attack by murdering all the prominent men of that race. Early in 1804 they carried out their plan. But the massacre of the Servian head-men provoked the Servian revolution; and, as the result proved, Alexa Nenadovich and the other victims of the Janissaries died for their country just as much as if they had fallen fighting on the field of battle. The news spread like wildfire; the people flew to arms; and, as usually happens when a leader is wanted, a leader was found in the person of George Petrovich, better known as Kara George.

Of the two great men, Kara George and Milosh, who have left a name in the history of modern Servia, the former was born about 1760 in the cottage of a peasant, who made a living by keeping bees. "Black" George, as his comrades called him, alike in Turkish and Serb, from his dark features, grew up in the grim Servian forest without learning to read or write. He served as a swine-herd and made a little money in what was then, as now, the chief branch of Servian trade. When the war seemed about to break out between Austria and Turkey in 1787, he fled with his family to Austria, and, as his father refused to quit his native land, either shot him, or had him shot, according to the most favourable version, at the command of his mother. He took part in the war with the volunteers on the Austrian side, became a brigand, and then, at the peace, fled again to Austria. Hajji Mustapha's mild rule attracted him back to Servia; and at this period he was living quietly as a pig-dealer in the village of Topola. When the *dahi* resolved upon the massacre of the principal Serbs, his was one of the names on their black list. But he escaped their attempts to kill him and became the saviour of his countrymen and the avenger of their wrongs.

In February 1804 a body of Serbs assembled at Orashatz and chose him as their chief. Kara George was unwilling to accept the post, for he felt that his ungovernable temper would disqualify him for the management of men. But his fellows would have no other leader, so he finally accepted their offer and at once issued an appeal to the Servian head-men, wealthy yeomen and tradesmen to join him. At first there was a tendency to view the rising with suspicion. The Serbs thought that the revolutionists might be only common brigands, who followed the approved Balkan method of robbing the people whom they claimed to liberate. In the district of Valjevo, however, two influential men, Jacob and Matthew Nenadovich, respectively brother and son of the Nenadovich murdered by the Janissaries, raised the standard of revolt, and spread the pious fraud that Kara George was the accredited agent of the Sultan, and that it was their duty, as his Majesty's loyal subjects, to aid the Servian chief against the rebellious Janissaries. This argument convinced the people that the movement had the Sultan's sanction, and no further incentives were needed. Selim was known to be a reformer and an enemy of the Janissaries; and it was against them, not against him, that the Serbs had a grievance. It is a striking proof of the peculiar character of the Servian revolution in its first stage, that the leaders everywhere ordered their followers to spare those Mussulmans who had no connexion with the Janissaries.

The latter at once saw their danger, and in vain tried to bribe Kara George, who refused alike their money and their promises, unless the latter were guaranteed by the Austrian government. At that time the Serbs regarded Austria as their natural protectress. She was their nearest neighbour ; she had occupied their country on more than one occasion; she had thousands of Servian subjects. To her accordingly the Servian leaders turned. Kara George even went so far as to offer the whole of Servia to the Emperor and to ask him to send some member of the Imperial house as a viceroy. The offer was tempting, but it was refused; and the Hungarian statesman who, in our own day, became the regenerator of Bosnia, thought the refusal a mistake. A more moderate suggestion— that Austria should attempt to reconcile the two parties in Servia—was, however, adopted ; and a conference was held at Semlin, under Austrian auspices, between the Servian leaders and the *dahi.* The conference was a failure, but the Austrians continued to favour the cause of the insurgents. The authorities at the frontier allowed arms and provisions to be smuggled across it; numbers of Hungarian Serbs joined the revolutionists; and, while the poet Obradovich placed half his property at their disposal, officers who had fought in the Austrian army furnished much-needed strategical knowledge. Everywhere the insurgents were successful; and, at last, the Sultan, becoming alarmed, resolved to send the vizier of Bosnia, who had already had experience in Servia, to restore order in that pashalik. At the vizier's approach the *dahi* fled to the island of Ada Kaleh in the Danube near Orsova, a fortress which is even now one of the curiosities of the near east. Here they were killed by the Serbs ; and with their death it might have seemed that the insurrection, having attained its object, would collapse.

But the Serbs, flushed with victory, were not content with what would have contented them a short time before. They insisted that an Austrian commissioner should be appointed to see that the agreement between the Sultan and his subjects was faithfully carried out, while the vizier declared such an interference by a foreign Power in the internal affairs of his master's dominions to be simply "impossible." No compromise seemed practicable, and the vizier returned to Bosnia, leaving matters much as they were before. Having little faith in the power of the Sultan to enforce reforms, and having failed to induce Austria to break her treaty engagements with Turkey and take their country under her protection, some of the Servian leaders now bethought them of the two Slav states, little Montenegro and big Russia. From Montenegro there was nothing to be obtained, so Matthew Nenadovich and two others set out on an embassy to the distant court of the great Tsar. Kara George had threatened Austria that he would apply elsewhere for help if she refused. The Metropolitan of Karlovitz, the spiritual head of the Hungarian Serbs, one of those intriguers common in the near east, who disguise the politician under the robes of the priest, had already prepared the way by submitting a memorandum to the Russian Minister for Foreign Affairs, in which he advocated the constitution of Servia, increased at Austrian expense by the addition of Syrmia and an outlet on the sea at Cattaro, as an autonomous, tributary Turkish province, governed by a Russian Grand-duke or a Protestant Prince. But the Minister was inclined to favour neither the scheme of the Metropolitan nor the prayers of the deputation. At that moment Russia regarded it as desirable to maintain the integrity of the Turkish empire; and the only advice of her Foreign Secretary was to petition the Sultan for a redress of grievances. But the incident is important as showing thus early the tendency of Servian politicians to play off Russia against Austria, which has, almost ever since then, been the key-note of their public affairs.

The Sultan, now thoroughly alarmed at the prospect of a dismemberment of his empire, resolved to finish with the too officious loyalty of his Servian subjects. The governor of Nish was appointed vizier of Belgrade and sent to restore order. Encouraged by the instigations of Constantine Hypselántes, Hospodar of Wallachia, and believing that, after all, Russia would help them, the Serbs resisted. A battle ensued, and for the first time the insurgents fought against their sovereign, and conquered. The eyes of the Mussulmans were opened, and it became clear to them, as to the Serbs, that the "loyal rising" had become a revolution against the Sultan. The latter employed the breathing-space which followed the Turkish defeat in forming a species of government for the management of their affairs. From the old days of Servian independence there had survived the custom of holding an assembly of the people, called *Skupshtina*; and such an assembly had been held by Kara George. A permanent Senate, or *Sovet*, was now formed by the election of a representative of each district into which the pashalik was divided. Even in our day the Servian parliament-house was not an imposing assembly; but that primitive senate, which met in a desolate monastery where there were no beds and no provisions but one sack of flour, was as far removed as possible from our idea of parliamentary institutions. Nor had it much real power, for Kara George was the practical ruler of the land.

Even now the Serbs had not thought of separation from Turkey, and made further appeals to the Sultan for peace and to the Emperors of Austria and Russia for intervention. But the Sultan was resolved to put down what he now regarded as a rebellion against his lawful authority, and his forces invaded Servia in 1806. The Servian victory at Mishar, near Shabatz, which has been glorified by the national bards, seemed likely to induce both sides to make peace. But the Russo-Turkish war began, and Napoleon advised the Sultan to refuse the moderate Servian demands. The Serbs gained one success after another, but marred their successes by the treacherous massacre of the Belgrade garrison. At the beginning of 1807 they were masters of the whole pashalik;

and for the first time in their history a Russian corps fought
side by side with them against the Turks.   And while they
had held their own, their former masters were fighting among
themselves.   Selim III had endeavoured to get rid of the
Janissaries, and they had got rid of him ; he had attempted
to reform his state, and, like all Turkish reformers, he had
failed.   His French sympathies, his European ideas, his military
system, made him unpopular with the old school of Turks.
The Mussulman religion was the natural ally of the conservative party in the capital.   Bigotry, vested interests, and brute
force won an easy victory over the well-meaning Sultan.   The
Sheikh-ul-Islâm issued an ambiguous decision, which was
interpreted as a justification of the sovereign's deposition.   A
captain of the Turkish pretorians emulated the conduct of the
Roman soldiery and placed Mustapha IV on the throne, whence
he had expelled Selim.   One palace revolution followed
another in rapid succession.   Selim and Mustapha both
perished by violence in 1808 ; and Mahmûd II, who was to
be the greatest reformer of modern Turkey, but had the
wisdom to conceal his plans till he was strong enough to put
them into force, ruled in their place.

Meanwhile the influence of Russia had become more
marked in Servian affairs.   In 1807 the first official agent of
the Tsar arrived in Belgrade as a proof that the ruler of All
the Russias had extended his paternal care to the Serbs.   A
convention was made between the two governments, by which
it was stipulated that the new state should be under the Tsar's
protection, and that the protector should keep up Russian
garrisons in the country and name all its officials.   But, when
the armistice caused a lull in the Russo-Turkish war, Russia
abandoned Servia, and was only induced to renew her protectorate when Austria made overtures of a similar kind to
Kara George.   Russian statesmen saw that Servia might be
useful to them as a means of keeping their rival, Austria, in
check ; and the unhappy little country had already begun to

be regarded as a mere pawn in the diplomatic game. When
hostilities recommenced, and the Turks, in spite of the heroic
defence of Deligrad, defeated the Serbs, the Russian agent
ran away, leaving his *protégés* unprotected. Two parties made
their appearance in the state, the one pro-Russian, the other
anti-Russian; and the sudden death of Milan Obrenovich, the
leader of the former faction, was ascribed by some to Kara
George, and considered by later writers as the beginning of
that feud between the Obrenovich and Karageorgevich families,
which was till 1903 the bane of Servia. Instead of acting
patriotically together, the peasant statesmen quarrelled among
themselves, and at times showed, like true Orientals, that they
regarded public positions not as places of trust, but as places of
profit. The Russophils procured the rejection of the Turkish
offer to give to Servia practically the same administration as
that of the two Danubian Principalities. But they soon found,
as the Principalities did, that the Tsar recognised no claims upon
his gratitude. We have already stigmatised the Russian treatment of the Roumanians at the peace of Bucharest in 1812; the
fate of the Serbs, who had co-operated with the Russian armies,
who had been led to expect help from the Russian protectorate,
was almost as bad. The eighth article of that treaty abandoned
them to such tender mercies as the Turkish government, now
released from the pre-occupation of the Russian war, might
mete out to them. The Turks were to occupy the old, and
the Serbs to demolish the new, Servian fortresses; the Porte
promised to the Serbs "the same advantages as those enjoyed by
the islanders of the Archipelago," "the management of their
internal affairs," and "moderate taxes, to be received directly
from themselves"; besides, there was a good deal of vague writing about "clemency" and other un-Oriental virtues. The
Russian regiment, which had been in garrison at Belgrade
during the latter part of the war, left the country; and Europe
was too much occupied with the great struggle against Napoleon
to concern itself about the fate of this little nation beyond the

Danube. The same memorable year, 1813, that marked the
freedom of Germany from Napoleon, witnessed also the re-
conquest of Servia by the Turks. Nearly all the native
chieftains, like Kara George, losing nerve, crossed into Austria ;
and no foreign intervention was possible. It has always been
so ; the eastern and the western questions cannot be solved
together ; when the great Powers are busy in flying at each
others' throats, the nationalities of the east must look after
themselves.

But it was at this moment that the second of Servia's two
modern heroes appeared on the scene, whence Kara George
and the other leaders of the late insurrection had fled. Milosh
Theodorovich Obrenovich had not played a very prominent
part in that movement. Nearly twenty years younger than
Kara George, he was the half-brother of that Milan whom
Kara George was suspected of having poisoned, and was so
devoted to him that he adopted his half-brother's surname,
Obrenovich, in which philologists trace the word *obrin*, the
Slav equivalent of the Avar race, which had once overrun the
Balkan peninsula. He, too, had begun life as a herdsman, had
come to riches and such honours as his native district could
bestow, and was raised to further distinctions by the returning
Turks as a reward for his aid in pacifying the people. The
new pasha of Belgrade, whose arm he had wounded in battle,
named him district official or *oborknes* of three districts, and
for a time he seemed to be content to use his influence in the
interest of the conquerors. Instead of heading an insurrection,
which broke out a year after the return of the Turks, he
actually suppressed it, thinking that the time had not yet come
for a successful uprising. But the cruelties of the victors
convinced him that nothing but force could avail against them ;
and the indignation of his fellow-countrymen showed him that
the moment had arrived for striking the decisive blow. On
Palm Sunday, 1815, he unfurled the banner of resistance
under the oak before the church at Takovo—a name ever-

memorable in Servian history, and to-day commemorated by one of the Servian orders. The assembled people swore to forget their differences and join in union against the common foe. The revolt spread all over the country, and some of the exiles began to return from their retreat in Austria. With the capture of the historic fortress of Passarovitz the insurgents gained the upper hand over the Turkish forces then on Servian soil. The state of western politics at this moment caused Mahmûd II to shrink from further hostilities, which might lead to Russian intervention. For Napoleon had now fallen; and the Russian ambassador in Constantinople had leisure to ask pointed questions of the Sultan and to remind him of the treaty of Bucharest. The British envoys to the congress of Vienna had declined to do anything for the Servian delegates, who had asked their aid; but Russia was nearer and more interested in the Balkans. An arrangement was made between the Turks and the Serbs. The latter retained their weapons, but acknowledged themselves to be the Sultan's vassals; the former allowed the Serbs to collect the taxes, and gave them a share in the administration of justice; a sort of national Senate was created at Belgrade for both these purposes. The insurgents had also gained the great advantage of having in Milosh a leader whose recent achievements had made him the representative of national feeling.

But personal jealousies have been the curse of the Balkan Christians. Milosh, great man as he was, could brook no rivals among his own countrymen; and his first acts after the restoration of peace were to remove all possible competitors. The first president of the new national Senate was, at his instigation, handed over to the Turkish pasha for summary execution. A haughty bishop, who treated Milosh with scant respect, was found murdered by robbers under suspicious circumstances. Black George himself met with a like fate. The former leader of the Serbs had secretly returned from his exile, full of hope that a fresh rising would free the land from the Turks, full of belief in the prospects of an organised insurrection in the Morea, which would divide the attention of the Sultan.   He urged Milosh to unite with him in the national cause.   But the crafty Obrenovich had no intention of sharing his glory with another.   He informed the pasha of Kara George's presence in the country ; the pasha bade him send the Liberator's head to Belgrade.   The order was carried out on June 24, 1817 by Vuitza Vulichevich, the mayor of Semendria, probably at Milosh's orders ; and the gory trophy, after having been identified to the satisfaction of the pasha, was dispatched to Constantinople for the edification of the Sultan.   Thus perished the first pioneer of Servian freedom, and by his death bequeathed to his countrymen a legacy of hate, which survived to the third generation.   At length, freed from all rivals, Milosh was recognised in November 1817 by all the head-men as their chief, who also conceded that, after his death, his next-of-kin should succeed him.

The first act in the drama of Balkan emancipation was over ; Servia had led the way ; now Greece was to follow, and compel the attention of the Powers to the eastern question.

CHAPTER IV

THE PREFACE OF GREEK INDEPENDENCE (1815-21)

THE settlement of Europe in 1815 affected those Greeks alone who inhabited the islands which down to 1797 had been in the possession of the Venetian Republic, and which since that date, except for their brief career as a "Septinsular Republic," had belonged to the French till one island after another had fallen into British hands. The convention of November 5, 1815, formed Corfù, Cephalonia, Zante, Santa Mavra, Ithaca, Cerigo, and Paxo with their dependent islets into "The United States of the Ionian Islands" under the protection of King George III and his successors. It was stipulated that a resident "Lord High Commissioner" should be appointed, who should convoke a legislative assembly for the purpose of drawing up a new constitution. Meanwhile the existing constitutional arrangements were to remain in force.

The southern islands of the Ionian group were already accustomed to the just, if autocratic, administration established there by their captor, Sir Hudson Lowe, the future gaoler of Napoleon ; while Sir James Campbell, to whom the French commander had surrendered Corfù in 1814, had gained such popularity with the Corfiotes, that they petitioned the British government to appoint him as first Lord High Commissioner. Instead, however, the government sent Sir Thomas Maitland, brother of Lord Lauderdale, and governor of Malta, where his despotic character had won him the nickname of "King Tom." The wisdom of this choice might well have been questioned ;

for the first Lord High Commissioner, if able and honest, was a rough soldier, who looked like a bull-dog, whose language surprised the elegant Ionians by its coarseness, and whose convivial habits disgusted a naturally abstemious people. Meanwhile, however, the Seven Islands greeted the new order of things with demonstrations of joy; Cephalonia addressed Maitland as "a new Aristides"; and an Ionic temple at Corfù, and monuments in other islands, still commemorate the services of the benevolent autocrat, to whom a strange fate had entrusted the poetic realms of Odysseus and Alkinoos.

Sir Thomas Maitland, who arrived early in 1816, came to the conclusion, as the result of recent experience and of his own personal temperament and observation, that the Ionians were not yet fitted for the management of their own affairs; and he therefore determined, as he must grant them a constitution, to give them the appearance, without the substance, of free institutions. He nominated a "Primary Council" of eleven Ionians under the presidency of Baron Emmanuel Theotókes, charged with the task of convoking the Constituent Assembly. The president was a member of a famous Corfiote family, which had already produced one of the regenerators of the Greek language in the person of his uncle, and the president of the Senate of the Septinsular Republic in that of his father. At once a patriotic Greek and a firm friend of Great Britain, Baron Theotókes was obviously indicated for the post. A Constituent Assembly of 40 members was formed, 11 being already members of the "Primary Council" and the remaining 29 elected by the Islands from a double list of candidates, submitted by that body. Thanks to this plan, borrowed by Maitland from that devised by the Ionian plenipotentiary of Russia in 1803, the High Commissioner was able to summon an Assembly which would be subservient to his wishes. To this body the "Primary Council" submitted the draft of a constitution, which was unanimously passed on May 2, 1817. This charter created a bicameral legislature—a "Legislative

Assembly," composed of 11 " integral " or *ex-officio* members, and of 29 members elected in the same manner as the Constituent: and a " Senate " of six persons, of whom four, representing the four larger islands, and one representing the three smaller islands by rotation, were elected by, and out of, the " Legislative Assembly," subject to the veto of the High Commissioner, while the sixth, or President, was nominated by the sovereign through the medium of the High Commissioner, from the ranks of the Ionian nobles.　Both Chambers received salaries and travelling expenses; the term of both was five years; that of the President of the Senate half that period. But this official, who could be re-nominated, bore in compensation the title of " Highness," was received with military honours, and was the most important person in the Ionian state after the High Commissioner, upon whose favour, however, he depended for his appointment and its renewal.　As the right of summoning the legislature in extraordinary session— it ordinarily met on March 1 of every other year—and that of advising the Crown to dissolve it resided in the High Commissioner, that official was practically omnipotent.　In the other six islands, he was represented by " Residents," while the Senate appointed their " Regents," usually local men, subject to his approval; and these " Regents " required that of his " Residents " for their acts.　The local municipal councils, of which the " Regents " were chairmen, were elected by open voting. The Senate elected, too, with his sanction, the two Ionian members of the " Supreme Council of Justice," while the two British judges were nominated by the Crown, and the High Commissioner and the President of the Senate were extraordinary members of this tribunal.　No printing-press, other than that of the government, could be erected without the consent of the Senate and the High Commissioner; and the official *Gazette of the United States of the Ionian Islands*, first published at Zante under a slightly different title in 1810 and subsequently transferred to Corfù, was long the sole Ionian newspaper.

This journal was printed for many years in Italian only; and, although the Greek Church and the Greek language were declared to be the predominant creed and idiom, English was employed in the police, sanitary, and postal departments, Italian in the legislature till 1849, and the national tongue was not made obligatory in the public offices till 1852. Such was the system, under which the Islands were governed for upwards of 30 years.

The Ionian constitution of 1817, illiberal as it may seem now, was characteristic of that age, and must be judged by its results. The Ionian Islands had for the previous 20 years been the sport of faction, and above all else needed repose and a just administration of the law. Maitland left the franchise, as he found it, the privilege of the nobles, while he benefited the peasants by prohibiting usurious loans which reduced them to the position of bondsmen, by facilitating the sale of land, and by beginning those splendid roads, which are the best monument of British rule in the Islands. His abolition of the ballot was a mistake, for it led to feuds and intimidation. Believing that well-paid officials have fewer temptations, he attached high salaries to the principal posts, and deliberately increased the offices in order to provide employment for the natives, to whom all professions except the church, the law, and medicine, were unfortunately closed, and for whom commerce had few attractions. The creation of the order of St Michael and St George, and the high-sounding epithets of senators and deputies, gratified the Ionian love of titles. Thus the nobles, especially at the seat of government, became the strongest supporters of the British protectorate.

An event soon occurred, however, which exposed the British to great odium and is still remembered in Greek lands as an error of British policy. The Russo-Turkish convention of March 21, 1800, had ceded to Turkey the former continental dependencies of the Ionian Islands, on condition of the observance of their ancient privileges; and the subsequent convention, which had placed the Islands under British protection, had made special allusion to this arrangement. By this time all the four continental dependencies, except Párga, had fallen into the hands of Ali Pasha of Joánnina. Párga, however, had been garrisoned by order of Napoleon, when the French recovered the Ionian Islands in 1807, on the ground that the treaty of 1800 had been annulled by Ali's violation of the clause which had guaranteed the ancient privileges of the ex-Venetian dependencies. Accordingly it was held by a French force till March 22, 1814, when Sir Charles Gordon, British Commandant of the opposite island of Paxo, occupied the place at the invitation of the inhabitants, anxious lest the French should hand it over to Ali[1]. The Parguinotes appear to have believed that their request for the union of their home with the Ionian Islands, as in Venetian times, had been granted. The Prince Regent approved the occupation of their town; a British officer was thenceforth stationed there; and it certainly seemed as if they, like the Islanders, were to enjoy the protection of the British Crown. Turkey, however, demanded the execution of the treaty of 1800; and Sir Thomas Maitland, who asserted that no "assurance of a more permanent connection[2]" had been given at the time of the occupation in 1814, and who calculated that the retention of the place would cost £50,000 a year, proceeded to carry out the cession.

Accordingly, early in 1817, Lieut.-Col. De Bosset, a Swiss officer in the British service, was sent to prepare the Parguinotes for the transfer of their home to the Sultan, and to inform all who desired to emigrate, that they would receive compensation for the loss of their houses and property, and a free passage to the Ionian Islands. The inhabitants unanimously expressed their resolve to leave their beloved home rather than become Turkish subjects, exposed to the tender mercies of the terrible pasha of Joánnina. The difficulty of arriving at a valuation of their property caused however, a long delay. The owners

---

[1] *Papers relating to the military occupation of Parga*, p. 3.

[2] *Papers relating to Parga*, p. 49.

assessed its value at nearly £600,000; the Ottoman commissioners at only £56,756; Corfiote valuers, judging by the standard of the islands, appraised it at £280,000; whereas Maitland insisted on deducting from this latter sum one-third, because the property was situated on the continent, and a quarter more, because the payment was to be in ready money. He, therefore, informed the Parguinotes that no more than £150,000 would be paid. After first digging up and burning the bones of their ancestors, the homeless population, save two families, abandoned Párga; and on May 10, 1819, the Turkish flag replaced (*proh pudor !*) the Union Jack, and the last free Greek community became extinct. But, on their arrival in Corfù, they did not receive their compensation without further deductions. As Ali had proposed to pay in depreciated coin, Maitland knocked off £8000 in consideration of payment in good metal, thus reducing the amount to £142,000, and provisionally retained a further sum of about one per cent. for freight and the expenses of the commission, the return of which sum the Parguinotes refused to accept as a definitive settlement. The government promised to build a church for them, and the exiles were provided with houses rent-free in the Corfiote suburb of Mandoúchio, where their descendants still reside. In the garrison-church of Corfù may still be seen the sacred pictures and the other furniture of the church at Párga, which had been placed there "until the day when the old home shall once more be free." Now that that day, long promised, but long postponed, has at last arrived, the cession of Párga, denounced in the Italian verses of Berchet and with greater force in the Greek of a famous ballad, will cease to rankle in the breasts of a high-spirited people, which had never forgiven the British for surrendering, albeit in strict observance of an international treaty, its altars and its hearths to the Turk.

Ali Pasha had now attained the object of his desires. But the Sultan had long been alarmed at his nominal subject's growing independence, and struck at the too powerful satrap in the person of his second son, Vely, already removed from the governorship of the Morea to that of Lárissa, and now further degraded to the less important pashalik of Lepanto. Ali saw in this deliberate stroke of policy the hand of a personal enemy, Ismael Pasho Bey, an Albanian and a former friend, who had fled to Constantinople and had there obtained the favour of the Sultan. Accustomed to remove every obstacle from his path, the pasha of Joánnina hired assassins to murder his foe. The attempt, however, failed; the assassins confessed; and the indignant Sultan declared Ali a rebel and an outlaw, and conferred his pashalik upon his intended victim. Thus threatened with destruction by his sovereign, Ali perforce appealed to the Greeks for assistance. There was nothing remarkable in this appeal to men of that race and creed; for the pasha, Mussulman though he was, had never trusted his Mohammedan retainers and had never founded a mosque, but had utilised the Greek bishops as his agents, had built churches for their flocks, had used their language as the means of his diplomatic correspondence, and had encouraged its study in the two colleges, which Greek patriotism and love of learning had erected at Joánnina, where Greek was spoken more grammatically than elsewhere. To the Albanians he spoke of independence, to the Greeks of a constitution; one of the former, Omer Vriónes, who had won fame and wealth fighting the Mamelukes of Egypt, and one of the latter, Odysseús, son of the famous klepht Androútsos, espoused his cause. But the Greeks as a whole showed little sympathy with the tyrant, whose cruelties had made him feared throughout Epirus. Everywhere the Sultan's troops were successful; Párga, Ali's last acquisition, submitted, and Ismael invited the exiled Parguinotes to return; Omer Vriónes deserted; even Ali's sons, Muktar and Vely, surrendered, the one Berat and Argyrókastron, the other Préveza; while the exiled Souliotes, mindful of the treatment inflicted upon their home, crossed over from Corfù, under Márko Bótzares, to assist the Turkish authorities against the rebel. Ali was besieged in his capital, and felt compelled to lay that flourishing town in ashes lest it should afford cover to the besiegers. But Ismael Pasho, the Turkish commander, irritated, instead of conciliating, the Christians of the province which had been conferred upon him as Ali's successor. His exactions made one chieftain after another abandon his side; and the Souliotes, still kept out of their promised home and their promised pay, consented to forgive the cruelties of their ancient enemy and entered the service of Ali Pasha. Convinced of Ismael's incapacity, the Sultan entrusted the supreme command to Kurshid Pasha, the governor of the Morea and a veteran who had had Egyptian experience. But the new commander had scarcely arrived at Joánnina when a fresh danger menaced Turkey on the eastern side of the Balkan peninsula.

During the previous six years a secret organisation, known as the *Philikè Hetairía*, or "Friendly Society," had been gradually working to promote a rising of the Greeks against Turkish rule. Founded in 1814 at Odessa by Nicholas Skouphâs, a native of Arta, Athanásios Tsakálof of Joánnina, and Panagiótes Anagnostópoulos of Andrítsaina in the Morea, it was composed of seven classes, ranging from that of the *Vlámides* (an Albanian word signifying "adopted brothers") up to that of "the chiefs of the initiated," and was governed by a mysterious committee, known as "the Supreme Authority." For the first three years of its existence, the Society made little progress, but thenceforth its "apostles" made many proselytes in the islands and in the Morea; Petrobey Mavromichále, the Prince of Maina, was among those thus initiated; it was even suggested that Ali Pasha should join the organisation; officials of the Society, called "Consuls," were nominated at Levádeia; others, under the title of "Ephors," were appointed to direct its affairs at Bucharest, Jassy, and Galatz. Meanwhile, it was felt that the leadership of the movement should be entrusted to some individual of commanding position. The thoughts of the Greeks naturally turned to Count Capo d'Istria, the distinguished Corfiote, who had played the part of Hampden during the French occupation of his native island, had abandoned the practice of medicine for public employment under the "Septinsular Republic," and, on the restoration of French rule, had entered the Russian service, in which he had risen by the favour of Alexander I and his own diplomatic talents with such rapidity as to represent his adopted country at the congresses of Vienna, Paris, and Aix-la-Chapelle. Capo d'Istria declined, however, the proffered position, whereupon Xánthos, the emissary of the Society, betook himself to Prince Alexander Hypselántes, eldest son of one Hospodar, first of Moldavia and then of Wallachia, and grandson of another. A major-general in the Russian army, he had lost his right hand at the battle of Kulm ; and his noble birth, his Russian connexion, and his personal bravery combined to indicate him as the fitting commander of a Greek revolution, which would thus appear to have the sympathy of the Tsar. Hypselántes accepted, and on June 27, 1820, was recognised as "General Commissioner of the Supreme Authority."

It was his first intention to raise the standard of revolt in Greece itself; but he ultimately decided to begin operations in the Danubian Principalities, with which his ancestors had been connected so long. To a superficial observer Wallachia and Moldavia might seem the most suitable basis for his attack ; for John Carageà, the former Hospodar of Wallachia, had been comprised in the Society, and Alexander Soûtsos, his successor, who was hostile to the revolution, died of poison, it is said, early in 1821; while Michael II Soûtsos, Hospodar of Moldavia, and the historian Rízos Neroulós, his Minister for Foreign Affairs, were in correspondence with Hypselántes. But the native population of the two Principalities regarded the Phanariote Greeks as tyrants rather than liberators ; the

Roumanian peasants felt no enthusiasm for the Hellenic cause; and it thus came to pass that the same movement which rid Greece of the Turkish yoke emancipated the Roumanians from their Greek princes.

Confident, however, of success, Hypselántes crossed the Pruth, since 1812 the boundary between the Russian and the Turkish empires, on March 6, 1821, attended by a few followers, and entered the Moldavian capital without opposition. The Hospodar's guards went over to the Hetairist chief; the few Turkish soldiers in Jassy were disarmed; and Hypselántes and Soûtsos met in the house of the Minister. But the exercise of authority soon revealed the deficiencies of the revolutionary leader. Full of noble sentiments, he lacked experience of men and affairs. A manifesto, announcing that "a terrible power was prepared to punish the boldness of the Turks and annihilate them," annoyed the Russian government; the massacre of Turks at Galatz and Jassy excited the fanaticism of their compatriots; the extortion of blackmail from a local banker in the interest of the cause frightened other capitalists. The Tsar, then engaged at Laibach in suppressing revolution at Naples, repudiated all sympathy with Hypselántes, and struck his name from the Russian army list; the Œcumenical Patriarch, under pressure from the Sultan, excommunicated the would-be saviour of Greeks and the Hospodar of Moldavia. Hypselántes slowly marched to Bucharest; Soûtsos fled into Russian territory, the last Phanariote prince who has actually ruled over a Roumanian land.

Arrived in Wallachia, Hypselántes found a further obstacle in the shape of a native, and indeed a nationalist, revolution. Upon the death of Alexander Soûtsos, a small noble, Tudor (or Theodore) Vladimirescu, so called from the Russian Order of St Vladimir which he had won in the last Russo-Turkish war, had raised a revolt in Little Wallachia against the nobles, Greek and Roumanian alike. This movement, at first social rather than political, became political and nationalist when its leader reached Bucharest. The native nobles saw that their best policy was to separate themselves from the Greeks, and divert the agitation, which seemed to savour of the French revolution, against the foreigners who had so long governed their country. Tudor came to terms with the "patriot" nobles, who disavowed all hostility to the Sultan; and thus his agitation was thenceforth diametrically opposed to that of Hypselántes. "Greece," he told the Hetairist chief, "belongs to the Greeks, and Roumania to the Roumans." Meanwhile, the Turks were making active preparations to retain it for themselves; a Turkish army entered Bucharest; and Hypse lántes, suspecting his rival of treachery, ordered his arrest, and then allowed him to be butchered without mercy. Denounced as a traitor by the Greeks, the murdered man is extolled as a patriot by his fellow-countrymen, who trace the re-establishment of their native princes to his revolution.

Hypselántes did not long maintain his position in Wallachia after the suppression of his native rival On June 19, the "sacred battalion," which he had formed out of young Greeks of the upper and middle classes, and which was under the command of his brother Nicholas, was cut to pieces, after a brave resistance, by the Turks at Dragashani. Upon receiving the news of this defeat, Alexander Hypselántes thought only of his own safety. By means of a forged letter, he pretended that he had been summoned to the Austrian frontier to discuss the military operations which the Emperor of Austria was, according to this fiction, about to undertake against the Turks. Abandoning his soldiers to their fate, he fled with two of his brothers into Austrian territory, from which secure position he issued an insulting proclamation to the men whom he had betrayed. For once, however, the policy of Metternich coincided with the requirements of poetic justice. The fugitive leader was arrested, and languished for six years the prisoner of the Emperor, in whose capital he died an exile in 1828.

The Greeks who remained behind behaved with a courage which contrasted with the conduct of their leaders. Prince George Cantacuzene, who commanded the insurgent forces in Moldavia, imitated his chief, and retired to Russia. But his young Greek soldiers resolved to strike a final blow for their deserted cause. At Skuleni, the spot where Hypselántes had crossed the Pruth, this band of some 500 heroes made on June 29 its last stand against the Turks. Of that number about one-fourth, after a desperate fight, escaped by swimming the river; the rest perished on the field or in the stream, while the Russians from the opposite bank applauded their resistance. Even then, Georgákes of Mt Olympus, a military leader and an enthusiastic patriot, who had commanded the troops of Wallachia in the time of its last prince, held out in the Moldavian monastery of Seku till, finding further resistance useless, he set fire to the powder-magazine, and was blown to pieces by the explosion. His comrade, the Macedonian Pharmákes, continued to defend the rest of the building for about a fortnight longer, when, on October 4, he was induced to surrender by the promise that his life should be spared—a promise violated by his subsequent beheadal at Constantinople. Thus, after having lasted six months, the attempt of the Hetairists in the Danubian Principalities ended in failure. Splendid acts of heroism illuminated this sorry preface of the Greek revolution; and against the incapacity of Hypselántes may be set the actions of Dragashani and Skuleni.

If the campaign of Hypselántes had little influence upon the course of events in Greece, it contributed to a complete change in the government of the Roumans. The Sultan had, indeed, already entrusted both the vacant thrones of Wallachia and Moldavia to Charles Callimachi, a former Hospodar of the latter principality. But the double revolution prevented him from setting foot in either province, where he was accordingly represented by two Greek governors. But the native nobility, anxious for the abolition of the Phanariote administration of their country, which had existed since 1711, were able to point to the Hetairist movement as an example of the danger to which the Sultan's empire was exposed by the employment of a hostile race in such important positions of trust.   When the Greek insurrection in the principalities had been crushed, the Roumanian *boyars* accordingly petitioned the Turkish government that the two Hospodars should thenceforth be selected from their own ranks.   Their petition was granted, and in 1822 Gregory IV Ghika, a Roumanised Albanian, and John Sturdza, member of an ancient Roumanian family, were appointed to the respective thrones of Wallachia and Moldavia. Thus ended the rule of the Greeks over the Danubian Principalities at the time when that of the Turks over Greece was drawing to a close.   Greek and Roumanian independence were born together.

CHAPTER V

THE WAR OF GREEK INDEPENDENCE (1821-9)

BARELY a month after Hypselántes had crossed the Pruth the revolution broke out in the Morea. The time and the place were both favourable to the movement. The Turks were occupied with two rebellions, one beyond the Danube and the other at Joánnina, whither the governor of the Morea had gone to crush Ali Pasha, and they had to conduct simultaneously a Persian-war. The Peloponnese, where the Christians were in a large majority, possessed in the native magnates leaders of wealth and position; and a committee of seven "ephors" had lately been formed there for the purpose of disseminating and organising the schemes of the Hetairists. In the early spring of 1821, the moment seemed therefore to have arrived for a general rising.

A picturesque tradition, which has obtained official confirmation by the consecration of that day as a national festival, dates the outbreak of the Greek revolution from April 6 (March 25, O.S.), when Germanós, Metropolitan of Patras, raised the sacred banner representing the death of the Virgin in the church of the monastery of Hagía Lávra near Kalávryta[1]. But, like most insurrections, the Greek rising began with isolated attacks upon Mussulmans, which became frequent towards the end of March. On April 2, the revolt became

---

[1] I inspected the original banner, which is not a Greek flag, as usually represented, at the monastery, in 1912. Cf. Δελτίον τῆς Ἱστ. καὶ Ἐθν. Ἐτ. iii, 428-45.

general; on that day the Greeks besieged the Turks in Kalávryta; on the morrow Petrobey surrounded the garrison of Kalamáta. Both places capitulated, and a solemn service of thanksgiving to Almighty God was celebrated on the banks of the Nédon, whence the Bey of Maina, elected president of a Messenian Senate, addressed a manifesto to Christian Europe. Simultaneously with the fall of Kalamáta, an outbreak occurred at Patras; and the popular song which declared that "not a Turk should remain in the Morea" was translated into action by the massacre of thousands of Mussulmans throughout the peninsula, where a victory at Valtétsi near Tripolitsá was proof of the prowess of the Greeks. Thence the movement spread across the gulf of Corinth, where Sálona, crowned by its fine medieval castle, once again became a Christian stronghold. Athanásios, known as Diákos (or the "deacon") from his early monastic life, who had been in the service of Ali Pasha, secured the surrender of Levádeia, whose Mussulman population shared the fate of their compatriots in the Morea. But the heroic "deacon" was overpowered in an attempt to hold the bridge of Alamán between Thermopylae and Lamia, where his statue now commemorates the courage with which the Leonidas of modern Greece confronted the tortures of impalement. Odysseús, equally brave and more fortunate, defended the pass of Graviá. The peasants of Párnes easily captured the town of Athens, then a place of some 10,000 inhabitants[1], the residence of a French and an Austrian consul, the seat of a Turkish *voïvode*, and defended by a small garrison and by a wall hastily constructed by the tyrant Hajji Ali the Haseki on the occasion of the Albanian raid of 1778. But the Akropolis, refortified by the Turks after the Venetian siege, resisted till midsummer of the following year. In the west, Mesolónghi and Vrachôri (now called Agrínion) joined the national cause, so that within three months from the commencement of the revolution the whole country south of the Maliac and the Ambrakian gulfs,

---

[1] In 1822 a census showed 1235 houses. Lámpros, Μικταὶ Σελίδες, 549.

except the fortresses, was in Greek hands. Even further north, Anthimos Gazês, a Hetairist who ten years earlier had founded at Vienna the first Greek newspaper ever published, kindled the flames of revolt in the villages that nestled among "the folds of Pélion"; and a provisional government, bearing the august name of "the Assembly of Thessalo-Magnesia," was formed to direct the affairs of that district. The three peninsulas which jut out from Macedonia into the sea embraced the Hellenic cause; and even the monks of Mt Athos armed for a contest which seemed to be religious no less than national. But internal quarrels soon reduced the Thessalians beneath the rule of Dramali Pasha, and Tríkeri at the mouth of the gulf of Volo alone resisted all attacks; while Aboulabad, the governor of Salonika, put an end before the year had closed to the insurrection in the three peninsulas by the capture of Kassándra and by the military occupation of the Holy Mountain. Of the islands Spétsai was the first to hoist the Greek flag; and a Spetsiote widow, the heroic Bouboulína, not only blockaded the gulf of Nauplia at her own expense, but took part herself in the blockade. Psará was not slow to follow; but Hýdra, owing to the reluctance of the wealthy primates, hesitated until a ship's captain, named Oikonómos, who was affiliated to the "Friendly Society," placed himself at the head of the people, and forced the local leaders to fit out a squadron under the Hydriote Tombázes. Samos proclaimed that union with Greece which was accomplished only nine years ago, whereas Syra, then wholly Catholic, preserved a neutrality which was the foundation of her prosperity. Crete, where the proportion—160,000 to 130,000—of Mussulmans to Christians was then much larger than at the time of the modern insurrections, received the tidings of the revolution with apparent apathy, despite the fact that it was then, in the phrase of Pashley, "the worst-governed province of the Turkish empire." The French consul at Canea, the only European representative who was then allowed to hoist his flag, reported that "the authority of the Pasha" was "null." The local authorities were powerless to control the Janissaries, who were there exclusively composed of Cretan Mussulmans, Greeks by speech and race, yet always the most fanatical members of the dominant creed. "No Christian," we are told, "was master of his own house"; while it was the custom to send bullets wrapped up in paper with a demand for blackmail—a demand quickly followed by the murder of the stubborn recipients of these significant missives. In short, "the horrors and atrocities which were almost of daily occurrence in Crete had hardly a single parallel throughout the whole extent of the Ottoman empire." The sole exception was the Sphakiotes, who had submitted to pay the capitation-tax only 50 years earlier. In the summer of 1821 a massacre of 30 Christians at Canea, and the butchery of the Metropolitan of Candia and five bishops at the altar of his cathedral, proved to the Cretans of the mountains what was in store for them. An order to the Sphakiotes to disarm had the effect of bringing them into the field. They rose against the Turks and blockaded Canea, while vessels from Kássos cut off its supplies by sea. But the Greek fleet, after burning a Turkish man-of-war, devoted itself to saving the Greeks of the flourishing Asiatic town of Aivali, instead of taking advantage of its supremacy in the Aegean. In that respect 1821 anticipated 1897, but not 1912.

Mahmûd II was not the man to allow his subjects to defy his authority with impunity, and he adopted the usual Turkish measure for punishing or preventing revolt—the massacre of the revolutionaries' fellow-countrymen. When he received the news of the slaughter of the Turks in the Principalities, he began to execute suspected Greeks; when there came the tidings of the wholesale slaughter of the Turks in the Morea, he beheaded Mouroúzes, the Greek dragoman of the Porte, and several other leading Phanariotes. Not content with these examples of his severity, he resolved to strike at the Greek race in the person of its most representative man, the venerable

Patriarch, Gregory V, a native of the Morea. On Easter Sunday the Patriarch was hanged from the gate of his palace, whence, after being exposed to the public gaze for three days, the body was dragged by the Jews, the inveterate enemies of Hellenism, and cast into the sea. The faithful recovered the body of the martyred Patriarch; it was interred at Odessa, and thence transported, fifty years later, to the Metropolitan Cathedral at Athens. Other executions followed that of Gregory. Charles Callimachi, whom the Sultan had appointed Hospodar of the principalities, was killed in prison; Greek heads were affixed to the battlements of Salonika; the Greeks of Smyrna, Rhodes, and Cyprus became the object of Mussulman fanaticism. Our generation, which has seen the Armenian massacres, can understand the motives and the methods of Mahmûd II. And the Greeks in 1821, like the Armenians in our own time, had no established Greek state, to which they could appeal. They could, however, beg the sympathy of cultured Europe in the name of those famous ancestors who have so often saved them; they might anticipate the protection of the Tsar on account of their common rebellion and the traditional policy of his house. But Alexander I was in a difficult position; as a member of the Holy Alliance, he could not consistently support a revolutionary movement; as the patron of the Orthodox inhabitants of Turkey, he could not acquiesce in their destruction. He contented himself with breaking off diplomatic relations with the Porte, and continued to vacillate for the next five years between his fear of revolution and his devotion to Orthodoxy. Thus, unaided by any foreign power, unassisted as yet by foreign volunteers, the War of Greek Independence had begun. In that war three phases may be traced: the first, lasting from 1821 to 1825, in which the Greeks were successful; the second, extending from the arrival of Ibrahim in the Morea in 1825, when the tide turned, down to 1827; and the third, which began with the intervention of Great Britain, France, and Russia, and which saw the last fight between Greeks and Turks, in 1829.

The early successes of the Greeks in the Morea had been won by leaders acting independently of any central authority. A "Messenian Senate" had, indeed, sprung into existence at Kalamáta, just as an "Assembly of Thessalo-Magnesia" arose on Pélion; but the need was felt for some council, which could at least conduct the business of the whole Peloponnese. Accordingly, on June 7, 1821, at a meeting held in the monastery of Kalteziaí, a "Peloponnesian Senate" of six, subsequently increased to eight, magnates and ecclesiastics, was appointed to exercise dictatorial powers, together with Petrobey, as commander-in-chief, until the taking of Tripolitsá. But twelve days after this appointment there arrived in Greece Prince Demétrios Hypselántes, a younger brother of the Hetairist chief, as the latter's representative. In an age of telegrams the futility of the new-comer's pretensions would have been promptly made public; for on the very day of his landing his brother's campaign was practically ended by the defeat of Dragashani. But news travelled slowly then; Demétrios Hypselántes was, therefore, able to impose himself upon the willing Greeks; and even Petrobey acknowledged as his superior officer this ex-captain of five-and-twenty, who had come from the service of Russia to ransom and rule Greece. When, however, the tidings of Dragashani arrived, the Peloponnesian Senators saw no reason why they should submit to the authority of one who represented a beaten and discredited leader; and nothing less than the threat of his departure and the consequent mutiny of the soldiers coerced them into accepting him as commander-in-chief. Yet, in spite of this jealousy between Hypselántes and the Senate, Monemvasía, the Gibraltar, and Navarino, the Portsmouth of Greece, were surrendered by their Turkish garrisons; the waters of that beautiful bay were reddened with the blood of the massacred Turks.

On the day when Monemvasía capitulated, another and an abler man arrived in Greece. Alexander Mavrokordátos was a member of the old Phanariote family which had given five princes to Moldavia and two to Wallachia, where he had himself held a court appointment. The outbreak of the revolution found him in exile at Pisa, whence he repaired to Greece to place his fortune and his services at the disposition of his race. Disgusted, however, at the quarrels between Hypselántes and the "Peloponnesian Senate" in the camp before Tripolitsá, he accepted an invitation to organise the administration of Aitolía and Akarnanía, and established at Mesolónghi under his own presidency an "Assembly of Western Continental Greece." Another Phanariote, Theodore Négres, created a more ambitious organisation for the eastern part of the Greek continent under the title of "Areopagos" with its seat at Sálona. Meanwhile, on October 5 the Turkish capital of the Morea had fallen, and a terrible massacre of its inhabitants ensued. It was estimated that at least 8000 Mussulmans and Jews perished in the assault and in the subsequent slaughter, while the sack of Tripolitsá made the fortune of more than one Moreote family. The outbreak of an epidemic was nature's revenge.

It had been stipulated that the functions of the "Peloponnesian Senate" should cease with the capture of the Peloponnesian capital; and Hypselántes gladly issued a proclamation to the people, convoking a National Assembly, which should, as he hinted in no obscure language, end the tyranny of the primates no less than that of the Turks. This Assembly met at Argos, but was speedily transferred to the village of Piáda not far from Epídauros, whence it derived the name by which it is known in history. There, on January 13, 1822, the Greek New Year's day, was proclaimed the Constitution of Epídauros —the first attempt to provide a central government for the whole of Greece. The constitution created a legislature of 70 annually elected members and an executive of five, of whom Mavrokordátos was appointed president and who named the "ministers," as they were called, of the eight departments. Universal equality before the law, religious toleration, freedom of an as yet non-existent press, and a republican form of government, were the characteristics of this organic law; they were scarcely suited to a country just emancipating itself from centuries of Turkish despotism and peculiarly attached to its communal organisation. The constitution, largely the work of an Italian, bears the marks of the Latin love of symmetry, which was so strangely at variance with the actual requirements of the Greeks. Indeed, the Moreote primates drew up a Peloponnesian Constitution of their own and formed a provincial senate of 20 members to watch over their local interests. For the moment, however, fortune seemed to smile on the Assembly. While it was still sitting, there came the news that Corinth had surrendered; and that admirably central position was chosen as the first capital of free Greece. Over Acro-Corinth were hoisted the newly chosen blue and white colours of the Greek nation.

While the Greek cause was thus triumphant on the Isthmus and to the south of it, the Turks defeated and slew Petrobey's eldest son, Elias, in Euboea, and were re-establishing their authority on a durable basis in the north-west. Khurshid's operations against Ali Pasha had been hindered by the outbreak of the revolution behind him. But in the autumn he had occupied the fortress of Litharítza, which the lord of Joánnina had built on a commanding height not far from the lake. The next step was the capture of the citadel, whence Ali retired to an island which is the summer-resort of the townsfolk. Ali had obtained a promise from Khurshid that his life should be spared; but Khurshid's successor, Mohammed, disregarded a pledge which he did not consider binding on his master. On February 5, 1822 he visited Ali in a little convent on the island, and, as he departed, stabbed him to the heart. But the present writer was shown the bullet-marks, which, according to the local tradition, were made by the missiles of the soldiers, who killed the old lion by firing through the wooden floor. Thus at the age of 82, perished the able but unscrupulous tyrant in the midst of that beautiful lake, which had witnessed the last struggles of so many of his victims and which a romantic poem has connected with the drowning of the fair Euphrosýne. The head of the old pasha, with those of his three sons and his grandson, after being exhibited at Constantinople, was buried beyond the Selymbría gate of the Turkish capital; and a tomb on the cliff above the lake of Joánnina and a Greek inscription outside the water-gate still preserve in his old residence the memory of one of the few Albanians whose fame has penetrated beyond the mountains of their savage native land.

If the dramatic punishment of Ali Pasha impressed European statesmen with the growing authority of the Sultan in Epirus, another event gained for the Greeks the sympathy of the whole civilised world. Of all the islands in the Archipelago the richest and most pacific was Chios, whose famous mastic-gardens were an appanage of the Sultan's wives. The prosperity and the character of the Chians rendered them unwilling to risk their lives and property in the doubtful cause of the revolution; and this conduct, without gaining them the confidence of the Turks, lost them the esteem of the Greeks. Against the express desire of the inhabitants, who had little wish to be saved from a tyranny which in their case was not oppressive, a Chian named Bourniás, who had served in the French army, and a Samian adventurer called Lykoûrgos Logothétes, who had become almost dictator of his native island, landed in Chios in March 1822, and occupied the capital. The capitan-pasha thereupon disembarked a large force at Chios; the Turks captured the town, and put to the sword every Greek whom they met; and nothing but a desire to preserve the mastic-gardens induced the capitan-pasha to offer an amnesty to the survivors. The two promoters of the abortive insurrection fled from the island, where 46 smoking villages, a ruined city, and a hecatomb of corpses testified to the rashness of their enterprise. Thousands of Chians were dragged away as slaves; thousands more begged their bread as penniless exiles. Their sufferings aroused the desire of their fellow-Greeks for vengeance; and a fleet under Andrew Miaoúles, a brave Hydriote who had issued from his hardly-won repose at the call of his country, sailed for the devastated island. On the night of June 18, while the capitan-pasha was celebrating the approaching moon of Bairam, Constantine Kanáres, a young sailor from Psará, steered a fireship towards the vessel of the Turkish admiral, which perished in the flames with nearly all its crew. Panic seized the rest of the Turkish captains, who cut their cables and fled, while their infuriated compatriots on the island avenged the death of the admiral, who had been borne ashore only to die of his wounds, by sacking the mastic-villages, which had been spared till then. This act of vengeance completed the ruin of what had been the most flourishing of Greek islands; it was calculated that of the 113,000 Christians, whom Chios contained in April, only 1800 remained there in August. Of the rest 23,000 had been slain, 47,000 sold into slavery, and the others scattered to every part of the Hellenic world. The destruction of Chios was the gain of Syra; for it was a body of Chian exiles who founded the new and Orthodox of Syra's twin towns, and introduced that delightful industry the manufacture of "Turkish delight," of which Syra has the monopoly. In 1825 the new town was christened by Luke Rhálles "Hermoúpolis" from the god of commerce, which was the main occupation of its industrious colonists[1].

In the spring of 1822 the Sultan, having already recovered possession of Thessaly and Joánnina, ordered the double invasion of Greece on the east and on the west. But before Dramali, who was entrusted with the command of the western army, had begun operations, the Turks who still held the Akropolis of Athens had capitulated. On June 21 the articles of capitulation, of which the second guaranteed the lives of the garrison, were signed; but the rumour of Dramali's advance

---

[1] Δελτίον τῆς Ἱστορικῆς καὶ Ἐθνολογικῆς Ἑταιρίας, iv, 481.

created a panic among the Athenians. Many fled, as of old, to Salamis, while the soldiery fell upon the Turks, of whom several hundreds were massacred and the rest escaped only thanks to the arrival of two French warships and to the courage of the consuls. The anarchy which prevailed there was ended by a summons to Odysseús to occupy the Akropolis, where till 1888 a bastion, which he built to protect the ancient Klépsydra and thus secure himself a supply of water, remained to associate the name of this revolutionary leader with the sacred rock. Meanwhile Dramali invaded the Morea with a pomp and circumstance which recalled the Turkish expedition to recover it from the Venetians 107 years earlier. But, although the Turkish commander at first carried all before him, although Acro-Corinth was abandoned by its garrison and he advanced as far as Argos, disease and the lack of forage compelled him to fall back upon the Isthmus. The Greek generalissimo was the celebrated leader of irregulars, Theodore Kolokotrónes, already a man of fifty-one at the outbreak of the revolution. Brought up in the Spartan rigour of Maina, where his father had sought refuge from his native district of Karýtaina from the Turks, he had pursued the career of arms as a brigand till the Morea was too hot to hold him. Escaping thence to Zante in the time of the "Septinsular Republic," he took part as a privateer in the last Russo-Turkish war; entering the service of the British, when they captured Zante from the French, he assisted in the assault upon Santa Mavra; and he was carrying on the trade of a cattle-dealer when the rumours of the revolution reached him. Returning from Zante to Maina, he was present when Kalamáta fell; and his skill in klephtic warfare, combined with his native common-sense, won him the first place among the military leaders. His plumed helmet, so familiar to every traveller in Greece, gave him a picturesque appearance; of all the chieftains of the War of Independence he is still the most popular; and his statues at Athens and Nauplia are the tribute of the people's admiration for his adventurous career and his patriotic services. But on this occasion the glory of a great victory was reserved for his nephew Nikétas. In the pass of Dervenáki, through which now runs the railway between Corinth and Argos, Nikétas fell upon the Turkish vanguard, and his personal prowess that day won him the name of the "Turk-eater." Dramali himself with the rest of his troops sustained a similar defeat, and died at Corinth before the year was over. Thus ingloriously ended the great Turkish invasion of the Morea in 1822.

On the west, however, whither Mavrokordátos had betaken himself, the Greeks were less successful. On July 16, the Greeks and a corps of Philhellenes, which had been formed two months earlier, were defeated at Péta a couple of miles above the famous bridge of Arta, owing to the treachery of a local chieftain. The Philhellenes, many of them seasoned warriors, were cut to pieces after a heroic struggle. On the same day Kyriakoúles Mavromicháles, brother of the Bey of Maina, was killed near the Epirote haven of Phanári in the attempt to co-operate with the Souliotes. These twin disasters induced them to capitulate, and they returned to the Ionian Islands, whither the terrified peasantry of Akarnanía also sought safety under the British protectorate. The most celebrated of the Souliotes, Márko Bótzares, remained, however, to fight and fall for the Greek cause on the continent. Thus freed from the dangers of an attack from the men of Soûli, Omer Vriónes, who had succeeded Ali as pasha of Joánnina, was at last able to march to the south and besiege Mesolónghi. But this first siege of Mesolónghi failed, whereas on the other side of Greece the close of the year witnessed the capitulation of the Turkish garrison of Nauplia, which was saved from pillage and massacre by the intervention of a British Philhellene, Captain Hamilton. In Crete, however, this second year of the insurrection had been unpropitious to the Christians. Hypselántes, at the request of the Cretans, had sent thither towards the end of 1821 a Russian Greek, who signed himself "Michael

Komnenós Afentoúlief" and boasted his descent from the Byzantine Emperors, as their leader and his representative. A diplomatist without military capacity is not the man to manage that turbulent island, whose tall warriors looked down with scorn upon this short and limping penman, who styled himself "Generalissimo and Administrator of all Crete." The murder of Anthony Melidónes, one of the most successful leaders, by a jealous Sphakiote chief, further weakened the Christian cause; a fresh organiser was sent to the island by the Greek government; and in the midst of this confusion an Egyptian fleet anchored in Suda bay. The Sphakiotes, who had begun the insurrection, were resolved to direct it; and the descendant of the house of Komnenós, "placed between the tiger and the panther," withdrew to Malta. In his place Manóles Tombázes, a member of the well-known Hydriote family, arrived as *Harmostés* (or Commissioner)—the first application of that since familiar term, already current among the Ionians, to the Governor of the great Greek island.

The mandate of the Greek legislature had now expired; and a second National Assembly accordingly met at Astros on the gulf of Nauplia early in 1823. After introducing a few modifications into the Constitution of Epídauros, the deputies appointed a new executive of five persons, of whom Petrobey was the president, Mavrokordátos being degraded to a secretaryship of state, while Hypselántes was ignored altogether. Unfortunately the discussions at Astros accentuated the differences already existent between the party of the primates, of which Petrobey was the leader, and that of the military men, headed by Kolokotrónes; while local and personal jealousies within the ranks of both parties demonstrated that human nature had changed as little as topography since the days of ancient Greece. It was already becoming apparent that a foreign prince would be the only possible head of the new Greek state, for no Greek would consent to recognise another Greek as his sovereign; and already men's eyes began to turn

to the ever-useful house of Saxe-Coburg, whose special function
it is to provide sovereigns of any religion for any throne.
Moreover, it was becoming obvious that public opinion in the
west of Europe would ultimately compel the governments to
pay attention to the claims of Greece. A Greek committee
was formed in London and affiliated with those of Germany
and Switzerland. The Congress of Veróna might, indeed,
refuse to admit the Greek delegates; but George Canning,
who had succeeded Castlereagh as Foreign Secretary, was
known to have Philhellenic sympathies. He recognised the
Greeks as belligerents, and assigned Kálamos, one of the
insular dependencies of the Ionian Islands, to the fugitives as
a place of refuge. The rigorous measures of Sir Thomas
Maitland could not prevent the Ionians from showing sympathy
with their fellow-Greeks of the mainland; but the violation of
Ionian neutrality in Cerigo, Zante, and Ithaca was severely
punished, and the consequent execution of several Ionians
rendered the protectorate unpopular. On the other hand,
Russia disillusioned any who still believed in the sincerity of
her Philhellenism by proposing in January 1824 the creation of
three separate vassal Greek principalities—Eastern Greece
(Thessaly, Bœotia, and Attica); Western Greece (Epirus and
Akarnanía); and the Morea with the possible addition of
Crete—under native officials, appointed by, and tributary to,
the Sultan. This arrangement, although it had the merit of
including Epirus and Crete, excluded the Archipelago, which
was to have the restoration of its old municipal privileges, and
would have left Greece in the position of the Danubian Principalities—weak, divided, and dependent upon Russia. The
leading Greek families would alone have gained; like the
Phanariotes in Moldavia and Wallachia, they would have
looked for advancement to the Sultan, while the Œcumenical
Patriarch, whom Russia suggested as the spokesman of the
three principalities at Constantinople, would have been his
creature.

The military operations of 1823 were less important than those of the previous years. At the outset the Turks were crippled by the conflagration of the arsenal at Constantinople —an outrage attributed to the Janissaries, anxious for a pretext for postponing their march against the Greeks. Nevertheless, the Sultan was now free from the distraction of the war against Persia, which had hitherto compelled him to fight in Asia as well as in Europe. His commanders subdued the last remnant of the insurrection in Thessaly by the reduction of Tríkeri, and plundered the village of Kastrí, which then (but now no longer) concealed the treasures of Delphi. From Scutari in Albania an army of Mohammedan Ghegs and Catholic Mirdites, the latter ever ready to fight against the Orthodox, descended into western Greece; and in a battle against these northern Albanians at Karpenêsi on August 21 the heroic Souliote, Márko Bótzares, met his death. His body was borne to Mesolónghi and there interred, amidst universal lamentation. His tomb may still be seen in the local " Herôon," where ere long the heart of one greater than he was destined to be laid to rest.

Lord Byron had arrived in Cephalonia in the very month of Bótzares' death; and his active participation in the defence of Greece contributed almost more than any other event to popularise the Hellenic cause in Europe. The great poet was no stranger to the Greeks or to their language. Twelve years earlier he had indited from the interior of the Choragic Monument of Lysikrátes, transformed into a study of Capuchin monks, his " Curse of Minerva " against the "plunderer " of the Elgin Marbles. He had translated the famous war-song of Rhégas, and had now come to prove that he could not only praise the virtues of ancient Greece but also imitate them. Yet Lord Byron, although a poet, had no illusions. He did not land in Hellas prepared to find it peopled with the impossible heroes of Plutarch; he expected the Greeks to be what centuries of Turkish rule might have been naturally anticipated to make them; and consequently he was neither disheartened nor disillusioned, when he had to do with men who were neither saints nor sages but human beings barely emancipated from a demoralising form of government, for which no adequate substitute had yet been found. In order not to compromise himself with any political party until he had studied the state of affairs, he remained for four months in Cephalonia. Meanwhile, negotiations for a Greek loan had been conducted. The first idea of the Greeks had been to raise money by restoring the island of Rhodes, its former seat, to the Order of the Knights of St John, to which Syra and three smaller islands were to be assigned provisionally. But this picturesque revival of Frankish Greece was abandoned for a more practical scheme, by which a nominal sum of £800,000 (really only £280,000) was raised in London.

While Lord Byron was still in Cephalonia, the Greeks obtained two successes. In the east they recovered the citadel of Corinth; in the west they compelled the Turks to abandon the siege of Anatolikón. But the quarrels between the military and the political parties in the Morea had developed into civil war, the first but not the last occasion when Greek fought Greek, instead of joining in an united attack upon the common foe. This fratricidal struggle, which Lord Byron endeavoured to compose, was provoked by Kolokotrónes, who, like another Cromwell, sent his son Pános to dissolve the legislature, then sitting at Argos, by force of arms. Most of the deputies reconstituted themselves a legislature at Kranídi opposite Hýdra, declared the executive deposed, and appointed a new committee in its place, with George Kountouriótes, a Hydriote, as its president. Thus Greece had two hostile governments, one established at Kranídi and supported by the shipowners of the Nautical Islands of Hýdra and Spétsai, the primates, and the military chiefs of continental Greece; and the other sitting at Tripolitsá, and deriving its authority from the prowess of Kolokotrónes and his personal followers. This struggle was proceeding when, on January 5, 1824, Lord Byron arrived at Mesolónghi; and what he both saw and heard confirmed his opinion that Greece in the throes of revolution required practical methods of government instead of the theories of Bentham. It seemed to him that the publication of newspapers, so eagerly recommended by the "typographical Colonel" Leicester Stanhope, who was with him, would inflame the party feelings, rather than edify the minds, of those who could read them. However Stanhope insisted on issuing, under the editorship of a Swiss Republican named Meyer, the first Greek newspaper published on Greek soil, if we except a few fly-sheets issued at Kalamáta three years before. Thus, on the mud-flats of Mesolónghi, began on January 12, 1824, with *The Greek Chronicles*, that press[1] which is so characteristic a feature of modern Greek life. Byron unhappily did not live to see the conclusion of even the civil war, which he had endeavoured to allay. On April 19 he died at Mesolónghi, where his heart still reposes. He had given his time, his means, and at last his life for the cause of Greece; and Greece has never forgotten his services. The historian Spyrídon Trikoúpes, himself a native of Mesolónghi, pronounced over his body a funeral oration, which is considered a model of Greek prose; statues have arisen in his honour; streets have been called by his name; and in many a remote island, in many a mountain village men still speak of Byron, as if he had died but yesterday—a happy exception to the cynical maxim of Lord Salisbury that there is no gratitude in international politics.

The year was not over before a second civil war had broken out, in which the English loan, instead of being devoted exclusively to the national defences, was frittered away in party jealousies. This " War of the Primates," as it was called, arose out of the antipathy felt by the Moreotes for an executive, the majority of whose members came from the Nautical Islands and

---

[1] Part of this printing-press is preserved in the Museum of "the Historical and Ethnological Society" at Athens.

the continent. The leaders of the Moreote party were the two Andrews—Zaïmes of Kalávryta, member of a family which has given more than one statesman to Greece; and Lóntos of Vostítsa, a friend of Byron, who had caroused with him when they were young; with them was Sisínes, or Sessini, of Gastoúni in Elis, whose name denoted his Venetian origin, who from the neighbouring Glaréntza jocularly called himself "Duke of Clarence" and kept up a style worthy of a Turkish pasha. The soul of the executive was John Koléttes, the future Prime Minister and diplomatist, a native of the Epirote village of Syrákou, who had begun life as physician to Ali Pasha's son Mukhtar and had learned statecraft at the court of Joánnina. Koléttes had already taken an active part in the revolution. After inciting his native village to revolt, he had become Minister of War under the Constitution of Epídauros; but this ex-doctor was a better politician than soldier; and, if he gained little renown in the field, his talents gained him a place on the executive, of which Kountouriótes was the nominal head. On this occasion his energy speedily crushed the rebellious primates; Kolokotrónes, who had espoused their cause, was imprisoned in Hýdra, and his son Pános slain; the two Andrews fled across the gulf of Corinth; Sessini was refused admission to Zante. The "War of the Primates" had ended with their complete failure.

While the Greek leaders were fighting among themselves, a new and formidable enemy had appeared in Greek waters. Unable to make headway single-handed against the insurgents, Mahmûd II had been forced to seek the aid of his vassal, Mehemet Ali, the pasha of Egypt, an Albanian who had risen from tobacco-dealing in his native Kavalla to the position of a modern Pharaoh. Mahmûd had already employed him against the Wahabis in Arabia; he now asked him to assist in subduing the Greeks, and appointed Mehemet's son Ibrahim pasha of the Morea. First, however, it was resolved to crush the islanders of Psará and Kássos, the former of which had gained world-wide fame as a nursery of bold and skilful seamen, while the latter had served as a base for maintaining the insurrection in Crete. Both these preliminary enterprises were successful. The Albanian troops of the pasha of Egypt effected a night-attack upon the rugged island of Kássos, slew the men and the old women, and carried off the young women and children into slavery. The Turkish soldiers of the capitan-pasha almost exterminated the male population of Psará, at that time increased by the refugees from Chios; and hundreds of heads and ears of the slain were exposed with a pompous inscription to the gaze of the faithful at Constantinople. The survivors fled to Aigina, Spétsai, and Syra, while some founded on the site of the classic Eretria a colony which they called New Psará. These two successive blows to the Greek cause were followed by a series of naval engagements, which retarded the arrival of Ibrahim in the Morea. On the way he put into Suda bay; but it was unnecessary for him to land in Crete, for the Cretan insurrection was by that time over, thanks to the importation of the Egyptian troops and the vaulting ambition of the Sphakiotes. Tombázes had left the island; and, amidst horrors such as the suffocation of hundreds of Christians by smoke in a cavern, the Cretan rising had smouldered out in the spring of 1824. Ibrahim pursued his course to the Morea; and with his landing there at the former Venetian colony of Modon on February 24, 1825, the second phase of the war began.

Ibrahim's first movement was directed against the two fortresses which commanded the bay of Navarino—the " new castle " at the south entrance, and the " old castle " at the north. But it became apparent that the key of the position was the island of Sphaktería, which lies, like some huge cetacean, across the bay, and which, at the eleventh hour, was occupied by Mavrokordátos with a chosen band of soldiers, among them the Piedmontese Philhellene, Count Santa Rosa, who, exiled for his attempts to establish freedom in his own country, had come to fight for that of Greece. An hour sufficed for the capture of this historic island, which, twenty-three centuries before, had witnessed the Spartan defeat, immortalised by Thucydides. The Italian historian of the modern battle on Sphaktería could not pretend to the skill of the great Greek writer, but at least in his friend and country-man Santa Rosa he found a hero, worthy of a place beside any Spartan. Although wounded, Santa Rosa refused to yield; and his name, with that of the Hydriote Tsamadós, who fell with him, is still associated with the bay of Navarino. A monument there preserves his memory; and 72 years later his heroism inspired another of his compatriots, Antonio Fratti, on the fatal field of Domokós. Mavrokordátos with difficulty escaped. The capture of Sphaktería was the prelude of the capitulation of both the "old" and the "new castles"—disasters for which the destruction of a part of the Egyptian fleet by Miaoúles at Modon only partially atoned. The loss of Navarino had at least one good result, that it convinced the Greek execu-tive of the necessity for union. Kountouriótes had displayed such a lack of energy in his measures for the defence of that important position, that it was felt that the Morea must be defended by the Moreote chiefs. Accordingly an amnesty was granted to the vanquished of the late civil war; the fugitive primates resumed their authority; Kolokotrónes was appointed commander-in-chief in the Morea.

The Egyptian successes, however, continued. The Archi-mandrite Dikaîos, better known as Papaphléssas, who had been the most energetic member of the "Friendly Society" in the Peloponnese, but whose courage and dissipation had led him to be styled the Alkibiades of the revolution, was cut down after a brave stand at Maniáki; Kolokotrónes was defeated in the pass of Makryplági, the scene of so many battles; and Ibrahim, despite a check inflicted upon him by Hypselántes at the mills of Lérna, marched towards Nauplia, then the seat of the Greek government. But the Egyptians were unable to undertake the siege of that strong fortress; so they returned to

Tripolitsá, whence, after again defeating Kolokotrónes, they proceeded to ravage the Morea with fire and sword till Ibrahim received orders to cross over into continental Greece and assist in the second siege of Mesolónghi, the most heroic incident of the whole war.

Reshid Pasha, the victor of Péta, had begun the siege towards the end of April; but it was not till the arrival of the Turkish fleet in July that he made sufficient progress to offer terms to the besieged. His offer was rejected; and the appearance of the Greek fleet dispersed the Turkish vessels, raised the maritime blockade, and re-victualled the town. It should then have been possible, as the besiegers had lost command of the sea, to cut off their communications by land. But, although George Karaïskákes intercepted some of their supplies, the leaders of the insurgents in continental Greece did little to save the place. The most famous of them, the klepht Odysseús, had met with a terrible end. This former favourite of Ali Pasha had been long suspected of scheming to obtain a province for himself from the Turks, who seemed more likely to appreciate his abilities than was the Greek executive. At last an overt act of treachery was discovered, and Odysseús forced to surrender to Gkoúras, his old lieutenant. The former master of Athens was dragged up to the Akropolis amid the execrations of the Athenians, and imprisoned in the Frankish tower, which then stood near the temple of Wingless Victory. There, on July 16, his corpse was found lying at the base of the tower, the victim not of a fall, as was pretended, but of his keeper's hand. The tower, and the bastion that he built, have both vanished; but the son of Androútsos still retains a place in the history of the city, which he had once governed, while his bust now stands in that "new Thermopylae" which he had made, the pass of Graviá—an exploit which should be set against his treachery. Trelawny, his son-in-law, for a time held out in a cave of Parnassós, where two British adventurers attempted to assassinate the friend of Shelley.

The arrival of Ibrahim before Mesolónghi put a new complexion upon the siege. In March, 1826, Anatolikón on an island in the lagoon, which had repelled a former attack, capitulated; and the loss of this outwork of Mesolónghi induced Sir Frederick Adam, who in 1824 had succeeded Sir Thomas Maitland as Lord High Commissioner in the Ionian Islands, to offer his mediation—an offer refused by the confident pashas, as was equally a summons from them to surrender by the stubborn defenders. Provisions had by this time begun to fail, so that the only hope was the return of the Greek fleet to relieve them. But Miaoúles, when he reappeared, was unable to enter the shallows near Mesolónghi and retired before the enemy's largely superior navy. No other alternatives remained to the garrison but surrender or a sortie. It chose the latter; and on the night of April 22, after signalling to Karaïskákes, who was to attack the besiegers in the rear, some 7,000 men, women, and children prepared to sally through the Mussulman lines. Only 3000 of them were combatants, while the rest of the 9000, who formed the total population of the town, were too old, too ill, or too much attached to their old home to leave it. The women wore male attire, the boys who could use pistols were armed; while those who remained shut themselves up in a ruined windmill and in the great magazine, where the powder was stored. Unluckily a Bulgarian deserter had betrayed the impending sortie to the enemy, who had therefore time to make preparations. For some time after crossing the ditch the garrison, commanded by Nótes Bótzares, Kítsos Tsavéllas, and Makrês, waited under fire till Karaïskákes should appear; then, when there was still no sign of his approach, they sprang, with shouts of "forward," at the besiegers, slew the artillerymen and cut their way into the open plain. The people behind them, however, seized with a panic, began to shout "back," and fled in confusion into the town. Those who had escaped from the besiegers' lines fell into an Albanian ambuscade, and the survivors with difficulty reached Karaïskákes' camp. Next morning Ibrahim's troops entered the town, only to meet with a determined resistance from those who had remained there, and who fired the powder-magazines rather than fall alive into their enemy's hands. It is calculated that about 2000 escaped to tell the tale of the great sortie, besides some 3000 prisoners. Among those who fell were Meyer, the editor of the Mesolonghiote newspaper, and the patriot magnate of Patras, Papadiamantópoulos. These men and others like them have conferred upon the little Aitolian fishing-town a fame which will last as long as the Greek nation. Every year a solemn procession of the inhabitants commemorates the heroic sortie ; and the second siege of Mesolónghi has taken its place among the famous sieges of history.

After the fall of this coveted place, the two pashas separated, Ibrahim returning to ravage the Morea, Reshid remaining to complete the pacification of western Greece. Meanwhile, the new turn that the war had taken since the intervention of the Egyptians made the Greeks desirous to obtain peace, provided that they did not lose their practical independence so dearly bought by five years of continuous fighting. External diffi-culties as well as domestic dissensions had convinced most of them that the protection of some great foreign Power was necessary to them; but, while one faction favoured Russia, and another suggested the Duc de Nemours as a French candidate for the throne, a third wished to place the whole country, like the Ionian Islands, under the suzerainty of Great Britain—a proposal actually passed by the Assembly at Nauplia in August 1825. This action strengthened the hands of George Canning, the British Foreign Secretary ; and Stratford Canning, the new British ambassador at Constantinople, met Mavrokordátos at Hýdra on his way out, to discuss the conditions of British mediation. The Assembly formally authorised the ambassador to treat on behalf of Greece, including Crete, on the basis of tributary autonomy under the suzerainty of the Sultan.

Meanwhile, the Duke of Wellington had induced the new Tsar Nicholas I to sanction the signature, on April 4, 1826, of a protocol, with the view of obtaining for the Greeks, on payment of an annual tribute to the Porte, the exclusive right of managing their internal affairs. This was the first effective diplomatic step of the Powers towards Greek independence.

In the summer of 1826 Reshid marched from western Greece into Attica to undertake the next important operation of the war—the siege of Athens. On August 15 he took the city by storm, forcing the Athenians to take refuge in the Akropolis, then commanded by Gkoúras. An attempt to recover the city was made by Karaïskákes, whom the newly-elected executive, presided over by Andrew Zaïmes, had appointed to the supreme command in eastern Greece, and by Colonel Fabvier, an experienced French officer, who had been entrusted by the Greek government with the organisation of a regular corps. The Turks repulsed the relieving force at Chaïdári near the monastery of Daphní, and proceeded to bombard the Akropolis, as Morosini had done 140 years before, and to mine the theatre of Heródes Atticus. The position of the garrison seemed to be desperate, when its commander was killed by a bullet as he was going his nightly rounds. But Kriezótes, a daring leader of irregulars, managed to traverse the Turkish lines and enter the fortress, whither Fabvier followed him with a considerable force on December 13. But this exploit increased the difficulties of accommodation, for the sacred rock was already crowded; and, despite a firman, obtained by Stratford Canning, which forbade the bombardment of the ancient monuments, the roof of the Eréchtheion collapsed and buried beneath its ruins the widow of Gkoúras and a number of Athenian ladies. One attempt after another was made to raise the siege. General Gordon, the historian of the revolution, occupied on February 5, 1827, the classic hill of Mounychía; while Colonel Boúrbaki, a Cephalonian who had served in the French army, approached Athens from the north-

west.   But this concerted attack failed; Boúrbaki was killed in
the plain near Kamaterón and his head sent to Constantinople;
Gordon was compelled to defend Mounychía.   Nor was Colonel
Heideck, the agent of the King of Bavaria, that warm friend of
the Greek cause, more fortunate in an expedition to Oropós.
The enterprise was then entrusted to two distinguished British
officers, Lord Cochrane, who had seen service in South America,
and Sir Richard Church, who had fought in Egypt, Italy, and
the Ionian Islands, where he had been wounded at Santa
Mavra and had made the acquaintance and gained the respect
of Kolokotrónes and other Greek chiefs.   In the spring of
1827 these two foreigners were appointed respectively to
command the naval and military forces of Greece.   Both
concentrated their efforts upon the Piræus, where Karaïskákes
co-operated with them.

Three successive misfortunes marked the course of these
operations.   A brilliant charge against the Turkish positions
round the Piræus was followed by the massacre of the Albanians
who had surrendered the monastery of St Spirídon under
promise that their lives should be spared.   In a subsequent
skirmish Karaïskákes, "at one moment," as he himself phrased
it, "an angel, at another a devil," but latterly more of an
"angel" than "devil," was mortally wounded at the spot where
his monument now stands; and with him expired one of the
most popular leaders of the revolution.   And on the morrow
of his death Sir Richard Church received a crushing defeat at
Pháleron, which compelled him to abandon his position at
Mounychía.   Thus, the garrison of the Akropolis was left to its
fate; on June 5 the capitulation was signed; a marble tablet
in the Odeîon of Heródes Atticus now commemorates Fabvier's
defence.   After a Greek occupation of five years and a Turkish
siege of ten months, the "castle of Athens" owned once more,
and that for the last time, the authority of the Sultan.   The
whole of continental Greece had been subdued; the capture of
Athens had completed what the siege of Mesolónghi had begun.

Happily for Greece, a month after the surrender of the Akropolis, Great Britain, France, and Russia signed the treaty of July 6.

While the Turks had been besieging Athens, the Greek politicians had convened a third National Assembly at Damalá, the picturesque village, a Frankish barony in the middle ages, which stands on the site of the ancient Troizén, whence this parliament takes its name. The convergence at this spot of the two rival factions—that of the government from Aigina, and that of the opposition under Kolokotrónes from Hermióne (the modern Kastrí)—was due to Lord Cochrane, who advised the latter party to read the first "Philippic" of Demosthenes and act upon the advice which it contained. There, in the romantic setting of a lemon garden, which served as a parliament-house, the Assembly on April 14 elected Count John Capo d'Istria President (Κυβερνήτης) of Greece, which was to include all the provinces that had taken up arms, for the term of seven years. Pending his arrival, a commission of three— George Mavromicháles (who was subsequently to be his assassin), Milaétes, and Nákos, all little-known and untried men—was to carry on the government. The election of Capo d'Istria was due to the Russophil party, of which Kolokotrónes was the leader, assisted by the Francophil section under Koléttes and Kountouriótes since the jealousy of Charles X for the house of Orléans had rendered the candidature of the Duc de Nemours impossible. The choice made by the Assembly, although it displeased many, had much at that time to recommend it. Capo d'Istria was the most distinguished living Greek diplomatist; he had influence with the Tsar; he was a proved patriot; but great diplomatists are rarely constructive statesmen, while patriotism loses practical value in one who, from years of absence abroad, has lost touch with his country. Capo d'Istria had known the Ionian Islands, but he did not know the rest of Greece, where society was very different from that of Corfù. Born under Venetian rule, he did not even write Greek correctly. But he was honest; he was indicated; even the British, men like Cochrane, Church and Hamilton recognised that he was inevitable. For every friend of Greece saw that what she wanted was unity; and the Corfiote Count seemed to be the only available person who could secure it. The result showed that Capo d'Istria brought not peace but a sword.

The acquiescence of the three Greek parties in his election was quickly followed by an agreement between the three Powers which they respectively favoured. On July 6, 1827, Great Britain, France, and Russia signed in London a treaty, pledging them to mediate and meanwhile to demand an immediate armistice from both Greece and Turkey. Tributary autonomy under the Sultan's suzerainty was defined as the form of the new Greek state that was to be created. An additional article provided that, if the Porte did not accept their mediation within a month, the Powers would establish consular relations with the Greek government; and that they would prevent, so far as possible, all collisions between the belligerents "without, however, taking any part in the hostilities." Instructions were sent to the naval commanders of the three Powers; and Admiral Codrington proceeded to notify the Greek government of the armistice, which was accepted by it, but refused by the Sultan. Yet, notwithstanding the armistice, Captain Hastings, the Philhellene, with his corvette, the *Kartería* (*Perseverance*), defeated a Turkish flotilla at the landing-place for Delphi and Sálona. Ibrahim, burning to revenge this attack, was compelled by Codrington to return to the bay of Navarino, where both the Egyptian and the Turkish fleets were blockaded by the three admirals. Ibrahim, if unable to issue from the bay, was, however, still free to ravage the country behind it; accordingly, warned by the approach of the stormy season and desirous of preventing the further devastation of the Morea, the three allied fleets entered the bay on October 20. Codrington's orders were that no cannon should be fired until the Turks began; but the Mussulmans saw at once that a battle was inevitable, and fired the first shot at the *Dartmouth's* long-boat, sent to parley. The *Dartmouth* and the French flag-ship retaliated with a discharge of musketry; an Egyptian vessel replied with a cannon shot, and the firing then became general; when the sun arose next morning, only 29 of the 82 vessels that had composed the Turkish and Egyptian fleets remained afloat. The defeated had lost 6000, the allies only 172 men, whose memory is preserved by three monuments on the spot. Never since Lepanto had the Turkish empire experienced such a naval disaster.

The news of Navarino caused immense rejoicings in Greece and among all those who sympathised with the Greek cause. In England, where Canning had meanwhile died, although the King was made to describe the battle in his speech from the throne as an " untoward event," he decorated Codrington and several of the officers who had won what Russell described as "a glorious victory." The Turks took the defeat with calm resignation, merely demanding compensation for the loss of their ships. The three Powers refused on the ground that they had not been the aggressors; and their ambassadors quitted Constantinople. Meanwhile the Greeks continued to act as belligerents. Church and Hastings were engaged in western Greece; Fabvier invaded Chios. But this second expedition to the mastic-island ended in failure; and its commander soon afterwards returned to France. Hastings, whose aim was the recapture of Mesolónghi, after some success, was mortally wounded before Anatolikón, thus adding another British victim to those of the fatal lagoon. Many years afterwards, the heart of this gallant officer was found by the late Arthur Hill in a box in the house of Hastings' friend and old comrade, the historian Finlay, at Athens. It now rests in the English church there, that pantheon of British Philhellenes, in which are commemorated the long and valiant career of Sir Richard Church and the brief but heroic life of Clement Harris, who seventy years after Hastings fell at Pénte Pegádia. The Cretans, too, rose again after Navarino, inspired by fugitives who had taken refuge on the rocky islet of Graboûsa off the west coast, a stronghold which the Venetians had retained after the Turkish conquest of Crete till 1691, and which had latterly become a nest of pirates. On that rugged cliff piracy was regularly organised; and the sea-robbers made their obeisances before a "klephtic Madonna." But the authorities of Graboûsa were patriots as well as pirates; the local municipality became the "Council of Crete"; and with its aid Hajji Micháles, an Epirote leader, stirred up a fresh insurrection. In 1828, however, he was defeated and hacked in pieces by the Turks; and the British cleared out the pirate republic of Graboûsa at the request of Capo d'Istria.

The President arrived in Greece in January 1828, and landed at Nauplia, where his mere presence sufficed to stop the civil war that had raged there for months between Theodore Grívas, the commander of the great fortress of Palamédi, and Strátos, who held Itsh Kaleh, the Akropolis of Nauplia. Thence he proceded to Aigina, whither the provisional government had removed from the range of Palamédi's cannon, and where he received the reports of the ministers for the several departments of state. They were certainly not encouraging. The Minister of the Interior informed him that the territory which actually acknowledged his authority consisted of no more than Aigina, Póros, Salamis, Eleusís, Mégara, and a few islands of the Aegean. The troops of Ibrahim held a large part of the Morea; continental Greece was almost entirely Turkish; Crete had risen in vain; Samos was practically independent under Logothétes, the promoter of the fatal expedition to Chios. Agriculture was at a standstill; the only profitable trade was piracy. The Finance Minister was not more comforting. He had, he said, neither treasure nor treasury; some of the revenues had been mortgaged a year in advance to pay the legislature; even the bills of the carpenters who had been at work on the presidential abode could not be met. The

Minister of War lamented the absence of an army, but his colleague of the Admiralty was not quite so gloomy ; as for justice, the head of that department remembered the adage that "the laws are silent in time of war," and was silent also. Such was the condition of Greece after nearly seven years of warfare.

Capo d'Istria began his career as President by a *coup d'état*. The Assembly, which had elected him at Troizén, had also drawn up a third constitution, which had declared Greece to be an independent, indivisible state, whereas the treaty of London aimed at the creation of an autonomous, tributary Hellas under the suzerainty of the Sultan. The President, as a diplomatist, knew that autonomy was not the same as sovereignty, and that the former was all that could be obtained for the present. He realised, too, that constitutions and representative bodies have a very relative importance in countries scarcely emancipated from an oriental despotism and still in a state of siege. He therefore persuaded the legislature to abdicate its functions, and in its place appointed a body, called the "Panhellénion," and composed of 27 members, forming three committees, administrative, financial, and judicial. At the same time he promised to summon a fresh National Assembly in three months' time. But, if the Greek leaders, who had borne the burden and heat of the struggle for independence, were prepared to accept the provisional dictatorship of the President, they saw no reason why they should submit to the authority of his unintelligent elder brother, Viaro, and of that brother's bosom friend, whom he summoned from Corfù and seated in the "Panhellénion." Viaro was his evil genius. As Commissioner of Aigina and the Nautical Islands, the home of powerful personages like Kountouriótes, he acted like a petty despot, arresting citizens, opening letters, exercising a censorship of the only newspaper then published in Greek, and threatening reprisals upon all who dared to criticise his very paternal orders. He ordered a petition of the Aiginetans to be burnt before their eyes, while the President was sufficiently tactless to describe the heroes of the revolution—men who had fought while he had only written—in unflattering language, calling the primates "Christian Turks," the military chiefs "brigands," the Phana- riotes "vessels of Satan," and the literary men "fools." In order to prevent the perpetuation of this last species, he drew up a strictly professional system of education—for priests at Póros, for farmers at Tíryns, for soldiers and sailors at Nauplia and Hýdra—and would not hear of the foundation of an Academy such as Lord Guildford had created in Corfù. He believed that character is more likely to build up a nation than learning, and that material prosperity is essential to the welfare of a state. But he forgot that he had to deal with a race which has a thirst for knowledge, and values the things of the intellect above all else. In short, Capo d'Istria, honest as he was in all his endeavours for the welfare of his country, sought to apply to a democratic, highly critical people methods which he had learnt in the Venetian society of Corfù and at the Russian court.

He began with finance. Greece had thus far had no national coinage ; he endowed her with a silver coin known as a *phœnix*, and bronze pieces of 1, 5, 10, and 20 *leptá*, and es- tablished a national bank, followed by an issue of paper notes[1] but his monetary unit was based upon a fluctuating value, and his bank was admittedly only a forced loan. Next he turned to the army, formed eight regiments of a thousand men each, and placed them under the command of Hypselántes in the east and of Church in the west. He divided the Morea into seven, and the islands into six provinces, governed by com- missioners, and thus weakened the municipal system which had so long flourished in Greece. But a long-expected event abroad soon over-shadowed these domestic reforms. On April 26, 1828, the Tsar declared war upon Turkey, and

---

[1] Lámpros, Μικταὶ Σελίδες, 654–64.

thus created a military diversion, which could scarcely fail to benefit the Greeks.

The moment seemed favourable for the accomplishment of Russia's traditional aim—the conquest of Constantinople. The Turkish fleet had been annihilated at Navarino; the Janissaries had been exterminated a year earlier on the Et Meidan, or "Meat Market," of Constantinople by the reforming Sultan; but the reformer had not had time to perfect his "new model," and the Greeks, under their Russophil President, were still unsubdued. But then, as so often, the power of Russia was over-estimated, and the resistance of the Turks surpassed expectation. Moreover, the Tsar, while fighting Turkey in the Balkans, was not a belligerent in the Aegean. Meanwhile, another of the three Powers which had signed the treaty of London rendered Greece a great service by ridding the Morea of the Egyptian troops. Ibrahim, owing to the withdrawal of the allied fleets, had already sent his wounded men with some thousands of Greek slaves to Alexandria; but the rest of his army had suffered severely during the winter; and in the summer of 1828 his Albanian garrison of Coron, one of the old Venetian colonies at the south of Messenía, mutinied and were allowed by the Greeks to leave the Morea for their own country. The French government thereupon offered to expel the remainder of Ibrahim's forces. The British cabinet accepted the offer; and on August 30 General Maison landed with a French army at Petalídi on the gulf of Coron to enforce the evacuation of the peninsula. Codrington had, however, already concluded a convention with Mehemet Ali for the removal of the Mussulman troops and the release of the Greek slaves. Ibrahim was willing to carry out his father's promise, but declined to hand over the Turkish fortresses of Modon, Coron, Navarino, Chloumoûtsi, Patras, and Rhíon, which had been specially excluded from the convention. The last-named, however, alone resisted; on October 30 it also surrendered. No hostile troops remained in the Morea, where the French, having thus easily cleared the fortresses, proceeded to clean them, to make roads, and to repair the ravages of Ibrahim. One of his last acts had been the complete destruction of Tripolitsá. So thoroughly did his Arabs carry out his orders, that of the former Turkish capital of the Morea the traveller can now find little but the foundations of what was once the *konak* of the pasha. In order to preserve the peninsula from a further invasion, the Allies by a protocol of November 16 placed it together with the adjacent islands and the Cyclades under their joint guarantee until a definite settlement of the Greek question, and allowed France to keep a certain number of troops in the Morea ; the rest returned home.

South of the Isthmus, the war was thus over ; north of it, the Turks were so much weakened by the Russian campaign and by an Albanian revolt, that the Greeks recovered lost ground. Hypselántes occupied Bœotia ; Sálona surrendered ; the castle of Vónitza on the Ambrakian gulf capitulated ; Lepanto and Mesolónghi followed. In Crete both parties accepted an armistice. Meanwhile, the representatives of the three Powers had been discussing the boundaries of the new Greek state at Póros, and their decisions were embodied in the London protocol of March 22, 1829. The northern frontier of Greece was to be drawn from the Ambrakian to the Pagasæan gulf, and was to include on the east Eubœa, the islands adjacent to the Morea and the Cyclades. The country thus delimited was to become an hereditary monarchy under a Christian prince to be chosen by, but not from, the dynasties of the three protecting Powers, with the consent of the Porte, which he was to acknowledge as his suzerain, from which he and his successors were to receive their investiture, and to which a tribute of 1,500,000 piastres (or some £30,000) should be paid. This arrangement displeased alike the Greek politicians and the President ; they resented the exclusion of Samos and Crete ; he intrigued against the nomination of a foreign prince who would take his place. On the other hand, the Sultan was willing to concede only the Morea and the adjacent islands. But had it not been for the Turcophil inclinations of Lord Aberdeen, then Foreign Secretary, the protocol would have been forced upon Turkey, and the kingdom of Greece would have become an accomplished fact. In these circumstances Capo d'Istria performed his long-deferred promise to convoke a National Assembly. In order to secure the election of a majority favourable to himself, he made an electoral tour of the Morea, where he was very popular. Many districts actually elected him as their representative; and, when this was declared illegal, mere delegates—"good Christians," as they were called—were chosen, who received written instructions from their constituents. Mesolónghi, always to the fore in the cause of freedom, protested against this caricature of representative government; the Nautical Islands naturally voted for the Opposition. From Greek lands still in Turkish hands, from Epirus and Thessaly, from Chios and Crete, came deputies to support him in the fourth National Assembly, which met on July 23, 1829 in the ancient theatre of Argos. A parliament thus elected provided a majority ready to carry out the President's behests. He received full powers of negotiation with the Allies; he appointed six, and selected from a list of 63 candidates submitted to him the remaining 21 members of the newly-created Senate, which was to take the place of the "Panhellénion," but with very limited authority; his name was to be engraved on the coins; he was to be the first, and for the present the only person, to wear the newly-created Order of the Redeemer. Only on one point, the ratification of the Allies' decisions, did the Assembly reserve its own rights, and this reservation proved a serviceable weapon in his hands; only one protest, a letter from Church, was raised against the nepotism which had made the President's younger brother, Agostino, his plenipotentiary in western Greece, and this protest was rejected. Capo d'Istria seemed to be at the summit of his power; Metternich, who had throughout

misjudged the Greek movement, regarded him as irremovable.

A few weeks after the close of the Assembly the long-drawn
war between Greeks and Turks ended. The advance of the
Russians towards Adrianople had compelled the Sultan to
withdraw all his available soldiers from Greece; and a body of
Albanians under Aslan Bey was ordered to escort the Turks
who still remained in Attica and Bœotia. On his way back
from Athens, Aslan had to traverse the then narrow pass of
Pétra between Levádeia and Thebes, then the Thermopylæ of
Bœotia, but now completely transformed by the draining of the
Copaïc lake. There he found Hypselántes prepared to dispute
his passage; and on September 24 Aslan sustained so severe a
defeat from the prince and Kriezótes, that on the morrow he
signed a capitulation, by which the Turks agreed to evacuate
all eastern Greece, except the Akropolis of Athens and the
fortress of Karababâ which commands the Euripus. Thus, in
Finlay's happy phrase, " Prince Demetrius Hypsilantes had the
honour of terminating the war which his brother had commenced on the banks of the Pruth."

CHAPTER VI

THE CREATION OF THE GREEK KINGDOM (1829-33)

THE War of Independence was over; it remained to fix definitely the dimensions and to appoint the ruler of the new state. Eleven days before the conclusion of the Greco-Turkish hostilities at Pétra, Russia had imposed upon the Sultan the peace of Adrianople, which included his recognition of the treaty of London and of the protocol of March 22. The effect of this treaty in London was such that the Duke of Wellington, then Prime Minister, abandoned the idea of making Greece a vassal principality, and became an advocate of an independent Greek kingdom. Twenty-five years later, his Foreign Secretary, Lord Aberdeen, confessed that Greece owed her escape from vassalage to complete freedom solely to the impression created by the treaty of Adrianople. The Duke believed the end of Turkey to be at hand; it was, therefore, useless to place Greece beneath a suzerain too feeble to defend her. On the other hand he foresaw the further aggrandisement of Russia, and he was accordingly anxious that Greece, believed to be Russophil, should not be too large. What the British Cabinet of that day wanted was a small, independent state; and such were the two leading ideas which inspired the fresh protocols, signed by the three Powers on February 3, 1830. They decided that Greece should be a completely independent state, governed by an hereditary monarch, selected outside the reigning families of Great Britain, France, and Russia, with the title of "Sovereign Prince of Greece." But in consideration of the advantage of independence, "and in deference to the desire expressed by the Porte to obtain the reduction of the frontiers fixed by the protocol of March 22," the frontiers of this principality were to be restricted to the mouth of the Spercheiós on the east, to that of the Achelôos on the west. It would have been difficult even for British diplomacy, whose geographical ignorance has provoked so many complications in the near east, to have drawn a worse frontier. The best that could be said of it was that it included Thermopylæ, the glory of ancient, and Mesolónghi, that of modern Greece. It sacrificed Akarnanía and a large part of Aitolía, whose inhabitants had borne a conspicuous part in the struggle ; and it thereby abandoned to Turkey the pass of Makrynóros, the Thermopylae of the west. It did, indeed, include Eubœa, the Devil's Islands, Skŷros, and the Cyclades, but it excluded Crete, and thus left to Europe a legacy of trouble and expense only recently finished. As usually happens, the best expert opinion could have been had for the asking, but was not considered. Colonel Leake was then in London ; yet the Foreign Office never consulted the famous traveller, who knew northern Greece as well as its clerks knew Downing Street. As ruler of the new principality the powers proposed Prince Leopold of Saxe-Coburg (subsequently first king of the Belgians). This was an excellent choice. The Prince, as he afterwards showed on the Belgian throne, possessed the qualities of a statesman ; he was forty years of age ; he had long been suggested as a sovereign for the Greeks ; five years earlier Kountouriótes had commissioned agents to sound him ; more recently he had himself sent an emissary to study the situation in Greece. No one was, therefore, surprised when, eight days later, he accepted. As the Porte likewise accepted these last protocols of the three Powers, and the Greek people was delighted at Prince Leopold's selection, it seemed as if the Greek question were settled ; so certain did this appear, that France abandoned into his hands her ancient protectorate over the Catholics in the

Cyclades. But the Allies had reckoned without the President. Capo d'Istria cherished the ambition of a life presidency for himself; he was disappointed that he had been overlooked, and he saw no reason why he should have sown that a foreigner might reap. He, therefore, deliberately set to work to paint the condition of Greece in the darkest colours, so as to deter the Prince from coming. Leopold himself was disappointed at the narrow frontiers of his intended principality; he had already written to Lord Aberdeen " that he could imagine no effectual mode of pacifying Greece without including Candia in the new state"; he had read Church's pamphlet on the strategic advantages of Akarnanía; he had even hoped to bring, like King George in 1864, the Ionian Islands as a present to his future subjects. Capo d'Istria harped upon the unpopularity of this restriction of frontier, with which Leopold would be identified; he cleverly availed himself of the decree passed at Argos that the negotiations must be approved by the legislature. He hinted that the Prince would do well to adopt the religion of his subjects, of which the President was a warm devotee. He tried to prevent addresses of welcome from reaching Leopold, and he treated the signatories as his enemies. All these things, combined with the remote prospect of a regency in England—for his dead wife had been the daughter of George IV—so affected the Prince, that he retracted his acceptance and in May definitely resigned the Greek throne. Leopold a year later became king of the Belgians; but he often lamented, amid the prosaic comforts of Brussels, the romantic career which might have been his at Athens. To-day the most instructive incident in his candidature is his prophetic warning about Crete.

Capo d'Istria had succeeded in thwarting the Coburg nomination, but there at once set in a reaction against himself. His own conduct and the revolutionary spirit, which spread to Greece from Paris as the result of the July revolution, both fostered the growing discontent. Success had made him more autocratic; and some of his acts were as arbitrary as those which had just cost Charles X his throne. To have signed an address to Leopold was considered a criminal offence, just as in later Italy it was sufficient proof of guilt to "have spoken evil of Garibaldi." He sent Russian ships to coerce the independent Mainates into payment of a tax; he was unable to procure the Turkish evacuation of the Akropolis and Euboea, because the Turks refused to budge till they received compensation for their private property and till the delimitation of the frontier was completed. But the President could not raise the money; and the Powers, distracted by the French and the Polish revolutions, tarried with the settlement of Greece. The Turkish garrison did not finally quit the Akropolis till March 31, 1833, nearly eighteen months after his death; the Athenians strongly criticised his administration; a military mutiny foreshadowed what was to follow. Worst of all, his refusal to pay the compensation demanded by the Hydriotes for their losses in the war aroused the stubborn opposition of that influential island. The Hydriotes started a newspaper, the *Aurora*, as the mouthpiece of their grievances; Capo d'Istria suppressed it, only to find that another journal, the *Apollo*, was being printed at Nauplia, whither the seat of government had been transferred from Aigina. Viaro smothered its first issue; but the editor transferred his operations to the indomitable island, where it at once became the organ of the Opposition, with "a Congress and a Constitution" as its programme. Hýdra then separated herself from the President's jurisdiction and became practically an independent commonwealth under a committee of local magnates. Syra, the most flourishing commercial community in Greece, galled by his mercantile regulations, supported Hydra. This was more than the President could stand; he ordered the fleet to punish Syra.

Before, however, the fleet had left the arsenal at Póros, the "constitutional committee" of Hýdra sent Admiral Miaoúles, who was one of its members, with Mavrokordátos as his adviser, to seize the arsenal. Miaoúles executed his task with his accustomed energy, and after trying to induce Kanáres, who was in command of a corvette there, to join the constitutionalists, put his old comrade under arrest. When the President heard of this *coup de main*, he forgot his diplomacy in his desire for revenge; and in the Russian admiral, Ricord, who was then at Nauplia, he found a willing instrument. The Russian officer sailed for Póros, and summoned Miaoúles to surrender the arsenal; the Greek admiral replied that he recognised no authority save the committee at Hýdra; the Russian blustered; the patriot retorted that he would do his duty. At this crisis the British and French commanders arrived by chance, but departed to Nauplia for instructions. Meanwhile Ricord's men came into collision with a vessel from Hýdra; and Capo d'Istria sent him a message, insinuating that he should strike before they returned. On August 13, 1831, he took up a position to cannonade the Greek fleet, whereupon Miaoúles sent him a message to the effect that he would blow it up rather than surrender. The Hydriote was as good as his word; a terrific explosion covered the beautiful harbour of Póros with the wrecks of the Greek ships; Miaoúles escaped with their crews to Hýdra; the troops of the President under Nikétas sacked the town of Póros, although it had previously capitulated, as if it had been a Turkish city, while the Russian admiral looked on. When all was over Capo d'Istria wrote to Ricord thanking him for his services. But the catastrophe of Póros was fatal to the President. The Greek Opposition considered him as a party chief; the British and French governments regarded him as a Russian proconsul.

The deeply wounded pride of a powerful family caused, within two months of the conflagration of Póros, the end of Capo d'Istria. The clan of the Mavromichálai was all powerful in Maina; since 1690 the name had been familiar; since 1769 it had been ennobled by the struggles of those who bore it in the cause of Greek freedom. In the War of Independence, at the taking of Kalama̓ta, at the battle of Valte̓tsi, in Eubœa, in Akarnani̓a, and in Epirus, the Mavromicha̓lai had fought heroically, sometimes with the loss of their lives, for Greece. But, notwithstanding these patriotic services, they represented Maina and all that Maina stood for—the blood feud, the ethics of a primitive society, defiance of a central and centralising authority. To Capo d'Istria it seemed that Maina must be "civilised" and raised to the level of the less Homeric parts of Greece; and the only way of achieving this object was the proscription of a family, whose word was law where his writ would not run. A local revolt, headed by Petrobey's brother John, had been suppressed through the intervention of the Bey's second son George at the request of the President, who had promised to arrange the disputes between the government and the clan, if John would come to Nauplia. John came, and was put under arrest, while prosecutions were set on foot against him and his son. His son fled to Maina, where Constantine, a brother of the Bey, headed the revolt of "the Spartans," as the Mainates loved to call themselves, against the gaoler of their chieftain's family. Thither the Bey himself likewise hastened, but was arrested and escorted back to Nauplia, where he was imprisoned on a charge of high treason and dereliction of his duty as a member of the Senate. Constantine and George were also conveyed to Nauplia and there placed under police supervision. These proceedings naturally aroused public sympathy with the persecuted family. The Bey's aged mother petitioned the President to release her distinguished son, who had been then nine months in prison untried; Admiral Ricord, the confidant of Capo d'Istria at Po̓ros, used his influence in the same direction. But the President remained obdurate; and, acting in accord with the Mainate code of honour, Constantine and George, who were merely "shadowed" by the police and not confined to prison, resolved to avenge their relative. On October 9, 1831, Capo

d'Istria walked, as was his wont, to attend early service at
the church of St Spirídon, the patron saint of his native
island, situated at the foot of Itsh Kaleh.   As he approached
the door, he noticed the two Mavromichálai standing on either
side.   He stopped for a moment, as if suspecting an attempt,
against which he had been warned; then, recovering his self-
possession, he walked on towards the church.   But before he
could reach the door, Constantine's bullet struck him in the
back of the head; George's dagger stabbed him through the
lungs; and he fell lifeless in the embrace of his one-armed
orderly.   His attendant laid the corpse upon the ground, fired
at Constantine and wounded him; another bullet from a
window struck the fleeing assassin; a third killed him; whereupon the crowd dragged his body through the streets and
hurled it into the sea.   Meanwhile, George had escaped into
the French residency, which was besieged by an angry mob
clamouring for his surrender.   Escorted by a French officer
he was ferried across to the island-fortress of Boûrzi, court-
martialled, and, on October 22, shot before the eyes of his
imprisoned father, who from the casemate of his prison saw
his son die, as he had lived, a true son of Maina.   The
portraits of the two Mavromichálai now adorn the Athenian
palace of the present head of the family, son of the ex-Premier
of Greece, where the visitor may distinguish the fierce mien of
George from the mild features of Constantine.

The lapse of three generations has enabled posterity to
form an unbiased judgment upon the career of Capo d'Istria.
No one will deny his private virtues, his austere life, his
sincere love of his native land, his services to it alike in the
days of his foreign employment and in those of his presidency.
But he tried to govern Greeks by the maxims, and with the
assistance, of the most autocratic of governments; he was to
the last a diplomatist, and revolutions need not diplomatists
but men of action.   Nevertheless, a grateful country has
recognised his public merits as well as his personal qualities.

Aigina, his first capital, and Corfù his birthplace, have both raised statues in his honour; the one island preserves in different form the orphanage which he founded, and the "government house" which was the first mint of Greece; the other cherishes in the Platytéra convent his murdered remains; a part of the University at Athens has been called since 1911 by his name; while his latest biographer has extolled the services to elementary education of the former ephor of the first public school at Corfù.

The assassination of Capo d'Istria awakened widely different feelings. The poet Alexander Soûtsos compared the assassins with Harmódios and Aristogeíton; the *Apollo* deplored the human tragedy, yet thought otherwise of the political tyrannicide; the friends of the murdered President mourned, and acted. The Senate at once met, and before mid-day of the fatal ninth of October nominated a provisional commission of three to carry on the government till a National Assembly met. The trio consisted of Agostino Capo d'Istria, the representative of the late President's family influence, Kolokotrónes, the leading Moreote chieftain, and Koléttes, the spokesman of continental Greece. Agostino, who was the chairman, unfortunately showed a complete lack of that conciliatory spirit which should have united all parties around the bier of his brother, and with the support of Kolokotrónes, he was able to outvote the more prudent Koléttes. Thus, when Syra offered to acknowledge the authority of the provisional government, and when Hýdra merely asked that two members of the Opposition should be added to the commission, an amnesty granted, and a freely elected Assembly held at some neutral spot, the olive branch of "the Constitutionalists" was rejected, in spite of a statesmanlike appeal by Andrew Zaïmes for union. Following blindly the policy of his late brother at Póros, Agostino employed the Russian fleet to blockade Hýdra, and showed his dislike for the French by dismissing one French general, and giving another a broad

hint that Greece could not afford the luxury of foreign troops
—a hint which led to the withdrawal of all French officers
from the Greek service. The most reckless charges were
banded about by the contending factions, each identified with
one or other of the three allied Powers; the Capodistrians,
or "Nappists," as they were called from a nickname of
Agostino, or from a follower of his brother, accused Great
Britain and France of complicity in the late President's murder;
the Hydriotes retorted that he had hired wretches to assassinate
the "constitutional leaders," and that his brother had sworn
to send the heroes of Póros to Siberia. Such was the atmosphere of mutual calumny in which the elections were held.
To make the Capodistrian majority secure, the Hydriote
deputies were prevented from landing at Lérna to take their
seats in the new Assembly at Argos; those of Maina were
arrested at Astros.

Koléttes saw that the time had arrived to sever his connexion with his two colleagues. His influence with the
Roumeliote or continental deputies enabled him to form a
formidable Opposition, which labelled itself as "constitutional,"
demanded the admission of the Hydriotes, and threatened, in
case of refusal, to hold a separate convention. Accordingly,
while, after taking the oath on December 17, the Capodistrians
held the fifth National Assembly in the schoolhouse at Argos,
the Roumeliotes met in another part of the town. Agostino
and Kolokotrónes went through the form of resigning their
posts; and on December 20 Agostino was elected President
(Προεστώς) of Greece. Koléttes, however, declined to resign;
and civil war ensued. Agostino summoned Russian assistance;
and after two days' fighting in the streets of Argos, which
Sir Stratford Canning, on his way to Constantinople, arrived
in time to witness, the worsted Roumeliotes retired beyond
the Isthmus, and at Perachóra near Corinth named a governing
committee, of which Koléttes, Zaïmes, and Kountouriótes
were members. Thus, Greece was once more distracted

between two rival authorities. A conference at the baths of
Loutráki failed. Agostino declared Koléttes and his confederates outlaws; Koléttes denounced Agostino as an usurper.
In vain a tardily published protocol of the Powers acknowledged
the latter as the legitimate President; in vain their Residents
caused him to publish a restricted amnesty; in vain Canning
counselled unity. What he had seen convinced him all the
more of the advantage of a foreign king over a native president,
who, as he wrote to Palmerston, "had neither knowledge, nor
the natural talent which replaces it."

At last, after two years' interval, the pre-occupied Powers,
on February 13, 1832, offered the crown to Prince Otho,
second son of the King of Bavaria. There seemed much to
be said for this choice. King Louis was an ardent Philhellene;
his name was well-known and popular in Greece; his country
was not important enough to arouse the jealousy of the Powers;
a German, Professor Thiersch, who had "discovered" Prince
Otho more than two years before, had since travelled about
Hellas as his unofficial agent, to sound public opinion and
prepare it for a Bavarian candidature. If the future ruler of
Greece was barely seventeen, it was pointed out that his lack of
experience would be more than compensated for by the greater
facility with which he would assimilate Greek ideas, while the
difficulties and unpopularity inherent in the existing administration would fall not upon the young sovereign but upon the
regency. On May 7 a treaty between Bavaria and the three
Powers settled the conditions of King Louis' acceptance for
his son. Otho was to bear the title of "King of Greece," an
independent, hereditary monarchy under their guarantee; in
case of his dying childless, his younger brother was to succeed;
but in no case were the Greek and Bavarian crowns to be worn
by the same person. On June 1, 1835, his twentieth birthday,
he was to come of age; and in the meanwhile three Regents,
appointed by his father, were to exercise full sovereignty. The
powers promised to guarantee a 5 per cent. loan of not more

than £2,400,000 to be raised in three instalments, the King of Bavaria to furnish a corps of Bavarian soldiers, "not exceeding 3500 men," with Bavarian officers for the organisation of a native army. The northern frontiers of the new kingdom, thanks to the efforts of Palmerston and the energy of Sir Stratford Canning, were ultimately advanced to the gulfs of Volo and Arta, and included the disputed district of Lamía, in consideration of which the indemnity to the Turks was fixed at £462,480, payable out of the loan. The Sultan accepted these arrangements and recognised Otho as King of Greece—a Greece much larger than that assigned to Leopold, but from which Samos and Crete were excluded. The former, after being organised by Koléttes, and proclaiming its independence, was coerced and erected in 1832 into an autonomous tributary Christian principality, from which troops were expressly excluded; the latter was united in 1830 to the Egyptian pashalik of Mehemet Ali as a reward for his services to the Sultan, while a liberal firman allowed the islanders a flag, free navigation, and the collection of their taxes by their bishops and captains. Strategically, however, the new frontier was, with one exception, favourable to Greece ; for it was so drawn as to give her the famous pass of Makrynóros and the whole eastern and southern shores of " Ambracia's gulf," save the fort of Punta and a strip of land behind it on the site of Actium. Thus Turkey retained the two keys—Préveza and Punta—of the gulf ; Punta she ceded in 1881, Préveza she held till 1912. The news of Otho's selection made the Constitutionalists at Perachóra resolve to attack the Capodistrians at once, in order to have their share of posts and honours when the king arrived. For the same reason the deputies who supported Agostino proclaimed him Regent till Otho's arrival, perhaps in the hope that he might continue to be Regent afterwards. In vain the excellent Thiersch was sent by the Residents of the Powers to hinder the advance of the Constitutionalists into the Morea. The ingenuous professor fell under the spell of Koléttes' diplomacy, convinced himself that justice was on their side, and went so far as to write on his own authority to the French commander, upon whom Agostino relied, bidding him allow them to cross the Isthmus. The Capodistrian cavalry posted at that dangerous passage, the scene of so many battles, dispersed at the first discharge, while the French, favourably inclined to Koléttes and fresh from a skirmish with the Capodistrians in Messenía, showed no disposition to fire upon the Constitutionalists. On April 8 Koléttes and his followers occupied Prónoia, the suburb of Nauplia, and a conflict seemed inevitable. Fortunately, however, a note had just arrived from London, stating that a "provisional government calculated to preserve the country from anarchy" was required. Armed with this document, the Residents presented themselves before Agostino, and informed him that he must resign. Agostino could not refuse ; but the Residents marred their success by causing him to ask the Senate to name the provisional government. The Senate responded by appointing an Administrative Committee of five, including, indeed, Koléttes, but leaving him in a hopeless minority. The Roumeliote leader, flushed with victory, naturally refused to accept this arrangement, but was induced to enter the town and discuss a compromise. His entry into Nauplia was a triumph ; such was the enthusiasm of the people, that Agostino, an unseen spectator of his enemy's reception, fled with his relatives, his brother's remains, and Mustoxidi, the Corfiote historian, on board a Russian vessel to Corfù, where he and Viaro joined the opposition to the British protectorate. After much discussion, a compromise was effected, by which the Committee's numbers were increased to seven, of whom only two were avowed Capodistrians, while all the seven ministers, subordinate to it, were Constitutionalists. But the device of a large quorum, always fatal to the transaction of business, was adopted, so as to paralyse the activity of the majority of the Committee. Thus, despite the resignation of Agostino, the

Capodistrian party continued to exist even without a Capo d'Istria.

Koléttes, in the hour of his triumph, was devoid of funds to pay his Roumeliote soldiery; and the latter resolved to pay themselves out of the plunder of the Morea. These strange "Constitutionalists," led by Theodore Grívas, and assisted by a band of Mussulman Albanians, soon caused the Moreotes, naturally jealous of "the continentals," to call upon their own famous chief, Kolokotrónes, to defend the peninsula. The old warrior cheerfully came to their rescue, and issued a proclamation declaring the acts of the Committee illegal, while his son, Gennaîos, stopped the march of the Roumeliotes. The government in its alarm begged the French to occupy Nauplia and Patras, and a French force actually garrisoned the great fortress of Palamédi; but before they could reach Patras, Kítsos Tsavéllas, the Souliote chief, who had headed a party in the heroic sortie from Mesolónghi, had seized the splendid castle, which he refused to surrender. He extended his jurisdiction over the twin forts which command the entrance to the gulf of Corinth, and held these strong positions till the arrival of Otho, whose Prime Minister he ultimately became. Tsavéllas was not a Moreote, yet he was not the only leader outside the peninsula who revolted against the government. Sálona was in the hands of the Opposition; and of the islands Tênos, Aigina, and Spétsai were unwilling, or unable, to acknowledge the authority of the Committee. The country was, in fact, in a state of complete anarchy; the "constitution" was a mere fiction; the people, as the poet Soûtsos bitterly complained, was "stripped" by the official "wolves."

It was necessary to hold a National Assembly before the king's arrival for the purpose of granting a general amnesty and of recognising his nomination. This Assembly of 224 deputies, including several Cretans, was considered as a continuation of that which had met at Argos, but assembled on July 26, 1832, in a wooden shanty at Prónoia, through the

interstices of which the free and easy representatives were
wont to inhale the tobacco from their protruding pipes ! The
Assembly did, indeed, pass the amnesty bill, and unanimously
recognised Otho ; but it abolished the Senate, and thereby
offended the Residents. One of the latter, Dawkins, the
representative of Great Britain, chanced to be out for a ride
in the direction of Areia, a village some two miles from Nauplia,
where the unpaid, ill-fed Roumeliote troops were quartered.
Spying the Resident, the penniless soldiery beset him with cries
for help and assistance. Dawkins in reply pointed with his
riding-whip to the shed, where the deputies were deliberating,
and added that it contained experienced paymasters. The
soldiers took the hint, broke into the midst of the Assembly,
dragged Notarâs, the aged chairman, from his seat, and carried
him off with seven of the richest members to Areia as hostages
for the payment of their arrears. As the government had no
money, the prisoners had to provide their own ransom. A
rump-parliament of 62 deputies, who remained in Nauplia,
after drawing up a protest, adjourned on September 1, till the
arrival of the king. But the outrage committed upon the
Assembly at Prónoia provided such an object-lesson to the
opponents of parliamentary institutions, that eleven years
elapsed before another Greek legislature met. It required the
revolution of 1843 to restore the liberties lost in 1832.

In September of that year Greece was left without any legal
authority to direct her affairs. The Assembly had been
dispersed ; the Senate had been abolished ; of the Committee
of seven, Demétrios Hypselántes had just died, after eleven
years spent in the service of Hellenism ; two of his colleagues
had gone to greet Otho˙ at Munich ; another had retired in
dudgeon to his native Hýdra. The three who remained—
Koléttes, Zaímes, and Andrew Metaxâs—could not form a
legal quorum. But it was felt that the coming king's government must be carried on ; so the Senate treated the decree of
the late Assembly as null, and recognised the triumvirs as the

supreme executive. Such was the confusion, that all the law-courts were temporarily abolished, and French troops summoned to keep order within the walls of Nauplia. But there was worse to come. The Senate, a creation of Capo d'Istria, preserved the Russophil traditions of its creator; and a section of its members desired that a Russian, instead of the Francophil Koléttes, should be in power when the king arrived. These senators fled with the government printing-press to Astros and thence to Spétsai, and offered the presidency of Greece to Admiral Ricord, whom public opinion held responsible for the burning of the Greek fleet at Póros. The admiral had frequently meddled in Greek domestic politics, but the presidency of the state he felt reluctantly obliged to decline; whereupon the senators nominated a fresh governing committee of seven, all military chiefs such as Kolokotrónes, Kriezótes, and Tsavéllas. At Nauplia and Kalamáta French bayonets supported the authority of "the constitution" and the triumvirs; elsewhere there would have been anarchy, had it not been for the action of the municipalities, which seeing the central government powerless to preserve order, took measures for its preservation themselves. The municipal institutions of the Greeks proved at this crisis more valuable than paper constitutions; native tradition is always more durable than imported ideas. Indeed, at that moment, the very name of "constitution" stank in the nostrils of the Moreote peasantry. They were taught to associate it alike with the French garrison of Kalamáta and with the Mainates who raided the fertile plain of Messenía; swineherds told travellers that "the constitution" had devoured their pigs; mothers told their naughty children that "the constitution" would come and take them!

One more tragedy was destined to afflict the unhappy country before the king at last arrived. As the day approached, the Senate and the military chiefs became all the more anxious to impose themselves upon the sovereign. Two of the latter, Kriezótes and the Argive Tzókres, accordingly resolved to

occupy Argos, so as to demonstrate their power in the neigh-
bourhood of Nauplia.   The triumvirs requested the French to
garrison Argos, and thither the French converged from Nauplia
and Messenía.   The Opposition had learned to hate the French;
and "Argive Vespers" were contemplated, which would rid
the peninsula of these foreign supporters of the government.
On January 16, 1833, the Greeks suddenly attacked them;
but the French cleared the streets, and then with their bayonets
drove their assailants from the houses.   Even the venerable
citadel, the ancient Lárissa, failed to shelter the fugitives from
the Corsican light infantry.   Kriezótes was taken, many of his
followers killed in the fight, two prisoners shot as an example.
The triumvirate thanked the French for their exertions; the
military chiefs deeply felt the defeat.   Happily time has
obliterated the feelings with which one Greek party then
regarded the nation which had rid the Morea of the Egyptian
troops.   A monument, erected by a patriotic Greek, now
commemorates on the quay at Nauplia the French who fell in
the War of Independence; while a lion, carved on a rock near
the suburb of Prónoia, bears impartial witness to the services
of the Bavarians who replaced them.   Sixteen days after the
conflict at Argos, the British frigate, *Madagascar*, with Otho on
board, arrived at Nauplia.   In the excitement caused by the
arrival of the long-expected king, the last incident of the
protracted reign of anarchy, which had begun with the murder
of Capo d'Istria, was forgotten.

While the rest of the Greek people had suffered so severely
from the war and its sequel, the Ionian Islands had made great
material progress under the British protectorate.   The three
currant-producing islands, Cephalonia, Ithaca, and Zante had
specially benefited from the destruction of the currant-fields in
the Morea.   As long as the war lasted, they had the monopoly
of the currant trade; and in 1829 the Cephalonians, in an
address to George IV, stated that in nine years the weight of
their currant crop had doubled.   "Our mountainous and rocky

island," they wrote, "has been, as it were, transformed into one
vast vineyard[1]." It was largely owing to the useful currant that
the revenue of the Seven Islands rose under Sir Frederick
Adam to £140,000. The new Lord High Commissioner was
thus able to expend large sums on public works. He constructed an aqueduct for the supply of water to Corfù; he
established a convalescent hospital and erected lighthouses; he
continued the road-building policy of his predecessor, and the
Residents in the other islands did likewise—Lord Charles
Fitzroy in Zante, Colonel Napier in Cephalonia. The latter,
during a long tenure of office, devoted all his efforts to the
development of that island, the "weak point," as he expressed
it, of the British protectorate. Cephalonia was always the most
restive of the islands; there the animosity of the nobles and
the peasants was intense; and, if the great currant-planters
were "glued to the English market," there was much less
money spent by the British officials there than at Corfù. The
Cephalonians and Zantiotes complained that Corfù was enriched at their expense; and Napier actually proposed that the
capital should be transferred to Argostóli. His own popularity
was shown by the repeated offer of the command of the Greek
army; but his methods, if well-meaning, were sometimes
arbitrary, as when he beat an Ionian noble, whom he found
beating his wife, and used his horse-whip on the peasants
engaged in making the roads. He endeavoured to prevent the
destruction of the Black Forest by the goats, and thereby
caused the indignation of their owners. He imported a colony
of Maltese to cultivate the south-east of the island, and thereby
aroused racial and religious jealousy. Complaints against him
reached the High Commissioner; the Napiers were not adapted
for a secondary station; and, despite his many services to
Cephalonia, he was removed. He took his revenge by
publishing a book, which is a violent tirade against Adam.

---

[1] Napier, *The Colonies*, 562.

The High Commissioner, despite his practical merits, was, indeed, guilty of extravagance. Maitland had gone to the opposite extreme, on one occasion walking into the Senate-hall with no other garments than a shirt, a red night-cap, and a pair of slippers! His successor spent the taxes of a small island on his gold-laced coat; and, not content with the palace erected by Maitland for his official residence and the meeting-place of the Senate, built the charming Villa of Mon Repos outside the town, whence the King of the Hellenes now gazes restfully across the sea at those Epirote mountains, which Europe in 1880 had intended should be his. Very popular with the Corfiote aristocracy, with which he had mingled before his appointment, he is still remembered with gratitude for his aqueduct, and deserved the statue which still stands in front of the palace. He abolished the system of road-building by forced labour, imposing a tax on imported cattle in its place. In 1824, the year of his appointment, the relations between the Greek Church in the Islands and the Œcumenical Patriarch were regulated; in the same year Lord Guildford founded the "Ionian Academy," where Greek was the vehicle of instruction. That ardent Philhellene, whose love of Greece led him to wear ancient Greek dress when he presided over the Academy, and to be baptised into the Orthodox Church, had wished, as Ugo Foscolo had suggested, to make Ithaca the seat of his University. But Corfù was chosen—an island of greater distractions and a more mixed population. Since the union the Ionian Academy has ceased to exist; but its library, a statue, and the name of a street still recall to the Corfiotes the memory of their enthusiastic benefactor. Besides the Academy he established Lancastrian schools; and in the time of Adam the Ionian treasury spent £7000 a year upon education --a great change from the days of the Venetians. As Foscolo had foreseen, the growth of an educated class, taught the principles of freedom from study of the Greek classics, would tend to undermine the British protectorate, while the lack of occupation in the restricted sphere of the Islands inevitably drove the youthful graduates into political agitation. Already in 1819 at Santa Mavra, and in 1820 and 1821 at Zante, there had been movements against the British. The formation of an independent Greek kingdom naturally increased the nationalist movement, and gave the Unionists a rallying-point. Already, in Adam's time, there were four parties in the Islands—the British, composed of the government officials and the majority of the land-owners; the Russian, which drew support from those nobles, whose feudal privileges had been restricted; the French; and the Greek, which hoped for ultimate union but was meanwhile content to live under the British protectorate till the young kingdom had become settled. As yet this party had no press for the expression of its feelings. Such was the state of the Ionian Islands when, in 1832, Sir Frederick Adam retired.

CHAPTER VII

THE BALKAN AND SYRIAN DIFFICULTIES
OF TURKEY (1822–45)

THE other Christian nationalities of the Balkan peninsula, with the exception of the Orthodox Albanians, showed little concern in the struggle of the Greeks for their independence. In vain Rhégas had appealed to the "tigers of Montenegro," the " Christian brothers of the Save and of the Danube," to "Bulgarians, Serbs, and Roumans" to rise as one people on behalf of the liberty of Greece. Had they heeded the poet's call, the Turks must have been crushed by the forces of the united Christians. But there was no probability of such an alliance of the Balkan peoples against the common enemy. The Roumans actually opposed, while Prince Milosh of Servia abstained from supporting, the Hetairist movement; not a few Serbs and Bulgarians, it is true, were among Hypselántes' followers in Wallachia, and a Bulgarian band was ready to co-operate with him beyond the Danube. But there was no general rising of the Christians. In 1821, as in 1897, the other Christian races sought so to shape their policy as to profit by the Greco-Turkish war. Not till 1912 did they unite.

The Roumans derived the greatest and speediest advantage from their Turcophil attitude by the substitution of native for Phanariote princes in 1822. The two Hospodars, as representatives of the national party, were delighted to execute the instructions which they had received from the Porte at the time of their appointment, to drive out the Greek monks, to replenish their empty treasuries with the funds of the Greek monasteries, and to close the Greek schools. French culture came more and more into fashion among the nobles; the resuscitation of their mother-tongue was the object of the patriots. Whereas, a few years earlier, Carageà and Callimachi had drawn up their codes in Greek, as being the language "used in the country," a society was formed for founding native schools, a national theatre, and a Roumanian newspaper. Although first Slavonic, in which the religious books were written, and then Greek had been so long the sole vehicles of ecclesiastical and secular culture, Roumanian had been adopted, owing to the lack of Slav priests, as the language of the Church in the seventeenth century, and had survived throughout even the Phanariote period in the poorer places of worship. Upon this basis, in the last decade of Greek rule, two fervent teachers, George Lazar and George Asaki, had begun to build a modest fabric of practical instruction in the vernacular. Hindered by the events of 1821, this work was now continued by Asaki and John Eliade Rădulescu, who may be regarded as the twin hierophants of the national idea in literature in their respective Principalities. Asaki derived his inspiration from a visit to his "ancestors" on the banks of the Tiber; Rădulescu was a pupil of Lazar, and therefore owed his education to the Roumanians of Transylvania, then more advanced than their brethren in the Principalities. The former was the first person to produce a play in Roumanian; the latter edited in 1829 the first Roumanian newspaper printed in the "bastard Latin" of the Danube, which was quickly followed by a second journal under his colleague's direction. Unfortunately, the spread of French among the nobles led to an intellectual and linguistic chasm being opened between the aristocracy and the people, which has not yet been fully bridged. The French language and French customs were considered the marks of a gentleman, just as at earlier periods a knowledge of Slavonic and Greek had distinguished the governing classes from the

peasants.   French schools were opened to supply the craving
for the idiom of society; and the frequent journeys of the nobles
to Paris embarrassed their estates and contributed to the
influence of the Jews, especially in Moldavia.

Roumanian historians date the national era of their history
from 1822.   But the appointment of native nobles as princes,
although so much desired, was not without its disadvantages.
The *boyars*, who were favourable in the abstract to the election
of a Roumanian as Hospodar, were jealous of the elevation of
one of their number over their heads.   Many of them had fled
into Russian or Austrian territory at the time of Hypselántes'
campaign; and these exiles complained to the Tsar of the
liberal policy of Sturdza in calling new and low-born men to
power in Moldavia.   When diplomatic relations between
Russia and Turkey were resumed, they returned, and wrung
from the prince a Golden Bull, exempting them, as of right,
from all taxes.   Moreover, if Roumanians had emancipated
themselves from their Greek rulers, they were overshadowed
by the great empire which had already incorporated one
Roumanian land and aspired to a protectorate over two of the
others.   The new Tsar, Nicholas I, had not been many
months on the throne when he massed his troops on the Pruth,
and haughtily demanded the evacuation of the Principalities by
the Turks, who still occupied them.   Great Britain urged the
Sultan not to provoke him; the destruction of the Janissaries
made it difficult to oppose him; and, on October 7, 1826, he
imposed upon Mahmûd II the convention of Akkerman,
which proclaimed the free navigation of the Black Sea, and
provided that the Hospodars should be elected from among the
oldest and ablest native nobles, with the consent of the Porte,
for seven years.   The consent of Russia was required for their
deposition or resignation; her counsels, expressed by her
consuls, were to be placed at their disposal; they were to draw
up a scheme of administrative reform for their much vexed
Principalities, which for the next two years were to be exempt

from the Turkish tribute, and were thereafter to pay in accordance with the sum fixed in 1802. Russia, it has been justly observed, gained more by this convention than by a war. But it was only the prelude to the war that soon followed. The battle of Navarino made the Tsar eager to attack an enemy whose navy had been shattered, before its army had been reorganised. Great Britain refused to join him, but the formal denunciation of the convention of Akkerman by the Sultan gave him the pretext that he sought. He concluded the war, which he had been carrying on against Persia, with a treaty which secured to him the possession of Edgmiatsin, the seat of the Armenian Katholikos, and on April 26, 1828 declared another war against Turkey. As usual, the first step was the occupation of the Principalities, which on this occasion lasted for six years. The two princes were replaced by a provisional government under Count Pahlen; the people, so long as the war lasted, experienced the horrors of the transport service, which the starving peasants were forced to undertake in place of their plague-stricken beasts of burden.

The second Russo-Turkish war of the nineteenth century was not the military promenade that the Tsar had anticipated. It was easy to occupy the Principalities; but Braïla and the great Turkish fortresses to the south of the Danube offered a long resistance. Varna was only obtained by treachery due to a palace intrigue against its commander; Shumla repelled repeated attacks; Silistria resisted a four months' blockade. In Asia the Russian arms were more fortunate. The Black Sea fortresses of Anapa and Poti fell; Paskievich, fresh from the Persian war, took Kars, Akhaltsykh, and Ardahan; Toprak Kaleh and Bayazid fell before the invaders. But the nett result of the year's operations was a diminution of Russian prestige, which rendered a second campaign inevitable. The Tsar, whose pride had been wounded by the stubborn resistance of the despised Turks, withdrew from the field, and entrusted the chief command in Europe to General Diebich,

an officer of German extraction. The Russian victory at
Kulevtcha, and the surrender of Silistria in June, 1829, marked
this change of direction. Diebich's army accomplished what
the Turks had regarded as the impracticable feat of crossing the
Balkans; and this double passage, from Pravadi to Aïtos and
from Varna to Bourgas, was performed almost without opposition and with an insignificant loss of life. On July 24 both
divisions met at Rumelikiöi, while the capture of Bourgas and
other places on the Black Sea enabled them to obtain supplies
from the Russian fleet. After engagements at Jamboli and
Sliven, Diebich marched on August 20 into Adrianople, "like
the commander of a new garrison entering a friendly town[1]."
The old capital of the Turkish empire had surrendered without
resistance to an army of barely 20,000 men. The audacity of
the Russian general and the ingenuousness of the Turks had
worked this miracle. Meanwhile, in Asia Paskievich had taken
Erzerum, and was preparing to march upon Trebizond. But
these striking military successes of the Russian arms were more
apparent than real. Mustapha, the reactionary pasha of
Albanian Scutari, reached Sofia with 40,000 Arnauts to save
an empire which he had hitherto allowed the Russians to
weaken; Shumla, the "virgin fortress" of Vidin, and Rustchuk,
were still held by Turkish garrisons. But the Russians had to
face an enemy more insidious than Turks or Albanians—the
plague and the other diseases, inseparable from the march of a
foreign army through regions notorious for their rapid and
enormous changes of temperature. In these circumstances
the Tsar was anxious to make peace, which Turkish statesmen,
ignorant of the true size and condition of the invading army
which they magnified to 60,000, and unaware of Mustapha's
march, were no less eager to conclude. They feared above all
else a revolution in Constantinople, which would cost them
their heads; and Baron von Müffling, the Prussian envoy,
exerted his great influence on behalf of Russia. Diebich, on

---

[1] Moltke, *Der russisch-türkische Feldzug*, p. 370.

his side, played to perfection the part of a victorious general; and when the Turkish plenipotentiaries, sent to negotiate peace at Adrianople, realised the true state of affairs and threatened to break off the negotiations, his advanced guard reached Chorlu, more than halfway on the road to Constantinople, while Aînos on the Ægean and Midia on the Euxine were held by the Russians. Simultaneously their fleets cruised off the mouth of the Bosphorus and menaced that of the Dardanelles, whither the British fleet would perhaps have followed the Russian flag and thus anticipated the Crimean war. The British ambassador joined the Prussian representative in urging the Sultan to yield; and Mahmûd II, with tears in his eyes, consented to the disastrous peace of Adrianople. Never in the history of the eastern question has the policy of "bluff" been so successful; never again till 1878 was a Russian army so near the goal of Russian ambition.

The treaty, which was signed in the old Turkish capital on September 14, 1829, did not diminish the territory so much as the prestige of the Sultan. The Tsar restored all the places occupied by his troops in European Turkey, so that the Pruth continued to be the Russo-Turkish boundary; but all the mouths of the Danube were lost to the Turks, and the Black Sea, the Bosphorus, and the Dardanelles were declared free and open to Russian merchantmen of any size, and to those of other Powers at peace with the Porte. In Asia, the Tsar restored Bayazid and Erzerum, but retained Anapa, Poti, and Akhaltsykh, so that the warlike population of the Caucasus was isolated. Turkey was to pay a war indemnity, subsequently reduced; and the Russians were to occupy the two Principalities and the fortress of Silistria till the whole of it should have been paid. Wallachia and Moldavia were to continue to enjoy their privileges, under the suzerainty of the Porte, but a separate act provided that the Hospodars should be elected for life, and should be removable for one reason alone, the commission of a crime. They were to direct the internal affairs of their respective Principalities in consultation with their extraordinary assemblies, or divans; and no Turkish fort nor settlement was to be permitted on the left bank of the Danube, where existing Mussulman property was to be sold within 18 months. The Principalities were exempted from furnishing corn, mutton, and wood to the Turkish government, but were to pay compensation for this exemption. On the death or removal of the Hospodar a sum equivalent to the annual tribute was payable; but the Principalities were freed from the latter for two years after their evacuation by the Russian army of occupation. Thus, the sole remaining ties between the Sultan and the Roumans were the investiture of their princes and the payment of their tribute. But, if the Turkish suzerainty had been diminished, the Russian protectorate had been increased, and the Russian occupation gave the opportunity of strengthening Muscovite influence.

Count Paul Kisscleff, to whom the Tsar entrusted the administration of the Principalities after the peace of Adrianople, bestowed real benefits upon their afflicted populations. He grappled successively and successfully with the plague, the cholera, and the famine, which befell them; and, after ensuring their material welfare, resumed the elaboration of that organic statute, which had been promised in the convention of Akkerman and had been begun during the war. This *règlement organique*, as it was called, was drawn up by a joint-commission of four Wallachian and four Moldavian nobles, under Russian auspices, and promulgated in the two Principalities in 1831 and 1832 respectively. As might have been anticipated from its origin, if it put an end to the prevalent anarchy of the administration, it left Roumanian society on a strictly oligarchical basis, of which the recognised exemption of the nobles from all contributions was the most remarkable proof. To retain the support of the nobles, Russia sacrificed the cultivators of the soil, whose position was made doubly worse by an increase in the days of compulsory work for the landlords and a decrease in the extent of land with which the landlords were obliged to furnish them in return. The peasants had thus all the burdens, the aristocracy all the honours, of public life ; but, in order to prevent either the *boyars* or the future prince from becoming too powerful, the Russians resorted to the plan, which they adopted in Bulgaria in 1879, of introducing a constitutional system of checks and balances so dexterously formed as to neutralise the power of the prince by that of the nobles, and the power of the nobles by that of the prince. Accordingly, an Assembly of *boyars* was to be elected, and had the right of complaining to the suzerain and the protecting Powers against him ; but he, on the other hand, might prorogue a seditious Assembly, and appeal to the two Imperial guardians of his Principality for leave to convoke another. In either case, the Tsar would be likely to be the arbitrator. Having thus organised the Principalities, the Russians withdrew in 1834, when a special arrangement between the Tsar and the Sultan provided that for this occasion only the two courts should name the princes. As such, Alexander II Ghika, younger brother of the prince of 1822–8, and Michael Sturdza were appointed for Wallachia and Moldavia respectively. Russia still, however, continued to exert her influence in the internal affairs of the Roumans by means of her consuls; she actually pretended that no change should be made in the organic statute without her consent and that of Turkey, and she opposed all attempts at propagating the national language. Her intrigues culminated in 1842 in the deposition of Ghika.

While Greece had been the theatre of one war, and the Principalities the base of another, Servia had been at peace with Turkey and undisturbed by the presence of Russian troops. Milosh, already recognised by his own people as their supreme and hereditary chief, was promised in 1820 the recognition of the Porte, which was also willing to fix the amount of the Servian tribute, if the Serbs would accept this as a final settlement. This offer was rejected, and a Servian deputation, sent to negotiate at Constantinople, was arrested, and kept under observation for five years. Further negotiations were suspended till the convention of Akkerman and the special act relating to Servia, which accompanied it, ratified and extended the previous Turkish concessions. The Porte undertook to execute without delay the eighth article of the treaty of Bucharest, to inform the Russian government of the fulfilment of this undertaking, and within 18 months to settle in concert with the deputies of the Servian people at Constantinople the points demanded by the latter. These included internal autonomy, the right to choose the chiefs of the nation, and the reunion with Servia of the six Servian districts, which had been comprised within the jurisdiction of Kara George, but had not taken part in the rising of Milosh. The Porte showed, however, no inclination to perform these pledges, given at Akkerman; and matters remained as they were until the conclusion of the Russo-Turkish war—a struggle in which, by the express desire of Diebich, anxious not to provoke Austrian jealousies or Turkish reprisals, the Serbs confined themselves to the work of hindering the junction of a Bosnian force with the Turkish army. In the treaty of Adrianople they had their reward; the Porte promised to execute "without the least delay" the annexe of the Akkerman convention, and more especially the pledge for the restoration of the six detached Servian districts. The Imperial decree to this effect was to be communicated to Russia in a month's time; but the usual procrastination of Turkish diplomacy deferred till 1830 the formal grant of Servian autonomy. No Turks, except the garrisons of the fortresses, were to live in Servia; Turkish estates there were to be sold, and the incomes of the *zaims* and *timariotes* assessed and paid to the Sultan, who would compensate his vassals for their lost privileges in the land. The Servian tribute was fixed, and was to be collected by the Serbs themselves; and, in place of Greek bishops, sent from Constantinople, they might choose men of their own race, subject to the approval of the

Œcumenical Patriarch. The entire internal administration was entrusted to "the Prince," as Milosh was officially designated, who was to exercise his powers in conjunction with the Assembly of the elders. That astute personage had offered to resign in favour of another, now that the work, which he had begun, seemed to be accomplished; the result of this mock abdication was his re-election by the Assembly and his formal investiture, on August 3, 1830, as hereditary Prince, by the Sultan. Still, however, the Porte hesitated to restore the six separated Servian districts, till Milosh selected a favourable moment, when Turkey was embroiled with Egypt, to foment disturbances among their inhabitants, and then invaded them to "restore order." Thus, at last, in 1833, the Turks recognised the logic of facts; and the Servian principality, enlarged by one-third, stretched as far as Aleksinatz on the south, the Drina on the west, and the Timok on the east—boundaries which it retained unaltered till the treaty of Berlin. Within these boundaries, however, there still remained the Turkish garrisons of the fortresses; and, by an ingenious quibble of the Ottoman government, supported by the Tsar, to whom the point was submitted for arbitration, the tumbledown defences of the town of Belgrade were held to constitute a "fortress," so that the Turkish population remained there. Accordingly, in 1833, Belgrade continued to be exempt from the fresh order which bade all Mussulmans outside the fortresses leave Servia within five years; and in 1838 there were still 2700 Turks in the town—a cause of continual friction, which 24 years later led to a sanguinary conflict.

With this exception, the principality of Servia was, so far as internal administration was concerned, free from the interference of the Turks in politics, of the Greeks in religion. A national government and a national church had replaced a system of alien rule, although absolute independence had not been obtained. But the peasants had not profited by this change of masters. They complained of being obliged

to provide provisions for the local chiefs on journeys, of forced
labour, and of other exactions; and their complaints found
vent in a revolt, which was suppressed by the powerful chief,
Vutchich, at the moment when the insurgents were actually
marching on Kragujevatz, where Milosh had fixed the seat of
government. The confirmation of his authority by the Sultan
made Milosh more autocratic than before. If he pretended
to adapt the *Code Napoléon* to the use of his subjects, he acted
as if his will were the only law. He took meadows and houses
at his own price; he allowed a suburb of Belgrade to be burned
down, in order to erect new buildings on the site; he made the
Belgrade shopkeepers put up their shutters to unload his hay.
By enclosing the commons, he tried to secure a monopoly of
the pig-trade, which was the staple industry of Servia; and
if, by refusing to grant fiefs, he benefited the cultivators of the
soil and saved them from feudal oppression, he thereby alienated many of his own friends. The discontent of the latter
led to a conspiracy against him in 1835; the conspirators
occupied Kragujevatz; and Milosh was forced to call an
Assembly and to promise a constitution. This first essay at
constitutional government in Servia, called from the place of
meeting, the "Constitution of Sretenje," created a ministry of
six persons, chosen from the Council of State, a committee
of leading men which dated from the early days of Kara
George's rising. The Prince was bound to sanction any law
thrice approved by the Council, which was to share with him
the legislative and executive power, as foreshadowed in the
Imperial decree of 1830, and of which all present and past
ministers were *ex officio* members. As an arbiter between the
Prince and the Council was instituted an annual Assembly, or
Skupshtina, of 100 deputies, to be elected by the people—a
provision which thus regulated and systematised the former
haphazard method of convoking such Assemblies. For the time
being, however, the jurisdiction of this body was practically
restricted to finance. The "Constitution of Sretenje" was,

however, suppressed almost as soon as it had been signed. Austria and Russia, aghast at the introduction of such principles in a state so near to one, and so dear to the other, protested; and the Sultan encouraged Milosh, who was nothing loth, to suspend it. The official press announced that he was the sole ruler in Servia, and he became more autocratic and more unpopular than ever. He established a monopoly of the salt which was imported from Wallachia, and spent the profits of this transaction in buying land there. Even his own brother Jephrem joined the Opposition, and was compelled, with Vutchich, to leave the country; while Russia viewed with disapproval the preponderance of the Prince's authority over that of the oligarchy and the consequent failure of her scheme to make the one counterbalance the other.

At that moment Milosh received support from an unexpected quarter. Lord Palmerston had come to the conclusion that to strengthen the small Christian states of the near east was the true policy of both Turkey and Great Britain. He saw, as Sir William White saw in our own time, that the Balkan peoples would thus become a barrier against Russian aggression. Accordingly, in 1837, Col. Hodges arrived in Servia as the first British consul ever accredited to that principality, and encouraged the Prince in his autocratic and anti-Russian attitude. Thus, the little Servian court became the scene of a diplomatic battle between the western Powers and the Tsar. The Sultan, then under the influence of Russia, with which he had concluded the humiliating treaty of Hunkiar Iskelesi in 1833 (see p. 147), could not, however, be persuaded by British diplomacy to support the authority of the Prince against the wishes of his own all-powerful protector. An Imperial decree of December, 1838, limited Milosh's sway by creating a Senate of 17 life members, corresponding with the 17 provinces of the principality. From this Senate four ministers were to be chosen, and all disputes between the Prince and this Council were to be referred to his suzerain.

Milosh was not the man to acquiesce in such a limitation of his powers. He stirred up the peasants, with the assistance of his brother John, by disseminating the statement that thenceforth they would have not one master, but seventeen. The Senate, however, ordered his enemy Vutchich to suppress this revolt ; and the triumphant leader, on his return to Belgrade, entered the Prince's house, and plainly told him that the nation had no further need of him. On June 13, 1839, the second founder of modern Servia abdicated in favour of his invalid elder son, Milan Obrenovich II, and crossed the Save. On July 9 Milan died, without even knowing that he had been Prince of Servia. Meanwhile, Vutchich, Jephrem Obrenovich, and the Turcophil Petronievich continued to carry on the government.

The Senate then decided to ask for the appointment of Milosh's younger son Michael Obrenovich III. The Sultan consented, but the patent of investiture omitted all mention of the hereditary character of the princely dignity. A Regency conducted affairs till Michael attained his majority on March 5, 1840; and even then the Porte forced upon him as advisers the two ex-Regents, Vutchich and Petronievich. This last act was in contravention of the recognised right of the Serbs to choose their own officials, and aroused widespread opposition. The peasants, preferring the rule of one man to that of several, clamoured for the prosecution of the two advisers, the recall of Milosh, and the restoration of the seat of government to Kragujevatz, a place less exposed to foreign influence than Belgrade, a Turkish fortress on the Austrian frontier. Michael consented to return to the former capital, and his advisers sought refuge with the Turkish commander of Belgrade, and subsequently in Turkey itself. Unfortunately the innate conservatism of the peasantry was alienated by the too progressive policy of Michael's Minister of Justice and Education, an Austrian Serb, who sought to convert this agricultural community of the orient into a civilised western state. Primitive peoples have always seen in a census a new engine of taxation, for to the oriental mind statistics are the prelude of the tax-collector; the social elevation of the clergy meant expense to the villagers, who shook their heads over the advantages of schools; while the Turkish authorities complained of the creation of a national theatre, where patriotic dramatists glorified the Servian hero who had slain Murad I on the field of Kossovo. Naturally this progressive policy cost money; and the most unpopular of all Michael's measures was the increase of the national tax, into which in 1834 all the various imposts had been consolidated. Moreover, the young Prince had foes in his own household; his mother wished for the restoration of his father; his uncle John was discontented. The recall of the exiles, who had sought shelter in Turkey, provided the Opposition with leaders. A "constitutional" party was formed against the Prince; and Vutchich, putting himself forward in August 1842 as the spokesman of all those who were dissatisfied from one cause or another with the government, demanded the dismissal of Michael's ministers and the reduction of taxation. The Prince, who had committed the mistake of returning to Belgrade, was abandoned by his troops when he marched against the insurgents; and, as the Turkish governor of that fortress favoured them, he had no option but to cross the Save on August 29, as his father had done three years earlier. Vutchich again entered Belgrade in triumph, and, as self-styled "leader of the nation," formed a provisional government, which summoned a National Assembly for the election of a Prince. This Assembly met on September 14, 1842, and elected Alexander Karageorgevich, younger but sole surviving son of Kara George, a man 36 years of age, who had been a pensioner of Milosh and an adjutant of Michael, and whose name and uncompromised past recommended him to the Serbs. The Porte ratified the election; Vutchich, as Minister of the Interior, remained the power behind the throne.

The Tsar, however, who regarded himself as the virtual protector of Servia, protested against this change of ruler as illegal and revolutionary, and demanded the deposition of Prince Alexander, a new election, the removal of the Turkish commissioner who had been present at the meeting of the Assembly, and the punishment of Vutchich and Petronievich. Lord Aberdeen, however, British Foreign Secretary, advocated the retention of Alexander; and a diplomatic compromise was made, by which the election was annulled on the understanding that the Tsar would not oppose Alexander's re-election. On June 15, 1843, he was re-elected; but the Russian autocrat would not be pacified until Vutchich and Petronievich had left the country, whither they shortly returned.

The Serbs of Bosnia had meanwhile been much less tractable than their fellows in Servia. The reforms of Mahmûd II met with a resolute opposition from the privileged aristocracy of that feudal land. The discontent of the Bosnian nobles, which had begun with the arrival of a Turkish governor, determined to deal out even-handed justice to all classes and creeds, broke out into open rebellion on the destruction of the Janissaries and the subsequent military reforms. Sarajevo had been a favourite station of the disbanded corps; and when its fanatical inhabitants learnt that thenceforth the Turkish soldier was expected to wear two crossed belts on his breast after the Austrian model, they exclaimed with sarcasm, that if they had to take the cross at all, it should be from the hands of the Austrian or the Russian Emperor. Under the leadership of Ali Pasha of Zvornik, the rebels drove out the governor sent by the "Giaour Sultan"; and the most vigorous measures on the part of his successor were required to re-establish his master's authority. But, when the conclusion of the Russo-Turkish war gave Mahmûd time to continue his well-meant reforms, the Bosniaks rose again against a movement, which they regarded as a double menace to their class privileges and their religious liberty. In Hussein-Aga, the headman of

Gradishka on the Bosnian bank of the Save, they found a natural leader. Hussein-Aga is one of the most romantic figures of Bosnian history. Young, handsome, and rich, he had the courage of a hero, and the reputation of a saint. His friends called him "the Dragon of Bosnia"; and, if he had been a real dragon, his enemies could. not have fled more rapidly before him. He had but to unfurl the green flag of the Prophet in Banjaluka, and the religious fanaticism of the country rose to fever heat. He marched at the head of his enthusiastic followers into Sarajevo; the Sultan's officials were either driven out of the towns or killed, and the governor only saved his life by flight. But even this did not satisfy the zeal of this new apostle. He meditated nothing less than a campaign against the Sultan beyond the boundaries of Bosnia. On the fatal plain of Kossovo, where four and a half centuries before the Bosnian Christians had fought in vain against the Turks, the leader of the Bosnian Mussulmans assembled his followers against the same foe. The discontented flocked to his standard from all quarters—the pasha of Albania, at the head of 20,000 warlike Arnauts from "bloody Scutari," the pasha of Sofia with a detachment from Bulgaria. So long as the three chiefs were united, they carried all before them; but the astute Grand Vizier, Reshid Pasha, succeeded in separating the Albanians from the Bosniaks and dealing with each apart. The newly appointed governor of Bosnia made himself master of Sarajevo, and set the native nobility at defiance by establishing his residence there, instead of at Travnik, the customary abode of the Sultan's representative. Hussein fled across the Save into Slavonia, where he was received by the orders of the Austrian Emperor with every mark of respect. But his presence so near the frontier was a source of embarrassment, for Bosnian bands were perpetually plundering the confines of the Austrian empire, and on three occasions the Austrian government had to take upon itself the duty of chastising the Sultan's rebellious subjects. Hussein was accordingly given

the choice of residing under closer supervision or of returning
to Turkey. He chose the latter, and died in exile on his way
to Trebizond. But the rising of 1831 was only the precursor
of further troubles. When the new Sultan, Abdul Mejid,
proclaimed the equality of all his subjects before the law in
the famous *hatti-sherif* of Gül-khâneh, the Bosnian reactionaries
once more displayed an obstinate resistance.

At last, in 1849, the rising had attained such formidable
dimensions that the Sultan resolved to make an end of the
feudal system altogether. He accordingly dispatched the
celebrated Omar Pasha, a Croatian renegade, and therefore
a Mohammedan Slav, like so many Bosniaks, to crush all
opposition to his will. The rebels were secretly abetted by
Ali Pasha Rizvanbegovich, the last great figure in the history
of the Herzegovina, who had taken the side of the Sultan in
the revolt of 1831, and had been rewarded with the governorship of that province. In his castle at Stolatz, and in his
splendid summer residence at Buna, near Mostar, Rizvanbegovich lived like an independent prince. He called the
Herzegovina "my province"; his subjects called him "a
second Duke Stephen" after the famous Vuktchich of the
fifteenth century, from the German form of whose ducal title
the Herzegovina received its modern name. He was, indeed,
the father of his people. He taught them to grow rice in the
marshes of the Narenta; he planted the olive and the vine;
he strove to extend the culture of the silk-worm. Severe
against the Christians who dared to revolt, he naturally sympathised with the refractory Mussulman nobles. But he was
no match for Omar in cunning. As soon as he had subdued
Bosnia, the generalissimo of the Sultan entered Mostar. Omar
invited his wily antagonist to his table, and when the old man
came had him dragged down to the famous *most* or "bridge"
over the Narenta, whence the town derives its name, and
placed upon an ass as a sign of his contempt. In this
humiliating position, Rizvanbegovich implored his captor to

send him to the Sultan for judgment. But Omar feared to
send so wealthy an enemy to the Turkish capital.   One of
those lucky accidents so common in Turkish history relieved
him of all anxiety. A gun—so the official version ran—chanced
to go off in the night, and the head of the captive happened
to be in the way of the bullet. Bosnia and the Herzegovina
were at Omar's mercy. The *begs* lost their old feudal privileges,
and their country was administered from Constantinople.   As
a token of his power, Omar in 1850 made Sarajevo, instead
of Travnik, the definite seat of government, and retained the
post of governor-general for nearly 20 years. But even his
authority was unable to restrain the mutual animosity of
Christians and Mussulmans. Whenever a Christian rising
took place in the Herzegovina the Montenegrins came to
the assistance of their brother Serbs, men of the same race
and religion as themselves.

Montenegro was, indeed, a continual source of trouble to
the Turks. The Prince-Bishop Peter I waged a successful
campaign against the governor of Bosnia in 1819; and the
repulse of a Turkish invasion from the side of Albania during
the Russo-Turkish war led to the recognition of Montenegrin
sovereignty over the Piperi tribe. When, in 1830, Peter I
ended his long reign of 48 years, he had the satisfaction of
having united to his little state the three districts of the Piperi,
the Kutchi, and the Bijelopavlich, so called after "the son of
Paul the White," a relative of the famous medieval hero,
Lek Dukagin. But not only had he nearly doubled Montenegro,
he had also given it a code, and obtained the payment of the
long-discontinued Russian subsidy of 1,000 ducats, and the
delimitation of the boundary between Montenegro and her
new neighbour, Austria. Future generations will perhaps
regard as the most important and fatal event of his long reign
this substitution of an active European Power for the moribund
Venetian Republic in the possession of Dalmatia. The French
annexation of that province was but an episode ; but the

Austrians came to stay, and their occupation of the Herzegovina in 1878 and their annexation of it in 1908 increased
the embarrassment of the mountaineers.

Peter I, who is venerated as a saint by the pious pilgrims
to his tomb in the monastery church at Cetinje, and who is
known as the "Great *Vladika*," was succeeded, according to
the usual custom, by his nephew, who took the name of
Peter II. The new Prince-Bishop, a combination of poet,
historical dramatist, and statesman, not uncommon in the
Petrovich dynasty, began by a series of reforms. He created
a police force, founded a printing-press, the successor of that
formed at Obod in 1493, established a paid, permanent
Senate (or *Soviet*) of 12 members and a president with
deliberative and judicial functions, and divided the enlarged
principality into eight districts (or *nahie*), of which the four
on the other side of the Zeta valley, known as the Brda (or
"mountains") gave to the ruler his second title. The population of the little state, thus reorganised, was estimated in 1846
at 120,000 souls. Peter II further abolished the dual system
of government, which had prevailed since 1516. From that
time the Prince-Bishop had always had at his side a lay official,
known as the civil "governor," originally chosen from among
the leading families of the Katounska district, in which
Cetinje is situated, and latterly always a member of the house
of Radonich. A dispute arose between Peter and the civil
governor; and the former settled the question in 1832 by
decreeing the abolition of the office and the banishment of
Vuko Radonich, its last holder. Thus, in Montenegro, as in
Japan, the spiritual authority suppressed the temporal; and
for the next 20 years Montenegro was a theocracy, but as
warlike as ever. In vain the Sultan tempted the Prince-Bishop
to recognise him as his suzerain by the offer of the city of
Scutari, a frontage on the Adriatic, and a part of the Herzegovina for himself and his heirs; but the pride and sturdy
independence of Peter II would not allow him to accept a

subordinate position such as that of Milosh. Consequently, a fresh Turco-Montenegrin campaign took place in 1832, in which the Turks were worsted; in 1835 a body of Montenegrins seized the ancient Montenegrin capital of Jablyak, which their ruler, however, thought it prudent to hand back to the Sultan; in 1840 a scheme for the capture of the still Turkish towns of Podgoritza and Spuj provoked another Turkish invasion. For several years, too, the indefinite status of the district of Grahovo on the Herzegovinian frontier involved the Monte-negrins in conflicts with Turkey. A treaty signed in 1838 had declared Grahovo to be neutral territory, under an hereditary *voïvode*, confirmed in his dignity by the Prince-Bishop and the governors of Bosnia and the Herzegovina; and this transitory state of things was continued by subsequent agreements. Finally, in 1843 the seizure by the Turks of the islands of Lessandria and Vranina in the lake of Scutari, by interfering with the fishing, severely injured the adjacent district of Montenegro. Several years of comparative peace with Turkey followed; but a sanguinary incident with the little country's other great neighbour had already arisen. The Pastrovich clan, inhabiting the Austrian littoral from Budua to Spizza, had sold its lands to the Montenegrins, naturally anxious for an outlet on the sea. Austria objected to this virtual occupation of her territory by her neighbours, and offered to buy out the purchasers. The valuation, however, led to a fatal collision between the Austrians and the Monte-negrins in 1838, and £40,000 barely compensated the latter for the loss of this strip of coast. More serious still was the civil war, a thing almost unknown in the history of Montenegro, which broke out in 1847, owing to the attempt of the Piperi and Crnitchka districts to secede from a principality which was afflicted by famine, and could not relieve them with the liberal rations of the Turks. The secessionists were subdued, and their ringleaders shot.

It was not in Europe alone that the reforming Sultan had

enemies to face. Scarcely had he ended the war with the Greeks and signed the treaty of Adrianople with the Russians than in 1830 his prestige was wounded in Africa by the French conquest of Algiers, which had acknowledged the nominal suzerainty of Turkey since 1519, but had been long practically independent under its Deys. Far more serious than this moral defeat was the revolt of Mehemet Ali, Viceroy of Egypt, in 1831, which threatened the very existence of the Ottoman throne. The ambitious Albanian was not satisfied with the reward which he had received for his services to his suzerain during the Greek war; Crete seemed to him an inadequate equivalent for the loss of the Morea; he in vain asked the Sultan to compensate his son Ibrahim with the pashalik of Damascus; and refusal made him all the more eager to obtain it. He knew that the reforms of Mahmûd II had rendered their author unpopular; religious fanaticism and vested interests had been alike wounded by the abolition of the Bektash dervishes, which had followed that of the Janissaries; one conflagration after another showed the dislike of the Conservatives at Constantinople to the new methods of their master; one insurrection after another in the provinces of Europe suggested a greater, and probably more successful, rising in Africa. Mehemet Ali could contemplate with self-complacency the condition of Egypt as compared with that of the rest of the Turkish empire. A French officer had organised his army; a French constructor had rebuilt his fleet; a French doctor had taught his physicians; he was the sole landowner, the sole manufacturer, the sole contractor in the country, where human lives were reckoned of as little account as in the time of the Pharaohs. The one thing lacking was complete independence, and the moment seemed propitious for its attainment. An excuse was readily found in the refusal of Abdullah, Pasha of Acre, to give up some Egyptian refugees, victims of Mehemet Ali's state socialism, who had taken refuge in the old city of the crusaders. Ibrahim thereupon invaded Syria; Jaffa and

Jerusalem were occupied by his troops; the Sultan's tardy resolve to declare his rebellious subject an outlaw was followed by the capture of Acre, the defeat of the Turkish troops and the surrender of Damascus. The diplomacy of the invading commander won for him the sympathy of the Syrian population; his strategy defeated the Ottoman generals, including Hussein Pasha, the commander-in-chief, in three successive battles. The victorious Egyptian troops crossed the Taurus mountains and entered Asia Minor; the Egyptian Viceroy demanded Syria, already conquered, as the price of peace. Mahmûd applied for the assistance of Great Britain, and sent Reshid Pasha, who had just pacified Albania, to crush the revolt of the greatest living Albanian. On December 21, 1832, Reshid was defeated and taken prisoner at Konieh; Constantinople itself seemed to be at the mercy of the rebellious vassal. The Sultan in vain opened negotiations with Mehemet Ali, at the suggestion of the French government; master of Syria, the Viceroy asked for Adana as well. This demand was refused; Ibrahim's reply was to order his advance-guard to occupy Brûsa, the ancient capital of the Ottoman empire. Then Mahmûd, finding the British government engaged with the affairs of Belgium and the French inclined to view with sympathy a ruler whose successes had been largely due to French organisation, threw himself into the arms of his hereditary enemy, the Tsar, whose army less than four years earlier had marched upon Constantinople. In February, 1833, a Russian fleet entered the Bosphorus; the "protector" of Roumans and Serbs against their sovereign had come to "protect" that sovereign against his vassal.

The arrival of the Russians in the Bosphorus caused far greater alarm in western Europe than the successes of Ibrahim. In their dealings with Turkey, the Christian Powers have always shown more zeal for what they believed to be their own interests than for those of either the Sultan or his subjects. It was a matter of less moment to the statesmen of London and Paris that an Albanian dynasty should displace the house of Osman than that the Tsar should obtain an exclusive influence at Constantinople.   But while British and French diplomatists wrote dispatches, the Russians strengthened their position.   A second Russian squadron entered the Bosphorus; a Russian army encamped on its Asian shore.   As the Russians had not yet evacuated Silistria and the Principalities, further forces were easily available.   Then Mehemet and Mahmûd came to terms; the Viceroy received for himself the whole of Syria, for his son the collectorship of Adana.   While he had thus obtained his price by attacking his sovereign, the Tsar was resolved to secure his reward for defending the latter. On July 8, 1833, at Hunkiar Iskelesi ("the landing-place of the manslayer") on the Asian shore of the Bosphorus was signed a Russo-Turkish treaty of mutual alliance and assistance. Russia pledged herself to provide troops for the Sultan in case of need; but a secret article stipulated that if "the need" were that of Russia, the Sultan, instead of providing troops, should close the Dardanelles to the war-ships of all nations. Thus, while Russia could intervene in the affairs of Turkey, the other Powers were excluded; and with a stroke of the pen Mahmûd II had signed away his own independence.   The British Foreign Office, taken unawares— for it did not receive an accurate text of the treaty till some months after the announcement of its signature by a London newspaper— pretended to ignore its existence; British and French influence sank at Constantinople, where Russia was all-powerful; nor was the Tsar greatly moved by the subsequent protests of the two western Powers, whose diplomacy he had outwitted.

The peace between the Sultan and his Viceroy did not last long, for neither was Mahmûd II the man to forget his humiliation, nor Mehemet Ali to forgo an advantage.   The Syrians soon became discontented with the rule of their new master.   Ibrahim, like everyone else who has attempted

to enforce the equality before the law of all races and creeds
in Turkey, aroused the opposition of the Mussulmans, long
accustomed to regard the Christians as their inferiors. By
his introduction of his father's system of monopolies he crippled
Syrian commerce; by the enforcement of conscription he
offended the mountaineers of the Lebanon, just as by a similar
policy the "Young Turks" of to-day have alienated those of
Albania. So early as 1834 he was obliged to repress a revolt,
which Mahmûd was prevented by foreign diplomacy alone
from assisting. Further risings followed, but an armed peace
was preserved till 1839, when Mahmûd could be restrained
no longer. Both adversaries had special motives for hastening
hostilities. Mahmûd had lately concluded with Great Britain
a commercial treaty, which, by repudiating the practice of
monopolies throughout the Turkish empire, struck a blow at
the economic system which Mehemet and his son had erected
in Egypt and Syria. It was, therefore, more than ever their
interest to sever their possessions from the other Turkish
dominions by a declaration of independence. Prudence
suggested the taking of this step before the Turkish troops had
been thoroughly re-organised by the Prussian officer who was
destined to plan the German victory of 1870, but who could
not hinder an Egyptian victory in 1839. Palmerston's remonstrances prevented Mehemet from becoming the aggressor;
but his warnings to Mahmûd were neutralised by the Turcophil
opinions of his ambassador, and by the passion of the dying
Sultan for revenge. On April 21 the Turkish army crossed
the Euphrates; two months later Ibrahim annihilated it at
Nezib. Mahmûd, fortunate in the opportunity of his death,
expired on July 1, 1839, without hearing the news of this
crushing defeat, the last blow of the many that had befallen
the empire during his long reign. He had witnessed the
independence of Greece, the autonomy of Servia, the loss of
Algiers, the revolt of his subjects in Bosnia, Albania, and
Egypt. He had seen the Russian frontier advanced to the

Pruth, the Russian protectorate extended first over his own Roumanian vassals, then over himself; he had signed the three humiliating treaties of Akkerman, Adrianople, and Hunkiar Iskelesi. Nor had his efforts as a reformer been very successful; if he had escaped the fate of his predecessor, the progressive Selim III, he had gained little but obloquy from those whom he had sought to improve in spite of themselves. Even to-day it is not yet certain whether Turkey be capable of reformation, whether the "Young Turk" be not merely the Old Turk in European clothes. No recent Sultan, however, has brought to this difficult task the energy and the indomitable force of will possessed by Mahmûd II.

The reign of his son and successor, Abdul Mejid, opened with a fresh disaster—the betrayal of the Turkish fleet by its admiral to Mehemet Ali at Alexandria. Thus defeated on land and deserted at sea, the Turkish government offered to make terms with Mehemet Ali, promising him the hereditary Viceroyalty of Egypt with Syria as an appanage for Ibrahim till such time as, in due course of nature, the latter should succeed him on the viceregal throne. The five Cabinets of Great Britain, France, Austria, Russia, and Prussia presented, however, a joint note to the Porte, urging that no final decision should be taken without their concurrence, inasmuch as the quarrel between Turkey and her vassal had become a question of European concern. But it soon became obvious that this striking unanimity of the five governments existed on paper alone, and not even on paper for long. While the British Foreign Secretary desired to reconfine Mehemet Ali within the boundaries of Egypt, the French Ministry could not resist the natural pressure of public opinion in favour of the Viceroy, who owed so much to France and from whom France might hope so much in return. Thiers, who became Premier at this juncture, went still further in support of Mehemet Ali; and the British and French governments drifted apart to such an extent, that, without the knowledge of the latter, the other four Powers concluded, in London on July 15, 1840, a convention pledging themselves to force Mehemet Ali to accept the terms arranged by them with the Sultan. These terms were the hereditary Viceroyalty of Egypt and the life governorship of southern Syria with the possession of the fortress of Acre, on condition that he submitted within ten days and evacuated the north of Syria, Adana, the holy places of Arabia, and Crete. At the end of that time the offer of southern Syria and Acre, at the end of ten days more that of the hereditary Viceroyalty of Egypt, would be withdrawn.

Great was the indignation of the French when this quadrilateral convention became known. Thiers, the historian of Napoleon, felt that it was "the Waterloo of his diplomacy"; the press, as usual, stirred up public excitement in a question which was supposed to affect the national honour; and even the middle-class monarch was constrained to speak of "unmuzzling the tiger" of revolution, in order to preserve his popularity. Patriots talked of invading Germany and Italy, of renewing the exploits of Napoleon, of exacting vengeance from his victors. Rival poets hurled challenges across the Rhine; bellicose newspapers exchanged threats across the Channel. Meanwhile, the allies were acting; the appearance of an Anglo-Austrian fleet under Sir Charles Napier off Beirût encouraged the mountaineers of Lebanon, deprived of their ancient privileges by the centralising despotism of Ibrahim, to rise against him. Beirût fell; Acre, which had resisted Bonaparte, was taken after a bombardment of three hours. Napier, while Ibrahim was retreating towards Egypt, concluded a convention with Mehemet Ali at Alexandria, promising to obtain for him the hereditary possession of that country as a pashalik of the Turkish empire, on condition that he made no further claims to Syria but restored the Turkish fleet. In the interval Thiers had fallen, and the return to power of Marshal Soult, who was highly appreciated in London, with

Guizot, fresh from the London Embassy, as his Minister of
Foreign Affairs, banished the fear of an European war, in which
the Tsar had promised to assist Great Britain. It only remained
to convince the Porte of the necessity of carrying out Napier's
promises. After the usual procrastination, the hereditary
pashalik of Egypt was conferred in 1841 upon Mehemet Ali
and his descendants in order of primogeniture, under pressure
from the Powers; his army was reduced to 18,000 men, and
its higher officers were to be appointed by the Sultan, whose
leave was necessary for the construction of an Egyptian navy,
and to whom the Viceroy was to pay an annual tribute of
£T.400,000. The Nubian conquests of Ibrahim were entrusted
to the Viceroy for life. The Sultan also conferred as an
appanage upon Mehemet the island of Thasos, where the
Viceroy's ancestors had once lived; but a Christian primate was
elected as the assessor of the Egyptian governor. Thenceforth Mehemet Ali troubled European diplomacy no more,
while France, returning to the European Concert, signed with
the other four governments at London on July 13, 1841,
the "Convention of the Straits," which closed the Bosphorus
and the Dardanelles, so long as the Porte was at peace, to the
vessels of war of all foreign Powers. This dangerous crisis in
the eastern question was over; and the young Sultan was able
to devote his attention to the difficult task of enforcing that
charter of reforms, which, on November 3, 1839, he had
solemnly published in the kiosk of Gül-khâneh. The lives,
property, and honour of all his subjects, irrespective of race or
creed, were guaranteed; the incidence of taxation was determined and its collection regulated; the European system of
recruiting introduced. Yet the evils of the Ottoman empire
have rarely proceeded from lack of good laws, but from the
want of their application. Nowhere are theory and practice
so far asunder as in Turkey, and nowhere is the saying of the
Roman historian truer, that the state is most corrupt, when
the laws are most numerous.

The Egyptian occupation of Syria had bequeathed a legacy of anarchy to the inhabitants of the Lebanon. The biblical mountain of the cedars had been ruled since 1697 as a feudal principality under the suzerainty of the Sultan by a prince of the family of Shihâb. In 1840, however, Beshîr-Shihâb, "the last great Prince of the Mountain," was deposed by the Turkish government, and sent into exile, and his relative Beshîr-el-Kassim Mulhem invested with the principality. It was the object of the Sultan's advisers to destroy the ancient autonomy of the Lebanon, and reduce that privileged mountain to the dead-level of a provincial governorship. They relied for the attainment of this policy upon the weak character of the new prince and the mutual animosities of the Maronites and Druses, who formed the majority of the inhabitants; for unfortunately this single area was peopled by different races of no less than six creeds. The Maronites, Roman Catholics whose services in the Crusades had gained them the promise of protection from St Louis himself, were under the special patronage of the French. At the instigation of France, Suleyman II had twice guaranteed to them the exercise of their religion; they had a special college in Rome; and in their churches at home a place of honour was reserved for the French consul, who was wont to hold his naked sword over the open book of the Gospel, in token of his sovereign's protection. The Druses, whose religious opinions were flexible but inclined on the whole towards a form of Mohammedanism, were the natural enemies of their Maronite neighbours, and in the opinion of French writers were considered to be the puppets of British policy in Syria. It did not, however, require any of those Machiavellian intrigues, which foreign publicists are fond of associating with our somewhat ingenuous statesmen, to induce the warlike Druses to rise against the feeble prince whom the Turks had set over them. In October, 1841, they rebelled against his authority and massacred the Christian villagers, with the complicity of the Turkish authorities, who then stepped in to restore order. Beshîr-el-Kassim was

deposed; and direct Ottoman government, in the person of
Omar Pasha, the former writing-master, and future Field-
Marshal of the Sultan, was installed on the Lebanon. This
remarkable man, who played so conspicuous a part in the
history of the near east, alike in the Lebanon, in Albania, in
the Danubian Principalities, in Bosnia, in Montenegro, in the
Crimea, and in Crete, was an Austrian subject and a Croat by
birth, whose real name was Michael Lattas. Deserting from
the frontier guard, he had fled to Vidin, learnt Turkish, and
embraced Islâm as a means of advancement. After acting for
some years as clerk to Hussein, then governor of Vidin, he
had gravitated to Constantinople, where he taught the future
Sultan, Abdul Mejid, calligraphy, and then, entering the army,
received his baptism of fire at Nezib. His old pupil naturally
considered him a fit governor of the Lebanon. The Powers,
however, protested against this violation of its privileges;
France, in the interest of her special clients, the Maronites,
urged the restoration of the local dynasty. The Porte, at the
suggestion of Austria, accepted a compromise; Omar Pasha,
an excellent and just administrator, was removed, and a
"provisional" organisation was adopted, which established a
dual system of government for the Lebanon. The Mountain
was divided into two administrative districts, one for the Druses
and one for the Maronites, each under a *kaimakâm*, selected
from the natives, but to the exclusion of the family of Shihâb.
Thus, for a single feudal hereditary chief were substituted two
prefects, appointed by, and removable at, the good pleasure of
the Ottoman authorities. The Lebanon, after the long enjoyment of practical independence, was humbled to the category
of county government. Nay more, in order to complete the
dismemberment of the former principality, the Turks severed
from the Maronite district and incorporated with the pashalik
of Tripoli the exclusively Christian territory of Djebaïl, which
comprised the ancient monastery of Kannôbîn, so long the seat
of the Maronite Patriarchs, the holy valley, and the famous

cedars. In the villages where a mixed population of Druses and Maronites lived together, two under-prefects, one for the Christians, the other for the Mohammedans, were appointed. These arrangements, however, failed to pacify the mountaineers. The break-up of feudalism had kindled in the breasts of the peasants the desire for equality with their lords ; and thus to the ancient quarrel of rival races and religions (for, besides the Druses and Maronites, the Mountain was inhabited by Greeks Orthodox and Uniate, by Mussulmans Orthodox and dissentient) there was added a new antagonism of classes, especially bitter when the peasant was a Maronite and the noble a Druse.

In the spring of 1845 the Druses, with the connivance of the Turkish military authorities, fell upon the Maronites and their French supporters. The French Capuchine monastery at Abeih was fired, and its superior, Père Charles de Lorette, massacred, while the American missionaries, who inhabited the same village, were left unscathed. Not only was the chief murderer acquitted by the Mohammedan tribunal, but Chekib-Effendi, the Turkish Minister for Foreign Affairs, who came in person to the Lebanon, ordered all European residents and travellers to quit the Mountain. When the French consul at Beirût sent his dragoman to protect the Christians, the emissary was arrested and thrown into prison. This last outrage to the law of nations brought Turkey to the verge of war with France; a French frigate prepared to bombard Beirût, unless the dragoman were set free; the French ambassador addressed an ultimatum to the Porte, demanding the restoration of French subjects to their abodes, the payment of compensation for the sack of Abeih, and the punishment of the authors of the massacres. As usual, the Porte yielded to the only argument which it understands—force—and accepted the French terms. The work of restoring order on the mountain still remained. Chekib maintained the dual system of administration, but, by way of concession to the Christians, created an administrative council of ten in either of the two districts; in both councils the Christians had a majority, so that they could at least make their complaints known. The Druses naturally murmured at this diminution of their authority; but the government was fortunate in its choice of the two *kaimakâms*, and for the next nine years the Mountain enjoyed a period of repose.

CHAPTER VIII

GREECE UNDER BAVARIAN AUTOCRACY (1833-43)

WHEN, on February 6, 1833, King Otho landed at Nauplia, there was a general feeling of relief. At last, it was hoped, the sorely-tried land, after eight years of warfare against the Turks and three more of internal convulsions, would obtain that repose which it so greatly needed. The monarch was young; he was unconnected with the factions and the intrigues of the politicians and the military chiefs; he was powerfully supported by three great nations; he was well endowed with the funds necessary for the organisation of a stable administration. The joy of the people, as portrayed in the well-known picture of his landing beneath the most beautiful of Venetian fortresses, was as natural as it was touching. Unfortunately, from the very outset difficulties arose, which, if they did not damage the popularity of the youthful King, estranged the loyal Greeks from the Bavarians who ruled in his name during his minority.

The treaty between the three Powers and Bavaria had entrusted the King of Bavaria with the appointment of the three Regents, who were to govern Greece for his son. King Louis' choice fell upon Count von Armansperg, a former Bavarian Minister of Liberal tendencies; Dr Maurer, a professor of law; and General von Heideck, who had already acted as the King's agent in Greece. To these three were added as a consultative supplementary member and secretary Councillor von Abel, and as director of finance Herr von Greiner. Armansperg was appointed President; and it was soon obvious that this pre-eminent position, combined with their incompatible temperaments and different social status, could not but create discord between him and his professorial colleague. The Count, an aristocrat and a diplomatist, despised the learned jurist as a commoner and a pedant; the professor, a serious scholar not free from the pettiness of German academic circles, regarded the Count as an elegant trifler who cared for nothing but society. The airs and graces of the Countess embittered their relations, of which the small world of Nauplia was soon informed. The discord of the Regents was the opportunity of the foreign representatives; and Dawkins, the British Resident, became the warm supporter of Armansperg. Moreover, no member of the Regency, except Heideck, had the smallest practical acquaintance with the country which they had come to govern. They were, therefore, compelled either to consult Greek politicians, who were naturally party men, or to adopt the usual German practice of evolving an administrative system out of their inner consciousness and their legal treatises. In these circumstances, the Regency could scarcely be successful.

The first problem which confronted it was the disbanding of the irregulars. At the end of every war there are in all countries numbers of "heroes," exceedingly useful when there is fighting to be done, but very embarrassing when society returns to its normal conditions. As it was in Greece after the war of 1897, so it was after the disturbances of 1832. It was comparatively easy to make the Moreotes beat their swords into ploughshares, for they had homes and land, to which they could easily return; but there were Souliotes and Macedonians, Cretans and Thessalians, whose abodes had been ravaged by the Turks and who had grown up to a distaste of any career save that of arms. When these men were suddenly placed before the alternative of either returning home or of enlisting in ten newly formed battalions of *Jäger*, their position was desperate. If they enlisted, they had to abandon their traditional dress for a Bavarian uniform; if they left the country, they had nothing before them but starvation or brigandage. Many took to the latter profession; and it was sad to see Arta sacked by Greek irregulars, German troops scattering veterans of the War of Independence, and young Bavarian officers receiving promotion over the heads of Greeks and Philhellenes, whose scars were more honourable than the smart uniforms of the Germans. An Opposition, which found a spokesman in Sir Richard Church, was at once created by this military policy; and the Greeks, who had hailed the Bavarian soldiers as a relief from the French, ended by contrasting French activity with Bavarian slowness.

The next step was the formation of a Greek Ministry under Trikoúpes, the historian of the Revolution, and the division of the kingdom into 10 nomarchies, which were subdivided into 42 eparchies, and those again into demes. As the demarch, or mayor, was nominated by the King, and could be suspended by the Minister of the Interior, a highly centralised western bureaucratic system was substituted for the ancient municipal liberties of the Greeks. What the Turks had respected, the Bavarians, like Capo d'Istria, sought to destroy. A similar policy of centralisation was adopted for the collection of taxes. Mavrokordátos, the Minister of Finance, made all the tax-collectors independent of the local authorities, claimed all pasture-lands as the property of the crown, and established a monopoly of salt. Such was the discontent at these measures, that they were speedily modified.

In respect of judicial reform and national education much was expected from a Regent, who was both a lawyer and a professor; but Maurer compiled codes too complicated for an eastern country in evolution, and drew up an educational scheme practicable only on paper, by which the young Hellene was forthwith to rise from the elementary school to the university. It was not till 1837, when he had ceased to be Regent, that the present university was founded. In its treatment of the

press, the Regency resembled Viaro Capo d'Istria. Editors
had to deposit so large a sum as caution money, and money
was so hard to raise at Nauplia, that the Opposition newspapers
then published there were obliged to cease publication, and
only the subsidised press of the Regency could live. Thus,
discontent was driven underground.

But the most unpopular measure of the Regency was its
ecclesiastical policy. It was obviously difficult to allow the
Orthodox Church in the free Greek kingdom to continue in
subordination to the Œcumenical Patriarch, who resided under the eye and influence of the Sultan. Accordingly, on
August 4, 1833, a decree, signed by 34 bishops, proclaimed
its independence, and created for its governance a synod of
five prelates, to be appointed by the King. The number of
bishops was to be reduced ultimately to ten, one for every
nomarchy; and all monasteries inhabited by less than six
monks were suppressed and their lands farmed as national
property. The opposition, which this policy, the work of
foreigners and schismatics, aroused, may be easily imagined.
The Patriarch, the dispossessed monks, those who objected
to the King because he was a Roman Catholic, those who had
regarded Russia as the great ally of Orthodox Greece, all
complained. It was not till 1850 that the Patriarch recognised
in a "Synodal Tome" the independence of the Orthodox
Church in Greece; it was not till 1852 that complete peace
was restored between the Patriarch and the Greek government.
Outside of the Greek kingdom his authority remained unim-
paired, till, in 1870, the creation of the Bulgarian Exarchate
dealt it a blow far more serious than that of the Regency.

The policy of the Regents and the exclusion of old Kolokotrónes from royal favour provided him with grievances which,
at first ventilated in the as yet unfettered press, soon found
an outlet in a conspiracy. A secret society, called the
"Phœnix," was formed to protect Orthodoxy and obtain
liberty, in imitation of the former *Philikè Hetairía*; and

the veteran conspirator circulated a sympathetic letter from Nesselrode, the Russian Minister of Foreign Affairs, as evidence of the Tsar's encouragement. A petition for the recall of all three Regents was signed for transmission to Nicholas I, while simultaneously a German interpreter petitioned the King of Bavaria to recall all the Regents except Armansperg. Thus, Nauplia was undermined by intrigues; the interpreter and Kolokotrónes were both arrested; the former was sent home without trial; the latter was condemned to death, together with Plapoútas, his fellow-conspirator, by an indecorous interference with the course of justice. To have executed the hero of Karýtaina and one of the men who had been sent to offer the crown to Otho would have been a blunder as well as a crime. The sentences were commuted to imprisonment for life, but the prisoners were released when Otho attained his majority. But Kolokotrónes and his friends were not the only active malcontents. Tênos refused to pay taxes; Maina rose in rebellion. Heedless of the warlike traditions of that Spartan race, the Regency had ordered the destruction of the towers which abounded there. The Mainates protested that their towers were a necessary protection for their lives and property; Maina was still a medieval land, and in the Middle Ages a man's castle was his house. A Bavarian corps, sent to execute the orders of the government, was surrounded and forced to capitulate; by way of showing their contempt the Mainates stripped their prisoners, and then demanded so much a head for them. Money, however, proved a more serviceable argument than force for the suppression of the insurrection. Some of the towers were destroyed, and tactful management enrolled the Mainates as soldiers, the best fighting material of the Peloponnese.

Before, however, the revolt of Maina had been suppressed, Maurer and Abel had been recalled. The relations between Armansperg and his colleagues had become so strained, that they had reduced his salary and asked for the removal of his chief supporter, Dawkins, the British Resident. Palmerston refused; but both he and Russia recommended the recall of Maurer and Abel. The King of Bavaria thereupon ordered their instant return and appointed Herren von Kobel and Greiner in their respective places, both old men, one of whom was unable to bear the privations of a young country. As Heideck was ordered to acquiesce in the President's decisions, from July 31, 1834 till he, too, was recalled in 1837, Armansperg was practically absolute. Maurer revenged himself by publishing the ponderous work on "the Greek people" which is the apology of his Regency.

Scarcely had he been recalled when another insurrection broke out, this time in Arkadía and Messenía, the districts where Kolokotrónes and Plapoútas were most influential. The leader of the revolt, a relative and namesake of Plapoútas, styled himself "director of the kingdom," and demanded the release of the two prisoners and the convocation of a National Assembly. The success of the insurgents so greatly alarmed Armansperg that he allowed Koléttes, the Minister of the Interior, to suppress it by the methods traditional with that statesman, the employment of Roumeliote irregulars. General Schmaltz, the new commander-in-chief of the army, then dispersed the rebels; Armansperg's plan had succeeded, but it had the natural result of reviving in the irregulars that taste for a roving life which it had been the first aim of the Regency to discourage. The disbanded irregulars in many cases became brigands, whom the municipalities of western Greece obtained leave to enrol as police, seeing that the central authority was unable to provide for the security of the provinces.

Meanwhile, on September 13, 1834, a decree was published announcing the removal of the seat of government from Nauplia to Athens. The choice of a capital lay between Nauplia, Corinth, and Athens. Economy and vested interests were in favour of the first; a central position, abundance of building land, and the proximity of two seas had induced the Bavarian architect to advocate Corinth; but historical associations, which must necessarily count for so much in Greece, decided for Athens. The Athens, however, which the King entered on December 13, 1834, was very different from that of Periklês, that of the Frankish Dukes, or the modern town, which in 1921 had reached a population of 292,991, and with its flourishing port contained 424,161 souls. The sieges and the struggles of the war had reduced the city to a heap of ruins, amidst which there arose majestically the ancient monuments. It was difficult to find accommodation for the court; even the King had to content himself with a simple one-storied house. Three wooden huts represented the bustling Piræus of our time. Under such depressing conditions Otho established himself in his new capital. Fortunately, the idea of imitating the Acciajuoli and building the palace on the Akropolis, which was suggested by Prince Maximilian of Bavaria, was vetoed by King Louis, who declared that the sacred rocks of the Akropolis, the Areiopagos, and the Pnyx must never be covered with buildings. Unfortunately, in laying out the new city, the Bavarians were less careful of the Byzantine antiquities, and not a few medieval churches were destroyed.

On June 1, 1835, Otho attained his majority; but Armansperg, with the title of "Arch-Chancellor," retained power. This appointment, followed as it was by the exile of Koléttes, the most powerful Greek statesman, who was sent as minister to Paris, caused dissatisfaction and proved that Bavarian administration had not ended with the King's majority. Otho was, however, only carrying out the advice tendered to him on this occasion by his father. The King of Bavaria had drawn up a whole programme for his son. "The Greeks," he admitted, "must not be made into Bavarians"; but, nevertheless, he considered that the time had not yet arrived when they could be governed exclusively by Greeks. If, therefore, he advised Otho to have none but Greek ministers —advice which his son did not then adopt—he urged the constitution of a Royal Cabinet under a German Chancellor with a consultative voice, and for this post he recommended Armansperg. The country, he added, was not yet ripe for a constitution, which would also offend the autocrats of Austria and Russia; but he suggested the promise of a Senate, to be nominated by the crown. The speedy dismissal of the German infantry; the distribution of lands to the pallikars; a due regard for proportion in the expenditure of the state, for example, the substitution of simple *chargés d'affaires* for ministers abroad (an economy partially introduced in 1910); and the restoration of the monastic property, concluded this paternal letter of advice[1]. Later in the year the writer visited Athens, to see for himself the condition of his son's young kingdom.

He found continental Greece cleared of brigandage, thanks to the energy of General Gordon; a portion of the public lands assigned to Greek families; a " Royal Phalanx" formed exclusively of Greeks, and mainly of veterans of the war; and a " Council of State " nominated by the crown, and endowed with the power to reject alterations of the fiscal system. But these prompt measures of the young King did not pacify public opinion. Early in 1836 an insurrection broke out in Akarnanía under three leaders, Dêmos Tsélios, Zervás, and Malámas, a former aide-de-camp of Agostino Capo d'Istria, men who were not brigands but political agitators, and who all agreed in demanding the expulsion of the Bavarians and the grant of a constitution. Armansperg suppressed this revolt by the favourite device of allowing chieftains such as Kítsos Tsavéllas and Theodore Grívas to enrol irregulars; while Sir Edmund Lyons, who had commanded the frigate that had brought Otho to Greece and had been appointed British minister at Athens on the King's attainment of his majority, made the insurrection the text for an appeal to Palmerston

---

[1] Trost, *König Ludwig von Bayern,* 127–32; Δελτίον τῆς Ἱστ. καὶ Ἐθν. Ἑταιρίας, ii, 516-20.

to advance the third instalment of the Greek loan, promised by the three protecting Powers in 1832. As the Tsar made his payment contingent on the indefinite postponement of the constitution, while France stipulated for the dismissal of all Bavarians, the formation of a national government, and the grant of the institutions necessary to its proper working, the British Foreign Secretary characteristically asked Parliament to guarantee the issue of the British share, without waiting any longer for the adhesion of the two other Powers. Meanwhile, his representative at Athens was instructed to support Armansperg.

After having laid the foundations of his son's palace on February 6, 1836, the anniversary of Otho's landing, on a site "sufficiently far from the sea to be out of range of a bombardment," as the careful father expressed it, Louis returned to Germany, whither later in the year Otho followed him. The object of the latter's journey was to find a wife; and, as his father strongly objected to a French princess or a Russian Grand-duchess, his choice fell upon Amalia, daughter of the Grand-duke Paul of Oldenburg, a high-spirited and energetic consort for the hesitating King, whose "native hue of resolution" was often "sicklied o'er with the pale cast of thought." But Otho brought back with him to Greece a Prime Minister as well as a Queen. During his absence Armansperg had become more autocratic and consequently more unpopular; and such continual complaints of the Arch-Chancellor's conduct had reached the King, that on February 14, 1837, he appointed another Bavarian, Herr von Rudhart, whom he had persuaded to accompany him, in place of Armansperg, but with the less pretentious attributes of Prime Minister and Minister of Foreign Affairs. Thus fell the last member of the original Regency. Rudhart's political career in Greece was much shorter and not more successful than that of the Arch-Chancellor. At the very outset, by a tactless visit to Metternich, he obtained the reputation of being a tool

of Austria and thereby the suspicion of the democratic Greeks
and the opposition of the British minister. An outbreak of
plague at Póros, the refusal of the merchants of Patras to pay
the tax imposed upon their business, and the promulgation
of a severe press-law, which the King of Bavaria had strongly
urged, made the Premier's position increasingly difficult, while
the expulsion of an Italian refugee, a certain Usiglio, who was
the bearer of a British passport, provoked the outspoken
British minister to one of the most violent letters in the history
of modern diplomacy. Embittered by these difficulties, the
well-meaning Bavarian resigned after ten months' experience
of his task; and his name is now only connected with the
opening of the University, which beginning in a hired house
at the foot of the Akropolis, was subsequently transferred to
the present handsome building. It is pleasant to note as a
proof of harmony between the two newly emancipated Balkan
peoples, that Milosh of Servia was among the subscribers to
what was at first "the Othonian," but has been rebaptised
"the National University of Greece."

Upon the resignation of Rudhart on December 20, 1837
only the Ministry of War was entrusted to a Bavarian; but
the King neutralised this elimination of the foreign element
by presiding over the cabinet councils, instead of appointing a
Prime Minister. The crown was thus held responsible by the
people for the mistakes of ministers, and could no longer
shelter itself behind them, while the unpopularity of Armansperg and Rudhart was transferred to the sovereign. Unfortunately, a series of untoward events contributed towards this
growing discontent. Riots broke out in 1838 at Hýdra,
occasioned by the application of military conscription to a
nautical population, which, in the words of a popular poem
of the day, "preferred suicide to the slavery of service," but
really caused by the heavy losses of the Hydriote shipowners
during the war and by the earthquake of the previous year.
A commercial treaty with Turkey, negotiated by Zográphos,

the Foreign Minister, in 1839, was denounced as a surrender. Previous to that date no Greek diplomatist had been officially received by the Sultan, and the relations between the two countries had been constantly strained. The immense enthusiasm caused by a private visit of Otho to Smyrna had led Mahmûd II to order the Œcumenical Patriarch to remove the too patriotic Metropolitan of that Hellenic city; and this step had been followed by the suspension of the Patriarch and the prohibition of a commemoration of Koraês, the literary father of the Greek revolution, at Constantinople. The Samians, too, provoked a Turkish blockade by their demands for union, and made loud complaints against Stephen Vogorídes, the first Prince sent to rule over them till British support secured the temporary settlement of their grievances. It was natural, however, that those Greeks, who believed in the enlargement of their restricted boundaries, should have hoped to profit by the difficulties in which Turkey found herself involved during her second struggle with Mehemet Ali and his victorious son. There is nothing more dangerous to the popularity of a Greek statesman than inability to satisfy the national demand for the redemption of "enslaved Greece" at a favourable crisis in the eastern question ; and, accordingly, in 1840, Zográphos, the author of the Turkish treaty, was forced to retire, and was thenceforth politically ostracised. Other difficulties also accrued from the Turco-Egyptian settlement of that year. France revenged herself for her diplomatic defeat by scheming against Great Britain in Greece ; and the Athenian court was thus converted into an international arena, where the representatives of the protecting Powers strove less for the welfare of the country to which they were accredited than for their own governments' interests. Greek statesmen were drawn into these rivalries ; and "British," "French," and "Russian" parties flourished under the respective leadership of Mavrokordátos, Koléttes, and Kolokotrónes.

At this moment, moreover, Crete, which was restored from

Egyptian to Turkish rule in 1840, rose and demanded union
with Greece. The islanders had suffered considerably under
the sway of Mehemet Ali. From the first, Christians and
Mussulmans alike had been disgusted at the subjection of the
island to Egypt; for the former had expected to shake off the
Turkish yoke for ever, while the latter, who hated the Egyptians,
had hoped to remain a law unto themselves, as they had been
before the insurrection. Mehemet, with the usual "kindness
of kings upon their coronation-day," had begun by promising
that the Cretans should pay "no taxes, except the tithe (which
was really one-seventh) and the poll-tax"; he had established
two mixed councils, respectively at Candia and Canea, for the
administration of justice; and till the autumn of 1831 the
phrase of his governor-general, that his "sole object" was
"to deliver the Christians from the vexations to which they
were formerly exposed," corresponded with facts. The law
was enforced as it had never been before, and the Christians
were, if anything, favoured by the Sultan's disloyal Viceroy.
But, just as Crete was beginning to recover from the ravages
of the insurrection, Mehemet sought to introduce his favourite
system of monopolies, thus treating a proud and warlike
mountain-people as if they were Egyptian fellaheen. He had
begun by taking over the tithes from the local *agas*, who had
been (in many cases) their hereditary proprietors, thus irritating
the Mussulmans; his next step was to make the councils his
subservient instruments. The secrecy of letters was violated;
new duties were imposed upon wine and other articles, and
that upon the export of oil increased; an octroi was created;
and all supplies to his government were to be furnished at
a low tariff. By these means £6000 a year more than before
was raised from the island. But the worst came, when in
1833, Mehemet Ali, accompanied by Col. Campbell, the
British consul-general, visited Crete, and issued a proclamation,
punishing all who left their land uncultivated, and confiscating
it after three years of such neglect. The diminished population,

only 129,000 at that time, was not sufficient to till the soil, which would therefore have passed into the Viceroy's hands; while a well-meant ordinance for the erection of two schools was regarded as a trap to kidnap the Cretan children and carry them off to Egypt. One of the traditional Cretan Assemblies, mainly composed of Mussulmans, met, some thousands strong, at Murniés, three miles from Canea, to ask for redress; and petitions were sent to the Residents at Nauplia and to the consuls of the three protecting Powers in Crete. Mehemet's Albanian governor, Mustapha, at first offered concessions, which a passing British naval officer, Sir Pulteney Malcolm, urged the Assembly to accept. But Mehemet insisted on making an example; and by his order Mustapha hanged ten of the assembled Cretans—an act of cruelty which cowed the others for the next eight years. The Christians had, however, no wish to exchange the rule of a Turkish Viceroy for that of the Sultan; and their desire for union with the Greek kingdom was increased by the speeches of Palmerston. A " Central Committee of the Cretans " was formed in Greece; and among the Greeks who hastened to assist the Cretan insurgents was the future Prime Minister, Alexander Koumoun-doûros. In 1841 the warlike Sphakiotes began the insurrection, and a provisional government was formed. But the Turks speedily suppressed the rising, the failure of which was included among the charges brought against Otho's government. Mavrokordátos, who was then Prime Minister, found it impossible to remain in office, owing to the constant intervention of the crown and the continued existence, under another name, of the privy council of Bavarians which stood between Otho and his ministers. Upon his resignation, the King resumed the practice of presiding in person over the deliberations of the cabinet. In vain Palmerston and Peel urged him to grant a constitution; his father told him that to concede it would be the ruin of his throne. The unpopularity of this system of personal government was enhanced by the demand of the Russian government for the payment of the interest on the loan, by the curtailment of official salaries from motives of economy and by the disappointed ambitions of those who had been leading politicians. All these things combined to cause the revolution of September 3/15, 1843.

The revolution was planned by the leaders of two out of the three parties, Andrew Metaxâs, who had succeeded to the direction of the "Russian" party on the death of old Kolokotrónes in February of that year, and Andrew Lóntos, who had guided the "British" since the fall of Mavrokordátos. Another ex-minister, Zográphos, co-operated with a movement which seemed likely to restore him to public favour ; but the "French" faction, whose chief was still in Paris, abstained from active participation in the plot. As usually happens in party politics, the two sections of the coalition had different objects. It is true that they both desired the expulsion of the Bavarians and other foreigners who had not taken part in the War of Independence ; but whereas the "British" section wished for a constitutional monarch, the "Russian" had long desired an Orthodox one. The leaders of both parties anticipated that, rather than yield, Otho would resign. The people, especially in the provinces, took little interest in the revolution, and it therefore became necessary to resort to the army. Accordingly, the political chiefs, having selected as their instrument Demétrios Kallérges, then a colonel of cavalry at Argos, procured his transference to Athens. Kallérges, still in his prime, belonged to the ancient Cretan family which had played so prominent a part in insurrections against the Venetians. Sixteen years earlier, he had been captured by the enemy at the battle of Pháleron ; and it was only the greed of his Albanian captor which saved his head and thus spared him to overthrow the absolute monarchy of Otho. After the assassination of Capo d'Istria, he had supported the Capodistrian party ; and his courage, coolness, and desire for distinction recommended him to the conspirators. Another officer, Colonel Makrygiánnes, who had won fame at the mills of Lérna and during the Turkish siege of the Akropolis, was selected as his collaborator. Twenty-four hours beforehand, news of the approaching revolution reached the ears of the King; but the orders given for the arrest of the ringleaders and their trial by court-martial were issued too late.

On the night of September 14, Kallérges, who had gone to the theatre, in order to allay the suspicions of the court, proceeded, at the end of the performance, to the house of Makrygiánnes. Finding to his surprise that his colleague was sitting peacefully in the midst of a few civilians, he resolved to act on his own initiative. Traversing the deserted streets, he directed his steps to the infantry barracks, where, stammering a few incoherent words, he drew his sword, and shouted: " Long live the Constitution !" The soldiers took up the cry, and followed him through the silent town to the great square in front of the palace, which now bears the name of "the Constitution." At the same time, having learned that the house of Makrygiánnes had been invested by the police, sent to arrest that officer, he detached a body of soldiers to raise the siege, and ordered others to open the prison and compel any citizens whom they met to join in the demonstration before the royal residence. It was one o'clock in the morning of September 15 ; and the King, as was his wont, was still hard at work in his study, when the military music and the shouts of " Long live the Constitution !" startled him from his desk. An aide-de-camp and the Minister of War, who went out to bid the soldiers disperse, were arrested by order of Kallérges, while the arrival of Makrygiánnes and his friends with the detachment that had repulsed the police increased the strength of the revolutionists. The King, despite the prayers of the weeping Queen, then showed himself at a window, and asked Kallérges what he wanted. The revolutionary leader replied that both army and people wanted a constitution, to which the King angrily answered by an order to the troops to disperse, whereupon he would consider their request. The troops, instead of dispersing, awaited the orders of Kallérges ; and the artillery, which the King had meanwhile summoned to his assistance, fraternised with them. The civilian ringleaders then appeared upon the scene, hastily summoned a meeting of the Council of State, and induced that body to send a deputation to the King, begging him to grant a constitution. While the deputation was still in the palace, the representatives of the five Powers drove up, and demanded to see the King. Sir E. Lyons had, however, already conveyed a significant hint to Kallérges not to allow the diplomatists to enter till Otho had promised a constitution, because Great Britain feared that their presence might make him obdurate and thus favour the schemes of the Russian party. Kallérges played his part with admirable composure and tact. He told the foreign ministers that they could not enter the palace till the audience of the deputation was over ; and, when the Austrian and Prussian representatives attempted to insist, he reminded them that "diplomatic etiquette required them to follow the example of their *doyen,* the Russian envoy." The King thereupon yielded, and signed decrees convening within 30 days a National Assembly, which consisted of 225 members, for drawing up a constitution ; dismissing all the foreigners from his service, except the old Philhellenes ; and appointing a new ministry under Metaxâs. The revolutionists were not, however, satisfied till he had also promised to decorate those who had taken part in the revolution, and had thanked Kallérges and Makrygiánnes. Then, at last, at 3 o'clock in the afternoon, the army marched past the palace with shouts of "Long live the Constitutional King Otho I!" Thus, by a practically bloodless revolution—for one man alone was killed in the fighting at Makrygiánnes' house—Greece became, after ten years of Bavarian despotism, a constitutional state. "Great credit," wrote Lord Aberdeen, "is due to the Greek nation for the manner in which they appear to have universally conducted themselves on this important occasion; so different from the example afforded by countries more advanced in civilization." The Greeks rightly regard the date of "September 3," as they call it in the old style, as the birthday of their parliamentary system—a system which, with all its faults, faults by no means peculiar to Greece, is the only possible form of government for so intensely political a people. The names of the chief square at Athens and of a leading street commemorate the grant of a "Constitution" through the revolution of "September 3"; the sword presented by the Athenians to Kallérges is still preserved; and the scene at the palace on that memorable morning is depicted in one of the most widely diffused of popular prints.

The Bavarian autocracy had failed; but its failure must not blind us to the real progress made by Greece in those ten years. In most countries, and not least in the south and east of Europe, the people prospers in spite of, rather than because of, its government. Intellectually, the advance of the Greeks was marked by the foundation of the Archaeological and other societies, and by the opening of the University; the scholar Buchon, who visited Athens in 1841, noticed the purification of the language from foreign words, and remarked that the country had already two public libraries. Materially, the improvement of the young state was shown in the increase of the land under cultivation, the consequent multiplication of the currant plantations, the considerable export of silk, the recovery of the mercantile marine from the damage inflicted upon it in the war, and the establishment, thanks to the enterprise of an Epirote, George Stávrou, of a National Bank. The marble quarries of Pentélikon had been re-opened to provide materials for the palace; the population of Athens had already reached a total of 35,000 souls; the Piræus, Patras, and Syra were becoming important commercial towns. Outside the narrow frontiers of the kingdom, patriotic and industrious Greek communities assisted the commercial and intellectual development. Their relations with the Greek

state formed one of the chief problems discussed by the
National Convention, which met on November 20, 1843,
but took its name from that memorable "Third of September" which had ended the government of Greece by an
absolute monarch and his alien advisers.   Thenceforth, the
fortunes of Hellas were in the hands of the Hellenes themselves,
and the foreign domination of centuries was over.

CHAPTER IX

THE GREEK AND IONIAN CONSTITUTIONS (1843-53)

THE first difficulty of " the National Assembly of September 3," which was opened on November 20, was to decide whom it was to include. In similar conventions held during the War of Independence representatives of Greek communities still under Turkish yoke had taken part; but to this Constituent Assembly the only delegates of external Hellenism admitted were those of Crete, Thessaly, Macedonia, and Epirus; and a vote was passed excluding from all official posts those Greeks of the Turkish empire who had borne no active share in the war. Thus, the Assembly drew a distinction between the "autochthonous" Greeks of the kingdom and the "heterochthonous" Greeks of the outside world. Similarly, the second article of the Constitution, while recognising the "dogmatic union of the Orthodox Church of Greece with the Great Church in Constantinople," declared the former to be "autocephalous and administered by a Holy Synod of Archbishops." Two other questions excited considerable discussion—that of the succession and that of the Senate. The 40th article of the Constitution provided, that the heir to the Greek throne must belong to the Greek Church; another series of articles created a Second Chamber. There were some who did not desire a Senate at all; there were others, chiefly adherents of the "Russian" party, who advocated the nomination of the senators for ten years instead of for life. Thus Greece was endowed with a bi-cameral system, which lasted down till 1864, consisting of a Chamber (or Βουλή) of never less than 80 members, all at least 30 years of age and elected for three years in proportion to the population by manhood suffrage; and of a Senate (or Γερουσία) of at least 27 persons, who had reached the age of 40 and whose members might be increased to half that of the Chamber, nominated by the Crown for life from fourteen categories, according to the present Italian method. Both senators and deputies received salaries. It was supposed that the Senate would act as a check upon the Chamber and become a Conservative force in the state. But, as a matter of fact, it was the medium of the first attacks upon Otho, and provided the Opposition with a permanent platform for the exposition of their views. On March 30, 1844, the King took the oath to the Constitution; and Lyons wrote enthusiastically about the way in which this "great political change" had been consummated. "Such self-command in a popular assembly, convoked under very exciting and critical circumstances," Aberdeen replied, "is highly creditable to the Greek nation."

It now became necessary to form the first ministry of the Constitutional Monarchy. Two politicians stood head and shoulders above the other public men of Greece at that moment —Mavrokordátos, the chief of the "English," and Koléttes, the leader of the "French" party. Both sought what they believed to be the welfare of the country which they had so long served, but their political programmes for attaining this object were widely divergent. Mavrokordátos held that it was the first business of the Greeks to make their kingdom a model of good government throughout the near east, and that then, and then only, when they had been faithful in a few things, would Crete and Epirus and Macedonia be added unto them. Koléttes advocated the opposite opinion, that the first aim of a Greek statesman should be the enlargement of the Greek frontiers, arguing that the additional forces which the contracted kingdom would thereby gain would prove the best means of

its internal development.   Unfortunately, the Epirote declined
to form a coalition cabinet with the Phanariote; and Mavrokordátos became Prime Minister without his co-operation and ere
long had to face his opposition.   Both politicians, reared under
systems of government very different from that just implanted
at Athens, considered the concentration of all power at the
centre as the best system of administration.   It is unnecessary
to examine the truth of the charges brought against Mavrokordátos by some of his contemporaries and repudiated by others,
of having used improper influence to obtain a majority at the
elections of 1844; for even to-day, in many, perhaps most
countries, the principle of freedom of election is more honoured
in political programmes than on polling-day.   But, in any case,
the Ministerialists profited nothing by this alleged pressure.
Mavrokordátos, like a much greater statesman a generation
later, was defeated at Mesolónghi; and the similar defeat of
Kallérges at Athens, where the hero of the late revolution
had lost his popularity and where his very candidature was
considered to be tainted with illegality, led to a disturbance
which provoked the King's intervention and the resignation of
the Cabinet.   Koléttes came into power, which he retained
till his death in 1847 by the skill and tact with which he
managed men.   While his spectacled rival was supported by
the more Europeanised Greeks, who wore black coats and discussed western theories of government, the former physician
of Ali Pasha's son, clad in the national dress and smoking his
long pipe, was surrounded by the far more numerous body of
fustanella-wearing Hellenes, by braves of the war whom he
had led across the Isthmus, by all the picturesque elements of
what was called "the National party."   From morn to eve his
closet was filled by men anxious for some post, some pension,
or some mark of distinction; and such was his consummate
skill that no one quitted his presence without an assurance
that the Minister would grant his petition.   Enjoying the confidence of the King to an unusual degree, and supported by

the French government with all its influence, Koléttes concerned himself little with speech-making in the Chamber,
whence a series of election petitions had excluded all but 12
members of the " English " party. His well-known policy of
territorial expansion had, however, the natural effect of arousing
the suspicions of the Turks ; and his three years' tenure of power
was marked by several serious incidents, which disturbed the
relations between Greece and her neighbour. The Turkish
government began by stopping the free circulation of the Greek
press in its dominions, because the newspapers preached the
" Great Idea." The attempt of a Greek to kill the Prince of
Samos increased the irritation, and in 1847 a diplomatic question
at Athens nearly provoked a crisis. Karatássos, an aide-de-camp
of Otho, applied for a Turkish *visé* to his passport in order to
visit Constantinople. Karatássos had long been suspected by
the Ottoman government, because he had invaded Thessaly six
years earlier ; and the Turkish Minister in Athens, Mousoûros,
whose Cretan origin made him the more zealous in the cause
of his employers, declined to grant the *visé*. This refusal was
reported to the King, who at the next court-ball loudly told
the diplomatist that he should have hoped that the Sovereign
would have merited more respect than to be treated in this
manner. The Turkish government demanded from Koléttes
a personal apology for this speech ; and, on the latter's refusal,
Mousoûros left Athens. A long diplomatic correspondence
ensued ; the Greek consuls were expelled from Turkey, and Greek
vessels forbidden to ply along the Turkish coasts. Relations were
still interrupted when Koléttes died, and it required the intervention of Russia before the honour of the Turks was satisfied.
Mousoûros returned to his post at Athens, but an attempt upon
his life convinced the Porte that his prolonged stay there might
lead to further difficulties. He was, therefore, promoted to
London, where he remained for more than a generation, the best-
known, and—as his translation of Dante into Greek proves—the
most cultured of all Ottoman ambassadors at the British court.

This tension with Turkey was not the only difficulty which encumbered the long administration of Koléttes. While the society of the Greek capital was distracted by the struggle for diplomatic influence between the British and French Ministers, the British government embarrassed the Francophil Premier by complaining of brigandage and by demanding payment of the interest on the loan. The last request was met by the generosity of Eynard, the Philhellene of Geneva, who advanced the £20,000 required to satisfy the British claim. But the disturbed state of the country caused much greater trouble. Koléttes, true to his old policy of converting the breakers of the law into its guardians, pacified Theodore Grívas, who had raised the standard of revolt in Akarnanía, by giving him a military post; but this remedy, as might have been expected, was only temporary; and ere long the veteran chieftain was again at the head of a band in the west, while Kriezótes, another survivor of the war, championed the discontented in Eubœa. After the death of Koléttes, his immediate successors Kítsos Tsavéllas, a Souliote chief of no political experience but a soldier of distinction, and George Kountouriótes found themselves compelled to grapple with a number of these risings, among which those of Pharmákes at Lepanto, of Tzamálas and Valéntzas (who invaded Greece from the Turkish frontier and burned a fine collection of manuscripts at Hypáte), by Perrotês at Kalamáta, and of Merendítes (who seized the fine castle of Patras, threatened to lay that flourishing town in ashes, and then escaped to Malta on a British ship with a large sum of money), aroused most attention. Yet, despite these disturbances, mostly due to personal motives, Thouvenel[1], a French diplomatist then at Athens, could write that, in 1849, Greece was "materially one of the happiest corners of the world." Ministries might come and go—for the repercussion caused by the French revolution of 1848 caused the fall of Tsavellas, and the

---

[1] *La Grèce du roi Othon*, 272; cf. his memoir on Greece in 1847, *ib.* 129-45.

Cabinets of Kountouriótes and the famous Admiral Kanáres were but short lived—but the people were little affected by political crises due to personal questions or court intrigues.

Early in 1850 an unfortunate dispute, which reflected little credit on Palmerston's diplomacy, temporarily embittered the relations between Great Britain and Greece. For some time past efforts had been made to obtain satisfaction of the claims of various British and Ionian subjects from the Greek government. Of these claims the largest was made by a certain Don Pacifico, a Gibraltar Jew, who had been Portuguese consul-general, and whose house at Athens had been pillaged by the mob during an antisemitic disturbance at Easter 1847, due to the prohibition of the customary burning of Judas Iscariot in effigy. The Athenians were not aware, until Don Pacifico drew up his bill of damages, how valuable the furniture of this unconspicuous individual had been. He sent in a claim for £31,534. 1s. 1d. for the loss to his property (including £26,618. 16s. 8d. for the vouchers of certain sums, alleged to be due to him from the Portuguese government), and for a further sum of £500 as compensation for "the personal injuries and sufferings" of himself and his family. The next claimant was a very different person, the eminent historian of Medieval and Modern Greece, George Finlay, who, after taking part in the War of Independence, had settled in Greece and in 1830 bought land at Athens. A portion of this land had been enclosed in the royal garden, and Finlay demanded 45,000 dr. as its price. Three other claims were put forward on behalf of Ionian subjects, some of whom asked 6000 fr. for the pillage of their barks at Selasína near the mouth of the Achelôos, while others sought compensation for ill-treatment at Patras and Pýrgos. A sixth item was based upon the arrest of some British sailors at Patras, for which an apology was asked. Finally, besides these personal claims, the British government asserted that the two islands of Cervi and Sapienza, which lie off the south coast of the Peloponnese, were not portions of the Greek kingdom, but belonged to the Ionian Islands. This last claim, which dated from 1839, was based upon the clauses of the treaties of 1800 and 1815, and upon a law of the "Septinsular Republic" of 1804, which regarded the insular dependencies of the Seven Islands. But Cervi had long been the property of the inhabitants of the Greek coast opposite, who had held it in Turkish times, while the geographical position of both islands rendered them respectively appendages of Vátika and Modon, rather than of the much more distant Cerigo.

The first six of these claims, lumped together in the same ultimatum, were presented to the Greek government on January 17, 1850, with a demand for a settlement within 24 hours, by Mr (afterwards Sir Thomas) Wyse, who had succeeded Sir Edmund Lyons as British minister in Athens in the previous year. This ultimatum was followed by a blockade of the Piræus, effected by a squadron under the command of Sir William Parker, which seized a Greek man-of-war and several merchantmen. These proceedings naturally excited against the British government public opinion abroad, ever in favour of the weak in a contest with the strong, while they made Otho very popular with his subjects. The conduct of the Greek authorities was patriotic without being aggressive. The officers of the Athenian garrison offered to resign half their pay, and many private individuals put their fortunes at the disposal of the nation; but the government avoided anything that might be interpreted as an act of provocation; and, except at Corfù, where British soldiers ran the risk of being insulted in the streets, the Greek people remained calm. Meanwhile, France and Russia, the two other protecting Powers, addressed representations to Palmerston, who, on February 12, accepted the "good offices" of the former. Baron Gros was thereupon sent to Athens to assess the amount due to the British claimants; but his award was rejected by Wyse, and the blockade renewed. At this, on April 27, the Greek government

yielded to Wyse's demands, viz., the payment of 30,000 *dr.*
to Finlay, of 12,530 *dr.* 49 *leptá* to the Ionians, and of
137,538 *dr.* to Don Pacifico *plus* a further sum of 150,000 *dr.*
as a deposit on account of the papers, constituting the proofs
of his claims on the Portuguese government. These sums were
all paid the same evening by the Greek government; and,
although a different arrangement had meanwhile been made
in London between Palmerston and the French ambassador,
the Athens convention was maintained, and the French ambassador consequently recalled, as a mark of his government's
displeasure. As Russia had also complained of the British
blockade and of the assumption that Great Britain could claim
Cervi and Sapienza without the consent of the other two protecting Powers, it was realised in London that Palmerston had
by his vehemence not only oppressed a small state, which
Great Britain had helped to call into existence, but had
estranged two great nations. Even Finlay admitted that "the
British government acted with violence, and strained the
authority of international law." *Punch*, with its usual shrewd-
ness in expressing the opinion of the average man, asked why
the British lion did not hit someone of his own size; and the
House of Lords passed a vote of censure upon Palmerston's
policy by a majority of 37. But the House of Commons
approved the principles upon which it was conducted, by 46
votes, after a debate memorable in the annals of parliamentary
eloquence for the Minister's citation of the famous declaration,
Civis Romanus sum. But when the rhetoric had died away,
and an Anglo-Franco-Greek Commission, sitting at Lisbon,
found the originals of Don Pacifico's alleged lost documents
in the Portuguese Archives, ascertained that during his residence
in Portugal he had never asserted his claims, and by the lurid
light thus thrown upon his case reduced his claims from
£26,618. 16s. 8d. to £150, people might well wonder whether
the championship of this cosmopolitan citizen of the British
empire had not been exaggerated. As for the question of

Cervi and Sapienza, which had been omitted from the ultimatum, it was quietly dropped.

Admiral Kriezês, who had been appointed Prime Minister just before the Anglo-Greek difficulty became critical and remained in office for more than four years, had the satisfaction of seeing his Premiership marked by the settlement of another long-standing problem—that of the relations between the Church in Greece and the Œcumenical Patriarch. The Church of the kingdom had been declared autocephalous in 1833 and by the constitution of 1844; but the Patriarch had never formally recognised its administrative independence, and Greek public life had accordingly been disturbed by the rival contentions of the extreme Orthodox party (of which Oikonómos was the leader, and which desired to obtain the Patriarch's recognition) and of the Archimandrite Pharmakídes, who represented the opinion that such recognition of an accomplished fact was alike unnecessary and undesirable. At last, in 1850, the Greek government availed itself of a favourable opportunity for asking the Patriarch to recognise its ecclesiastical arrangements. Thanks to Russian influence, the recalcitrant divines, assembled at Constantinople, gave way; and on July 11 a "Synodal Tome" was read there proclaiming the Church in Greece autocephalous. The "Tome" provided that the Metropolitan of Athens should be president of the Holy Synod of the Greek kingdom; and that in all questions of administration the Church in Greece should be independent; but that it should receive the holy oil from the Œcumenical Patriarch, whose opinion should be asked on grave questions of dogma. The sad coincidence of the assassination of Korphiotákes, Minister for Ecclesiastical Affairs, on the day when the "Tome" was read aloud in all the churches of the kingdom, and the continued opposition of Pharmakídes, did not prevent the final acceptance of this settlement; and in 1852 the Greek Chamber enacted the above-mentioned provisions. Thus the chief ecclesiastical problem of Greece was solved.

Another theological agitation, the so-called " Phil-Orthodox " movement, headed by a monk named Papoulákos, who went about denouncing the Catholic king and praising the Orthodox Tsar, was suppressed by his incarceration at Andros. That beautiful island of lemon groves and rushing waters provided a theological martyr in the teacher Kaïres, whose prosecution for unorthodox ideas and death in prison attracted notice in England.

The conflict between the British and Greek governments in the case of Don Pacifico was not the only cause of friction between the two countries at this period. The events of the last twenty years in the Ionian Islands had culminated in an open agitation for union. In 1832, with the appointment of Lord Nugent as Sir F. Adam's successor, Liberal ideas for the first time found an exponent in the person of a Lord High Commissioner, whose political career at home encouraged the Ionian reformers to hope for his support. Nugent began by a promise of reforms, but his first attempt to perform it was the illegal substitution of the system of election from a triple list of candidates for that from a double list, as provided by the Constitution of 1817 ; and this extension of the freedom of choice led to the dissolution of the Assembly by the Crown long before its natural term had expired. The appointment of young and untried officials of Liberal views to administrative posts increased the influence of the Liberal party ; but the High Commissioner was fortunately a good man of business, who conferred practical benefits on the Islands by employing the pension-fund, created by Maitland, in loans at an easy rate of interest to the peasants, by limiting to £35,000 the annual sum payable by the Ionians to the protectorate, and yet bequeathing a large surplus to his successor, Sir Howard Douglas. The fourth Lord High Commissioner, a strong Conservative, reverted to the benevolent despotism of Maitland and Adam, believing that the Ionian people was not yet ripe for a more Liberal form of government. This reaction from Nugent's

rule naturally exasperated the Liberal party; and the presence
of so doctrinaire a Whig as Lord John Russell at the Colonial
Office during the latter part of Douglas' Commissionership
tempted the eminent Corfiote historian, Mustoxidi, to address
a memorandum to him on the condition of the Islands.
Mustoxidi admitted that the Islanders preferred the British
protectorate to any other political connexion, for independence
was still unobtainable; but he demanded in their name the
grant of a freer system of election, annual sessions of the
Assembly, and a free press.   This memorial made some impression upon the Colonial Secretary, who, however, loyally
supported his subordinate; and no essential change of policy
ensued during the remainder of the latter's term of office.
Ecclesiastical difficulties, however, accumulated in his path.
A conflict with the "Phil-Orthodox" party increased the unpopularity of his administration.   An attempt to reform the
table of kindred and affinity excited the opposition of the
Œcumenical Patriarch, who protested that the Orthodox
religion was in danger, whereupon the British ambassador at
Constantinople obtained his deposition by the Sultan.   The
indiscretion of a Protestant missionary caused the accusation
of proselytism to be levelled against the Commissioner, who
prevented the re-establishment of a Roman Catholic see at
Corfù.   Finally, his rashness in seizing the papers of Mustoxidi
and of Viaro and Agostino Capo d'Istria, whose brother
George had been mixed up with the "Phil-Orthodox Society,"
discovered at Athens in December 1839, gave the historian
and the members of that family, ever the foes of Great Britain,
a plausible ground for complaint of his illegality—for the
papers obviously contained nothing treasonable, or they would
have been published.   Another summary dissolution of the
Assembly, disapproved by the Colonial Secretary, incensed the
Opposition.   Nevertheless, despite Mustoxidi's long indictment
of him to the Colonial Secretary, Douglas had the solid
interests of the Islands at heart, as his improvement of the

Corfiote aqueduct, of the roads, the prisons, and the educational system proved—benefits, however, which entailed the first public debt of the Islands under the British protectorate. He continued in two respects the work of his immediate pre-decessor—the reduction of the annual contribution of the Ionian treasury, and the preparation of a new code, while he ordered British officials to learn Greek. His popularity with the landed classes, who naturally preferred stability for their property to aught else, is still manifested by the obelisk which commemorates him at Corfù; and, after his retirement, by becoming a member of the House of Commons, he was able to advocate their interests, and thereby embarrass his Liberal successor, Mackenzie.

The new Commissioner's rule was abruptly closed by the result of a conflict with the Senate. A convinced reformer, he found that body, and more especially Petritsópoulos, its President, opposed to his ideas. Accordingly, when the President's term of office expired, he availed himself, for the first time in Ionian history, of the power of non-reappointment conferred by the Constitution, and nominated a moderate Liberal, Count Delladecima. The Conservatives were then in power at home, and Lord Derby, the Colonial Secretary, disapproved of this act. In vain did Count Delladecima chivalrously tender his own resignation, in order to save the Commissioner; Mackenzie resigned after barely two years of office, during which he had done little but reduce the debt initiated by his predecessor. In 1843 his place was occupied by Lord Seaton, whose rule was, for weal or woe, the most remarkable of the whole protectorate.

A military man, a Tory peer, and the victor of the Canadian insurgents could scarcely have been expected to develope into a Radical reformer. And for the first five years of his rule, despite the September revolution in Greece, Seaton gave no outward sign of his intentions, but followed the traditional policy of the protectorate, promoting education, establishing district courts for the hearing of petty cases, mending the roads, beginning a canal at Santa Mavra, and planning a model farm for the teaching of agriculture. But the revolutionary movements of 1848 in other countries appear to have converted the Conservative soldier into an advanced democrat. Immediately after they began, he obtained the sanction of the home government to three reforms—a free press (which, he trusted, would counteract the attacks of the Maltese and Athenian newspapers, hitherto the usual organs of aggrieved Ionians); the right of the Assembly to vote the extraordinary expenditure; and the free election of all municipal authorities. Not content with these reforms, Seaton proposed to render the Assembly more democratic, although Earl Grey, his chief, warned him to proceed gradually, and to await the results of the concessions already given before granting more. The disturbed state of Cephalonia, always the most Radical of the Seven Islands, might have been supposed to justify the Colonial Secretary's advice. Class as well as national feeling was more rife there than among the other Ionians; and Baron d'Everton, a British official of Italian experience, who was then Resident of the island, could not trust his police. A riot during the procession of the Cephalonian saint, Gerásimos, increased the local discontent; the Resident reported the existence of a secret society for the emancipation of the Greeks; and on September 26, 1848, a band of peasants attacked Argostóli. Their attack was repulsed, but shortly afterwards the decree for the freedom of the press came into force; and its immediate effect was the publication of a swarm of newspapers, of which four appeared in Cephalonia alone, written in the vernacular and for the most part hostile to the protectorate. An article in one of these journals led Seaton to order the arrest of two Cephalonian politicians, Zervós and Livadâs, and their banishment to Paxo; but neither this result of his own measure nor the disturbances in Cephalonia deterred him from carrying out the rest of his

programme. On April 26, 1849, he announced a drastic
reform of the Constitution of 1817; and a Radical charter
was approved, which sanctioned the direct election by ballot
of the members of the Assembly, increased from 40 to 42,
by an electorate more than thrice as large as that which had
hitherto possessed the suffrage. On the other hand, the
Senators were to be appointed from among the members of
the Assembly by the Lord High Commissioner—an arrangement more Conservative than that of 1817. Indeed, the
authority of the government over the Second Chamber was
made doubly sure by an amendment, introduced by Seaton's
successor, which allowed the Lord High Commissioner to
choose two Senators from outside the ranks of the Assembly.
Moreover, as the latter body was summoned only every other
year, and the only financial reductions which it could make
were in the salaries of the native officials, its practical powers
were still limited. But Seaton had provided the Ionians with a
means for airing their grievances such as they had never possessed
before; and it was thenceforth possible for them to express
their desire for union with Greece alike in the Assembly and
in the press. The murder of Captain Parker, the official in
charge of the forest in Cephalonia, barely a fortnight after
Seaton had announced his reforms at Corfù, was an ill omen
of their success.

Seaton bequeathed to his successor, Sir Henry Ward, who
had sat as a Liberal in the British Parliament, the difficult
task of superintending their working, for his own term of
office ended a little more than a month after their introduction.
The Liberal commoner proved at once to be more Conservative
than the Tory peer, and his first official act was to inform the
Assembly that his predecessor's reforms must be regarded
as a final settlement of the question; when that body showed
signs of demurring, it was prorogued. Further disturbances
in Cephalonia of both a local and a political character followed,
on August 26, his grant of an amnesty to the insurgents of the

previous year and the release of the two exiled politicians. The peasantry rose and burnt the country-houses of the land-owners, one of whom perished in the flames, and the head-man of a village was shot as he stood by the Lord High Commissioner. Martial law was proclaimed—a singular preliminary to the exercise of a wide suffrage and vote by ballot; Zervós was again sent into banishment; numbers of peasants were flogged with the "cat"; and 21 persons, including the two ringleaders, Vláchos and a priest called Nodáros, but nicknamed "Father Brigand" by his own countrymen, were executed. A section of Liberals in England endeavoured to obtain a vote of censure upon these methods of repression; but their attempt failed; a second amnesty had already been granted, and no further riot occurred in Cephalonia during the protectorate.

The first Assembly elected under the reformed system met in March 1850. Of the three parties, which divided the Ionians—the "Radicals," the more moderate "Reformers," and the reactionary or "Subterranean" party, which supported the protectorate—the Reformers had a majority, and only 11 out of the 42 members were Radicals. But the Radicals, if a minority, were the noisiest and most popular party, especially in Cephalonia and Zante. Among those chosen by Cephalonia were two Radical editors, Zervós and Mompherrátos, whose election was largely due to their banishment by the authorities—for the political "fortune of a Radical," as a Cephalonian satirist remarked, "was made when the high police knocked at his door." In fact, six out of the ten deputies of that democratic island belonged to the Radical party, while Corfù returned only one. Many members were new to parliamentary life. From the very outset the Assembly gave a taste of its quality by its desire to omit the word "indissoluble" from the oath, which described the bonds between the Islands and the protectorate by that adjective. The epithet was omitted, with the assent of the Lord High Commissioner, who drew up a new form of oath; but, in spite of a protest signed by five members, four of them Cephalonians, the allusion to the "treaty of Paris" and to the "rights of the Protecting Sovereign" was maintained in this second formula. To the High Commissioner's advice that the Assembly should devote itself to such practical reforms as the improvement of ecclesiastical administration and of the status of the clergy, the reorganisation of education, and the completion of the Santa Mavra canal, the Speaker replied by censuring the policy of the British government in the Don Pacifico case, by blaming the protectorate for the decline of Ionian trade and agriculture, by demanding further reforms, and by alluding to the union in one body of all the scattered members of the Greek family. It was thus apparent from the beginning that the democratic changes of 1849 had whetted, instead of satiating, the appetite of the Ionian politicians. The only difference between the two Liberal parties was this, that while the Reformers advocated constitutional reforms which would not prejudice the ultimate removal of the protectorate, the Radicals desired nothing short of immediate union with Greece. Consequently Radicals and Protectionists alike opposed reforms, because the former feared lest they might make the protectorate popular, the latter because they feared to lose their privileges. When a motion by the Cephalonian Typáldos on December 8, expressing the "will" of the islanders for union, was proposed, the Assembly was abruptly prorogued for seven months, and, before the year 1851 had closed, was dissolved. Ionian historians still regard this short-lived legislature as the first historic landmark on the road towards union. Its successor, in which the Lord High Commissioner believed that he had secured the support of the Reformers, whereas he had thereby alienated many Protectionists, and to which for the first time his speech was read in Greek, instead of in Italian, proved to be almost equally unmanageable. Banishment had decimated the Radicals; Count Caruso, Regent of Cephalonia, "supervised" the elections there; and only one Radical of importance, Constantine Lombárdos, a Zantiote doctor, sat in this Assembly. Nevertheless, by a majority of one vote it rejected the reforms proposed by the government; before it met for its second session, a general crisis in the east had begun, and Ionian nationalism received a yet further stimulus from the events which led to the Crimean War.

The Revolution of 1848, which had indirectly influenced the politics of both Greece and the Ionian Islands, produced far more violent effects in the Roumanian countries. Upon the deposition of Ghika in 1842, George Bibescu, the scion of a noble family who had held office as secretary of state, and who was an enthusiastic admirer of the great Roumanian hero, Michael the Brave, was elected Prince of Wallachia. Before long, however, a quarrel with the Assembly, arising out of the grant of a mining concession to a Russian subject, led to the suspension of that body; and the Prince, free from the opposition of his legislature, was able to devote himself to such practical measures as the making of roads, the draining of marshes, and the establishment of a customs-union with Moldavia—the first step towards the political union of the two Principalities. In Moldavia the exceptionally long reign of Michael Sturdza, which lasted for 15 years, was a period of social reform. The sanitation of the towns, the establishment of strict ordinances against infectious diseases, the creation of a police force, and a series of measures tending to improve the lot, and protect the interests, of the peasants, were the work of this active prince. He removed from Moldavia, as his colleague removed from Wallachia, the last taint of slavery by the emancipation of the gypsies, who were the property of the state and of the monasteries. Most difficult task of all, he attempted to grapple with the Jewish question, which is still one of the gravest problems of Roumanian statesmanship. The Jews, already numerous in Moldavia at the beginning of the 19th century, had become in the time of Michael Sturdza, owing to the opening of the Black Sea to the commerce of all countries, an important element in the population. Alarmed at their increase, he forbade them to reside in his principality, unless they either possessed a certain amount of capital or had learned a trade; he treated as vagabonds those Hebrew travellers who came unprovided with passports; and he compelled them to close their shops on Sundays and feast days. But while, on the one hand, he thus endeavoured by direct means to diminish their numbers and influence, on the other, by allowing them to become members of the local commercial associations without payment of the charges payable by the Christian members, he gave them an enormous advantage over the native traders. At that period, trade was generally regarded as fit for foreigners alone; but a day arrived when the Roumans looked back with dismay at this fiscal exemption of the Moldavian Jews. Naturally, the liberal measures of both Bibescu and Sturdza procured for their authors the animosity of the greater nobles, always inclined to resent the domination of a prince who had been but yesterday one of themselves. Both rulers were forced in self-defence to cripple as far as possible the power of these haughty magnates. Bibescu, by a strict enforcement of an article of the *règlement organique*, excluded the great nobles from his new Assembly on the ground that they did not reside in their electoral districts but were absentees at the capital; Sturdza aimed at weakening their power by a profuse creation of magnates from the ranks of the lesser nobility. But the discontented usually found support from the Russian consul, and it was against the constant interference of this foreign Power in their affairs that the Roumanian edition of the Revolution of 1848 was mainly directed.

The spirit of nationalism had developed apace during the 14 years of the *règlement organique*. Michael Kogălniceanu and others, who had studied history abroad, returned home to describe the glories of the Roumanian race's past and the

degradation of its present condition.   The Colleges of St Sava
at Bucharest and the Academy at Jassy, founded by Michael
Sturdza and called by his name, enabled those who did not
belong to the aristocracy to obtain the same education as their
social superiors.   The sons of the nobles were often defeated
in the class rooms by the children of those whom they despised ;
and the opening of public posts to those who had gained
a diploma was equivalent to a social revolution.   The Russians
and their clients, the native magnates, took alarm ; and excuses
were found for suppressing the upper classes of the two
Roumanian colleges.   But a generation had been prepared
for the Revolution of 1848, and when that movement passed
over Europe, it did not stop at the Carpathians.

In Moldavia, where the revolution broke out on April 8, it
was speedily suppressed by the Prince, without the aid which
Russia offered him.   There the demands of the ringleaders
were confined to the redress of certain abuses in the administration, and the agitation left the masses cold.   A more advanced
programme of reforms put forward by Kogălniceanu, in
which the latter attacked the *règlement organique* and the
Russian protectorate and demanded a national constitution
with the union of the Principalities, led to the exile of
its author.   But in Wallachia events of a more stirring
character took place.   So little was the movement there directed
against the Prince, that the members of the revolutionary
committee invited Bibescu to put himself at their head.
Bibescu, too weak or too well informed to champion a cause
which was sure to incur the opposition of the Tsar, declined
their overtures ; and the revolution began at Islaz, a village
near the Danube.   On this, the Prince arrested several of the
committee ; but an attempt upon his life and the slowness of
the army in responding to his orders convinced him that he
could not check the movement which he had refused to lead.
On June 23 a great crowd surrounded his palace, and forced
him to sign a constitution which annulled the *règlement*

organique; whereupon, the Russian consul-general protested, and bade him quit the country. Bibescu obeyed and abdicated, leaving the revolutionary committee in possession of the government. But, as always happens on such occasions, there were two parties among the leaders—a moderate section, of which Eliade Rădulescu was the chief, and which carefully refrained from touching the suzerain rights of Turkey, contenting itself with emancipation from the Russian protectorate, with agrarian reform, and with a liberal constitution ; and a Radical wing, which aimed at the immediate establishment of an united and independent Roumania, without reflecting that such an attempt would involve a disastrous war against Turkey, Russia, and Austria simultaneously. Of these two schools of thought the Moderates were successful in obtaining the chief influence in the provisional government, which was formed after the abdication of Bibescu.

Neither the agrarian nor the foreign policy of the provisional government was successful. Of the great noble families only seven took part in the revolution ; and the land commission, appointed to examine the condition of the peasants, to abolish forced labour, and to make the cultivator of the soil in some measure its owner, was a failure. The Metropolitan called down the thunders of the Church upon what he described as "the ruin of the family and of private property"; the Russians invited the Turks to come forward as the champions of those institutions. The Turks fell into the trap laid for them by Russian diplomacy, and occupied Wallachia. The provisional government was dissolved at the bidding of the Turkish commissioner, and a Lieutenancy set up, consisting of Eliade Rădulescu and two other members of the moderate party. The Sultan was satisfied ; not so the Russians ; they insisted upon a further enquiry, in which the Turkish commissioner should be "assisted" by a Russian general, while the Radical party by its violent attacks upon Russia in the press played unconsciously the Russian game. The excuse for the employment of force was afforded when the manuscript of the precious *règlement organique* was publicly burned by the people of Bucharest after having been previously dragged in a mock funeral procession past the windows of the Russian consulate. The Russian authorities in the town thereupon begged of Omar Pasha, the Turkish commander, to protect them; a collision between the Ottoman troops and the local firemen led to bloodshed; and the Russians once again occupied the Principalities to restore order. A final attempt of the Radicals was abandoned on the advice of the British consul. The Lieutenancy of three was abolished, and a rich noble, Constantine Cantacuzene, appointed sole Lieutenant-Governor. On May 1, 1849, Russia and Turkey concluded the Convention of Balta Liman, which limited the duration of the Princes' reigns to seven years, abolished the Assemblies, and substituted for them divans (or Councils) named by the Princes. A considerable Russo-Turkish army was to occupy the Principalities till their complete pacification; and a Russian and a Turkish commissioner were to assist the Princes to reorganise the administration. Michael Sturdza, who had preserved his throne throughout the revolution, declined to reign any longer on these terms, and retired to Paris, the usual exile of Roumanian rulers in retirement. In his place Gregory V Ghika, who had taken part in the movement of the previous years, was appointed Prince of Moldavia; while Bibescu was succeeded in Wallachia by Barbe Stirbeiu, his brother, who had exchanged the family name for that of his adopted father, and had had a large experience of public life during the late reigns.

The Roumanian revolution of 1848, suppressed though it had been, left its mark upon the history of the people. Abroad, the exiled revolutionaries stirred up public opinion in favour of their nationality; and western Europe learnt, to its satisfaction, that in that distant corner of the continent there was a race, neither Slav nor Greek, which might, if supported in its aspirations, became a buffer-state between Turkey and Russia. This discovery made most impression upon the two Liberal Powers, France and Great Britain, so soon to engage in a common struggle against Russia; and, whilst French and French-speaking Roumanian writers enlightened the first of Latin nations on the lot of this oppressed scion of the Latin family, Palmerston himself raised the Roumanian question in the House of Commons. At home, the two Princes, instituted on the ruins of the revolution, continued, in a quieter manner, the work of its authors. Both Stirbeiu and Ghika re-established the system of instruction in the vernacular, and encouraged the publication of the national history. Both grappled with the agrarian question, which the Wallachian ruler endeavoured to solve by reducing the daily hours, while increasing the days, of the peasant's compulsory labour for his landlord, and by substituting a money payment for the old practice of forced work upon the roads. The reorganisation of the army and the reduction of the debt incurred by the occupation, which ended in 1851, were due to his policy; his Moldavian colleague was less wise in permitting the Jews to open drink-shops in the villages, thus laying the foundation of a grave social evil, which modern legislation has sought to diminish. But the work of both Princes was prematurely interrupted by the outbreak of hostilities between their great neighbours in 1853. Russia informed them that they might retain their thrones on condition of severing their connexion with their suzerain. The Princes, well knowing that this time Turkey would have the western Powers behind her, refused to accept this order, and fled to Vienna, there to await the tide of affairs which should restore them to their respective states.

Servia, although in a much less degree than the Roumanian Principalities, was affected by the European convulsion of 1848. Alexander Karageorgevich, whose throne remained unshaken by an attempt at an Obrenovich restoration in 1845, was naturally well-disposed to Austria and Turkey, the two Powers which had supported him. These good relations between Austria and Servia were greatly strengthened by the action of the Serbs during the revolution in the Austrian empire. On May 13 a National Assembly of the Austrian Serbs met at Karlovitz, the seat of the Metropolitan, and demanded the nomination of a Patriarch and a *Voïvode*, naming to the latter dignity Colonel Shuplikatz, an officer who had served in the Napoleonic wars. Under the banner of "Emperor and Nationality" they aided the Austrians against the Magyars, and were joined by many volunteers from the principality, despite the remonstrances of the Turkish government. So far as the Serbs of Austria were concerned, they gained little but the addition of the title of "Grand *Voïvode* of the Servian *Voïvodina*" to the already numerous designations of the Austrian Emperor; but this co-operation of the two neighbouring branches of the Servian race led many of the Austrian Serbs to enter the service of Prince Alexander, where their experience was valuable to the principality, and kept the foreign policy of Servia within the orbit of Austria at a critical period of the eastern question.

Montenegro, like Servia, was stirred by the movement of the Austrian Serbs. Peter II offered the aid of 10,000 of his subjects to Jellatchich the *Ban* of Croatia; but the latter declined to allow the Montenegrins to take part in the civil war between Hungarians and Croats. A series of frontier skirmishes between the mountaineers and their Turkish and Albanian neighbours provided, however, that military exercise which was the chief occupation of the *Vladika's* subjects. In these circumstances Peter II died, on October 31, 1851, the last ruler of the Black Mountain who united the chief ecclesiastical and political functions in his own person. His remains repose on the summit of the Lovtchen—the lofty mountain, recently so famous, which commands the sea of stones that he had ruled so wisely; and his name is preserved in Servian literature by two dramas, "The Mountain Garland,"

and "Stephen the Little," and by a series of poems, in which
he extolled the heroism of his subjects.

The dying *Vladika* had nominated his nephew Danilo, then
absent in Vienna, as his successor, charging Pero Tomaso
Petrovich, President of the Senate and likewise uncle of the
young heir, with the duty of governing the country till the
latter could arrive.   Pero was, however, acclaimed by the war-
party, which wished for a vigorous policy against the Turks;
and, when his nephew reached Cetinje, he found the usurper
installed in his palace.   Danilo promptly appealed to the
people for the execution of the late ruler's testament, and his
uncle was constrained to acknowledge him as his sovereign.
Instead, however, of pardoning the bellicose chiefs who had
endeavoured to rob him of his heritage, Danilo warned them
that he would punish their disloyalty, thus from the outset
creating a party against his authority.

The new ruler began his reign by changing the theocratic
system of government, which had prevailed in Montenegro
since 1516.   He was young, he was in love with a fair damsel
of Trieste, he wanted to marry, he desired to found a family,
he had no calling for an ecclesiastical life.   Already the late
Vladika had shown by moving his residence from the
Monastery to the so-called "Billiard-table," that the separation
of a Montenegrin sovereign's dual attributes was impending.
Danilo sent a message to the Senate, proposing this change in
the ancient constitution.   In 1852 Montenegro was declared to
be an hereditary, temporal principality; the succession to the
throne was to be by order of primogeniture in the male line;
and another member of the Petrovich family or of the Montenegrin aristocracy was to be appointed head of the Church.
Communication of these changes was made to the Orthodox Tsar, who approved them; Austria had already been consulted; Turkey alone resented the erection of Montenegro
into a secular principality, especially as her suspicions were
aroused by this practical recognition of the Tsar as patron of

the newly-created Prince. Omar Pasha, the Croatian who had been in the Lebanon and in the Principalities, but was then Governor of Bosnia, tried to detach the Piperi from the rest of Montenegro by the promise of fiscal exemption and a grant of lands; a band of Montenegrins again seized the ancient capital of Jablyak by a *coup de main*; nor did its evacuation by the prudent Prince prevent the indignant Turks, anxious for war, from invading the Black Mountain. Attacked simultaneously by five separate Turkish forces, Danilo begged Austria and Russia to intervene, while he held the Turks at bay. Austria, incensed against Turkey for her recent hospitality to Polish and Hungarian refugees, played the game of Slavonic Orthodoxy by supporting Montenegro. An Austrian envoy, Count Leiningen, informed the Sultan that the Austrian Emperor was bound as a Christian sovereign to intervene on behalf of his Christian neighbours; the Sultan consented to desist from hostilities; and on March 3, 1853, peace was signed on the basis of the *status quo*, after the Turks had sustained serious losses. Austria had performed a service to the little state, which came to regard her as a more dangerous foe than Turkey; and the Austrian envoy had insisted by a reference to the Turkish firman of 1799 that the Prince of Montenegro was not a vassal of the Sultan. Danilo personally thanked the Austrian Emperor for his intervention; and, peace being restored, his own marriage, and the appointment of another member of the Petrovich clan as bishop, completed the change of the ancient constitution.

CHAPTER X

THE CRIMEAN WAR (1853-6)

THE war between Turkey and Montenegro had scarcely ended, when another and a far more serious conflict began, which involved the western Powers and ended the long period of peace, unbroken, so far as Great Britain was concerned, since the battle of Waterloo. Russia, regarding herself as the special protectress of the Orthodox Church, had intended to make a Turkish refusal to conclude peace with Montenegro a *casus belli*. But the prompt and vigorous action of Austria and the sudden acceptance of Count Leiningen's summons by the Porte had removed this ground of complaint. The Balkan Slavs in general, and the Montenegrins in particular, had in the spring of 1853 no special need of Russian intervention on their behalf.

There was, however, a more distant part of the Orient, where the unhappy divisions of Christian doctrine engaged the attention of diplomatists and furnished an excuse for the activity of fleets and armies. By one of those tragic circumstances, which make the believer sigh and the cynic smile, the holiest spot on earth, the scene of Our Lord's birth, had become the subject of a theological dispute between monks of opposing sects, and was soon to be made the occasion for a war between monarchs of rival races. By the Capitulations of 1535 the custody of the Holy Places had been entrusted to French Catholics; and this French protectorate, reaffirmed in 1673, had been solemnly confirmed and enlarged by the famous Capitulations of 1740. Articles 33 and 82 of that instrument, the Magna Carta of the French in the Levant, provided that the French religious Orders should not be disturbed in their occupation of the church of the Holy Sepulchre at Jerusalem, and that, whenever the fabric of the Holy Places required repair, the requisite leave should be granted at the request of the French ambassador. These exclusive privileges of "the eldest daughter of the Church," derived from a period when the Russian empire had not yet sprung into being, had been undermined by certain firmans conceded to the Greek Church from 1634 onwards, at times when France was either hostile to Turkey, or indifferent to ecclesiastical questions and to that political importance which they always assume in the east. The Orthodox naturally gained ground during seasons when pure reason directed French foreign policy, for it is a result of anticlericalism in Latin countries that it cripples the national influence otherwise exercised by the Church abroad. When, however, Louis Napoleon became President of the Second French Republic, the support of the French Catholics was essential to him. Alike in Rome and at Jerusalem he came forward as the champion of the Catholic cause and instructed his ambassador at Constantinople to insist upon the strict execution of the Capitulations of 1740, thus, in the words of the British Foreign Secretary, "making the tomb of Christ a cause of quarrel among Christians." The Porte, embarrassed by the rival claims of France on behalf of the Latin, and of Russia in favour of the Orthodox monks, endeavoured to please both parties. By a note of February 9, 1852, it directed that keys of the north and south gates of the great church at Bethlehem and of the grotto of the Holy Manger "must be given" to the Latins, "as of old," and they were allowed to erect a silver star adorned with the French arms in the shrine of the Nativity. By a firman, issued under Russian pressure, it reaffirmed the custom of giving keys of these sanctuaries to the Greeks, Latins, and Armenians, and provided that "no change" should "be made in the present state of the gates of the church of Bethlehem." The French were naturally indignant that the Porte had ratified the privileges of the Greeks, which they considered as an infringement of their own treaty rights. The Russians wished that this confirmation of their clients' contention should be publicly announced at Jerusalem; the French were equally desirous that what they regarded as a diplomatic defeat should not be proclaimed aloud.

The unpleasant task of communicating the decision of the Porte to the rival sects of the Holy Land was entrusted to Afif Bey, who followed the Fabian policy for which Turkish diplomacy is famous. This Mussulman, whom the irony of history had made a judge between warring Christians, delivered a series of the usual platitudes on the relations between the Sultan and his Christian subjects. When these beatitudes failed to satisfy the impatience of the Orthodox party, he adjourned the assembly to Gethsemane, and there read an order of his master, permitting the Latins to celebrate mass once a year in the church of the Virgin, provided that the altar and its ornaments remained undisturbed. This permission irritated the Latins, without appeasing the Greeks. The former declared it impossible to celebrate mass "upon a schismatic slab of marble, with a covering of silk and gold,... and before a crucifix which has the feet separated"; the latter observed, that the firman, which Afif had been presumably sent to read, had not been read. Pressed by the Russian consul-general, Afif sought refuge in subterfuges, and finally admitted that he had no instructions to read the firman at all. Thus, the Greeks were defeated, and their defeat was rendered all the more galling when, on December 22, the silver star of the French was placed by the Latin Patriarch in the sanctuary of the Nativity, and the keys of the great door of the church of Bethlehem and of the sacred manger were handed over to the adherents of the *filioque* clause. The

Russian government, in the name of outraged Orthodoxy and injured autocracy, called for "an act of reparation," and ordered an army corps to advance to the frontiers of the Danubian Principalities—the usual prelude of a Russo-Turkish war. Thus the Russian "heir of Byzantium" in the true spirit of Byzantine history, had found in a quarrel of theological schools a pretext for armed intervention. If the Tsar could no longer come forward as the protector of the Montenegrin mountaineers, whose grievances had been removed, he might still pose as the champion of the humiliated Orthodox monks of Palestine. In this frame of mind, he sent Prince Mentschikoff, a Chauvinist without diplomatic training, on an extraordinary mission to Constantinople, to demand not only a prompt settlement of the question of the Holy Places, but, as subsequently transpired, a Russian protectorate over the whole of the Orthodox Church in the Ottoman empire.

Mentschikoff's methods of diplomacy soon convinced the Turkish government that coercion, not conciliation, was his aim. He began by refusing to call upon the Turkish Minister for Foreign Affairs, who at once resigned. The Grand Vizier, in alarm, begged Col. Rose (afterwards Lord Strathnairn), then British *chargé d'affaires*, to summon the British fleet from Malta to Vourlá near Smyrna. The British government disapproved its agent's request; but, just at the moment when its disapproval seemed likely to mollify the Tsar, the French fleet was suddenly ordered to anchor off Salamis. The Emperor Napoleon III, as the Prince-President had now become, had personal no less than political reasons for pursuing a vigorous foreign policy towards the Tsar. Trifles count for much in the highest and most august circles, where the fate of nations is often decided; and the *parvenu*, who had assumed the Imperial style and was eager for the recognition of the long-established sovereigns of Europe, was stung to the quick by the Tsar's description of him in official correspondence as "my dear friend," instead of the customary

phrase of monarchs, " my brother." Moreover, the brand-new
Emperor, still fresh from the *coup d'état* and not yet securely
established on the throne, had need of some striking success
abroad, which would divert the minds of his discontented
and critical subjects from domestic politics. If he could obtain
this success by co-operation with a great Power of old-standing
and unimpeachable reputation, such as Great Britain, he would
raise himself in the social scale and make people forget his
origins and his methods—the ridiculous failures of Strassburg
and Boulogne, the prison of Ham, the exile in London, and the
second of December.

So far the British government had not been involved in
the question at issue between France, Russia and Turkey; nor
did there seem to be any adequate reason why it should be.
Great Britain was the protectress of neither the Roman
Catholics nor the Orthodox in the near east; and, as the
greatest commercial community in the world, she was assumed
to be specially desirous of peace. Her Prime Minister at this
time, Lord Aberdeen, was not only a friend of peace but a
friend of Nicholas, whom he had met in London nine years
earlier. On that occasion the Tsar had discussed the eastern
question with the future Prime Minister, then Foreign Secretary,
and urged upon him the desirability of a mutual understanding
between their two countries. A memorandum of the supposed
common interests of Great Britain and Russia in the near east
was drawn up; and the Tsar left with the impression that he
could rely upon Aberdeen's co-operation, and left behind him
the conviction that he was a man of his word, upon whom
strict reliance could be placed. Accordingly, when his friend
became Prime Minister, the Tsar felt that he was sure of
his support; and a month after Aberdeen's Cabinet had been
formed, he spoke freely with Sir Hamilton Seymour, the
British ambassador to his court, on the state of Turkey. "We
have on our hands," he said, "a sick man—a very sick man;
it will be, I tell you frankly, a great misfortune if one of these

days he should slip away from us, especially before all necessary
arrangements were made." He disclaimed Catherine the
Great's dreams of territorial expansion, but alluded to his
rights and duties towards the Christian subjects of the Sultan,
and suggested that, in the event of the dissolution of Turkey,
Servia and the Bulgarians should receive the same form of
government as the Danubian Principalities, and that Egypt
and Crete should become British possessions. As for Constantinople, he stated that he would neither allow Great Britain
to establish herself there, nor would he annex it himself; as
to a temporary " occupation " of the Turkish capital, that was
another matter. These overtures were politely rejected in
London. Our only interest in Egypt, Sir Hamilton Seymour
said, was one of transit to India; the other Turkish territories
Great Britain did not covet. Nor did the Cabinet believe
that the end of Turkey was nigh. In this it was right.

But, while the Tsar's desire to co-operate with Great Britain
and his friendship with the head of the British government
seemed to augur well for the preservation of good relations
between the two countries, the ambassador whom the British
Cabinet now bade return to Constantinople was a man whom,
of all diplomatists, Nicholas hated most. Lord Stratford de
Redcliffe, as he now was, had played a great part in the tortuous
politics of the Levant. We have seen him intervene with
authority in the affairs of Greece; he had already won an overpowering influence at Constantinople. But the Tsar had once
slighted him by refusing to receive him as ambassador at
St Petersburg; and this affront, like that to Napoleon III,
intensified the strength of "the Great Eltchi's," as of the French
Emperor's, opposition to the Russian plans. In those days an
ambassador was not what he is said now to have become—a
clerk at the end of a telegraph wire. Lord Stratford did not
merely repeat his instructions, he sometimes ignored them; and,
while a hesitating Cabinet in London was making up its mind,
he had already made history, and made it irrevocably. But

the great ambassador was not only "the voice of England in
the east"; he stood behind the trembling Turkish Ministers
and gave them courage and advice, so that they left his presence
men and statesmen. Before his arrival on April 5, 1853,
Mentschikoff had already unfolded to the Turkish government
the real scope of his mission, which went far beyond the
question of the Holy Places. Russia through her envoy offered
the Turks the aid of her fleet and 400,000 men against any
western Power in return for an addition to the fatal treaty of
Kutchuk-Kaïnardji, placing the Orthodox Church entirely
under her protection. This proposal was to be kept secret
from Great Britain; but, within four days of his return to
Constantinople, the British ambassador was aware of its nature.
He at once advised the Turkish Ministers to keep the question
of the Holy Places distinct from that of the general protectorate,
to remove any grievance that Russia might have by the prompt
settlement of the former, and to decline to entertain the latter,
without, however, refusing the spontaneous redress of any
abuses. Thus, the ground of legitimate complaint would be
completely cut away from under Mentschikoff's feet. The
Turks acted upon his advice; and by his timely interposition
between the Russian envoy and the new French ambassador
he managed on April 22 to secure the settlement of the original
cause of dispute, the question of the Holy Places. It was
arranged that, while the key of the church of Bethlehem and
the silver star should not be removed, their presence there was
to be understood to confer no new right upon the Latins; that
the doorkeeper of the church should continue to be a Greek,
but should not prevent the ingress of people of other creeds;
that Greeks, Armenians, and Latins should have daily precedence in that order at the tomb of the Virgin; that the
gardens of the convent of Bethlehem should remain under
the joint care of the two rival sects; and that the repairs to the
cupola of the church of the Holy Sepulchre should be carried
out by the Sultan on the lines of the existing plan; while the

windows of the buildings overlooking its terraces should be walled up. Thus, both the Montenegrin and the monkish questions had been settled; the peace of Europe might seem assured.

But, nine days earlier, fresh Russian dispatches, penned under the influence of the news that the French fleet had been ordered to Salamis, had reached Mentschikoff. In obedience to the pressing orders of his incensed master, the Russian envoy demanded from the Turkish government a treaty guaranteeing to the Orthodox clergy and Church in the Ottoman empire all their ancient privileges and all the advantages accorded to other Christian bodies. Such a treaty, in the words of the Turkish Minister of Foreign Affairs, "would be giving to Russia an exclusive protectorate over the whole Orthodox population, their clergy, and their churches." Whenever an Orthodox bishop—and in the Turkish empire the bishops are usually politicians first and spiritual pastors afterwards—had any grievance, he would have appealed to the Tsar, who would thus have had an excuse at any moment for interfering in the internal affairs of Turkey. An *imperium in imperio* would thus have been erected, compared with which the intervention of the Papacy in English politics under the Plantagenets or the existing French protectorate over the comparatively few Roman Catholics of Turkey were as nothing. For the Tsar was near at hand, and at the head of armies and fleets, while the Orthodox subjects of the Sultan were legion, and numbers of those who were officially labelled as "Greeks," because they belonged to the Greek Church, were Slavs of a race akin to that of the Russians. The Turkish government consulted Lord Stratford as to their policy, and decided to reject the proposed Russian treaty. Meanwhile, the settlement of the question of the Holy Places had placed the Tsar in a far worse position, as that of a man who was bent upon picking a quarrel with his neighbour. Mentschikoff, unable to go back, repeated his demand in the form of a convention, which he

requested the Turkish government to accept.   Once again the
British ambassador, now the real power behind the Turkish
throne, counselled firmness, and, in a private audience with
the Sultan, informed him that, in the event of imminent danger,
the British Mediterranean squadron would be held in readiness.
Mentschikoff, after further attempts to wring consent from the
Sultan and his Ministers, thus causing a Ministerial crisis at
Constantinople, orally received from Reshid Pasha, the new
Foreign Minister, on May 18, a refusal to grant the protectorate
over the Greek Church in Turkey, demanded by the Tsar.
In vain, at Lord Stratford's suggestion, the representatives of
the other three Powers joined him in expressing to Mentschikoff
their regret at the threatened rupture of Russo-Turkish relations.
He merely consented to accept the promise of the protectorate
through the less formal channel of a note, in place of a convention or a treaty.   When the Turkish government rejected this
ultimatum, he left Constantinople with his staff.   His Imperial
master attributed his defeat to the supremacy of Lord Stratford,
and filled the European courts with his complaints of the
British ambassador.   These complaints were not without some
foundation, for the latter is said to have boasted openly that
the Crimean war had been his revenge for the Tsar's refusal to
receive him.   Yet, while the Tsar recognised that behind the
Sultan stood the commanding figure of "the Great Eltchi," he
could not believe that either the British government, presided
over by his friend Aberdeen, or the British people, immersed
in commerce, would permit their ambassador to lead them
into war.   In this Nicholas was wrong, though a superficial
survey of our recent history might have tended to confirm him
in this fatal error.

The British people is almost always a riddle to foreign
statesmen ; and at that time public utterances had more than
usually obscured its real character.   Two years earlier the
Cobdenite School, still in the glory of the Free-trade triumph,
had foretold that the Great Exhibition would mark the end of

wars, and that the British lion would lie down with the
Manchester lamb. In 1853 nearly 40 years of peace had
passed over the heads of the British people, and a generation
had grown up which knew the horrors of war from books alone.
This last fact was, in reality, a danger rather than a hopeful
sign ; for we have learnt in our own day that, when the Crimean
war had ceased to be a personal recollection, the populace was
eager for a great colonial campaign. But the Tsar believed
that he knew the pacific nature of Great Britain, just as 45
years later sapient German politicians vowed that the British
would never go to war for the sake of a distant colony. He
was misled by the undue prominence given to the utterances
of the peace party, forgetting that the vast, silent mass of the
British public rarely takes part in public meetings, but quietly
decides the fate of governments on polling-day. He did not
foresee that the mere fact of Cobden's and Bright's rooted and
high principled antipathy to all wars would inevitably destroy
their influence in opposing any particular war, whereas the
opposition of a Liberal to a particular Liberal measure is of far
more value than that of a Conservative, the enemy on principle
of all Liberal proposals. The middle classes, whom Nicholas
had studied at a distance during his visit to England, seemed
to him sunk in material prosperity ; the British Jeshurun had
waxed fat, he was not likely to kick. So reasoned the Tsar ;
and the peace party honestly, but unfortunately for its own
cause, did all that it could to confirm him in this strong
delusion.

Confident that Great Britain would not fight against him,
the Tsar, on July 2, 1853, ordered his forces to cross the Pruth
and occupy the two Danubian Principalities, whose Princes
were informed that they might keep their thrones, on condition
of breaking off all relations with the Porte. The Princes,
ordered by the latter to disobey the Russian orders and to
pay their tribute as usual, as soon as they became convinced
that the Turks would be supported by the western Powers,

refused to carry out the Tsar's behests, and in October fled
to Vienna. The Russian occupation was followed by a manifesto, declaring the Orthodox Church to be in danger,
disclaiming "the intention to commence war" or to make
conquests, and protesting that the Tsar regarded the Principalities merely as a "security" for "the restoration" of his
rights. Thus, war was even yet not officially declared; but,
as the Tsar had given to his operations the colour of a crusade,
the Turks retaliated by preaching a religious war. As for
the Powers, Austria naturally felt alarm at the occupation of
territories on her own frontier, inhabited by the same race
as some of her own subjects; Prussia, whose romantic sovereign,
Frederick William IV, was the Tsar's brother-in-law, and
whose foreign policy had been hitherto subservient to that
of Russia, united with Austria; and Great Britain and France,
while they sent their fleets to Besika Bay near the mouth of
the Dardanelles, consulted with the two chief German states
at Vienna as to the best means of averting a conflict. There
their representatives approved with some modifications a
document, which had originated in Paris but which came to
be called from the place of their meeting, "the Vienna Note."
This document stated that "whereas, if at all times the
Emperors of Russia have evinced their active solicitude for
the maintenance of the immunities and privileges of the
Orthodox Greek Church in the Ottoman Empire, the Sultans
have never refused to confirm them;...the government of
His Majesty the Sultan will remain faithful to the letter and
to the spirit of the treaties of Kaïnardji and Adrianople relative
to the protection of the Christian religion, and His Majesty
considers himself bound in honour...to cause the Greek rite
to share in the advantages conceded to the other Christian
rites by convention or special arrangement." The Tsar, as
was anticipated, accepted this note; and Lord Clarendon, the
British Foreign Secretary, ordered Lord Stratford to procure
"the assent of the Turkish government thereto."

The powerful ambassador had already persuaded his colleagues in Constantinople to approve a note inspired by himself, informing the Russian government that the Sultan had issued firmans in confirmation of the privileges of the Orthodox Church. He none the less executed his orders as the agent of his government, but at the same time let the Turkish Ministers see that his mind did not approve what his tongue was bound to utter. They amended the note by making the above-cited passages run as follows: "Whereas, if at all times the Emperors of Russia have evinced their active solicitude for the Orthodox Greek religion and Church, the Sultans have never ceased to provide for the maintenance of the immunities and privileges which they have spontaneously granted at different times to that religion and to that Church in the Ottoman Empire, and to confirm them;...the government of His Majesty the Sultan will remain faithful to the stipulations of the treaty of Kaïnardji, confirmed by that of Adrianople, relative to the protection by the Sublime Porte of the Christian religion, and...His Majesty considers himself bound in honour... to cause the Greek rite to share in the advantages granted, or which might be granted, to the other Christian communities, Ottoman subjects." Russia rejected the note, as thus amended; and this difference of phraseology, which was, indeed, more than merely verbal, caused the final rupture. The Porte summoned the Russian general to evacuate the Principalities within 15 days; and, as he disregarded this summons, on October 23, the third Russo-Turkish war of the century formally began. A day earlier, and therefore, in technical violation of the convention of 1841 (unless the Russian occupation of the Principalities were considered as constituting a breach of the peace), the British fleet had, at the request of France, entered the Dardanelles. Russia protested at this breach of the "Convention of the Straits"; and for the first time the Tsar was brought face to face with the hard fact of a probable war against Great Britain. The probability was increased by the substitution of a separate Anglo-French understanding for the concert of the four Powers. While Austria, the Power nearest, most directly concerned, and most capable of striking quickly, held back, and Prussia followed Austria, the French Emperor and the forward party in the divided British Cabinet, headed by Palmerston and Russell, pushed Great Britain into war. A spark was now alone needed to cause an explosion of popular indignation, no less dangerous because it was unreasonable.

Five days after the two empires were in a state of hostility, Omar Pasha, commander-in-chief of the Ottoman forces in Europe, crossed the Danube at Vidin, and entrenched himself at Kalafat in Wallachia ; a few days later the Russian occupants were defeated at Oltenitza. The Tsar's reply was to send out his Black Sea fleet ; on November 30, his admiral annihilated the Turkish fleet in the port of Sinope. An outburst of rage against the Tsar and the British Premier greeted the news of this affair in London. Aberdeen durst not show himself in the streets ; Palmerston, with his unerring comprehension of what the average Englishman of the middle classes wanted, resigned his seat in the Cabinet, nominally on an internal question, really because he saw that strong measures were what the country demanded. Yet, there were both precedent and justification for the destruction of the Turkish fleet at Sinope. At Navarino, 26 years earlier, we had aided in destroying another Turkish squadron ; and we had not then the excuse of being, as the Tsar was, at war with Turkey. Yet Sinope was called a " massacre," Navarino an " untoward event." The blame, if any, attached to the British and French commanders, who had been authorised to engage, if necessary, in defensive operations in the Black Sea. But the British Cabinet adopted the suggestion of the French Emperor to notify the Russian government "that every Russian ship thenceforward met in the Euxine would be requested, and, if necessary, constrained, to return to Sebastopol." Thereupon,

Palmerston, the war advocate *par excellence*, rejoined his former colleagues. The Tsar, on receipt of this notification, recalled his ambassadors from London and Paris, just at the moment when the representatives of the four Powers at Constantinople had drawn up a fresh note and persuaded the Porte to accept it. Nor were the prospects of peace improved by the visit of a deputation from the Society of Friends to St Petersburg. The worthy Quakers were charmed with the simplicity of an Autocrat, who spoke of Her Imperial Majesty the Empress as "my wife," but they did more harm than good to the cause which they had at heart. The majority of their countrymen wanted war, and the Cabinet "drifted" into it.

If a war against Russia were to be successfully and speedily conducted it was obviously desirable that the four Powers should act together; for Austria, from her geographical position, could at once pour troops into the Principalities, while Prussia would be tolerably certain to follow the lead of Austria. If, on the other hand, war could by any means have been avoided at that eleventh hour, then the close union of the four Powers offered the best guarantee for a pacific settlement; for even the Russian Autocrat would scarcely have cared to oppose the unanimous decision of the European Areiopagos. Moreover, Count Buol, the Austrian Minister of Foreign Affairs, actually offered on February 22, 1854, to support Great Britain and France, if they would fix a period within which the Russian troops should evacuate the Principalities under pain of hostilities. There is no reason to doubt that the Austrian Emperor, despite the services rendered to him by Russia against the Hungarians in 1849, would have been as good as his word, and that Austria, in the famous phrase of Schwarzenberg, would have "astonished the world by her ingratitude." For national gratitude, with a few rare exceptions, chiefly to be found in the Balkan states, has little practical value, however useful it may be to an after-dinner speaker, while national interests are always powerful motives with statesmen. Austria, with her millions of Slav subjects, could not contemplate with indifference a Russian campaign, undertaken on behalf of the Slavs of Turkey; nor could she, the greatest of all Danubian states, acquiesce in the occupation by another great Power of the Danubian Principalities, inhabited by kinsmen of her own Roumanian people. Unfortunately, the British Ministry telegraphed for confirmation of Count Buol's offer and a clear statement of Prussia's intentions. The Austrian and Prussian replies—the former merely a repetition of Count Buol's proposal, the latter characteristically undecided—were of no practical value, for the simple reason that, on February 27, the day before they arrived in London, the British ultimatum had been dispatched to St Petersburg. Thus, the impatience of the British public, excited by the press, and the pressure exercised by the French Emperor, who had actually taken upon himself to write to the Tsar in the name of Queen Victoria and in reply had received for his pains a cutting allusion to the retreat from Moscow in 1812, hustled the British government into taking an irretrievable step, before it had even received answers from two possible allies.

The British ultimatum informed the Russian government that its refusal or omission to send an answer within six days from the date of delivery, promising to withdraw all its troops from the Principalities before April 30, would be regarded as a declaration of war. A French ultimatum, couched in the same terms, was sent at the same time. As the Russian government refused to answer, simultaneous messages were sent by the British and French sovereigns to their respective Parliaments on March 27; and on the morrow the British declaration of war was published. It enumerated the successive phases of the various questions which had led up to the final arbitrament of the sword; but it did not explain why Great Britain and France alone had decided to champion a cause which concerned Prussia equally with, and Austria even more than, themselves; for the question which was the gist of the ultimatum was the occupation of the Principalities, and that was an Austrian rather than a Franco-British concern. On April 11 the Tsar replied, and twelve days later, in a manifesto to his people, gave a religious colour to the impending war.   Prince Gortchakoff, the commander of his army of occupation, and himself a warm admirer of the British, had already, on March 24, crossed the Danube and entered the dreary Dobrudja, reviving in the classically educated politicians of that day memories of those lachrymose " Pontic Epistles," which the exiled Ovid had composed in that dismal region.   Already, also, two treaties had been signed—one between the two western Powers and Turkey, pledging Great Britain and France to defend the Ottoman empire and Turkey to make no separate peace with Russia ; the other between Great Britain and France for common action against the Tsar.   Cynics, reading of these alliances, may have recalled with a smile, how the French Emperor had said not long before, that "the Empire means peace," and how the peace party had been identified by the Tsar with the British people !   As for Austria and Prussia, they on paper supported the " step taken directly by France and England...as being founded in right," guaranteed one another's territories against attack, and, while desiring " to avoid every participation in the war," deprecated "the indefinite continuance of the occupation of the territories on the Lower Danube."   Only in the event of a Russian annexation of the Principalities, or in that of a Russian "attack on, or passage of, the Balkan," would the two German Powers act on the offensive.   These contingencies never arose.   But, on May 23, the four governments were still protesting "that the integrity of the Ottoman Empire, and the evacuation of that portion of its territory which is occupied by the Russian army," were, and would be, the objects of their united endeavours.

Meanwhile, amidst immense enthusiasm, a British fleet, under Sir Charles Napier, the hero of Acre, had set sail for the Baltic, escorted by the Queen in person from its moorings. But this Baltic expedition proved to be a bitter disappointment; and the capture of a single island was small compensation for the failure to take the Russian fleet and attack the Russian arsenal of Kronstadt. But it was not in the north that the northern Colossus was vulnerable. The allied armies, the British commanded by Lord Raglan, a pupil and secretary of Wellington, the French led by Marshal St Arnaud, whose Algerian reputation had been confirmed in his master's eyes by his co-operation in the *coup d'état*, encamped by the Dardanelles not far from the spot where, five centuries before, the Turks had made their first settlement in Europe. Thence, in the month of June, they moved to Varna, now the first harbour of Bulgaria, and then the chief port of European Turkey on the Euxine. But the early successes of the Turks were due not to the armies of the Allies, but to the energy of three young British officers. The veteran Paskievich, the famous commander of the last Russo-Turkish war, had advised the Tsar to direct his forces first against Silistria, the fortress taken by the Russians 25 years before; and thither in May he had himself marched to execute his plan. But the conqueror of Erivan found himself baffled by Capt. Butler and Lieuts. Nasmyth and Ballard, who had assumed the direction of the defence and had inspired that devotion which Mussulmans often feel for British officers. Then, for the first time the Arab Tabia earthwork, notorious in the diplomatic negotiations of 25 years later, became a household word in England, where the exploits of its gallant defenders were read with all the more pride because they were our fellow-countrymen. When Butler was mortally wounded, Ballard took his place; and so spirited was the resistance that on June 22 the old Russian strategist raised the siege. A fortnight later, Ballard and six other young British officers crossed the Danube with the Turks, and defeated the Russians at Giurgevo; nor did Gortchakoff dare to retrieve this defeat in the presence of a little squadron of British gunboats. He retreated upon Bucharest, leaving the Turks masters of the lower Danube ; on August 2 the last Russian soldier recrossed the Pruth.

To this ignominious retreat the threatening attitude of Austria had contributed even more than the bravery of the Turkish soldiers and the pluck of a handful of British officers at Silistria and Giurgevo. On June 3, Austria had summoned the Tsar to evacuate the Principalities ; and the ease with which her army could invade them lent weight to her summons, which Prussia was ready to support. Eleven days afterwards, the Austrian Emperor signed a convention with the Porte, pledging himself " to exhaust all means," even force, "to obtain the evacuation of the Danubian Principalities,...to re-establish the legal state of things " there, and to withdraw his army as soon as peace was concluded. In further pursuance of this aim, the Austrian government sent an officer to the British headquarters to concert a joint plan of campaign. Before significant measures of this kind the Tsar could but yield, unless he wished for a war against Austria, in which she might be supported by Prussia and the minor German states. With the departure of the Russian army ceased the provisional administration which the Russian generals had created on the flight of the two Hospodars. During this interregnum two Russian " presidents" had held office, Kalkinsky at Bucharest, Urusoff at Jassy; but their conduct was far milder than that of former Russian armies of occupation. Efforts were made to gain the sympathies and utilise the services of the local aristocracy, but the burden of supporting the costs of the occupation fell upon the two countries. The Princes returned with the Austrian army, which remained there, despite Russian protests, till March 1857, long after the termination of the war. Thus, with the Austrians encamped in the Principalities, Russia could not, as in 1828 and 1877, march through them to attack the Turks beyond the Danube. A Balkan campaign was excluded; and with little bloodshed and without a blow from the allied armies, the object of the British ultimatum—the evacuation of Wallachia and Moldavia—had been attained. Common-sense would have suggested that this was the moment for peace.

Before following the allied armies from Varna to the Crimea, whither the national craving of the British for a sensational triumph and the desire of the French Emperor for that "glory" which is the foundation of brand-new dynasties were about to send them, it is desirable to note the effects of the struggle upon the Balkan Christians. While the Roumanians, as usual, had had to bear the brunt of the Russian passage to the Danube, the stolid Bulgars, whose fortress of Silistria and port of Varna had been the scenes of a Russian defeat and a Franco-British encampment, remained indifferent to the operations conducted in their midst. Servia, whose geographical position was more difficult and whose historic consciousness was more awake than that of the plodding Bulgarian peasants, was placed in a situation of no slight embarrassment. Turkey was her suzerain, Russia her protectress, while Austria was not only her neighbour but had acquired influence and sympathy among her leading men, many of whom had been Austrian subjects and had aided against the Hungarians during the revolution of 1848. Alexander Karageorgevich owed much to the support of Turkey and Austria ; nor had he forgotten, that, while the Tsar had opposed his election, the British Premier, when Foreign Secretary in 1843, had instructed Lord Stratford to keep him on the throne. But Russia had numerous adherents among the peasants, who even spoke of the Orthodox Tsar as " our Emperor." Such were the tendencies of the Servian public men and populace, when the three Powers most nearly concerned demanded the intentions of the little principality. Mentschikoff, with his usual violence, ordered Alexander to dismiss Garashanin, a representative of modern ideas, who had succeeded Petronievich as his chief adviser. But this was Russia's sole diplomatic success in Servia. A

Turkish army approached the southern frontier of the principality and extracted from the Prince a pledge of armed
neutrality, while, at Lord Stratford's suggestion, the Sultan
issued a new firman, guaranteeing the Servian privileges.
An Austrian force was massed along the frontier to prevent
a Russian occupation; and the importation of war material
through Austrian territory was prohibited. Nevertheless, the
Serbs resolved to be prepared to defend their country, if it were
menaced—and the menace seemed to many to come rather
from the Austrian force on the Save than from the Russians on
the lower Danube. The principality was militarily organised;
Austria showed signs of impatience; and both the British and
French governments urged the Servian envoy, Marinkovich, to
give her the satisfaction that she sought by disarming. All
excuse for alarm of a Russian invasion disappeared with the
withdrawal of the Russian troops across the Pruth. Austria
dominated the councils of the Prince; Russia had the sympathies of the people; but neither Prince nor people moved a
step.

From Montenegro the Tsar had stronger reason to expect
support. Despite the fact that one war against Turkey was
barely over, a considerable party at Cetinje, headed by
Danilo's uncle, George Petrovich, was anxious for another.
Danilo, however, at the advice of Austria, which had just
rendered him so considerable a service, again resolutely opposed
a warlike policy, at the risk of his popularity and even of his
throne. A conspiracy was formed against him, in which his
uncles George and Pero were implicated; and the agitation
for war became acute when the Turks massed troops along the
Herzegovinian frontier, thus provoking the bellicose mountaineers. Some urged an attack upon Antivari, others raided
the Herzegovina. Danilo protested that he could no longer
keep in his subjects; and their discontent rose to such a pitch,
that the Piperi, the Kutchi, and the Bijelopavlich districts
of the Brda, comparatively recent and still unamalgamated

acquisitions of the principality, proclaimed themselves, in July 1854, an independent state.   Danilo was forced to take the field against his rebellious subjects ; some fled into Turkish territory, others submitted, and were made to pay an indemnity for the civil war which they had caused.   But, while maintaining neutrality, the Prince thought it prudent to conciliate both his subjects and the Tsar by ordering a three days' fast for the success of the Russian arms.   The Catholic Mirdites, on the other hand, under their Prince Bib Doda, followed Omar Pasha to the Danube, as they had followed him a year before against Montenegro.

The effects of the Russo-Turkish quarrel were far more serious in Greece than in the Slav states of the near east. The Greeks inevitably sided with Orthodox Russia against Catholic France in the question of the Holy Places; they also considered that the moment when Turkey was involved in war with Russia would be favourable to their national aspirations for the annexation of Epirus and Thessaly.   " Nine-tenths of the Greek nation," it was said by a competent observer, sincerely sympathised with Russia ; nor could this sympathy be matter for wonder when she was fighting their hereditary and apparently only enemy—for, at that time, the danger to Hellenism of an independent Bulgaria did not exist.   It was believed at Athens that all the Orthodox subjects of the Sultan, whom it was still the official usage to classify collectively as Greeks, because they belonged to the Greek Church, would rise at a given signal.   Both the King and Queen, and especially the latter, considered that the time had come for that expansion of their kingdom's narrow borders, in which they both fervently believed, and identified themselves with a cause which was at once national and popular.   " Do not all the Greeks beyond our frontiers without exception desire their liberation ?   Do not we all without exception desire the unity of the Nation?" said the King to his doubting advisers.   During the winter of 1853 money was collected, and bands were enlisted at Athens under the Queen's undisguised patronage, in view of a rising in the spring; while, when the time for the expected insurrection arrived, a number of Greek officers resigned their commissions in order to join the bands on the frontier, among them the sons of Karaïskákes and Theodore Grívas. Secret societies were formed in the Ionian Islands; and despite British efforts to keep the Ionians neutral and the imprisonment of several priests, a body of Cephalonians and Zantiotes crossed over to join the insurgents in Epirus.

On January 27, 1854, Radovítzi near Arta raised the standard of revolt; Arta itself was besieged; but the Turkish relief forces, although twice repulsed at Pénte Pegádia, the famous "Five Wells" between Joánnina and Arta which gained notoriety in the war of 1897, managed to enter the town by sea from Salaóra on the Ambrakian Gulf. On March 15 a first battle at Péta, the scene of the defeat of 1822, resulted in the victory of the Greeks, while Theodore Grívas entered Métzovon. But these successes were not permanent. Grívas was forced to evacuate Métzovon and retire to Thessaly; a second battle at Péta on April 25 drove the Greeks from that position; a third attack upon the "Five Wells" dislodged them thence; an enthusiastic Radical deputy from Zante was beheaded by the Turks, and the insurrection in Epirus was over. Meanwhile, in the middle of February, bands, of which Christódoulos Hajji Pétros was the principal leader, had entered Thessaly from the then frontier town of Lamía; but, on April 22, the Greeks failed to take Domokós—the scene, 43 years later, of the fatal battle—their failure, as at Péta, being due to divisions between their own leaders. Hajji Pétros, however, fixed his camp at Kalabáka, the present terminus of the Thessalian railway, close to the famous monasteries "in Air," the Metéora of medieval and modern times, whose inmates celebrated a *Te Deum* to commemorate a victory which he won at that spot. But this success bore no fruit, owing to the intervention of Great Britain and France at Athens; and Blunt, our consul

at Salonika, warned the Thessalian insurgents of the futility of
further bloodshed. As for Macedonia, the landing of Karatássos, the hero of the incident with Turkey in 1847, near
Mt Athos, was paralysed by a French man-of-war, which sank
a vessel bearing his ammunition. As usually happens in
irregular warfare of this kind, the combatants did not always
distinguish between friends and foes ; and it is probable that
the material losses inflicted upon the Epirotes and Thessalians by those who had come to deliver them cooled their ardour.

Meanwhile, on March 19, the Porte had sent an ultimatum to the Greek government, demanding the recall
within ten days of all Greek officers then participating in the
insurrection, the closure of the frontier to armed bands and
the punishment of officials concerned in the agitation, the
public repudiation of the collection of money for the insurgents,
the moderation of the nationalist press, and an enquiry into
the release of the inmates of the gaol at Chalkís that they
might serve against Turkey. As the Greek reply was considered unsatisfactory, diplomatic relations between the two
countries were broken off, and all Greek subjects were ordered
to quit the Ottoman empire within 15 days. Otho at once
commanded his troops to prepare for an advance to the
frontier, and at one moment resolved to put himself at their
head. A tent with the royal colours was actually pitched near
the palace garden ; and the Queen, who was the soul of the
war party, regarded with indifference a possible occupation of
Athens and a blockade of the Greek ports by the Powers,
provided the King could enter Thessaly. But the majority of
the Kriezês Cabinet, and especially the Ministers of Justice
and Finance, Pélikas and Proveléngios, as well as the Greek
representatives in London, Paris, and Constantinople, urged
the expediency of peace. The opposition of the Ministers
roused the high-spirited Queen to a fury of indignation.
"Europe," she told the two leaders of the peace party in the
Cabinet, " in giving the throne of Greece to Otho, imagined

that she would have him here as a simple instrument of her own interests and her own policy; but Europe was mistaken. Otho has identified his fortunes with those of the Nation." "The only safety for the Greek government, the Nation, and its future," she added, "lies in the progress of the insurrection[1]."

But Greece, however enthusiastic, could not withstand the pressure of the Powers, who addressed a collective note to her. The King of Bavaria and the Austrian Emperor privately warned Otho of the difficult position in which his patriotism was placing him; Wyse, then British minister in Athens, insisted in regarding this national movement as entirely financed with Russian roubles, although Pélikas told him that for the Greeks it was "a question not of Russian conquests but of Greek freedom"; and his French colleague, Baron Rouen, did not hesitate to tell Otho, that if he, as a Catholic, was afraid of taking up an attitude hostile to Orthodoxy, Napoleon III would send him an army to protect him against his own subjects. As this argument was naturally repudiated by a sovereign, who, though a foreigner by birth, was no less ardent a nationalist than his subjects and nobly scorned to support his throne on foreign bayonets, the French Emperor considered the advisability of dethroning him—a scheme in which he had been encouraged by Kallérges, the hero of the September revolution, who was then in France. The British government was not prepared to take so violent a step; but, on May 10, the British and French ministers addressed notes to the Greek government, threatening the strict enforcement of the treaty of 1832, which had placed Otho on the throne, and which provided that he should "appropriate to the payment of the interest and sinking fund...of the loan," guaranteed by the protecting Powers, "the first revenues of the State," should these revenues be employed in attacking Turkey. This threat was not enforced, but towards the end of May the allied troops occupied the Piræus. Otho was made to declare that he

---

[1] Ἀπομνημονεύματα τῆς ὑπουργίας Σ. Πήλικα, 154–5.

would "observe faithfully a strict and complete neutrality," and would call to his "counsels new ministers most competent to carry this engagement into execution." This "Occupation Cabinet," as it was called, was presided over by Alexander Mavrokordátos, the veteran statesman of the War of Independence, at that time minister in Paris, who alone enjoyed the full confidence of the two western Powers. But Mavrokordátos, as not infrequently happens with diplomatists, had lost touch with his own country ; he had not held office there for ten years; and he returned to the ungrateful task of executing an unpopular policy, forced upon court and country by the bayonets of a foreign army of occupation. His most active colleague, Kallérges, who became Minister of War, was specially unpopular at the palace, where his share in the revolution of 1843 had not been forgotten, and where his unconcealed desire to dethrone the King must have been known. As Mavrokordátos did not arrive immediately, while Kallérges was already in Athens, plotting against the King and giving it out that the western Powers desired his dethronement by a national movement, there was some danger of a conspiracy until the arrival of the Prime Minister and his uncompromising loyalty kept his anti-dynastic subordinate in check. Thus, the King and Queen underwent a terrible ordeal. Otho and Amalia may have acted undiplomatically, perhaps unwisely, in 1854, for, alas! the great Powers have one law for weak states and another for the strong. Italy might take Mohammedan Tripoli, but Greece might not touch Greek Thessaly. Now, however, in the land which he loved not always wisely but too well, there is recognition of the patriotism of Otho and his noble Queen at the crisis of the Russo-Turkish war ; and a modern dramatist has portrayed in a brilliant historical play, "The Occupation," the agony within the palace.

The Franco-British occupation of the Piræus, like the Austrian occupation of the Danubian Principalities, lasted till

1857. The French commanders at the outset unnecessarily humiliated the royal couple by marching their troops past the windows of the palace—an affront which made Otho more popular than ever with his people, who regarded him as a martyr of the national idea. The French also broke up the type of a Russophil newspaper, arrested its editor, and insisted upon the prosecution of another journal. But these inroads upon the dignity of the Crown and the liberty of the press were less serious than those of the cholera, which, imported into the Allies' camp in the summer of 1854, spread from the Piræus to Athens. The classic plague, described for all time in the prose of Thucydides and the verse of Lucretius, seemed to have returned to a city long immune from its visitations—for cholera rarely scourges Greece. For five months it ravaged Athens, decimating the population, then some 30,000, and slaying many of the refugees who had emigrated thither from Turkey. Many citizens fled; the streets were deserted; even politics were hushed; no sound was heard save that of the cars conveying the sick to the hospitals, the dead to the cholera-pits, the survivors to the country or the sea. But amid the general panic, the King and Queen nobly did their duty, comforted the bereaved, and stood by the dying. Another scourge was added to the cholera. Many adventurers, who had been engaged in the insurrection, took to the road when the bands were dispersed; and even on the highway between Athens and the Piræus two French officers were robbed, and an artillery captain carried off to the mountains. Meanwhile, however, official relations with Turkey had improved. The first act of the "Occupation Cabinet" had been to resume them; and in the following year the commercial treaty of Kanlijeh, at the "bloody village" on the Bosphorus, bloodlessly regulated the mutual trade of the two countries. But Hellenism, alike in Constantinople as at Athens, was compelled by force to repudiate all sympathy with the Orthodox Autocrat. The Œcumenical Patriarch, the official head of the Greeks in Turkey, has always been liable, from his place of residence, to pressure from the Sultan; and at this crisis, Abdul Mejid, true to the policy of Mohammed II, ordered Anthimos VI to issue an encyclical, denouncing the Tsar's motives as hypocritical.

The bellicose passion, kindled in the breasts of the British, had received very meagre satisfaction from the operations on the Danube and in the Baltic. It was not so much a good peace, but a good war, that was wanted in England in the summer of 1854; and the people thought that an army and fleet should not have been assembled for nothing. War correspondence, then a novel form of excitement, enabled the public sitting comfortably at home to witness, as in a theatre, the movements of soldiers in the field; and the sporting element, which plays so large a part in our popular politics, found a still finer arena in an offensive war. The Crimean harbour of Sebastopol, of which Catherine the Great had been quick to recognise the potentialities, had been indicated to the Tsar by his Corsican counsellor Pozzo di Borgo, a quarter of a century earlier, as the probable goal of a hostile British fleet; the traveller Oliphant in 1853 had first drawn the attention of the British public to this remote spot; and, before the siege of Silistria had been raised, the *Times* and Lord Lyndhurst had advised its capture, as the best means of crippling Russia. The *Times* wrote with peculiar animation, because Nasmyth, the hero of Silistria, was its special correspondent. In the Cabinet, the Minister of War, then the Duke of Newcastle, shared the opinion of these amateur strategists, who professed to speak in the name of the British people. The rest of the Cabinet yielded to pressure from outside, and approved on June 28, it is said, while in a state of post-prandial drowsiness, an urgent dispatch to Raglan, instructing him "to concert measures for the siege of Sebastopol." St Arnaud had already received from Paris cryptic orders not to advance towards the Danube but to anticipate the transport of his troops from Varna by sea. Raglan sent for Sir George Brown, who commanded the Light Division, and asked for his opinion on the question, whether such an undertaking, as the dispatch put it, could "be undertaken with a reasonable prospect of success." Brown replied that, as they had no information about the strength of the forces in Sebastopol, the Duke of Wellington in their place would have refused so heavy a responsibility, but that the tone of the dispatch showed the determination of the government that Sebastopol should be besieged, if not by their present Commander-in-Chief, then by someone less scrupulous. Raglan allowed his deference to the government of civilians at home to outweigh his own better judgment as a soldier. St Arnaud and his staff, likewise opposed to so rash an undertaking, had orders to concur with the decision of his British colleague; and thus, against the wish of both commanders, the war was transferred to the Crimea. Nearly two months, however, were spent at Varna before the expedition sailed; for, besides the time required for preparing the means of embarkation, nature protested against a prompt departure. Fire destroyed many of the British military stores; the crowded cemetery at Varna still bears silent witness to the ravages of cholera among the allied troops. It was not till September 13 that the allied fleets reached the Crimea; and on the following day a body of British troops occupied without opposition the port of Eupatoria. The main force landed near the lake of Kamishlu; and soon 37,000 French, 27,000 British, and 7000 Turks were encamped upon the shores of what was to most of them an absolutely unknown land. Only the Turks could claim some connexion with the country, for its natives shared their faith, and from 1475 in the time of Mohammed II till the latter part of the eighteenth century Crim Tartary, once the seat of Genoese colonisation, had been a part of the Ottoman empire. Only as recently as 1783 had it been finally incorporated by Catherine II in the Russian dominions. Thus in the Crimea began that secular strife between Turk and Muscovite, of which this war was not to be the last phase.

On September 19 the allied armies started for Sebastopol.
Their march led them to the stream of the Bulganak, where the
first skirmish between the western forces and their enemy
took place. Next day, on the banks of another river, since
then more famous than many a greater stream, the Alma, they
fought and won their first great battle. The Russians, commanded by Mentschikoff, who was now called to support his
blustering diplomacy by force, were obliged to retreat after a
struggle in which the British took the principal part, owing to
the slowness of the French commander. A similar delay after
the victory was even more dangerous ; for, had Raglan's
proposal to march on at once to Sebastopol been adopted, it
was believed that that fortress would have succumbed without
resistance to the Allies within five days of their landing, and all
the losses and labours of twelve weary months would have been
spared. Indeed, alike in London, Paris, and St Petersburg, it
was thought that Sebastopol was lost. St Arnaud, however,
refused, on the ground that his men were tired and that it was
too costly a sacrifice to attack the Russians in the position
which they were said to occupy. Two whole days were spent
in embarking the wounded, and it was not till the 23rd that
the march was resumed. Even then, however, the invaders
did not go straight to the point where Sebastopol was most
vulnerable. Months before, two British naval officers, who
knew the place, had pointed out that, in the event of an invasion
of the Crimea, the Russian arsenal should be attacked from the
north side, the Severnaya, as the Russians called it, and had
argued that the capture of the Star fort, which stood above
that shore of the roadstead, would lead to the immediate fall
of the town and the forts on the south bank and to the
destruction of all the shipping in the harbour. Moreover, it
was the opinion of the Russians that an occupation of the
north would have enabled the Allies to cut off all communications
with the outside, and thus, if they could not capture Sebastopol
by immediate force, they could prevent reinforcements from

relieving the garrison. The great engineer, Todleben, who contributed so much to the defence of the town, stated afterwards that, had the Allies attacked the Star fort at once, they must inevitably have taken it. This was also the plan advocated by Raglan and Sir Edmund Lyons, who, after his experience of diplomacy in Greece, was then commanding the in-shore squadron off Sebastopol. But St Arnaud, already suffering from the disease which a few days later proved fatal, declined once more to adopt the scheme of his British colleague ; and, as the task of attacking the fort would have naturally devolved upon the French in virtue of their position opposite to it, the British commander reluctantly suggested a flank march right round Sebastopol, crossing the Tchernaya, which flows into the harbour, and thus attacking the place from the south. This alternative, strongly supported by Sir John Burgoyne, the British engineering expert, was accepted by St Arnaud.

Accordingly, the Allies set out upon a venture into the unknown ; for, with the usual carelessness of the British War Office, little previous study had been made officially of the land defences of a town which a British engineer had first seriously fortified for Nicholas 24 years earlier and which had been recently strengthened. A report by a British officer, written 19 years before the war, had been almost neglected ; and the recent book of a private traveller was the best guide which our generals had to the Russian stronghold. Moltke, it may be surmised, would not thus lightly have besieged a fortress. On the march round to the south a surprise occurred, which, had it not been for Raglan's presence of mind, might have been a disaster. Suddenly, the British commander, while executing a reconnaissance, found himself in sight of a Russian force. The surprise was mutual, for neither army was aware of the movements of the other. What had happened was that Mentschikoff, after his defeat at the Alma, convinced that Sebastopol must fall and that his communications would be cut off, had ordered the closing of the roadstead, in which the Black

Sea fleet lay at anchor, by sinking some of the ships. This
desperate measure, bitterly resented by the naval officers who
had toiled to create and hoped to use this instrument of war,
was executed by the reluctant Admiral Korniloff, who thus saw
seven of his vessels scuttled and the rest imprisoned by their
sunken hulls. Having thus liberated the crews for the defence
of the town, Mentschikoff marched out with his main army
along the high road which led to the interior of Russia, in-
tending to hang upon the flank of the Allies. It was the rear
of this army upon which Lord Cardigan had suddenly come;
and only the arrival of the British cavalry and the ignorance of
Mentschikoff prevented what might have been a serious British
defeat. Fortunately the Russian rear-guard retreated; the
Russian opportunity was lost; and next day both the British
army and the co-operating fleet occupied, after a few shots, the
small harbour of Balaclava to the south of Sebastopol. Thus,
after the lapse of centuries, this old Genoese colony, formerly
the see of a Latin bishop, fell once more under the sway of a
western Power.

A further delay in beginning the siege now intervened;
and three weeks elapsed between the occupation of Balaclava
and the first attack upon Sebastopol. Raglan and Lyons
urged immediate action, but Burgoyne advised first landing
the siege-trains; and General Canrobert, who had succeeded
St Arnaud in the command of the French, was of the same
opinion. Todleben, the Russian engineer of German extraction,
who was the brain, as Korniloff was the soul, of the defence,
used this respite to strengthen the Malakoff tower and other
outworks of the town, and thus the scientific organisation of
the one completed the religious enthusiasm of the other; the
engineer believed in grape-shot, the admiral in the God of
battles. But an immediate attack, in the opinion of Todleben,
would have prevailed over his science and the soldiers' enthusiasm. Thus a third chance of prompt success was allowed
to slip; and when, at last, on October 17, the siege began,

the place was in a far stronger position than three weeks earlier. Encamped on the south, the Allies could not, as would have been possible from the north, spare sufficient forces to prevent communications from the interior of Russia with the beleaguered town. Mentschikoff, stung by Korniloff's heroism and suspecting his formal remonstrances, was thus enabled to throw 16 battalions back into the place, so that, when the bombardment began, the total number of its defenders was equal to the available forces of the Allies. Ere long the Russian troops rendered available by the evacuation of the Danubian Principalities swelled the hostile numbers in and round Sebastopol to nearly double those of the besiegers. Nor was the first day's bombardment decisive; Korniloff, indeed, was mortally wounded while going his rounds, but the fleets failed in their attack, sustaining some material and no little moral damage.

For the next week the bombardment was continued without much effect; and on October 25 the assailants were themselves assailed. Mentschikoff had resolved to regain possession of the port of Balaclava, whence the British drew their supplies; and early on that day, Liprandi, one of his subordinates, attacked the redoubts which Sir Colin Campbell, who was in command at Balaclava, had caused to be thrown up hastily on the causeway to the north of the harbour. The Russians drove from the redoubts the Turks who manned them; and, had it not been for the bravery of the 93rd Highland regiment, the Russian cavalry would have seized the little town. But the battle of Balaclava is chiefly memorable for the two great charges—that of the Heavy and that of the Light Brigade—both celebrated, and the latter immortalised, by Tennyson. The exploit of General Scarlett, who at the head of a small squadron of heavy cavalry wedged himself into the centre of a large Russian force, and in eight minutes forced it to retreat, resembled the deeds of warriors in days when battles were decided by hand-to-hand combat, and

generals strove to win the *spolia opima* from the rival commanders. The Russians, however, still held the captured
redoubts; and Raglan ordered Lord Lucan, who was in
command of the cavalry, to send them "rapidly to the front,
and try to prevent the enemy carrying away the guns." Lucan
misunderstood this order, and believed that his chief had
commanded the cavalry to attack the Russian guns at the end
of the north valley beyond the causeway—a task of extraordinary
danger, because the attacking horsemen would be exposed to
a fire from "cannon to right of them, cannon to left of them,
cannon in front of them." Nevertheless, he ordered his
brother-in-law, Lord Cardigan, who was in command of the
Light Brigade, to execute this terrible operation. Cardigan
was a formalist, who always executed his instructions in the
most literal sense; he had just preserved a strict neutrality
while the Heavy Brigade had been engaged, because he had
not been ordered to attack; he now, although well aware
that "someone had blundered," rode with his six hundred
"into the valley of death," which was flanked on either side by
Russian forces stationed on the causeway and the Fedioukine
heights and raked by the battery at the end. The brigade,
or that portion of it which survived this murderous ride,
charged into the jaws of this battery, seized it, and made its
way back with diminished danger, owing to the chivalrous
and successful attack of the Chasseurs d'Afrique, which silenced
the guns on the Fedioukine heights. Of 673 horsemen, 113
had been killed, 134 wounded, and 475 had had their horses
slain. The leader of the brigade described his act of heroism
under misapprehended orders as "a mad-brained trick," but the
just appreciation of the charge fell from the lips of General
Bosquet, who summed it up in a phrase which has become
classic: *C'est magnifique ; mais ce n'est pas la guerre.* Despite
these two exploits, the battle was not decisive. The Russians
were left in undisturbed possession of the captured redoubts,
and the moral confidence of the garrison in Sebastopol was

proportionately increased. Eleven days later took place the third and last great battle of the war in which the British were engaged. The ruins of what was once the "magnificent citadel" of Inkerman, the creation of Greek princes, lay a little to the east of the besieged stronghold. The name was now immortalised by the struggle on a not distant hill, where, on November 5, Sir J. Pennefather held the British position for hours in the mist against a vastly superior Russian force, while officers and soldiers fought Homeric battles, man against man, till the intervention of the French assured the victory to the Allies.

But now more insidious foes than the Russians attacked the armies of the besiegers, little more than half as numerous as the besieged. On November 14 a cyclone destroyed 21 vessels laden with stores for the British and tore in pieces their tents and canvas hospitals, while a biting snow-storm gave the soldiers a foretaste of the Crimean winter. Men and horses alike died from the consequent exposure on the wind-swept downs, where the British, owing to the lack of an efficient War Office, suffered more than the better organised and more experienced French army. Cholera and other diseases helped to diminish the number of the combatants; and in seven months 10,053 of our men died from sickness alone. The deplorable condition of the expeditionary force was depicted in trenchant language by Russell, the war correspondent of the *Times*, whose messages aroused the intense indignation of the people against the authorities. When the newspaper denounced our military system as "that huge imposture," and deplored the "destruction of the British army," the public became furious with its rulers. As soon as Parliament met for the session of 1855, Roebuck gave notice of a motion for a Committee of Enquiry; and before the discussion upon it began, Lord J. Russell resigned. The adoption of the motion by a large majority involved the fall of the Aberdeen Ministry; and Palmerston, the choice of the nation, became Prime Minister, with Lord Panmure as Secretary of State for War.

The British people rejoiced that a strong man who knew his own mind was at the head of the government, instead of the statesman who had ruined his reputation by his tenure of the Premiership. Always fortunate, Palmerston profited by improvements already beginning at the seat of war; a road, and even a railway, at last facilitated the transport of stores from the tiny port of Balaclava; in the person of Florence Nightingale a human angel combatted and almost subdued the "angel of death," the "beating" of whose wings had been heard in the hospitals at Scutari.

Meanwhile, diplomacy had been striving to end the war. After the battle of Inkerman the Tsar authorised Prince Gortchakoff to discuss the question of peace on the principles, known as "the four points," postulated by Great Britain, France, and Austria, viz. the cessation of the Russian protectorate over Moldavia and Wallachia and the application of a collective guarantee of the Powers to all the three Danubian Principalities; the freedom of the navigation of that river; the revision of the treaty of July 13, 1841, so as to terminate Russian preponderance in the Euxine; and the abandonment of Russia's claim to protect the Orthodox subjects of the Sultan. Austria, however, on December 2 concluded a treaty with the two western Powers to meet the event of the Tsar's refusal to accept these "points"; and the danger of her armed intervention induced him to agree to participate in a conference at Vienna. But before it met, Nicholas I was dead. "Russia," he had boasted, "has two generals, upon whom she can rely, Generals January and February." One of the finest cartoons ever published in *Punch* represented "General February turned traitor," and laying his icy hand on the proud Autocrat. The news that the despised Turks had repulsed his troops at the harbour of Eupatoria on February 17 aggravated the seasonable malady which fell upon him; and on March 2 he died, bequeathing the war and the peace negotiations to his son, Alexander II. Thirteen days later the conference of Turkey and the Powers (with the exception of Prussia, excluded by the hesitation of her King to resort to war in case of failure) met. Agreement on the first two " points " was soon attained; but the third naturally aroused Russian opposition, while the Russian amendment, proposing to throw the Straits open to the fleets of all nations, as naturally met with a refusal from the Porte and the Powers. Gortchakoff was ordered by the new Tsar, desirous of peace but afraid to purchase it by the loss of prestige, to decline any reduction of the Black Sea fleet; and with this answer the peace negotiations practically ended. An Austrian proposal to establish a collective guarantee of the Ottoman empire, a system of counterpoise in the Euxine, and the limitation of the Russian fleet there to the number of ships maintained before the war, was approved by Russell, the chief British delegate, and his French colleague, but rejected by the British government and the French Emperor. At this rebuff, Austria, considering that the responsibility for the continuance of the war rested upon the Allies, reduced her armaments and accorded to France and Britain nothing more substantial than her " moral support." They had, however, gained an unexpected increase of strength in 15,000 Sardinian troops, which Cavour had sent under La Marmora to take part in the war, with the object of thus enabling Sardinia to be represented at the ultimate peace negotiations. This act of far-sighted statesmanship, opposed by the Piedmontese unofficial press, led to the raising of the Italian question at the Congress of Paris; and thus the unity of Italy is perhaps the only lasting result of the Crimean war.

Even before the diplomatists had ceased to confer at Vienna, the bombardment of Sebastopol was resumed; in May the Allies captured the stores laid up at Kertch and Yeni Kaleh in the east of the peninsula, and penetrated through the Cimmerian Bosphorus into the Sea of Azov, where they destroyed a flotilla of transports sailing over what had till then been a Russian lake. Two places in Circassia fell, thus completing the rapid and easily-won success of this expedition, which contrasted so markedly with the long-drawn siege of Sebastopol. On June 18 the assaults on the two defences known as Fort Malakoff and the Redan proved abortive; and this disappointment hastened the end of the British commander. General Simpson, Raglan's successor, and Pélissier, who had relieved Canrobert in the command of the French, pressed on the siege; but the victory of August 16 over the Russians on the river Tchernaya was largely the work of the Sardinian troops, who thereby redeemed the disastrous defeat of Novara and popularised the policy of Cavour in sending them to fight in a cause which had seemed to be none of theirs. The French, by a second and successful assault upon the Malakoff, more than compensated for another British failure to carry the Redan; and on September 9 Sebastopol fell. The object of the Crimean expedition having been attained and with considerable glory to his arms, Napoleon III, who had at one time wished to command in person, now showed a desire for peace. If the British public, disappointed at the lack of dramatic British triumphs since Inkerman, wished for a continuance of the war, it soon became clear to statesmen that Britain would have to fight without her French ally. The Tsar, too, might now seek peace without loss of honour; for on November 28, Kars had succumbed to famine after a gallant defence by Fenwick Williams, and for the second time a Russian army entered that famous fortress. Austria, stepping in as a mediator, presented an ultimatum to the Tsar, approved by France and (with certain reserves) by Britain, which was accepted by Russia; and, on February 25, 1856, a Congress, at which Clarendon, the Foreign Secretary, represented the British government, met in Paris. Hostilities were promptly suspended, and such was the desire for peace that an agreement was easily reached.

On March 30, 1856 was signed the solemn instrument, which regulated, at least, in their main outlines, the affairs of the near east till the next great European Congress met at Berlin in 1878. The treaty of Paris left the map, with one exception, exactly as it stood before the war. The conquests of the Allies in the Crimea and at Kinburn, and the Russian acquisition of Kars, were restored, this last for the second time, to their previous owners ; but, as recompense for the restoration of the Crimean towns and ports, and "in order to secure the better the free navigation of the Danube," the Tsar ceded to the Principality of Moldavia the southern part of Bessarabia and the delta of the Danube (the islands forming the latter, however, were "replaced under the immediate sovereignty of the Sublime Porte" by the treaty of June 19, 1857), thus restoring a portion of what Russia had annexed in 1812. The mouths of the Danube, although thus re-included within the Turkish empire, were put under the authority of a commission, upon which each of the signatories was represented by a delegate, for the purpose of removing obstacles to the traffic from Isaccea to the sea. At the conclusion of this task, the powers of this body were to be transferred to a permanent commission, composed of a delegate apiece from each of the seven riverain states—Württemberg, Bavaria, Austria, Turkey, Servia, Wallachia, and Moldavia, the delegates of these last three vassal Principalities being approved by the Porte. The navigation of both the Danube and the Black Sea was declared free, subject only to necessary police and sanitary regulations. The Black Sea was neutralised, and its waters and ports were closed to the navies of both the riverain empires and of any other Power ; consequently the establishment of naval arsenals on its shores became unnecessary, and both the Tsar and the Sultan pledged themselves neither to create nor to maintain them there. Turkey was admitted to the dubious privileges of participation in the public law and the Concert of Europe ; and the other signatories undertook "to respect the independence and the territorial integrity of the Ottoman Empire," guaranteed "in common the strict observance of this

engagement," and promised to " consider every act calculated
to do injury thereto as a question of general interest." Should
any threatening disagreement arise between the Porte and one
or more of the Powers, the Porte and its opponent were to
invoke the mediation of the other signatories, before resorting
to force.

Other clauses of the treaty provided for the welfare of the
Sultan's Christian subjects. Abdul Mejid communicated to
the other high contracting parties the firman of February 18,
which had proclaimed liberty of worship, civil equality of all
Ottoman subjects, admitted Christians to military service, and
reorganised (on paper) the fiscal system. " The high value
of this communication," naïvely observed the Powers, impressed
them so strongly that they disclaimed any right to collective
or separate intervention between the Sultan and his subjects.
As regards the Principalities, Wallachia and Moldavia (the
latter slightly increased in size) were to enjoy, under Turkish
suzerainty and the guarantee of the Powers, their previous
privileges. No exclusive protection over them should thenceforth be exercised by any one of the guarantors ; no special
right of interference in their internal affairs would be allowed.
Russia's pretentions having been thus repudiated, the Porte
undertook to maintain there " an independent and national
administration," no less than full liberty of worship, legislation,
commerce, and navigation. A special commission, composed
by the Powers, with a Turkish commissioner, was to " meet
without delay, at Bucharest " for the revision of their existing
legislation, the study of their condition, and their future
organisation. The Sultan promised to convoke at once in
each of the two Principalities an Assembly, or " divan *ad hoc*,"
so composed as to represent most exactly the interests of all
classes, with the function of expressing the wishes of the
population concerning their definite organisation. The commission, " taking into consideration the opinion expressed by
the two divans," was to " transmit, without delay, to the present

seat of the Conferences, the result of its own labours." A convention, to be concluded at Paris between the high contracting parties, was to sanction the final agreement with the Porte; and, in conformity therewith, an Imperial ordinance was to " constitute definitely the organisation of these provinces, placed thenceforth under the collective guarantee of all the signatory Powers." A national army would maintain peace in the interior and on the frontiers of the Principalities; and no armed intervention, even by their suzerain, for the purpose of maintaining or restoring internal repose, was permitted except after previous agreement with the Powers. Servia was to continue in the same position as before, her "rights and immunities" being "placed thenceforth under the collective guarantee of the contracting Powers"; her "independent and national administration, as well as full liberty of worship, of legislation, of commerce, and of navigation," was preserved. The Porte retained the right of garrison, but no armed intervention was to be made without the previous consent of the Powers.

Two conventions, signed the same day, regulated the questions of the Straits and of the Black Sea. The former merely recapitulated the treaty of 1841, with the addition that the passage of the Dardanelles and the Bosphorus would be permitted to the light craft, not more than two apiece, which the Powers were authorised to station at the mouths of the Danube; the second convention provided that Russia and Turkey might each keep six small steamers and four light craft in the Black Sea for the service of the coasts.

Of the historic treaty of Paris not much has stood the strain of time, national sentiment, and interests of state. The creation and complete independence of Roumania and the independence of Servia have made of merely antiquarian importance the clauses concerning the vassal Principalities of 1856; Russia, so early as 1870, availed herself of the defeat of one of her Crimean opponents to repudiate the Black Sea clauses of the treaty; Sebastopol saw in 1886 the rebirth of the Black Sea fleet; while Batûm, still Turkish in 1856, has become a fortified port of the Russian Euxine. The strip of Bessarabia, ceded to Moldavia at Paris, was handed back to Russia at Berlin; Kars has long been a Russian town[1]. How the signatories of the treaty of Paris have observed their undertaking "to respect the independence and the territorial integrity of the Ottoman Empire" may be seen by the Austrian annexation of Bosnia and the Herzegovina, the Italian annexation of Tripoli, and the British occupation of Cyprus and Egypt, while the clause which pledged Russia and Sardinia to invoke the mediation of their co-signatories in the event of a disagreement with the Porte was disregarded by Russia in 1877 and by Italy in 1911, and Cavour's signature thus dishonoured. The blessings promised to the Sultan's Christian subjects, which seemed of such "high value" to the diplomatists of Paris, have proved to be absolutely worthless, even when disguised under the form of a Constitution. Of all the provisions of the treaty those for the regulation of the Danube have proved to be most useful. The powers of the European commission were extended in 1871 for 12 further years, and at the expiration of that period for 21 years more; and the removal of piracy no less than sandbanks has been its work. As usual, the least showy section of this great international document has been the most successful.

Looking back upon the war which was ended by the treaty of Paris, we may well ask ourselves whether the gain was such as to compensate us for the death of 28,000 men and the addition of 30 millions to the national debt. Lord Salisbury years afterwards told his countrymen that in 1854 they had "put their money on the wrong horse." For the free Balkan states have arisen as a barrier to a Russian advance upon Constantinople by land, while that city no longer possesses for us the supreme importance that it occupied in public esteem before we held the keys of the Suez Canal. A British statesman who, after the Armenian massacres, the Macedonian

[1] Batûm is temporarily occupied (April, 1922) by Georgian Bolsheviks, Kars by the Kemalists; all Bessarabia is now Roumanian.

muddle, and the fiasco of the "Young" Turkish constitution, should think it desirable to draw the sword of the British empire in defence of Turkey, would, indeed, have learned little from history. Year by year it has become more evident that the Turks must leave Europe; nor is it likely that Russia will take their place. That belongs to the Balkan states.

Besides the subjects contained in the treaty of Paris, two others affecting the near east were discussed in the sittings of the Congress. Austria, in the 14th protocol, obtained from the Russian delegates a disclaimer of any such Russian protectorate over Montenegro as the Tsar had formerly claimed to exercise over the Danubian Principalities. Mutual sympathy was declared to be the sole bond of union between the Muscovites and the mountaineers; while Aali Pasha, on behalf of Turkey, stated that the Porte regarded the Black Mountain as an "integral part of the Ottoman empire." This statement in direct violation of the firman of 1799, of the Turco-Montenegrin treaties of 1838 and 1842 and of the hard facts of many a Turkish defeat at the hands of the mountaineers, was warmly repudiated by Prince Danilo in a memorandum addressed to the signatory Powers on May 31. He pointed out with considerable exaggeration that, with more reason he might claim "half Albania and all the Herzegovina," on the ground that the Balsha dynasty, which ruled over the Zeta in the fourteenth and fifteenth centuries, had once possessed those lands, while the Turks had never possessed Montenegro; that "for 466 years," that is, since the battle of Kossovo, "the Montenegrin people had never been subjected by any Power"; that "for four and a half centuries it had waged continual warfare with Turkey"; but that, notwithstanding these services to Christendom, Montenegro, owing to the theocratic constitution which had only recently been abolished, had never been received officially within the family of European states. The Prince claimed the official recognition of Montenegrin independence, the expansion of the

Principality at the expense of Albania and the Herzegovina, the delimitation of the Turco-Montenegrin frontiers, and the concession of the town and harbour of Antivari, which his predecessor the *Vladika* Danilo had tried to secure a century and a half earlier, and which was a commercial necessity for a people, deprived by the loss of Cattaro in 1814 of all access to the sea. In support of this memorandum, Danilo, who in 1855 had married Darinka Kuechich, daughter of a Serb merchant of Trieste, visited Napoleon III in 1857. The French Emperor, who two years before had established a French vice-consulate at Cetinje and sent thither as his representative M. Hecquard, the well-known writer on Albania, received the princely couple with the honours due to an independent ruler. But the only immediate result of this visit was a Turkish offer to bestow upon the Prince a part of the Herzegovina with a civil list and a Turkish title, and to open all Turkish ports to his subjects, on condition that he did homage to the Sultan as his suzerain. Danilo, who in the previous summer had refused the wish of the people of Nikshich to become his subjects, from fear of provoking a fresh war with Turkey, was disposed to accept the Turkish offer, which his warlike people considered a disgrace. Nothing eventually came of the proposal; but Danilo's unpopularity, already demonstrated by another rising of the Kutchi against his tax-collectors, became such that a conspiracy against his life was discovered and two of the ringleaders shot.

The second Oriental question which, though excluded from the treaty, found a place in the 22nd protocol, was the unhappy condition of Greece. Walewski, Napoleon's Minister, observed that the Franco-British occupation of the Piræus could not end without serious inconvenience, so long as the abnormal situation of that country continued. Clarendon supported his French colleague with the argument that, before withdrawing her troops from Greece, Great Britain must have "solid guarantees for the maintenance of a satisfactory state of things." Russia, through her spokesman, willingly joined the other two protecting Powers in all measures calculated to improve the condition of the Hellenic kingdom. The "Occupation Cabinet" had ere this ceased to exist; for the refusal of the Queen to receive a lady friend of Kallérges had led to the final retirement of Mavrokordátos and the appointment of the Hydriote D. Boúlgares as Prime Minister in October 1855. The veteran statesman, who thus quitted the political stage, had made the mistake of increasing the salaries of the deputies and senators, and thus attaching to the irremovable Second Chamber an odium which led to its abolition after the revolution of 1862. But he had maintained Greek neutrality in spite of the national enthusiasm for Russia; and his withdrawal from public life, followed by the death of Metaxâs, and the absence of Trikoúpes at the London legation, removed all the old leaders and with them the three "foreign" parties from the arena, leaving it clear for a new and self-reliant generation, which had grown up since the War of Independence. Boúlgares, whose flowing robes and inherited dignity won him the nickname of Artaxerxes from the Queen, was an honest man, who endeavoured to grapple with one of the two plagues of the country which had aroused the concern of the protecting Powers at Paris—brigandage and financial disorder. A Greco-Turkish convention was signed for the suppression of the former; and the peasants, convinced that the government meant business and that brigands would not be protected in high places, co-operated with the authorities in hunting them down, shooting them whenever possible to make sure of their removal. It was then that the bold lieutenant Mégas slew, and was slain by, the brigand Davéles at the classic "crossroads," where Œdipus had slain his father Láïos. The three Powers, on their part, created a financial commission, composed of their representatives at Athens, which met in February 1857. On the 27th of the same month the occupation ended.

CHAPTER XI

THE UNION OF THE DANUBIAN PRINCIPALITIES
(1856-62)

THE Congress of Paris had not ended the difficulties of the near east. On the contrary, it had expressly provided, in a series of articles, for the regulation of the two Principalities. The Roumanian question at once became the order of the day; and public attention passed from the Crimea to the lower Danube.

The union of Wallachia and Moldavia had been gradually maturing. Two articles of the *règlement organique* had anticipated its possibility; and Cavour had recalled this fact to the memory of his colleagues at the Congress. Bibescu, initiating a policy which led afterwards, in the hands of Bismarck, to the unity of Germany, had suppressed the fiscal barrier between the two Principalities, so that thenceforth "the impotent stream of the Milcov" no longer divided their mutual trade. The Revolution of 1848 had further strengthened the unionist idea; and the refugees in Paris had influenced the mind of Napoleon III, who saw in the union a barrier against the advance of Russia. A Roumanian pamphlet, published in Paris, advocated the election of the same ruler for both the Roumanian states; and, at the conferences of Vienna in 1855, the French government put forward their union as the best solution, while Turkey, supported by Great Britain and Austria, opposed it. During the Congress of Paris, Napoleon III expressed the opinion that the only means of satisfying the Moldavian and

Wallachian peoples was to unite them under a foreign prince, while preserving the suzerainty of the Sultan. Queen Victoria likewise advocated an hereditary monarchy; and Clarendon agreed with the Emperor that such a plan might perhaps be the best solution for the Principalities, but that the selection of a foreign prince would create a second Greece close to the Russian frontier; for, argued the British statesman, a foreign ruler, if a Catholic, would be forced by the attacks of his Orthodox clergy to lean upon Russia, and, if Orthodox, would voluntarily gravitate towards her. However, when Walewski raised the question in the Congress of Paris, and advocated the union, Clarendon and Orloff supported him, while the Turkish and Austrian spokesmen naturally opposed. The latter suggested that the population of the two provinces should be asked their opinion; and this idea was adopted. From that moment the result depended upon the electoral skill of the rival parties and upon the amount of pressure which the Turkish government could exercise and the French permit.

The seven years' term of office, which the convention of Balta Liman had prescribed for the two Princes, expired in 1856; and in the room of Stirbeiu and Gregory Ghika, both disinterested adherents of the union, the Porte nominated two lieutenant-generals, Alexander Ghika, the old and incapable Hospodar, deposed in 1842, and Theodore Balsh, whose zeal against the union was increased by his desire to become Prince, as the reward of his services to his employers. It was obvious to everyone that the real struggle would be fought out in Moldavia, which, as the smaller Principality, would have most to lose by the union, involving, as it must, the degradation of Jassy from the rank of a capital to that of a provincial town. Before quitting office there, however, Gregory Ghika had prepared the way for the unionist idea by appointing its partisans as prefects, while his Wallachian colleague addressed a memorandum to Napoleon III in favour of the appointment of a foreign hereditary Prince. Balsh undid his predecessor's work by substituting Separatists for Unionists as prefects, and by collecting signatures against the union. Behind the scenes stood, as usual, the consuls of the Powers, the Austrians assisting the Separatists, the French representative Place protecting the Unionists, and himself protected by Thouvenel, whom we last saw at Athens but who then held the French embassy at Constantinople. The death of Balsh, the evacuation of the Principalities by the Austrian troops, and the arrival of the international commission, created by the treaty of Paris, in March 1857, did not diminish the conflict. The new lieutenant-general, Nicholas Vogorídes, son of the similar official of 1821-2 who had afterwards been first Prince of Samos, disregarded his promise to respect the manifestations of the people's will. Two divans *ad hoc*, composed respectively of 112 Wallachs and 84 Moldaves, were elected; but the Moldavian registers were manipulated in such a manner that the landed proprietors and professional men were decimated, while a solid block of 167,222 ignorant and malleable peasants swamped all the other voters. Napoleon protested, and threatened to recall his ambassador from Constantinople; Russia, Prussia, and Sardinia supported him; but the British government was opposed to the union, which it had come to regard as the first step towards the dismemberment of Turkey. A compromise was effected during a visit paid by Napoleon to Osborne; Great Britain joined France in causing the Porte to annul the elections in both Principalities; France gave way on the question of their union. This time Vogorídes was impartial; and the Moldavian divan, thus freely elected, contained only two Separatists. By this overwhelming majority a motion was carried, embodying the four points of the Moldavian charter: the autonomy and neutrality of the two Principalities, their union in a single state, the selection of their ruler from among the reigning dynasties of Europe on condition that his heirs should embrace the national religion, and the creation of a single representative Assembly. The same four points were formulated by the Wallachian divan, in which the two ex-Princes, Bibescu and Stirbeiu, patriotically sacrificed their own chances in favour of a foreigner whose nomination would silence local rivalries. The divans had thus answered the Austrian and Turkish objection, that the peoples of the two Principalities desired to remain separate. It was now the duty of the Powers, according to the treaty of Paris, to examine the report of the commission and draw up a convention for the definite organisation of the two provinces.

This convention, signed at Paris on August 19, 1858, was based upon the Osborne visit rather than the votes of the Danubian divans. In vain both Gladstone and the future Lord Salisbury had advocated union; both Disraeli and Palmerston opposed it. Thanks to the compromise arranged between the British and French governments, a scheme of organisation was adopted, which was neither union nor separation. The two provinces were thenceforth to be known as " the United Principalities of Moldavia and Wallachia," and were to remain under the suzerainty of the Sultan and the collective guarantee of the signatories of the treaty of Paris. Fokshani, from its position the mutual frontier, was selected as the seat of a Central Commission, composed of eight Wallachs and eight Moldaves, for the preparation of laws common to the two Principalities, and of the federal Court of Appeal. The two armies were to receive the same organisation, and to be united in case of need under one commander, nominated alternately by either Prince; but their flags were to remain separate, with the addition of a blue streamer common to both! These more or less Unionist provisions were counterbalanced by such frankly Separatist arrangements as the election of two Hospodars for life, and the creation of two Assemblies elected by a new septennial act, to which the voting of laws peculiar to either Principality was entrusted. The Turkish tribute was fixed at 1,500,000 piastres annually for the smaller, and 2,500,000 for the larger province; and such approved western principles as the equality of all citizens before the tax-collector, and the abolition of all feudal privileges, exemptions, and monopolies, were combined with the admission of all Christians to full political rights. Agrarian reform was forthwith to improve the lot of the Roumanian peasants. Pending the election of the new Princes by the respective Assemblies, the provisional government was entrusted to three Commissioners, named in virtue of their official positions, in either Principality. Thus diplomacy imagined that it had solved the question of the lower Danube.

But human nature is stronger than parchment bonds ; and the astute politicians of Bucharest and Jassy found a means of eluding the cunning devices of the Powers for keeping them divided. The Convention of Paris had provided for many contingencies, but not for that which actually happened—the election of the same person as Hospodar by both Assemblies. At first such a choice did not occur even to the Roumanians themselves, for in Wallachia all the three Commissioners, whose duty it was to hold the elections, were opposed to the union and favoured the elevation of either of the two former Princes, Bibescu or Stirbeiu, to the throne ; while in Moldavia two of the three were Unionists, but neither Unionists nor Separatists could agree upon their respective candidate. The fatal day had almost arrived and would have found the Unionists still undecided, when at a party meeting at Jassy Pisoski put his back against the door with a pistol in his hand, and threatened to shoot himself, if his colleagues did not make up their minds before leaving the room. At the same time he proposed a new candidate, Colonel Couza, a Moldave of Galatz descended from a small noble family, which had given two victims to its country. Couza, then Minister of War, was in his thirty-ninth year ; he had studied law in Paris, served on the bench and in the army, and had won popularity during the lieutenancy of Vogorídes by resigning the prefecture of Galatz as a protest against the illegalities of his chief. Galatz had just elected him to the Assembly; the Assembly, on January 17, 1859, unanimously elected him Prince. It now remained to secure his election by the Wallachian Assembly, in which Bibescu's partisans had a majority. Fortunately, the Wallachs had waited to see how the Moldaves would vote; and a Moldave agent now assured them that France and Russia were favourable to Couza and would recognise the accomplished fact of his double election. On the day of the vote at Bucharest, the Unionists organised a popular demonstration in his favour; the mob invaded the galleries of the Chamber, and the butchers whetted their knives in an unmistakeable manner. This practical argument was enforced by an appeal to patriots to vote for the Union in the person of Couza and to the partisans of Bibescu, its former advocate, to support it. Pressure and principle prevailed; the Wallachian Assembly on February 5, unanimously elected Couza. The Prince took the title of Alexander John I. The personal union was accomplished.

The election had occurred at a most favourable moment of international politics. Austria, one of the two chief opponents of the union, could not intervene owing to the Italian war; and Couza even concluded a secret arrangement with an agent of Kossuth for co-operation with the Hungarian patriots, of which the occupation of the Bukovina was to be the reward. Great Britain withdrew her opposition; towards the end of 1861 Couza was received at Constantinople, and the signatories of the treaty of Paris recognised the union. The Central Commission of Fokshani was suppressed; the two Assemblies and the Ministries, which had existed since Couza's election, were fused into one; and the seat of government was transferred to Bucharest. In 1862 the first united Roumanian Assembly met there. Looking back, we must admit that Gladstone and Salisbury were right in advocating the union, which has led to the creation of the present strong and flourishing kingdom of Roumania.

Almost at the same time at which Couza was raised to the

throne of the united Roumanian Principalities, Alexander
Karageorgevich was forced to abandon that of Servia. His
neutrality during the Crimean war had, as he told his people,
found its reward in the favourable Servian clauses of the treaty
of Paris, which largely nullified the Turkish right of garrison.
But his Austrophil policy, which had won him the sympathy
of the western Powers but had not commended itself to his
people, was now less pleasing to one of the former, owing to
the close relations between France and Russia after the war.
Thus, while the French and Russian consuls at Belgrade were
now united against Austrian influence, a plot for Alexander's
removal, on the ground that he was an Austrian puppet, was
discovered among the senators. Regardless of the article in the
Charter of 1838, which proclaimed that senators could not be
punished without the consent of the Porte, the Prince arrested
the conspirators, who were tried for high treason, and of whom
eight were sentenced to death—a sentence commuted into
imprisonment for life. This illegal act provoked the intervention of the Porte, which sent a commissioner to Belgrade to
hold an enquiry. Thereupon the Prince gave way, released
the prisoners, restored the fallen senators to their dignities, and
called a Francophil Ministry, of which Vutchich and Garashanin
were the leading spirits, to his counsels. But the Senate, having
thus vindicated its rights against the Prince, sought to humiliate
him, and to change the Servian government into a Venetian
oligarchy. A proposal, thrice approved by the Senate, was to
become *ipso facto* law, even without his approval, so that his
veto would be practically abolished. At this moment, an
incident between the British government and the Porte
increased the difficulties of the situation. The British consul,
Fonblanque, was one day sitting on the glacis of the Turkish
fortress of Belgrade, the beautiful promenade so well-known
to every modern visitor under the Turkish name of Kalimegdan.
While feasting his eyes on the magnificent view of river and
plain which stretches out before the gaze, he was attacked and

wounded by a Mussulman soldier belonging to the Turkish garrison.   Other Albanians tried to pull down the flagstaff from the front of the consulate; and Sir Henry Bulwer, our ambassador at Constantinople, who chanced to be at Semlin, demanded and obtained satisfaction from the Porte.   But Bulwer's action did not stop there; he had a colloquy with the Servian leaders, and is said to have advised them to summon a National Assembly—the usual British panacea—to discuss the evils from which their country was suffering.   No such Assembly had been held for ten years; no Assembly, elected by the tax-payers in European fashion, had ever been convened before.   But, despite Austrian and Turkish opposition, this parliament, called from the day of its meeting, " the *Skupshtina* of St Andrew," and composed of 500 deputies, was held at Belgrade; and the senators fondly believed that by its aid they would get rid of the Prince and place in his stead one of the oligarchy, perhaps Garashanin.

The result was very different from what the Senate had anticipated.   The Assembly had no desire to substitute oligarchical rule for that of the Prince; what it wished was the substitution of a strong man for the existing ruler.   After demanding that it should be thenceforth annually summoned for the consideration of all the government's acts, it criticised the Prince's neutral policy during the Crimean war, and requested his abdication.   Ministers and senators alike advised him to yield; but he fled to the Turkish fortress, whereupon the Assembly, to the dismay of the oligarchs, insisted that old Milosh, the hero of the second War of Independence, should be recalled from his exile at Bucharest.   For a moment the army meditated a reaction against the Assembly in the joint interest of the two former rivals, the Prince and the Senate.   But the citizens supported the Assembly; the consuls advised the Prince to disavow the army.   Thereupon the Assembly declared Alexander Karageorgevich deposed, and appointed a provisional triumvirate pending the return of Milosh. The people had thus abandoned the Prince; there only remained the Powers. Russia, never his friend, maintained the right of the Serbs to choose their own ruler; Turkey, afraid of the spread of discontent among the Southern Slavs, and Austria, desirous that the fortress of Belgrade should not fall into Servian hands yet afraid to violate the treaty of Paris by armed intervention, both abandoned him; Bulwer's influence was on the side of peace. Accordingly, on January 3, Alexander abdicated and crossed over to Semlin; but his wily old successor declined to accept the dignity, thus restored to him by his fellow-countrymen, until he had obtained the consent of his suzerain. The Porte did not hesitate to ratify his election, merely passing over in silence the hereditary character which the Assembly had impressed upon it. Then, on February 6, Milosh re-entered in state, with his son Michael, the country which he had left an exile 20 years before, and began his second reign.

Milosh was 79 years old when he returned to power, and his character was no longer capable of adapting itself to restraint. He at once resumed the arbitrary methods of his former reign, dissolved the Assembly, banished his chief opponents, and threw Vutchich into prison, where that powerful chief died under circumstances suggestive of poison. When the Porte demanded an autopsy of the body, Milosh refused it; when the consuls paid him official visits, he treated them with the barest courtesy, telling the British representative, that in Servia the Prince's will was the law, and that neither the Porte nor the Powers should command there. In accordance with these autocratic principles, he quashed the decisions of judges and increased his own civil list, while carefully excluding from the Assembly which he convened the representatives of European culture. In foreign affairs, however, he showed much greater prudence, abstaining from exploiting the anti-Austrian and pro-Sardinian sympathies of his people during the war of 1859, and promising to send back the fugitive Bosniaks who implored his aid on condition that the Porte recognised the Servian Princedom as hereditary in his family. In view of his great age and of the prospects of a disputed succession at his death—for already there was a rumour of a Karageorgevich restoration in the person of Alexander's son, the subsequent King of Servia—both the Serbs and the Powers were anxious for a settlement of this thorny question. A Servian deputation was sent to Constantinople, and pointed out in a memorandum that Mahmûd II had granted the hereditary dignity of Prince to Milosh and his descendants in 1830 and in 1838, that this privilege had not lapsed in consequence of the change of dynasty, and that it constituted an "anchor of safety" for the country. The deputation further requested the enforcement of the Imperial ordinance of 1830, which forbade Mussulmans to reside in Servia, unless they formed part of the Turkish garrisons. This provision had been violated by another ordinance in 1833, which allowed the Mohammedan inhabitants of Belgrade to remain indefinitely (because a Turkish quibble and a Russian award had declared the then town of Belgrade to be a "fortress"), and those of the other parts of Servia for five more years. Indeed, till after 1860, a squalid Mussulman population still lingered on beneath the shadow of the fortress, the cause of frequent quarrels and the object of conflicting jurisdictions. Finally, in place of the charter of 1838, the germ of conflicts between the Prince and the Senate, the Serbs asked for leave to work out a constitution by themselves suited to their requirements. Before these requests had been granted, Milosh died, on September 26, 1860, in the house which he inhabited among the trees of Topchider, the park of Belgrade. The house has been preserved as it was at the time of his death, and there the traveller may still see the collection of wax fruits and the garments of modern Servia's second founder—a man with the defects of his age and country, but still one of those masterful personalities who on a larger stage would have received from historians the epithet of " great."

Michael Obrenovich III, who, after the lapse of 18 years, a second time ascended the throne, represented a new era in the history of Servia. The Prince was now a man in the prime of life, who had travelled to European capitals and imbibed ideas very different from those of his rugged sire. His proclamation told his people, that in his reign the law would be supreme ; and the legislation of his first Assembly, establishing an universal income-tax, a national militia of 50,000 men with a French officer as Minister of War, and a legislature, based on the payment of taxes and destined to meet every three years, displayed a desire for the reorganisation of the country which aroused the suspicions of the Porte. Availing himself of the European conference, held in 1861 at Constantinople for the formal recognition of the Union of Wallachia and Moldavia, he raised the Servian question, and specially insisted that those Turks who still resided in Servia outside the fortresses should be subject to the jurisdiction of his courts. Turkey complained to the guaranteeing Powers ; and Lord Russell, then our Foreign Secretary, espoused the Turkish cause, from fear lest Servian independence should endanger the integrity of the Turkish empire. Ere long, however, an event occurred which demonstrated the practical justice of the Servian argument. A few hours' cannonade proved, as usual, more eloquent than any notes.

Cunibert, the physician of Milosh, had predicted years before that one day the presence of Turks and Serbs, side by side in Belgrade, would inevitably provoke a sanguinary conflict between them. The British traveller Denton, who visited Belgrade in the spring of 1862, observed the anomaly of a guard, half Turkish, half Serb, which nightly patrolled the decaying " fortifications "—" four dilapidated gates," a " partly palisaded " ditch, and " the remains of some earthen entrenchment "—which marked the boundaries of the old, or Turkish town, the *dortjol*, as it was called. So much had Belgrade grown by that time, that the Constantinople gate, "the ruinous arch" which alone offered "any show of defence," was "in the centre" of the town. The Turkish quarter itself was invaded by Christian houses; and nothing kept the remaining Turks in Belgrade but the policy of the Porte, which regarded every Turkish shopkeeper in Servia as a possible artilleryman in case of need, whose services were paid in anticipation by a small annual retaining fee. Naturally the Servian government, as it became more independent, found this state of things intolerable. The regular garrison of 4000 regulars was less obnoxious than the existence of this Turkish preserve in the heart of the Servian capital.

On June 15, 1862, a scuffle ensued at a well near the boundary between the Turkish and the native quarters, in which two Serbs were killed by two Turkish soldiers. Servian policemen arrested the soldiers, and were conducting them to the Turkish police-station, when a volley of musketry from that building was discharged with fatal effect into their ranks. A general conflict then began, and the populace broke into the Turkish shops. The Prince was absent from Belgrade, but Ilija Garashanin, the Prime Minister, and the consular corps exerted themselves to restore order; and Longworth, the British representative, at last succeeded in persuading the pasha in command of the fortress to withdraw his police from the town, on condition that Garashanin guaranteed their safe transit. The rest of the Mussulman population followed them; quiet seemed to be restored. On the morning, however, of the 17th, at the very moment when the consuls were on their way to visit the pasha, the fortress suddenly opened fire upon the town, and for five hours bombarded Belgrade. The Prince hastened back to his capital; the pasha was induced by Austrian representations, and ordered by his government, to cease firing; and, to restore confidence, the British and French consuls-general went under canvas in full range of the Turkish and

Servian guns. The pasha was recalled, an Ottoman commissioner sent to Belgrade, and a conference of the Powers
convened at Constantinople. Between the two extremes of
the Turkish demand for the restoration of the *status quo* and
the Servian claim for the withdrawal of all Turks from Servia
a compromise was effected. Russell had already pointed out
that the logic of facts forbade the acceptance of the Turkish,
the 29th article of the treaty of Paris that of the Servian
contention; Bulwer at the conference carried out his chief's
instructions; his Austrian colleague pointed out that the
evacuation of the fortress of Belgrade would excite the Austrian
Serbs. It was finally agreed that the Turks should abandon
the Turkish quarter of Belgrade, retaining the fortress, and
evacuate the fortresses of Sokol near the Bosnian frontier and
Ujitze—the latter of special strategic importance as commanding
the communication across the *sanjak* of Novibazar with Montenegro. These two fortresses were dismantled and are now
picturesque ruins; the Turkish quarter of Belgrade with the
exception of the Jewish houses, two mosques (one of them
now used as a gasometer!), an occasional fountain and the
crumbling remains of the Constantinople gate—*tanti nominis
umbra*—was pulled down; and the Turkish garrisons held
nothing but the river fortresses of Shabatz on the Save,
Belgrade, Semendria, Fetislâm, and the island-castle of Ada
Kaleh on the Danube, and the position of Little Zvornik on
the Drina, opposite the larger Bosnian town of the same name.
The Mussulman residents were to sell their property and leave
Servia as soon as possible. Bulwer's suggestion that the Servian
army, which he considered too large for a vassal state, should
be reduced to 12,000 men, was rejected, thanks to the diplomatic activity of John Ristich, the future Regent and Premier.

Michael had been induced to accept this compromise by
the result of the conflict which the sister Servian state had
been waging contemporaneously against the Turks. Since
the presumed pacification of the near east at Paris, the

Montenegrins had fought two campaigns with their hereditary enemies. Despite Danilo's efforts to maintain peace, the murder of a Montenegrin priest, whose head was fixed on the ramparts of the frontier-fortress of Spuj, followed by a cattle-lifting raid of its inhabitants, necessitated a formal protest. The Turkish reply was to concentrate its Herzegovinian garrisons on the Montenegrin frontier. The people of the Sutorina, the long, narrow tongue of the Herzegovina, which Ragusan fear of Venice had caused to be ceded to Turkey at the treaty of Passarovitz, and which then ran down to the sea as an enclave of Dalmatia, successfully opposed, with Montenegrin aid, the Turkish advance; one or two villages of the Adriatic coast proclaimed their union with the Principality; and a Montenegrin senator seized for a moment the adjacent fortress of Spizza on the bay of Antivari, destined to such European notoriety 20 and 50 years later. Danilo appealed to Paris, Vienna, and St Petersburg, with the result that a French squadron and a Russian frigate arrived off Ragusa to watch events. Meanwhile, Hussein Pasha received orders to occupy the territory of Grahovo, which by the compromises of 1842–3 had been declared neutral ground. On the rocky plain of Grahovo the Prince's elder brother Mirko, in two successive engagements of May 12 and 13, completely routed the greatly superior Turkish force; an Austrian officer a little later counted 2237 skeletons on the field; and many Turkish standards, cannon and rifles fell into the hands of the Montenegrins, while British medals, won before Sebastopol, went to adorn Cetinje. Grahovo is considered to have been the Marathon of Montenegro; and 50 years later Prince Nicholas solemnly celebrated the jubilee of his father's victory. The Turks withdrew; and a conference of ambassadors at Constantinople in the autumn led to a rectification of the Montenegrin frontiers, by which the districts of Grahovo with the adjacent Rudine, Jupa, and the Upper Vasojevich were added to the Principality. To Danilo's reign might thus be

ascribed some increase of Montenegrin territory, as well as
the secularisation of the theocratic government; he had
introduced in 1855 a new code, which punished brigandage,
even when it was justified in popular estimation by being
practised against the Turks, and severely reprobated theft;
he had supplemented his predecessor's corps of *perianiks*,
or body-guards, by establishing a regular system of conscription and a military hierarchy; and he had established a sort
of college in his own palace, where he sometimes acted as
professor. But he was not popular, and he met his end by
the usual fate of Balkan rulers—assassination. On August 13,
1860, the Prince and Princess, who were taking the baths
at Perzagno on the Bocche di Cattaro, had been walking in
the cool of the evening on the quay of Cattaro, when a
Montenegrin exile, one Kadich, shot him as he was handing
the Princess into his boat. The victim expired next day;
his assassin was hanged, without revealing his accomplices.
Some ascribed his crime to political motives, others to private
revenge; the gossip of Cetinje attributed it to the rage of
an injured husband. The Princess, without delay, accompanied the corpse to the capital, where it lies within the
monastery church; and, as Danilo had only left one little
daughter Olga, the succession passed, as he had arranged,
to his nephew Nicholas—for Mirko, the latter's father, was
regarded as too bellicose and too destitute of European culture
to govern Montenegro at so critical a time. The hero of
Grahovo, whom people called "the sword of Montenegro,"
patriotically stood aside in favour of his son, as nine years
before he had acquiesced in the election of his younger
brother, and was content to serve the new Prince as President
of the Senate, representing in his councils the old, exclusive
Montenegrin spirit, which regarded with distrust French influences and European education, represented by the cultured
and ambitious Princess-Dowager Darinka.

Nicholas I was not quite nineteen years old when he began

his reign—the longest and most glorious of any Montenegrin ruler. Sent as a child to reside in the family of the future Princess Darinka at Trieste, he had completed at the college of Louis-le-Grand in Paris, thanks to the generosity of Napoleon III, the education begun at the cosmopolitan seaport. But like all true Highlanders, his heart was always in his own country, and his devotion to his rugged mountains enabled him to blend successfully in a transition period the old national traditions with the culture of the west. Over a young Prince, reared in her own home and educated in France, the Princess-Dowager hoped to exercise her sway; but, the old Montenegrin party, which saw in the foreign marriage of the late ruler a cause of the national discontent with his rule, hastened the marriage of the new sovereign with Milena, the daughter of a native chieftain; and ere long the Princess-Dowager retired to Paris, Corfù, and St Petersburg, leaving the little court of Cetinje free to steer its way through the sea of politics. Finally she settled, like the last Princess three centuries before her, at Venice.

The Prince had been barely a year on the throne when the Herzegovina rose once more against the Turks. The victory of their Montenegrin brethren at Grahovo had excited the Serbs of the ancient "Duchy"; and the Christians of the Sutorina, Nikshich and other frontier districts, under the leadership of Luka Vukalovich, defeated in 1861 the troops of the redoubtable Omar Pasha. The Montenegrins were naturally filled with enthusiasm at the success of their kinsmen; and, if the decision had depended on the people, war would have begun at once. Nicholas himself could not but sympathise personally with the Herzegovinian insurgents. Born at Njegush, the first village which the traveller on the way up from Cattaro to Cetinje passes, whither his family had emigrated from the Herzegovina centuries before, he regarded the Herzegovina as the cradle of his race; a lover of his native language, he knew that it was there spoken in its greatest purity ; a student of the national history, he might desire the re-union of the scattered members of the Serb race under one sceptre. But diplomatic considerations and the advice of the Powers constrained him to preserve, at the risk of his popularity at home and in the South Slavonic world, more than a strict neutrality ; for, if his subjects daily joined the insurgents as volunteers and the rumour of a violation of the Montenegrin frontier was eagerly welcomed as an excuse for war, he allowed the Turks to revictual the fortress of Nikshich by sending supplies from Albania across his own territory. None the less, Omar Pasha, having put down the insurrection, blockaded Montenegro during the winter, and in the spring of 1862 invaded the Principality on the pretext of re-establishing order on the frontier. The Turkish plan of campaign was to take advantage of the unfavourable conformation of the little state, invading it at either end of the short Montenegrin funnel (then only 12 miles long) which connected Albania with the Herzegovina, viz. through the Zeta valley and the Duga pass, while a third corps created a diversion in the Brda to the east of this passage. Although greatly outnumbered, Mirko and the Prince's father-in-law, Vukotich, held the Turks in check for two months, till they at last outflanked Vukotich, took Mirko between two fires, and compelled him to leave the fertile Zeta valley at their mercy. Montenegro was thus cut in two by the Turkish forces ; but, while they ravaged the valley, Mirko reorganised the resistance in the mountains to the west of it, and, when they resumed the offensive, defeated them at Zagaratz and Kokoti.

Meanwhile, the Powers looked on at this unequal struggle ; for France, hitherto the protectress of Montenegro, was occupied in Mexico, while Palmerston, usually the friend of struggling nationalities, regarded the mountaineers as rebels whom the Sultan was justified in chastising. There was talk of an Italian expedition to Antivari in support of Montenegro ;

but only the Pope showed such sympathy as he could give, by forbidding the Roman Catholics of Albania to aid the Turks, and at Athens subscriptions for the Montenegrins were opened. Omar again renewed the attack, this time along the Rjeka which flows into the lake of Scutari. A long-disputed battle below the picturesque little town which takes its name from the river convinced the Montenegrins that further resistance was useless, and the Prince, who had providentially escaped assassination during the war, accepted the Convention of Scutari, dictated by the Turkish commander. The frontiers of 1859, and the internal administration of the Principality remained intact. Turkey allowed the Montenegrins to import and export whatever they pleased, except arms, through the haven of Antivari, and to rent agricultural lands in Turkish territory—concessions intended to remedy the two chief Montenegrin grievances, the lack of access to the sea, and the lack of arable land. In return, the mountaineers were to abstain from frontier raids, from the support of insurrections of Turkish subjects, and from erecting frontier forts. The two severest clauses—that which exiled Mirko for ever, and that which authorised the Turkish troops to occupy and fortify strategic points on the Montenegrin route between Scutari and the Herzegovina—were fortunately annulled by mutual consent. For five years more Mirko, the bard as well as the warrior of the nation, remained by his son's side till cholera slew the hero who had defended the cavernous monastery of Ostrog from the Turks, who had won the fight of Grahovo, and twice merited the praise of the Roman poet: *Imperium asseruit non sibi, sed patriae.* These years were devoted to repairing the ravages of the war, while the Prince, in 1866, almost succeeded in achieving the greatest aim of Montenegrin policy for half a century—a seaport. The Sultan had actually consented to cede to him a strip of coast at Novasella near Spizza; but France and Great Britain, fearful lest it should become in Montenegrin hands a mere Russian haven, opposed the cession.   British statesmanship 14 years later repaired this injustice at Dulcigno.

The year 1862 had been eventful in south-eastern Europe. Besides the bombardment of Belgrade and the war in Montenegro, a revolution had driven Otho from the Greek throne. Five years earlier, such a disastrous termination of his reign seemed improbable, for the occupation had made the King extremely popular.   For some time after the departure of the allied armies this state of things continued; and the year 1858, in which Otho celebrated the 25th anniversary of his accession, was quietly occupied with practical economic works, such as the opening of the Euripus to traffic and the laying of a cable between Syra and the Piræus.   Meanwhile, the financial commission of the three protecting Powers was engaged in examining the financial resources and administration of the country.   Its report, drawn up in 1859, suggested that in lieu of the sinking fund and interest on the allied loan of £2,400,000 Greece should be compelled to pay an annual sum of £36,000, which was to be increased as her resources improved.   It also advocated some modification of the system of collecting the tithe and the publication of accounts.   There was, however, one question which caused the court serious difficulty, that of the succession.   The constitution of 1844 had indicated as heir Otho's next brother, who must become a member of the Orthodox Church.   But, as the Convention of 1832, which conferred the crown on Otho, had said nothing about his successor's change of religion, an agreement was made in London in 1852 between Greece, Bavaria, and the three Powers, imposing upon the heir the necessity of his conversion.   The Bavarian representative, however, added a minute, that either the heir should not be forced to change his religion till the moment of his accession to the throne, or else he should obtain on his conversion a guarantee that he would succeed to it; otherwise he might have abandoned the faith of his ancestors for nothing.   Otho's next brother,

Luitpold (afterwards Prince-Regent of Bavaria) resigned his rights; and the succession seemed to lie between his son Lewis, and Luitpold's next brother Adalbert, who had, however, married a Spanish, and therefore, Roman Catholic, princess. The reluctance of the Bavarian princes to change their religion so greatly impressed some Greek politicians, that their thoughts fell upon Peter of Oldenburg, the brother of the Queen. Amalia, whose popularity had been further increased by the speed with which she transacted business as Regent during her consort's absence in " Europe "—as a French wit remarked : " he read documents without deciding, she decided without reading "—felt flattered by this idea, which thenceforth divided the court into two factions and neutralised the influence of Bavaria at Athens at a critical moment.

For two years after the departure of the Allies Otho's popularity continued; but the outbreak of the Austro-Italian war of 1859 placed him in a difficult position. Crispi, visiting Athens in that year, found the people enthusiastic for the Italian cause; and a *Te Deum* was sung after every Italian victory. But the King, as was natural in a Bavarian, sympathised with Austria, and even desired to extend the protection of the Greek flag to the Austrian vessels. But, while his people accused him of Austrian sentiments, the British and French governments suspected him, as in 1854, of favouring an insurrection in Turkey, proclaimed by Karatássos, the aide-de-camp, who had been the cause of the Greco-Turkish incident of 1847. The Opposition, eager to embarrass the government, made capital out of Otho's Austrophil views; and a riot due to the students' protests against the sale of expensive straw-hats was magnified into a political question. The elections were, indeed, favourable to the Cabinet of Athanásios Miaoúles, a son of the admiral, and a devoted loyalist, who had come into office after the occupation; but at the historic Mesolónghi the idol of the Athenian youth and subsequent author of Otho's deposition, Epaminóndas Delegeórges, entered parliamentary life.

The Syrian massacres of 1860 diverted attention for a time from these internal affairs; but the achievements of Garibaldi in southern Italy rekindled the democratic feeling. The defeat of the Ministerial candidate for the Speakership was followed by the seizure of Opposition newspapers and the dissolution of the Chamber. These acts irritated the Opposition; and the newly elected body received the nickname of " the Chamber of Mayors," from the number of those officials whom government influence sent to sit in it. A large batch of new senators was created, in the hope of securing that branch of the legislature also. In vain Sir Thomas Wyse pointed out the danger of thus shutting the safety-valves of public opinion, while a combination of circumstances at this time rendered not only the Bavarian Court, but also the three protecting Powers hostile or indifferent to the King's preservation—Russia for the opposite reason to that of Bavaria; Great Britain because she suspected him of designs against both her protectorate over the Ionian Islands and the integrity of Turkey, which she still cherished as the secret of her Indian empire; France because her advice had been disregarded and perhaps from the personal influence of Kallérges, then Greek minister in Paris, over the Emperor. Thus, in 1861, all the stars in their courses seemed to fight against Otho.

In May a plot was discovered in the army; and the government made the mistake of sending the ringleaders to Nauplia, which thus became the headquarters of the revolutionary movement. Meanwhile, the Opposition became more systematic; the new men, who had entered public life, notably Delegeórges, were supported by the students, whose heads were full of the theoretic beauties of the French revolution and who were veritable missionaries of their ideas because they propagated all over the Greek world the anti-dynastic principles which they had imbibed at Athens. Thus was realised the prophecy of shrewd old Kolokotrónes, who years before, pointing to the newly founded University and to the palace, remarked : " this house will eat up that one ! " As usually happens, the more advanced democrats placed in front of them an elderly champion of unquestionable respectability, the venerable Kanáres, whose fame and popularity, won in the War of Independence and recently confirmed by his independence in the Senate, they exploited for their own purpose. In the press they found two powerful exponents of their programme in the *Future of the Fatherland* and the *British Star*, the latter a Greek newspaper founded in London by Stéphanos Xénos, a brilliant novelist, who was one of the first persons to name, so early as 1859, Prince Alfred (subsequently Duke of Edinburgh) as the best successor to Otho. An attempt to assassinate the Queen, on September 18, by a lad named Dósios during the King's absence abroad, created a violently royalist reaction ; but six weeks later a plot of some cavalry officers to kidnap the returning monarch showed that it was merely temporary. Miaoúles, conscious that public opinion demanded the change of a Ministry over which he had presided since 1857, tendered his resignation ; and Kanáres, the most popular man in Greece, was summoned to the palace in January 1862. But the task of forming a Ministry proved that it was easier for the old seaman to fire a Turkish ship than to steer his way through the shoals of politics. His programme was excellent, but his list of Ministers caused such a revulsion of feeling that the King was able to withdraw his mandate. Miaoúles remained in office, and the events of the next few months earned for his Cabinet the name of " the Ministry of blood."

On February 13, 1862, the garrison of Nauplia revolted. That city, where 29 years before Otho had been received by his subjects with such enthusiasm, was the seat of the discontent ; and the eloquent and charming widow of a senator, Mme. Kalliópe Papalexopoúlou, and the Belgian consul Zavitzános, were the ringleaders there. The insurgents demanded the abolition of the "system" identified with the existing Ministry, the dissolution of "the Chamber of Mayors," and the convocation of a National Constituent Assembly, and addressed a petition to the ministers of the three Powers. On the same day a revolt took place at Argos; Tripolitsá and Kyparissía followed these examples; but the only serious danger was presented by the risings at Nauplia and Syra, where, however, the Catholic town remained loyal. The government formed a camp on the Isthmus under General Hahn, a veteran Swiss Philhellene, who occupied Argos and Tíryns and besieged Nauplia. Although the garrison found aid from a Cretan colony established in the suburb of Prónoia, where the Assembly had sat in 1832, the royalist troops soon carried the outworks; but the refusal of the King to grant a general pardon united the garrison in the resolve to resist, and the dauntless Kalliópe stood on her balcony as the shells whizzed past her, shouting that "Mesolónghi secured the nation's independence, Nauplia will secure its liberties!" An amnesty for all but 19 conspirators was at last accepted; the excepted persons were removed on French and British steamers; and on April 20 Hahn entered Nauplia. Order was restored in Syra by Tsîros, a well-known brigand-hunter, who met and defeated the insurgents in Kýthnos. There was no enthusiasm at these victories of Greeks over Greeks; a sea-girt graveyard at Nauplia guards the remains of those who fell in 1862; the slain of Kýthnos were hymned as martyrs. A secret memorandum of the Minister of the Interior to the King depicted the discontent in the provinces, except among the working-classes, the growth of an intellectual proletariat, spoiled for manual labour but unable to obtain posts in the civil service, and the danger which he ran, unless he changed his "system," allowed freedom of election, and settled the vexed question of the succession, by proclaiming to his Orthodox subjects an Orthodox heir-presumptive. These representations were supported by Mr (afterwards Sir) Henry Elliot, the extraordinary envoy of Great Britain, who communicated his chief's desire for a change of Ministry, a dissolution, and the observance of the constitution. Otho fulfilled the first of these wishes ; and on June 7 the long lived Miaoúles administration gave place to a Cabinet, the last of the reign, under the Court Marshal, Gennaîos Kolokotrónes, son of the famous klepht, and himself more of a soldier than a statesman. The new Premier likewise urged Otho to decide the question of the succession, while Russell advised the Greek and Bavarian representatives in London to send one of Prince Luitpold's sons to reside in Greece while he was still of an impressionable age. Otho, however, preferred that his nephew should not be required to change his religion till he came of age in the following January. But ere that date Otho had ceased to reign.

Informed of the discontent at home, the King now tried to divert attention to " the Great Idea," of which he had been so fervent an apostle at the time of the Crimean war. Emissaries were sent to negotiate with Garibaldi for his co-operation in creating an insurrection in Turkey ; subscriptions were opened for the Montenegrins then struggling against the Porte ; the King hoped that Servia would declare war on the Sultan. So serious did the agitation appear to Russell, that he ordered Scarlett, the new British minister at Athens, to "inform the King of Greece that war against Turkey will precede for a very short time his deposition and abdication." Nor did our Foreign Minister use threats alone ; he offered the Ionian Islands to Otho, on condition that he promised not to raise the eastern question. Otho refused, and his refusal did him honour, for he argued that the Ionians were the subjects of a civilised European Power, whereas the enslaved Greeks of Thessaly and Epirus lived under an Asiatic despotism. Believing in the success of Montenegro and an alliance with Servia, he was doomed to complete disappointment. Garibaldi, instead of landing in Epirus, was wounded at Aspromonte ; the Montenegrins made peace ; the Serbs accepted the decisions of the conference at Constantinople. All hopes of a diversion in

Turkey disappeared. Then the Queen, ever impetuous, urged her consort to undertake a long tour in the provinces at the moment when prudence advised his continued presence in the capital.

An insurrection in Akarnanía under the auspices of Theodore Grívas, the veteran leader of irregulars whose exploits went back to the anarchy of 1832, was foretold by the British vice-consul at Mesolónghi for the beginning of October. The time passed without anything untoward occurring; and on October 13 the royal couple, believing that the alarm was groundless, started on what was to be the last of their many Greek cruises. The King seems to have had some foreboding of his coming deposition, for on the day of his departure he said to Nicholas Dragoúmes, his Minister for Foreign Affairs: "I have read that the people consider it unlucky to reign more than 30 years. My 30 years are almost accomplished." The royal yacht had been gone but three days when Grívas caused the garrison of Vónitza, a place on the gulf of Arta that had been conspicuous in the medieval, and now made a page in the modern history of Greece, to raise the standard of revolt. Mesolónghi, Patras (at the instigation of the former Minister, Venizélos Roúphos), and other places quickly followed. Otho received at Kalamáta, on his voyage round the Morea, the news of the revolt of Vónitza, and at once gave the order to return. But, before his yacht could reach the Piræus, Athens had risen. On the night of the 22nd the garrison revolted; the Premier, who had come to the conclusion that the deposition of Otho was inevitable, made no effort to save the throne, and refused to order the arrest of the conspirators. As in 1843, the streets were deserted; and even the civilian ringleaders of the revolution thought it more prudent to remain indoors until dawn. Then they proceeded to the artillery barracks, where Delegeórges, using a cannon as a desk, scribbled on a scrap of paper a proclamation, declaring the fall of Otho's sovereignty and the formation of a provisional government, composed of Boúlgares, Kanáres, and Roúphos, which should hold office till a National

Convention should have elected a new King. A rush was made upon the defenceless palace, where Hahn offered no resistance; the King's effects were mostly spared, but his correspondence was carried off and read by the provisional government. The dethroned King's letters were found to be animated by feelings of the warmest love for Greece; and it is related that Kanáres, who had been persuaded to join the government against his will, wept with remorse at their perusal.

Boúlgares, the president of the triumvirate, then formed a Cabinet, in which Delegeórges and two other future Premiers, Koumoundoûros and Thrasýboulos Zaïmes, had seats. Order, however, was not restored for two days; armed men discharged their rifles in the streets, in sign of joy; several innocent people were killed by accident; several shops were plundered; the museum on the Akropolis lost some of its treasures; and the prison was relieved of some of its less valuable inmates. On the evening of the 23rd the royal yacht was signalled, and anchored just outside the entrance of the Piræus. A crowd, whose revolutionary sentiments were manifested by shouts and shots, had already assembled to prevent the sovereigns from landing. A copy of the proclamation and a fatal shot, fired from the shore at a loyal officer, who had ventured to shout "Long live the King!", convinced them that disembarkation was impossible. A hasty council was held on deck; the Queen urged an instant return to Kalamáta or Liméni, where they had just received enthusiastic receptions; Otho, as usual, hesitated to make up his mind till he had received more detailed information. A modern Greek historian has expressed the opinion that the Queen's advice, if modified by a return to loyal Gýtheion, might perhaps have saved the Bavarian dynasty. But meanwhile the diplomatic corps arrived, and unofficially counselled resignation. That night Otho spent in the classic waters of Salamis, meditating on his decision. Next morning he informed the British minister of his intention to quit Greece, and, after writing a farewell proclamation to his people, in which he recalled his love and labours for their land, and declared that he left it to avoid further bloodshed, he embarked, as he had come nearly 30 years before, on board a British ship, the *Scylla*, for Venice. The last drop in his cup of bitterness was the spectacle, as the vessel rounded the Morea, of the blazing arch of triumph, which the people of Kalamáta had erected only a few days before to welcome their now exiled monarch. The new state of things was accepted everywhere. The protecting Powers raised no voice against his deposition; and Liberal Britain, by the mouth of Russell, declared, in accordance with the Whig principles of 1688 so dear to that statesman, that Greece, being " an independent nation," had the right " of changing its governing dynasty upon good and sufficient cause." This condition the British government, always severe to Otho, believed to exist.

Time has, however, modified the judgment of that day upon the first King of Greece. That Otho was a great ruler, no one will pretend; that he was a bad man, his worst enemy could not assert. His faults were those of a weak and pedantic character, absorbed in details and unable to arrive at rapid decisions; his misfortune was that he had no heir. If he had governed his country less, and had been blessed with offspring, possibly his descendants would be still sitting on the Hellenic throne. Time has, however, yet more clearly demonstrated his ardent, if at times impolitic, patriotism; even in his retirement at Bamberg, where he died in 1867, he continued to wear the Greek dress and to interest himself in the fortunes of Greece. His former subjects have generously recognised his merits; modern Greek literature has depicted him and his Consort in a more favourable light; the son of one who was prominent in overthrowing him admitted that perhaps his expulsion was a mistake; and a Greek statesman confessed that he had made a pilgrimage to his tomb in the Theatiner church of Munich and stood in meditation over the last remains of one who never ceased to love Greece.

CHAPTER XII

THE CESSION OF THE IONIAN ISLANDS (1862-4)

THE revolution of 1862 had been as bloodless as that of 1843; but the mere removal of Otho did not necessarily mean the immediate reign of law. "The troops at Athens," wrote an eye-witness, were in a state of complete insubordination; they "broke into houses, and robbed passers-by in broad daylight"; a British watchmaker was plundered; and liberated gaol-birds, taking to the road, displayed their " constitutional " principles to the harmless Bœotians and Megareans. But the town was speedily patrolled by a civic guard, composed of students and leading citizens, and the richest Athenian banker was seen shouldering a musket in the defence of property and order. Shops were re-opened, and the British minister reported that there had "probably never been a general rising attended with so little bloodshed and resistance."

Every moment, however, the arrival of Theodore Grívas with his myrmidons and the consequent deposition of the provisional government were expected; but the death of that dreaded chief removed its fears. The elections for the promised National Assembly, in which representatives of the Greek colonies abroad were allowed to sit, while every constituency in Greece elected twice the usual number of deputies, took place; and on December 22 this, the second National Assembly held at Athens, met. Meanwhile, the selection of a King had been occupying the diplomatists of the three protecting Powers. The most popular candidate in Greece was Prince

Alfred, second son of Queen Victoria, who had made an excellent impression some three years before during a visit to Athens, where a secret petition in his favour had been signed before Otho's deposition.   It was believed in Greece that, if elected, the British Prince would not arrive empty-handed, but would bring the Ionian Islands and perhaps Thessaly and Epirus with him.   British capital, it was pointed out, would follow in his train, and the lean years of Bavarian rule would be thus followed by fat years of Anglo-Saxon enterprise. Portraits of " our Alfred " were circulated at Athens; he was actually proclaimed King at Lamía; popular demonstrations were organised in front of the British Legation; and a deputation entered to interview the British minister, no little embarrassed by the lack of instructions from home.   The British government was, in fact, more anxious to defeat the Russian nominee, the Duke of Leuchtenberg, who, as the grandson of Eugène Beauharnais as well as the nephew of Alexander II, was also the French candidate, than to secure the election of Prince Alfred.   Russell pointed out that the Prince then stood next to the Prince of Wales in order of succession to the British throne, that he was heir-presumptive to the Duchy of Saxe-Coburg, and that the Queen had resolved to refuse her consent to his acceptance of the Greek crown. In order to prevent the election of the Duke of Leuchtenberg, the British government had already invited Russia and France to respect the protocol of February 3, 1830, which excluded members of the reigning families of the three protecting Powers from the Greek throne, and had asked Russia to state whether she considered the Duke as such.   When it had become clear that their candidate had no chance, Russia and France assented, with the view of annulling Prince Alfred's election, in case the Greeks should persist in voting for him despite the official British disclaimer; and Russia promised to regard an eventual election of the Duke as null and void. Such was the attitude of the three Powers, when from December

6 to 15 the voting for a sovereign took place, not, as in the case of the Roumanian Principalities, in the National Assembly, but by the more democratic and imposing method of a popular *plébiscite* of Greeks at home and abroad.   When the urns were opened, it was found that the Greeks had ignored the disclaimer of the British government in their zeal for a British King, and that 230,016 Hellenes had voted for Prince Alfred, 2400 for the Duke of Leuchtenberg, and smaller numbers for various royal personages.   Only 93 desired a Republic; only six voted for a Greek; the same number for the Danish prince who was destined to be King.   Not a vote was recorded for a Bavarian, although the Bavarian consul canvassed for Otho's nephew, Lewis.   On February 3, 1863 the National Assembly ratified the election; but the British government adhered to its statement, undertaking, however, by way of compensation, to find a king.

Elliot, who meanwhile had arrived on a second mission to Athens, informed the provisional government that, if the Greeks chose a constitutional king agreeable to Great Britain and respected the integrity of Turkey, Great Britain would reward them with the Ionian Islands.   The eyes of the British were, of course, first cast upon the inevitable house of Saxe-Coburg, which, in the phrase of a witty Frenchman, "has candidates for all thrones of all religions."   Two Coburgers were suggested—the former King-Consort Ferdinand of Portugal and Duke Ernest II of Saxe-Coburg-Gotha.   Both of them fulfilled Russell's requirement that the choice should fall not upon "a prince under 20 years of age, but rather a prince of mature years and of some experience."   But there were objections to both; for the former was a Catholic, and the latter childless.   As Duke Ernest's heir was Prince Alfred, the British government had to find another successor.   A close study of the *Almanach de Gotha* revealed the existence of another Coburger in Austria.   But eventually all three Coburg candidatures collapsed.   The ex-King-Consort of Portugal declined to renew his kingship in Greece. The reigning Duke of Saxe-Coburg discovered that his people would not let him leave his Duchy and that he could not promise to be always sound on the integrity of Turkey; he wanted larger boundaries, while retaining his position as a German prince. The Austrian held that it was better to lose Otho's crown than omit the *filioque* clause. Meanwhile, the National Assembly was even more distracted than the British government. Personal factions took the place of parties with well-defined policies; and, in imitation of the French Revolution, the followers of Kanáres and Demétrios Grívas were styled "men of the mountain," those of Boúlgares "men of the plain." The military took sides, for discipline was at an end; the 6th battalion under Leotsákos, brother of one of the victims of Kýthnos, was for Boúlgares, the rest of the army supported the "mountaineers." Local chiefs, who had seats in the Assembly, were accompanied by bands of armed retainers who occupied the lobbies or the courtyard of the house where it met. With so much inflammable material about, it did not require much to produce civil war. Four ministers and the triumvir Kanáres resigned; the formation of a new Ministry by his two colleagues was branded by the "mountain" as unconstitutional; their adherents outside fortified a strong position in the town; a collision occurred, and, in proper French fashion, the October revolution was followed by the "days of February." Pending a definite decision, the Assembly assumed the executive power, which it exercised through its vice-president, Moraïtínes. His first act was to call out the recently-created national guard; a committee of leading politicians interposed its good offices between the combatants; the Assembly elected a new Ministry under Bálbes; and the army, drawn up in the appropriately-named Concord Square, swore before the Assembly to obey its orders.

At last, after the Greek crown had been hawked about Europe for three months, the Premier was able to announce,

on March 30, that the three protecting Powers had proposed
as king Prince Christian William Ferdinand Adolphus George,
second son of Prince Christian of Schleswig-Holstein (a few
months later Christian IX of Denmark), and that King Frederick
VII of Denmark had given his conditional consent. The
British choice had fallen upon one who could not possess the
experience which Russell had considered desirable—for he was
at the time a young lieutenant of 17 in the Danish navy. But
the Greeks in the Assembly knew that none of themselves would
be allowed by the jealousy of their compatriots to reign, like
the Obrenovich dynasty in Servia, or like Couza in Roumania,
over the young state. They resolved, therefore, to repeat,
under more favourable auspices, the experiment of a youthful
foreigner as sovereign, and unanimously elected the Danish
prince as " King of the Greeks " (not, as Otho had been, " of
Greece "), adding a rider to the effect that his heirs should
belong to the Orthodox Church. A deputation, composed of
Kanáres, Zaïmes, and Grívas, departed for Copenhagen to offer
him the crown. Several weeks passed, however, before the
King of Denmark's conditions had been rendered acceptable ;
on June 6 the crown was finally accepted ; and on July 13,
despite two Bavarian protests, the arrangements, already
tabulated in protocols, were set forth in a treaty between the
three Powers and the King of Denmark. This treaty provided
that the new sovereign should bear the title of " George I King
of the Greeks " (subsequently altered to " Hellenes "), that his
kingdom should be increased by the union of the Ionian Islands,
that the crowns of Greece and Denmark should never be united
on the same head, that King George's successors should belong
to the Orthodox Church, and that his majority might be
accelerated by a decree of the National Assembly. Very
favourable financial provisions were made for the new monarch.
Besides the civil list which he would receive from his subjects,
the three Powers each relinquished the annual amount of
£4000 out of the sums which the Greek government had

agreed in 1860 to pay them, in accordance with the findings of the financial commission; while Great Britain promised to advise the Ionian government, at the moment of the union, to set aside £10,000 a year for the new King. A secret Anglo-Danish treaty pledged him to refrain from promoting insurrectional movements against Turkey in return for the Ionian Islands.

While the negotiations between the Powers and the Danish court were proceeding, Athens was left in a state of anarchy. The strife between the two rival factions in the Assembly became bitterer as the moment of the new King's arrival drew nearer; for, as before the advent of Otho, the leaders of either party wished to be in power at the moment of his coming. Brigands penetrated to the outskirts of the capital, while the abduction of an Austrian circus-rider by a band of soldiers provoked a diplomatic incident. In the absence of any constituted authority, cabinets were elected by a vote of the Assembly; and thus the election as Minister of War of Pános Koronaîos, one of the conspirators of Nauplia, commander of the national guard, and a prominent "mountaineer," was regarded by himself as a means of securing the executive power, by the Opposition as a danger against which force was the only remedy. Both factions appealed to arms. Kyriákos, a brigand in sympathy with the "men of the plain," occupied the monastery of the Holy Angels, the ancient Kynosárges, near the road to Marathon; Leotsákos, the most formidable rival of the would-be military dictator, when ordered to dislodge the brigand, fraternised with him in the style of the officer in *Le Roi des Montagnes*. Koronaîos thereupon arrested his insubordinate officer; the latter's men retaliated by capturing two Ministers as hostages for his release. These reprisals were the signal for civil war. Again, in French revolutionary fashion, Athens having had her "days of February," now had her "days of July." At dawn on July 1 the fighting began between the Ministerialists under Koronaîos and the "men of the plain" under Papadiamantópoulos, an artillery officer who had taken a prominent part in the October revolution. The "mountaineers" occupied the palace, the school which takes its name from its founder Barbákes, and the Akropolis; their rivals bombarded the palace and killed its defender, Aristeídes, son of Admiral Kanáres. A deputation of three members of the Assembly obtained an armistice of 24 hours; but complete anarchy continued to prevail, for half the ministry had resigned, and the sole constituted authority was D. Kyriakoû, the President of the Assembly, who could not secure a quorum of deputies to confer legality upon his efforts to restore peace. Next day the fighting was renewed; Koronaîos besieged the National Bank, whose director belonged to the opposite faction, and whose strong-room contained a large sum in specie. The "mountain" artillery swept Stádion Street, one of the chief thoroughfares of Athens, and from the "Frog's Mouth" the Opposition howitzers replied. In the evening the ministers of the three Powers sent their secretaries to the President of the Assembly and the two rival leaders, and induced them to conclude an armistice of 48 hours, threatening to leave Athens unless this proposal were adopted. Some 200 people had fallen; and Koronaîos alone offered any further objection to a peace, which he rightly interpreted as his political extinction. The Assembly then met in the Barbákeion; Roûphos reconstituted the Ministry with men of so little influence as to allay suspicion; and this "Cabinet of Affairs" held office till the arrival of the King. The army was ordered to leave Athens, which it quitted on July 5; its rival leaders resigned, whereupon their submissive forces were exiled respectively to Mesolónghi and Sparta. The security of the capital was confided to the national guard. Thus, the reign of disorder, which had prevailed more or less continuously since Otho's deposition, came to an end—a struggle for place not for principle, which the ministers of the three Powers unanimously stigmatised in the strongest language as a conflict of "culpable ambitions."

Modern Greek historians have joined in this condemnation; but, after all, revolutions are rarely made with rose-water.

The coming of King George had been delayed by a tour of the European courts in the company of Count Sponneck, a Danish ex-Minister, who had been attached to his person as a political mentor, but who, even before he had ever set foot on Greek soil, offended the whole class of Greek public men by proclaiming his own position to be "so exalted that no one in Greece could overshadow it." Great was the joy, when at last the young King arrived at Athens on October 30. The rejoicings of Nauplia upon Otho's arrival 30 years earlier were renewed under the shadow of the illuminated Akropolis; but a British diplomatist could not refrain from wondering how this "slight, delicate stripling," whom he saw take the oath in the National Assembly, and whom he heard proclaim that he would aim at "making Greece a model kingdom in the east," would succeed in the task that lay before him. This observer lived to admit that the experiment of choosing for the second time a youth to wear the Greek crown had turned out far better than even optimists could have expected. King George had difficult crises to face—the war of 1897, the military uprising of 1909; but he not only kept his throne and founded a dynasty, but saw his country—what Otho yearned in vain to see—thrice enlarged.

The first of these acquisitions—that of the Ionian Islands —was the present brought by the King to his own subjects. The British government, after 50 years' experience, had come to the conclusion that it was desirable to sever its connexion with the Seven Islands. The repressive measures adopted during the Russo-Turkish war, culminating in the suppression of the sole remaining Liberal paper in Corfù for its criticisms of British sympathy with Turkey, had kept alive the discontent of the priests and people. Many of the nobles and gentry were still attached to the protectorate; but, owing to the reforms of 1849, the Assembly was in the hands of the Opposition, whose

election and the salary attached thereto depended upon the
Orthodox zeal of the clergy and the new-born freedom of the
enfranchised peasantry.   The children in Cephalonia used "to
write, as a copy, a prayer for the expulsion of the English "; and
Ward declared that the system of government bequeathed to
him by Seaton "was not to be worked by any human power."
From outside, too, came criticisms of the British administration
—-from the press of autocratic Russia and Napoleonic France,
neither of which countries enjoyed a tithe of the real
liberty accorded by British statesmen to the Ionians.   Even
an Austrian minister defended the Neapolitan Bourbons by
citing British methods in the Islands.   It is true that, when
Sir John Young, who had succeeded Ward as Lord High
Commissioner in 1855, held a general election at the close of
the following year, the measures taken by his predecessor
against the Cephalonian Radicals proved so efficacious that all
the ten members returned by that island, the birthplace of
Ionian Radicalism, were ministerialists, and Lombárdos of
Zante was the leading representative of Unionism.   But this
eleventh Assembly had not been long in session, when a rumour,
subsequently proved to be well-founded, aroused a storm against
the protectorate.   Young, at the suggestion of Bowen, his
secretary, who knew the language and was supposed to know
the habits of the islanders better than most British officials,
proposed to the home government, that the Ionian question
should be solved by the cession of the five southern islands to
Greece and the conversion of Corfù and Paxo, the most
important strategically, the most attached to the protectorate,
and the least difficult of management, into a British colony.
When a report leaked out at Corfù that a petition with this
object was being surreptitiously circulated, and that three Ionian
signatures had actually been obtained, a gust of patriotic
indignation swept over the Assembly.   That body, disregarding
the official denial of the Attorney-General, who was entitled to
speak, without voting, on behalf of the government, applauded

vociferously the invective of Lombárdos, and unanimously
adopted a motion for the appointment of a committee of
enquiry, on which every island should have a representative.
The suspicions thus aroused had begun to subside when, on
November 12, 1858, the *Daily News* published Young's
dispatches, dated June 10 of the previous year and July 14,
1858, containing the colonisation scheme. The publication
of these despatches, abstracted from the pigeon-holes of the
Colonial Office, was, in the phrase of the Colonial Secretary,
"an inconceivable misfortune"; for they not only rekindled
excitement in the Islands but alarmed the other signatories of
the treaty of 1815. Worst of all, the event occurred at the very
moment when the most Philhellenic of then living British
statesmen was on his way as "High Commissioner Extraordinary" to enquire "into the administration of the Ionian
Islands under the Charter."

The Derby Ministry, then in office, had in its chief a
translator of Homer, in its Colonial Secretary the novelist
Bulwer Lytton. To these literary statesmen the suggestion
of Lord Carnarvon, Under-Secretary for the Colonies, that
Gladstone, another Homeric scholar, should be sent out on
this mission naturally commended itself. Gladstone's political
friends were almost unanimously opposed to his acceptance
of the offer. Aberdeen shrewdly doubted whether Homer
would be a war-horse strong enough to carry his rider through
this Ionian Iliad; Sidney Herbert only trusted that the result
of the mission would be to hand the Islands over to Greece.
But to Gladstone, the scholar and the churchman, the proposal
was welcome as an opportunity of visiting the scenes of the
"Odyssey" and studying the Orthodox Establishment. To
the existing Lord High Commissioner his coming was scarcely
acceptable. For Young, despite the tempest aroused by the
rumour of his colonisation scheme, could truthfully affirm that
during his tenure of office "the power of the high police" had
"not been resorted to in any single instance," while, at this

time not a single Ionian was "in exile, in confinement, or
any kind of legal process, for a political offence." Trade was
growing; the effects of the cholera at Zante had been obliterated by a splendid olive crop and the consequent reduction
of the debt. The only recent incidents had been a display of
anti-Turkish feeling by the municipal officer superintending
the market of Corfù in forbidding the supply of bread to Turkish
troopships, and the refusal of himself and his colleagues to halt
before the palace during the procession of St Spirídon, the
patron-saint of the island. It was, therefore, a surprise, as
disagreeable to the Lord High Commissioner as it was agreeable to the Ionian Unionists, to learn that his old schoolmate
and colleague in Parliament was coming out to examine his
work. The task, difficult for anyone unacquainted with the
peculiar conditions of the Islands, was rendered harder by
the indiscretion of the London Liberal newspaper; and Gladstone, then in Vienna, had to make, not for the last time,
a practical apology to the Austrian government. When,
accompanied by his Neapolitan friend Lacaita, upon whose
knowledge of this old Venetian colony he relied, the eminent
statesman arrived, on November 24, 1858, at Corfù, he soon
found that the stolen dispatches, the policy of which was
repudiated alike by Young and himself, had done their work.
In vain he told the Senate and the ten Corfiote deputies that
there was no question of altering the treaty of 1815, and that
he had come not to discuss the British protectorate but to
examine how it could be harmonised with local interests.
In vain he offered Radical reforms in place of union. At
Santa Mavra, whither he proceeded from Corfù, the Greek
authorities reiterated their abhorrence of Young's unlucky
dispatches, and heard without conviction that union was an
Utopia which was the main obstacle to practical improvements.
At Ithaca the memories of the "wily Odysseus" may have
interested the scholarly Commissioner more than the plaints
of his political descendants. At Cephalonia he was greeted,

to his disgust, with cries of " Down with the Protectorate ! "
as well as shouts of " Long live the Union ! " while copies of
the historic vote of December 8, 1850, were thrust into his
carriage.   He attributed this bitterness of Cephalonian feeling,
which the local politicians formally disavowed, to the repressive
measures of 1849, but was impressed with the tragic appeal
of the aged Archbishop for union of "this unhappy island"
with Greece.   In Zante, the constituency of the protectorate's
most vehement opponent, he was constrained once again to
point out the impracticability of union in the then condition
of Europe, but was received with the habitual courtesy of the
Ionians towards a friend of their race.   Thence he went to
Athens, where he received the impression that there was no
general desire for the annexation of the Islands—an impression
somewhat disproved by the relations believed to exist between
Otho and a leading Unionist newspaper there.   To the influence of the press Gladstone attributed the Unionist sentiments which he found in Paxo, where two exiled Corfiote
editors had employed their compulsory leisure in propaganda
against the protectorate.

After paying this cursory visit to all the outlying islands
except remote Cerigo, Gladstone settled down to work at
Corfù, besieged by needy Ionians who regarded him as an
earthly providence able to provide places for themselves
and even dowries for their daughters, and regarded by the
British as a political Jacob, the supplanter of the rightful
Lord High Commissioner.   Having decided on a plan of
reforms as an antidote to union, which he considered detri-
mental to the Islands so long as Otho ruled over Greece,
Gladstone advised Young's recall and offered himself as temporary successor to introduce the reform scheme.   There was
no room for two High Commissioners at Corfù ; Young left
on January 25, 1859; and, on the same day, Gladstone, whose
offer had been gladly accepted by the Queen, entered upon
his office and opened the extraordinary session of the Assembly.

Two days later, that body passed a motion, "that the sole and unanimous will (θέλησις) of the Ionian people has been, and is, the union of all the Seven Islands with the Kingdom of Greece." Gladstone told the Assembly that its only legal means of expression was by petition; and, when the motion was repeated in that form, he characteristically quibbled about the meaning of the word θέλησις, which he insisted upon translating "disposition," instead of the obvious signification. The Ionians were doubtless amused at this not uncommon pretention of a foreign scholar to know more about their own language than they themselves, while his scholarly chief was probably edified by the philological criticism, which accompanied his transmission of their petition to the Queen. The royal reply, as was expected, was a flat refusal "to abandon the obligations" laid upon the British monarchy by the treaty of 1815, or to "permit any application to any other Power in furtherance of any similar design." Thereupon, the eminent statesman in his best Italian introduced into the Assembly his Ionian reform bill. His study of Ionian affairs had convinced him, that, while union was undesirable, "not Cherubim and Seraphim could work" the existing system; he saw that, although, as Greek and French writers admitted, the material prosperity of the Ionians was greater than that of the free Greeks, the fiscal system weighed heavily on the peasantry, crippled the export trade and discriminated unfairly between town and country. The civil service, as he remarked, was "disproportionate to the number of the population, and to the work done"; for "the paid servants of the public" were "above 2200 among 240,000 inhabitants," and had increased by one-quarter since the reforms of 1849, so that the Ionians were the most official-ridden people in Europe. The nobles and the gentry naturally liked to have it so, just as the deputies were glad of their salaries, which Gladstone found excessive and sought to halve and pay only while the Assembly was sitting. He could, therefore, scarcely expect either the officeholders, who were the mainstay of the protectorate, or the Radicals, who were its fiercest enemies, to approve of a retrenchment which would touch their vested interests.

Nor were his political reforms calculated to win the favour of either British or Ionians. His proposed transformation of the Senate from an executive body into a partly-elected, partly-nominated Second Chamber pre supposed the existence of a wealthy and powerful aristocracy. But the Ionian nobles had neither the means nor the moral courage to oppose a strong resistance to the measures of a democratic Assembly, which, under the Gladstonian scheme, would have met annually to vote the budget, could have impeached all officials before the Senate, and with that body would have enjoyed the revived Venetian privilege of petitioning the Crown against "grave malversation" on the part of the Lord High Commissioner. The proposed Ministry, to which the executive powers of the Senate were to be transferred, would have owed its nomination to that official; but the authority over the high police, with which he had been invested since 1817 and which empowered him to banish whomsoever he chose, was abolished. Frequently exercised by earlier High Commissioners, it had never been used by Young. These proposals, regarded by the British and their friends as likely to increase the power of the Ionian democrats, were feared by the democrats as an indefinite postponement of the union—a "national suicide," as a Zantiote Radical journal called their acceptance. Count Dusmani, the future historian of Gladstone's mission, a Protectionist who had been 30 years in public life, warned their author that they would be rejected. A few voices, those of Count Flamburiari, the president of the Assembly, of Sir Peter Braïlas, of Sokrátes Kourês, were raised in their defence. One deputy, whose name Padovan showed his Venetian origin, spoke for two whole days against them—a feat worthy of the great parliamentarian himself. Meanwhile, the would-be legislator of the Ionians had showed a strange ignorance of the laws of his own country.   He had ignored the constitutional rule that the acceptance of the Commissionership had vacated his seat in Parliament and disqualified him from seeking re-election.   Upon learning that he was no longer a member of Parliament, he had formally resigned the Commissionership on February 1, leaving his friends at home to solve the nice problem in truly Gladstonian fashion by first appointing Sir Henry Knight Storks, an Italian-speaking colonel of Ionian experience, as High Commissioner, and then making him name Gladstone as his temporary deputy.   During this brief interregnum the debate dragged on, till, on February 16, 1859, the evening of Storks' arrival, the Assembly adopted with only one adverse vote and nine abstentions a motion rejecting the whole scheme.   Three days later, Gladstone left Corfù, after having demonstrated that local knowledge is more valuable than genius in the near east, and that neither a great name nor high station imposes upon the Greek democracy.   His biographer has admitted that the Ionian mission was a failure, which, if it did not injure the temporary Commissioner's future at home, prejudiced the position alike of his predecessor and of his successor in the Ionian Islands.

The tenth and last Lord High Commissioner, at the time of his appointment a simple colonel, chiefly known for his management of the hospitals at Scutari during the Crimean War, found that the Assembly was not disposed to let the question of union slumber.   The outbreak of the Italian War (April 1859) had a natural influence upon Ionian politics.   Corfù was the traditional refuge of Italian exiles; it was thence that the Bandiera brothers had started on their fatal expedition to Calabria in 1844; a Greco-Italian society, the "Great Brotherhood," had suffered imprisonment under Ward; Ionian Radicals were members of similar bodies in Italy; and a central committee in Zante was in correspondence with Garibaldi through the restless Lombárdos, whose inspiration might be traced in the writings of the French scholar and traveller, Lenormant,

against British rule. But the Unionists founded some of their
most specious arguments upon the utterances of British
ministers. When Russell, in his famous dispatch of Oct. 27,
1860, proclaimed "the Italians" to be "the best judges of their
own interests" and spoke with enthusiasm of "their liberties"
and "independence," the Ionian Dandolo invited him to
apply these doctrines to the Greeks of the Seven Islands.
When, four months later, the Assembly met early in 1861,
an attack upon Gladstone's mission was followed by proposals
to submit the question of union in Italian fashion to a *plébiscite*
and to appeal to the parliamentarians, governments, and
philanthropists of Europe for their co-operation. After warning
it of the unconstitutional character of these motions, Storks
prorogued it for six months—a weapon robbed of half its
terrors by the practice of paying the deputies' salaries even
when parliament was not sitting. This incident led to a
debate at Westminster, which gave both the Duke of Newcastle,
then Colonial Secretary, and Gladstone, then Chancellor of
the Exchequer, an opportunity of upholding the protectorate.
Cession to Greece, argued the great Philhellene, would logically
involve that of Crete, Thessaly, and Epirus, and would at
the same time be a reckless waste of public money spent on
fortifications and "a crime against the safety of Europe."
These words were spoken on May 7, 1861 ; on December 8,
1862, the same Cabinet, of which the speaker was a member,
decided, with the solitary opposition of Lord Westbury, to
give up the Islands—only one of many examples of British
inconsistency in the eastern question. Palmerston himself,
the head of the government, consented to the cession of
Corfù, whose surrender he had declared in 1850 to be an
act of folly, whose retention, even if the southern islands were
ceded, he had again urged in 1851 as an act of wisdom. Such
is statesmanship !

The statements of Newcastle and Gladstone had some
influence upon Ionian politics. When the twelfth Ionian

Assembly met in 1862, it learnt with surprise that its newly-elected President, Zervós, the fervent Cephalonian Radical and exile of earlier days, had toned down into a "Reformer," so moderating was the effect of office, so slight seemed the prospect of union on the very eve of its accomplishment. The Radicals, however, under Lombárdos, continued their protests against the protectorate, in some cases blaming the British authorities for what, since the reforms of 1849, was really the fault of their own free municipalities. If since that date the roads were no longer kept up and the splendid forest of the Black Mountain inadequately protected, it was because those local bodies allowed politics to enter into their work and feared to punish the authors of forest fires in view of the next municipal election. In order to remedy these abuses, Storks persuaded the Senate to restrict, through the Regents of the islands, the powers of the municipalities, while he threw open to competition the smaller posts in the public service. It was too late, however, for a system of benevolent despotism. Already, in this very year, Russell had offered the Ionian Islands to Otho on condition that he abstained from causing trouble in Turkey. After his deposition, the election of Prince Alfred, who had visited Corfù in 1859 and whose elder brother had landed in Cephalonia in the summer of 1862, caused Great Britain to be much more popular than before, except among the extreme Radicals; while Elliot's promise that the Ionian Islands would be the reward of the Greeks for choosing a suitable monarch, who would respect the Greek constitution and the integrity of Turkey, was the first official announcement to the Ionians of the new British policy. The Queen's speech of 1863 repeated the offer, provided also that the Ionians themselves expressed their definite desire for union—a desire only doubted by those who regarded the local aristocracy and the officials as the sole representatives of public opinion, and by cynics who believed, to the last, that the Radicals would shrink from an act that would put an end to their salaries and close the political career of most of them for ever. At Westminster, however, the abandonment of the Islands was strongly criticised by Lords Derby and Carnarvon and by Disraeli, while Palmerston contended that the cession of the protectorate was the affair not of Parliament but of the prerogative.

Article 4 of the treaty of July 13, 1863, relative to the accession of King George, between the three protecting Powers and the King of Denmark, provided for the union of the Islands with Greece, when it should "have been found to be in accordance with the wishes of the Ionian Parliament," and should "have obtained the consent of the Courts of Austria, France, Prussia, and Russia." These Powers in a protocol of August 1 agreed to this revision of the treaty of 1815, of which three of them had been signatories; a newly-elected Ionian Assembly on October 5 voted with only three dissentients for the Union of the Seven Islands and their dependencies with Greece. The Anglo-Ionian honeymoon was, however, of short duration. In his message to the Assembly, Storks had stated five conditions, whereas the late elections had been fought on the cry of "Union without conditions." Of these conditions the most important were the preservation of the British cemeteries in the Islands—a question raised in 1902, when it was proposed to erect a casino on that at Corfù—the annual charge on the Ionian revenues of £10,000 in augmentation of the new King's civil list, and the abandonment of all Ionian claims in return for the quittance for a debt of £90,289 due to the protectorate "for arrears of military contribution." These conditions were accepted, although the payment made by the Ionians to their future sovereign aroused the just criticism that the expiring protectorate had no right to mortgage the future of an integral part of his kingdom. But a still greater surprise was in store for them. By a treaty between Great Britain and the above-mentioned Powers, signed in London on November 14, 1863, the Ionian Islands were declared neutral territory, and consequently the forces maintained there were to be limited, and the fortifications of the island of Corfù and its immediate dependencies were to be destroyed before the departure of the British troops. The announcement of these further conditions caused indignation alike in the Islands and in Greece. The Greek plenipotentiary, Charílaos Trikoúpes, son of the historian, and himself a future Premier, who thus made his first appearance in public life, arrived in London after the treaty was signed, and described the imposition of these conditions as "the immolation of Greece to Austria." Both Austria and Turkey regarded the fortifications of Corfù as a danger, the one to the Adriatic, the other to Epirus, while Palmerston defended the treaty by the precedents of the demolition of the Belgian fortresses and the neutralisation of Chablais and Faucigny. The Greek government pointed out that the neutrality of such islands as Cerigo and Santa Mavra would be nonsense, because they were geographically continuations of the Morea and Akarnanía, and cited the British bombardment of Copenhagen as a proof of what neutrality was worth in the event of war between two strong naval Powers. A compromise was made and embodied, on January 25, 1864, in a protocol which neutralised only the two northernmost islands—Corfù and Paxo with their dependencies, and removed the limit imposed upon Greek forces in all of them. These terms were incorporated in the definite treaty of union, signed on March 29, 1864, by the three protecting Powers and the King of the Hellenes, who took over the existing contracts with the Ionian Bank and the Austrian Lloyd, and promised to pay the pensions and compensations, enumerated in a separate convention and amounting to £10,676, due to certain British subjects and Ionian officials, whose services would be no longer needed. This last condition the Greek government considered unreasonable, for thus not only had the Ionians to pay £10,000 as an annuity to their new King, but the Greeks the same sum in pensions to the old Ionian establishment. Great Britain acted generously in ceding the

Islands ; she need not have spoiled her splendid act of self-sacrifice by petty pecuniary considerations.

The last sad act in the drama of the protectorate now began—the destruction of the Corfiote fortifications. Fortunately, the picturesque "Old Fort," from whose κορυφώ (or "twin peaks") the island received its present name, was spared ; but the marine defences of the "New Fort," the adjacent "Fort Abraham" and the fortifications of the islet of Vido, which commands the entrance of the harbour, were blown up. Ionians argued that the British had no right to destroy these works without consulting them, because about two-thirds of their cost during the protectorate had been paid out of Ionian money. The great blocks of masonry, on one of which the author read the date of 1837, still cumber the islet of Vido ; and such was the force of the explosion that an officer in charge of it told him that it broke all the windows in the opposite houses of Corfù. The destruction of these fortifications embittered the local press against the departing protectors ; but when, on the last morning of British rule, June 2, 1864, two of our men were told off to sever the statue of Britannia from the Phaiakian gallery, which still stands on the top of the palace, a friend heard some native bystanders exclaim, "she never did us any harm." At noon, Thrasýboulos Zaïmes took over the Islands as extraordinary envoy of the Greek government ; and four days later King George landed at Corfù, subsequently visiting the other six islands. It is pleasant to relate, on the authority of the British diplomatist who accompanied him, that at Santa Mavra alone was any bitterness exhibited towards the dethroned protectorate. The last scene in the drama of union was the entrance of the 84 Ionian deputies, or twice the ordinary number, elected for the first time by manhood suffrage, into the National Assembly at Athens on August 3. From the Corfiote deputation the landed class was wholly excluded ; the country swamped the town.

Thus ended the connexion of half a century between Britain and the Ionian Islands. The lapse of more than another half century since the union enables us to form some opinion upon the step then taken. The question may be considered from various standpoints. From that of the Greeks of the kingdom the union was an advantage, not only because it gave them seven beautiful islands, all in a better material condition, so far as roads and public works were concerned, than the older provinces, but also because the Ionians furnished a cultured and aristocratic element to the state, which was due to the long Venetian domination. The Ionian Islands have produced one Prime Minister, several prominent politicians, and some distinguished diplomatists to Greece, while the great natural beauty of Corfù has favoured the growth of art there. To the Ionians themselves the union was an ethical gain; for most nationalities, and not least the Hellenic, prefer to be governed even less well by their own fellow-countrymen—and in the east the rulers should also profess the same faith as the ruled—than to be governed better by strangers, especially if these be of a different creed. The moral key-note of the Ionian agitation for union was not so much liberty as nationality and religion, the two coefficients of Hellenism. Moreover, as Lytton pointed out, there were social, as well as political, difficulties. "The cordial amenities of bearing, and the judicious consideration for national pride, and even national prejudices," which he recommended in a memorable dispatch, were not always found among our officials. An Englishman, wrote a French observer, repeats that he is an Englishman twenty times a day, but once extra in the Ionian Islands. But from the material point of view— and ordinary mortals do not live by great ideas alone—the Ionians, and more particularly the Corfiotes, who benefited principally by the British occupation, have suffered since the union, as they soon discovered. Life in Corfù was a very different thing under the British from what it is to-day.

Then a number of highly-paid officials spent their money freely in the town, trade was brisk, and the station was known as "the soldier's paradise." Posts there were in plenty for the Corfiotes, while the amusements which always follow the British officer attracted natives and strangers alike to the place. No doubt this concentration of interests in the town had the bad effect of inducing the landowners to leave their estates in the interior of the island, in order to have their share in the social gaities and lucrative employments which the capital offered. So far the Greek government has not done as much as was expected for the Ionian Islands, and there is a melancholy air about the untenanted residences of the former High Commissioners, which was only dispersed when the annual visit of the German Emperor to Gastouri attracted Greek royalty to *Mon Repos*. Lastly, there remains the strategic and political aspect of the cessions. Napoleon, Nelson, and other commanders placed a high value upon Corfù, while Bismarck considered the withdrawal of our protectorate as a sign of weakness. Certainly the German statesman did not usually err on the side of generosity; and it may be doubted whether an enlarged and grateful Greek state be not more to our advantage than the protectorate over one discontented section of a hostile nationality. To sum up: the union will be differently judged by political economists, who ignore flesh and blood, and by politicians, who, being patriots themselves, admire patriotism in other nations.

The traces of the British occupation have not quite died away. The initials "G.R." and "V.R." may still be seen in the palace at Corfù; the townspeople still drink the excellent water which Adam brought from Benizze; and the square which now bears his name was so called because of the solemn doxology held there to commemorate the opening of the aqueduct. Roads and monuments to High Commissioners, a few graveyards and a few gray-beards remind the islanders of their former benefactors; the Ionian Bank still carries on

business; and cricket is still played at Corfù, where a few
scraps of English have been incorporated in the vernacular.
But the generation is fast passing away which knew the protectorate; to most the British history of the Islands has passed
into that chapter of our national renunciations, which records
the lost possessions of Britain in the Mediterranean—Tangier
and Port Mahon.

The entry of the Ionian deputies into the National Assembly
enabled that body to begin the discussion of the new constitution, of which a draft had been prepared by a committee.
During the nine months since the young King's arrival the
Assembly had used up three more Ministries; and party spirit
ran so high that the decision of the Ionian members to give
a patriotic support to the government of the day soon gained
for them the reproaches of the Opposition. One deputy protested against the interference of Sponneck in the deliberations
of the Assembly; and the discussion of the articles proceeded
so slowly that the royal mentor begged the British government
to use its influence with the Opposition—a request which
evoked the excellent, if somewhat tardy, recognition of the
principle, that the less the three Powers intervened in Greek
politics, the better would it be for Greece. The complete
unification of the Ionian Islands with the rest of the kingdom
proved to be an apple of discord even among the Ionians
themselves; for, while the Corfiote and Cephalonian deputies,
supported by the Opposition, desired the full and immediate
application in the Islands of the Greek legal and fiscal system,
the other Ionian members followed the government, then
headed by Kanáres, in supporting the gradual adoption of
uniformity. The result was that the Ionians retained their
fiscal system, introduced in 1803 and preserved during the
British protectorate, by which an export duty of 22·2 per cent.
on wine and oil represented the sole contribution of the
inhabitants to the state. As weeks and months were still
passing, the King, at the advice of the French minister, sent

a message to the Assembly on October 18, reminding it that nearly a year had elapsed since his arrival, that more than two months had gone by since the arrival of the Ionian deputies, and that the delay in voting the constitution was causing discontent among the people and embarrassment to the Crown. He, therefore, requested the Assembly to vote upon the rest of the constitution in ten days, reserving full liberty of action to himself in case of its non-completion within that period. This hint at his possible departure from the country had its immediate effect. Despite Opposition protests, the Assembly, which was still engaged in the discussion of the 71st article when the royal message arrived, voted that and the remaining 39 by October 29. One verbal amendment relating to the Roman Catholic priests in Greece was accepted at the suggestion of the Crown to please the French government; and on November 28 the King took the oath to the constitution and the President declared the labours of the Assembly over. Thus, after sitting for nearly two years, the second National Assembly held in Athens had provided the kingdom of Greece with a second King and a second constitution, the sixth drawn up since 1821, which, however, lasted longer than any of its predecessors.

The constitution of 1864 created an uni-cameral system. The Senate was abolished by a majority of 211 to 62, although the leaders of both the government and the Opposition were favourable to some sort of Second Chamber. The difficulty of forming such a body in a country, where there was (except in the Ionian Islands) no aristocracy, where democracy is engrained in the blood, and where large fortunes were then very rare, argued for a single Chamber, while the practical experience of the Othonian Senate had discredited that branch of the legislature in the eyes of the people. It is true, that the first parliamentary criticisms of Otho had been made in the Senate; but what specially damaged the senators in popular estimation, usually based on the attitude of the governing classes towards their salaries, was the extension of the senatorial sessions so as to obtain remuneration for the largest number of months, and the subsequent conversion of the monthly wage, fixed by the constitution of 1844, into a larger annuity. Sponneck's attempt to introduce into the constitution a paid Council of State, as a check, was only temporarily successful, for the articles creating it were repealed next year. The Senate having been thus abolished and the Crown restricted within the limits of constitutional monarchy, which King George was very careful not to overstep, the Chamber of Deputies became omnipotent, and parliamentarism was installed in all its latest developments. The *Boulé*, as it was classically called, was composed of deputies, elected for four years by universal, secret, simultaneous suffrage, in proportion to the population. Its numbers, in no case less than 150, have been as high as 234, but were reduced in 1905 to 177 and were 181 in 1912[1]. The unfortunate proviso, which fixed the quorum at so great a figure as half the total number of deputies *plus* one, gave opportunity for obstruction by means of abstention on a large scale, which at times paralysed public business. Members were paid 2000 *dr.* (about £80) for each ordinary session of not less than three or more than six months, and their travelling expenses alone for any extraordinary session. In 1884 this salary was altered to 1800 *dr.*, which was occasionally increased in case of a very long extension of the sittings, while in practice a compensation of from 1500 to 2000 *dr.* was paid latterly for attendance at an extraordinary session. But Ministers, pensioners, or officers already in receipt of state pay, were only entitled to the difference between the legislative and their official salary. Special representation was continued in the electoral law of 1864, which accompanied the constitution, to the people of Hýdra and Spétsai and to the colonists of New Psará—as Erétria had been re-baptised—in gratitude for the services of the Nautical Islands in the War of Independence; and similar feelings

[1] Now 369.

of pity and patriotism awarded Greek citizenship to the
refugees of Párga, Soûli and Hagiá. The restriction of election to men of 30 prevented, as in Italy, the accession of
young and enthusiastic politicians to power; and the provision
that a deputy must be either a native of, or at any rate settled
for at least two years in, his constituency, tended to narrow
the choice of the electorate to local magnates and to the
exclusion of national statesmen, who, as often happens,
chanced to be unpopular in their native place. Salaried civil
servants and mayors were further declared ineligible, but
officers of the forces were allowed to become deputies, being
placed in retreat during the whole period of the legislature. This last provision scarcely tended to the maintenance
of discipline, for the army might have the spectacle of a
subordinate officer criticising his superiors from his place
in Parliament. But the insertion of this clause, which had
not existed in the constitution of 1844, is traceable to the
military character of the revolution of 1862, of which this was
the reward. Later legislation endeavoured to diminish the
evil by regarding the period of an officer's parliamentary life
as so much lost time in his military career. A Cabinet of
seven Ministers, not necessarily members of the *Boulé*, in
which, however, they all had a right to speak, continued to
carry on the work of government. On five occasions King
George availed himself of the privilege to form extra-parlia-
mentary Cabinets; on six he dismissed a Ministry which had
not been forced by the Chamber to resign. But these were
exceptions to the normal working of the ministerial system.
Excluding the £12,000 a year paid to King George by the
three protecting Powers, the civil list was fixed at 1,125,000 *dr.*,
inclusive of the £10,000 contributed by the Ionian Islands.

The relations of Church and State caused considerable
debate. The Orthodox Ionian deputies desired the maintenance of their union with the Œcumenical Patriarch, which
had been sanctioned by the Ionian charter of 1817 and which

they regarded as a national, no less than an ecclesiastical, question. But the Orthodox Church in Greece was once more proclaimed autocephalous, in an article, identical, save for one adverb, with that of the constitution of 1844; and an arrangement was made with the Patriarch respecting the cession of his jurisdiction over the Ionians, and allowing the chief Corfiote ecclesiastic to retain for his life the coveted title of "Metropolitan." It was provided that the heir to the Greek throne, simply styled "the successor" (for the "European" title of "Duke of Sparta" is not used in Greece) must belong to the Orthodox Church. Finally, it was enacted that a revision of the constitution could only take place, if, after the lapse of ten years, the *Boulé* in two successive legislatures requested by a majority of three-quarters of its whole number the revision of specified provisions. In that event, a revisionary Chamber, composed of twice the ordinary number of deputies, was to be specially convened. An exception, however, was allowed in the case of article 83, which created a Council of State; the revision of this article was permitted in the next legislature, if three-quarters of the members demanded it. The Council of State of from 15 to 20 persons, nominated for ten years by the Crown on the proposal of the Cabinet for the purpose of preparing and examining bills, had formed no part of the original draft; but it had seemed to Sponneck to provide a possible check on democracy, and had therefore been recommended to the Assembly. But to the Greek democrats it smacked of Bavarian autocracy—for Otho had had a similar Council of State from 1835 to 1844—and it was accepted as part of the constitution by only a small majority. Scarcely had the constitution been passed than a large group of deputies signed a protest against the restoration of this institution; and in the next legislature it was abolished, and the four articles of the constitution relating to it consequently annulled, by 120 votes to 26. When, however, a thorough revision of the constitution was imperatively demanded in 1910, the Crown did not—perhaps could not—wait till two successive legislatures had demanded revision by a three-quarters' majority. It was felt that the country could not afford the time for the nice performance of those preliminary obligations.

The constitution of 1864, with that one exception and a few smaller changes, regulated Greek public life for 46 years. Nowhere has the democratic ideal been more clearly expressed in writing; whether the national interests were equally well interpreted by it, is another question.

CHAPTER XIII

REFORMS AND THEIR RESULTS: THE LEBANON AND CRETE (1856–69)

Sanguine statesmen, who had undertaken the Crimean war to maintain the integrity of the Ottoman empire, hoped that the sacrifices of the western Powers would be at least rewarded by the reform of Turkish administration and by the amelioration of the conditions under which the Christian subjects of the Sultan lived. Believers in paper reforms were encouraged in this belief by the publication, on February 18, 1856, a week before the meeting of the Congress at Paris, of an "Illustrious writing," or *Hatti-Humayûn*, confirming the promises made at Gül-khâneh in 1839. This second charter, granted by Abdul Mejid to his people, ratified all "the spiritual privileges and immunities" accorded "to all Christian communities or to other non-Mussulman religions." Patriarchs were to be nominated for life, and thus the scandal of frequent changes avoided; their revenues were to be fixed, and the temporal affairs of their respective communities placed under the control of a committee, chosen from among them. The fabric of churches schools, and hospitals might be repaired, provided—it was added with a fine respect for archaeology, which no one would have expected from the Turks—that "the primitive plans" were followed! All injurious appellations, tending to wound the susceptibilities of this or that creed or race, were to be severely punished; compulsory conversion was prohibited; office was thrown open to every nationality; civil and military education was offered to all who complied with the regulations. Justice was to be administered in public, and witnesses were to swear in the fashion of their respective creeds; codes of law were to be prepared and translated into all the languages of the empire; any corporal punishment approaching to torture was abolished; the police was to be reorganised in a manner to inspire confidence and security. Christians were declared admissible to the army; and equality of rights was stated to involve equality of taxation. Reform of the tithe-system and abolition of the tax-farmer were promised; an annual budget was to show how the taxes had been spent; roads and canals were to be made, banks founded, European capital attracted for the development of the Sultan's dominions. In short, an Asiatic despotism, based upon the Koran and which in Europe was still rather in the nature of a garrison than a settlement, was to be transformed by a stroke of the pen into a western empire. The history of the next half-century is the best commentary on the Utopian programme contained in this optimistic document, which was communicated to the signatories of the treaty of Paris—a communication which they ingenuously declared in article 9 to be of "high value" and yet as not authorising their collective or separate intervention in the internal affairs of Turkey. In other words, the charter was treated as the "spontaneous emanation of the Sultan's sovereign resolve" to govern on European lines but without European control.

No one acquainted with the Turks, or indeed with any nationality accustomed for centuries to regard itself as a governing and superior race, could have expected these reforms to be palatable to the Mussulmans. A reaction naturally set in; and little more than two years had passed, when an outbreak of fanaticism—repeated at the same place in 1895—resulted in the murder of the British and French consuls at Jedda, the active intervention of the two late allies of the Sultan, and the bombardment of the town by a British vessel. Ere long the horrors of the Lebanon aroused the attention of Europe and occasioned the dispatch of a French expedition to Syria. A little while more, and Crete rose against her masters.

The settlement of the Lebanon in 1845 had secured peace as long as the Emir Haydar, who governed the Maronite section of the Mountain, lived. But, upon his death in 1854, the Porte selected as his successor a certain Emir Beshîr-Ahmed Bellamah, whose appointment not only divided the British from the French government, but was also challenged by other native chiefs. A social revolution was at this time developing among the Maronites, the fertility of whose wives was in striking contrast with the barrenness of the soil. As a natural consequence of this disproportion between the Christian population and the land available for its support, the young Maronites found themselves compelled to emigrate or obtain such an agrarian law as would end, or at least modify, the feudal system then still prevailing on the Lebanon. In this agitation, the peasants found leaders, as usually happens, in the younger sons of the nobility, who, excluded by primogeniture from the advantages of the first-born, "took the people into partnership," like the aristocratic Athenian demagogue of old. The priests, too, sprung from the loins of the people, espoused the popular cause, under the leadership of the bishop of Beirût; while the new governor of the Maronite district was glad to exploit for the destruction of his rivals the socialistic sentiments of the peasantry. An agrarian insurrection began, and a peasant commonwealth was formed with a gigantic farrier as its president. So far the movement had been confined to the Maronites, for the Druse nobility was at first inclined to side with the Maronite aristocracy against the peasants, who seemed to be the common enemy of the upper class, whether Maronite or Druse. But the fabric of feudalism among the Druses was more substantial than among the Christians; and the Turkish authorities, glad of an excuse to abolish the local autonomy, were able to direct the Druses, peasants no less than chiefs, against the Maronites, by whom they regarded themselves menaced. Fanaticism was met by fanaticism; and, while French diplomacy naturally blamed the Druses, British accused the Catholic Maronites. But the latest and most exhaustive study of the question points to the Turkish authorities rather than the Maronite priests as responsible for kindling the inflammable material accumulated by racial, religious, and class hatred on the Lebanon.

On April 27, 1860, the Druses began the massacres of the Maronites; a month later 32 blazing villages illuminated the Mountain. Sites familiar to Christendom from the Bible, Sidon and "Baal-gad, in the valley of Lebanon under Mount Hermon," were turned into shambles, where defenceless refugees were butchered; in Deir el-Kamar, the lofty "monastery of the moon," the ancient palace was strewn with the corpses of Maronites, slowly done to death by the Druses under the eyes of the Turkish soldiers. Even the pasha of Beirût professed his regret at these horrors; and, owing to his influence, on July 6 the Druses and Maronites signed a treaty of peace. But "the Syrian atrocities" were not yet over. Three days later, the Mussulmans of Damascus, whither numbers of fugitives had fled, attacked the Christian quarter; for ten days the pillage lasted, and the British consul reported that 5500 Christians perished there. The carnage would have been greater, had it not been for the noble conduct of Abd el-Kâder, the Skanderbeg of Algeria, then living in exile at Damascus. The brave defender of northern Africa against the French strove to prevent and, when he could not prevent, to mitigate the massacre, even at the risk of his life. His retainers escorted hundreds, who would otherwise have been killed, to Beirût beneath the shadow of the foreign consulates. Thither, as soon as the news of the massacre reached him, Thouvenel, then French Minister of Foreign Affairs, resolved to send an expedition. Such a policy was defensible on political no less than humanitarian grounds, for France was the special protectress of the Maronites, and her Emperor hoped to recover in Syria those clerical sympathies which he had lost the year before in Italy. Russell, however, fearing the creation of a French principality or protectorate in Syria, desired the proposed intervention to be regulated by a special convention, which Russia, already dissatisfied with the progress of the promised Turkish reforms, wished to extend to the general condition of the Christians in Turkey, to the Balkans no less than to the Lebanon. The Russian suggestion was rejected; a Greek offer to send a detachment of *évzonoi* and two warships was declined; and on August 3 the signatory Powers of the treaty of Paris, with the exception of Sardinia, signed in that capital a protocol, which was converted a month later into a convention. A body of not more than 12,000 European troops, of which Napoleon III at once furnished 6000, was "to contribute to the restoration of tranquillity," but this occupation was not to exceed six months. This "active co-operation" of the Powers with the Sultan was justified by that very article 9 of the treaty of Paris, which seemed to exclude their intervention in the internal affairs of his empire. Before, however, the French expedition under General Beaufort d'Hautpoul, an officer of Syrian experience, had arrived, Fuad Pasha, the Turkish Minister of Foreign Affairs, whom the Sultan had sent as his commissioner extraordinary to Syria on the news of the massacres, had exacted exemplary punishment at Damascus. By his orders, 111 soldiers were shot, 57 civilians hanged, the pasha himself secretly executed, and Abd el-Kâder decorated. But when the French proceeded to clear the Lebanon, the Druses were allowed to escape through the connivance of Fuad or the stupidity of his agents; and the French expedition thus became merely "a charitable promenade." Thouvenel strove to obtain an extension of its duration. Russell, however, fearing Napoleonic designs against Syria and Egypt, opposed it; and it was finally arranged that by June 5 the evacuation of the country should be complete. Beyond increasing the popularity of the Napoleonic

song, *Partant pour la Syrie*, the nine months' French occupation of Syria had not achieved much. International jealousy
had again favoured the Turks; and in the commission which
had been sitting at Beirût Lord Dufferin's championship
of the Druses tempered their punishment with mercy; 245
Druses were exiled to Tripoli in Africa, and others to the castles
of Belgrade and Vidin; the pasha of Beirût escaped death by
transportation to Constantinople; indemnities were paid by the
Ottoman authorities, of course irregularly, to the Christians of
Damascus and the Lebanon, and were supplemented by a French
subscription.

It now remained to reorganise the administration of the
Mountain. The international commission decided that the
Lebanon should form an autonomous province under an
Ottoman governor-general, chosen from among the Sultan's
Christian subjects. The frontiers of this province were restric-
ted by the exclusion of Beirût and several villages; it was divided
into six districts, three administered by Maronites, one by a
Druse, one by an Orthodox Greek, and one by an Uniate.
The capital was fixed at Deir el-Kamar, a Christian enclave in
the Druse district, from which it was detached. Advisory
provincial and district councils, a local police, and a tribute,
upon which the Mountain had a first charge, completed the
charter of 1861. Its signature was almost the last act of Abdul
Mejid; on June 25, 1861 he died, leaving behind him the
memory of a humane ruler, who had attempted, if in vain, to
continue the reforms of his father, and bequeathing to his
brother Abdul Aziz, till then regarded as the hope of the
reactionary party, an embarrassed exchequer, an unfulfilled
policy of progress, a threatening situation in the Balkan
peninsula, and an untried organisation on the Lebanon, which
satisfied none of its inhabitants.

The first Christian governor-general of the Mountain, a
Catholic Armenian of learning and experience alike in diplomacy
and administration, was received with suspicion and discontent.

The Maronites had demanded a governor-general of their own race ; the Druses had lost their feudal privileges and were placed in an inferior position to the Greeks ; the Greeks, who might appear to be the chief gainers by the reorganisation, regarded Daoud Pasha as an enemy, because he was an Armenian. The democratic section of the Maronites refused to pay taxes to an autocratic foreigner, who relied on the local aristocracy. But the clever Armenian triumphed over all these obstacles. First, he secured by a ruse the deportation of the Maronite tribune, Karam ; then he removed the Turkish soldiers, and traversed the Mountain to hear in person the grievances of its inhabitants. Confidence was thus gradually restored ; private vengeance gave way to law ; and all was going well when, in 1863, the release of some of the exiled Druses brought back to the Lebanon the authors of the massacres. Daoud solved even this difficulty by a scheme of land purchase ; the Druses sold their real property and emigrated in such large numbers to the fertile Haurân, the Bashan of the Bible, that the district has obtained the name of "the Druse Mountains." These successes secured the governor-general's unanimous re-nomination at the expiration of his three years' term. But experience had disclosed defects in the practical working of the theoretical organisation, compiled by diplomatists ignorant of the peculiar conditions of the Lebanon. Accordingly a new statute was drawn up and signed by the representatives of Turkey and of the five Powers at Constantinople on September 6, 1864, which modified and simplified that of 1861. The Lebanon continued to be administered by a Christian governor, nominated by the Porte ; and Daoud's tenure was prolonged for five years. In order to give to the Maronites, the most numerous element of the population, a representation proportionate to their numbers, a seventh district, administered by a Maronite, was created ; the district councils were annulled ; and the provincial council was so reorganised, that out of its 12 members four were Maronites, three Druses, three Greeks of the two rites, and two

Mussulmans—one Sunnite, or Orthodox, the other a *Metâwileh*, or dissenter.   All feudal privileges and the right of asylum, enjoyed by ecclesiastical establishments, were abolished, but litigation between ecclesiastics was left within the sole jurisdiction of the ecclesiastical authorities.   Each village became a commune, whose mayor and petty justice of the peace was a local sheikh.   A body of police was responsible for the preservation of order ; and it was reiterated that the 3500 purses (£14,583. 6s. 8d.), at which the tribute was assessed for the time being, should be devoted to local requirements, any surplus being paid to the Imperial treasury.

This statute, which could not be altered without the consent of the Powers, remained, for more than half a century[1], the charter of the Lebanon, and has likewise served as a model for Crete.   With the exception of an insurrection headed by the escaped Maronite democrat, Karam, in 1866, and terminated by the severity of Daoud and the final deportation of its leader, the Mountain has enjoyed unbroken peace.   A succession of strong governors, notably Rustem Pasha, subsequently ambassador in London, a firm and economical administrator, kept both Maronites and Druses in order.   Their mutual hatred has almost disappeared; and emigration has reduced the Druses to the third place numerically among the inhabitants of the Lebanon, which, according to the latest figures, contains 229,680 Maronites, 54,208 Orthodox Greeks, 49,812 Druses, 34,472 Uniates, and 30,422 Muslims.   The policy of the Sultan's representative has been to rely upon the aristocratic and conservative element, thereby checking the democrats and the clergy.   The most pressing question on the Lebanon is now agrarian, for, despite the large numbers of emigrants, land can scarcely be purchased on the Lebanon, where more than one-third of the soil, and that the best, is owned by the monasteries.   Mortmain is the curse of the Mountain, because the peasant, even if he return from abroad with his little pile, cannot gratify his earth-hunger.   If he

[1] The French, as mandatories of Syria, published a new constitution for the Lebanon in 1922.

wish to cultivate the land of his beloved Mountain, he must do so as a monk or a *métayer*. Nevertheless, the Lebanon is, on the whole, the most successful example of autonomy applied to a Turkish province. Samos had frequent difficulties with her princes; Eastern Roumelia was soon merged in Bulgaria; Crete would never rest till she had obtained union with the Greek kingdom.

The "great Greek island" had enjoyed—if for the Cretans it could be called "enjoyment"—an unusually long period of repose after the abortive insurrection of 1841. In 1858, however, 8000 islanders mustered together, and an Assembly, convened at Peribólia near Canea, threatened to resort to force unless the reforms promised at Gül-khâneh and re-affirmed in the *Hatti-Humayûn* of 1856, were realised. The fiscal burdens of the Cretans were not onerous, for besides the tithe of agricultural produce, estimated at an average of 10s. per head, they paid only one tax, that in commutation of military service. But the collectors of this tax, not in itself heavy (for it was only £5560 for the whole island, or about 8d. per head), demanded the simultaneous payment of two years' arrears, and some too zealous agents threatened the introduction of other taxes, of which the recent census seemed to be the preliminary. Vely Pasha, the governor-general, a native of Crete, and a son of Mustapha, for so many years *váli* of the island, had acted humanely and liberally on the system which he had learned when ambassador in Paris; but his road-making policy, at first hailed with enthusiasm, had made him unpopular with the peasants, who had to provide the labour and pay 9s. per head, and his toleration of changes of religion had led to squabbles about proselytism. But underlying all these causes was the desire of the Christians for union with Greece, or at least for a Cretan principality under Kallérges, the hero of the revolution of 1843 and himself of Cretan extraction[1]. The moment was favourable to the Cretans, for France was on their side and the

---

[1] Consul-general Longworth's report of 1858 in *Parliamentary Papers* 1867-8, vol. lxxiii, No. 3965, 1.

Turks were occupied with the Montenegrin war; and thus the
Servian highlanders rendered their first, but not their last,
service to the Greek islanders, equally attached to liberty and
equally ready to fight for it. The Porte, therefore, before much
blood had been shed, wisely replaced the well-meaning but
obnoxious governor by a milder official, Sami Pasha, promising
provincial councils and other concessions on the lines of the
Hatti-Humayûn of 1856.

But these promises, which had stayed, or rather postponed,
the insurrection, were disregarded by the next governor-
general, Ismail Pasha, whose objects were to increase his
fortune and advance his own career. A petition to the
Sultan in 1864, setting forth the Cretan grievances, was
neutralised by a counter-petition, so that discontent, increased
by two bad crops, continued to spread until, in May 1866,
some 4000 Christians met at Peribólia to discuss the situation.
On May 26, a fresh petition, resembling that of 1864, was
drawn up for presentation to the Sultan. The Christians
complained of the exorbitant duties levied since 1858 upon
various articles of food, upon the sale of wine, upon tobacco,
and upon salt—this last a special grievance, because it crippled
the Cretan staple manufacture of soap; nor were they pacified
by the Turkish argument that the rise in these taxes was
intended to compensate the treasury for the loss entailed by
the reduction of the export dues throughout the empire. They
further complained of the vexatious system of farming the taxes,
of the want of bridges and roads—for the Turks had done
practically nothing to improve the communications of the island
in the two centuries of their occupation—and of the undue
interference of Ismail in the elections to the "Councils of the
elders," as they were picturesquely called, despite the promises
made eight years earlier. They asked for a bank to prevent
the usury of the oil-merchants, to whom alone the farmers
could apply for loans; they claimed judicial reform—for the
awards of the courts were issued in Turkish, not in the tongue

understanded of the people, the evidence of a Christian was unavailing against that of a Mussulman, imprisonment was often indefinitely protracted, and it was the custom to arrest the relative of an escaped or contumacious culprit as a hostage. The lack of schools, the closing of all the Cretan ports save three, and the restrictions upon religious freedom, which compelled a converted Mussulman to quit the island, completed the list of grievances.

So far reform, not revolution, was mentioned; it was only later that the Cretans petitioned Queen Victoria, Napoleon III, and the Tsar for union with Greece, or, if that were impossible, for a reformed political organisation. Clarendon, then at the Foreign Office, replied that reforms should be granted, but that "the condition and prospects of the Ionian Islands ought to deter the Cretans from wishing to be united with Greece." The Foreign Secretary's opinion was based upon the discouraging reports[1] which he had received from his consuls in the three principal islands since the union, and especially from Corfù, whose inhabitants felt that they had been treated "as a conquered people," or, in the words of a Corfiote, as "a fief of the politicians at Athens." The wholesale dismissal and reduced payment of Ionian officials, the abolition of imprisonment for debt—the only guarantee which the landowner had for the fulfilment of contracts by his tenants—and the assimilation of the legal system to that of the rest of Greece, caused the landed proprietors of the island to petition the King, and Padovan, so lately the leader of Corfiote Unionism, to quit the *Boulé* in disgust at what he called "the slaughter of the Seven Islands, and particularly of Corfù." While a "state of penury and despondency reigned in that island," and the six rural deputies openly advocated the extinction of all private debts—the χρεῶν ἀποκοπαί of the ancients—by means of a heavy property tax and heavy import-duties, the Metropolitan

---

[1] Contradicted by M. S. Dragoúmes, the subsequent Premier, then a judge in Corfù.

of Cephalonia protested against the separation of the Ionian
Church from the Patriarchate and its union with that of the
Greek kingdom, finally accomplished in 1866. Still, the British
Minister's argument was not convincing, for it took no account
of the sentiment of nationality ; moreover, the Ionians had had
the material advantages of the British protectorate for nearly
half a century, while the Cretans had obtained practically no
benefits, material or other, from the uncovenanted mercies of
the Turk, whose administration even the most ardent defender
of "the integrity of the Ottoman Empire" would scarcely place
on a level with our own.   However, both Lord Stanley, who
succeeded Clarendon on the fall of the Liberal government (June
1866), and his French colleague, continued to bolster up Turkish
rule in Crete, thereby prolonging for over 30 years a question
which only ten years ago was definitely solved.   Upon Stanley,
in particular, lies a heavy responsibility for the Iliad of woes
which this procrastination has involved.

The dilatoriness of the Porte and its ultimate refusal to
remit taxes, the exhortations of the militant priest Parthénios
Kelídes, the influence of Cretans in Athens and of unofficial
Greek agents, and the warlike preparations of Ismail, who
gathered the Mussulmans into the three chief fortresses of the
island, brought on an insurrection, which might have been
prevented, or at least again postponed, by a prompt redress of
Cretan grievances.   The Porte was, indeed, anxious to provoke
an armed rising, which would enable it to transfer the troublesome island to its vassal, the Khedive Ismail, to whose famous
predecessor it had been subjected from 1832 to 1840 ; and this
plan was not unpleasing to France, then extending her influence
in Egypt by the construction of the Suez Canal.   Egyptian
troops were landed, as in 1823 ; and Egyptian offers of a bank,
schools, and roads were made to the Cretans, if they would
consent to union with Egypt.   Instead of accepting them, a
"General Assembly of the Cretans" held at Sphakía, on September 2, declared Ottoman rule abolished and proclaimed

union with Greece. Already blood had begun to flow; an Egyptian defeat at the Springs of Apokórona led to the recall of Ismail and the appointment as special commissioner of Mustapha Pasha, a severe but just, if merciless Albanian, who had hanged the Cretans at Murniés in 1833 and from his previous 30 years' governorship of the island was known as "Kiritli" (or "the Cretan"). He was assisted by the Egyptian Minister of War, himself a Cretan, converted to Islâm.

The Cretan insurrection of 1866 naturally aroused the keenest sympathy in Greece, and profoundly affected Greek politics. Since the adoption of the constitution, Greek public life had been agitated by constant ministerial changes, chiefly due to the disturbing presence of Sponneck, as the power behind the young King. With his aid, in March 1865, Alexander Koumoundoûros succeeded in displacing his chief Kanáres as Prime Minister, and thus beginning his series of Premierships; but the first parliament elected under the new constitution resulted in a confusion of parties which rendered it impossible to form a stable administration. Five Cabinets followed one another in almost as many weeks; and even Sponneck's departure did not completely allay the apprehensions of Europe or the discontent of the Greeks. Such was the state of affairs, when the news that "the great Greek island" had risen reached Athens. Delegeórges, then Minister of Foreign Affairs, was at first desirous of not only assisting unofficially the Cretan insurgents but of encouraging another insurrection in Thessaly and Epirus. But the King, whose position was difficult, and the Premier Boúlgares, realising that Greece was not then prepared for war with Turkey, decided not to repeat the experiment of 1854, but to restrict the co-operation of the government to a passive attitude towards the volunteers who were flocking to Crete, and who found capable leaders in Koronaîos, commander of the national guard and chief of the "Mountaineers" during the street fighting at Athens in 1863, and Zymbrakákes, a Cretan officer of the Greek army,

educated in France. The insurgents divided the island into
three military commands—the western held by Zymbrakákes,
the central by Koronaîos, and the eastern by the Cretan chief
Kórakas, while a little steamer, the *Panhellénion*, worked by
British engineers, fearlessly ran the Turkish blockade. Possible
complications with Servia, anxious to be rid of the remaining
Turkish garrisons, were added to the calculations of Ottoman
statesmen.

The crushing defeat of the insurgents under Zymbrakákes
by Mustapha at Baphé on October 24 caused the temporary
subsidence of the insurrection, and some of the Sphakiotes
even came to terms with the Turks. But Koronaîos restored
the enthusiasm of the islanders by his successes in the centre,
where he had established his headquarters at the monastery
of Arkádion, a strongly-fortified building near Rethýmne,
destined to be the scene of this insurrection's most heroic
drama. Within its walls a number of women and children
had taken refuge ; and, in the absence of Koronaîos, its
defence had been entrusted to Demakópoulos, another Greek
officer. Against this sacred fortress Mustapha directed his
attack ; but its massive construction proved superior to the
force of his mountain artillery, while within soldiers and monks,
with the cry of "Liberty or death" upon their lips, defended
the position for two whole days. "Never in their recollection,"
said the islanders, "had such a battle been fought in Crete."
At last, on November 21, the Turks forced the iron gate ; the
Egyptians, pressed on by the bayonets of their comrades,
effected an entrance into the courtyard ; then Máneses, the
abbot, put a match to the powder-magazine, uniting defenders
and assailants in one common hecatomb. The survivors,
who had surrendered their arms on a promise that their lives
should be spared, were mostly massacred ; the refectory ran
red with the blood of women and children ; and a British
correspondent, visiting the monastery some months later,
found the charred and mutilated remains of the victims still

strewn on the floor. The heroic garrison of Arkádion did not die in vain. The verses of the poet Paráschos commemorated their resistance, worthy of the best days of ancient Sparta ; public opinion abroad was deeply stirred by the recital of the siege ; a fund for the Cretan refugees was started in London ; a committee of British residents, including the historian Finlay, was formed in Athens ; and, to the embarrassment of the Turcophil Cabinet of St James, the transport of 315 fugitives by H.M.S. *Assurance* from Sélino Kastélli caused pro-British demonstrations in Greece, where Koumoundoûros, again at the head of affairs, found a neutral attitude increasingly difficult, owing to the sympathy of the Greeks with the Cretans. So strong was this feeling, that a riot broke out at the Piræus, where the people attacked and drove back into the sea a body of returning and disillusioned volunteers, transported on Turkish and French vessels.

In January 1867 the two Cabinets hitherto most favourable to Turkey suddenly modified their Cretan policy. Stanley, while still obdurate on the question of union, suggested the application to Crete of the system of autonomy, recently adopted for the Lebanon. The Marquis de Moustier, the new French Minister of Foreign Affairs, who as ambassador at Constantinople had been Turcophil and on a recent visit to Athens had used to the King and government language frank to the verge of brutality, went much further. " It would be far better," he said on January 24, " for the Porte to give up Candia " than to grant autonomy. He declared that " the country was lost to Turkey," and added that " Crete had become a permanent sore limb of the empire, and it was better to amputate it than to allow it to become the nucleus of gangrene, which might spread to every part of the empire." Union, in his opinion, " was the only plan to be now adopted," while he " would not hesitate also to abandon Thessaly." Gortchakoff, on behalf of Russia, likewise advocated union as the remedy ; and, on March 30, all the Powers, except

Great Britain, supported the French proposal to allow the Cretans to decide by a *plébiscite* on the future form of government—Samian autonomy, the Moldo-Wallachian system, or union with Greece. Never had there been so favourable a chance for solving the Cretan question; well might Fuad Pasha, the Turkish Foreign Minister, remark, that his sole consolation was the refusal of the British government to join in this suggestion.

The changed attitude of the Powers and the heavy losses of Mustapha, of whose army, originally 17,850 strong, only 6000 had returned to Canea, induced the Porte to promise a commission in Constantinople, to which the Cretans were invited to send delegates, for the purpose of drawing up a new system of government. This scheme proved to be futile; for the delegates went reluctantly to the capital, and seven of them prematurely quitted it as a protest. Meanwhile, a provisional government was formed by the insurgents at Sphakía in the name of King George; and Demétrios Mavrokordátos, ex-Minister of Education, was elected governor of the island. Dissatisfied with Mustapha, the Porte sent Omar Pasha, the famous Croatian general, to take command. But Omar was now an old man, full of his own importance, and disposed to underrate the difficulties of a Cretan campaign after his Montenegrin experiences. His plan of driving the insurgents into the mountains of Sphakía and annihilating them there, cost him, despite the discord between the Cretan leaders, two defeats, avenged by savage outrages. The diary of a German officer, who accompanied him, told how the Croat "ordered the division to ravage and rape," and how "all prisoners were murdered or worse." By his orders, one of the horrors of the insurrection of 1823 was re-enacted, and a body of fugitives was stifled in a cave by the smoke of a huge fire, kindled at its mouth. Still, the insurgents, though lacking in unison, remained unsubdued. Koronaîos nearly destroyed Omar's army in a ravine between Rethýmne and Candia; Hajji

Micháles Jánnares, son of the likenamed leader of "the great insurrection" and himself the most remarkable figure of this, displayed the picturesque bravery and manly stature of a Cretan chief in many a skirmish; while a second blockade-runner, called the *Arkádion* from the famous monastery, and bought by the Greek colony in England, made one trip after another, and, when its crew had at last to burn it to avoid capture, was speedily replaced by another vessel, the *Enosis* (or *Union*). If at the end of his three months' campaign, the Sultan's favourite general had destroyed 600 villages, he had lost more than 20,000 men. Trikoúpes, the Greek Minister of Foreign Affairs, protested against his outrages; Gortchakoff sarcastically remarked that Britain "had on other occasions been disposed to support the aspirations of a people struggling for independence." Then the Sultan himself resolved to try conciliation, granted an amnesty, and, as his foremost strategist had failed, sent his Grand Vizier, Aali Pasha, to create a new Cretan organisation. The provisional government protested against the amnesty, and under the influence of a deputation from Athens, rejected Aali's offers, declaring that a mixed international commission and a *plébiscite* to determine the wishes of the population provided the only satisfactory solution. Aali, however, summoned a General Assembly of four delegates from each district to meet him; and his proposals were formulated in the "Organic Statute of 1868," which was the law of the island for the next ten years. Under this arrangement Crete was divided into five provinces and sub-divided into 19 districts; the two principal authorities were a governor-general (or *váli*) and a commander-in-chief, who were to be usually distinct persons but who on occasion might be one and the same individual. The *váli* had two assessors, of whom one was to be a Christian, and was to be assisted by a Council of Administration, likewise composed of Christians and Mussulmans, partly elected, and partly consisting of *ex officio* members, such as the Greek Metropolitan. Similarly, each provincial governor (or *mutessarif*), if a Christian, was to have a Mohammedan assessor (or *mouavin*), if a Mussulman, a Christian; and he was to be assisted by an administrative council. Official correspondence was to be conducted in both languages. A General Assembly, consisting of four delegates elected by the "Council of the Elders" of each district, and of four from each of the three towns, all paid a salary for their services, was to meet at Canea in an annual session of not more than 40 days for the discussion of measures of public utility. Religious questions were to be discussed in special sittings, in which the members of the particular religion could alone participate. While no fresh tax was to be imposed, those already existing were specified to be the tithe, the payment for exemption from military service, the duties on liquor, salt, and tobacco, and the customs dues. The tithe was to be remitted for the next two years, and reduced by one-half for two more[1].

The half-regretted decision of the provisional government to continue the insurrection involved Crete in another year of desultory warfare. Hussein Avni Pasha, who had succeeded as both civil and military governor towards the end of 1867, neither gained nor lost any decisive battle. Koronaîos had returned to Greece, whither, after an ineffectual attempt to defend the lofty plateau of Homalós, Zymbrakákes followed him. A last attempt to keep the insurrection alive was made at Athens, whence towards the end of November the veteran Mainate chief, Petropoulákes, set out with a body of volunteers for Crete. This incident almost led to war with Turkey. On December 11, 1868, a Turkish ultimatum was presented to the Greek government, demanding the dispersion of the volunteers, the disarming of the three blockade-runners or their exclusion from Greek ports, and protection for all Cretan refugees who sought to return home. Five days'

---

[1] *Parliamentary Papers*, 1867–8, vol. lxxiii, 469–83.

grace was given, and the expulsion of Greek subjects from Turkey was threatened.

Public opinion in Athens, as the British minister reported, was "unanimous in wishing for a rupture." The Greeks had from the outset sympathised with the Cretans; and no sooner did Koumoundoûros, who had taken part in the insurrection of 1841, become Premier at the end of 1866 than he began warlike preparations and sent an emissary to Belgrade to conclude an alliance with Servia, while Trikoúpes, his Foreign Minister, issued a circular asking for Crete, Thessaly, and Epirus. The King's marriage, however, in October 1867, with the Russian Grand-duchess Olga had hindered the Pan-hellenistic designs of the war-party; and, when the King returned to take up the reins from his uncle John of Glücksburg, who had been Regent in his absence, his first act was to dismiss Koumoundoûros, although the Premier had a large majority in the Chamber. The Russian ideal was a general rising in the near east under Muscovite auspices; and at this moment the Russians were preparing to give to Hellenism the greatest blow which it had received since the creation of the Greek kingdom—the erection of the Bulgarian Exarchate. Boúlgares, who returned to office in 1868 after a Cabinet of Affairs had been tried, was Russophil and indifferent about foreign policy; anxious for peace, he would have gladly stifled the insurrection, and refused to allow the Cretan deputies to sit in the newly elected Greek parliament. His Foreign Minister, however, Peter Deligiánnes, was openly in favour of union with Crete, for which he had tried to obtain British support. When, in December 1868, Gladstone became Prime Minister, the hopes of the Greeks revived, for they believed that the great Philhellene, who had contributed towards giving the Ionian Islands to them, would also support the annexation of Crete. Clarendon, his Foreign Secretary, in vain informed them that his chief, because he was anxious for the progress of Greece, condemned aggressive action as likely to injure the country financially. But, like the Ionians in their attitude towards union with Greece, the Greeks have always regarded union with Crete not as a question of cash but as one of national sentiment—a quality too often ignored by diplomatists as a factor in politics. Accused by Koumoundoûros of deserting their Cretan brethren, and forced to support nearly 50,000 Cretan refugees, the Greek ministers were in a difficult position; Karam, the Maronite leader, then in Athens, offered to raise a revolt in the Lebanon, while Peter Deligiánnes, who directed Greek foreign policy, continued to advocate the Cretan cause. Accordingly, the Greek government's reply amounted to a practical rejection of the Turkish demands; and Photiádes Bey, the Ottoman minister, left Athens on December 17. Three days earlier a fresh incident had occurred, which made the situation still more critical. The famous blockade-runner, *Enosis*, when summoned to stop, fired at a ship commanded by Admiral Hobart Pasha, a British seaman in the Turkish service; the admiral demanded that the authorities of Syra (where the *Enosis* had taken refuge) should treat her as a pirate, and blockaded her in the harbour; whereupon the Greek government dispatched a corvette with orders to invite Hobart to raise the blockade, and, in case he persisted, to attack him. It has been suggested that in this affair there was collusion between the Greeks and the Turks; at any rate, the corvette returned to the Piræus, while Hobart remained outside Syra watching the *Enosis* for nearly six weeks, until the nomarch of the Cyclades had promised that she should be detained there until the legal proceedings against her were over. The blockade-runner was ere that harmless, for on December 26 the elder Petropoulákes, with 600 insurgents, had surrendered at Askýphon in Sphakía; the insurrection was obviously dying, unless a Greco-Turkish war reanimated it.

Meanwhile, at the proposal of Bismarck, a Conference of the signatory Powers of the treaty of Paris was held there on January 9, 1869, for the purpose of settling the Greco-Turkish dispute. Despite an initial difficulty, due to the claim of the Greek delegate, to whom had been accorded a merely consultative voice, to be placed on an equal footing with the Turkish representative, although Greece had not been a signatory of the historic treaty of 1856, Peter Deligiánnes submitted to the Conference a written statement, complaining of the dismemberment of the Hellenic race, and asking for the definite settlement of the Cretan question and the rectification of the land frontiers of the Greek kingdom. This radical solution had already been excluded, and the Conference, having persuaded the Turkish government to suspend its measures of expulsion, drew up a declaration on January 20, requesting Greece to abstain from tolerating the formation of armed bands on her territory and the equipment of armed vessels in her ports with a view to aggression against Turkey. The Turkish government agreed to this declaration, and Russia urged King George to accept it. At this juncture a Cabinet crisis at Athens brought Thrasýboulos Zaîmes into power; and Theodore Deligiánnes (the future Premier), his Foreign Minister, on February 6 adhered to the declaration, while proclaiming that the country was unprepared for war. Turkey then cancelled her hostile dispositions against Greek subjects, and diplomatic relations were resumed. The situation at Athens had been aggravated by a decree for the issue of treasury notes for £535,414—a measure which was withdrawn on condition that the National and Ionian Banks consented to a forced loan to the government of £756,000. The Cretan insurrection, now that all hope of Greek intervention had disappeared, died a natural death. Sphakianákes and Hajji Micháles held out for a little longer in the east, but in the spring the three years' struggle ended. A nominal amnesty was granted; a liberal governor-general, Mehemet Ali, the Prussian pasha afterwards murdered in Albania, was appointed; and for the next four years Crete slept the sleep of exhaustion.

CHAPTER XIV

THE ROUMANIAN AND SERVIAN QUESTIONS
(1862-75)

THE Cretan insurrection was not the only event which drew public attention to the east of Europe in 1866. The Roumanians did not long remain content with the native officer whom they had elected Prince of the united Principalities in 1859. Couza had succeeded in gaining the recognition of the Porte and the Powers; but he found it impossible to pacify the politicians of his own country. The Roumanian Assembly was the battle-ground of three parties—the Conservatives or "Whites," the Radicals or "Reds," and the Moderate Liberals, whose views coincided with those of the Prince. The country, a large proportion of whose inhabitants were peasants unable to read or write and totally ignorant of political questions, was unsuited for parliamentary government, which in practice degenerated into the "management" of elections by the party in power and the manufacture of disturbances by the party in opposition. Couza had been little more than a year on the throne when the "Reds" roused the people of Craïova and Ploeshti against the coalition government; in 1862 the land bill of the Conservative statesman, Barbe Catargi, based on the liberty alike of property and of labour, excited the violent opposition of the "Reds." The latter, conscious that they were in a minority in the Assembly, announced their intention of convening a mass-meeting on June 23, the anniversary of the revolution of 1848, in close proximity to the house of parliament. The government replied that it would prohibit the meeting; but the Premier, driving back from the Assembly, was shot by an assassin—a foreigner, it was said, hired by his enemies. The murderer has never been brought to justice; for when Constantine Rosetti and John Brătianu, the "Red" leaders, were haled before the police court, the former threatened the Prince that he would denounce the real culprit, unless the proceedings were stopped. Couza was never proved to have instigated the crime; but, in any case, he gave orders to hush up the enquiry. This interference with the course of justice failed, however, to remove the hostility of the "Reds." They accused the Prince of being a Russian agent, and thus discredited him in the eyes of the French, because he ordered the disarmament of Polish volunteers crossing his territory on their way to aid their insurgent fellow-countrymen during the Polish rising of 1863. In the same year a "monstrous coalition" of "Whites" and "Reds" was formed against the Prince's favourite minister, Kogălniceanu, and addressed a memorial to the Powers, praying for Couza's removal. The story is told that the Prince considered the memorial of so little importance as to subscribe towards the travelling expenses of the politician who was to be the bearer of it. But events proved that he had under-estimated the gravity of the campaign against him, not only in Paris, but also at home. His bold policy of reforms, while benefiting the peasantry, only exasperated the politicians.

Brief as was his reign, Couza's name is associated with three acts of the first importance—the secularisation of the monasteries, the agrarian law, and free education. The monastic question in Roumania had long exercised the ingenuity of native statesmen. The country was dotted over with numerous religious establishments, founded by the piety of former princes and nobles, who, in order to secure their endowments, had "dedicated" their foundations to the Holy Places of Jerusalem, to Mounts Athos and Sinai, and to other ecclesiastical

corporations dependent upon the Œcumenical Patriarchate. It
was calculated that one-fifth of the Roumanian soil, including
some of the most fertile districts, was the property of these
" dedicated " monasteries, whose surplus revenues went abroad
and whose abbots, being Greeks, were regarded as foreigners
by Roumanian nationalists. Accordingly, after the downfall
of Phanariote rule, successive efforts had been made to solve
this economic, ecclesiastical and national question. Gregory IV
Ghika had expelled the Greek abbots and assigned two years'
revenues of the Wallachian monasteries to pay the national
debt; the Porte, under Russian influence in 1827, had restored
the abbots, who successfully resisted the attempts of the
Russian organisers and of the native princes who followed to
compel them to devote a considerable proportion of their
income to the schools, hospitals and other public establishments
of the Principalities. Couza, after fruitless negotiations at
Constantinople and Bucharest, resolved to settle the matter
finally; and a decree of 1863 transformed nearly all the
monasteries into hospitals or prisons, expelled the abbots, and
secularised their property. By way of compensation, a lump
sum of £1,080,000 was set aside for the benefit of the Holy
Places, but by the authorities of those establishments indignantly
refused. The Orthodox Church was furious at what it considered to be an act of sacrilege and confiscation; and its
indignation was increased by the Prince's proposals for making
the Roumanian Synod more independent of the Œcumenical
throne.

The agrarian law, the second item in Couza's daring
programme, was greeted with a vote of censure. Thereupon,
the Prince, on May 14, 1864, ordered a battalion of infantry to
clear the hall in which the deputies were assembled, and
dissolved parliament. A proclamation justified this Cromwellian
coup d'état, and invited the people to choose by a *plébiscite*
between "the Elect of the Roumanians" and "a factious
oligarchy." The *plébiscite* by 682,621 votes against 1307 ratified

Couza's acts; and both the Porte and the ambassadors of the Powers were convinced by his arguments and his personal charm at Constantinople.   In accordance with what he interpreted as the popular wish, he "developed" the convention of Paris of 1858 into a new "Statute," or constitution, by the creation of a Senate largely nominated by himself, and of a Chamber elected by manhood suffrage.   In the then condition of Roumania, such an arrangement would have placed both branches of the legislature at the disposition of the Prince, for his prefects would take care that the peasants should vote for government candidates, while the nominated senators, having to retire by lot every two years, would likewise be his creatures. There was only one element in the state which could overthrow this benevolent autocracy—the army; and as soon as Couza lost its support, he fell.   Meanwhile, he strove to popularise his *coup d'état* by "the rural law" of 1864, which abolished forced labour, tithe, free transport of wood for the landlord, and similar feudal burdens, on payment of an annual sum to the state during a *maximum* of 15 years, and established a peasant proprietorship with a fixed rate of compensation to the former owners.   To prevent the Jews from acquiring the control of the peasants' holdings, these were declared inalienable, nor could they be mortgaged except at the end of 30 years.   Couza's land scheme was welcomed by the peasants, but it has had the defect of not providing for the growth of the peasants' families, for a plot of ground sufficient for one man has been found inadequate for his numerous offspring.   Moreover, despite repeated prohibitions, the small owner has evaded the provisions against sale and mortgage, so that Couza did not solve the most difficult Roumanian problem—that of the land.   Still his name has become legendary with the Danubian peasants, who long after his death expected his return to pacify their earth-hunger by a fresh distribution of estates.   A third law, establishing free education, nominally compulsory in its elementary stage, opened, six years before Forster's act in England, the path of civil and military employment to the peasants' sons. To this reform the growth of Roumanian democracy and of an intellectual proletariat is mainly due.

It was not to be expected that the politicians would quietly acquiesce in the *coup d'état*. A society was formed "for the defence of constitutional government"; and the leaders of the Opposition pledged themselves, "in case of a vacancy on the throne, to support by every means the election of a foreign prince belonging to one of the reigning families of the west." The "Reds," whose chiefs were Rosetti and Brătianu, sought to bring about the "vacancy" which they desired to see filled by a foreigner, and excited a rising in the capital during Couza's absence abroad in 1865. An amnesty was interpreted as an act of weakness by the Radicals; while the aristocracy, from which the politicians then mainly sprang, viewed with jealousy the "new man's" appointment of foreigners to well-paid posts and his adoption of two illegitimate sons whom he had had by a Roumanian lady, Princess Marie Obrenovich, the mother of the future King Milan of Servia. "Reds" and "Whites" thus sank their mutual differences in a common desire to rid themselves of the "tyrant," whose successor Brătianu set out to Paris to find. He had not long to seek, for the name of Prince Charles Lewis of Hohenzollern-Sigmaringen had already been suggested to Napoleon III by Mme Hortense Cornu, an intimate friend of both the French Emperor and the Hohenzollern family. While the "Red" leader prepared European opinion for the deposition of Couza by a pamphlet denouncing him as surrounded by Russian instruments, and thus played upon French suspicion of Russian designs in the east, the committee of Conservatives and Radicals, which had been formed to upset the throne, acted at Bucharest. A number of officers were induced to put their services at the disposal of the conspirators, who decided to dethrone Couza and proclaim the Count of Flanders, brother of Leopold II King of the Belgians, on the night when the chasseurs, Couza's favourite corps, were on guard at the palace, that is to say, on that of February 22, 1866. Early on the fatal evening the Prince was warned of the approaching revolution; but he paid no heed to the warning beyond informing the chief of police, who reported the city quiet. The Prince retired to rest, confident in his beloved chasseurs; but about four on the morning of the 23rd he was aroused by an officer of the guard, who, followed by other officers and some civilians, entered his bedroom. Seeing that the army had abandoned him, he signed a document abdicating, and "deposing the reins of government in the hands of a lieutenancy and of a ministry elected by the people." Having obtained his signature, the conspirators helped him to dress, and led him by a back-door to a house, where he remained a prisoner till the evening, when in a carriage with the blinds down he quitted his capital for ever. Couza never saw Roumania again, for his petition to be allowed to return as a private citizen in 1867 was refused; but seven years after his fall his remains were laid to rest in the soil, which he had striven to win for the peasant and of which he had been the first sole ruler. In 1912, amidst enormous enthusiasm, his successor unveiled his statue at Jassy. Of Couza it may be said, that the good which he did lives after him. Too late his public merits were appreciated, and, if his private life was not above reproach, the most recent Roumanian historian describes him as a "beneficent and noble autocrat."

The people of Bucharest accepted the revolution without protest. When they woke up in the morning, they found already installed a provisional government, composed of Lascar Catargi, a Conservative, Golescu, a Liberal, and Colonel Haralambie, representing the officers, while a new ministry promised them a foreign prince in the place of him who had "deceived their expectations." The same day Count Philip of Flanders was acclaimed Prince of Roumania. The Count, however, at once declined the difficult task of reigning over "the Belgium of the lower Danube"; and both the Porte and the Tsar protested against Couza's deposition. A conference of Turkey and the Powers accordingly met in Paris on March 10, in which the Turkish representative objected to both a foreign prince and an hereditary Hospodar. But the Powers deliberated slowly; and, while they were discussing the fate of Roumania, the question was settled outside the conference room by the irrevocable logic of facts. Brătianu proceeded to Düsseldorf, where the Prince of Hohenzollern-Sigmaringen then was, told him that Napoleon III had suggested the candidature, and offered the crown to his son. King William I of Prussia, as head of the family, was asked for his approval, which he was loth to give; but Bismarck, who saw that a Prussian beyond the Carpathians might be an embarrassment to Austria, advised Prince Charles "to go at once," for, argued the great statesman, "if you are once in Roumania, the question will be soon solved"; as for the Powers, they would protest, "but a protest exists only on paper." Bismarck added that there would not be "much to fear" from Austria, which would otherwise try to wreck his candidature, for he intended "to keep Austria occupied for some time to come"—an allusion to the impending Austro-Prussian war. Even in case of failure, he concluded, "you will always remember with pleasure a *coup* which can never be a reproach to you." Meanwhile, the candidature had become known in Roumania, where, despite a separatist riot at Jassy, which had suffered economically by the union, a *plébiscite* on April 20 adopted Prince Charles by 685,969 to 224 votes. The conference declined to accept this decision, because it had already adopted a motion to the effect that the future Prince must be a native and elected by the Assembly,— the Constituent Assembly did, indeed, ratify the result of the popular vote. Furnished, however, with leave of absence from his military duties as lieutenant in the Prussian dragoons, Prince Charles travelled under the name of "Hettingen" and on the pretext of business at Odessa, to the Hungarian port of Báziás on the Danube, in whose modest inn he overheard his fellow-guests discussing the probable failure of his mission and prophesying for him the fate of Couza. Here he was joined by Brătianu, but it was not till he first set foot on Roumanian soil at Turnu-Severin on May 20 that his future Premier publicly recognised in the spectacled second-class passenger by the Danube boat the Prince of Roumania. Fifteen days later the conference separated without having arrived at any decision, after both the British and French delegates had opposed coercive measures. Clarendon, then our Foreign Minister, suggested that it might be wiser for the Porte to recognise Prince Charles, provided he paid homage to the Sultan, than to have a Russian intervention. The Cretan insurrection happily divided the attention of the Turks, who contented themselves with massing troops at Rustchuk; the outbreak of the Austro-Prussian war prevented, as Bismarck had predicted, the Austrian schemes; indeed Magyar and Servian emissaries tried to persuade Prince Charles to create a diversion against the Austrians; Sardinia, as the ally of Prussia against Austria, favoured a Prussian prince; while Napoleon III looked with satisfaction on one who was connected through his mother with the Imperial family of France. To the Roumanian politicians the liberal tendencies displayed by his father when Prussian Premier were a further recommendation.

The new Prince's position was not, however, easy. He found himself practically alone among a people of whose language and customs he was ignorant, whose finances were in a desperate condition, whose officials had been mostly unpaid for months. First appearances were not encouraging; the Roumanian soldiers made a bad impression on the prim Prussian officer, who realised that with such material he could not fight Austria; there was not a mile of railway, and not many roads, in the whole country; the streets of the capital were a "bottomless morass"; he could scarcely believe that a one-storied building looking out on a dirty square was the "palace." Still, he was young—27 years old at the time—he was hopeful, he was a Hohenzollern, and he surmounted all his difficulties.

The first problem that awaited solution was the passing of the new constitution, for which a Constituent Assembly had been elected by the provisional government. The two most salient features of the charter of 1866 were the Prince's right of absolute veto, upon which he insisted, and the famous article 7, which provided that "foreigners of Christian denominations can alone obtain naturalisation." Brătianu and Rosetti, the two Radical members of the Prince's first Cabinet, which was composed of both "Whites" and "Reds," had proposed that "religion is no obstacle to naturalisation in Roumania," and had promised a special law for the naturalisation of the Jews. This proposal aroused a storm of indignation among the Moldave deputies. An anti-Semite editor roused the rabble of Bucharest against the ministry; the synagogue of the capital was destroyed; and article 7 was substituted for the original draft. Thus early in his reign Prince Charles had proof of the feeling against the Jews in Moldavia. His reconstruction of the synagogue out of his privy purse did not satisfy the powerful Jewish communities of western Europe. In 1867, Brătianu, abandoning his tolerant policy in order to win Moldave support for the reorganisation of the army, revived the Russian regulation against Jewish publicans and leaseholders, thus calling down upon his head the remonstrances of the British and French governments. A year later 31 Moldave deputies introduced a still stronger measure against the Jews, absolutely prohibiting their residence outside the towns, their acquisition of real property, and their acceptance of national or municipal contracts. The expulsion of the Jewish publicans began; anti-Semite riots followed; Sir Moses Montefiore visited Bucharest; and the British government twice—in 1868 and 1872—accused Roumania of violating article 46 of the convention of Paris, which had declared "all Moldaves and Wallachs equal before the law." As the Prince's father wrote, "the Jewish question is a *noli me tangere*, for the Jews have money and the whole press." Ten years afterwards the treaty of Berlin again impressed this hard fact upon the Roumans.

The constitution settled, the next question was the recognition of the Prince by his suzerain. To a Hohenzollern the notion of vassalage was peculiarly repulsive; indeed, the existence of such a bond had been one of the reasons for which King William had objected to his relative's acceptance of the throne. But, while already determined to sever the last link that bound him to Turkey at the first favourable opportunity, the Prince had meanwhile to eat his leek. Thanks to the influence of John Ghika, who, as a former Prince of Samos, was popular at Constantinople, the Sultan was induced to receive him; and during the audience the proud vassal contrived so to comport himself as to save his own dignity while conveying to his suzerain that the days of Phanariote humility were over. On October 24 he received the firman of investiture, which recognised him as Hereditary Prince of "the United Principalities," as the Turks were still pleased to style Roumania, with the right of a separate currency but without that of making separate treaties or of conferring decorations; the annual tribute was to be increased; the army not to exceed 30,000 men. Six months had thus sufficed to regulate the Prince's anomalous position.

In his adopted country however, his situation was long uncertain. Although the former Hospodars, Bibescu, Michael Sturdza, and Stirbeiu, acknowledged him, his first general election showed that the Couzist and Separatist party was still strong in Moldavia, for one-third of the new members was chosen on that programme. Already a deputation of officers had put his tact to the proof, by begging him to dismiss for a breach of discipline their comrades who had deposed his predecessor. In 1870 Couza was elected to the Chamber, and the French government offered him its assistance in recovering his throne—an offer which the patriotic Rouman haughtily declined, refusing to owe his restoration to foreign intervention.

Napoleon III had speedily repented the part which he had played in placing a Prussian prince on the lower Danube. The victory of the Prussians at Sadowa had revealed to him the growing power of his future adversary; the Prussianising of the Roumanian army, the organisation of which had hitherto been confided to a French military mission, convinced him that French influence over "the little Latin sister" in the east was waning. In the meeting which he had in 1867 at Salzburg with the Emperor of Austria, the idea, suggested immediately after the fall of Couza by Nigra, the Italian representative in Paris, that Austria should be compensated for the loss of Venice by the occupation of Roumania, was revived. Accordingly, on the advice of Bismarck, the Prince drew close to Russia, and endeavoured to assuage the alarm felt in Hungary at the Roumanian propaganda there. This change of foreign policy lost him the support of the "Reds," who represented him as Bismarck's agent, ready to sacrifice the interests of his adopted to those of his native country. His marriage in 1869 with Princess Elizabeth of Wied temporarily restored his popularity; but riots broke out at the "exclusively Red" commercial town of Ploeshti, and a conspiracy was discovered, in which the national guard was involved. At this moment the outbreak of the Franco-Prussian war, arising out of the candidature of the Prince's brother for the Spanish crown, rendered the situation still more critical. The sympathies of the Roumans and their foreign Prince were diametrically opposed; they, as Latins, naturally hoped for the success of the French; he, as a former Prussian officer, was heart and soul with his old comrades of the Danish war.

The French government avowed its intention of treating him as an enemy; his own Minister of Foreign Affairs declared that Roumanian interests and sympathies were with the French colours. The "Reds" only awaited the news of a Prussian defeat to proclaim the republic at Ploeshti. But the tidings of the Prussian victories, the arrest of the "Red" leaders, and the birth of a princess somewhat calmed the agitation. The conspirators, however, were acquitted; and the scandals arising out of the concession of the contract for the Roumanian railways to Strousberg, a Prussian, caused a fresh outcry against the Prussian Prince. It had been his object from the first, as he himself wrote, to develop "the material welfare of these richly-endowed lands"; and he had "taken as the basis" for this work "the construction of a network of roads and railways[1]." Accordingly, he had entered with perhaps too much zeal and too little knowledge of financial and technical details into the schemes of the Prussian railway-king, whose refusal to pay the coupon of January 1871 was a blow alike to the shareholders, who were mostly Prussians, induced to invest in the stock on the security offered by the presence of a Prussian ruler at Bucharest, and to the Prince, whose government was requested by Bismarck to pay the interest in lieu of the defaulting contractor. The fact that the Roumanian railway commissioner, appointed by the Prince, had formerly been in the service of the Hohenzollern family, was interpreted by the Opposition as a proof of jobbery; and the Prince, who had already expressed in a circular to the Powers his inability to cope with party passion any longer, poured forth the bitterness of his soul in a letter to a correspondent, published in a German journal. A leading Roumanian statesman declared that at that moment the Prince had "no one in the country for him," while the British ambassador at Constantinople began already to talk of a Turkish commission to the United Principalities. The climax was reached on March 22, 1871, when the German colony in Bucharest, assembled at a banquet under the chairmanship of the North-German consul-general to celebrate the Emperor's birthday, was bombarded with stones by the mob while the police looked on complacently. Next morning the Prince sent for the two members of the provisional government of 1866 who were then in the capital, and informed them that

---

[1] *Aus dem Leben*, ii, 270.

he wished to hand back to them the authority which he had received five years earlier. Lascar Catargi, one of the two, implored him to think of the country, and undertook the responsibility of forming a Cabinet. The Prince consented; and at midnight the Conservative chief was able to announce the formation of a ministry of resolute men, which remained in power for five years—a thing till then unknown in Roumanian public life. The recalcitrant Chamber was dissolved; a docile majority was obtained in the new legislature by "moral suasion" at the elections; and Rosetti, the editor of the anti-dynastic *Romanul*, finding an agitator's occupation gone, left for France, the haven of all Roumanian politicians out of work, whether deposed princes or uncrowned demagogues. The crisis was over, and the Prince noted with pleasure that his strongest supporters were precisely those who had supported his predecessor—men of principle, who believed in the stability which monarchy affords, even irrespective of the person of the monarch. His chief embarrassment was now his former friend Bismarck, whose appeal to the Porte to force its vassal to settle the claims of the Prussian shareholders, by wounding Roumanian national feeling in its most sensitive spot, only increased the bitterness against the Prussians; but an arrangement was made through Austrian mediation. This step marked the beginning of better relations with the Dual Monarchy, of which a commercial treaty signed in 1875, the centenary of Austria's annexation of the Roumanian Bukovina, was the first fruit. This act, however, offended both the Porte, which declined to recognise the claim of its vassal to conclude international treaties, and the coalition of the Opposition leaders, some violently opposed to Austria-Hungary, all eager for office after five years in the wilderness. Once more, the throne was attacked; and rumour was busy with the name of a Colonel Dabija, to whom the crown had been offered. Then came the revolution in the Herzegovina and therewith the revival of the eastern question, which was destined to make Roumania an independent kingdom.

The neighbouring principality of Servia, whose friendship Prince Charles was careful to cultivate, had already made an important advance on the same road. Prince Michael's object was to obtain the withdrawal of the Turkish garrisons from the fortresses in Servia, which they still occupied after the settlement of 1862. While he devoted his energies at home to the improvement of his army, his wife, Princess Julia, and Philip Christich were sent to London to influence British opinion, hitherto ill-disposed towards Servia. Favourable speeches in parliament by Cobden and Gregory, a member much interested in the eastern question, and an attack upon Michael by the *Morning Post* drew attention to the Servian question, and a subsequent mission of the Servian diplomatist, Marinkovich, elicited from Clarendon the admission, that the British government would have no objection to see the remaining fortresses in Servian hands, provided that the Porte consented. The decline of Austrian influence owing to the Prussian victory of 1866 and the Cretan insurrection were favourable to Servia, as to Roumania; and a correspondence took place between Ristich and Koumoundoûros on the subject of a Serbo-Greek alliance. Although neither King George nor the Boúlgares ministry considered an alliance desirable, the possibility of such a general rising of the Balkan peoples as it would have provoked so greatly alarmed Russia and France that they prevailed upon Austria and Great Britain to support Michael's request for the evacuation of the remaining fortresses. The decision, as in most Servian questions, really depended upon Austria; and Beust, who then directed her policy, found, in his anxiety to give her repose after her recent defeat at Sadowa, that Belgrade in Servian hands would not be a menace to her interests. Michael assured the Porte that a contented Servia would be a better defence to the Turkish empire than the fortresses on the Save and on the Danube; Stanley argued, erroneously as subsequent history has shown, that a free Servia would probably care but little how the Bosniaks or Bulgars were governed; he added that Turkish honour might be salved by the maintenance of the Turkish flag on the walls of Belgrade. Thus abandoned by Austria and Great Britain, the Porte yielded, and on March 3, 1867, expressed its willingness to "confide the guard of the fortresses" to Michael, completely withdrawing the Mussulman garrisons, on condition that the Turkish and Servian colours should wave together from the ramparts.   Michael then visited his suzerain; on April 18 the keys of the fortresses were handed to the Servian authorities; and on May 6 the last Turkish soldier quitted Servian soil. Even externally, save for its one mosque, Belgrade is no longer a Turkish town; even the Constantinople gate has been destroyed since 1867.

Michael's moderation had rendered a signal service to his country, but he had failed to content the rasher politicians who dreamt, like Garashanin, of a Balkan confederation, and regarded his journey to Constantinople as an act of servility. Great projects were in the air of Belgrade; the Mohammedan Serbs of Bosnia offered their neutrality, in case the Servian army should enter their country, if their lands and faith were respected; Michael visited Roumania, and signed treaties of alliance with Prince Charles and Prince Nicholas of Montenegro; a pact was made with the Bulgarian committee, whose seat was Bucharest, for the resurrection of a Bulgarian state. The dismissal of Garashanin indicated, however, that Michael was not disposed to go so far as his Prime Minister wished in foreign policy, while his internal administration was too autocratic for the admirers of parliamentary institutions, who clamoured for a modern constitution.   Their opposition to him was focussed by the *Omladina* ("Youth"), a secret society, originally founded for literary objects by a body of Servian students at Pressburg, which advocated the union and independence of the Servian nation, and carried on from Neusatz in southern Hungary a journalistic propaganda, all the more vehement after the prohibition of its meeting in Belgrade in 1867.   To these enemies was added the exiled dynasty, living and plotting in the neighbouring Dual Monarchy against a prince, who, like Couza in Roumania and Otho in Greece, had no legitimate heir of his body. Anxious to provide for this contingency, Michael, who had separated from his gifted consort, meditated a second marriage with his cousin Catherine Constantinovich. While walking with that lady and her mother Anka in the park of Toptchider on June 10, 1868, where three years before he had celebrated the jubilee of Takovo, three men fired at him and his companions. Michael fell dead upon the ground, Anka was killed, her daughter wounded. The actual assassins, criminals from the neighbouring prison, were only the tools of more influential persons. Public opinion held the Karageorgevich family responsible for this brutal murder of the best ruler that modern Servia has yet had ; the public prosecutor accused Alexander, the politicians his more ambitious wife, Persida, acting, it was supposed, in the interest of her son Peter, the subsequent King of Servia. Others believed that Radovanovich, Alexander's business manager in Belgrade, planned the deed, hoping by means of a draft constitution, compiled by himself and signed by Prince Peter, to become the power behind the young pretender's throne, and thence distribute the spoils to his own family and friends. The plot was, however, only half successful. The ex-Premier, Garashanin, who chanced to be taking the air at Toptchider, was attracted by the cries of Michael's attendant, and hastened with great presence of mind to the city to warn the authorities. On the way he came up with a carriage, the pace and inmate of which aroused his suspicions. By ordering his arrest, he prevented communication between the murderers and their confederates in Belgrade. The Ministry and the Senate at once met, and a provisional government was formed, consisting of Marinkovich, the President of the Senate, Leshjanin, the Minister of Justice, and Petrovich, the President of the Appeal Court. They acted with promptitude and energy, arrested Radovanovich, summoned a Grand *Skupshtina*, and sent Ristich, then Minister of the Interior, to

fetch the late Prince's next-of-kin, Milan, from Paris, where he
was studying.   It was rumoured at first that Michael had left
his natural son Velimir his heir, and the Dowager Princess
once thought of adopting him and playing the part of Regent;
but, as no will was forthcoming, the crown passed to Michael's
cousin, then not yet 14 years old.   Consequently, the Grand
Skupshtina, a practical body, whose 523 members included
only one lawyer, proclaimed Milan Obrenovich IV, and elected
three Regents—Colonel Blaznavatz, Minister of War, Ristich,
and Gavrilovich, a Senator and geographer—for three years,
with a further extension of their Regency in case of need.   A
Liberal Cabinet was formed; the Regents declared that they
would keep Michael's maxim "the law is the highest will in
Servia"; and it was arranged that a *Skupshtina* should meet
annually.   The assassins were tried; 13 persons were shot as
principals or accomplices; and Alexander Karageorgevich,
acquitted by an Austrian court, was sentenced in default by a
Servian tribunal, and he and his family were forbidden to enter
Servian territory.   Alexander died an exile in 1885, and it was
only after a still more awful tragedy, enacted on the 35th
anniversary of Michael's murder, that his son mounted the
blood-stained throne of the last Obrenovich.   Happily a new
pretender did not arise in the person of Michael's bastard, who
lived and died an artist in Bavaria.

The murdered Prince had been considering the desirability
of granting a larger measure of liberty to his people; and the
Regency, despite a law forbidding all modification of the
existing form of government during a minority, accordingly
produced a constitution in 1869, which remained in force for
the next 20 years.   The single chamber, or *Skupshtina*,—for
Ristich confessed that he could find no elements for a second
—was to be three-quarters elective, and one-quarter nominated.
Not only officials but also lawyers were declared ineligible
(just as they were excluded from the "unlearned parliament"
of our Henry IV), but the Prince could nominate any Serb of

30 years of age, who paid 30 *dinara* in direct taxes. This assembly could be convoked where, and dissolved when, the Prince chose; and its members had no right to initiate legislation. As the government could, and often did, suspend acts dealing with the liberty of the subject, of speech, and of the press, in case of danger, the constitution of 1869 has been described as "a thinly-veiled autocracy," against which the Radicals, first organised in 1881, began at once to agitate. A national currency removed the previous confusion of foreign coinage; Ministerial responsibility was established; and the Regency devoted much attention to internal politics during the lull in the eastern question. The three Regents, representing what were called in Servia "Liberal," but what we should consider as moderate Conservative, principles, remained in power till, on August 22, 1872, Milan came of age, and assumed the reins of government.

Milan possessed excellent natural abilities, but his birth and education did not promise well for his reign. His father had died at 33 of the fast life which he had led in Vienna; his mother, a Catargi, had been Couza's mistress, and had been found in the palace at Bucharest on the night of the Roumanian Prince's deposition. A Parisian education is not the best moral tonic for a Balkan heir; and the royal pupil once remarked, that if he was what he was, his Regents and Ministers had only themselves to blame. Brought to the corrupt atmosphere of Belgrade at an age when most boys are at school, isolated in the palace without brothers, sisters, or playmates of his own age, early initiated into the arts of intrigue, and taught to believe that most things can be had for money, he came to be regarded as the type of the man of pleasure. Visits to Vienna and Paris soon after his accession turned his head; he, too, desired in little Servia to repeat the luxury of the Austrian and French capitals, with the natural result that within three years of his majority he was loaded with debts; and such was his unpopularity at Belgrade, that a strong party desired the candidature for the Servian throne of that far wiser and more serious ruler of the sister-state, Nicholas of Montenegro. Meanwhile, the intrigues of the exiled dynasty and the jealousy of the family of Garashanin, always envious of the Obrenovich clan, to which it had hoped to provide a successor in Ilija's son, Milutin, rendered Milan's position still more difficult, until, when the great Balkan crisis began in 1875, competent observers saw that there were only two courses before him—war or revolution.

CHAPTER XV

THE BULGARIAN EXARCHATE (1870–5).

HITHERTO the history of the Balkan peninsula during the nineteenth century had been occupied with the formation and development of Servian, Greek, and Roumanian states out of the Ottoman empire, and with the struggles of the Montenegrins to maintain their freedom. Now, however, under the influence of Russia, a long-forgotten, silent nationality, destined to play an important part in the events of the last third of the century, sprang into independent ecclesiastical existence—the prelude of its resurrection, after the lapse of nearly five centuries, as a Balkan state.

Despite the literary efforts of Bulgarian patriots, such as the historian Paysij of Samokov and his disciple, Sofronij, bishop of Vratza, author of the first printed book in modern Bulgarian, the stolid Bulgars had remained comparatively unmoved by the stirring events of which their own and the neighbouring lands had been the theatre. They lacked local leaders, such as the Serbs and Greeks possessed; their ecclesiastical authorities belonged to a foreign race; their practical experience of warfare was small. They took little part in the Russo-Turkish war of 1806–12; but in 1821, instigated by the Greek clergy, many of them had enlisted with the Hetairists in Wallachia, and subsequently others had aided the Greeks in Greece. The Russo-Turkish war of 1828–9 aroused their active sympathy to a greater degree than its predecessor. A captain of volunteers, Mamartchov of Kotel—

the town which, from Sofronij downwards, has given so many
patriots to Bulgaria—believing that the hour of his country's
redemption had struck, called his fellow-townsmen to arms,
but was arrested by Cossacks while attempting to unfurl the
banner of a free Bulgaria at Trnovo, the medieval capital.
A deputation to Diebich found the treaty of Adrianople
already signed; the permission to emigrate to Bessarabia,
Wallachia and Moldavia, the institution of a Russian consulate
at Sliven, and the maintenance of a Russian garrison at
Silistria till the payment of the war indemnity in 1836, were all
the advantages that the Bulgars reaped from this struggle in
their midst. Russia had clearly shown that she did not desire
an independent Bulgaria; the people of Sliven soon expressed
their dislike of the Russian consul's patronage; but a British
visitor to Sliven and Kotel had foreshadowed the later policy
of Lord Salisbury two generations afterwards—that it was the
interest of Britain to create a Bulgarian buffer-state between
Russia and Turkey. Between the peace of Adrianople and
the epoch of the Crimean war a few isolated and local risings
alone broke the quiet of the land. In 1836 the energetic
Mamartchov, who had meanwhile held a post under the
Russians at Silistria, planned an insurrection at the monastery
of Kapinovo; but the secret was betrayed to the Greek
Metropolitan of Trnovo, who informed the Turkish commander in time to seize the conspirators. Some were executed,
Mamartchov exiled. Five years later the oppression of the
tax-collectors aroused a rebellion of the Bulgars on the Servian
frontier; Europe received through a French emissary a foretaste of the " Bulgarian atrocities " of 1876; but the change of
dynasty in Servia prevented an extension of the movement.
Similar exactions produced in 1851 a rising in the district of
Vidin. Unprovided with firearms—for Alexander Karageorgevich prevented their importation from his adjacent principality—the insurgents nevertheless attacked the strong natural
fortress of Belogradtchik, only to be repulsed. More massacres

followed, but this hopeless insurrection, the most serious that had occurred, convinced Turkish statesmen of the desirability of making some concessions to this hitherto unrecognised nationality.

A powerful agency of nationalism had begun to exert its influence over the Bulgars. The perusal of a book on "The old and new Bulgarians" by the Slavonic scholar Venelin inspired Aprilov, a merchant of Gabrovo, to found in 1835 the first purely Bulgarian school at that flourishing little town, whose traders were the first Bulgars to do business with Russia. The Bell-Lancaster system was adopted; the school-books were printed in Servia; and ten years later 53 Bulgarian schools were already at work. Well might the Bulgarian colony at Odessa inscribe upon the tomb of Venelin the sentence, that he had "recalled to memory the forgotten, but once famous and mighty people of the Bulgars." The first national school was followed in 1844 by the first national periodical, published at Smyrna; but books and newspapers continued to be printed abroad, for down to 1877 what is now Bulgaria contained only one printing-press. Nevertheless, such was the zeal of the Bulgars for education, that books and schools prepared them to become ecclesiastically independent of the Greek Patriarchate and politically independent of the Turkish empire.

The former of these two movements began with the demand for national bishops; and its first success, due to the Archimandrite Neofyt Bozveli and to Stephen Vogorídes, the first prince of Samos, both natives of Kotel, the cradle of the Bulgarian nationalist movement, was the erection of the first Bulgarian church at Constantinople in 1848. The next step was the omission of the Patriarch's name from the prayers in this church—an example speedily followed throughout Bulgarian lands, where the demand for separation from the Patriarchate became so general that the Grand Vizier was ordered by Abdul Mejid to hear on the spot the complaints of the Bulgarian peasants. Meanwhile others, taught by the

failures of the Russians during the war in Bulgaria and in the
Crimea, turned their eyes towards Rome, just as the Bulgarian
Tsars had done in the thirteenth century, and for a similar
reason. Dragan Zankov, the literary leader of this party,
pleaded in his journal *Bulgaria* for union with the Roman
Catholic Church, in the hope of obtaining thereby the protection
of France, traditionally extended to the Eastern Catholics.
Zankov proceeded to Rome at the head of a deputation ; and
in 1861 Pius IX consecrated Sokolski, an ex-brigand turned
monk, Archbishop of the Bulgarian Uniate Church. It was,
however, at once evident that comparatively few Bulgars
thought French protection worth a mass ; Sokolski mysteriously
disappeared to Russia ; and the plan of including the Bulgarian
people within the papal fold remained unrealised. Still, the
Œcumenical Patriarch was seriously alarmed by these movements. While rejecting the Bulgarian demands—the so-called
"seven points"—for a national hierarchy and ecclesiastical
autonomy under an elected archbishop, who should acknowledge his supremacy, the Patriarch was willing to appoint
Bulgarians or at least Bulgarian-speaking bishops in purely
Bulgarian dioceses, and to make other concessions. These
the Bulgars rejected ; eight more "points" were presented,
and refused ; the demands of the Bulgars rose ; they declined
to accept the Patriarch's offer of a semi-independent "Exarchate of all Bulgaria" beyond the Balkans, made to them
under the influence of the Cretan insurrection in 1866 ;
nothing would content them but an independent national
Church, not limited to the district between the Balkans and
the Danube.

Besides the Greek bishops and the Turkish pashas, two
other elements combined to spread discontent among the
Bulgarian peasants during the early sixties. In 1861 some of
the richest villages were assigned to 12,000 Tartars, who had
emigrated from the Crimea. It was not the first time that
Tartars had settled in the Balkan peninsula ; the Thracian town

of Tatar-Pazardjik still preserves the name of its founders; the Balkan village of Vrbitza had been colonised by another band of emigrants from the Crimea. Encouraged by the Turkish government for political reasons, the newcomers were a fresh burden to the peasants, who had to yield up to them the best portions of their fields and to build houses for them without payment. Lured by Russian promises, 10,000 disgusted Bulgars emigrated to occupy the sites which the Tartars had abandoned, only to return disillusioned the following year. But the Crim Tartars were, at least, mild and laborious; whereas the second batch of immigrants, the Circassians, who arrived in 1864 after the Russian conquest of their native mountains, were a terror to the natives, once again forced to build houses and relinquish land for the use of their unwelcome guests. Nature, however, came to the aid of the Bulgars. While there are still Tartars in Bulgaria, the Circassians in 14 years had almost entirely disappeared; disease, war, and emigration account for the fact that of the 40,000 families which entered Bulgarian districts, nearly all have vanished. But such immigrations, supervening upon the ecclesiastical difficulty, naturally provided material for patriotic agitators. In 1862, excited further by the bombardment of Belgrade, where the Bulgarian journalist Rakovski organised a legion of his fellow-countrymen, and by the warlike movements in Montenegro and the Herzegovina, a band of political brigands under Panajot Hitov held the Shipka pass. Like the great klephtic leader of the Greek War of Independence, Hitov has left memoirs of his adventures, which were, however, cut short by the arrangement of the Serbo-Turkish differences.

In 1864, the Turkish empire was divided administratively into 28 *vilâyets*. Consequently, the creation of one great *vilâyet* of the Danube out of the previous small pashaliks, and the appointment of Midhat Pasha as governor with residence at his native town of Rustchuk, which thenceforth remained the seat of the Turkish administration, were real boons to the

Bulgars. Midhat's governorship, which lasted for four years, was undoubtedly a great success. There has, perhaps, been no period in the Turkish history of that troublesome region when so much was done for the development of its natural resources; but free Bulgaria has achieved, during its 44 years of practical independence, far more than even the most enlightened of modern Turkish statesmen could accomplish. So far as the Balkan provinces of Turkey were concerned, Midhat came too late to save them for the Turkish empire; but it is not so much good laws, as good, honest administration such as was his in the Balkans, such as was Rustem's in the Lebanon, that Turkey wants.   Under him the "model *vilâyet*" of the empire was that of the Danube. He made military roads; he saw an English company construct the first railway in Bulgaria from Rustchuk to the port of Varna, which thus became the link between Constantinople and the west; he began another line, intended to connect Plevna with the Danube; he built the great bridge of Bela over the Yantra; he began the quay at Rustchuk, founded an orphanage at Sofia, a school at Shumla, a hospital at Plevna and a town at Orchanieh. A service of diligences and an establishment of fire-engines were due to his initiative; he created savings-banks and tried to improve the system of agriculture; in fact the traveller Kanitz found that, wherever he went, such progress as he saw was the work of Midhat.   But the "Pasha of the Giaours" was not content with material progress alone. He treated the Christians as human beings; he made a serious attempt to realise the promises contained in the *Hatti-Humayûn* of 1856; his police no longer insulted the Bulgars; his officials were sometimes natives. Thirty years earlier, when, in 1837, the reforming Sultan Mahmûd II had made a royal progress through Bulgaria, the timid Christians, whom he had come to benefit, had bowed their heads to the ground at the passage of the Great Lord, upon whose face it was not meet for them to look   But if Midhat knew how to treat the Bulgars as men, he knew also how to treat them as rebels.

Since the time of the Crimean war a number of Bulgarian exiles, discontented with the small prospects which the Turkish rule offered to educated men in their own country, had emigrated to Bucharest. The emigrants were divided into two camps, the "old" Bulgars—men of some substance who intrigued with Russia and were called "Christian Turks" by their opponents—and the "young"—mostly students, who preferred the programme of the Servian *Omladina* and the methods of conspirators, and were despised as "vagabonds" in the "old" Bulgarian press. While some advocated a South Slavonic federation with Servia, the "Secret Bulgarian Central Committee," influenced by the Austro-Hungarian *Ausgleich* of 1867, sent a memorial to the Sultan, begging him to assume the medieval title of "Tsar of the Bulgarians," to grant Bulgaria a constitution, and to establish a Turco-Bulgarian Dual Monarchy. Meanwhile, the party of action among the emigrants raised the ancient lion-standard of Bulgaria on Bulgarian soil. In 1867 two small bands under Panajot Hitov and Totjov crossed the Danube; but the coldly calculating peasants showed no belief in the success of this movement, which was suppressed with extreme severity. A few survivors cut their way over the Servian frontier; a bloody assize was held at Svishtov; but Midhat's temerity in shooting two passengers on an Austrian steamer, accused of complicity, led to the protests of the Powers and his recall. The Porte was not sorry for an excuse for removing so independent a governor, while the Christians saw with mixed feelings the departure of one who had been the greatest supporter of their material interests, yet at the same time the strongest opponent of their national aspirations. Five successive governors ruled over the province during the next six years, of whom one alone attempted to continue the work of Midhat. A second revolutionary movement, the product of Michael Obrenovich's plans for a general Slavonic rising, was not checked by the Prince's assassination. The Servian Regency, occupied with domestic politics, vainly strove to restrain the Bulgarian emigrants at Bucharest; a band of well-drilled volunteers again unfurled the lion-banner between the Danube and the Balkans ; and, though they were almost annihilated, their bravery impressed both Turks and Christians alike. Among those inspired by their fate to work out the salvation of his country was the future Prime Minister of Bulgaria, Stambulov, then a lad at Trnovo.

The Cretan insurrection and the hostility of Greece made Turkish statesmen adopt the advice, given by Fuad Pasha in his political testament, " to isolate the Greeks as much as possible from other Christians," and "to withdraw the Bulgarians from the domination of the Greek Church." Aali Pasha, fresh from Crete, supported the opinion of Fuad ; Ignatyeff, the Russian ambassador at Constantinople, advocated the foundation of a separate Bulgarian Church in the interest of Panslavism. The Patriarch, when pressed, referred the Turkish Ministers to the Canons of the Church ; the Turks, invited to decide a nice point of Christian theology, preferred to consider arguments of statecraft. On March 11, 1870, a firman created a Bulgarian Exarchate, comprising the whole *vilâyet* of the Danube, except notoriously non-Bulgarian towns and villages such as Varna, but including the now Servian towns of Nish and Pirot. The firman further stated that other places might pass under the authority of the Exarch, if two-thirds of their inhabitants so desired. The Exarch was to obtain a *berat* from the Sultan, to mention the name of the Patriarch in his prayers, and to receive from him the holy oil. Both races at once saw the importance of this act, which laid the foundations of a new power in the east; Christian and Greek were thenceforth no longer synonymous in European Turkey. The Bulgars thanked Aali for his boon; the Patriarchate struggled against the execution of the firman,

and succeeded in postponing for two years the appointment of the first Bulgarian Exarch. Then, finding further
resistance impossible, the Patriarch excommunicated the
Exarch and his clergy as schismatic. From that moment
there was war to the knife between Patriarchists and Exarchists ; and Macedonia became the battle-field of the rival Greek
and Bulgarian propaganda. Bishoprics became pawns in the
political struggle, and peasants killed each other in the name
of contending ecclesiastical establishments. The Bulgarian
Exarchate had brought not peace, but a sword. The Exarchs
since 1872 have resided at neither Trnovo, the seat of the
medieval Patriarchs, nor at Sofia, the modern capital, but
at Constantinople, thus accentuating their claim to ecclesiastical
jurisdiction over the "unredeemed" Bulgars of the Turkish
empire.

The creation of the Exarchate did not pacify the Bulgarian
revolutionists of Bucharest, whose leaders were, since the
death of Rakovski, the ex-deacon Vasil Levski and the novelist
Ljuben Karavelov, whose motto was that Bulgaria must free
herself, and that what she wanted was not an Exarch but a
leader of insurgents. In 1870 a secret congress, held in
Bucharest, drew up a programme for the liberation of the
Bulgarians by a revolution, which was to be directed not
against the Turks as such, but only against the Turkish
government ; alliances were to be made with the other Balkan
states ; local committees were formed in Bulgaria, which
"Apostles," headed by Levski, traversed in all directions.
This organisation, which recalls the Greek "Friendly Society,"
spread rapidly ; numbers of peasants and small tradesmen were
initiated ; and all went well till a cosmopolitan adventurer, who
had joined the society, fatally compromised it by an act of
brigandage, committed on a Turkish convoy. The authorities
discovered that the criminals were not only highwaymen but
conspirators ; Levski was wounded and taken ; on the spot,
where he was hanged at Sofia, his monument now stands.

Karavelov's complicity was discovered, and his expulsion from Roumania demanded by the Turkish government. Accused of malversation by his younger comrades, he abandoned revolutionary journalism for literature.

Russia obtained another diplomatic triumph besides the creation of the Bulgarian Exarchate in 1870. Availing himself of the Franco-German war and of the consequent inability of the French to offer opposition, Gortchakoff announced in a circular of October 31, that Russia would no longer be bound by the Black Sea clauses of the treaty of Paris. Earl Granville, then our Foreign Secretary, pointed out that one party to a treaty could not declare its conditions to be no longer binding without the consent of the other parties. This high-handed action on the part of Russia provoked much indignation, especially in the United Kingdom, where the memories of the Crimea were still green ; and it was felt that Gortchakoff would not have thus defied Europe, if he had not assured himself of the support of Bismarck. For the sake of form, the Prussian statesman proposed a conference, which met in London in January 1871, and at which all the signatory Powers of the treaty of Paris were represented, except France. The articles of that treaty regarding the neutralisation of the Black Sea were abrogated ; the Sultan was allowed to open the Dardanelles and the Bosphorus in time of peace to the fleets of his friends and allies ; the European Commission of the Danube was prolonged for 12 years, and the works already created there were neutralised, subject to the right of the Porte to send vessels of war into the river. Thus the audacity of Gortchakoff, aided by circumstances, was successful ; the last benefit to Great Britain from the Crimean war was lost only 15 years after that costly conflict had closed ; while in 1911 another signatory Power of the treaty of Paris might have cited Gortchakoff's circular as a precedent for declaring that she, too, was no longer bound by that instrument.

The creation of the Bulgarian Exarchate was not the only

misfortune which befell the Greeks in 1870--a year full of import for eastern as for western Europe. On April 11 a party consisting of Lord and Lady Muncaster, Mr and Mrs Lloyd and their child, Mr Vyner, Mr Herbert, secretary of the British, and Count de Boyl, secretary of the Italian legation at Athens, with an Italian servant and a Greek courier, made an excursion to the battle-field of Marathon. Previously to their departure, Erskine, the British minister, had enquired of the chief of police whether there was any danger, but no hint of insecurity had been given by that official. Four mounted gendarmes, however, accompanied the excursionists. On the return journey, at Pikérmi, 13 miles from Athens, a band of 21 brigands fired out of the wood; two of the gendarmes fell wounded, whereupon the brigands hurried up the mountain side with the tourists and the other two gendarmes. Six infantrymen, who had been unable to keep pace with the horses, then came up, and fired upon the brigands; but, finding that their fire made no impression and fearing to wound the prisoners, they desisted from their attempt at rescue. The brigands, not wishing to saddle themselves with unnecessary encumbrances, told the two ladies that they might return to Athens with the child, the Italian servant, and the two unwounded gendarmes, whither, on April 13, Lord Muncaster was sent to arrange for the payment of the ransom, originally fixed at £32,000, but reduced to £25,000 *or* an amnesty—a demand quickly expanded into £25,000 *and* an amnesty. The two chiefs, Tákos (or Demétrios) Arvanitákes and his brother Christós, who managed all the negotiations for the band, attached more importance to the amnesty than to the ransom, because Tákos was a man of means, who had been an outlaw since 1857 and wanted to return to society; while they were encouraged to insist upon the amnesty by emissaries from Athens, who, in Erskine's phrase, were "believed by Zaïmes [the Premier] to have been despatched by some of the leading members of the Opposition," with the object of making the government commit an unconstitutional act and of then turning it out.   In fact, by article 39 of the Constitution, specially framed to prevent the wholesale remission of punishment to brigands, the King possessed the prerogative of granting an amnesty for political offences only.   Erskine accordingly wrote to the brigands as follows: "There will be no difficulty as to the payment of the money, but you must not insist on an amnesty, which government have not the power to grant.   Persons will be sent to treat with you, and in the meantime both the King and the President of the Council [who had both just returned from the Archipelago] have assured the English minister that you shall not be molested.   Make your prisoners as comfortable as you can. You can even put them under cover in some rural habitation without any fear."   There was, therefore, never any doubt about the payment of the ransom; the only question was, whether the brigands could be induced to waive their demand for the amnesty.   Curiously enough, both the British Secretary for Foreign Affairs and the brigand chief thought that the amnesty should be granted, despite the fact that it was unconstitutional.   Clarendon, when referred by the Greek minister in London to the law, replied: "I could not admit the validity of the constitutional objection....The Greek Constitution had so often been violated by the government...that I could not listen to a plea founded on it as an excuse."   "The representatives of England and Italy," remarked the chief brigand, "should say to the Greek government, that they do not care at all how the thing is done, whether by amnesty or no, whether an amnesty be legal or not."   At the same time this high constitutional authority was willing to provide means of keeping within the letter of the law.   He suggested, that, if so much fuss were made about the unconstitutional nature of the act, a fresh National Convention should be summoned, and the Constitution amended to meet his requirements! Or again, playing upon the double meaning of the word "political," which in Greek also means " civilian," he would beg to point out that, as all the persons concerned were civilians, His Majesty could constitutionally grant the amnesty! The Greek government, on its part, offered to close its eyes while a British man-of-war gave the brigands the means of leaving Greece, or to promise them a pardon after a trial at Athens. The brigands were, however, not particularly anxious to enjoy an affluent exile at Malta—the place suggested—while they absolutely declined to trust their lives in Athens; they were willing, however, to submit to a trial at Oropós, whither they had in the meantime transferred themselves and their prisoners, provided that it was followed by a pardon. The leading lawyer of Greece declared this original idea of a sham local assize to be impossible, and thus for some days negotiations went on without result, while the prisoners, except for the inclement weather, had no cause to complain of their treatment. The brigands took them to church on Sunday, and introduced them to the parish priest; there were dances, jumping, and throwing the stone, and one brigand, the scholar of the party, read history for two hours one evening!

The British minister had urged General Soûtsos, Minister of War, and the latter had promised, not to send troops against the brigands, who in that case would be certain to kill their prisoners. The government was therefore compelled to treat with the robbers as if they had been an independent state. The King "showed the most eager wish to place himself in the hands of the brigands," and emissaries of increasing rank were sent to argue with them. Frank Noel, the squire of Achmétaga in Eubœa, who had two brothers of the chiefs in his employ, and who possessed a great knowledge of the people among whom he and his family had lived for three generations, generously went, at considerable personal risk, to interview the captors. At last, on April 18, the Cabinet commissioned Col. Theagénes, aide-de-camp of General Church, and a man of great probity, who had traversed the Turkish lines during the siege of the Akropolis in 1827, to parley with them. His instructions were to tell them that the ransom was at their disposal, and that they could leave Greek soil by land or sea (in the latter case, on an English vessel), but that they could not be amnestied, and that meanwhile under no pretext must they leave Oropós; otherwise the government would feel itself released from the obligation taken not to pursue them. On April 20 Theagénes communicated to Tákos at Oropós the above terms, but without any result beyond irritating him. When allusion was made to the necessity of remaining at Oropós, the chief produced Erskine's letter, and contended that the promise of immunity, which it contained, was absolute and not conditional, so that he claimed the right to go whithersoever he pleased. Then, turning to the prisoners, he bade them write to their ministers that, if this affair were not terminated by the following evening, he would cut their throats, "for that," he added, "is the colonel's desire, since he threatens us with the detachments." Theagénes then departed, and next day proceeded, in accordance with the orders of the government, to shut the brigands within Oropós. But hearing that they had crossed the river Asopós with their prisoners to the neighbouring village of Sykaminón, he changed his plans, and resolved to surround that village, and thus force them to accept the proposals made to them. At the same time a Greek gun-boat lay at anchor off the *skála* of Oropós. A despatch from the Cabinet, ordering Theagénes not to attack them at Sykaminón, but simply to blockade that place, and only to attack, if they attempted to leave it, arrived too late. When the brigand chief saw the soldiers, he sent Anemogiánnes, the Greek dragoman of the prisoners, with Erskine's letter, to Theagénes, and ordered the emissary to warn the colonel not to allow his men to approach nearer. Theagénes, on receipt of this message, told the dragoman to inform the brigands that they would not be molested at Sykaminón, where they would receive the money. Anemogiánnes, however, under pretext of finding a horse, delayed his return to the brigands, so that this message was never delivered. While this conversation was going on, Theagénes saw the robbers with their prisoners escaping in the direction of Délisi (the ancient Délion), with the ultimate intention of gaining the fastnesses of Agrapha. The soldiers set out in pursuit; and at Délisi, Herbert, who could run no more, was cut down and then shot by the brigands. Infuriated at this spectacle, the soldiers fired, whereupon, 40 paces beyond the spot where they had massacred their first victim, the brigands stabbed and shot Lloyd. They then divided, one party, under Christós (who was shot by the troops) running towards the sea, the others towards Skimatári, the present junction of the line to Chalkís. Near Skimatári, Vyner and Boyl gave out, and were shot by the brigands, more fortunate than their two comrades in the manner of their deaths, for no yataghan mangled their bodies. Of the brigands 7 were killed, 4 wounded and captured, while 10, including the chief, escaped. The heads of the 7 slain malefactors were exhibited on the Plain of Mars at Athens.

The news of the massacre of the prisoners caused an immense sensation in England. Debates took place in both Houses; newspapers published articles of incredible violence, and nothing short of the destruction of Greece would satisfy some of the most vehement critics. Gradually people came to see that it was unjust to blame a whole nation, because 21 brigands, of whom only two were Greeks and the rest Albanian-Wallachs, had murdered a party of distinguished Englishmen. The whole affair, as Noel, the Englishman who knew the country best, pointed out, had been grievously mismanaged. The brigands had threatened and meant to kill their prisoners, if pursued, and had relied for immunity on the British minister's letter; while, as Noel wrote on the morrow of the massacre, "had the government suspended hostilities, everything would have been arranged," for they had told him that they would accept the ransom alone, and leave the country, if they failed to obtain their demand for an amnesty. A month after the murders, the trial of the four men concerned in them, and of other brigands, including two former members of this band, began at Athens, and a sensation was created when two wounded robbers were borne into the court on litters. All four were condemned to death, and three of them, together with two others, were publicly guillotined on the Plain of Mars. No less than 111 persons were accused of complicity in this affair, and 62 of them were committed for trial, among the latter, to the general amazement, Noel; but the court eventually decided that there was no case against him. It was generally felt, as the President of the Criminal Court had said, that the national honour could "be vindicated only by the speedy and complete extirpation of brigandage"—a plague, which had diminished between 1856 and 1862 but had revived after the revolution and the anarchy that followed. Accordingly, a circular against it was issued; and, although a Greek deputy was captured later in the year, Granville was able, before it closed, to express the satisfaction of the British Cabinet at the energetic measures of the Greek government. Gladstone's prophecy that this sad affair appeared "likely to be a great event in the history of Greece" has been verified; for, since the capture of Lord Muncaster's party, no foreigner has been taken by brigands in Greece. The murder of a Greek near Lamía in 1894 was a repetition on a much smaller scale of "the drama of Oropós"; but that incident was a rare exception to the public security of the country.

In another way, Gladstone's remark was true. Four deputies protested against the alleged remark of Zaḯmes about the communications between "some of the leading members of the Opposition" and the brigands; the resignation

of General Soûtsos was followed by that of the rest of the
Cabinet; and a series of short-lived ministries ensued, one of
which, under the guidance of Koumoundoûros, carried a
drastic measure against brigandage.

The excitement caused by "the drama of Oropós" had
scarcely subsided, when the question of the Lávrion mines
became acute.   Lávrion is just such a place as the political
economist loves ; for it reproduces, as far as it is possible to
do so beneath the blue sky and in the sun of Greece, the
conditions of our own "black country."   It is essentially a
workmen's town, where alone in Greece the thin edge of a
labour question sometimes makes itself felt.   Yet the prose
of mining is, at least, refined at Lávrion by the tradition of
over two thousand years.   Aeschylus wrote that the Athenians
had "a fountain of silver, a treasure of their land"; and
Herodotus relates how Themistoklês, like the shrewd statesman
that he was, persuaded his fellow-citizens to devote the profits
of the Lávrion silver-mines, which were to have been divided
among them, to the building of 200 ships—the origin of the
naval power of Athens, which saved Greece at Salamis.   Soon
after the Roman conquest we hear of an insurrection of slaves
employed there ; but a little later the mines were supposed
to have been worked out; and Pausanias describes Lávrion
as a place "where once were silver mines."   For nineteen
centuries they were abandoned ; but in 1864 an Italo-French
company bought lands at Lávrion with the object of pursuing
mining operations.   The reasons which led to its formation
were quite romantic.   The late Lord Sherbrooke once remarked in the course of one of his sallies at the expense of his
classical education, that in his Australian days he was walking,
without knowing it, upon hidden gold-fields, which a scientific
training would have enabled him to discover.   But—so the
story runs—it was the study of the classics which led a certain
Signor Serpieri to found his company for the exploitation of
the long-neglected mineral wealth of Lávrion.   This gentleman

had read the passage of Strabo[1], in which the great geographer, writing some 30 years before Christ, said that, though the ancient silver mines had given out, yet the workmen were still able to extract the precious metal by smelting over again the refuse and the scoriae. He then proceeded to Lávrion, examined the heaps of old refuse that were lying about, and returned to "Europe" with some specimens in his pocket. A concession was granted to him and to M. Roux of Marseilles to work the mines, but a question arose as to the right of the company to extract ore from the refuse which Strabo had mentioned. The disputes which followed formed a not inconsiderable part of Greek political history during the next few years, and led to some unpleasantness between the Greek government and the representatives of France and Italy. Like everything else in Greece, the Lávrion mines became a political question; and the Opposition of the day sought to extract political capital from the ancient refuse. The newspapers represented the spoil-banks of Strabo as a second California, which ought to have belonged by natural right to the nation but were being exploited by greedy foreign capitalists. The real value of the minerals was immensely exaggerated; public opinion became excited; and a law was passed in 1871, declaring the refuse-heaps to be national property. France and Italy protested against this law, and, when the Greek government replied that the Greek courts were open to the aggrieved company, threatened force, and appealed to the other Powers. Austria proposed, and the Greek government refused, arbitration with the company; and matters had come to a deadlock, when in 1873 the company sold its rights, and a new company, of which Sig. Serpieri was again the leading spirit, obtained a concession to work the minerals, on condition of paying a heavy royalty of 44 per cent. on the ore extracted from the refuse and slag. As this was soon found to be heavier than the mining company could

[1] ix, 1, 23.

bear, it was subsequently reduced, but not before the Athenian public had paid the usual penalty of speculators in such ventures.

The next two years, which preceded the great crisis of the eastern question, were occupied in Greece with parliamentary and constitutional struggles. Politicians, like Delegéorges and Boúlgares, who had played an important part in the overthow of Otho, found when they became Prime Ministers that it was not easy to translate into practice the advanced democratic doctrines which they had preached when in opposition. Liberals in power often turn conservative, but they thereby lose their popularity with their former admirers. Poetic justice decreed that Delegéorges, who had risen to office by the agitation about the mines of Lávrion, should fall by the same agency, and that the idol of the students in 1862 should become the object of their hostile demonstrations in 1873, because he declined to reconstitute the phalanx created in the revolutionary year. Boúlgares, his successor, was accused of violating article 56 of the constitution, because at the sitting of December 12, 1874, he considered as legal a quorum composed not of half the total number of deputies *plus* one, but of half the total number of deputies actually living and elected *plus* one. The leaders of the Opposition thereupon declared the constitution to be in danger; 19 newspapers of Athens appealed to the people to save it; the names of ministerial deputies who formed this irregular quorum were pilloried, and the nickname of στηλῖται ("dishonoured") applied to them, while two members of the Cabinet were accused of bribery in connexion with the appointment of several archbishops. The Ministry was compelled to resign in 1875; and Charílaos Trikoúpes, who had recently been arrested for a strong article, supposed to reflect upon the Crown, became for the first time Prime Minister. Son of the former minister in London and historian of the Greek revolution, he had learnt as his father's secretary of legation to appreciate British methods, had sat in the National Assembly, had been sent to London to negotiate in the matter of the Corfiote forts, and had gained his first experience of office as Minister of Foreign Affairs during part of the Cretan insurrection. Trikoúpes' hour, however, was not yet come; but the elections which he held were free from all government interference, and it was reserved for his successor Koumoun-doúros to obtain from the new Chamber a vote annulling all laws passed by the unconstitutional quorum. In 1876 the whole Boúlgares Cabinet was impeached for a breach of the constitution, and two of its members were tried and convicted of bribery; the archbishops were punished for simony. But the international situation in the east diverted the attention of the Greeks from these internal problems and united rival politicians in a common bond of patriotism.

CHAPTER XVI

THE BALKAN CRISIS OF 1875-8.

In the summer of 1875 a revolt in an obscure village of the Herzegovina, judged at the outset to be merely "an internal affair of Turkey," was the beginning of a movement which spread all over the Balkan peninsula, involved three of the Balkan states, as well as Russia, in war with Turkey, and terminated in the most important Congress that has ever met to settle the affairs of south-eastern Europe. Except for the revolt of the highlanders of Krivoshije, the mountainous district above Risano on the Bocche di Cattaro, in 1869 against service in the Austrian army, that corner of the South Slavonic world had not attracted the attention of diplomatists since the Herzegovinian insurrection of 1861 and the Turco-Montenegrin war that had arisen therefrom. Despite a poetic appeal to their brethren of Montenegro and the Herzegovina, the men of Krivoshije had not found allies; but even so they had amazed Europe by the vigour of their resistance to the army of a first-class Power. Prince Nicholas, anxious not to offend his great neighbour, had then preserved a strict neutrality, while three years later his diplomacy smoothed over a frontier incident at Kolashin between his warlike subjects and the Turks. But, if the Herzegovina had remained quiet, the Christians were far from contented. The Cretan insurrection of 1866-9 had set an example which was not lost upon them—for the social condition of the two countries was not unlike. In both there were practically no Turks, except the officials, sent from Constantinople and usually changed before they had time to learn the language or study the needs of the people; in both the native Mussulman oppressors belonged to the same race and spoke the same tongue as their Christian victims. The latter had benefited but little from the formal declaration of equality before the law, made so ostentatiously by Abdul Mejid. Whatever the theory might be, the Christians of Bosnia and the Herzegovina, which formed one government, were virtually debarred from giving evidence in the higher courts, and could only obtain justice against members of the dominant creed by enormous bribes. " All provincial authorities," wrote the British consul some years before the final insurrection broke out, " with rare exceptions, act according to the inspirations of their own personal interest "; and he added the significant warning that " without some powerful intervention, Bosnia and the Herzegovina might soon witness scenes similar to those which have lately terrified Europe in Syria." No Christians were employed in the administration; the police purchased their places, and reimbursed themselves by extorting money from those whom they were supposed to defend; and, worst of all, the exactions of the tax-farmers were such that the peasant, when all was paid, seldom kept for himself more than one-third of his crop.

The harvest of 1874 had been very bad, yet the tax-farmers did not on that account diminish their demands; what little had been yielded by the green oases in the stony plateau of Nevesinje, a village some 25 miles from Mostar, lay rotting on the ground; for the peasants could not gather it into their barns till the dilatory publicans, a Christian and two Mohammedan Serbs, had assessed it. Unable to obtain redress against their tardy and exorbitant assessment, 164 inhabitants fled to Montenegro in February 1875, whence they did not return for some months. Meanwhile, two events had excited the Christian population. The slaughter of a band of Montenegrins by the Turks at Podgoritza in October 1874 had provoked a protest from Prince Nicholas, to whom the Orthodox Serbs of the Herzegovinian border looked as their natural champion; the visit of the Austrian Emperor to Dalmatia in the spring of 1875 encouraged the Catholic clergy, who had long looked to Austria for aid; and oppressed subjects of the Turks told their tale of woes to the powerful ruler of their Dalmatian kinsmen. Thus, a rising, of which the origin was traceable to internal maladministration, was encouraged by circumstances in two neighbouring states. Finding the fugitives from Nevesinje a burden on his exiguous treasury, Prince Nicholas obtained leave for them to return to their homes, which in some cases were burned over their heads. Outrage succeeded outrage, till at last, on July 1, Nevesinje rose, refusing either to pay taxes or to admit the police. After two Turkish commissioners had failed to pacify the insurgents, the consuls of the Powers were sent to disclaim all active sympathy with the insurrection, and Server Pasha, who had played the same part in Crete, was commissioned " to redress abuses."

These missions likewise failed, for the Christians, often deceived, had no faith in the Turks. The insurgents, however, laid before the consuls a statement of their grievances. They complained that the ancient tithe had been increased to $12\frac{1}{2}$ per cent. upon grain, tobacco, vegetables, fruit, and hay, which in practice had become still more. For the tax-farmers were in the habit of living for several days at the expense of the peasants, while the latter could not touch the fruits of their fields until the tax had been paid. Tobacco and the juice of the grape were liable to a further excise; every Christian male had to pay 30 piastres a year as poll-tax for exemption from military service; taxes on land, houses, pasture-lands, small animals, hogs, and beehives were added; and the peasants' burdens were made still heavier by compulsory work on the roads and by horse service for the conveyance of troops. Besides these grievances against the

government and its agents, the Christians complained of the
feudalism of the landowners, or *agas*, mostly Mohammedan
Serbs, converted to Islâm after the fall of the old Bosnian
kingdom in 1463 and of the " Duchy" of S. Sava, whence
the Herzegovina takes its name, some 20 years later. These
landlords treated their Christian tenants, or *kmets*, as serfs,
and extracted from these struggling cultivators of the stony
Herzegovina a quarter of the produce, an annual animal of
the flock, a large amount of gratuitous labour, and free food
whenever they descended upon the peasants' huts.   Thus,
between the Imperial tax-farmer and the native *aga*, the lot
of the Christian was intolerable. Before the law he was always
at a disadvantage ; the chief functionaries were Turks, ignorant
of Serb ; the language of the courts was Turkish, which he
did not understand ; in short, the petitioners summed up their
condition in the sentence that they had "no security for life,
for honour, or for property." Nevertheless, at that stage of
the insurrection, they still wished to remain subjects of the
Sultan, and, with the exception of those who inhabited the
frontier districts, did not desire union with Montenegro. They
demanded lands in some foreign country, to which they could
emigrate, or autonomy under a foreign Christian prince, or
else a foreign occupation till justice had been accorded to
them.   For Turkish reforms, without European intervention
as a guarantee of their performance, had been proved to be
valueless.   Thus, at first, just as in Servia in 1804, the revolt
was not against the Sultan, but against the local authorities,
who misgoverned in his name, and the native Mohammedan
landlords, in whom pride of birth was combined with the
arrogance of apostasy.

The insurrection spread to an extent which seriously
alarmed the statesmen of Constantinople. The Krivoshijans,
who had beaten the Austrians in 1869, poured across the
frontier. On August 15, 1875, a similar movement, likewise due
to the extortions of the tax-farmers, had begun at Kozaratz near

Prjedor in north-west Bosnia, where the two religions had lived more harmoniously than in the Herzegovina. This Bosnian revolt extended rapidly eastward to Brod and Dervent, while the bulk of the Turkish troops, reduced below their proper strength before the outbreak in the Herzegovina, was engaged in grappling with the latter. Consequently the native Mussulmans took the law into their own hands; and in Bosnia there raged a civil war, in which the combatants were of the same race and speech but of different creeds. The theatre of this struggle being near the frontiers of the Dual Monarchy, the Slavs of Hungary could assist their brethren of Bosnia, while the Herzegovinian insurgents pitched their head-quarters in an old monastery some three hours from Ragusa, where the survivors of the massacre, perpetrated on the Catholics of the neighbouring plain of Popovo, found refuge, and where the Christian combatants found sympathy and supplies. A distributing committee sat at Castelnuovo on the Bocche di Cattaro, and rifles were landed in the Sutorina. The pass of Muratovitza proved to be the Marathon of the Herzegovina, where a local chief, Lazar Socitza, drove back the Turkish army with signal success; and on December 12 the Sultan issued a new firman, completing the *Hatti-Humayûn* of 1856, and promising administrative reforms. But as Count Andrássy, the Austro-Hungarian Foreign Minister, pointed out in the note which he drew up on December 30, the Turkish reforms were vague and inadequate, while the Turkish arms had been unsuccessful. There was "no district of European Turkey," he wrote, "where the antagonism which exists between the Cross and the Crescent takes such an acrimonious form." He therefore suggested the immediate suppression of tax-farming, the expenditure of the amount raised by direct taxation in the country, religious liberty, a special commission of Christians and Mussulmans in equal numbers to superintend the reforms, and the amelioration of the rural population. Lord Derby, then our Foreign Secretary, gave a general support to these proposals; and the Porte accepted all but the second point. But neither the Andrássy note, nor the conference of Baron Rodich, the Slav governor of Dalmatia, with the insurgent chiefs in the Sutorina, nor yet the Berlin Memorandum of the three Imperial Cabinets—which proposed an armistice and a mixed commission, adding that the Christians should be allowed to retain their arms, and that the Turkish troops should be concentrated—availed to stay the insurrection. The Berlin Memorandum met with no support from the Turcophil government of Great Britain. The imprisonment of Ljubibratich, one of the insurgent chiefs, an agitator rather than a guerrilla leader, by the Austrian authorities as a concession to Magyar hatred of the Slavs, could not cripple a movement with which the two neighbouring principalities of Servia and Montenegro were about to announce their co-operation.

From the outset it was to have been expected that a prolongation of the insurrection would involve those two states. At first, indeed, neither of the Princes was anxious for war with Turkey. Milan, when a deputation from his parliament presented him with an address, expressing the impossibility of Servian indifference to the fate of the Bosniaks and Herzegovinians, had replied by dismissing Ristich, his bellicose Premier, and the leading advocate of the " great Servian " idea. But the Prince of Servia soon found that he had to reckon with two outside competitors for his shaky throne as well as with the war-party in his own country. Peter Karageorgevich, son of the exiled Prince, and a man of far more military capacity than himself, placed at the disposal of the Bosnian insurgents his experience gained during the Franco-German war, and distributed medals bearing his image and a telling allusion to the historic plain of Kossovo. Nicholas of Montenegro, a born leader of men, after sending the wily old warrior, Peko Pavlovich, to quiet the insurgents, had allowed him to become one of their most active chiefs, while numbers of his subjects crossed the frontier, whence his own father-in-law directed operations. Embarrassed by the comparisons which were drawn between his attitude and that of his two rivals, Milan recalled Ristich to power in the spring of 1876, and accepted the services of Tchernaïeff, a Russian general, who appeared in Servia nominally as correspondent of a Pan-slavist journal. Nicholas' next step was to send a memorandum to Lord Derby, pointing out the "intolerable position" in which the insurrection had placed him ; nor was the advice of the Tsar and the British government, that the Turks should placate the two Servian rulers by ceding a port and a little territory to Montenegro and Little Zvornik to Servia, adopted in time to prevent war. Ristich demanded that the adminis-tration of Bosnia, which was still in revolt, should be entrusted to Milan in return for a fixed payment ; and on June 30 the Prince of Servia issued a manifesto to his people, in which, after allusions to the medieval Tsar Dushan and to Milosh, he announced that his army was "about to enter the disturbed provinces in self-defence." On July 1, Servia, and on the morrow Montenegro, declared war against Turkey on behalf of their brother Serbs. The moment had at last come—so Prince Nicholas told his subjects—to restore the Servian empire, which had fallen with the first Murad and should revive with the fifth, who had just ascended the blood-stained Turkish throne.

The situation of the Turkish empire in the summer of 1876 might, indeed, justify the sanguine rhetoric of the poet-Prince of the Black Mountain. The insurrection in the Herzegovina had not only aroused the sympathies of the two neighbouring Serb states, but had quickened the national feeling of the Bulgars. A fresh revolutionary committee was formed in Bucharest ; and the failure of Stambulov, the future Premier, and of Stojanov, the future Speaker of the *Sobranje,* to rally the peasants to his flag at Stara Zagora only redoubled the efforts of the ardent patriots. Giurgevo became their head-quarters ; in the winter nights they would cross the frozen

Danube to the Bulgarian bank; wooden cannon were hollowed out of cherry-trees: a congress of conspirators was held in a clearing of the forest. The Bulgarian leader, known as "Benkovski" from the name on his Polish passport, fancied himself a second Napoleon; but this "revolt in the Sredna Gora," or "middle range of mountains" between the Balkans and the Thracian plain, which began on May 2, lasted only 10 days, and was repressed with terrible severity. In the words of a British official, the Turks committed "cruelties worthy of Red Indians" at the sack of Panagjurishte. At the sight of the ruined town, the insurgents separated in despair; "Benkovski," betrayed by a shepherd, was killed by the Turks. But, although unimportant in itself, this insurrection incidentally caused the eyes of the whole civilised world to be directed to Bulgaria. The national movement had spread across the Maritza to Mount Rhodope, where the Christians fought against the Mohammedan Bulgars, or *Pomaks*, who were, like the Mohammedan Serbs in Bosnia and the Mohammedan Greeks in Crete, the most fanatical adherents of Turkish rule. The village of Batak on the northern spurs of Rhodope was preparing to join the national movement, when a force of Bashi-Bozuks under the command of Achmet Aga of Dospat and his colleague, Mohammed Aga of Dorkovo, arrived there. After some attempt at defence, the villagers surrendered on the distinct promise that their lives should be spared. Then began what Mr Baring, the British Commissioner, stigmatised in his official report, drawn up after a visit to the spot, as "perhaps the most heinous crime that has stained the history of the present century." Achmet Aga and his men spared neither age nor sex. When the terrified Christians, to the number of over a thousand, took refuge in the church and churchyard, the Bashi-Bozuks fired through the windows, and then, tearing off the tiles, threw burning rags dipped in petroleum among the helpless fugitives below. Only one old woman would seem to have escaped from within those desecrated walls; and when, more than two months later, the British Commissioner visited the spot, the stench of the unburied corpses was overpowering. "In the streets at every step," wrote Mr Baring, "lay human remains—here a skull of an old woman—there the false tress of some unhappy girl." It was estimated that 5000 out of a population of 7000 had perished at Batak alone, while the Christians slaughtered throughout Bulgaria in that fatal month of May made up a total of 12,000. But the massacred Bulgars did not die in vain; their death was the birth of their country.

The "Bulgarian Atrocities" aroused the indignation of the whole Christian world. To the correspondent of the *Daily News* belongs the credit of having first disclosed the infamies of Batak; the British and American Commissioners confirmed his story. Gladstone left his theological studies on "Future Retribution" to write on the "Bulgarian Horrors"; and his famous pamphlet, sold by tens of thousands, awakened the righteous anger of the British people against the system of government, which could not only allow, but reward, such crimes—for Achmet Aga had been decorated for his conduct. The great Liberal statesman, whose services to the eastern Christians did more to raise British prestige in the Balkan peninsula than our fleets or armies, urged "the extinction of the Turkish executive power in Bulgaria." "Let the Turks," he wrote, "now carry away their abuses in the only possible manner, namely by carrying off themselves. Their Zaptiehs and their Mudirs, their Bimbashis and their Yuzbashis, their Kaimakams and their Pashas, one and all, bag and baggage, shall, I hope, clear out from the province they have desolated and profaned." Even the Conservative Foreign Secretary telegraphed to Constantinople that "any renewal of such outrages would prove more disastrous to the Porte than the loss of a battle," and admitted, that "any sympathy which was previously felt" in Great Britain for Turkey had "been completely destroyed by the lamentable occurrences in

Bulgaria." His ambassador at Constantinople, Sir Henry Elliot, might callously remark that "we have been upholding what we know to be a semi-civilized nation," and that it did not matter how many Bulgars had been butchered, provided British "interests" were maintained. But the feeling of the British public towards the Turkish government was no longer that which had prompted the Crimean war; indeed, a former member of the Aberdeen Cabinet was now the leading opponent of Turkey. "Even if Russia were to declare war against the Porte," Lord Derby added, "Her Majesty's government would find it practically impossible to interfere." An Ottoman official, perceiving when it was too late the full political import of the Batak massacre, asked one of its authors, how much Russia had paid him for a deed which would furnish her with a fresh excuse for intervention on behalf of the persecuted Slavs of the Balkan peninsula. Since that day there have been atrocities in the Turkish empire on a far larger scale, but the Armenian massacres had much less effect upon politics than the butchery of Batak.

Western governments are generally less moved by the massacre of Christian subjects of the Sultan than by the murder of one of their own consuls. But the ferment of May 1876 produced both these incentives to intervention. A Bulgarian girl of dubious antecedents, who had embraced Islâm, was seized by some Greeks at the Salonika railway-station; her *yashmak* was torn off, and she was taken to the American consulate. An excited mob of Mussulmans vented its fanaticism upon the French and German consuls (the latter a British subject), who were forcibly detained in a mosque and murdered on May 6. The six murderers were promptly hanged; but the movement of unrest was not confined to the provinces. The National party at Constantinople, discontented with the weakness of the Russophil Grand Vizier, raised the cry of "Turkey for the Turks"; several thousand *softas*, or theological students, forced the Sultan to dismiss his Minister.

The British fleet arrived in Besika Bay; and on May 29 the
new Grand Vizier and his confederates, having obtained a
fetvah from the Sheikh-ul-Islâm authorising the deposition of
Abdul Aziz on the ground of his incapacity and extravagance,
declared the throne vacant and on the following day proclaimed
his nephew Sultan under the title of Murad V.   Four days
later the death of Abdul Aziz prevented all danger of a
restoration.   The nature of his end has been much contested ;
five years afterwards Midhat Pasha and others were tried and
convicted of the Sultan's assassination ; but the trial, held
under the shadow of Yildiz, was an absurd travesty of justice,
and the late Dr Dickson of Constantinople, who saw the dead
man's body, informed the present writer that Abdul Aziz
committed suicide by cutting his arteries with a pair of scissors.
The removal of his uncle did not, however, long confirm
Murad on the throne.   The tragedy of his sudden elevation
to power affected a mind naturally feeble ; the National party
soon recognised that he was not the man to direct the fortunes
of the empire in a time of dire distress.   On August 31 he
was deposed in his turn, and his brother Abdul Hamid II
took his place.   Murad vanished in the palace of Cheragan
on the Bosphorus, which had witnessed his uncle's tragic death.
There he remained a prisoner till his death in 1904, but it
was not till the revolution of 1908 that his wives were allowed
to leave the mysterious palace, which had been isolated for
over 30 years from the outside world.

Seldom had a Sultan begun his reign under greater difficulties than the astute diplomatist who thus ascended the
throne.   He found Bosnia and the Herzegovina in revolt
against his authority, Servia and Montenegro fighting on their
behalf.   The Servian army, increased by a body of volunteers,
was under the command of Tchernaïeff, whose plan of campaign
was to invade the Turkish territory on the south and east by
the valleys of the Morava and the Timok, while at the same
time despatching detachments to the frontiers of Bosnia and

of the *sanjak* of Novibazar. But the Russian commander's strategy was neutralised by the inferior material of which the Servian forces were composed. Unlike the warlike Montenegrins, between whose Prince and their own there could be no unity of purpose, the Serbs had been at peace for two generations with their former masters, for whom they were no match in the field ; while the Bulgars, cowed by the massacres, did not rise, as was expected, and a Bulgarian legion retired in disorder. Tchernaïeff, indeed, crossed the Turkish frontier to the south, and carried the Turkish camp by a sudden attack. But, while one Ottoman general checked the Servian advance to the east at Zajetchar and laid the important strategic post of Knajajevatz in ashes, another descended the valley of the Morava, and completely defeated the retreating army of the south at Aleksinatz. Milan, from his headquarters at Parachin, had already invited the Powers to intervene. An armistice was granted, but the negotiations for a settlement were hindered by his ill-timed proclamation as King at Deligrad on September 16, at Tchernaïeff's suggestion, and the fighting was resumed. The Serbs made a desperate stand at Djunis, but in vain ; Aleksinatz was lost ; all southern Servia was in the power of the Turks, and the road was open to Belgrade. Then the Tsar intervened to save Servia from annihilation. General Ignatyeff handed a Russian ultimatum to the Porte, demanding the conclusion of an armistice within 48 hours with both Servia and Montenegro. The Turkish government yielded ; and on November 1 an armistice of two months was signed, which was subsequently extended till March 1, 1877, when a definite peace was concluded between Milan and the Sultan. Servia neither lost nor gained by the war of 1876 ; her territory was left undiminished ; her finances were unencumbered by a war indemnity.

Meanwhile the Montenegrins had fought with far more success than their Servian allies. The forces of the Black Mountain were divided into two armies, that of the north,

which, under the command of the Prince, invaded the Herzegovina, and that of the south, under Bojo Petrovich, his cousin
and subsequent Prime Minister, whose instructions were to
watch the Albanian frontier.   The northern army defeated the
Turks with great loss at the village of Vutchidol, and the
advance guard reached the old castle of Duke Stephen only
a few miles from Mostar.   But the Austrian military attaché
warned the Prince not to enter the Herzegovinian capital, and
bad news from the south compelled him to hasten back to the
defence of his country, only to find that his cousin had twice
routed the enemy at Medun near Podgoritza.   Another Montenegrin victory at Danilograd in the Zeta valley and the
capitulation of Medun concluded the campaign of 1876.
Montenegro signed an armistice with the Porte on the basis of
uti possidetis; Bojo Petrovich was sent to Constantinople to
negotiate peace, with instructions to ask for an increase of
territory, including the cession of the then Turkish fortress of
Spizza.   The Porte was willing to cede Spizza, to which Austria
and Italy, as Adriatic states, objected; but it declined to give
up Nikshich, whereupon the Prince recalled his envoy and
prepared for a second campaign.

European diplomacy did not remain idle while Servia and
Montenegro were keeping their truce with Turkey.   Despite
the despatch of the British fleet to Besika Bay and a bellicose
speech from Lord Beaconsfield, Lord Salisbury, least chauvinistic of our Conservative statesmen, was sent to represent Great
Britain and modify the Turcophil attitude of her ambassador
at a conference of the Powers for the settlement of the eastern
question, which met at Constantinople in December.   Salisbury's
instructions were to take the integrity of Turkey as a basis; to
endeavour to obtain for Bosnia, the Herzegovina, and Bulgaria
such local autonomy as would give the inhabitants some control
over their affairs; to preserve, with the addition of Little
Zvornik, the Servian *status quo*; and to enlarge Montenegro by
the Herzegovinian districts of Piva, Drobniak, Banjani and

Zubci and by the port of Spizza—districts which yielded
nothing to the Ottoman treasury but would, it was thought,
appease Prince Nicholas. The conference, however, was
doomed to failure. On December 23, while the delegates were
at work, salvos of artillery suddenly distracted their attention
from their papers and protocols; and they were informed that
the cannon were announcing to the people the proclamation of
a constitution, which created a bicameral legislature—a Senate
named for life and a Chamber of Deputies elected in ratio of
1 to 50,000—and declared all "Ottomans" (for such was
thenceforth to be the official name of all the Sultan's subjects
of whatever creed) to be equal before the law. Salisbury was
not deceived by the specious arrangements of "Midhat's
Parliament," as this first Turkish legislature was called after
the Liberal statesman who had just returned to power. When
the Turks argued that the reforms proposed at the conference
were unnecessary, because there was now a constitution, the
shrewd British statesman pointed out that constitutions require,
even in western Europe, some time to bear practical fruit, and
that there was "no probability of the appearance of popular
leaders," who, even if they did appear, could be exiled by the
mere word of the Sultan. But the Turkish delegates showed
that they were versed in at least one parliamentary art, that of
obstruction. In the name of the integrity of the Ottoman
empire, which formed the corner-stone of their new constitutional edifice, they rejected, or declined to discuss, the
chief proposals of their foreign colleagues. When "Bulgaria"
was mentioned, they first professed not to know what the word
meant, and then said that it was a geographical term for the
region north of the Balkans. They strenuously refused to
settle the long-vexed question of Little Zvornik, even though it
was pointed out that that hamlet had been assigned to Servia
by the delimitation which followed the treaty of Adrianople
and by the Imperial ordinance of 1833; that it had lost all
strategic value; and that the Sultan might still keep his

suzerainty over it.   In vain Salisbury recalled to Midhat the lessons of 1828 and the loss of Greece; a National Council, convoked for the purpose, refused to accept the proposals of the conference, of which the chief were the rectification of the Montenegrin frontier, and the autonomy of Bulgaria, Bosnia, and the Herzegovina, under governors-general to be named by the Porte with the consent of the Powers.   On this the conference broke up, in January, 1877; and Gortchakoff, in a circular note to the other governments concerned, asked what measures they now proposed to take for enforcing the decisions of Europe.   Salisbury remarked before he left Constantinople, that he and his colleagues had "all tried to save Turkey, but she" would "not allow" them "to save her"; from that moment he regarded war as certain.   Still, his journey to the Turkish capital had not been in vain; his eyes had been opened to the fact that the average British consul, through whose eyes our government looked at the Balkan peninsula, had taken his information almost wholly from Turkish officials, and he vowed that he would reform the service.   From that resolve dates its re-organisation; even now the British Foreign Office relies too much upon non-British consuls; but the obvious bias, which strikes the reader of the voluminous blue-books of 35 years ago, has almost entirely disappeared.   This is not the least of Salisbury's many services to the near east.

The British government made one further attempt to preserve peace.   A fresh conference was held in London; and on March 31 the representatives of the Powers signed a protocol, taking cognisance of the conclusion of peace between Turkey and Servia, asking for a rectification of the Montenegrin frontier with the freedom of the river Bojana, which flows out of the lake of Scutari, and begging the Porte to place the Turkish army on a peace footing.   Meanwhile, Midhat Pasha had fallen, and with him all hope of serious reform had disappeared; the parliament, which he had created, had neither experience of public life nor independence of the government, and supported the latter in rejecting the London protocol. War was now inevitable; Russia signed a military convention with the Prince of Roumania for the passage of her troops across his territory; and on April 24 the Russian troops crossed alike the European and the Asiatic frontiers of Turkey. The fourth and last Russo-Turkish war of the century had begun. Five days later Montenegro re-opened hostilities.

Both Turks and Russians realised that Roumania was the key of the situation. Powerless in the Black Sea, where the Turkish fleet was then superior, the invaders could attack Turkey by land alone; and in Europe every facility for doing so was placed at their disposal by the Principality. Prince Charles had always chafed at the legal fiction of vassalage, which affected his people far less than himself, and had, from the moment when he accepted the throne, resolved to shake off that irksome yoke as soon as possible. But the "Reds," suspecting already that the independence of Roumania would be purchased by the sacrifice of that part of Bessarabia which had been restored in 1856, just as the independence of Italy had been bought by the sacrifice of Nice and Savoy, had opposed the Prince's desire, till, in 1876, he contrived to rid himself of the irresolute Conservative Cabinet, which had been five years in office, and placed Brătianu in power. As usually happens, the responsibilities of place changed the ideas of the Radicals; and Brătianu began to negotiate with Russia for the participation of the Roumanian army in the coming war. The convention was not submitted to parliament until the Russians had actually entered the country, and even then voted only after considerable opposition. Some pointed out that it was an infraction of the treaty of Paris, and that the Russian pledge which it contained "to maintain and to protect the actual integrity of Roumania" was an inadequate guarantee. Others, while approving the principle of the convention, opposed the active co-operation of the army with the invaders. Upon this, however, both Prince and Premier insisted; and, although

Gortchakoff haughtily replied that Russia had "no need of the assistance of the Roumanian army"—a piece of arrogance for which Plevna was soon to be the punishment—they ultimately carried their point. The Porte, which had invited the co-operation of its vassal against the Russians, not only protested, but also ordered the bombardment of the Roumanian town of Kalafat—an act which provoked the declaration of war by Roumania, and the proclamation of Roumanian independence on May 21. But, as Gortchakoff, whose lesson was yet to come, still declined his aid, the Prince continued to mass his troops on the left bank of the Danube; while, a month later, the Russian army crossed the river almost without opposition at two points, one facing the Dobrudja, the other opposite Svishtov, and Bulgaria thus became the theatre of the war. Alexander II, confident of the success which seemed to await him in this Slavonic province, attended a solemn thanksgiving in the church of Svishtov; and General Gourko surprised Trnovo, the former residence of the Bulgarian Tsars, traversed the Balkans by the low pass of Hainköi, entered the valley of the Tundja, and took the Shipka pass in the rear. It seemed as if this daring officer would reach Adrianople, or even appear at the head of his cavalry before the walls of Stambûl. A panic broke out at the Turkish capital. Mehemet Ali, the German renegade of French extraction, whom we last saw as governor-general of Crete, was appointed Ottoman commander in Europe, while Suleiman was recalled from Montenegro to Thrace. Then the fortune of war turned; Gourko, despite the desperate bravery of his Bulgarian allies, was defeated at Stara Zagora and driven back to the Balkans; Osman Pasha, hitherto stationed in compulsory idleness at Vidin, occupied Plevna, whose defence was to be the most heroic episode of the campaign. That small town, easily captured in the first Russo-Turkish war of the century, proved to be the chief barrier to Russian success in the last.

The siege of Plevna began on July 20 with a Russian

repulse, which was followed ten days later by a second and far more crushing defeat. Then the Grand-duke Nicholas telegraphed in despair, begging Prince Charles to lead his despised army across the Danube. But the Prince declined to move until his conditions were accepted. His desire was to assist the Russians as the chief of an independent army; the Roumanians were, however, fused with the others, but, as compensation, their Prince was appointed commander-in-chief of the allied forces before the beleaguered town. On September 11 they attacked the strongest of all the defences of Plevna, the "indomitable Grivitza redoubt," and after three attempts placed the Roumanian colours on its summit. But the assault upon a second redoubt failed. Unable to take Plevna by storm, the allies shut in the garrison so closely on every side that at last Osman's supplies ran out. He was compelled to resort to a general sortie, and, after performing prodigies of valour, surrendered on December 10 with all that was left of his gallant army. Next day the Tsar and the Prince entered the town, and the former returned to Russia. Meanwhile, the Turks had in vain endeavoured to dislodge the Russians from the Shipka pass, and in Asia had lost, for the third time in history, the strong citadel of Kars, captured by an Armenian general, Loris Melikoff. On the west of the Balkan peninsula the Montenegrins, for whose cause the letters of Stillman in the *Times*, an article by Gladstone and a poem by Tennyson had aroused interest in England, managed to defeat the usual Turkish tactics of invading the principality simultaneously through the Duga pass on the north and the Zeta valley on the south, thus cutting the little state in two, by repulsing the southern army; and, when Suleiman, after great losses, reached Spuj from the north, he was called away to oppose the Russians in Bulgaria. Mehemet Ali, who was to have started from the south-east and met his colleagues at Danilograd, was likewise defeated, and summoned away, as we saw, to command on a more important field. Thus relieved from all danger of an attack upon his capital, Prince Nicholas was able to devote his energies to the wearisome siege of Nikshich, which at last surrendered, on September 8, after having been almost continuously blockaded by insurgents or Montenegrins ever since the revolt in the Herzegovina began. The fortress of Bilek speedily hoisted the white flag; the Montenegrins had thus conquered an important piece of the Herzegovina. But Austria and the autumn rains vetoed an advance on Trebinje and Mostar; so the mountaineers, turning back towards the sea, which it had so long been their object to reach by diplomacy, occupied Spizza and began the siege of Antivari. Thus everywhere, in Montenegro, in Bulgaria, in Asia Minor, the Turks were worsted. Two days after the fall of Plevna, the Porte invoked the mediation of the Powers.

A fresh enemy simultaneously appeared in the field. On the very day of the vain Turkish appeal, Servia again declared war against her old masters. More fortunate than in their previous campaign, the Serbs defeated the Turks at Pirot, whilst Milan, amidst general enthusiasm, entered the ancient Servian town of Nish. All the Slavonic armies, Russian, Servian, and Montenegrin, continued to advance, while the Roumanians blockaded Vidin. Gourko recrossed the Balkans, took Sofia, and routed Suleiman near Philippopolis; Skobeleff and Radetzky surrounded the Turkish army, which had fought so valiantly in the Shipka pass, at the neighbouring wood of Shéjnovo on January 9, 1878; eleven days later the Russians, as in 1829, entered Adrianople. The terrified Mussulmans fled before them to the fastnesses of Rhodope; and the brutality of the Cossacks towards these refugees almost equalled that of the Turkish irregulars to the Bulgarians in 1876. A third Servian victory by General Belimarkovich at Vranja brought the arms of the modern principality to the verge of the plain of Kossovo; the Montenegrins occupied Antivari and Dulcigno; and their poetic ruler expressed in an ode to the sea the joy which he felt at having at last cut his way to the Adriatic. The advance of the Serbs into Old Servia and of the Montenegrins upon Scutari in Albania, and the Roumanian siege of Vidin, were only cut short by the news of the armistice, which, like the treaty of 1829, had been signed at Adrianople on January 31, 1878.

It seemed as if, unaided, the Turkish empire must this time collapse before the combination of Russia and her three Balkan allies. But the Russian advance had alarmed the other great Powers specially interested in the solution of the eastern question. Austria-Hungary, expelled from Italy in 1866, had looked since then upon the western half of the Balkan peninsula as her sphere of influence; the Emperor Francis Joseph had, indeed, promised his neutrality during the war at his meeting with the Tsar at Reichstadt on July 8, 1876, on condition that the occupation of Bosnia and the Herzegovina should be his reward; but the Austrian government feared lest this condition should not be observed by the victorious Russians, who would thus have been accused—as they were, in fact, accused 30 years later—of betraying the cause of the Slavs. In Great Britain, the Prime Minister was an avowed friend of Turkey—an attitude attributed by his friends to political insight, by his foes to his Jewish blood and his Asiatic imagination; while public opinion, so deeply moved by the Bulgarian atrocities that Derby had doubted in 1876 whether even a Russo-Turkish war would revive the old Crimean sympathy with Turkey, was in 1877 less influenced by the sufferings and aspirations of Christian nationalities rightly struggling to be free than by fear of a Russian occupation of Constantinople. Even Gladstone in private admitted the decline of humanitarian enthusiasm; his second pamphlet, "Lessons in Massacre," made little impression; his five resolutions against support of Turkey and in favour of local self-government, moved in the House of Commons in a speech of extraordinary grandeur, describing England as the former hope of the oppressed all the world over, frightened timid Liberals. As the Russians

became more successful, the British public became more
warlike; the press and the music-halls pandered to, and thus
increased, the revived desire for a new Crimean war; and the
language of politics was enriched with the word " Jingo," which
denotes a state of mind likely to last as long as human nature
and certainly fostered by hysterical democracy.   As usual, the
violence of extreme men like Professor Freeman, who professed
his willingness to see India perish rather than Turkey saved,
damaged the cause for which that eminent historian had done
so much.   Not yet entrenched in Egypt, even though she had
half the Suez Canal shares in her pocket, Great Britain still
regarded the Russians at Constantinople as a menace to her
Indian empire, nor was much importance attached to the fact
that the Tsar had expressly discountenanced the occupation of
the New Rome; for he had returned to Russia, leaving generals
in the field who might be tempted to set diplomacy at defiance
and win eternal glory by planting the cross once more over
Santa Sophia.   The Conservative Cabinet was, indeed, divided ;
but its most powerful member was in favour of war, which in
the early weeks of 1878 seemed to be inevitable.   The British
fleet was ordered to Constantinople—a destination at once
altered, after the resignation of Lord Carnarvon, the Colonial
Secretary, for its former station of Besika Bay—and parliament
was asked to vote six millions for armaments.   The Russians
moved their lines close to the Turkish capital; a part of the
British fleet was ordered to enter the sea of Marmara for the
protection of British life and property there.   Thus, the forces
of the two rivals of the Crimea were once more separated by
a few miles only; the Grand-duke Nicholas established his
headquarters at the maritime village of San Stefano, ten miles
from Constantinople; the British admiral was stationed off the
island of Prinkipo.   In the general confusion, on February 14,
Abdul Hamid dissolved his parliament, and suspended the
constitution, which remained in abeyance till July 24, 1908.
   At this moment the intervention of another eastern

nationality threatened to complicate the situation still further. The Greeks had hitherto taken no part in the struggle.   The insurrection of the Slavs in Bosnia and the Herzegovina, and the first Servian and Montenegrin campaigns, had found the Hellenes merely interested spectators; the brief Bulgarian rising could scarcely have been expected to command their sympathy. Koumoundoûros had merely thought it prudent, in view of an extension of the movement in the Balkan peninsula, to buy arms; and in the autumn of 1876 a popular demonstration, held on the classic Pnyx, after protesting against the neglect of Hellenic rights by the advocates of Bosnian and Bulgarian autonomy, urged the Cabinet to make further military preparations.   Similar meetings took place in the provinces; yet the politicians continued to play the party game of ins and outs. But when Russia, the great Orthodox Power, which had been one of the three protectresses of the young Greek kingdom, entered the field, the position changed.   There were some who wished to avail themselves of this Russo-Turkish war, as they had desired in that of 1854, to excite insurrections in the Greek provinces of Turkey; while the national pride rejected the idea of a fresh, and perhaps final, settlement of the eastern question, in which "the Hellenic factor," as Gladstone called it, should be ignored.   It was felt at Athens that party dissensions must cease in the face of this crisis, in which the future of Hellenism, the realisation of "the Grand Idea," might be at stake.   A coalition Cabinet, an "Œcumenical government," as it was called, was formed in June, 1877, under the presidency of old Admiral Kanáres, who more than fifty years before had fired the capitan-pasha's ship at Chios, and who had as colleagues no less than four ex-Premiers.   Such a "Ministry of All the Talents," from which Boúlgares was the only leading statesman excluded, has never been constructed in Greece before or since; and Freeman, looking down from the Akropolis on the spectacle of a people demanding "that personal and party jealousies should be put aside," rejoiced that there was

"still life" in Greece. Trikoúpes, who occupied the Foreign
Office in this "Great Ministry," at once declared his readiness
to prevent, as far as he could, outbreaks among the Greek
subjects of Turkey, provided that the British government
recognised, when the time for a settlement arrived, that there
was "an Hellenic question before Europe." Derby was willing
to concede equal "administrative reforms or advantages" with
those likely to be granted to other Christian nationalities, but
declined to promise his support of territorial aggrandisement.
Nevertheless, despite the employment of Albanian irregulars
by the Turks in Thessaly and the pressure of the "Brotherhood" society in Greece, the majority of the Cabinet, following
the advice of the British government and the national dis-
inclination of the Hellenes to identify their cause with that of
the Balkan Slavs, declined the Russian invitation during the
siege of Plevna to join in the conflict and share in the spoils.
But when the news of the Russian advance on Adrianople
arrived, the excitement of the populace became intense. The
"Œcumenical government," whose chief was already dead,
resigned; the populace demanded war; Koumoundoûros, who
formed the new Cabinet, had to satisfy public opinion by
supporting insurrections in Epirus, Thessaly, and Crete; and
his Foreign Minister, Theodore Deligiánnes, announced on
February 2, 1878, that the government had "resolved to occupy
provisionally with its army the Greek provinces of Turkey."
But the news of the Russo-Turkish armistice checked this
invasion. Earlier in the year it might have been good policy,
as Trikoúpes had suggested, to obtain a seat at the coming
Congress of Berlin by participating in the Balkan war, just as
Cavour had won a place for Sardinia at the Congress of Paris
by sending her troops to the Crimea. Greece had, however,
waited too long; if she attacked Turkey after the armistice,
she would fight alone. The Greek troops were stopped by the
government, when they had reached Domokós, and recalled
on condition that "an Hellenic question be discussed at the

Congress"; but the insurrections went on, and volunteers crossed the frontier. The movement in Epirus was soon suppressed; but that in Thessaly was more serious. The picturesque villages which gleam on the slopes and nestle in the folds of Pélion rose in rebellion; a provisional government was formed, which proclaimed union with Greece; and from the classic rocks of Olympus another band of insurgents announced to the Powers "the annexation of Macedonia," as a protest against its inclusion in Bulgaria. The Turks, however, captured the two headquarters of both these organisations at Litóchoron on Olympus and at Makrinítza on Pélion. The fall of the latter place is still associated with the death of Ogle, the *Times* correspondent, who was beheaded by the barbarians on his way to save its inhabitants, but whose name is still preserved by a street at Volo. At last, British intervention through consuls Blunt and Merlin ended the Thessalian insurrection in May by telling the insurgents that "Hellenic interests" would "not be injured by acceding to English advice," and by proposing an amnesty, a year's remittance of taxes, and the separate administration of Thessaly from Epirus. The Porte accepted these proposals, and the other insurgent leaders laid down their arms.

In Crete also there had been desultory fighting. In May 1876 the Cretans, after seven years of comparative repose, broken only by a threat to take up arms against a new tax, demanded such modifications of the Organic Law of 1868 as would make it consonant with that "self-government" promised by Aali Pasha. The demand was repeated in 1877, but the Porte refused; and a meeting of Cretans was held in Athens, which determined on a revolt. Hajji Micháles landed in the island; a committee was formed there under the style of "the General Assembly of the Cretans"; and, owing to the excitement caused by the Russian advance, this body demanded complete autonomy, a chief of the executive elected by the people, the payment of an annual tribute of 500,000 piastres,

and a guarantee of these concessions by the Great Powers.
There was among the Christians a large party of peace, which
had not forgotten the hardships of the last insurrection; and
the influence of the women was thrown into the scale against
war; but the returned chiefs were in favour of fighting. On
February 15, 1878, the General Assembly, having had no answer
from the Porte to its demands, declared all negotiations at an
end, and appealed to the Powers. Fighting began, and the
Panhellénion (p. 314) re-appeared off the coast; but a truce was
quickly concluded, because the Turks had so few troops in the
island, owing to their late Balkan campaign, while the insurgents
had little food. After the arrival of reinforcements, the Turks
broke this truce; but the British government mediated on
behalf of the Christians with the Porte, which promised that
it would, "in concert with England, make arrangements for a
new form of government for Crete, in accordance with the
legitimate demands and requirements of the island." The
provisional government of seven members, which by this time
had been created, agreed on May 26 to accept British mediation
with an armistice on the basis of *uti possidetis*; and the ripening
barley harvest increased the desire of the Mussulmans, who
had fled, as usual, to the towns, to return to their farms.
British consuls had thus made peace alike in Thessaly and
Crete.

The treaty of San Stefano, which had meanwhile been
signed by the Russian and Turkish delegates on March 3, was
not calculated to satisfy Hellenic aspirations. That abortive
instrument, long regretted in Bulgaria, would have restored the
Bulgarian empire of the Middle Ages, and, while hopelessly
dismembering Turkey, would have put a final end to Greek
ambitions in Macedonia. It provided for the creation of a
vassal principality of Bulgaria with a frontage on both the
Euxine and the Aegean, with an inland frontier which marched
with the Danube on the north and comprised the Macedonian
lakes of Prespa and Ochrida, once the home of the Bulgarian

Tsars and the seat of the Bulgarian Church. To Servia, as the reward of her two campaigns, was assigned a considerable slice of territory, which included Nish and Little Zvornik, while her south-western frontier was drawn in so favourable a manner as almost to touch the enlarged eastern boundary of Montenegro. The two Serb states would thus have practically joined one another ; and an all-Servian railway might have united Belgrade with the Adriatic, and thereby provided the Switzerland of the Balkans with an outlet on the sea. To these territorial advantages were added the recognition of Servian independence and the cessation of the tribute, which since 1867 had been the last vestige of Turkish suzerainty. Montenegro was more than trebled in size, and doubled in population ; she was to retain her recent conquests ; Nikshich, Bilek, and Gatzko in the Herzegovina, Spizza, Antivari, and Dulcigno on the Adriatic, Spuj, Podgoritza, Plava, Gusinje, and the medieval Montenegrin capital of Jablyak on the side of Albania, and Priepolje in the *sanjak* of Novibazar, were included in the enlarged principality. Montenegrin independence, which had really existed for five centuries, and had been already thrice acknowledged by the Turkish firman of 1799 and by the Turco-Montenegrin treaties of 1838 and 1842, yet subsequently ignored by the Turks, was formally recognised by the Sultan. Roumania, which had rendered such splendid service to Russia at Plevna and had isolated the garrison of Vidin while the Slavs advanced towards Constantinople, was treated far less generously than the Bulgars, whose country had, indeed, been the theatre of operations, but who had played a much less important part in the actual fighting. While the independence of Roumania was admitted by the Porte, Russia acted with base ingratitude towards her Latin allies. She was resolved to re-acquire at all costs, preferably at that of her Roumanian neighbours, the southern part of Bessarabia, which had been taken from her and joined to Moldavia in 1856. She, therefore, obtained from Turkey in lieu of part of the war indemnity the *sanjak* of Toultcha, which comprised a large part of the barren Dobrudja, as well as the islands of the delta and the Isle of Serpents, with the object of exchanging them compulsorily for that far more desirable strip of Bessarabia. Further, in lieu of a portion of the war indemnity, Russia stipulated for the cession to herself of Ardahan, Kars, Bayazid, and Batûm with a strip of coast in Asia, so that Trebizond and Erzerum would become the first important towns within the new Turkish frontier. In order still further to cripple her adversary, she insisted on the demolition of all the Danubian fortresses and a war indemnity, which after the above deductions amounted to 310,000,000 roubles, 10,000,000 payable at once and the rest according to a subsequent understanding. On behalf of the Christian populations still left under Turkish rule, she demanded autonomy for Bosnia and the remaining portion of the Herzegovina under a Christian governor-general, subject to modifications thereafter to be made by Turkey, Austria-Hungary, and herself. In Crete the Porte promised "to apply scrupulously the Organic Law of 1868," and to introduce "an analogous law adapted to local requirements into Epirus, Thessaly, and the other parts of Turkey in Europe." Finally, by article 16 Turkey engaged "to carry into effect, without further delay, the improvements and reforms demanded by local requirements in the provinces inhabited by Armenians, and to guarantee their security from Kurds and Circassians." The subsequent Armenian massacres form a striking commentary on this article.

The treaty of San Stefano was a wholly Slavonic settlement of a question which concerns other races as well. It would have given the final blow to the Turkish empire in Europe by cutting the remaining Ottoman territory in two separate parts, and by imposing a Bulgarian barrier between the two chief cities of European Turkey. More than that, it would have aggrandised the Bulgarian at the expense of the Greek nationality in Macedonia and Thrace, and would have sacrificed the

Albanians to the aggrandisement of Montenegro and Bulgaria. From every part of the ceded districts came protests against this flagrant violation of justice and ethnology. The Greeks addressed an erudite disquisition to the British government on this complete disregard of their historic claims; the Mussulmans appealed to Queen Victoria as the Empress of a hundred million Moslem subjects; the Lazes begged for British protection to prevent the cession of Batûm and the consequent ruin of Trebizond; the Serbs protested against the inclusion of Servian regions in Bulgaria; the Albanians formed a league to "resist until death" any attempt upon the inviolability of their land; the Roumanians bitterly reproached Russia for having treated them with such base ingratitude, and contended that no modification of the treaty of Paris, the charter of their country, could be legally effected by two of the signatories without the consent of the others. The British government replied sympathetically to both the Greek and Roumanian claims to be represented at the Congress, and told the Greek Cabinet that it was "prepared to exert all its influence to prevent the absorption into a Slav state of any Greek population." But the chief motive of British opposition to the treaty was the conviction that the "big Bulgaria" of San Stefano would be merely a Russian province, a constant menace to Constantinople, and a basis for a future Russian attack upon it. The idea of the late Sir William White had not then gained acceptance in England, that our true policy in the east is the formation of strong and independent Balkan states, which would serve as a barrier between Russia and her goal and might even become the allies and the outposts of a reformed Turkey against Muscovite aggression. Yet close observers of the attitude of the Bulgars during the war might have noticed that the "little brothers," whom the Russians had come to free, were very glad of freedom, but had no desire to exchange one despotism for another, even though the latter were Orthodox and Slavonic.

"Liberated nations," wrote Bismarck some years later, "are not grateful but exacting"; and that most realistic of then living statesmen supported his thesis by the examples of the Greeks, the Roumanians, the Serbs, and the Bulgars. "All these races," he pointed out, "have gladly accepted Russian help for liberation from the Turks; but since they have been free they have shown no tendency to accept the Tsar as successor of the Sultan....Even if the peace of San Stefano had been carried out intact" the permanent dependence of Bulgaria on Russia "would probably have proved false." But at that moment all the appearances justified the British suspicions. The past policy of Russia towards the eastern Christians had not been disinterested; her past relations with Greece proved that what she did not want was the erection of a really strong Christian state on the ruins of Turkey. All the circumstances attending the birth of the new Bulgaria pointed in the same direction—the Prince to be "freely elected by the population," and the future administrative organisation to be drawn up by an assembly of notables, "under the superintendence of an Imperial Russian Commissioner," who would watch for two years over its application. Nor was Great Britain the only Power opposed to the treaty. Austria-Hungary had greater interests in the Balkan peninsula; she had been promised at Reichstadt the occupation of Bosnia and the Herzegovina; she contemplated that *Drang nach Osten*, which would have been as effectually barred as the Greek advance to Constantinople by a "big Bulgaria," cutting her off from Salonika; and, if Hungarian sympathies were with the Turks as the foes of the Slavs, Andrássy in 1869 had recalled the rights of the Crown of St Stephen over medieval Bosnia. In France, Waddington, the new Foreign Minister, educated at Rugby and Cambridge, had strongly British predilections.

Even before the treaty of San Stefano, Austria-Hungary had proposed the summons of a conference at Vienna, which

DIAGRAM TO ILLUSTRATE THE TREATY OF SAN STEFANO

REFERENCE:
The territory restored to Turkey by the
Treaty of Berlin is shown thus
English Miles
0 10 20 30 40 50   100

BLACK SEA

Bosporus

RUMANIA

BULGARIA

Tributary Principality

SERVIA

Accession to Servia

Bosnia

Herze-govina

Accession to Montenegro

MONTENEGRO

AUSTRIA

ADRIATIC SEA

Albania

Epirus

Thessaly

GREECE

AEGEAN SEA

Dardanelles

Thrace

R. Maritsa

R. Danube

Portugalia
Accession to Rumania

BULGARIA

Macedonia

RUMELIA

subsequently became the Congress of Berlin—the capital of the Power least interested in the eastern question, and the abode of the great statesman who had both the frankness to offer himself as " an honest broker" and the authority to secure the acceptance of his friendly offices.   Russia was willing to entertain the proposal, provided that she might select what clauses of the treaty she pleased for discussion at the Congress.   The British government, on the other hand, demanded the examination of the treaty as a whole, and followed up its demands by action.   Derby, indeed, declined to be responsible any longer for a warlike policy, with which he had long been out of sympathy, and resigned the Foreign Office to Salisbury, fresh from his practical experience of Turkish tactics at the Constantinople conference, who lived to make the sorrowful confession that in her pro-Turkish policy Great Britain had "backed the wrong horse."   Beaconsfield then called out the reserves, and ordered a force of native Indian troops to Malta, while his new Foreign Secretary in a circular addressed to the other Powers summed up the British government's objections to the treaty of San Stefano. The mobilisation of the Austrian army, the indignation of Roumania at Russian ingratitude, the discontent at home, all contributed to induce the Tsar to listen to the British arguments.   Through the mediation of Count Schouvaloff, the Russian ambassador in London, a secret agreement, which speedily found its way into print, was made between the two governments for the modification of the " big Bulgaria," and the way was paved for the meeting of the European Areopagos at Berlin.

The Congress of Berlin, which opened on June 13 and closed on the same day of the following month, was the most important gathering of statesmen that had met since the last great liquidation of the eastern question at Paris 22 years earlier.   All the Great Powers were represented by their leading statesmen—Great Britain by the Prime Minister and the Foreign Secretary; Russia by Gortchakoff and the Russian ambassador in London; France by Waddington; Austria-Hungary by Andrássy and Haymerle; Italy by Corti, her Minister for Foreign Affairs; Germany by the "Iron Chancellor," who was elected president of the Congress. Each Power was also assisted by the counsels of its ambassador in Berlin; while Turkey, the object of this surgical operation, found in Alexander Karatheodori and Mehemet Ali, respectively a Greek and a German, characteristic advocates of Moslem interests. In pursuance of the British pledge to see that Greek claims should not suffer from Greek neutrality in the war, and of his favourable reply to the Roumanian note, Salisbury championed the admission of both Greece and Roumania. He pointed out that the creation of the Bulgarian Exarchate had made the Greeks and Bulgars rivals, and that, while the latter enjoyed the protection of Russia, the former were unrepresented at the council which was about to decide on the future of the east. With his customary irony he added that, "after having heard the delegates of a nation which claimed the provinces of another state, it would be equitable to listen to the representatives of a country which demanded territories already belonging to it." The Congress decided, however, that the Greek delegates, Theodore Deligiánnes and Alexander Ragkavês, like the Roumanian representatives, Brătianu and Kogălniceanu, should be merely admitted to state their views without the right of voting. Thus, none of the small states immediately concerned in the settlement were allowed direct representation at the council-board; and the discussion was conducted by men personally unacquainted for the most part with the geography and racial characteristics of the vast and complicated region which they were about to partition, much as Pope Alexander VI partitioned Africa, without having seen it.

The Congress, in spite of the threatened departure of the British delegates at a critical stage of the negotiations, accomplished its work, and drew up on July 13 what for 34 years was, at least on paper, the charter of the Balkan peninsula. The treaty of San Stefano was almost entirely nullified by the treaty of Berlin. Instead of a " big Bulgaria " stretching from the Danube to the Aegean and from the Black Sea beyond the Macedonian lakes, it created a small "autonomous and tributary principality under the suzerainty of the Sultan," which was bounded by the Danube, the Balkans, the Black Sea and the Servian and Macedonian frontiers, and had a harbour at Varna. South of the Balkans there was artificially formed an autonomous province, known by the diplomatic name of "Eastern Roumelia," and placed "under the direct political and military authority of the Sultan," but administered by "a Christian Governor-General" "named by the Porte, with the assent of the Powers, for a term of five years." The recent history of Moldavia and Wallachia might have suggested the reflection that national feeling will sooner or later join together what diplomacy has severed. But for the moment the separation of Bulgaria into two sections was regarded as a triumph of British statesmanship and a diminution of Russian influence. Such is the short-sightedness of the ablest diplomatists, that when the union of the two Bulgarias was accomplished only seven years later, it was the British government that supported, and the Russian that condemned it. It was further provided that the Prince of Bulgaria should be "freely elected by the population and confirmed by the Porte, with the consent of the Powers," and that no member of any great reigning dynasty should be eligible. Until a Bulgarian "Assembly of Notables" should have drawn up an organic law for the principality, a Russian commissioner was to direct the administration, but the duration of this provisional arrangement was limited to nine months. The organisation of Eastern Roumelia, on the other hand, was entrusted to an European commission, to which three months were assigned for its labours.

While the articles affecting Bulgaria were, intended to minimise Russian influence in the eastern Balkans, the clauses regarding the Serb population were favourable to the growth of Austria in the west.   In pursuance of the Reichstadt agreement, and on the proposal of Salisbury, without any protest but merely "with some apparent reluctance" on the part of the representatives of Italy (which 30 years later expressed such popular indignation at their annexation), Bosnia and the Herzegovina were to be "occupied and administered by Austria-Hungary," which thus became what she had been for two decades of the eighteenth century—a Balkan state.   Arguments, alike practical and historical, could be advanced for this arrangement.   Even the author of the *Illyrian Letters*[1], Mr (now Sir) Arthur Evans, no friend of Austria, had admitted that it was "the only solution within the sphere of practical politics."   The two provinces contained few Turks, and were distant from the Turkish capital; while the co-existence of two Slav races and of three religions, Orthodox, Roman Catholic, and Mussulman, suggested the administration of a strong foreign Power as a better means of securing order and good government than the annexation of part of Bosnia to unsettled Servia, and of the Herzegovina to a principality so devoid of material resources as Montenegro, which an exclusive attention to the doctrine of nationalities might have demanded.   Austria-Hungary had already a number of Croats and Serbs among her subjects; Dalmatia was the natural frontage of Bosnia; and, besides the Hungarian claims to the medieval Bosnian kingdom, the north of it had been annexed by Austria so recently as 1718.   Moreover, the British Secretary for Foreign Affairs saw in an Austrian occupation the best means of preventing a chain of Slav states from stretching across the Balkan peninsula.   In a secret Austro-Turkish agreement, signed on the day of the signature of the Berlin treaty, the Austrian plenipotentiaries declared that the above-mentioned article contained nothing derogatory of "the

[1] Pp. 239–40.

Sultan's sovereign rights," and that "the occupation" would
be "considered as provisional."

This was not the only blow dealt by the Berlin treaty at the
hopes of Servian and Montenegrin patriots. Article 25 further
gave to the Dual Monarchy "the right of keeping garrisons
and having military and commercial roads" in the *sanjak* of
Novibazar, which remained as a Turkish wedge between the two
Servian states, a funnel through which Austrian influences and
perhaps Austrian armies (unless the Morava route were preferred)
could penetrate into North Albania and Macedonia. A further
convention, dated April 21, 1879, between Austria-Hungary
and Turkey, while confirming this treaty right, stated that
Austrian troops would only be placed at the three points of
Priboj, Priepolje, and Bijelopolje, which last place was almost
immediately exchanged for Plevlje. In accordance with
Austrian wishes, the territorial additions made to modern
Servia at Berlin were not in Old Servia, the heart of the
medieval Servian kingdom, which still remained Turkish,
but at Nish and Vranja, and in the Bulgarian-speaking district
of Pirot, thus increasing the principality by one-fourth. Servia
also obtained the formal recognition of her independence;
but, like the other two Slav states, she was to pay her share
of the Ottoman debt for these new possessions. Montenegro,
at last definitely recognised by everyone as a sovereign state,
had to be content with twice, instead of thrice, her original
territory. She kept Nikshich, and received the districts of
Piva and Banjani with the Duga pass on the side of the
Herzegovina, Podgoritza, Spuj, Jablyak, and the towns of
Gusinje and Plava with their dependent villages on that of
Albania. She obtained an outlet on the sea at the bay of
Antivari, but was forced to restore Dulcigno to Turkey and to
cede Spizza to Austria. The former of these grievances was
redressed in 1880; the latter has never been forgotten, for the
guns of what was from 1878 to 1919 the southernmost village
of Dalmatia commanded the bay and dominated the King's

palace on the shore. Yet further to prevent Antivari from becoming a possible naval base for Russia, article 29 provided that all Montenegrin waters should "remain closed to the ships of war of all nations," that the principality should have neither fleet nor naval flag, and that the maritime and sanitary police of the small strip of Montenegrin coast should be in the hands of Austria-Hungary. These inexorable conditions, feebly criticised by one of the Italian representatives and maintained intact for 31 years, were a bitter disappointment to Prince Nicholas. He saw the Herzegovina, the cradle of his race, the stony land where he had fought so valiantly against his hereditary enemy, occupied by his arch-foe—that *Erzfeind* which was then so much more feared at Cetinje than the *Erbfeind* of other times. He saw, too, Spizza, the poor man's "ewe lamb," as his ardent admirer, Freeman, called it, taken from him, its captor, by a Power to which it had never belonged. These acts, especially the latter, he never forgave, nor were his people likely ever to forget.

A still greater injustice was perpetrated by the articles dealing with Roumania. Roumanian independence was made conditional on the retrocession of South Bessarabia to Russia in exchange for "the islands forming the delta of the Danube as well as the Isle of Serpents," which had been transferred from Moldavia to immediate Turkish sovereignty in 1857, "the *sanjak* of Toultcha," and "the territory situated south of the Dobrudja as far as a line starting eastward from Silistria and terminating in the Black Sea, south of Mangalia." Against this cruel condition, first foreshadowed and denounced by Rosetti at the end of 1875, and plainly advanced at the Russian headquarters in Roumania in 1877, Prince Charles and his high-spirited people protested in vain. Russia insisted on thus rewarding the splendid services of her Latin allies, to whose assistance her victory had been largely due, while the extra piece of land given as a consolation to Roumania was benevolently taken from Bulgaria. In the phrase of a

Roumanian statesman, it was "not vanquished Turkey who paid Russia for the expenses of the war, but Roumania." The empire of the Tsar was thus once more bounded by the " accursed stream," the Pruth which, after 22 years of union, again separated the free Roumanians from their brothers in Bessarabia, a region historically and ethnographically Roumanian, while the Dobrudja contained large Bulgarian and Turkish elements, as well as Turkish-speaking Gagauzes, Christianised descendants of the Cumans, and was still as desolate as when Ovid had lamented that it was his place of exile. Moreover, the consignment of a Bulgarian population to Roumanian rule tended, and was perhaps intended, to sow discord between the two adjacent states. Roumanian energy has, indeed, made the best of this compulsory and unpopular exchange; the splendid bridge of Cernavoda now spans the Danube, uniting the trans-Danubian province to the rest of the country, and making the barren Dobrudja a highway, by the now flourishing port of Constantza, from Berlin to the Bosphorus. But the ingratitude of Russia long rankled in the minds of the Roumans, and soon had the effect of driving that Latin country into the orbit of the Triple Alliance. The other and much more plausible condition of her independence— the abolition of Jewish disabilities—Roumania has sometimes evaded and sometimes ignored. It is argued by Roumanian statesmen that in their country, and especially in Moldavia, the Jewish question is not religious but social and economic, and that the admission of these Semitic outlanders to full rights would swamp the native population. In order, however, to obtain recognition by the Powers, the Roumanian government had to revise article 7 of the constitution, which permitted the naturalisation of Christian aliens only ; but even then the naturalisation of the Jews was limited by various legal restrictions, with which a pre-occupied Europe did not trouble to interfere. Roumania received a seat on the European commission of the Danube, whose powers continued "as far as

Galatz in complete independence of the territorial authorities."
From there to the Iron Gates the regulations for the river
were to " be elaborated by the European commission, assisted
by delegates of the riverain states," while to Austria-Hungary
was entrusted the removal of the Iron Gates, accomplished in
1896.

Greece received by the Berlin treaty no increase of territory.
Deligiánnes told the Congress that, in view of the general
desire of a pacific settlement, his government would be content
for the time being with the annexation of Crete and of the
Turkish provinces bordering on the Greek kingdom—an
arrangement which, as he justly argued, would be a guarantee
of peace. Accordingly, the Congress, on the proposal of
Waddington, invited the Porte, in its 13th protocol, so to
rectify the Greek frontier as to make the northern boundary
of Hellas march with the Peneiós on the east, and with the
Kalamâs, which flows into the sea opposite the southern half
of Corfù, on the west. The 24th article of the treaty reserved
to the Powers the right of their mediation to facilitate this
settlement, which had been originally suggested by Salisbury
in a despatch of May 28, and for which the Greek Premier
expressed his gratitude to England. Crete, on the other hand,
was to remain Turkish, the Porte promising to apply the
Organic Law of 1868; and the Cretans, who had hoped more
from the collective wisdom of the Powers at Berlin than from
British intervention, were so keenly disappointed that the
General Assembly requested the mediation of the British
government with the Porte, while petitions for a British
protectorate were sent to consul Sandwith by Cretan Christians.
The rest of the Turkish empire, for which no special administration was provided, had to be content with the prospect of
an organisation similar to that which had failed to satisfy the
Cretans, the details being left to "special commissions,"
representing the native populations. This article, destined
to cover Macedonia, Thrace, Albania, and the larger part

of Epirus, has remained a dead letter, and thus, in 1912,
provided a *casus belli.*

Such were the main provisions of this new charter of the
near east, so far as it affected Europe.   In Asia, the Black
Sea frontier, as fixed at San Stefano, was preserved at Berlin ;
the Porte ceded Ardahan, Kars, and Batûm to Russia, but
retained Bayazid ; while the Tsar promised that Batûm should
be made "a free port, essentially commercial."   Eight years
later his successor, despite the protests of the British government, repudiated this solemn promise, thus affording a further
example of Russian good faith.   Finally—most futile of all
these pledges—by article 61 the Porte undertook "to carry
out, without further delay, the ameliorations and reforms
demanded by local requirements in the provinces inhabited
by the Armenians, and to guarantee their security against the
Circassians and Kurds."   Periodical statements of these
reforms were to be made to the Powers, who would "superintend their application."   A special responsibility for the
protection of the Armenians devolved upon Great Britain in
virtue of the Cyprus convention, which had been hastily
signed on June 4, and the publication of which during the
Congress came as a thunder-clap upon the diplomatic world.
By this convention Great Britain engaged to join the Sultan
in the defence of his Asiatic dominions against any further
Russian attack, and the Sultan promised, in return, "to
introduce necessary reforms" there, in consultation with his
ally.   In order to enable the latter to fulfil her engagement,
he assigned to her "the island of Cyprus to be occupied and
administered by" her as "a place of arms" in the Levant,
on payment of an annual tribute, calculated by the average
surplus of the five previous years, and on the understanding
that a Russian evacuation of the recent Asiatic conquests
should be followed by a British evacuation of Cyprus.   Thus
Beaconsfield "consolidated" the Turkish empire by assigning
the administration of Bosnia and the Herzegovina to Austria-

Hungary and that of Cyprus to Great Britain, with which its sole historical connexion had been the ephemeral conquest by Cœur-de-Lion nearly seven centuries earlier. The Turks were indignant at this pacific cession of their territory; Cypriotes and British now alike condemn the financial arrangements. But the Premier's own opinion of these diplomatic achievements was summed up in the memorable phrase, in which he told the British people on his return from Berlin, that he had brought them "peace with honour."

The experience of the generation that has elapsed since the signature of the Berlin treaty forces us, however, to qualify the estimate which the British plenipotentiaries formed of its provisions; the victories of the Balkan League and the Entente have destroyed the *status quo* which it created. But even before the great upheaval of 1912 it had not proved in any sense a permanent "settlement of an eternal question"; it had not secured the peace of the Balkan peninsula; it had not ensured the just treatment of the Christian races which it left under Turkish rule. Almost every signatory Power, and more than one small state, had violated some provision of this solemn international instrument. Turkey had broken articles 23 and 61 by doing nothing to reform the lot of the Macedonian and Armenian populations, while no Power had taken effective steps on behalf of the latter. Russia had torn up article 59 by closing and fortifying Batûm; Austria-Hungary had arbitrarily extended the provisions of article 25 by annexing Bosnia and the Herzegovina. Italy by her annexation of Tripoli and the Cyrenaica had ignored article 63, which proclaimed the maintenance of the treaty of Paris. Bulgaria had already contemptuously and successfully annulled two whole series of clauses by the union of Eastern Roumelia and the declaration of Bulgarian independence. Roumania had defied article 44 by her persecution of the Jews; the Albanians article 28 by their refusal to be included in Montenegro. The Montenegrin frontier had been modified by an armed demonstration,

whereas Greece had received only a portion of the territory
indicated as hers in the 13th protocol, and Crete had protested
against article 23 to such purpose, that after four of the
signatory Powers had placed her under the government of
a Greek commissioner, she proclaimed her union with Greece.
Two short but desperate wars, one of them fratricidal,
a third barely averted, various insurrections in Crete and
Albania, and the sanguinary conflict of rival propagandas in
Macedonia, had demonstrated the futility of supposing that
the paper panaceas and parchment bonds of western diplomacy
would heal the racial and religious jealousies or restrain the
racial ambitions of centuries in a part of Europe—if Europe
it can be called—where the claims derived from medieval, and
even ancient, history are constantly invoked as if a thousand
years were but as yesterday. Yet, if the treaty of Berlin
presents a still more lacerated appearance to-day, it nevertheless marked an advance towards the ultimate solution of the
eastern question, for it greatly diminished Turkish rule over
the Balkan Christians, now wholly destroyed by the Balkan
Christians themselves. Whatever Servian nationalists may say,
the 41 years of Austrian administration in Bosnia and the
Herzegovina, with which we may compare the British occupation of Egypt and the French protectorate of Tunisia, had
converted two wild Turkish provinces into a civilised Balkan
state, even if the subjects did not love their civilisers; free
Bulgaria has proved to be a triumphant success ; while the
exemption of the Macedonian Greeks from Bulgarian rule
led Greek politicians to bless the name of Salisbury for his
services in helping to destroy the treaty of San Stefano. But
to regard the tattered Berlin treaty as an inviolable law of
nature was to ignore the fact that, in the imperfect world of
politics, international arrangements are only binding, so long
as the contracting parties choose to be bound by them, or the
populations concerned are weak and disunited. When, for
the first time in history, the "little neighbours" of Turkey

joined hands against her with the double strength of enthusiasm and organisation, the treaty of Berlin, like all artificial creations, succumbed before the great forces of nature ; and the principle of "the Balkans for the Balkan peoples" proved to be stronger than the barriers, erected by the Powers in their own interests, between the free and the unredeemed members of the same family.

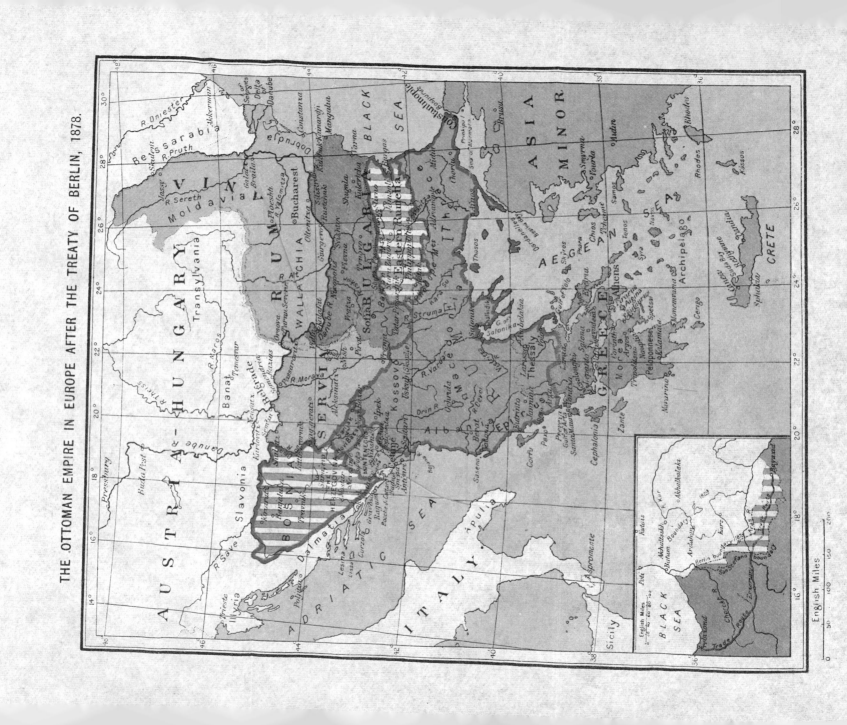

THE OTTOMAN EMPIRE IN EUROPE AFTER THE TREATY OF BERLIN, 1878.

English Miles

CHAPTER XVII

THE UNION OF THE TWO BULGARIAS (1878-87).

THE three years immediately following the Berlin Congress were occupied with the delimitation of the new frontiers and the establishment of the new order of things, which in the cases of Roumania, Bosnia, Montenegro, and Greece proved to be more difficult than had been expected. The Roumanian authorities took possession of the Dobrudja in November 1878, but nearly two years elapsed before the boundary between this trans-Danubian province and Bulgaria was fixed. Article 2 of the Berlin treaty had laid down that this boundary was to be drawn " to the east of Silistria," and a struggle now ensued between the Russian delegate and his colleagues on the European commission with regard to this line. While he strove to remove the Roumanian frontier as far away as possible from the celebrated fortress, they desired to fix it so close to the walls as to leave the town slaughter-house in Roumanian territory ! While this point was being argued, the Roumanian government occupied the Arab Tabia redoubt, rendered famous by the exploits of our countrymen in the siege of 1854 ; and this act so greatly irritated Russia that she insisted upon the evacuation of the position by her late allies— a second humiliation which naturally wounded the pride of a young and valiant nation. At last, in June 1880, the frontier was definitely drawn, so as to give the celebrated redoubt to the Roumanians, who also evaded the obligation of building their bridge so close to Silistria as to be at the mercy of its

Bulgarian garrison. Thus the Bulgaro-Roumanian frontier was unsatisfactory to both parties: it gave to Bulgaria the strong fortress which dominated the Dobrudja, it gave to Roumania valuable appurtenances of that place. Further difficulties arose out of the regulations for the Danube between the Iron Gates and Galatz. Austria-Hungary, although not a riverain state in this portion of the Danube, succeeded in obtaining the presidency of, and a casting vote on, a mixed commission of those states instituted for its regulation. Against this interference of the Dual Monarchy in the Servian, Bulgarian, and Roumanian reaches of the river, Roumania protested. It was not till 1883 that the treaty of London, signed by the signatory Powers of the treaty of Berlin, finally decided this question. The authority of the European commission, prolonged to 1904 and thereafter automatically renewable for periods of three years, was extended as high as Braïla, but removed from the Kilia arm of the river, which was partly Russian and partly Roumanian; while from Braïla to the Iron Gates simultaneous jurisdiction was exercised by a mixed commission, composed of five delegates, selected from Austria-Hungary, the three riverain states, and the European commission, under the chairmanship of the Austrian delegate and with its seat at Giurgevo. The three riverain states were excluded from this conference; Great Britain alone had pleaded for the admission of Roumania to its discussions.

Ere this, Roumania, on March 26, 1881, had been proclaimed a kingdom, on the proposal of the same General Lecca who had been instrumental in dethroning Couza 15 years earlier. The Roumanian crown was made from a Turkish cannon captured at Plevna, in token of the manner in which the country's independence had been won. A few months earlier, the succession to the throne had been settled—for "Carmen Sylva's" only child had died in 1875—by the adoption as heir of Ferdinand, son of that Leopold of Hohenzollern, whose candidature to the Spanish crown had been the occasion of the Franco-German war. The marriage of this nephew of King Charles with Princess Marie, daughter of the late Duke of Coburg, and grand-daughter of Queen Victoria, has connected the Roumanian dynasty with that of Great Britain. With the Germanic Powers the political relations of Roumania became close. After the conclusion of the Triple Alliance in 1882, Brătianu, following the foreign policy already advocated by the "Junimists," or "Young" Conservatives of Moldavia, had interviews with Kalnoky and Bismarck in 1883, thus bringing the Latin nation on the Danube within the orbit of the three central states, in opposition to Russia and France. This connexion involved the abandonment of Roumanian Irredentism at the expense of Austria-Hungary, just as Italy's partnership in the Triple Alliance had necessitated official discouragement of the corresponding Italian movement. Thus Roumania then became, under a German sovereign, a representative of German interests in the near east, and Bucharest a fortified outpost of the Triple Alliance.

Sixteen days after the signature of the Berlin treaty, the Austrian troops under Baron von Philippovich crossed the Save in four columns to take possession of Bosnia. The chief column followed the historic route along the Bosna valley which Prince Eugene had taken on the occasion of his famous dash on Sarajevo in 1697. But the Austrians had reckoned without the fanaticism of the Bosnian Mussulmans. On August 3 the Moslems of Maglaj treacherously cut to pieces a squadron of hussars; and a series of skirmishes followed, until the second column, having captured the ancient city of Jajce, where the last Bosnian king had met his death in 1463, effected a junction with the main body and pressed on to Sarajevo. When the Austrians approached, an insurrection broke out in the capital; the Turkish governor was deposed; and a fanatic, named Hajji Loja, preached a holy war against the Christians. On the 19th the Austrians opened fire upon the city, which,

after a desperate resistance, fell into their hands; a large part
of the town perished in the flames, and the grave of many an
Austrian soldier still bears silent testimony to the fury of the
defenders.   Meanwhile, a guerrilla warfare had broken out in
the rear, under the command of Muktija Effendi, an Albanian
from Novibazar, who was joined by some Turkish regulars.
The Bosna valley was once more the scene of constant conflicts;
and the Herzegovina, which had at first submitted to Baron
Jovanovich almost without a blow, became restive.   It was
necessary to send four more corps to the relief of the army of
occupation.   The valley of the Bosna was then cleared; the
Herzegovina was subdued by the end of September; and on
October 20 the last stronghold of the Bosnian insurgents
surrendered.   In 1882, however, another insurrection broke
out in the Herzegovina; and it was not till the appointment of
Baron von Kállay, the historian of the Serbs and former
consul-general at Belgrade, to direct the destinies of "the
Occupied Territory," that the constructive work, which has
gone on till recently, began.

The military occupation of the three points in the *sanjak*
of Novibazar began with the entrance of the Austro-Hungarian
troops into Plevlje on September 10, 1879.   The Austrians sent
only one civil official thither; and the Turkish administrative,
judicial, and financial authorities continued to co-exist with
them, while Turkish troops were stationed in the same towns
as the Austrian garrisons.   The delimitation of the Novibazar
frontier, in which Germany supported the Turks, was a cause
of Russian resentment; but friendly relations between the
Austrians and the Turkish authorities were largely maintained
during the period of this mixed occupation by the tact of Ferik
Suleiman, the perpetual pasha of Plevlje, who was appointed
soon after this strange and hybrid arrangement began.   The
exclusion of Turkish irregulars from the *sanjak* by the Austro-
Turkish convention of 1879 also had an excellent effect; while
Ottoman pride was characteristically salved by the diplomatic

device of forming the three towns and the four small intervening
watch-posts occupied by the Austrians into a new and smaller
sanjak of Plevlje.   But with the natives of this district, mostly
Serbs—for here was Rascia, the nucleus of the old Servian
monarchy—the "Europeans" were never popular.   These
"enslaved" Slavs were never allowed by their free Servian and
Montenegrin neighbours to forget the treaty of San Stefano;
and they regarded the Austro-Turkish wedge which prevented
the union of the two states on either side of them as an obstacle
to that dream of a revived Servian empire, which, after the
lapse of five centuries, was still ever present to the imaginative
minds of the scattered Serbs.   In 1881, however, M. Mijatovich,
then Servian Minister for Foreign Affairs, signed a secret convention with Austria, promising to discourage Servian agitation
in Bosnia, on condition that Austria promised to support
Servian pretensions to territory in Old Servia, or rather "in the
direction of the Vardar valley."   This convention, which
expired in 1889, is said to have been described by King
Alexander as "an act of treason."

While Austria was thus taking up her new position as the
"sentinel of the Balkans," her neighbour, the Prince of Montenegro, was unable to obtain the two Albanian districts of
Gusinje and Plava, which had been assigned to him at Berlin.
Their inhabitants were first-class fighting men, who cared for
neither the Congress nor the Sultan, and objected to have their
homes and themselves transferred without their consent to
another state, which, being admittedly better governed than
their own, might interfere with their time-honoured privileges
of lawlessness.   The fact that the Gusinjiotes could almost all
speak Serb and were converts from Orthodoxy to Islâm only
increased the hostility between them and their Montenegrin
neighbours, while the alleged "pagan" origin of the dwellers
by the lake of Plava may account for their fierce defiance of
both Turkish officials and Montenegrin braves.   The Sultan's
first envoy, sent to induce the Albanians to obey the orders of

the Berlin Congress, was Mehemet Ali, one of the Turkish plenipotentiaries; but the Arnauts were no respecters of persons, and they set fire to his house at Djakova and murdered him as he fled from the blazing building in September 1878. A second emissary failed to make them yield. Accordingly, in 1879 hostilities broke out between them and the Montenegrins; and the "Albanian League," which had been formed to combat the treaty of San Stefano, was revived, probably at the suggestion, certainly to the satisfaction, of the Porte, which was thus able to make the national sentiment of a race, which had had no separate existence since the days of Skanderbeg, and no great local leader since Ali of Joánnina, an excuse for not carrying out its inconvenient engagements. A compromise, suggested by Count Corti, the Italian ambassador at Constantinople, according to which Montenegro should receive instead of the towns of Gusinje and Plava a portion only of the former district and a larger strip of territory between Podgoritza and the lake of Scutari (including a part of the Gruda tribe with the town of Tuzi, famous during the Maltsori[1] insurrection of 1911), was accepted on April 12, 1880, but proved incapable of execution, owing to the determined opposition of the Albanians. Those who inhabited this region were Roman Catholics; and, if the Mussulman Albanians had objected to Prince Nicholas as a Christian, the Catholics repudiated him as what was worse—an Orthodox one. Prenk Bib Doda, the Mirdite Prince, whose territory to the south of the Drin was not menaced by the proposed aggrandisement of Montenegro, marched at the head of his tribe to the aid of his brothers in faith; and ere long 10,000 men were on the frontier. Meanwhile, Gladstone had returned to power in England, and his well-known Montenegrin sympathies facilitated a solution of the question. The plenipotentiaries of the Powers met in conference at Berlin in June to consider the best means of securing the performance

[1] This appears to be the correct spelling of the word usually spelt "Malissori."

by Turkey of the unfulfilled engagements made there two years before, and proposed in lieu of Count Corti's scheme, that Montenegro should receive the town of Dulcigno and a strip of seaboard as far as the river Bojana. This proposal the Porte refused to accept on the ground that Dulcigno contained a Moslem population, and secretly urged the Albanians to resist its cession. Thereupon, at the suggestion of the British government, a naval demonstration of the Powers was held in September before the old Venetian colony, while Montenegrin troops approached it by land. As the Porte still held out, and the admirals were anxious not to bombard the town, this existence of *Dulcigno far niente*, as Beust wittily called it, might have continued indefinitely, had not the British government suggested the seizure of the rich custom-house at Smyrna. The mere suggestion had the desired effect; Dervish Pasha, the Turkish commander, drove out the Albanians, and at last, on November 26, the Montenegrins peaceably occupied Dulcigno. Prince Nicholas publicly expressed his gratitude to Great Britain, and he never forgot the part which she played in procuring for him this fresh outlet on the sea. Dulcigno is not, however, the natural frontage of the Black Mountain, but of Albania, as the Arnauts still remember; it is an apple of discord between them and the Slavs, while the latter have not developed it; indeed, it is a mere open roadstead, and the neighbouring bay of Val di Noce has never been exploited. But, at any rate, if Montenegro still lacked a good harbour, if her haven of Antivari was till 1909 still bound by Austrian fetters, she had a seaboard of 30 miles, and she owed its extension, as she owed her brief occupation of Cattaro in 1813, to the aid of a British fleet. Dulcigno, however, has been our last service to the Black Mountain. Gladstone's successors cared nothing about the "smallest among peoples"; for years they left their country unrepresented at Cetinje, published no reports on its progress, and took no part in its Sovereign's Jubilee, thus allowing British prestige to decline in one of those states

where it stood highest. Dervish Pasha completed the pacification of northern Albania by inviting Prenk Bib Doda to visit a
Turkish man-of-war, then lying off San Giovanni di Medua.
The young Mirdite Prince unsuspectingly accepted the invitation ; but he was no sooner on board than the vessel got up
steam and carried him off to a 28 years' exile, mostly spent at
Kastamuni in Asia Minor, whence he returned in 1908. A
corps of gendarmes, the so-called "Mirdite zaptiehs," was
formed for the preservation of order in his native land ; but
during the exile of the Prince and the absence of his mother
and sister from the ruined home of the family at Oroshi, the
Mirdite capital, all real authority was exercised by the Mirdite
Abbot, who had learnt in Newfoundland and Bombay what
freedom and civilisation meant. Other leaders of the "League"
were exiled, but a fresh bond was formed in 1883 between the
four Catholic tribes of Kastrati, Hoti, Gruda, and Skreli, to
oppose the definitive delimitation of the Montenegrin frontier.
Even in 1911 there were two points where the boundary of the
principality was undefined—at Muzechka on the Albanian, and
near Grahovo on the Herzegovinian side ; and this purely
political line had been so badly drawn in other places, that
men of the same family and of the same rights in pasture-land
had been placed on opposite sides of this most unscientific
and anti-ethnographic frontier. Hence may be traced most
of the subsequent disputes between the Montenegrins and
Albanians, disputes apt to be magnified into international
incidents.

The rectification of the Greek frontier, suggested at the
Berlin Congress, gave even more trouble than that of the
Montenegrin boundary. Beaconsfield had told Greece that
she had a future, and that she could accordingly afford to wait.
She had to wait three years before she obtained one portion of
the new territory indicated as her due ; she waited over 30 for
the remainder. The Porte pursued its usual dilatory policy ;
the Turkish military authorities maintained that the Peneiós-

Kalamâs line would not be defensible; and the "Albanian
League" made its appearance in Epirus, as well as in northern
Albania. When the Porte appointed its commissioners, the
Epirote village where they were to meet their Greek colleagues
could not be found upon the map; when the meeting at last
took place in February 1879 at Préveza, the commissioners
could not agree. The Greeks considered inadequate and in-
consistent with the Berlin protocol the frontier offered by the
Turks, which ran from a point between Halmyrós and Volo to
the valley of the Aspropotamós, thus leaving a large portion of
the gulf of Volo Turkish, while ceding Halmyrós, Domokós
and portions of the districts of Kardítza and Phársala to Greece.
Accordingly on March 18 the commission broke up, while
Albanian delegates visited the chief European capitals and petitions and counter-petitions rained upon the British government
from the Greek and Albanian inhabitants of what the former
called "Epeiros" and the latter "Albania," the former begging
for union with Greece, the latter declaring their intention to fight
rather than permit the cession of Préveza, Arta, and Joánnina.
Waddington then proposed that the negotiations, broken off at
Préveza, should be renewed at Constantinople, under the supervision of the ambassadors of the Powers; and Salisbury in a
masterly despatch pointed out that the frontier of 1832 had been
badly chosen, that it had been largely responsible for brigandage, and that the territory in question was "rather a source of
weakness than of strength to the Sultan." Accordingly, a fresh
Greco-Turkish commission met on the Bosphorus in August, but
with the same result as before; nor was Salisbury's proposal of
a frontier commission more fortunate. The accession of Gladstone to power in 1880 was welcomed in Greece, as in Montenegro, for the new Prime Minister was gratefully remembered in
connexion with the last extension of Hellas 16 years earlier.
Great Britain and France thereupon co-operated in convening a
conference of the Powers at Berlin in June for the settlement of
the Greek and Montenegrin questions. The frontier there

adopted on the proposal of the British and French delegates was very favourable to Greece; it ran from the mouth of the Kalamâs on the Ionian Sea to the eastern extremity of the crest of Olympus on the Aegean, leaving both Joánnina and Métzovon to Greece; indeed France wished to include the whole of Olympus, the abode of the Greek gods, in Greek territory. Athens went wild with excitement at the news; Trikoúpes, who had again succeeded Koumoundoûros as Prime Minister, at once accepted the proposal of the conference, and, when the Porte rejected it, mobilised the Greek army. A change of ministry in France, however, seriously injured the Greek cause. Hitherto the British and French governments had been the best friends of Greece; but Barthélemy St-Hilaire, the new French Minister of Foreign Affairs, whom the Greeks had ingenuously regarded as a Philhellene because he had translated Aristotle, adopted arguments which his British colleague qualified as those of the Turks, in opposition to those of the Powers.

The result was that the Porte, finding the Powers disunited, made a firmer resistance, while Greece went on with her military preparations. A French proposal for an arbitration of the Powers on the frontier question failed, because neither of the parties directly concerned desired to pledge itself beforehand to accept the award of the arbitrators. The Porte instead suggested a conference at Constantinople between itself and the representatives of the Powers; and this gathering, from which Greece was excluded, ultimately decided the question. Had the Greeks so desired, they could probably have had Crete, which Bismarck desired to give them instead of the Mussulman population of Epirus, and which the Turkish delegates actually offered, together with a narrow strip of continental territory along the existing boundary and "a few little islands" thrown in, on March 14. But it was naturally the policy of Greece to prefer an increase of territory on the mainland, where there were other Christian competitors, to the union of Crete, which, containing a wholly Greek population, was certain sooner or later to be joined to the Hellenic kingdom. Goschen, the British delegate, pleaded for the strategic frontier of Olympus and would have wished to secure Préveza for Greece, while Granville admitted that, after what had happened, "the Greek people" had "the amplest justification for holding that there ought to be a rectification, based on a line traversing the valley of the Kalamâs and that of the Peneiós." But it was clear from the outset that the Turks would make the cession of Préveza a *casus belli*; and, while all the Powers wanted peace, Greece was not prepared for war.   Finally, on May 24, 1881, a convention was signed, drawing the frontier line from near the defile of Karalik-Dervend, a little north of the vale of Témpe and about three miles south of Platamôna, to the river of Arta, and thence along the course of that river to its mouth on the Ambrakian gulf. Thus Greece received nearly the whole of Thessaly and that portion of Epirus which formed the district of Arta, whose famous bridge became, and long remained, the boundary between the free Greeks and their Epirote brethren—in all a territory of some 14,000 square kilomètres.   Punta, the "point" at the mouth of the Ambrakian gulf opposite Préveza, with the strip of Turkish territory behind it, was ceded; and thus one of the two keys of the gulf, which had been specially left to Turkey in 1832, was given to Greece.   Both there and at Préveza the fortifications were to be dismantled, and the navigation of the gulf was to be free. The religious property, or *vakouf*, and the religion of the Mussulmans were to be respected; Greece was to take over "a part of the Ottoman public debt proportionate to the revenues of the ceded territories."   The frontier was not ideal; the summit of the most typical of all Greek mountains was excluded from Greece, in which Pélion and Ossa were included; while Arta became Greek, the fields of its inhabitants remained Turkish; and Goschen admitted that Greece deserved a larger share of Epirus, where a journey from Arta or Préveza to Joánnina will convince the traveller of the predominantly

Hellenic character of that then unredeemed district.   But the arrangement was probably the best that could be made in the circumstances, nor has Great Britain cause to be ashamed of her part therein.   Koumoundoûros, who was in his last Premiership, accepted it ; and thus Greece gained the valuable plain of Thessaly and the historic capital of the medieval Despotat of Epirus.   Fighting, however, ensued in the following year for the possession of Karalik-Dervend, seized by the Turks in defiance of the convention, but definitely assigned to Greece by a mixed commission.   Thus ended the long-drawn question of the northern frontier, which had cost Greece from first to last two loans, amounting altogether to 180 millions of *drachmaí*, caused an aggregate deficit of 140 millions in her budgets, and led to the introduction in 1877 of the forced paper currency.   Trikoúpes accordingly during his long administration of over three years devoted his attention to economic questions. In 1884 he was able to abolish the forced currency ; but the higher taxes, which he had imposed, produced a re-action, and, in 1885, raised his rival, Theodore Deligiánnes, for the first time to the Premiership.   For from the death of Koumoundoûros in 1883 to that of Trikoúpes in 1896 Greek politics were a duel between those two men, the one a great statesman, the other a consummate parliamentary manager.

Crete, still left under Ottoman domination, had to content herself with a modification of the Organic Law of 1868.   This modified charter, called the Pact of Halépa, from the consular suburb of Canea, where it was signed in October 1878, provided that the Governor-General should hold office for five years, and should be assisted by an adviser of the opposite religion; that there should be a General Assembly sitting publicly for 40, or at most, 60 days in the year, and composed of 49 Christians and 31 Mussulmans; that Greek should be the language of both the Assembly and the law-courts; that natives should have the preference for official posts; and that, after the cost of local administration had been deducted from the insular revenues, the surplus should be divided in equal shares between the Imperial treasury and the houses of detention, schools, hospitals, harbours, and roads of the island, upon which practically nothing had been spent since the days of the Venetians, for Vely Pasha's well-meant effort to make a road from Rethýmne had led to his recall in 1858. Paper money was prohibited; salaries were to be paid in specie; newspapers were allowed; and an amnesty and the remission of arrears of taxation promised. In theory, at any rate, the Pact of Halépa was the high-water mark of Ottoman concessions to Crete. The bulk of the Christians were better satisfied than the Mussulmans; and during the seven years governorship of Photiádes Pasha, formerly Ottoman minister at Athens and himself a Greek of conciliatory disposition and administrative capacity, the island had little history. If the Christians desired the Greek government to accept the Turkish offer to cede the island in place of Thessaly in 1881, they acquiesced in its refusal for the sake of the future aggrandisement of the whole race; for advice from Athens usually has much weight in Crete.

The most important creation of the Berlin treaty—the principality of Bulgaria—was entrusted to Russian hands during the interregnum which lasted until a Prince could be elected. The Russian Commissioner, Prince Dondukov-Korsakov, was a rich man who kept open house and was personally popular, but he treated the country as a Russian province. All the chief posts were filled by the Russian "liberators," regardless of the fact that the Bulgarian peasants are extremely suspicious of foreigners. At first, while the memories of Turkish rule were fresh in men's minds, recognition of Russia's services reconciled the natives to this alien domination; but political gratitude, even in the Balkans, is usually short-lived, and ere long the Bulgarians began to show that they had not ceased to be Turkish *râyahs* in order to become Russian subjects. Yet further to strengthen the hold of Russia, the Commissioner prepared the draft of a constitution, at once ultra-democratic and ultra-conservative, which was so devised that the Prince could be checkmated by the people and the people by the Prince, while the real power would remain with the Tsar; unfortunately, paper constitutions never produce in practice the results which they are intended to achieve. It never occurred to the astute framer of the Bulgarian charter, that he had not provided against one contingency which actually arose—the union of Prince and people against their "liberators." Meanwhile, Bulgaria, a land of peasants without the smallest experience of parliamentary institutions, was suddenly endowed with a single Chamber, or ordinary *Sobranje*, elected by manhood suffrage, with free, compulsory, elementary education, equal electoral districts, payment of members, and a free press. As against these democratic provisions, the Ministers were made independent of the Chamber and creatures of the Prince, who was given the further power of dissolving the *Sobranje* whenever he chose. No second Chamber was instituted, nor would it have been easy to devise one in a land without an aristocracy, without great fortunes, and without a leisured or a highly cultured class. But for great changes, such as the election of a Prince, the nomination of Regents, the extension, cession, or exchange of territory, or the revision of the constitution, an extraordinary assembly, or Grand *Sobranje*, was declared necessary. This body was formed of twice the number of members composing the ordinary Chamber. The constitution was passed by an Assembly of Notables, held not at Sofia, the newly-chosen capital, but at the ancient Imperial city of Trnovo on April 28, 1879. Next day, Prince Alexander of Battenberg, son of Prince Alexander of Hesse and nephew of the Tsar, was elected first Prince of Bulgaria. Two months later the new ruler set foot in his principality and took the oath to the constitution at Trnovo.

Prince Alexander, at the time of his election, was only 22 years of age; but he had already seen service in the land of his adoption. He had taken part in the Russo-Turkish war,

had crosed the Danube at Svishtov and the Balkans with
Gourko; he had fought at Nova Zagora and had stood in the
trenches at Plevna; at the time of his election he was serving
as a Prussian lieutenant at Potsdam. If, however, his military
experience and his tall, martial bearing fitted him for one part
of his duties, his complete lack of both political education
and statesmanlike capacity were serious drawbacks to the
performance of the other. He was obstinate, talkative, and apt
to quarrel with his advisers, and he had the great disadvantage of
having to trust for some time to interpreters in his intercourse
with them. A stranger to the tortuous politics of a newly-
emancipated oriental land, in which personal questions naturally
played a prominent part, he was certain to make mistakes in
council, which, however, he fully redeemed on the field of battle.

For the first two years of his reign, the Prince, who had
ascended the throne as the nominee of Russia, naturally inclined towards the Russophil, or Conservative party, although
the Nationalists, or Liberals, were in a majority. Finding himself
unable to work with his parliament, in 1881 he suddenly issued
a proclamation announcing his resignation unless irresponsible
authority were conferred upon him for seven years, and appointed the Russian general Ernroth president of the provisional
administration. A packed Assembly, held at Svishtov under
threat of the Prince's instant departure on the steamer which
lay ready in the Danube, conceded his demands; the *coup
d'état* had succeeded, and he was, to all appearance, master
of the country. But Russia was the power behind the brand-
new Bulgarian throne; two more Russian generals, Sobolev
and Alexander Kaulbars, arrived from St Petersburg to assume
the posts of Premier and Minister of War; and representative
institutions were reduced to a small Chamber which had no
function beyond that of voting the budget. Both the
Prince and his people soon resented the tactless conduct and
imperious ways of the Russian generals, who treated the free
Bulgarians as Asiatics, and loathed their ruler as a German.

Accordingly, in 1883, he restored the constitution of Trnovo; and his two Russian Ministers retired to their own country. From that moment Russia began to intrigue against the too independent Prince, who was compensated by the affection of his hitherto indifferent people for the loss of Russian patronage.

Meanwhile, the International Commission had drawn up the Organic Statute for Eastern Roumelia; and in 1879 Alexander Vogorídes, son of the Roumeliote who had been first Prince of Samos, and himself a Turkish official, was appointed the first Governor-General. Aleko Pasha, as he was called in the Turkish service, thus represented in his own person the three nationalities of the province—Bulgarians, Greeks, and Turks—whose languages were all declared to be official. The Roumelian constitution was more conservative than that of the neighbouring principality. The local assembly consisted of 56 members, of whom 36 were elected on a property or educational franchise, while the others were either nominated or *ex officio* members. Politics were excluded from its discussions, which were occupied with financial and administrative questions; the "spoils system," apt to be the curse of the Balkan states, was avoided by a permanent civil service; and the chief posts were filled by well-to-do Roumeliotes of good family. Six Directors conducted the administration, the chief of whom, the Secretary-General, Gavril Krstjovich, was, like the Governor, a Roumeliote with Samian experience. In these circumstances, Eastern Roumelia was materially better off than the principality; the Thracian plain is naturally the richest part of the two Bulgarias; and the absence of political agitation is the greatest of blessings that any Balkan land can enjoy. Only in the Rhodope mountains, where a half-English, half-Polish adventurer, named St Clair, owner of a hunting-box near the coast of the Black Sea, had been hailed as a "saviour" by the Mussulman insurgents at the close of the war, 22 communities of 19,000 Bulgarian Moslems formed the so-called "Pomak Republic," independent alike of Turkey and of Eastern Roumelia, to which the Berlin treaty had assigned them. One of the authors of the massacres of 1876 maintained himself as the chief of this band of fanatical robbers, until, in 1883, the Porte, heedless of the Berlin treaty, annexed the "Republic" by the cheap device of decorating and giving official uniforms to the leading "Republicans."

Nationalist feeling was maintained, despite the prosperity of Eastern Roumelia, by the Bulgars of Sliven, the industrial town which regarded the capital as cosmopolitan; and, when the first Governor-General's five years of office expired, there was an Unionist party, which advocated the nomination of Alexander as his successor. For the moment, however, the Unionists were defeated, and the Russophil Krstjovich was appointed under the name of Gavril Pasha. But the tactless exercise of the Porte's right of veto on Roumeliote legislation, and the wish for a Bulgarian customs union, increased the desire for political unity. A secret gathering fixed the coming revolution for September, 1885; and on the morning of the 18th, Majors Nikolajev, Filov, and Mutkurov surrounded the Pasha's *konak* at Philippopolis, while Stojanov, the leader of the Unionist agitation, entered his room and told him that he was a prisoner. The aged Governor-General yielded to superior force; he was drawn round the town in mock triumph with a Bulgarian schoolmistress holding an unsheathed sabre by his side, and then sent away to Sofia, and thence to Constantinople. Not a single drop of blood stained the revolution; the Union of the two Bulgarias under Alexander was proclaimed; and a provisional government, of which Dr Stranski was the head, was formed to await his decision. The Prince had been forewarned of the conspirators' plans, but he hesitated at first to defy Turkey and the Powers by accepting their offer. Stambulov, then Speaker of the Chamber, told him, however, plainly, that, if he did not advance to Philippopolis, he must retire to Darmstadt; for Bulgarian opinion wanted the Union, and would abandon a

Prince who had not the moral courage to achieve the national desire. Alexander, accordingly, ordered the mobilisation of the army, and on September 21 entered Philippopolis. The *Sobranje* at once approved the Union, and voted an extraordinary credit for its defence.

To the general surprise, the Sultan contented himself with protests and merely defensive preparations, hesitating between the fear of complications in Albania and Macedonia and that of offending the Moslems. The Powers, especially Russia, professed to be scandalised at so flagrant an infraction of the Berlin treaty; but Great Britain, where Salisbury, then in power, was convinced that the movement was national and anti-Russian, insisted that the wishes of the Roumeliote population should be consulted. One of the first acts of the provisional government and of the people of Philippopolis was to implore British aid and to appeal to British love of liberty; and our consuls were ordered to recognise that body as the *de facto* authority. The Tsar Alexander III was so indignant at his cousin's audacity, that he struck his name off the army list, and recalled all Russian officers from Bulgaria. Still more violent was the opposition of Bulgaria's two rivals in the Balkans, Greece and Servia. Both countries demanded territorial compensation for the aggrandisement of the principality; and the Cretans proclaimed once more their union with Greece. Servia sought to obtain the former *sanjaks* of Vidin and Sofia as far as the river Isker; three members of the Deligiánnes Cabinet advocated immediate naval action in Crete and the seizure in Epirus of the frontier proposed at the Berlin conference. But their policy was not adopted; and, while Greece went on with her preparations, a conference of the ambassadors of the Powers met at Constantinople to consider the Eastern Roumelian question. Salisbury, in direct opposition to the policy adopted after the treaty of San Stefano, strongly supported the Union, realising that Bulgaria was not, as had been feared in 1878, merely a Russian outpost. His instructions to Sir William

White, who represented Great Britain in the conference, were to induce the Sultan to abstain from military intervention, to secure, if possible, the appointment of Alexander as Governor-General of Eastern Roumelia for life, and to resist all proposals for his deposition.   The fact that the Prince was a Battenberg assured to him the sympathy of Queen Victoria.

The only serious danger was on the side of Servia.   On March 6, 1882, Prince Milan, to show the superiority of his position, had been proclaimed King, and Servia raised to the dignity of a kingdom.   But the glamour of this title did not make King Milan popular; his life was attempted in the Belgrade cathedral; his peasant subjects rose in rebellion against the arbitrary measures of his "iron Minister," Christich; while the Karageorgevich pretender was more threatening because he had married a daughter of Prince Nicholas of Montenegro.   Dynastic reasons, therefore, suggested a spirited foreign policy as the best means of raising the prestige and increasing the popularity of the Obrenovich family.   Nor were there lacking other motives for a conflict.   The Bulgarians coveted Pirot, the Serbs desired Vidin; and the river Timok, by changing its course, had created a delicate question of frontier between the mutually jealous neighbours.   A tariff war yet further embittered their relations, so that the news of the Philippopolis revolution found both King and people predisposed for war.   Financially in a desperate position—for she had spent much on her railways—Servia had little to lose; as Garashanin expressed it in a pithy Servian proverb "a naked man will jump far."   All parties were unanimous for war, and the clergy inflamed the peasants.   The result was a complete surprise.   When, on November 14, Servia began hostilities, the general belief was that the "King of Servia and Macedonia," as the Belgrade populace styled Milan, would have a triumphal march to Sofia.   Appearances pointed to such a conclusion, for the Bulgarian army was denuded of its Russian instructors, whose places had been hastily taken by young officers, while

the Servians had had the experience of two campaigns. But
the Bulgarians were fired with zeal for the national cause; even
the Moslems of the principality rallied to the side of a leader
who had shown them toleration; recruits from Macedonia
crossed the frontier; and the main body of the Servian army,
when on November 16 it approached the picturesque village of
Slivnitza, which lies on the direct route to Sofia, found Prince
Alexander facing it at the head of his hastily collected forces.

The battle of Slivnitza, which lasted for the next three days,
was the Bulgarian principality's baptism of fire. The night
before the battle, the raw Bulgarian levies were still doubtful;
but, when the fighting began, the splendid example of the
Prince inspired them with firmness. The critical moment
was reached on the third day, when a rumoured march of the
Serbs on the capital from the south caused a panic at Sofia and
the Prince had to reassure the terrified citizens by his presence.
The alarm proved to be false; the Serbs were defeated at Slivnitza;
their siege of Vidin proved fruitless; King Milan asked in vain
for an armistice; and the Bulgarians, after a two days' battle
at Pirot, occupied that coveted town. The road to Belgrade
lay open to the invaders, but next day Austria intervened to
save her *protégé*; and Count Khevenhüller informed Prince
Alexander that, if he advanced further, he would find an
Austrian army before him. Thus, on November 28, ended
this fourteen days' fratricidal war; an armistice was signed in
Pirot; and on March 3, 1886, the treaty of Bucharest restored
the *status quo*. Bulgaria gained from Servia neither territory
nor money, neither Pirot nor pigs; but she had established that
right which comes of might to the possession of Eastern Roumelia. Meanwhile, the conference had been interrupted; but
the Bulgarian Foreign Minister, Tsanov, had negotiated terms
with the Porte, and on April 5 the revived conference ratified
this arrangement. The government of Eastern Roumelia was to
be "entrusted to the Prince of Bulgaria, in accordance with
article 17 of the treaty of Berlin"; so long as the administration

of Bulgaria and Eastern Roumelia remained in the same hands, the Mussulman villages in the canton of Kirdjali and the adjacent home of the Pomaks in the Rhodope (hitherto excluded from the administration of Eastern Roumelia) were to be administered directly by Turkey, in lieu of the Porte's right (as set forth in article 15 of the Berlin treaty) to provide for the defence of the Eastern Roumelian frontiers by raising fortifications and keeping troops on them; and a commission, appointed by the Prince and the Porte, was to examine the Organic Statute of Eastern Roumelia, with a view to its revision. The diplomatic cleverness of this settlement is obvious. The letter of the Berlin treaty was preserved; the Turkish annexation of the "Pomak Republic" was legalised; in the eyes of Turkish theorists, Eastern Roumelia remained a separate province, united by a limited personal union with the principality; while the practical Bulgarians regarded it as "Southern Bulgaria," whose administration was merged in that of the north, and whose 91 representatives sat with their northern brothers in the same National Assembly. Thus, Alexander was a Prince for life at Sofia, a pasha for five years at Philippopolis—a position somewhat galling to his dignity but of little real disadvantage to his people.

The Bulgarian triumph at Slivnitza had yet further increased the excitement in Greece. Deligiánnes had reintroduced the forced paper currency, abolished in 1884, and raised a "patriotic" loan of 30 millions of *drachmaí*. Two collective notes, addressed, at Salisbury's suggestion, by the representatives of the six Powers to the Greek Premier, the former inviting him to disarm, the latter informing him that "no naval attack by Greece upon the Porte could be admitted," produced no effect upon him, but were, on the contrary, followed by warlike demonstrations in various provincial towns. The advent of Gladstone to power at this juncture, with Lord Rosebery at the Foreign Office, in no wise modified Salisbury's Greek policy; and men-of-war began to concentrate in Suda bay. Deligiánnes called up two more classes of the reserves, and, on hearing of the decision of the conference to permit the practical union of the two Bulgarias, reiterated the necessity of conceding to Greece the frontier promised to her at Berlin, as a means of "re-establishing the equilibrium between the various races of the Balkan peninsula." On April 26, the Powers, with the exception of France, who restricted herself to friendly advice, invited the Greek government to place its forces on a peace footing. As Deligiánnes' replies were not considered adequate, on May 8 the five Powers, whose ministers left Athens, proclaimed the blockade of the Greek coasts from Cape Malea to the north-eastern frontier and of the entrance to the gulf of Corinth. By the irony of fate, the chief command of the blockading squadron off the island of Kéos was entrusted to the Duke of Edinburgh, who, as Prince Alfred, 23 years earlier had been elected king of the country that he was now coercing. Upon the establishment of the blockade, Deligiánnes resigned; and, after a brief Cabinet of affairs under Bálbes, Trikoúpes returned to power. Meanwhile, skirmishes had taken place on the frontier, where the two armies were facing one another; but an armistice was arranged and a disarmament decree issued by the new Ministry. Thereupon the blockade was raised on June 7. The military preparations of this lengthy crisis cost Greece deficits to the amount of 95 millions of *drachmaí* and a forced currency, destined to remain in circulation for many years, while it temporarily diminished the popularity of Gladstone in the Hellenic world. A long period of repose ensued in Greece, where Trikoúpes, installed in power for the next four years, reduced the number of deputies to 150, developed the railway system, strengthened the navy, and spent freely upon public works.

Prince Alexander did not long enjoy his triumph. An enemy more insidious than Turkey or Servia was scheming for his overthrow. Russia had not forgotten his audacity in achieving for himself what she had failed to accomplish for her own ends at San Stefano; even before the union she had

sought to rid the principality of a ruler, whose motto since
1883 had been "Bulgaria for the Bulgars." In May a plot
against his life, organised in the Russian interest, was discovered
at Bourgas; and in many other towns of Eastern Roumelia the
centralising tendencies of the Bulgarian government, which
dismissed or transferred local officials, replacing them by men
from the principality, caused dissatisfaction. In the army there
were discontented officers, whose services had not been adequately rewarded and who were ready to play the Russian
game, certain to be disavowed in case of failure, sure to be
recognised in case of success. Of these the chief were Major
Grujev, the head of the Military Academy, and Capt. Benderev,
the Acting Minister of War. The conspirators, some 80 in
number, selected the moment when Sofia was almost denuded
of troops in consequence of an alarm on the Servian frontier,
and at two in the morning of August 21, 1886, entered the
palace, and forced Alexander, by pointing their loaded revolvers
at his head, to sign a paper abdicating the throne. Three
hours later he was driven with his brother Francis Joseph to
the monastery of Etropol and next day to the Danube, where
he was conveyed on board his yacht, and on the morning of
August 23 landed at the Russian port of Reni, whence he was
allowed to proceed to Lemberg. Thus, the first Prince of
Bulgaria, like Couza 20 years earlier, was kidnapped and
deposed before Europe could say a word. Despite railways
and telegraphs, the Balkan states still furnished materials fit
for medieval romances.

As soon as the officers had successfully performed their part
of the plot, the civilian element made its appearance, under the
leadership of Dragan Zankov, who had been in his time merchant, journalist, schoolmaster, Turkish official, and Bulgarian
Prime Minister, and who had never forgiven Alexander for
having once dismissed him from office and arrested him as an
agitator. In former days an advocate of ecclesiastical union
with Rome, latterly a Liberal but a partisan of Russia, he held

a meeting of youths, idlers, hawkers, and professional politicians
—for the mass of the population was apathetic—at which the
late Prince was denounced as "a German foreigner who had
tried to estrange" Bulgaria's natural protectress and to ally her
"with her hereditary enemy." The meeting was then adjourned to the cathedral, where, as not infrequently happens in
Balkan states, an intriguing churchman was found, in the person
of the Metropolitan Clement, ready to pronounce the blessing
of Almighty God upon the band of traitors. The next move
was to the Russian agency, in front of which the free Bulgars
were ordered by their leaders to go down on their knees in the
mud, while the Metropolitan, addressing the representative of
the Tsar, begged that Russia would "take the interests, liberty,
and future of Bulgaria under her high protection at this grave
moment, and defend her from danger." After this degrading
scene, the conspirators proceeded to form a provisional government. As Peter Karavelov, who was Radical Prime Minister
at the time, declined to have anything to do with them and
strongly repudiated the use which they had made of his name
to lend a colour of authority to their *coup d'état*, the supple
Metropolitan assumed the Premiership, with Zankov at the
Ministry of the Interior; and a proclamation was issued, informing the people that "the mighty Russian Tsar, the protector
of Bulgaria," would not leave their "fatherland without his
powerful protection." Sofia remained, however, for only three
days in the hands of the conspirators. Stambulov, then Speaker
of the *Sobranje*, held his native city of Trnovo for the Prince,
and thence issued a counter-proclamation, declaring Clement
and his colleagues to be outlaws, appointing Mutkurov, who was
at Philippopolis, Commander-in-Chief, and invoking the aid of
the whole nation against the traitors. The threat of the provincial regiments to march on the capital, the tepid response
of Russia, and the dislike of the Bulgars for the interference of
ecclesiastics in temporal affairs, caused the Metropolitan and
his colleagues to resign. Popov, a loyalist officer, occupied the

palace; Karavelov resumed office, with Stoilov, who had been
Alexander's private secretary, as Foreign Minister; but Stambulov declined to co-operate with the restored Premier, whose
sincerity he doubted; and the country was governed by a
Regency, composed of Slavejkov, Stranski, and himself. As soon
as the whereabouts of the kidnapped Prince had been discovered,
a telegram was despatched to him, begging him to return to
his faithful people. Alexander accepted the invitation, and on
August 29 set foot on Bulgarian soil at Rustchuk, where he was
enthusiastically received. After confirming the arrangements
made by the Regency, he was so weak as to transmit to the Tsar
through the Russian consul, who had met him on his landing,
a telegram, containing the fatal words: "Russia having given
me my crown, I am ready to return it into the hands of her
sovereign." The Tsar personally disliked his cousin, and
had grown distrustful of one whose independence was resented
as ingratitude by the Russians. He therefore replied, that he
could not approve the Prince's return, the consequences of
which would be disastrous for Bulgaria; that he should abstain
from all intervention in its affairs, so long as the Prince
remained there; and that he reserved his decision as to his
own future action. This fatal mistake cost the Prince his
throne. Despite his warm welcome in his capital, and the
pressing arguments of Stambulov, he publicly announced his
abdication on September 7; and, after appointing a Regency
composed of that energetic statesman, Mutkurov, and Karavelov
(subsequently replaced by Jivkov), with a strong coalition
Ministry under Radoslavov, next day left Bulgaria for ever.
Under the name of Count Hartenau, the first Prince of "the
peasant state" lived for seven years more the happier life of an
Austrian officer—another example of the historic truth that
assassination or abdication, execution or exile, is the normal fate
of Balkan rulers.

Russia, having got rid of Alexander, made a bold but
mistaken attempt to recover her lost influence. As her agent

for this purpose she selected Major-General Nicholas Kaulbars, brother of the former Minister of War, ostensibly to "assist" the Bulgars at this crisis.   But the methods of this strange diplomatist did more than aught else to alienate the sympathies of the stubborn peasants from their Russian patrons.   While the Regents wisely desired the interregnum to be as short as possible, Kaulbars demanded in peremptory language the immediate raising of the state of siege, the immediate release of all the conspirators, and the postponement of the elections for the Grand *Sobranje*, which was to choose the new Prince. With this object he stumped the country as an Imperial antielection agent, only to find that his interference had aroused the national spirit of the country.   When, despite his efforts, the elections were held, he declared that the Russian government considered them to be illegal, and expressed his "strong censure" of the Bulgarian government—a piece of impertinence which drew upon him the well-deserved retort that "the Bulgarian Ministers accept censure only from the representative National Assembly, as is the custom in all constitutional countries."   Another Russophil conspiracy at Bourgas failed; and on November 10 the Grand *Sobranje* unanimously elected at Trnovo Prince Waldemar of Denmark, brother of Queen Alexandra and of the King of the Hellenes and brother-in-law of the Tsar.   Not meeting with that autocrat's approval, the Danish Prince, who had been mentioned as a candidate in 1879, declined the offer; and the ineffable Kaulbars took his departure, followed by all the Russian consuls.   Meanwhile, without Russian aid, the Regency had conducted the internal affairs of the country with a success that won for Bulgaria the admiration of British statesmen, while it had concluded an arrangement with Servia for the settlement of the Timok boundary question by an exchange of territory, and the construction of the Bulgarian railway to the frontier.   It only remained to find a Prince.

For the next six months the Bulgarian crown went a-begging,

while Russian plots, continued at Silistria and Rustchuk after
the departure of Kaulbars and his staff, but suppressed by the
patriotism of the national guard, rendered the appointment of
a definite form of government all the more desirable.   A deputation, consisting of Grekov, Stoilov, and the Roumeliote
deputy Kaltchev, set out on an European tour in quest of a
Prince.   St Petersburg refused to receive them, but in London
Lord Iddesleigh, then at the Foreign Office, congratulated
Bulgaria "on possessing statesmen so well qualified" for their
difficult task.   Various names were suggested for the throne.
Russia would have liked to see the election of the Prince of
Mingrelia, a college-friend of the Tsar and a Russian subject;
but Grekov, in the name of the deputation, declared that no Assembly would elect a man with such antecedents.   Oldenburg
and Leuchtenberg candidatures—the usual resource of Muscovite diplomacy when oriental thrones are vacant—met with an
equally cold reception.   At one moment, a personal union
under the King of Roumania was suggested; at another,
Alexander was invited to return to his faithful people; and,
when he refused, there was talk of a single temporary Regent,
such as Aleko Pasha, the deposed Governor-General of
Eastern Roumelia, or Von der Goltz Pasha, the German
organiser of the Turkish army.   Meanwhile, Zankov, despite
the smallness of his following, was intriguing at the Porte to
obtain the suppression of the Regency—a step to which the
British government stated plainly that it would not be a party,
and which would have been repudiated by the vast majority of
Bulgars.   At last a Prince was found willing to accept the
crown.   So early as December, Prince Ferdinand of Coburg
had received the deputation at Vienna, his name having been
suggested to M. Kaltchev at the marble-topped table of a
Viennese circus.   The successful candidate was the youngest
son of Prince Augustus of Saxe-Coburg and descended through
his mother from King Louis-Philippe.   Except in point of age
—he was at this time 26 years old—the second Prince of

Bulgaria bore no resemblance to the first; by training and temperament he was the exact opposite of his future subjects. A poor horseman and an officer only in name, he was fonder of botany than of sport; he was a Roman Catholic, while they were preponderantly Orthodox; he was a stickler for etiquette, while they were convinced democrats. But he was well-connected, wealthy, and willing; and, accordingly, on July 7, 1887, he was elected at Trnovo Prince of Bulgaria. The news of his election was received "without any marked enthusiasm" at Sofia; and his pedantic reply to the deputation which notified it to him produced a chilling effect. Natchevich, however, the Minister of Foreign Affairs, induced him to come without further hesitation to Bulgaria, leaving time to legalise his position. From the ancient capital of Trnovo the Prince issued a proclamation announcing that he had mounted "the throne of the glorious Bulgarian Kings," and concluded with the cry of "free and independent Bulgaria." Thus, from the outset he connected his name with the medieval Bulgarian empire and indicated the ultimate aim of his policy—an aim attained at Trnovo 21 years later. Russia, however, protested against his election, proposed General Ernroth as Regent, and long withheld her consent to the Prince's recognition—a course which involved his social boycott by the Powers but had no other serious consequences. In fact, the absence of a Russian agent was a positive advantage. Salisbury, who at first adopted an attitude of reserve, gradually acquiesced in the rule of a "Coburger," and therefore a relative of Queen Victoria. The Prince, who was one of the ablest of Balkan diplomatists, bided his time; and for nearly seven years his great Minister, Stepan Stambulov, defied Russia and won the admiration of Great Britain as "the Bulgarian Bismarck."

CHAPTER XVIII

ARMENIA, CRETE, AND MACEDONIA (1887—1908)

THE Armenian, Cretan, and Macedonian questions were the most serious problems which Europe had to face in the near east between the arrival of Prince Ferdinand in Bulgaria and the revolution which overthrew the Hamidian system in Turkey. The first concerned the Powers and the Sultan; the second involved Greece in war with Turkey; the third aroused the mutual jealousies of almost every Balkan state, which saw in Macedonia to a greater or less extent "the promised land" of its future expansion.

The Armenian question differed totally from Balkan problems. The Armenians were in a different position from all the other Christian races of Turkey. While the Greeks, Bulgars, Serbs, and Koutzo-Wallachs could look for support to Athens, Sofia, Belgrade, and Bucharest, the Armenians had no Armenian state to which they could turn for protection. In that respect they resembled the Albanians, but with this important difference, that the Albanians were first-rate fighting-men who could defend themselves, while the Armenians, with the exception of a few in the Russian service, were not. Unfortunately this unwarlike race has as its neighbours the savage Kurds, the Albanians of Asia Minor, who treat it much as the Arnauts treated the Serbs of Old Servia. Divided between Russia, Turkey, and Persia, deprived for more than five centuries of the last remnant of national independence, split up ecclesiastically into Gregorians, Catholics and Protestants, with the spiritual head of the

Gregorian Church under Russian, and its Patriarch under Turkish, authority, the Armenians, in a secret petition presented to the Congress of Berlin, had disclaimed political ambition and had begged for an arrangement modelled on that of the Lebanon, under a Christian governor. Instead of this, the collective wisdom of Europe was content with a vague promise of security and reforms. Great Britain did indeed send consuls to report on the condition of Asia Minor ; but even Gladstone, when he came into power in 1880, dropped the Armenian question at a hint from Bismarck. A so-called "Armenian constitution," granted in 1863, which entrusted Armenian affairs to a "National General Assembly" meeting biennially at Constantinople under the presidency of the Patriarch, with two smaller councils for religious and civil business, alone represented Armenian nationality in Turkey.

Down to 1889 the question attracted no further attention. But in that year the first news of outrages in the Armenian provinces of Turkey reached England. Abdul Hamid II had meanwhile established a system of highly centralised personal government; Midhat's short-lived parliament had long been dissolved, and its author had died in exile; the Palace had superseded the Porte ; and the Sultan's favourites had more influence in the affairs of the empire than his Ministers. At the same time the Armenians had become the objects of suspicion to the Sultan and the Tsar alike, and both Russians and Turks professed to discern an "Armenian peril" in the material progress of these clever and industrious, but unpopular, men of business. When the cry of oppression was raised, the Turkish authorities merely prosecuted Moussa Bey, a Kurdish chief, who was acquitted, but ultimately exiled. The Armenians, on their part, were already agitating; their societies, of which the chief bore the significant name of *Hindchak* ("the Bell"), sounded the alarm in the ears of somnolent diplomacy. The Kurds, reinforced by the fanatical Mussulmans whom the events of 1878 had driven "bag and baggage" into Asia, redoubled their exactions; conflicts arose, and the Armenian massacres began.

For three weeks in the late summer of 1894 the district of Sasun in the province of Bitlis became the scene of horrors which recalled those of Batak. The Kurds, aided by Turkish troops, under the command of Zekki Pasha, destroyed 24 villages, and butchered, with the most revolting cruelty, every Armenian whom they could find. Zekki was decorated for his "services"; but Great Britain demanded the appointment of a commission of enquiry, which British, French, and Russian delegates should accompany. The commission, officially designated as intended "to enquire into the criminal conduct of Armenian brigands," conducted its proceedings with the partiality which might have been expected from this statement of its object, and proved as dilatory as most Turkish institutions. In vain, the three Powers presented a scheme of Armenian reform; in vain, great meetings were held in London and Paris on behalf of the Armenians. An Armenian demonstration at Constantinople on September 30, 1895, only resulted in a massacre of many in the capital and of many more at Trebizond. But this was nothing compared with what was to come. While the ambassadors were presenting a new scheme of reforms to the Sultan, which he promised to see carried out faithfully, a gigantic massacre was taking place in Asia Minor. During part of October and the whole of November the Armenians were murdered wholesale; and the murders were organised by the Sultan's officials, headed by Shakir Pasha. The British ambassador wrote home that "over an extent of territory considerably larger than Great Britain" all the large towns save three and almost all the villages had suffered, and that a moderate estimate put the loss of life in those six weeks at 30,000. Still, however, the massacres continued. The cathedral of Urfa, the Edessa of the Crusaders, was the scene of a human holocaust, in which nearly 3000 persons perished; Van, hitherto spared, was selected for the next great crime; while the Powers, fearful of reopening the eastern question by active intervention, which would have aroused mutual suspicions, left the Armenians to their fate and contented themselves with demanding the presence at Constantinople of a second *stationnaire* for the protection of their own subjects.   But Europe was soon to learn that under the very shadow of the embassies the unhappy Armenians could be butchered with impunity.   A body of the latter, more desperate than the rest, indignant at the supineness of the Powers and infuriated at the forced resignation of the Armenian Patriarch and the irregular appointment of his successor, seized the premises of the Ottoman bank and only left them under promise of a safe conduct and the protection of the ambassadors.   Scarcely had they been shipped on board a French steamer, than the infuriated Sultan took a terrible vengeance upon their innocent compatriots.   For the next two days, August 27 and 28, 1896, the streets of Constantinople were the theatre of an organised massacre.   The Armenian quarter was attacked by gangs of men, armed with clubs, who bludgeoned every Armenian whom they met, and forced their way into the houses of Armenians or foreigners who had Armenian servants, in pursuit of their victims.   Police officers and soldiers aided, and even directed, this Turkish St Bartholomew ; and it was not till the representatives of the Powers, who had seen with their own eyes what had occurred, sent a strongly-worded note to the palace, that the order was issued to stop the slaughter.   Some 6000 persons perished in this horrible carnage ; and, in the words of a British diplomatist, it seems to have been "the intention of the Turkish authorities to exterminate the Armenians."   The perfect organisation of the shambles was proved by the fact that scarcely anyone who did not belong to that race perished, and that those few exceptions were due to such accidents as will happen even in the best regulated massacres.

The "disturbances at Constantinople," as they were euphemistically called by diplomatists, convinced even the most incredulous that the previous massacres in remote parts of the empire had not been mere inventions. Gladstone, once more sallying forth from his retirement, as he had done at the moment of the Bulgarian atrocities, made his last great public utterance at Liverpool on behalf of the Armenians, and branded Abdul Hamid II as "the Great Assassin," while French writers pilloried him as "the Red Sultan." But no steps were taken to punish the author of the Armenian horrors. Germany, anxious for concessions in Asia Minor, constituted herself his protrectress, and reaped the reward of her selfish and inhuman policy. Austria-Hungary was too deeply interested in the Balkan peninsula to risk action, of which it was difficult to foresee the results. Russia had cynically declared through the mouth of Lobanov, that she did not, after her experiences in Europe, desire the creation of another Bulgaria in Asia Minor. Salisbury, again in power, solemnly and publicly warned the Sultan of the consequences of his misgovernment, and suggested the eventual necessity of employing force; the French ambassador at Constantinople advocated the despatch of a fleet as the only means of intimidating Abdul Hamid; and among British residents there the opinion was expressed that Great Britain should, and could, have acted with more vigour. The most that can be said is that, having, in virtue of the Cyprus convention, greater responsibilities towards the Armenians than any other signatory of the Berlin treaty, she did a little more to support them. Further, but smaller, massacres at Tokat formed a sequel to the atrocities. Then Crete supplanted Asia Minor in the attention of the European public; and the sufferings of the Armenians were forgotten till in 1909 the massacres at Adana renewed them.

The presence of the European squadron in Cretan waters in 1886 and the collapse of the warlike movement in Greece had restricted the movements of the Christian islanders to a Platonic declaration of union at that crisis; and it was not till 1889 that a fresh insurrection took place, which differed, however, in its origin from those which had preceded it. On this occasion the quarrel was not, in its inception, between the Christians and the Moslems, but between two political parties, described as Liberals and Conservatives, but really only actuated by the desire to obtain, or retain, office with the spoils attaching thereto. The Liberals, having obtained an overwhelming majority at the elections of that year, excluded their adversaries from all the available posts ; whereupon five Conservative deputies brought forward a motion for union with Greece, in order to embarrass their opponents. Trikoúpes, who was still in power at Athens, through M. Grypáres, the Greek consul at Canea, did all that he could to discourage an agitation which he considered inopportune, and pointed out that Crete was only a part of the general Hellenic question. But the magic word of union, once uttered, rekindled the latent enmity of the rival creeds; what had been originally a party quarrel between two gangs of place-hunters became a religious struggle between Christians and Moslems. The mission of an Imperial special commissioner, with power to offer £T.20,000 and an agricultural bank, only alarmed the Mussulmans without contenting the Christians. Murders occurred; retaliation ensued; one sect fired the villages of the other; Moslem peasants crowded into the coast-towns; Christian refugees fled to Athens; and, while the Porte sent troops by driblets, Trikoúpes urged the Powers, and especially Great Britain, to act. The Sultan, having recalled his Polish *vâli*, issued a firman on November 24, which virtually repealed the Pact of Halépa, declared the office of Governor-General to be unlimited by time, reduced the numbers of the Assembly to 57 members (of whom 35 were to be Christians), announced the formation of a *gendarmerie* from natives of other Ottoman provinces, established a fixed sum in lieu of the tithe of oil, and gave a preference to those who knew Turkish (which is not the language of Crete) in official appointments. This firman created widespread disappointment, while its democratic proviso, that judges should continue to be popularly elected, perpetuated one of the worst evils in the island. The insurrection ceased; but desultory outrages continued, and an outlaw, named Liápes, who had many murders to his account, was depicted as a hero to the Athenian populace, till Deligiánnes, who had ousted Trikoúpes in 1890, but who pursued his rival's pacific policy, prohibited this cult. Meanwhile, three Mussulmans successively held the post of Governor-General, to the manifest advantage of the minority, until the Sultan, in 1895, at last yielded to the violent importunities of the Cretans, and appointed Alexander Karatheodori Pasha, a Christian who had been Prince of Samos, as *váli*. The increase of the numbers of the Assembly, which had not met since 1889, to 65—40 Christians and 25 Mussulmans—seemed to have dissipated the dangers of further disputes.

But the Cretan Moslems, like most minorities accustomed to the exercise of power, were resolved to demonstrate the futility of attempting to govern Crete through the medium of a Christian. Murders of Christians began; a Christian Committee of Reform was founded and embittered the situation; while Karatheodori, who had made himself personally popular with the Mussulmans, was deprived by his government of the means of paying his *gendarmerie*. The re-appointment of a Mussulman as his successor, instead of satisfying the Moslem party, disgusted both sides, for the Mussulmans wanted a military governor, while the Christians desired another Christian. Such was the state of tension when the insurrection, which was to end in the practical destruction of Turkish rule over Crete, broke out on May 24, 1896, with a sanguinary conflict in the streets of Canea. Too late, the Sultan accepted the advice of the Powers, revived the Pact of Halépa, promised to summon the General Assembly and to grant an amnesty, and appointed a Christian governor in the person of George Berovich, who also had been Prince of Samos. One commission, comprising European officers, was to organise the *gendarmerie*; another to reform the tribunals. This arrangement, accepted by the Christians, was regarded by the Mussulmans, who derived their inspiration from the palace, as one of the usual paper reforms which they were expected to resist; and the arrival of the Turkish officer, who had been connected with the Armenian massacres at Van, encouraged their resistance. The customary delay in beginning the work of organising the police made the Christians also suspicious; and a Mussulman outbreak at Canea on February 4, 1897, followed by the burning of a large part of the Christian quarter, renewed the civil war. The Christians occupied Akrotéri, the "peninsula" between Canea and Suda bay, and proclaimed union with Greece.

Meanwhile, the news of a massacre at Canea had caused immense excitement at Athens, where, since the last Cretan outbreak, the politicians had been mainly occupied with economic questions, culminating in the financial crisis of 1893, and the currant, and likewise the currency, crisis of 1894–5, when the exchange went up to 46 *dr.* 87 *l.* to the £. Trikoúpes, who had counselled quiet at the time of the last insurrection, was now dead; and Deligiánnes, the bellicose Minister of 1885, was once more in power. But even the greatest of Greek statesmen could no longer have resisted public opinion. Greece had incurred enormous expenses for the maintenance of the Cretan refugees at Athens, while there were numbers of Cretans established in Greece, whose influence was naturally in favour of intervention. Prince George, the King's second son, left the Piraeus, amidst enthusiastic demonstrations, with a flotilla of torpedo boats to prevent the landing of Turkish reinforcements; and on February 15 a Greek force under Col. Vássos, with orders to occupy Crete in the name of King George, to restore order and to drive the Turks from the forts, landed a little to the west of Canea. The same day the admirals of the five European Powers, whose ships were then in Cretan waters, occupied the town, whence the last Turkish governor of the island had fled for ever. The insurgents on

Akrotéri then attacked the Turkish troops, until the admirals forced them to desist by a bombardment, which caused intense indignation at Athens and some disgust in London among those who remembered Navarino. A note of the Powers promising autonomy on condition of the withdrawal of the Greek ships and troops met with an unfavourable reply; and, though the admirals issued a proclamation of autonomy, they followed it up by a blockade of the island, and by another bombardment of the insurgents at Maláxa above Suda bay.

The conflict between Hellenism and its hereditary foe could no longer be confined to "the great Greek island." In Greece a body called the "National Society" forced the hand of the government; an address from 100 British members of parliament encouraged the masses, ignorant of the true conditions of British politics, to count upon the help of Great Britain; the King, in a speech to the people, talked of putting himself at the head of an army of 100,000 Hellenes. The secret history of the weeks immediately preceding the war is still only a matter of surmise; but the opinion is now held in Greece, that King George expected the Powers to prevent hostilities at the last moment; he could then have yielded to their pressure without risking his position with his subjects. Neither he nor the Sultan wanted a war, from which the latter knew that, if successful, he would gain nothing; and at the outbreak of hostilities he was less unpopular at Athens than the German Emperor, whose officers accompanied the Turkish army, whose policy throughout had been bitterly hostile to the country, of which his sister would one day be Queen, and who is still held largely responsible for the war. Among the Greeks, who had had no war with Turkey since that of Independence, but who had wished to fight in 1854, in 1878, and in 1886, there was intense enthusiasm, unfortunately as yet unaccompanied by organisation. Greece is a profoundly democratic land where the soldier does not recognise a social superior in his officer, where the critical faculty is highly developed, and the national tactics were aptly described by the phrase "klephtic war" (κλεφ-τοπόλεμος), while the military qualities of the Turks were then universally recognised, and their army had been schooled by German instructors. Thus, the contest was unequal, even though a band of red-shirted "Garibaldians" of various nations, under a son of the great captain, came to the aid of the Greeks and money poured into the war fund from abroad.

On April 9 armed bands of the "National Society" crossed into Macedonia; further conflicts occurred on the Thessalian frontier; and on April 17 Turkey declared war. True to his traditional policy of dividing the Christian races of the near east against each other, the Sultan secured the neutrality of Bulgaria and Servia by an opportune grant of bishoprics, commercial agents, and schools in Macedonia. An Austro-Russian note to the Balkan courts warned them not to interfere in the struggle. Thus any hopes of common action by the Christians were dissipated, and the ring was confined to the two combatants. The "Thirty Days' War" was an almost unbroken series of Greek disasters. The Greek navy, which was superior to that of the Turks, and upon which great hopes had been placed, effected nothing except the futile bombardment of Préveza, the capture of a cargo of vegetables at Santi Quaranta and that of a Turcophil British member of parliament. This inaction of the fleet was doubtless due to the influence of the Powers. A bombardment of Smyrna or Salonika would have mainly damaged the Greek populations of those cities; but Turkish islands could easily have been taken, as by the Italian and Greek fleets in 1912, and better terms thereby obtained at the peace. Thus, Greece was deprived of her most valuable arm. On land, the campaign naturally fell into two divisions, one in Thessaly, the other in Epirus. In Thessaly Edhem Pasha, the Turkish commander, after severe fighting in the Meloûna pass, and an obstinate battle at Revéni, occupied Lárissa, whence the Crown Prince's troops had fled in disorder; in Epirus the battle of Pénte Pegádia, the "Five Wells," between

Arta and Joánnina, where the Greeks had twice defeated the Turks in 1854, saved the latter town, and cost the life of Clement Harris, a British Philhellene. The Turkish advance across the Thessalian plain aroused a reaction at Athens. The indignant crowd marched on the unprotected palace ; and the King owed the preservation of his throne to the prompt intervention of Demétrios Rhálles, a democratic politician, who had formed a party of his own in Attica and had become the most influential leader of the Opposition, and the idol of the Athenians. The scene of Kléon, demanding to be entrusted with authority, was re-enacted; and Rhálles was forthwith appointed Prime Minister on April 29. Next day Col. Smolenski, "the hero of Revéni," who had fought in Crete as a volunteer in 1868, and was the one officer who had distinguished himself in the war, repulsed the Turks in a first attack on Velestîno, the site of the legend of Alkêstis, but had to yield in a second battle ; the classic field of Phársalos was the scene of one Greek defeat, and the unknown village of Gríbovo in Epirus that of another; and the climax was reached when, on May 17, the battle of Domokós, in which the Italian Fratti renewed the heroic tradition of Santa Rosa, as Harris had that of Byron, opened to the Turks the Phoûrka pass which leads down to Lamía. A panic seized the Athenians at the news; the royal family durst not show itself in the streets; the royal liveries were changed; pictures of Smolenski replaced the royal portraits in the shop-windows. Then the Powers intervened; an armistice was signed on May 19 and 20 in Epirus and Thessaly; and Col. Vássos, who had already left Crete, was followed by the rest of his men. A treaty of peace was concluded at Constantinople on December 4, which provided for the evacuation of Thessaly by the Ottoman troops, and the cession for the second time of that province to Greece, except one village and certain strategic positions, which brought the Turkish frontier very near Lárissa. Greece was ordered to pay a war indemnity of £T.4,000,000, and submitted to an International

Commission of Control over "the collection and employment of revenues sufficient for the service of the war indemnity loan and the other national debts." The six Powers were each represented by a delegate on this Commission ; and the government monopolies of salt, petroleum, matches, playing cards, cigarette paper, and Naxian emery, the tobacco and stamp dues, and the import duties collected at the Piraeus were ear-marked for its disposal. In the following year the Turkish troops left Thessaly and with them almost all the remaining Moslem landowners; of this brief second Ottoman occupation a series of Turkish postage-stamps is almost the sole record. Soon, in Thessaly, as at Chalkís, a few mosques—the finest has perished by fire—will alone remind the traveller that there for nearly five centuries the Turk held sway.

The final settlement of the Cretan question long vexed the diplomatists of Europe. Eighteen months were spent in the search for a governor. A Swiss Federal Councillor, a Luxemburg colonel, a Montenegrin minister were in turn proposed. Meanwhile, Germany, followed by Austria, had retired from the European Concert on the Cretan question ; and the forces of the four other Powers, supported by their fleets under the command of the Italian Admiral Canevaro, had occupied the coast-towns, the British holding Candia, the Russians Rethýmne, the French Sitía and the islet of Spinalonga, the Italians Hierápetra, and all four Canea. In these places, especially within the cordon of Candia, the Mussulmans were herded, while the Christians held the whole of the open country, and a migratory assembly, presided over by Sphakianákes, issued decrees under the seal of Mínos. An attack upon the British in the harbour of Candia and the murder of their vice-consul on September 6, 1898, hastened a settlement of the Cretan question. Admiral Noel's energy achieved what diplomacy had long striven to obtain ; the ringleaders were hanged, and two months after the affray at Candia the last detachment of Turkish troops left the island ; the fort

on the islet in Suda bay was thenceforth alone occupied by
Ottoman soldiers.   On November 26, the representatives of
the four protecting Powers at last met at the palace at Athens,
and offered to Prince George of Greece the post of their
High Commissioner in Crete for three years, under the
suzerainty of the Sultan.   Each Power promised to advance
£40,000 for the initial expenses of the new administration.
Their offer, due to the influence of the Tsar Nicholas II
(whose life Prince George had saved in Japan), was accepted;
and on December 21, the Greek Prince landed at Suda.   Five
days later the admirals left; and, though the troops of the four
Powers still remained, the High Commissioner was the sole
responsible authority in the island, while their representatives
in Rome under the presidency of Admiral Canevaro, who had
become Italian Foreign Minister, formed a Cretan Areopagos,
before which the affairs of the island were still discussed.   The
Prince's appointment, originally made for three years, lasted
for nearly eight; and for the first five Crete remained tranquil.
Naturally popular with the Christians, he endeavoured to
reassure the Mussulmans; and, if he made a pilgrimage to the
historic monastery of Arkádion, he also visited the chief
mosque at Canea.   Even the Sphakiote chiefs were induced
to give up their weapons.   A mixed commission, under the
chairmanship of Sphakianákes, was appointed for the purpose of drawing up a constitution; and in 1899 the first
Assembly of Autonomous Crete, composed of 138 Christians
and 50 Moslems, met to examine its draft.   In accordance
with this constitution, as definitely accepted, the Prince
appointed five "Councillors" (one a Mussulman), while he
was allowed to nominate 10 members of the Chamber of
Deputies, a body otherwise elected biennially, which was to
meet every year.   Sphakianákes, who had played so prominent a part in the emancipation of his country, then retired
into private life.   "For the first time for 1900 years, since
the Roman conquest by Metellus," wrote an enthusiastic

Athenian journal, " Crete possesses a completely autonomous government." Finally, the Russian authorities retired from Rethýmne and the British from Candia; the disarmament of this, the most dangerous district of the island, the complete extinction of crime there, the institution of a postal service, and the increase of the provincial revenue had all been achieved at Candia by Sir H. Chermside and his assistants.

The departure of the British gave a further impetus to the Moslem emigration, which was encouraged by the Sultan; and the census of 1900 showed that the Mussulmans had dwindled to only one-ninth of the population, and that they were mainly confined to the three chief towns. A *gendarmerie* of Cretans organised and officered by Italian carabineers, took the place of the Montenegrins in the preservation of order. A Cretan flag, postage-stamps, and small coins were further steps towards independence; and M. Eleuthérios Venizélos, the ablest of the Prince's Councillors, suggested the formation of the island into a principality, like Samos, at the end of his three years' term. This proposal naturally aroused indignation at Athens, where it was then feared that Crete, having once tasted the sweets of complete independence, might no longer desire union with Greece; and the consequent dismissal of the presumptuous Councillor caused a serious breach between him and the High Commissioner. The election of mayors and the censorship of the press, both of which the Prince wished to have in his own hands, led to difficulties with the Assembly; and early in 1904 discontent became rife in the island. The Italian Foreign Office warned the Prince to act constitutionally; but a crisis was reached when, in March, 1905, the Opposition took to the mountains and established its headquarters at Thérisso, a strong position already famous in the annals of Cretan warfare. The insurgents there declared themselves a provisional National Assembly, proclaimed union with Greece, and held out till winter forced them to surrender to the European consuls. The following summer Prince George, weary of Cretan politics, resigned, despite a petition of many deputies in his favour. Thereupon the four Powers entrusted to King George the selection of a new High Commissioner. His choice in September, 1906, fell upon M. Alexander Zaïmes, the most Conservative and most silent of Greek statesmen, who had been Premier at the time of the conclusion of peace in 1898. Little more was heard of Crete under his sway. The Powers, while peace reigned, allowed the island to become more and more hellenised. In pursuance of their promises, made on July 23, Greek officers out of active service replaced the Italian carabineers in the command of the *gendarmerie* and were summoned to organise the militia. As soon as those two bodies should have been formed, order restored, and the safety of the Moslems assured, the international troops were to be gradually withdrawn. Accordingly, on May 11, 1908, in answer to an appeal from M. Zaïmes, who showed that their conditions had been realised, they announced that the evacuation of the island would begin that summer and would be concluded within a year from the departure of the first detachment, which took place on July 29. Such was the condition of the island when on October 7, 1908, the news of the annexation of Bosnia and Bulgarian independence once more provoked the proclamation of union with Greece.

Armenia and Crete had scarcely ceased to occupy the attention of Europe when a third question, more complex than either of them, became acute. Macedonia was the land of conflicting races and overlapping claims. During a large part of its history it had been entirely Greek; in the Middle Ages it was alternately under the hegemony of Bulgarian, Servian, and Byzantine Emperors, until the all-conquering Turk ground these respective empires to powder. But in the tenacious traditions of the near east their memories have survived; and, while no Englishman would found a claim to large portions of France upon the conquests of Edward III, Serbs speak of his contemporary, Stephen Dushan, as if his coronation as Tsar at

Üsküb had been but yesterday, and Greeks of Alexander the Great as if the centuries that have elapsed since his death were a watch in the night. A fourth propaganda, mainly the work of a certain Apóstolos Margarítes, had evolved from the "Lame" or Koutzo-Wallachs, previously regarded as Greeks, "Macedonian Roumanians," brothers of the Roumans beyond the Danube; while in Salonika and other towns the Jews, descendants of the Hebrew emigrants from Spain, formed a large and Turcophil element. Religious differences revived these racial hatreds. The firman creating the Bulgarian Exarchate in 1870 provided that, outside of what soon became Bulgaria, a petition by two-thirds of the inhabitants could secure the transfer of a district from the Patriarch to the Exarch; and "Patriarchists" and "Exarchists" thenceforth represented respectively the Greek and the Bulgarian cause in Macedonia, while Servia and Roumania, seeing the political advantages of an ecclesiastical propaganda, began to agitate for the restoration of the Servian Patriarchate of Ipek and the erection of a separate Roumanian Church. Schools and churches became the favourite weapons of the rival nationalities; so early as 1869 Prince Charles of Roumania had sent books for the Koutzo-Wallach pupils; from 1885, the millenary of Methodios, the apostle of the Slavs, dates the great spread of Bulgarian schools in Macedonia. The treaties of 1878 naturally made the Balkan states regard Macedonia as their promised land. Servia, cut off from expansion in Bosnia and the Herzegovina by the Austrian occupation, and bound by a secret treaty not to agitate there, looked to the south of the Shar mountains, to Üsküb, and even to Salonika; Bulgaria remembered the frontiers which were awarded her at San Stefano; Roumania saw that by first fostering and then sacrificing the Koutzo-Wallachs, she might claim compensation nearer home; while Greece regarded these newer nationalities as upstarts who had no rights in the land redeemed from "the barbarians" by Basil II, who had celebrated in the church, which had once been the Parthenon, his triumph over the Bulgars. Austria-Hungary, from selfish reasons, was glad to divert the attention of Servia from the Bosnian Serbs, and that of Roumania from the "unredeemed" Roumans of the Dual Monarchy; while, at the same time, established in the *sanjak* of Novibazar, she could contemplate a descent upon the valley of the Vardar and Salonika, until her military authorities discovered that it would be better strategy to march towards the Aegean through the valley of the Morava, than to traverse the cut-throat defile of Katchanik. Similarly, the Turkish government saw that to increase the confusion of the Macedonian races was its best chance of retaining a country where genuine Turks, as distinct from Mohammedan Albanians, Circassian immigrants and nomad Tartars, were, except in two or three districts, comparatively few. So the Porte favoured now the Bulgar, now the Serb, now the Greek, and now the Koutzo-Wallach, according to the weakness or importunity of each. Thus in 1890, despite the opposition of Russia but with the approval of Salisbury, the boldness of Stambulov wrung from the suzerain, by the covert threat of proclaiming the independence of the principality, two *berats* for the appointment of the first Bulgarian bishops of Macedonia at the sees of Ochrida and Üsküb. Great was the indignation of the Œcumenical Patriarchate, in vain it demanded that the Bulgarian clergy should wear a distinctive garb, as the badge of their "schism"; in vain it closed, as a protest, the Orthodox churches throughout Turkey. In 1894 two more Bulgarian bishops were appointed; and further concessions to the Bulgars rewarded the neutrality of that principality during the Greco-Turkish war of 1897, when Bulgaria, by cutting the railway between Constantinople and Salonika, might have hindered the despatch of troops to Thessaly. Thus, too, the appointment of a Serb as bishop of Üsküb in 1902 divided the Slavs, while the protest of the Koutzo-Wallachs against the cession of Thessaly to Greece was recompensed in Macedonia, and in 1905 theirs was again the propaganda favoured by the Turks. In fact, whenever Greece was troublesome to the Porte, the Bulgars and the Koutzo-Wallachs benefited, while the latter, as having of all the Christian races least to gain and most to lose by an immediate liquidation of the Macedonian question, were consequently almost as much interested as the Jews in the maintenance of Ottoman rule. In Macedonia, as elsewhere, that rule meant misgovernment ; of the reforms stipulated in article 23 of the Berlin treaty none was carried out.

The Greco-Turkish war of 1897 seemed to idealists an excellent opportunity of uniting the Christian races of the Balkans in a struggle against the common enemy. But, under the pressure of their mutual jealousies and conflicting ambitions, and in consequence of the Austro-Russian agreement, which aimed at preserving the *status quo* and withheld the two great Powers most directly interested from exercising a separate influence in the Balkan peninsula, the Macedonian question was stifled. Two years had not, however, elapsed before a Macedonian Committee, which had its seat at Sofia, and summarised its programme in the phrase " Macedonia for the Macedonians," addressed a memorial to the Powers in January 1899, advocating the formation of an autonomous province of Macedonia with Salonika as its capital, under a governor-general " belonging to the predominant nationality," who should hold office for five years. It was believed that this nationality would be Bulgarian ; and it was hoped that an autonomous Macedonia under a Bulgarian governor would be a step towards the " big Bulgaria " of San Stefano. As this memorial proved, however, to be waste paper, and a Macedonian congress at Geneva came to nothing owing to internal dissensions, the party of action took the field. Bulgarian bands crossed the frontier, and conflicts with the Turks took place. But it was soon apparent that the Turks were not the only objects of the Committee's hostility. In 1900 one of its emissaries shot at Bucharest a Roumanian professor who

edited a newspaper favourable to the Roumanian claims in
Macedonia. Thereupon the Roumanian government, already
at variance with Bulgaria about an islet in the Danube, demanded the punishment of the Committee. The Powers and
the Porte supported the Roumanian demand; and Boris
Sarafov, the president of the organisation, was arrested with
other leading members. The court, however, under the influence of public opinion in Bulgaria, whose army, schools,
and press were largely officered by Macedonians, acquitted the
accused. A split then occurred in the Committee, the extreme
section under Sarafov favouring force, the moderate men
preferring legal means and an educational propaganda. The
former were aware of the fact that the European press was only
concerned with the Balkan races when they were either cutting
each other's throats or inflicting damage upon some foreigner;
and the whole world became aware of the existence of a
Macedonian question, when Miss Stone, an American missionary, was captured by a gang of political brigands. Meanwhile, Old Servia was the scene of Albanian feuds, culminating
in the murder of Mollah Zekko, a donkey-boy who had risen
to be the leader of a movement for an autonomous Albania,
and whom even the Sultan, always the patron of the Albanians,
feared and conciliated. So serious was the state of things,
that the Sultan appointed Hilmi Pasha Inspector-General of
Macedonia, while Moslems as well as Christians were agreed
"that the provinces of Turkey in Europe cannot be allowed to
remain in their present deplorable condition."

Austria-Hungary and Russia, the two Powers most immediately interested, were of the same opinion; their Foreign
Ministers met at Vienna and drew up in February, 1903, a
modest scheme of reforms for the three Macedonian *vilâyets* of
Salonika, Monastir, and Kossovo, which the other Powers
supported. They recommended the Sultan to appoint an
Inspector-General for a fixed number of years; to re-organise
the *gendarmerie* with the aid of foreign officers, composing it

of Christians and Moslems in proportion to their respective numbers; and to establish a separate budget for each of the three *vilâyets*, upon the revenues of which the cost of local administration was to be a first charge. The Sultan accepted the Austro-Russian reform scheme, but its sole result was to increase the disorder. The Albanians of Kossovo, suspecting interference with their liberties, rose in rebellion, shot the Russian consul at Mitrovitza, and held up the Sultan's envoys at Ipek; a gendarme shot another Russian consul at Monastir. The Bulgarian bands, despite the dissolution of the Macedonian committees by the Bulgarian government, blew up railway bridges, placed bombs on steamers, and mined the Ottoman bank at Salonika. The Greeks were terrorised by the Bulgarian committeemen and plundered by the Turkish irregulars. The former seized Krushevo, a largely Patriarchist town, and levied blackmail on its inhabitants; when the latter recovered it, "a golden powder rose round the Turks and prevented them from seeing" (and sacking) the Bulgarian quarter. These occurrences nearly provoked a Turco-Bulgarian war. The position of the Bulgarian government was extremely difficult. Nearly one-half of the population of Sofia consisted of Macedonian emigrants and refugees, of whom there were no less than 150,000 in the whole principality, while a military conspiracy complicated the situation. While Prince Ferdinand sought to pacify his suzerain by appointing the Turcophil General Petrov Prime Minister, Austria and Russia in October, 1903, issued a second edition of their reform scheme, called, from the place of signature, the Mürzsteg programme. This programme, accepted by the Sultan, attached Austrian and Russian civil agents to Hilmi Pasha, the Inspector-General, entrusted the reorganisation of the *gendarmerie* to a foreign general, aided by military officers of the Powers, who would divide Macedonia among them; and demanded the reform of the administrative and judicial institutions of the country with the participation of the Christian population. General de

Giorgis, an Italian officer, was appointed to command the *gendarmerie*; and his successor was another Italian, Count di Robilant. All the Powers, except Germany, sent a small contingent of officers, subsequently slightly increased; and Macedonia was, for police purposes, divided up into five *secteurs*, the British taking Drama, a rich district almost wholly peopled by Pomaks, the French Serres, the Italians Monastir, the Austrians Üsküb, and the Russians Salonika. Most of the *vilâyet* of Kossovo, the worst of all, and part of that of Monastir, were excluded from this arrangement. An agreement between Bulgaria and Turkey for the prevention of armed bands helped to improve the condition of Macedonia in 1904, while a British committee did much to relieve its distress.

But in the autumn of that year a new disturbing element arose. Unable to obtain protection for their fellow-countrymen against the Bulgarians, the Greeks organised bands in their turn; and Paul Melâs, one of their leaders, who fell in Macedonia, became a national hero, commemorated by a monument at Athens. The rival parties, which took their titles from the Greek Patriarch and the Bulgarian Exarch, and were secretly encouraged by consuls and ecclesiastics, murdered one another in the name of religion, which in Macedonia was a pretext for racial patriotism; while the Sultan widened the breach between Greece and Roumania by recognising the Koutzo-Wallachs as a separate nationality, with the right of using their language in their churches and schools. These national quarrels spread beyond Macedonia. The Bulgarians destroyed the Greek quarters of Anchialós and Philippopolis, and the inhabitants of the former sought a new home in Thessaly; the Roumanians demonstrated against the Greeks resident in their country; a common danger caused Greeks and Serbs to fraternise; and an Athenian street received a Servian name. Meanwhile, the British government, disgusted with the slow progress made by the Mürzsteg programme, proposed in 1905, with the approval of the Macedonian congress at Sofia, its extension to the *vilâyet* of Adrianople, and the appointment of a commission of delegates, nominated by the Powers, under the presidency of the Inspector-General, for the purpose of framing financial reforms. The Sultan at first refused to allow foreign interference in his finances ; but the occupation of the custom-house and telegraph-office at Mitylene by an international fleet on November 26 and of the Kástro of Lêmnos ten days later forced him to recognise the four financial experts whom the other Powers had already sent to Salonika as colleagues of the Austrian and Russian civil agents. In March, 1908, all the arrangements made for the pacification of Macedonia—the appointments of Inspector-General, civil and financial agents, and *gendarmerie* officers, originally made for two, were prolonged for six years. Meanwhile, Sir Edward Grey, in the name of the British government, had caused remonstrances to be made at Athens and Sofia against the continued passage of Greek and Bulgarian bands into Macedonia, and secured the recall of the Metropolitan of Drama and the Greek consul at Kavalla, as active propagandists. Towards the end of 1907 Sarafov was murdered at Sofia by a Macedonian, at the instigation of Sandanski, leader of the terrorist section of the organisation, and advocate of an entirely independent Macedonia. But still the bands increased, while the British proposal to augment the *gendarmerie* met with no support from the other Powers, mainly occupied with the rival railway schemes of Austria and Servia. In short, the result of European intervention in Macedonia had been ineffective. If the taxes had been better collected and administered, if the Turkish troops had committed fewer outrages, the strife between Greeks, Bulgars, and Koutzo-Wallachs had been bitterer than ever. Such was the situation when the Turkish revolution of 1908 broke out.

The Macedonian question naturally affected the internal, as well as the external politics of the Balkan states. But it was not the only difficult problem which they had to solve during the period of 21 years which separated the election of Prince Ferdinand from the Turkish revolution. Bulgaria was governed for the first seven years of the new reign by the ex-Regent, Stambulov, the most considerable statesman whom Bulgaria has so far produced.

Alike in his methods and in his fall, the son of the Trnovo innkeeper resembled the great German Chancellor. During his long tenure of the premiership, he was absolute master of Bulgaria; for the Prince was at first much in the position of our George I, ignorant of the language and the customs of his subjects, and Stambulov was consequently for some years indispensable to him. The Minister had no constitutional scruples; he held that his end—the maintenance of Bulgarian freedom—justified his means, which included the manipulation of elections and the persecution of political opponents. He saw clearly that it was the interest of Bulgaria to establish friendly relations with Turkey; he was thus able to secure Turkish support against Russian schemes and to establish Bulgarian schools and bishoprics as the nucleus of a Bulgarian propaganda against the Greeks and Serbs in Macedonia. When Trikoúpes proposed to him a Balkan Federation, he betrayed the Greek statesman's offer to the Porte, in order to conciliate it. Supported by both Salisbury and Crispi in his opposition to Russian attempts to secure the diplomatic removal of Prince Ferdinand, he suppressed Russophil conspiracies with the utmost severity. A Montenegrin raid near Bourgas failed; and Major Panitza, who had trusted that Russia would save him from paying the penalty of treason against his Prince, was tried by court-martial and shot as a traitor. Brigandage, which had discredited the country by the seizure of two Austrians at the Bellova railway-station, he put down with as firm a hand as the intrigues of Orthodox churchmen against the Catholic Prince. Political assassination became the weapon of the discontented; Beltchev, one of Stambulov's colleagues, was shot by his side at Sofia; Vulkovich, his agent, was stabbed in the street at Constantinople. These acts of violence rendered it imperative to provide for the future of the throne; accordingly, the Prince, in 1893, married a Bourbon Princess, Marie Louise of Parma—an union which necessitated a modification of article 38 of the constitution, permitting the baptism of the heir in the Roman Catholic faith. Stambulov not only succeeded in obtaining the adoption of this amendment by the Grand *Sobranje*, but shut up the recalcitrant Metropolitan Clement in a monastery for having opposed it publicly. This marriage, by providing an heir who received the name of the ancient Bulgarian Tsar Boris, strengthened the throne, but proved to be the cause of the great statesman's fall. United to a Bourbon, the Prince naturally desired diplomatic society for his wife and social recognition for himself, while by this time he had acquired sufficient knowledge of the language and character of his people to feel competent to govern without his too powerful and most unceremonious minister. The relations between Prince and Premier became more and more strained; Col. Petrov, the Prince's favourite, was forced upon the unwilling Premier as a colleague; and a princely telegram, accusing his First Minister of "vulgarity," caused the latter to resign. On May 31, 1894, Stoilov succeeded him, and for nearly five years remained in office. Unfortunately, the fallen statesman, like his German prototype, vented his spleen in newspaper interviews, which provoked his prosecution for defamation. The end came on July 15, 1895, when he was brutally assaulted by three assassins; three days later he died of his wounds, and the tardy trial of his murderers of whom only Hallio Stavrev, the principal, was condemned to death and then sentenced instead to 15 years' imprisonment, cast suspicion upon the government and discredit upon the country.

Freed from all control, the Prince then made his peace with Russia. Alexander III was now dead; and a few days before Stambulov's murder, a deputation, of which Mgr Clement and Stoilov formed part, had gone to St Petersburg to lay a wreath

on the dead Tsar's grave and to effect a reconciliation with his
successor. The Russian conditions were the conversion of
Prince Boris to the Orthodox Church; and this solemn farce
was enacted in 1896, after a more than usually unseemly
theological controversy. Nicholas II acted as godfather by
proxy; Russia formally recognised Prince Ferdinand as the
reward of this apostasy; the other Powers followed; and the
Prince *de jure*, as well as *de facto*, basked in the smiles of his
suzerain and his protector. Thenceforth his policy became
steadily Russophil. The officers implicated in the kidnapping
of his predecessor were reinstated and those appointed under
the anti-Russian *régime* removed; Russian training was encouraged in the army; a Russian admiral and a Russian
financier visited Bulgaria. Russian Grand-dukes came to
celebrate the 25th anniversary of Shipka and the 30th of
Plevna; and Ignatyeff urged the Bulgars to transmit to their
children the sacred duty of realising the treaty of San Stefano,
thus exciting their desire for Macedonia. Notwithstanding
that agitation and the instability of Bulgarian Cabinets after the
fall of Stoilov in 1899, owing to dissatisfaction with his financial
and railway policy, the principality made substantial progress,
thanks to the grit of its inhabitants. In Bulgaria it is necessary
to distinguish between the people and the politicians. Unlike
the Greek, the Bulgarian peasant dislikes politics, and wishes to
cultivate his field in peace; while political parties, increased
from two to eight without any corresponding difference of
principles, fight for office in the name of this or that party
leader. The politicians are mainly recruited from the towns-
men and especially from the lawyers; and it was noted as
significant that in 1908, thirty years after the creation of
Bulgaria, nearly one-third of the deputies were graduates, and
Sofia had nine daily papers. Consequently, the kaleidoscopic
succession of nine Cabinets, now Russophil, now Stambulovist,
in the same number of years, scarcely affected the stability of
the country; nor did such public scandals as the impeachment

of four Ministers for the violation of the constitution in their personal interest reflect discredit on the laborious masses, who had no concern with lucrative contracts. But lavish expenditure on railways and harbour-works inevitably caused financial difficulties; and these, aggravated by bad harvests, forced the government in 1900 to impose a tithe on agricultural produce, which provoked a serious peasant riot near Rustchuk. A new tariff, intended to protect native industries, raised the cost of living, while free and compulsory education produced, as usual, an overflow of professional men and a consequent supply of professional agitators. Hence, even in "the peasant state," which had seemed to British observers in the early nineties to be an almost ideal country for the tillers of the soil, a Socialist movement has arisen in the last 20 years. There, too, as in older communities, the students became so troublesome that in 1907 Stambulov's successor, Petkov, the "Haussmann of Bulgaria," closed the University, only to fall a victim to assassination by a discharged official. These were signs that progress in Oriental countries, if rapid, had its drawbacks, and that there was much of the old Adam still latent beneath the surface of their European civilisation. The history of Servia since the Bulgarian war tells the same tale.

For some years after that event Servian history mainly con-sisted of the domestic squabbles of the royal family. Milan, though an able man, had the usual vices of the Europeanised Oriental, while his beautiful wife, Queen Natalie, possessed a strong will of her own. International politics widened the breach between the royal couple, for the King was an Austrophil, while the Queen, as befitted the daughter of a colonel in the Russian army, was an adherent of the Tsar. Servian public life reflected these tendencies, for the Radicals, or rural party, were Russophil, and of the urban parties, the Progressives and the Liberals, the former was pro-Austrian. At last Milan obtained a divorce from his wife, and followed this domestic victory by summoning a commission, on which all the three political parties were represented, and in the labours of which he himself took part with marked ability, for drawing up a constitution far more Liberal than that of 1869. Its most important article was that which made all classes of the community, and not peasants alone, eligible as deputies, but one-fourth of the National Assembly was still to be nominated by the King. Freedom of the press and a lower suffrage were granted; and Milan informed the deputies that they must accept the constitution as a whole without amendment—a threat which induced them to pass it *en bloc* on January 2, 1889. Scarcely, however, had this new charter come into force, than he abdicated in favour of his son, Alexander, on March 6, 1889. As the young King was only 13 years of age, three Regents, all Liberals, were appointed to govern the country, the chief of them being Ristich, the ablest Servian statesman, who 21 years before had been one of Milan's own guardians; the others were Generals Protich and Belimarkovich. The bickerings of the divorced couple and the Queen's assertion of her right to reside in her son's capital kept Servia, however, in a constant ferment; an attempt to expel her was at first frustrated by the mob and the students; blood was shed in the scuffle; but next day Ristich ordered the police to break into her house and escort her to the station. At last both the ex-King and Queen not only consented to live abroad for their country's good, but made up their private differences in order to save the throne from the Karageorgevich pretender. Meanwhile, Alexander, who had been hitherto apparently immersed in the study of constitutional history, suddenly amazed his Regents by ordering their arrest at his dinner-table on April 13, 1893, proclaiming himself of age, and dissolving the National Assembly. The success of this *coup d'état* directed against the Regents encouraged him to make another against the Radicals. Accordingly, on May 21 of the following year, he abolished the constitution of 1889 and restored that of 1869. This drastic act was followed, five years later, by a wholesale proscription of the

Radical and Russophil party, which the Court sought to implicate in the attempted assassination of Milan, then commander-in-chief, by a certain Knezevich, said to be an agent of the pretender; and the way in which this "Servian Dreyfus case" was conducted aroused general indignation.

In August, 1900, Alexander, who had hitherto been successful, committed the serious political mistake of marrying a lady-in-waiting of his mother, Madame Draga Mashin, widow of a Bohemian engineer and herself of "Bohemian" tendencies, which Belgrade gossip at once exaggerated. This union proved his ruin. The Tsar, indeed, hastened to congratulate the King; and in the following year the death at Vienna of Milan, who had retired in disgust, removed one of the constant irritants of Servian public life and Russia's greatest enemy. But the lack of an heir, the suspicion that Queen Draga was scheming to secure the succession for one of her brothers, Nikodem Lunjevitza, and the petty jealousies of Belgrade society rendered the King's position insecure. In vain he granted an amnesty to the proscribed Radicals; in vain, in 1901, he celebrated the anniversary of the Turkish evacuation of Belgrade by the issue of a constitution more Liberal than that of 1869, less Radical than that of 1889, giving the country the safeguards of a second Chamber for the first time in its history and a Council of State. He described this new charter as "the result of an understanding between the sovereign and the leaders of the three political parties"; and the first elections held under it aroused unusual interest. But still discontent grew apace in a soil so congenial to political intrigue as is that of the Servian capital. The first sign of the coming tragedy was the proclamation of Peter Karageorgevich as King by an adventurer at Shabatz in 1902. To secure himself against similar conspiracies Alexander appointed a military Cabinet under General Tsintsar-Markovich, and on April 7, 1903, perpetrated a third *coup d'état*, by which he suspended the new constitution until he had rid himself of his old enemies,

the Radicals.   After having repealed all obnoxious laws by his
own authority, abolished the Council of State, the ballot and
the freedom of the press, and dismissed the senators and the
Radical judges, he appointed a new batch of life-senators and
Councillors, all innocent of Radicalism, and then at once
restored in this form the suspended constitution, which he had
so arbitrarily revised, with the object, as he told his people, of
maintaining "order, unity, and peace."   The result was the
very opposite.   Cut off by the abolition of the ballot from the
sure support of their peasant adherents, and thus deprived of
their constitutional remedies, the Radicals sought refuge in the
usual Balkan device for desperate emergencies—a palace
revolution.

The spring of 1903 was ominous for the royal couple.
A scullion in the palace kitchen was suspected of trying to
poison their food; a plot was formed to shoot the King at the
door of the cathedral on Palm Sunday, the national festival.
Ultimately, another and more appropriate anniversary was
selected for the deed—June 10, the day when Michael had
been assassinated thirty-five years before.   The conspirators
were officers who had taken the oath to Alexander; and their
leader was Colonel Mashin, brother of the Queen's first husband
and her personal enemy.   Others, it was said, were well paid for
their murderous work; while behind the actual assassins stood
the smug, black-coated politicians, ready to profit by what was
cynically proclaimed to be a "glorious revolution."   On the
night of June 10, 1903, the conspirators met at the "Servian
Crown" to arrange their plans; the 6th regiment occupied the
approaches to the palace; the door was exploded with dynamite;
and in the ensuing darkness the murderers groped about for
two hours till at last they found the royal couple hiding in a
cupboard where the Queen kept her dresses.   The wretches
who wore the King's uniform showed no mercy to their
sovereign.   Pierced by over 30 bullets the last Obrenovich fell,
clasping his wife in his arms, while the ruffians who profaned

the name of officer stabbed and outraged the body of the Queen. Throwing the two mangled corpses out of the window, the assassins continued their work in the city. The Queen's two brothers, the Prime Minister and the Minister of War, were shot in cold blood; the Minister of the Interior was seriously wounded; the occasion was seized for gratifying private revenge; and Belgrade proved to the world that she was still, after a century of practical freedom, inhabited by thinly polished barbarians. Nor was this impression diminished, when, in the morning, the capital was decorated with flags, the church bells rang, and dance music enlivened the squares. When night fell, two carts conveyed the bodies of the King and Queen to their last resting-place in the church of St Mark, where the second and least conspicuous Obrenovich Prince had been buried. No friend was present at their humble funeral. A few hours after the tragedy a new Ministry under Avakumovich, of which the chief conspirator was a member, issued a proclamation temporarily reviving the constitution of 1901 and summoning the National Assembly for the election of a king. The country had but a short interregnum. Prince Peter Karageorgevich may not have been privy to the murders, but it was he who profited by them, for on June 15 the National Assembly unanimously elected him King. The new sovereign, who nine days later mounted the blood-stained Servian throne, had spent 45 of his 57 years in exile—now in Hungary, now at the court of his Montenegrin father-in-law, now at Geneva— and was therefore practically a stranger to the land, over which his father Alexander had ruled for sixteen. He had fought in the Franco-German war and in the Bosnian insurrection, and was therefore more of a soldier than his two predecessors; he had translated Mill *On Liberty*, but the English philosopher's speculations were scarcely adapted to the society of Servia. Even before his arrival, the politicians had restored, with some alterations, the constitution of 1889. This constitution of June 18, 1903, which till 1921 remained in force, provided for a

single chamber, elected by citizens who paid 15 *dinara* a year
in direct taxes, and convened annually in the capital on October
10. Election was to take place by departmental *scrutin de liste*,
thus embodying the principle of proportional representation;
and it was provided that in each department there must be two
candidates furnished with an University degree or the diploma
of a high school. A Grand *Skupshtina* of twice the usual number
of deputies was to be summoned to decide upon a regency,
the succession to the throne, a modification of the constitution,
or any cession or exchange of territory. The new sovereign
took the oath to this constitution, and unlike Milan and
Alexander, he kept his promise to be "a true constitutional
King of Servia." A day before, the time-serving Metropolitan
had invoked the divine blessing upon the new, as he had
already invoked it upon the murderers of the late King, in the
self-same cathedral where he had baptized and married his
murdered sovereign. But, if the head of the Servian Church
could thus apologise for assassination, foreign governments
were more scrupulous. Italian officers sent back their Servian
decorations; the King of Roumania withdrew his name from
his Servian regiment. Austria and Russia, traditional rivals for
influence in Servia, alone recognised King Peter; but the
Austrian Emperor stigmatised the act, to which he owed his
throne, as "a heinous and universally reprobated crime."
The British and other ministers were withdrawn; and the
humorous element, never wanting in Balkan tragedies, was
supplied by the author of the Armenian massacres, who
expressed his horror at the midnight murders committed by his
Christian neighbours.

Boycotted by Europe, King Peter soon had to face internal
difficulties. He was the prisoner of the regicides, who occupied
all the best posts and whom he dared not offend. Both they
and the politicians intended that he should be merely a puppet,
while even in Servia there was still a party which cherished the
memory of the old dynasty; and the conspiracy of the garrison

of Nish, where it had always been popular, and the existence of a bastard son of Milan at Constantinople, menaced the early days of the new. The presence of the Crown Prince of Montenegro, when Peter was anointed at Jitcha in the ancient coronation church of the Servian kings, seemed to secure him the support of a dangerous rival; but the marriage of Prince Nicholas' second son Mirko, with Mlle Natalie Constantinovich, the nearest relative of the murdered King, might prove an embarrassment to the new, as it had proved to the old dynasty. Moreover, in his own family the new ruler had a source of anxiety in the person of his heir, Prince George, a youth of violent temper, whose antics soon kept Belgrade gossip busy with the doings of the palace. Foreign diplomatists not unnaturally declined to sit down with assassins at the royal table; a reaction against them began, and a " league for " their " legal punishment " was formed; but it was not till 1906, when the chief regicides were placed on the retired list, that Great Britain resumed official relations with Servia, whose export trade to the United Kingdom had entirely disappeared since their rupture. Still the antagonism between regicides and anti-regicides, who formed a " Nationalist party," continued; the former attacked two Nationalist deputies in the street; and two anti-regicide officers were murdered without the culprits being brought to justice. One foreign potentate, indeed, the Prince of Bulgaria, exchanged visits with King Peter almost in the year after his accession; and this fraternal feeling was the forerunner of a Serbo-Bulgarian convention in 1906, which, as the first step to a customs union of the two Slav states, caused a tariff war with Austria-Hungary and the usual embargo upon the export of Servian swine into the Dual Monarchy. But this conflict was not an unmixed evil, for it led to the discovery of other outlets for Servian live-stock and tended towards a better understanding with Great Britain, of which the effect was seen in the eastern crisis of 1908. When, too, the Austrian Foreign Minister, Baron Aehrenthal, earlier in that year

announced that leave had been asked to survey the route
for a railway across the *sanjak* of Novibazar, uniting the
Bosnian terminus at Uvatz with the Turkish station of
Mitrovitza, a Servian counter-proposal for a line from the
Danube to the Adriatic at San Giovanni di Medua obtained
Italian and Russian support. Thus, under the Karageorgevich
restoration, Servia ceased to pursue the Austrophil policy of
Milan ; the Progressive party almost disappeared ; the Liberals
were merged in the new Nationalist group ; and the " Old "
Radicals, under M. Pashich, the veteran democrat of the
eighties, became, with the " Young " Radicals, the most
important factors in public life.

Prince Nicholas of Montenegro was occupied, after the
definite enlargement of his principality in 1880, with the
problem of adapting a Homeric state of society, where fighting
had been the main occupation of the men for nearly five
centuries, to the changed requirements of a modern community. Excellent roads were made ; trade was encouraged,
tobacco cultivated, and each mountaineer ordered to plant a
vine. The first Montenegrin public library and museum, and
a theatre, where the Prince's two plays were performed amidst
loud applause, increased the intellectual resources of the little
capital ; and the 400th anniversary of the first Slavonic printing-
press, celebrated in 1893, reminded the world of Montenegrin
aspirations after knowledge in the past. Five years earlier, a
new code, the work of M. Bogoshich, was promulgated.
Meanwhile, the Highlanders had kept their hands in by
repeated brushes with the Albanians on the frontier ; and in
1895 the Prince made the experiment of a standing army.
Famines continued, however, to tax the resources of the
country ; and many Montenegrins emigrated to Servia.

The mountain principality, so long cut off from the world,
has become much more closely connected with western Europe
since 1896. On October 24 of that year, the Prince's fourth
daughter, Elena, married the heir to the Italian throne, who four

years later became King of Italy. This union, which recalls the marriages of the Montenegrin Black Princes with fair Venetians in the 15th century, was a love match, but has none the less had important political and economic results for the little mountain state. It not only brought the Petrovich dynasty, the bicentenary of which was celebrated a few months later, within the family circle of " European " Courts, but induced Italians to regard the country of their Queen as a field for economic enterprise and incidentally to take more interest in Balkan politics. Two other Montenegrin Princesses had married Russians, so that, after the accession of another son-in-law to the Servian throne, Prince Nicholas became on a small scale the "father-in-law of Europe"; while the marriage of his second son, Mirko, might conceivably unite the two Servian states in one hand. Finally, two other marriages, that of his fifth daughter to Prince Francis Joseph of Battenberg, and that of his eldest son to the Duchess Jutta of Mecklenburg-Strelitz, brought his family into special favour with the late Queen Victoria, whom he visited at Windsor in 1898. It was, perhaps, as much in virtue of his exalted connexions as to commemorate the fortieth anniversary of his accession that Prince Nicholas assumed the style of " Royal Highness" at the close of 1900, and that of King at his Jubilee in 1910. But the increased importance of the reigning house considerably augmented its expenditure, while the usual discord of married brothers who live in the same small place was aggravated by the lack of an heir to the Crown Prince, whose brother Mirko had offspring.

In 1905, the Prince amazed Europe by issuing two edicts, announcing the grant of parliamentary institutions and liberty of the press to his people. A Liberal in theory, especially in British politics, the Prince had always been an autocrat in practice, although in 1868 he had transferred some of his functions to the Senate, increased to 16 members, and in 1874 had created a Ministry. But neither the Senate nor the Ministry had any real power. Consequently this sudden new departure seemed a dangerous experiment. The example of Russia, the growing desire of those young Montenegrins who had been educated at Belgrade to have a share in the government of their country, and the reflection that the change, if inevitable, had better be made in his own lifetime rather than in that of his much less experienced successor, doubtless influenced so shrewd a ruler as Prince Nicholas in his decision, although his official explanation was that he had been actuated by the Liberal ideas imbibed at Paris in his youth. The constitution —a lengthy document of 222 articles—was borrowed, however, from Servian sources, especially the Servian constitution of 1889. The Prince continued to represent the state in all its foreign relations ; primogeniture in the male line was declared to be the law of the succession to the throne ; the Senate was preserved ; the country was divided into departments (*oblasti*), districts (*capitanie*), and communes (*opshtine*) ; the Church was proclaimed autocephalous, and all other cults free ; a free press and free compulsory elementary education, a Council of State of six, and a Court of Accounts of three members, formed parts of the charter. A National Assembly (*Narodna Skupshtina*), partly elected by universal suffrage, and partly composed of *ex officio* nominees of the Prince, was to meet annually on October 31. This body, the term of which was four years, was composed of 62 members elected by the 56 districts and the six towns, and of 14 nominated or *ex officio* members, viz. the Metropolitan, the Roman Catholic Archbishop of Antivari (who bears the title of " Primate of Servia "), the Mohammedan *Mufti*, the six Councillors of State, the presidents of the Grand Tribunal and of the Court of Accounts, and the three brigadiers. Deputies must be at least 30 years of age and pay 15 *kronen* in taxes annually. The first general election under this constitution was held in November, 1905. On December 19 the first Montenegrin parliament met ; the old Ministers who had so long executed their master's edicts resigned ; and a new Ministry of younger

men took their places. "Nothing," said the Prince, "would
afflict my heart more than to hear it said: 'the old Prince,
though meaning well, has acted with precipitation, and esteemed
his people to be more advanced than it really is'." In fact,
however, parliamentary government was not a success. Until
the appointment of M. Tomanovich as Premier in 1907
Cabinet crises were frequent; a group of Socialists made its
appearance; the country was divided into factions; and,
whenever a personal ruler's strong hand is withdrawn, it
may be found that parliamentarism, at present more or less a
comedy, is a dangerous gift to a poor and primitive Balkan
state. Already, at the general election of 1907, feeling ran so
high that the office of a Radical journal was wrecked, the
Radicals refused to take part in the voting, and all the deputies
elected were consequently Conservatives. Then came the
discovery of bombs from Servia in Montenegro. Montenegrin
ex-ministers were prosecuted; a democratic ex-Premier was sent
to prison at Podgoritza; and accusations were made against the
Servian government of complicity in a plot against Prince
Nicholas, which led to a rupture of diplomatic relations between
the two sister-states, whose rulers had private reasons for not
greatly loving one another.

Another influence which was tending to modernise Montenegro was that of the emigrants who returned from the United
States. This was a comparatively new feature in the social life
of the Black Mountain, whose sons, if they emigrated, usually
went, till recently, to some other part of the near east. It is
calculated that there are now some 30,000 Montenegrins in
America; and their country is thus drained of its young men, with
evil results to the damsels who remain behind. These emigrants,
on their return, like the "intellectuals" whom the government
sent to study abroad, are apt to become discontented with their
highland home. Nor was it without risks for a small and poor
state to allow foreigners, and those mainly of one nationality, to
conduct its chief commercial enterprises. Commercially modern

Montenegro was practically an Italian colony. Italians managed the tobacco monopoly; they conducted, under the Montenegrin flag, the navigation on the lake of Scutari; they controlled the Marconi station at the haven of Antivari. No wonder that this system of foreign concessions, perhaps inevitable in a country where capital was scarce, was causing some to raise the cry of "Montenegro for the Montenegrins." Still, despite these disadvantages of progress, the country had reaped advantages also. Since 1906 it has had its own coinage, based on the silver unit, called, with a fine flavour of the Middle Ages, a *perper*. As a natural corollary, a bank has been founded. A railway was inaugurated in 1908, which connects Vir Bazar on the lake of Scutari with the harbour of Antivari; a motor-service joins the capital with Cattaro and Podgoritza; telephones enabled the Ministers to issue their orders from the new offices, whither they had emigrated from the old "billiard-table"; and the village-capital, grown in size, is lighted by electricity. Princes and officers dressed in khaki represented, among giants clad in the splendid national costume, the transition stage upon which Montenegro had now, for weal or woe, inevitably entered.

Roumania continued, during the quarter of a century which followed her practical accession to the Triple Alliance, a course of peaceful progress, broken by occasional political disturbances and by serious social upheavals. When, in 1906, the Jubilee exhibition, held to commemorate the fortieth anniversary of the sovereign's first arrival in his adopted country, enabled visitors to compare the present with the past, they saw that Roumania had assumed, in little more than a generation, all the externals of western civilisation. A railway system of nearly 2,000 miles facilitated travelling where, at the Prince's coming, there had not been a single train. The Iron Gates had been blasted, and a noble bridge spanned the Danube at Cernavoda, which, by uniting the rest of the kingdom with its newly-won haven of Constantza, has given importance to the despised Dobrudja and made Roumania the highway from Berlin to Constantinople. The credit of the Government was such that it could borrow at a trifle over 4 per cent.; the production of petroleum in large quantities had tended to modify the purely agricultural character of the country, which, with a population of between six and seven millions, was the largest, as it was likewise the steadiest, of the Balkan states. But of this population 80 per cent. depended upon the land for their living; and about one-half of the land belonged to a comparatively small number of large proprietors, who in many cases let their property to middlemen, often Jewish capitalists. The peasant, whenever his rent was raised, had either to borrow at usurious interest, or to pay by labour what he could not pay in cash. He was thus reduced to the condition of either a debtor or a serf, unless he chanced to be a small proprietor himself. Even then his prospects were not rosy, for ignorance and sometimes physical weakness prevented him from making his little plot of land feed his large family. Even after the second revision of the constitution, proposed by Brătianu in 1884, he was almost wholly excluded by the electoral system from parliamentary representation, while the time of the legislature was too often wasted in the barren conflicts of Liberals, Conservatives, and "Young" Conservatives or "Junimists"—meaningless party labels without underlying principles. Thus the peasantry became the natural victims of the glib agitators, whom free education had provided in its customary fashion. The great peasant risings of 1888 and 1907 were the results—the latter a veritable Roumanian *Jacquerie*, in which many lives were lost and much machinery was destroyed. A corollary of this agrarian movement was the continued Anti-Semitic agitation, which had so greatly embarrassed the earlier years of the reign. In 1897 Anti-Semitic riots took place; and in 1902 the United States addressed a note to the signatories of the Berlin treaty on the subject of the persecution of the Roumanian Jews and their consequent exodus in large numbers, in direct contravention of article 44 of that famous instrument.   But, except for the exclusion of the Roumanian minister in London from the Guildhall banquet, nothing was done in response to this appeal, and the Roumanians could retort that almost every nation concerned had broken some article of the Berlin treaty.

Foreign policy had been throughout under the direct control of the King, and therefore pro-German and at times pro-Turkish.   Since the visit of the Austrian Emperor to Bucharest in 1896, after the opening of the Iron Gates in the presence of the three riverain sovereigns, this connexion with the three central Powers, begun by Brătianu and Bismarck in 1883, had become closer.   A military convention had bound the fortunes of the Roumanian army of 200,000 men to those of Austria-Hungary under certain conditions; and on one occasion Roumania mobilised at the bidding of Germany, in order to save the embarrassed Turks from denuding their Asiatic provinces of troops.   The fortification of the capital by General Brialmont further strengthened the barrier which Roumania could offer to a Russian advance on Constantinople.

Her friendship with Austria-Hungary had had, however, the effect of forcing Roumania to interest herself in the Macedonian question, thus offending the susceptibilities of the only other non-Slavonic Christian state in the near east—Greece. Compelled to relinquish, at least for a time, the idea of redeeming the "unredeemed" Roumanians of the Dual Monarchy, she had cast her eyes afar upon the long-forgotten Koutzo-Wallachs of Macedonia and Epirus, whom Roumanians state to be Roumanians and Greeks assert to be Greeks.   Whenever this propaganda has been relaxed, the Latin and the Greek races of the peninsula have fraternised, as when their two governments concluded a commercial convention, their two rulers met at Abbazia, and the students of Bucharest visited Athens in 1901.   But the Greco-Roumanian honeymoon ended, when, in 1905, the Roumanian ministry obtained from the Porte the recognition of the Koutzo-Wallachs as a separate nationality, with the right of worshipping in their own language.   Anti-Greek riots took place in Roumania ; and diplomatic relations between the two countries, already inter-rupted between 1892 and 1896 owing to the fact that the Roumanian courts had declared illegal the legacies of the brothers Záppa, the founders of the Záppeion at Athens, were again broken off for several years.

Greek internal politics were comparatively uneventful during the eleven years which followed the evacuation of Thessaly.   It was the calm between two periods of excitement. After M. Zaïmes, the most conservative of modern Greek statesmen, had settled the various questions arising out of the war, Theotókes, a former lieutenant of Trikoúpes and the first Ionian who had reached the chief place in Greek politics, became Prime Minister in 1899; and his four Premierships, two of them unusually long, altogether filled up a large portion of this period.   His first resignation, towards the close of 1901, was due to popular indignation at a translation of the Gospels into a very vernacular form of Greek, which caused a fatal riot among the students of the University and an attack upon two newspaper offices.   The incident was instructive, as showing the importance attached by the Greeks to the original text of the New Testament, which they justly regard as one of the most valuable portions of their national heritage.   A similar agitation arose in 1903, when Rhálles, then in office, was forced by the students and one of the professors to stop the performances of the *Orésteia* of Æschylus, because certain phrases in the version of M. Soteriádes did not please the purists.   Disturbances, arising out of another difficult question, that of the currants, cut short the second Theotókes adminis-tration in 1903; and two years later the hand of an assassin removed Deligiánnes from the stage of Greek politics, where he had so long played a leading part.   The crime was not due to political motives, but to the suppression of gambling-hells at the orders of the veteran statesman, the "grandfather," as he was popularly called, of public life. His death had the effect of splitting the so-called "National party," of which he had been the chief, into two sections, one following Rhálles, the other Mavromicháles, with the natural result that Theotókes, at the head of an united party, attained and kept the Premiership for more than three and a half years till July, 1909. During his long administration the second celebration of the revived Olympic Games at Athens in 1906, in the presence of the late King Edward VII, concentrated there the representatives of the whole Hellenic world as well as of other nationalities. A year later the census proved the great development of Athens and the Piræus, and the remarkable increase of Volo since the Thessalian port had been united with Greece. But the figures of some country districts showed that emigration to the United States—a phenomenon non-existent before 1891 —was responsible for the large decrease in the excess of males over females, which, strange as it seems to Englishmen, had been a marked feature of Greek life. To the remittances of these emigrants was partly due the great reduction in the rate of exchange, which from 46 *dr.* 87 *l.* to the £ at the time of the currant crisis of December, 1894—January, 1895, was in 1913 reduced practically to par (i.e. 25 *dr.* to the £ sterling). To their return to their own country may be traced in due course of time the permeation of new ideas. Already the traveller is startled by being addressed in English with a strong American accent in remote villages of the Morea and at the discovery that one-fifth of the population of a town in central Greece has emigrated. These "Americans" fought well in 1912.

This review of the Near East down to the Turkish revolution of 1908 may be completed by some reference to the history of those islands which occupied a position of autonomy or of vassalage to Turkey, yet unlike Crete, have had only occasional connexion with the general trend of the eastern question.   Cyprus, under British control since 1878, is scarcely a source of satisfaction to observers.   The island was handicapped economically from the outset by the absurd arrangement, by which the British government agreed to pay to Turkey an annual tribute, calculated on the average excess of revenue over expenditure during the five previous years, or in other words, £92,800. This mode of assessment was peculiarly inappropriate, because the Turks, as is their wont, had spent little upon public works, and the whole revenue of the island at that time was only £147,281.   Thus, the British took over an island where everything was still to create, and at the same moment a huge liability wholly disproportionate to its resources.   But the full injustice of this obligation became patent four years later, when nearly £82,000 of the tribute was earmarked to pay the interest on the repudiated Turkish loan of 1855, which Great Britain and France had guaranteed and which was largely held by their subjects.   Thus, the Cypriotes were made to defray the liabilities of the whole Turkish empire towards the bondholders and to meet what had been a joint guarantee of the two western Powers.   The result has been that annual surpluses in the colonial budget have been converted into deficits, without any corresponding advantage to the suzerain.   Irrigation, the most pressing need of the island, and other public works, which could have been undertaken if Great Britain had made a better bargain with the Turk, have been largely neglected, and the island has only one small railway, while the government spent only £5,000 on education.   In short, to quote the phrase of an expert in the *Times*[1], the tribute, abolished in 1914, was "a millstone round the island's neck."   From yet another point of view Cyprus has failed to warrant the praise bestowed upon Lord Beaconsfield 49 years ago. Occupied originally on strategic grounds, and first governed by so eminent a soldier as Sir Garnet (afterwards Lord) Wolseley, it has ceased, since the British occupation of Egypt

[1] May 24, 1912.

in 1882, to have the military value which it had previously possessed. Moreover, we are having in Cyprus much the same political experience that we had in Corfù; the Greeks, who form the vast majority of its 310,709 inhabitants, desire union with Greece. The British government, aware of this fact, so arranged the constitution, which was granted to Cyprus in 1882, that the nine Christian elected members of the Legislative Council could be outvoted by the High Commissioner and the six *ex officio* members with the aid of the three elected members who represented the 61,422 or 19·4 per cent. of Mussulmans. The Christian deputies are in permanent opposition to the government, and in April, 1912, resigned in a body as a protest against the refusal of the High Commissioner to increase their numbers and to spend the taxes exclusively in the island. Nevertheless, something, even under these disadvantages, has been done for Cyprus. The plague of locusts has been checked; justice is fairly administered; and the Christians enjoy liberty and security for their lives and property, which they lacked in the Turkish times. But most races, emancipated from the Turks, become discontented when they have had time to forget the grave evils of Turkish rule. A generation has grown up in Cyprus which does not remember the joy with which the British flag was welcomed there. Education has made the Christians more critical and inclined to regard the British occupation "as a merely transitory episode in their history," while they warmly repudiated the contention of the British government prior to 1914 that, if Great Britain evacuated Cyprus, it would be handed back to Turkey.

The privileged "Twelve Islands" of the southern Sporádes— Ikaría, Pátmos, Léros, Kálymnos, Astypálaia, Nísyros, Têlos, Sýme, Chálkeia, Kárpathos, Kássos and Megíste (or Kastellórrizon—of which the first four, united in one Greek province with Samos during the War of Independence, had received a confirmation of their former charters from Mahmûd II in 1835, and paid nothing, except a collective sum of 80,000 piastres, to the treasury, were threatened in 1867, during the Cretan insurrection, and again in 1869, with the forcible loss of their rights. At the instigation of Stanley, however, to whom their inhabitants appealed, Turkey withdrew her troops. To Clarendon she offered excuses; but a fresh attempt to reduce the *Dodekánesos* to the common level of Turkish provinces was made 20 years later. Sýme was blockaded and starved into surrender, and in 1893 several of the chief men were imprisoned[1]. The "Young" Turks completed this work; but the Italian occupation of 10 of these islands, together with Leipsó, Kôs and Rhodes, in 1912, restored their liberties. In 1902 the Turks made similar encroachments upon the privileges of Thasos, where an occupation by Turkish troops followed a protest against new taxes; and the Egyptian ascendancy there (see p. 151) was restricted to the woods and mines, a part of the *vakuf* of Kavalla, whose administrator was the Khedive.

Samos had accepted unwillingly her position of dependence upon Turkey in 1832, and it required a blockade of the port of Vathý before she acquiesced in autonomy as a substitute for union with Greece. Her first Prince, Stephen Vogorídes, whose reign lasted for nearly 20 years, only once visited his principality, which he governed by means of successive lieutenants, no less than 11 in number. His absence and their maladministration caused such discontent, that in 1849 a revolution broke out, the Prince's representative was expelled, and in 1850 the Prince at last resigned. A fresh "Analytic Charter" was then issued, confirming the privileges conferred in 1832, but substituting the indirect for the direct election of the Assembly. The new Prince, however, Alexander Callimachi, never once set foot in Samos, which he administered by his agent Koneménos, until, at the instigation of Stratford de Redcliffe, John Ghika, the subsequent Roumanian statesman, was sent there, at the critical period of the Crimean war, first as lieutenant and then as Prince. Ghika suppressed

---

[1] An "elder" of Kálymnos in the *Secolo* of June 2, 1912.

the piracy and brigandage which ravaged the island, improved
the administration of justice, and, although a poor Greek
scholar, connected his name with the foundation of a high
school, appropriately called the " Pythagóreion " after the most
famous son of Samos.　His next four successors continued to
encourage public works, and during the great crisis of the
eastern question between 1875 and 1878 Samos remained
undisturbed.　Scarcely, however, was it over than the Assembly
telegraphed to Constantinople, requesting the re-appointment
of Adosídes, a former Prince, in place of the too passive ruler
who had governed the island during those years.　The immediate resignation of the well-meaning Photiádes, who had
done much in a quiet way for education in the island and is
still remembered as the founder of a seminary for priests,
taught the Assembly the dangerous lesson that it could un-
make Princes.　This has been responsible for much of the
subsequent instability in Samos.　The power of the Assembly
became greater, when Alexander Karatheodori, the well-known
statesman, became Prince in 1885.　He allowed the majority
of that body to direct his policy and his public appointments,
so that office became the reward of party services.　Measures
taken against the phylloxera, which was ruining the famous
Samian vineyards, made his administration unpopular ; force
was used to repress the disorder ; several peasants were killed
and wounded, and the arrival of Turkish troops, in contravention of the firman of 1832, so greatly increased the
discontent that in 1894 he resigned.

So far the princely reigns had been of long duration, for in
60 years Samos had had only 8 Princes.　But in the next 18
years there were no less than 10.　After the strict rule of
the Albanian Berovich, who was afterwards celebrated for his
flight from Crete, Stephen Mousoûros, subsequently ambassador in London, found the Assembly resolved to usurp the
princely functions.　The complaints of the Samians were again
heard at Constantinople ; and a radical reform in 1899 reduced

the princely office to a shadow.   Till then the Prince had had
the right of choosing his four councillors (or βουλευταί), one
for each division of the island, out of a list of eight submitted
to him ; but he was now forced to accept those four whom the
Assembly, a body of 39 members *plus* the Metropolitan, chose
to elect, without the power of either dismissing them, or of
dissolving or even proroguing it.   Placed between the exigencies
of the Porte and the claims of the Assembly, and invested
with a limited veto, he was at once the creature of Constantinople and the sport of Samian faction.   The palace at Vathý
was thus no bed of roses.

Princes now followed each other in rapid succession.   One
was recalled for having accused the Samians of demanding
that Prince Nicholas of Greece should be their ruler, just as
his brother was of the Cretans; another, whose chief adviser
was his barber, fell into disgrace at Constantinople for allowing
the councillors to exceed their powers ; a third, a member of
the well-known family of Mavrogénes, after founding a technical
school and encouraging both agriculture and the excavation of
the Heraîon, found the local politicians too strong for him.
At last, in 1907, the Sultan sent as Prince a Cretan, Kopásses,
of markedly anti-Hellenic opinions, whose reign was the most
turbulent in the history of the island.   In 1908 he refused to
summon the Assembly, and threatened to employ Turkish
troops to disperse it, if it met spontaneously.   The people
blockaded him in the palace, and fired upon the troops, whereupon the Turkish navy bombarded Vathý.   M. Sophoúles,
the scholarly leader of the Opposition and the most influential
man in Samos, was forced to flee to Syra, and addressed a
memorial to the three protecting Powers, in which he declared
that Turkey wanted "to make Samos a Turkish province."
It was pointed out that the Prince had further violated the
constitution by increasing the Turkish garrison, and by allowing
the Turkish, instead of the Samian flag, to be hoisted over the
barracks—thus eventually provoking in 1912 the otherwise

unjustifiable bombardment of this autonomous island by the Italians.   The crisis of October, 1908, in the near east led the Samians, like the Cretans, to agitate for union with Greece, for, if geographically close to Asia, they are racially and religiously all Greeks, and on March 23, 1912, Kopásses was assassinated. His successor, Vegléres, was deposed by M. Sophoúles, who had returned with a body of volunteers.   Availing itself of the Balkan war, the Samian Assembly proclaimed union with Greece on November 24.   The prudent Greek Premier accepted this decision with reserve at the time, in view of the peculiar international position of the island.   But, on March 15, 1913, a Greek force took official possession of Samos, which thus, after 80 years of autonomy, became, with its 68,949 inhabitants, an integral part of the Hellenic kingdom.

CHAPTER XIX

THE TURKISH REVOLUTION (1908–12)

THE eastern question suddenly entered on a new and acute phase in the summer of 1908. The "Young" Turks, or party of reform, whom diplomatists had hitherto been wont to regard as dreamers, had long carried on a secret propaganda, which had made great headway in the army. A Committee had been formed under the title of "Union and Progress" at Geneva in 1891, and thence transferred to Paris, and in 1906 to Salonika, where it met with the ardent support of the Jews and Freemasons, who form an important element in the population of the great Macedonian seaport. It was the intention of the Committee to begin the revolution on the anniversary of the Sultan's accession, August 31; but events caused it to hasten its action. The meeting between Edward VII and the Tsar at Reval made it fear foreign intervention; Abdul Hamid, informed by his spies of the agitation among his Macedonian troops, had made preparations to crush it; and an incident, which in any other country would have had no political importance, secured for the conspirators the co-operation of the Albanians, whom of all his subjects the Sultan had humoured, feared, and trusted most. This incident was nothing more alarming than an excursion, organised for the benefit of the Austrian school at Üsküb, to a wood near Ferisovich on the line to Mitrovitza. But the Albanians of that district considered the proposed entertainment, of which dancing was to have been an item, as bad for public morals, already contaminated by the music-halls of Üsküb; while the rumoured display of Austrian flags aroused their political suspicions. Accordingly, they burnt the platform erected for the dancers, and threatened to fire upon the excursion-train if it attempted to traverse the cut-throat gorge of Katchanik. This threat alarmed the Committee of Union and Progress, which feared that an Albanian attack upon Austrian subjects would be made the pretext for an Austrian invasion of the country, and that consequently its own scheme would be frustrated. Some of its members parleyed with the Albanians of Ferisovich to such purpose that the latter threw in their lot with the revolutionary movement, and telegraphed to the Sultan demanding the revival of the constitution of 1876. Meanwhile, several occurrences had shown the spread of the agitation among the officers of the 3rd army corps. At Resnja, near the lake of Prespa, on July 3, Major Niazi, after seizing the military chest and a number of rifles, took to the mountains as the chief of a "Young" Turkish band; and Shemshi Pasha, who was sent to suppress him, was killed at Monastir. Other assassinations of reactionary officers followed in quick succession; the Sultan, realising that he could rely upon neither the Albanians nor the army, on July 22 appointed as Grand Vizier "little" Said Pasha, the Liberal statesman who had once fled for refuge to the British Embassy. It was too late, however, for half-measures; on the morrow Major Enver Bey and the Committee proclaimed the constitution at various places in Macedonia, and the 2nd and 3rd army corps threatened to march upon Constantinople. On the 24th a decree of the Sultan announced the restoration of the constitution, which had been suspended since 1878. The censorship of the press and the spy system were abolished, and a Chamber of 280 deputies, elected by grand electors, themselves chosen by every group of from 250 to 750 adult males above 25 years of age, was summoned to meet.

Great was the enthusiasm of the people, when they found

that the news was true. For some days Macedonia seemed
to have become Utopia. Enver Bey exclaimed that "arbitrary
government" had "disappeared." "Henceforth," cried this
enthusiastic leader of the revolution, "we are all brothers.
There are no longer Bulgars, Greeks, Roumans, Jews, Mussulmans; under the same blue sky we are all equal, we glory in
being Ottomans." At Serres the president of the Bulgarian
Committee embraced the Greek Archbishop; at Drama the
revolutionary officers imprisoned a Turk for insulting a Christian;
in an Armenian cemetery a procession of Turks and Armenians
listened to prayers, offered up by their respective priests, for the
victims of the Armenian massacres; at Samsûn the Turks
saluted the beard of a Greek prelate; at Tripoli Turks and
Arabs joined in thanksgiving services. The Bulgarian bands
surrendered, and the brigand Sandanski was received like the
prodigal son. Even the cautious British government, which
might have been expected to regard with scepticism the results
of this sudden conversion of an Oriental autocracy into a
constitutional monarchy, hastened to prophesy, through the
medium of Sir Edward Grey, that "the Macedonian question
and others of a similar character will entirely disappear." The
magic word "Constitution" had, indeed, an extraordinary
effect upon British Liberals. Without pausing to consider
whether the "Young" Turk would not prove to be merely
the "Old" Turk with a varnish of Parisian culture and without
a belief in religion, they welcomed enthusiastically the Committee of Union and Progress. Pro-Bulgarians became in a
moment pro-Turks; an Ottoman deputation met the British
ambassador on his arrival at Constantinople; and the popularity
of Great Britain rose in Turkey to a point which it had not
attained since the time of Beaconsfield. There were, however,
some persons who foresaw that the position of the Christians
of Turkey would be worse, instead of better, under the new
system, which would inevitably aim at reducing them all to
one dead level. The Greeks were suspicious from the outset;

while here and there, in Arabia and Armenia, reactionary
pashas struggled, but in vain, against the new order. On the
other side, the triumphant revolutionaries naturally increased
their demands. They insisted on the removal of the Sultan's
favourite, Izzet, and accused Said of having violated the constitution by reserving to his master the nomination of the
Ministers of War and Marine. Accordingly, Said made way
for Kiamil, likewise an Anglophil but of a more advanced
Liberalism, who included both a Greek and an Armenian in his
Cabinet. Sweeping changes were made in the administration;
and several of those who had battened on the Hamidian misgovernment were made to disgorge. In the house of one
ex-Minister, who had been in office for no more than 18 months,
£170,000 were found and appropriated to the public service!
The new men and the new methods inspired such confidence
in the Powers, that they decided to remove the vestiges of
foreign control, as the Committee of Union and Progress
desired, from Macedonia. The foreign officers were recalled;
the International Commission of Finance ceased to exist;
"Young" Turkey was to act by herself.

There were two governments, however, ready to seize this
opportunity of profiting by the internal difficulties of the state,
from all connexion with which they had both long desired to
emancipate themselves. The grant of constitutional liberties
to the subjects of Turkey proved a serious embarrassment to a
Christian Power like Austria, whose wards in Bosnia and the
Herzegovina did not enjoy similar privileges, especially as the
Turkish press suggested the extension of the constitution to
such "integral parts" of the Ottoman empire as the two
occupied provinces and Eastern Roumelia. A strike on that
section of the South Bulgarian lines, which Stoilov had tried to
obtain amicably nine years before but which still belonged to
the Oriental Railways Company, provided the Bulgarian
government with an excellent excuse for seizing and retaining
it, on grounds of public safety. A diplomatic incident, arising

out of the omission to ask the Bulgarian representative to an
official dinner at Constantinople, was construed as a reminder
that a vassal was not meet to sit at table with the envoys of
sovereign states.   The act was peculiarly foolish, because
Bulgaria had had separate representation at the Hague, and
her Prince had been accorded sovereign honours at foreign
Courts.   It wounded the national pride, and gave the Prince
just the pretext that he needed for declaring his independence.
At Buda-Pesth he met the Austrian Emperor, himself anxious
to seize the psychological moment for annexing Bosnia and the
Herzegovina.   Prince Ferdinand, who had lost his first wife
nine years before, had become particularly acceptable to the
Austrian court by his recent marriage with a Princess of Reuss.
Personal claims and public policy led to an understanding
between the two violators of the oft-broken treaty of Berlin.
It was arranged that the one should support the other, if
Servia protested by force against this mortgage on her future.
Having secured the consent of Austria, and well knowing that
his army was ready and that "Young" Turkey was weak, the
Prince returned to Bulgaria; and at Trnovo, her medieval
capital, in the church of the Forty Martyrs on October 5, 1908,
he was proclaimed "Tsar of the Bulgarians"—a title re-
miniscent of the old Bulgarian empire, which had embraced
other regions besides modern Bulgaria.   To increase the
solemnity of this act, the proclamation was repeated on the
citadel hill, where once had stood the palace of the Tsars.   Two
days later Austria-Hungary formally annexed the two provinces
which she had occupied for 30 years; and Crete thereupon at
once proclaimed her union with Greece.   While Sig. Tittoni,
the Italian Minister of Foreign Affairs, described the annexation
of Bosnia and the Herzegovina as merely the destruction of
"a diplomatic fiction," his fellow-countrymen loudly demanded
compensation elsewhere, and his British colleague blustered
without being able to do anything, because Germany was
well known to be behind Austria-Hungary.   The annexation

naturally provoked a formal protest from the Porte, the boycott of Austrian goods in Turkey, and the fiercest resentment
in the two Serb states. At one moment Servia, where the
Crown Prince led the anti-Austrian party, seemed to be on the
brink of war with Austria-Hungary; and Montenegro was
spoiling for a fight, encouraged by the speeches of British
Ministers and left without any other official British guidance than
that of a hastily-sent diplomatist, whose knowledge of Spanish
was not of much service at Cetinje, whither for three years
Sir E. Grey had omitted to send a resident representative.
Milovanovich, the Servian Minister of Foreign Affairs, made
a political tour abroad, demanding a strip of Bosnia which
would unite Servia with Montenegro; the President of the
Montenegrin parliament sent a message of thanks to the Lord
Mayor of London; and Prince Nicholas announced that, if the
Austrian annexation were allowed, he would consider himself
released from the restrictions imposed by article 29 of the
Berlin treaty upon the bay of Antivari.

Meanwhile, the elections to the Turkish parliament were
held. Efforts were made to gerrymander the constituencies
so as to favour the Mohammedan element, and the majority
of the deputies elected were Mussulmans; but 18 Greeks,
4 Bulgars, 2 Serbs, 2 Jews, and 2 Armenians sat in the
legislature; whereas the Greeks protested at, the Armenians
acquiesced in, the results of the polls; and, while Jerusalem sent
three Mussulmans, Salonika returned M. Carasso, a leading
Jew and Freemason. On December 10 the Sultan opened
parliament in person with a speech, in which he alluded to the
encroachments of Austria-Hungary and of the " *Vâli* of the
province of Eastern Roumelia "—a phrase considered " pro-
vocative " in Bulgaria—and announced that his intention to
govern constitutionally was "unalterable." All real power was,
however, in the hands of the Committee; and when Kiamil
made a show of independence by dismissing the two Ministers
of War and Marine, who were its nominees, it revenged itself

by procuring the adoption of a vote of no confidence in him and his consequent fall. The Committee was, however, still opposed by another organisation, the "Liberal Union," of which the leader was Ismail Kemal Bey, and which advocated decentralisation. Assassination removed the Albanian editor of the "Liberal Unionist" organ; but on April 13, 1909, a counter-revolution broke out at the capital, the combined work of reactionaries and constitutionalists and inspired by Abdul Hamid, who believed that with the aid of the former he could restore the system of absolute government. Soldiers, led by an Albanian, occupied the parliament-house, and killed two officers who belonged to the Committee; most of the garrison joined in the revolt; Hilmi Pasha, the Grand Vizier, made way for Tewfik; the Minister of Justice was killed, and the Minister of Marine wounded, whereupon the Sultan granted a free pardon to the mutinous troops. Simultaneously with this revolt in Constantinople a massacre of the Armenians at Adana in Cilicia, in which several thousands, including two American missionaries, perished, completed the iniquities of the "Red Sultan's" long reign. If Abdul Hamid did not actually order this massacre, it is significant of the reactionary cause, with which it was associated in the popular mind, that cheers were given for him, and an arch at Adana, commemorative of the constitution, was pulled down. No rebellion, no conspiracy to restore the Armenian kingdom could be proved in partial justification of the horrors which ensued not only at Adana, but at Tarsus and other places in Cilicia—a district almost wholly spared at the time of the previous Armenian massacres. Fire completed the work of destruction; and special care was taken to destroy the account-books, in which the Armenians had registered the liabilities of their Moslem debtors. Neither the *vâli* nor the military commander of Adana showed the least energy in attempting to stop the massacres; while the troops, summoned from Salonika at the news of the first outbreak of savagery, by firing upon the

Armenians provoked the second. Nor can the "Young" Turks be acquitted of culpable weakness at the least in allowing the two principal officials of Adana to escape with light sentences ; if many guilty Mussulmans were hanged, at least three innocent Armenians shared their fate.

The day of reckoning for Abdul Hamid was at last nigh. When the news of the counter-revolution reached Salonika, the Committee of Union and Progress refused all compromise with Constantinople, and Mahmûd Shevket led the Macedonian troops to the capital in defence of the constitution which he had sworn to uphold. The senators and deputies met at San Stefano, the scene of the abortive treaty of 1878; and both houses of the legislature, sitting as a National Assembly, agreed in recommending obedience to the orders of this commander. His terms included the proclamation of martial law, the punishment of the mutineers, and the reduction of the garrison of Constantinople. These conditions were accepted, and on April 25 the avenging army entered the capital. Five hours' hard fighting and the employment of cannon were required to reduce the rebellious soldiers who held the Taksim and Tashkisla barracks—men who had been sent from Salonika some months before to replace the Sultan's favourite Albanian guards, but had been won over by the reactionaries. Exemplary vengeance was taken upon the authors of the counter-revolution ; 40 of the ringleaders were hanged publicly ; and on April 27 the National Assembly met with closed doors to decide the fate of the Sultan, whom public opinion regarded as their accomplice, if not their instigator. The *fetvah* of the Sheikh-ul-Islâm, enumerating his misdeeds, was read ; and the Assembly unanimously voted his deposition, and proclaimed his younger brother Reschad under the title of Mohammed V. Next day the fallen Sultan, who had so long befooled the diplomatists of Europe, was removed to Salonika, and interned in a villa there, whence he was till his death removed to Constantinople. He was allowed to solace himself with his ladies ; the treasure, amounting to over a million sterling, found in his palace, was claimed by the Ministry of Finance for the nation which he had so long misgoverned.

The new Sultan was a mere puppet in the hands of the Committee. Of the world he could know little, for he had been confined by his brother within the gilded cage of his palace, and he is said to have declared "that he had not read any newspaper for 20 years." But the authors of the revolution obtained in him what they wanted—a figure-head. The dawn of the new reign was not, however, auspicious ; an attempt to levy taxes in northern Albania provoked disturbances in that lawless region, where "village Hampdens" protested by force against this interference with their time-honoured custom of paying exactly what they chose ; and a new Mahdi appeared in the Yemen.

Mohammed V found, however, at his accession, that two of the three external difficulties, which had arisen in October, 1908, had been already settled. The suggestion of Sig. Tittoni for a conference on the eastern question at Naples came to naught ; and it became obvious that everyone would have to recognise the accomplished fact of the Austrian annexation of Bosnia and the Herzegovina. Servia and Montenegro, despite the renewal of their diplomatic relations and the conclusion of a military convention, were too weak to stand alone against their powerful neighbour, especially as the Servian capital was within range of his guns. Great Britain could not help a wholly inland state, while the appearance of her fleet off the Montenegrin coast might have provoked war with Germany, the real mistress of the situation. Russia, not yet recovered from her exhausting struggle against Japan, was informed from Berlin that, if she aided Servia, Germany would support Austria. M. Isvolski, the Russian Minister of Foreign Affairs, perforce admitted that Russia had "not legally the right to protest alone"; his Austrian critics contended that his hands were tied by a previous secret agreement between

Austria and Russia, by which the latter had given to the former liberty of action in the two occupied provinces. Italian indignation, displayed by Fortis in a great speech in the Chamber, was forgotten in the disaster of the earthquake at Messina and Reggio. Thus, force triumphed. On February 26, 1909, an Austro-Turkish agreement was signed, by which Austria-Hungary renounced all her rights in the *sanjak* of Novibazar, whence she had withdrawn her troops on October 28, while Turkey formally recognised the annexation of Bosnia and the Herzegovina. The name of the Sultan as Khalif was to be still used in the public prayers of the Bosnian Mussulmans, whose spiritual chiefs would continue to depend upon the Sheikh-ul-Islâm. Turkey accepted £T.2,500,000 for the domain lands in Bosnia and the Herzegovina; and Austria-Hungary promised to abolish *pari passu* with the other Powers her post-offices in Turkey and to assist the Porte in securing the abolition of the capitulations. On April 6, the Ottoman parliament ratified this arrangement; and thus, so far as Turkey was concerned, the question was over. The Turks lost practically nothing by the annexation of two provinces which had really ceased to belong to them for 30 years, and over which, even before that time, their hold had been precarious. For Servia and Montenegro, however, the recognition of the incorporation of so large a Serb population within the Dual Monarchy meant the destruction of their own hopes for the future. At this national crisis, as at Athens under similar circumstances in 1877, a Coalition Cabinet, in which three ex-Premiers sat, was formed at Belgrade. Finding no prospect of material support from the Powers, Servia sent a note on March 9 to the signatories of the Berlin treaty, stating that she demanded no compensation for the annexation, which was a matter for them. A peaceful solution was facilitated by the action of the bellicose Crown Prince, who on March 25 resigned his right of succession in favour of his brother Alexander, in consequence of the death of a servant, alleged to

have been due to his violence.   Austria declared that she had
no intention of contravening the independence of Servia ; and
another Servian note to Vienna promised that the army should
be replaced on a peace footing.   As a reward of Montenegrin
acquiescence, article 29 of the Berlin treaty, which regulated
the bay of Antivari, was considerably modified.   The clause
prohibiting Montenegro from having either ships or flag of war
was suppressed ; the port of Antivari was no longer closed to
the warships of other nations, although it was to retain its
purely commercial character ; and the rest of this article was
entirely cancelled.   Thus, Montenegro might now erect fortifications between the lake of Scutari and the coast ; her
maritime and sanitary police was no longer entrusted to Austrian
boats, nor was she forced to adopt the Dalmatian maritime code.
Still the bay of Antivari was dominated by the guns of Spizza,
and an Austrian fleet could now enter it.   Nor was the withdrawal
of the Austrian garrisons from the *sanjak* considered by the
Serbs to be much compensation.   For, while Turkey still
retained that strip of territory and thus divided them, Austria,
thanks to the Bosnian railway, now constructed to Uvatz, could
re-enter the *sanjak* whenever she pleased, and her officials were
known to have surveyed a future line across it.   Besides, her
military authorities then believed that a future march to the
Ægean had not been hindered by the withdrawal from the
sanjak, for, in their view, the best route to the south was not
through the Katchanik defile but across Servia.   All the Powers
having finally accepted the new order of things in April, 1909, it
only remained to perform the promise of a constitution, announced to the people of the two annexed provinces, which,
together with the historic connexion between Bosnia and the
Hungarian crown, had been officially alleged as a motive for
their annexation.   In February, 1910, the promised constitution
was granted ; and on June 15 the first Bosnian diet was opened
at Sarajevo, its numbers corresponding fairly accurately with
the relative strength of the various religious elements in the

population. Out of 73 elected and 17 *ex officio* members, 37 represented the Orthodox Serbs, 29 the Moslems, 23 the Catholic Croats, and one the Jews. But no measure could be so much as discussed until it had been first approved by both the Austrian and the Hungarian cabinets. Thus Bosnian liberty was still, as was perhaps necessary for a time, in leading-strings.

The settlement with Bulgaria mainly depended upon finance, although at one moment the Bulgarian army was mobilised. The Turks demanded £5,000,000 as compensation; the Bulgars offered £3,280,000. Russia then stepped in with a proposal which satisfied both parties. Turkey still owed to her 74 annual instalments of the last war indemnity; she agreed to cancel 40 of these, so as to enable Turkey to borrow the £5,000,000 which she claimed from Bulgaria. The latter, instead of paying £3,280,000 to Turkey, agreed to pay this sum to Russia in annual instalments of £200,000. If the operation cost Russia some material sacrifice, it regained for her prestige and perhaps gratitude in Bulgaria. It was further agreed between Bulgaria and Turkey, that a Chief *Mufti* should reside at Sofia to look after the interests of the Bulgarian Moslems; that the kingdom should continue to set aside a sum for the maintenance of its Moslem schools and mosques; and that such buildings should " be demolished only in case of imperious necessity." On April 19 the Porte recognised " the new political situation " of the kingdom, which was formally sanctioned by all the Powers in the course of the next few days. King Ferdinand had realised his ambition, and to him personally and socially the declaration of independence was a gain. But frugal Bulgarian democrats realised that this increase of social status would involve greater expense in the representation of their country abroad, and the loss of some of the material advantages derived from their nominal vassalage. National sentiment was, however, favourable to national independence. Thus, the last vassal state of the

Sultan in the Balkans was fully emancipated, and the nominal and the real frontiers of Turkey in Europe became identical.

There remained still to be solved the Cretan question. At the moment of the proclamation of union, M. Zaïmes was absent from the island, to which he has never returned. The proclamation had been signed by the three Christian Councillors; and an extraordinary session of the Chamber was at once held for the purpose of ratifying their action and of appointing an Executive Committee of five persons, of which M. Michelidákes was president and M. Venizélos a member, to carry on the government provisionally in the name of the King of the Hellenes, until his officials should have taken it over. The Greek Constitution was adopted; Cretan stamps were surcharged with the word *Hellás*; the official note-paper was headed "Kingdom of Greece"; the civil servants took the oath to King George; appeals from the insular courts were sent to Athens. The Greek government, however, of which Theotókes was then head, declared that it was extraneous to the events which had occurred in Crete and made no reply to the Cretans. The opinion was expressed by many persons at the time and is now generally held, that, had the Greeks immediately taken Crete, instead of preserving an unimpeachably "correct" attitude, that island would have remained part of the Greek kingdom. Turkey was then involved in difficulties with Austria and Bulgaria; a Greco-Bulgarian alliance would have made it difficult for her to invade Thessaly; while the new state of things in the Turkish empire was not yet consolidated. Above all, Abdul Hamid was still on the throne; and it was notoriously easier to treat with him, especially on the basis of a pecuniary compensation, than with a strongly chauvinist Turkish parliament. It was, indeed, objected by cautious Greek diplomatists, that the Powers still had troops in the island. But the attitude of the Powers was remarkably encouraging. The British minister at Athens stated, indeed, that the principle of his government was "to do nothing which

could prejudice the new *régime* in Turkey[1]"; while the Italian
Minister of Foreign Affairs indulged in the platitude that
"without the consent of all the Powers, no change in the
political situation of Crete can be taken into consideration."
But the two most reactionary of them—Austria and Germany—
were ready to support the union, if some other state would
take the initiative[2]. When, on October 28, the official communication of the four protecting Powers was made, its tone
gave satisfaction alike at Canea and at Athens. They considered the union as dependent upon their assent, but "none
the less they would not be averse from regarding with good-will
the discussion of this question with Turkey, if order be
maintained in the island and if the security of the Mussulman
population be assured[3]." Meanwhile, they authorised their
consuls to enter into "administrative" relations with the
provisional government.

The latter took every care that the two conditions of the
Powers should be fulfilled, although the Mussulmans, stimulated from outside, sought to provoke difficulties and then
presented complaints, which the consuls dismissed as futile.
But the delay, as months wore on, became embarrassing to
both the provisional authorities in Crete and to the Cabinet of
Athens, where public opinion fretted at the postponement of
a definite solution and the Premier thought that he detected
a consequent feeling against the Crown[4]. Matters became
worse, when, after the suppression of the counter-revolution in
Turkey, the military party became predominant, and sought
to divert attention from the mistakes committed by the
"Young" Turks at home, by picking a quarrel with Greece.
As the nationalist spirit in Turkey became stronger, the
Turkish demands increased. First, the Porte asked for the
postponement of the promised withdrawal of the international
troops; next it sought the suppression of various concessions,

---

[1] *Libro Verde: Creta* (1911), p. 32.
[2] *Ib.* p. 33.   [3] *Ib.* p. 36.   [4] *Ib.* p. 45.

made by the Powers to the Cretans, and desired to establish a
sort of limited autonomy, or, in other words, to set the clock
back to the time previous to 1898. Then it expressed the
wish to send a *stationnaire* to Cretan waters. While the
Powers negatived these proposals, and announced their
intention of maintaining the *status quo*—whatever that might
be—and of "concerning themselves with good-will in the
Cretan question," Theotókes, on July 17, 1909, felt compelled
to resign, in order to prevent a threatening demonstration
against his attitude towards Crete. Rhálles, his successor, a
politician popular at Constantinople, was at once placed in
the difficulty which had prevented him from accepting office
three months earlier. He wanted to dissolve parliament, but
the threat of the Cretans to elect deputies to the new Greek
Chamber would, he knew, be regarded by Turkey as an un-
friendly act; he would, therefore, find himself in the dilemma
of either excluding the Cretan representatives or of risking a
war with Turkey by admitting them—a dilemma solved by the
tact and firmness of M. Venizélos in June, 1912. Rhálles,
therefore, decided to postpone the dissolution till the following
year, and assured the Turkish minister in Athens of his intention to "re-establish good relations with Turkey" and "as
regards Crete, to accept loyally the decisions of the Powers[1]."
No one who knows that statesman's frank character can doubt
that he meant what he said.

But events in Crete provided the Turkish military party
with a further pretext for demands upon Greece. On July 26,
in accordance with their promises, the four Powers withdrew
the rest of their troops from the island. As soon as they were
gone, the Cretans hoisted in the place of the Cretan emblem
a Greek flag on the bastion of the fort at the entrance of the
port of Canea. Warlike demonstrations in Turkey ensued;
and on August 6 the Turkish government ordered its minister
in Athens to demand from Rhálles a written disavowal of

[1] *Ib.* p. 87.

the Cretan agitation for union and a further repudiation of any such design on his part; in case of delay in replying to this peremptory note, Naby Bey was to leave Athens. At the same time preparations were made for sending a Turkish fleet to Kárpathos, or even Suda, while a boycott of Greek goods began in Turkish ports. Three days later, Rhálles replied that " Crete being in deposit in the hands of the protecting Powers, the Greek government can only leave the solution to them and conform itself with their decision." He repeated that Greece would continue to observe her " correct " attitude, and added that not a single Greek officer was at that moment on Turkish territory, for those in Crete had left the Greek army. This reply was considered unsatisfactory by the Porte ; and on August 13 a further note was presented to him, complaining of the presence of Greek officers in disguise in Macedonia, observing that " Greece has nothing to do " with the Cretan question, and that, " as the attitude of the Greek government in foreign affairs has not been beyond reproach," a further "clear and frank declaration " was desired. Greece at this appealed to the Powers to prevent war; and on the 18th Rhálles again replied to Turkey, reiterating the intention of his government to conform to their decision and to abstain from encouraging any Cretan agitation. Meanwhile, in Crete the Executive Committee, finding itself unable to secure the removal of the offending flag, in face of the general opposition, resigned, whereupon the Chamber nominated three local magistrates as a provisional government. At last, as no Christian Cretan could be found to haul down the flag, the Powers each landed a company of marines, who, amidst perfect order, on August 18 cut down the flagstaff. A part of it is now preserved in the Museum of the Historical Society at Athens, together with the last Turkish flag that floated over the battlements of Canea and with fragments of the shells fired by the fleets of the Powers at Akrotéri, as memorials of the Cretan question. The Powers on the same day drily

pointed out to the Porte that both the Cretan and the Macedonian questions were matters of European concern.   The
Porte then disclaimed bellicose intentions towards Greece, and
all fear of war was dissipated.

But the humiliation which Greece had undergone produced
a strong feeling of disgust in that country.   For some time
past the conviction had been growing that the national interests
had been sacrificed to the exigencies of party politics.   Even
so early as May 1909, the young officers had begun to form
a "Military League," which, being at the moment the only
organised force in Greece, made itself the organ of the people
in its struggle against the politicians.   As Rhálles refused to
accept a note embodying their proposals, the officers composing the League, over 500 in number, marched out of
Athens on the night of August 27/28, and formed a camp at
Goudí, under the leadership of Col. Zorbâs, a distinguished
officer.   All efforts to break up the League failed; two officers,
who tried to seduce the cavalry from their allegiance to that
organisation, were arrested; and the mayor was sent in vain
to parley with the chiefs.   Rhálles resigned, and Mavromicháles on August 29 became Prime Minister under the
control of the League.   The Leaguers then returned to Athens,
and issued a manifesto, demanding radical reforms, and more
especially the reorganisation of the army and navy, the
exclusion of the Royal Princes from their military commands,
and the bestowal of the two Ministries of War and Marine
upon officers.   The former of these posts was conferred upon
Col. Lapathiótes, a member of the League, whose chief at the
same time protested its devotion to the Crown.   Popular
demonstrations in different provincial centres expressed support
of the League's programme ; and the trade guilds of the capital
appealed to the people to support it as the best means of
ending "political corruption."   There was, however, a strong
opposition in the Chamber, which manifested itself when the
government, at the bidding of the League, proposed the

removal of the Princes from their commands. The League threatened to occupy the legislative building by force; but the intervention of the King, who desired his sons to resign their commissions, anticipated this act of violence, and on the morrow the Chamber passed the bills for their removal, and for the abolition of the Crown Prince's post of Commander-in-Chief, together with 23 other measures, without debate.

The success of the Military League emboldened the junior naval officers to demand the removal of many of their seniors, and the re-admission of a sub-lieutenant, who had been punished for insubordination during the war of 1897. On the refusal of the government, Commander Typáldos, the leader of this second agitation, seized the naval station at Salamis, and, with the aid of three small vessels, resolved to show fight. The new "battle of Salamis" lasted less than half an hour and cost only six lives; the government was victorious, and Typáldos and his supporters were sentenced to prison but subsequently pardoned. The League became more and more exacting. Its representative in the Cabinet plainly told the deputies that they were there only to obey its orders; but, although Col. Zorbâs ordered the dismissal of this unparliamentary Minister, two officers of the League shortly afterwards appeared in the Chamber, and demanded the immediate adoption of the budget with 27 other bills, and the recall of the Greek representatives from four European capitals. The Chamber, coerced by the knowledge that the troops were under arms, accepted these demands, and 160 laws were added to the statute-book in 55 hours! Still the League was not satisfied, and it insisted upon the dismissal of the Minister of the Interior, who had incurred its displeasure.

At this moment a new and powerful figure arrived upon the stage of Greek politics. Several officers of the League had made in Crete the acquaintance of M. Venizélos, the Cretan chief, whom we last saw in collision with Prince George. Long before the birth of the League, M. Zaïmes had prophesied that, if M. Venizélos could be induced to collaborate with the Royal family, he would become the saviour of Greece. The League accordingly invited the Cretan politician to Athens as its political adviser, and from his arrival the marvellous re-generation of the country is usually dated. No better choice could have been made, for the newcomer's strength lay in his great force of character, his complete detachment from the old parties, and the independence of mind which made him refuse to flatter the people. He saw that the anomalous state of affairs could not continue; he, therefore, proposed the summons of a National Assembly to revise the constitution. The politicians accepted this proposal, on condition that, as a corollary, the League should be dissolved; the King, after some hesitation at the convocation of a National Assembly without the elaborate forms provided by the constitution (see p. 296), reluctantly consented. A veteran lieutenant of Trikoúpes, M. Stephen Dragoúmes, accordingly became Premier at the end of January, 1910, with General (as he had now become) Zorbâs as his Minister of War, and with a mandate to summon the proposed Assembly. The League stifled all expressions of public opinion hostile to this plan; the Chamber passed the necessary bill, and, after "purging" the University, ended its labours. The League thereupon, in a manifesto to the nation, declared the interference of the army in politics to be over and announced its own dissolution.

The National Assembly, composed of 358 deputies, was opened on September 14. Among those elected were M. Venizélos and four other Cretans; and the Porte at once protested against their election. M. Venizélos and one of his colleagues were, however, technically Greek subjects; and they accordingly entered the Assembly, resigning their positions in Crete, where M. Venizélos was then chief of the provisional government, while the other three patriotically declined the seats offered them, so as not to embarrass the Greeks. The Assembly was at once divided by the question whether it was a Constituent or only a revisionary body. The difficulty was too great for M. Dragoúmes, who resigned; and on October 18 the King took the heroic step of appointing Prime Minister the famous Cretan, hitherto chiefly known at the palace as the opponent of his son. Of the many services rendered by King George to Greece this was not the least. From that moment he gave his whole confidence to his First Minister, who immediately pronounced in favour of the revision of the non-fundamental articles of the constitution. Five days later, however, the abstention of the old parties and the advocates of a Constituent Assembly left him without a quorum on a vote of confidence. His prompt resignation provoked a mass meeting, organised by the trade guilds and the University, in his favour; and, on his advice, the King dissolved the Assembly. The appeal to the country, in which the leaders of the old parties refused to participate, gave M. Venizélos an overwhelming majority. The officers were ordered to devote themselves exclusively to their profession; the elect of the nation was dictator. No Greek statesman had ever been so popular, or wielded such authority.

The "Second Revisionary National Assembly," which met on January 21, 1911, adopted the revised constitution on June 11. After a vehement discussion an addition was made to article 2, forbidding the translation of the Scriptures without the consent of the Church in Greece and the Œcumenical Patriarch. Elementary education, declared compulsory, was to be provided gratis by the state. The expropriation of proprietors for purposes of public utility was defined, with special reference to the sale of the large estates and the creation of a peasant proprietary in Thessaly. The quorum of the Chamber was reduced to one-third of all its members; parliamentary vacancies were not, unless very numerous, to be filled in the last year of a legislature; military men were declared ineligible as deputies; election petitions were transferred from the Chamber to a special tribunal; the pay of members was fixed at 1000 *dr.* every three months (except those resident in Athens or the Piræus, who received 800 *dr.*); and frequent absence without leave was to involve the deduction of 20 *dr.* per sitting. The Council of State was revived; public officials, with few exceptions, obtained security of tenure; and the official language was declared to be that in which the constitution was drawn up. The Assembly further passed a bill creating the post of Inspector-General of the Army, despite the opposition of General Zorbâs, and thus restoring the Crown Prince to his military command. With the close of this National Assembly the normal state of things returned; and at the general election for an ordinary Chamber, on March 25, 1912, M. Venizélos obtained the support of 150 out of 181 members. All the deputies from Attica and Bœotia (where Rhálles, the once powerful *Atticarch*, was defeated) were Venizelists; north of the Isthmus every member but one belonged to the Premier's party; while even in Corfù, the stronghold of Theotókes, a Venizelist headed the poll. Once again the Cretans elected deputies, 69 in number, to the Chamber. But the Premier declared that he would resign rather than allow them to take their seats, as Greece needed a period of repose, in order to reorganise her army and her internal administration; and such was his influence, that he prevented those of them who had eluded the ships of the Powers from entering the Chamber, which he then adjourned till October. Meanwhile, he had been quietly working to promote a better understanding with the other Balkan states. Despite a fresh Greco-Roumanian incident at the Piræus, he renewed diplomatic relations with Roumania in 1911; Bulgarian students visited Athens; the Greek Crown Prince visited Sofia; and, with the aid of Bourchier, the *Times* correspondent and a friend of both countries, the bases of an agreement were laid between those two former rivals, Greece and Bulgaria.

But nothing proved to be such a potent cause of union

between the Balkan Christians as the policy of "Turkification,"
adopted by the chauvinistic section of the "Young" Turks,
whose plan of reducing the various races and regions of the
empire to one dead level of Turkish uniformity provoked
general discontent.   The Bulgars of Macedonia protested
against the immigration of Bosnian Moslems, renewed their
revolutionary organisation in self-defence, and invited the
Powers to resume their control.   The Druses revolted in the
Haurân, a new Mahdi, Said Idris, appeared in the Yemen ;
the Greek bishop of Grevená was murdered, and the Œcumenical Patriarch proclaimed equality to be a mere phrase and
declared the Greek Church to be in danger.   The representatives of the "Twelve Islands" complained that their
privileges were annulled; the Cretan Christians protested
against the attempt to send Moslem judges ; the Moslems of
northern Albania objected to the payment of dues, of which
they saw no result in their own country, to the census, to
military service in the distant Yemen, and (like the Mainates)
to the destruction of their fortified towers.   In 1909 fighting
had taken place at Ljuma, a place noted for the independent
spirit of its inhabitants, between the Turkish troops and Isa
Boletin, an influential chief; in the following year the imposition of an *octroi* for "urban improvements" rekindled the
insurrection.   The Albanians held up a trainload of troops in
the Katchanik defile ; but the Turks ultimately disarmed the
north of the country.   Despite the consequent lack of rifles,
however, the five mostly Roman Catholic tribes of Hoti,
Gruda, Kastrati, Skreli, and Clementi, known collectively as
the Maltsori, or "mountain-men," and inhabiting the territory
between the lake of Scutari and the ill-defined Montenegrin
frontier, began a fresh insurrection early in 1911, and inflicted
severe losses upon the Kurdish troops, of whose savage
methods of "restoring order" the author was an eye-witness.
Great excitement was caused in Montenegro, whither many
Albanians found refuge among their Albanian relatives, and

war was only prevented by the influence of King Nicholas, while in the Mirdite country a "provisional government of Albania" was formed by Sig. Tocci, an Albanian from Calabria. After severe fighting round Tuzi, an armistice was granted by Turgut Shevket Pasha; and in August King Nicholas, upon whose exchequer the refugees were a heavy burden, advised, and, indeed, compelled the insurgents to accept the Turkish terms—an amnesty, the limitation of military service to Europe, freedom from taxes for two years, permission to bear arms outside the towns, roads, Albanian schools, and compensation in maize and in cash, to which the Sultan, who paid a state visit to the plain of Kossovo, contributed £T.10,000.

Scarcely was the Albanian insurrection over when Turkey found herself suddenly plunged in a foreign war. The Italians had long coveted Tripoli, which they regarded as their share of the Turkish empire, especially since the French occupation of Tunisia had precluded all hope of acquiring that country. For some time the Turks had placed obstacles in the way of the "peaceful penetration" of Tripoli by Italians, who were refused archæological and other facilities, readily granted to other nationalities. But, so late as June 9, 1911, the Italian Minister of Foreign Affairs had declared in the Chamber that his policy had "as basis the maintenance of the territorial *status quo* and the integrity of the Ottoman empire" in Africa as well as elsewhere. Still later, at the beginning of July, the Ottoman heir-apparent had been received with honours in Rome; while during the Maltsori rising the Italian government had strictly prevented the export of arms and the passage of volunteers across the Adriatic. Accordingly, the world was taken by surprise, when on September 26 Italy sent an ultimatum to the Turkish government; nor were the reasons alleged in that document—"the state of disorder and neglect" in which Tripoli and the Cyrenaica had been left, the "opposition to every Italian initiative," and "the agitation against the Italians"—generally considered adequate for the employment

of such an extreme remedy. The King and the Premier,
Sig. Giolitti, were unfavourable to war, but the Nationalist
party, the Sicilians in the Cabinet and in the country, a
financial house which possessed great interests in Tripoli, and
the general desire for a national triumph overcame all opposition, and war began. The fighting in "Libya"—as the two
provinces were called in Italy—resulted in the loss of Turkey's
last direct possessions in Africa, which by a royal decree of
November 5, 1911, subsequently converted into law, were
"placed under the full and entire sovereignty of the kingdom
of Italy." But the war only affected the Levant in a secondary
degree. At the outset the Italian government sent a message
to its agents in the Balkans, reiterating its adherence to the
principle of the territorial *status quo* in that region and dis-
countenancing "any movement in the Balkan peninsula
against Turkey"; and, when the Italian fleet bombarded
Préveza and San Giovanni di Medua, it was promptly recalled
on the remonstrances of Austria-Hungary. When it was
found, however, that progress was slow in Libya, the fleet sank
some Turkish ships in the harbour of Beirût, bombarded the
Turkish barracks at Samos, and the mouth of the Dardanelles,
sent a flotilla of torpedo-boats a long way up that dangerous
strait, and occupied in April and May, 1912, Rhodes, Kôs,
Leipsó, and 10 islands of the *Dodekánesos*. A congress of
insular delegates, held at Pátmos, expressed, however, on
June 17, their desire for union with Greece, and meanwhile proclaimed the autonomous "State of the Aegean" with a flag of
its own—a proceeding strongly discountenanced by Italy. Thus,
the Italian occupation raised an Aegean question. When, on
October 18, the treaty of Lausanne ended the war, the Italians
promised to evacuate the islands, whose inhabitants were to
have full pardon, immediately after the Turkish evacuation of
Libya. Meanwhile, the Italian troops remain in them.

CHAPTER XX

THE BALKAN LEAGUE AND ITS RESULTS (1912–14)

THE Turks were induced to sign the treaty of Lausanne by the knowledge that another struggle was impending. The Balkan peninsula had remained comparatively quiet during the greater part of the Libyan war; but in August, 1912, symptoms of the coming storm began to manifest themselves. Sanguinary incidents occurred on the Montenegrin frontier, causing the Turkish minister to quit Cetinje; there were massacres at Berane in the *sanjak* and at Kotchana in Macedonia; and this latter outrage, following a previous massacre of the Bulgars at Ishtip, provoked the demand for war throughout Bulgaria. The grant of a sort of administrative autonomy to Albania was a blow to the national aspirations of the four Balkan states in the proposed autonomous territory. Servia complained that the Turks had seized her munitions of war in transit, Greece that a Greek vessel had been subject to violence in the port of Samos, while Bulgaria saw a menace in the Turkish manoeuvres in Thrace. In vain Count Berchtold, the Austro-Hungarian Minister of Foreign Affairs, sent a circular to the other Powers on August 14, inviting their opinion on the desirability of advising Turkey to adopt a programme of decentralisation and the Balkan states to adopt a policy of moderation. Diplomacy was powerless to check the movement when once the four Balkan kingdoms, forgetting their mutual jealousies, united against the common enemy

The dream of Rhégas was at last a reality; a Balkan League was formed against the Turks. The authorship of this marvellous work, hitherto the despair of statesmen, although attempted by Trikoúpes in 1891, has been ascribed chiefly to M. Venizélos. Fortunately at that moment each of the four allied states was governed by a man of character, while the negotiations were conducted with such secrecy that neither Turks nor European diplomatists suspected what was coming.

So early as April, 1911, the Greek Prime Minister, with the approval of King George, who was the only other Greek statesman originally in the secret, had cautiously sent to Sofia through an Englishman living in Vienna a proposal for a Greco-Bulgarian defensive alliance against Turkey in case of an attack upon either of the contracting parties, and for common action in defence of the Ottoman Christians. Simultaneously, private letters to King Ferdinand and M. Gueshov, his Premier, urged the need, and pointed out the future possibilities, of this agreement. For months, however, Bulgarian caution and distrust delayed the acceptance of the Greek offer, while a Montenegrin plan for a mobilisation of all the Balkan states on the outbreak of the Libyan war found them unwilling or unprepared.

Rizov, then Bulgarian Minister in Rome, had also in September, 1911, urged his Government to avail itself of the Libyan war to attack Turkey before she could reorganise her army, and while the Italian fleet could prevent the transport of Turkish troops across the Aegean. He was instructed to sound the Servian Premier, Milovanovich, at Belgrade, where he had been Minister and his Montenegrin wife had relatives. His soundings were satisfactory; and at a secret conference of Bulgarian diplomatists with M. Gueshov in Vienna, where the King of Montenegro was then on a visit to the Emperor, further steps were taken. At Rizov's suggestion, M. Gueshov secretly travelled across Servia with Milovanovich, and discussed the question on the journey. These negotiations culminated in the Serbo-Bulgarian treaty of alliance on March 13, 1912, signed by both sovereigns.

This instrument provided, at the suggestion of M. Pashich, who had been taken into the secret by Rizov, an arrangement for the partition of the territory eventually to be conquered from Turkey. To Servia were assigned "the territories to the north and west of the Shar range"; to Bulgaria "all those to the east of the Rhodope range and of the Struma river." Bulgaria was desirous that "the intermediate territory" should form an "autonomous Macedonia"; but, in case this should prove to be impracticable, "a line was drawn from the point where the Servian, Bulgarian, and Turkish frontiers met at the north of Egri Palanka...to Struga, at the northernmost extremity of Lake Ochrida, leaving Kratovo, Veles, Monastir, and Ochrida to Bulgaria, while the ultimate disposal of certain districts lying mainly north of this line and south of the Shar range"—consisting of the districts of Kumanovo, Skoplje, Krushevo, and Dibra, and the sub-district of Struga—was "reserved for the arbitration of the Tsar," which both parties agreed "to accept as final." This Serbo-Bulgarian treaty was supplemented by a military convention on May 12, drawn up under the impression that the principal theatre of war would not be in Thrace but in Macedonia, and accordingly pledging Bulgaria to send 100,000 of her 200,000 men thither. Later, however, the staffs of both countries realised that Thrace would be more important; and on September 28 they agreed that the Bulgarians should operate there, the Servians, who were to furnish 150,000 men, in Macedonia.

M. Venizélos had authorised M. Panâs, his Minister at Sofia (at the request of M. Gueshov, conveyed through Bourchier), to open formal negotiations in the last week of February, which culminated in the signature, on May 29, of the Greco-Bulgarian treaty. It pledged both parties to mutual aid, should either be attacked by Turkey, to secure "the peaceful co-existence" of the Greek and Bulgarian populations of Turkey, and to co-operate in securing the rights of those nationalities.

The treaty was to remain in force for three years, and, unless denounced six months previous to that date, to be considered as automatically renewed for a year. Its contents were to be kept secret. An annex provided that, in the event of a Greco-Turkish war arising out of the question of the admission of Cretan deputies to the Greek Parliament, Bulgaria should merely preserve a benevolent neutrality. A military convention followed four months later. Montenegro made verbal arrangements, "at first purely defensive," with Bulgaria and Greece; and in September, 1912, a Serbo-Montenegrin treaty was signed in Switzerland, providing "for separate military action," so that "no Turkish town or village was to be occupied jointly by Servian and Montenegrin troops[1]."

The Allies now began to mobilise and to demand the enforcement of article 23 of the Berlin treaty; the Porte, with a death-bed repentance, resolved to apply to European Turkey the law of 1880 for provincial reforms, hitherto a dead letter. When Austria and Russia, as mandatories of the Powers, informed the Balkan courts that they would "allow, at the end of the conflict, no modification of the territorial *status quo*," the Balkan rulers politely replied that diplomatic intervention was too late. On October 8 Montenegro, which alone had claimed a rectification of frontier, declared war; and the Montenegrins at once showed that they had not degenerated during the long years of peace. Next day Prince Peter fired the first shot in the most important conflict waged in the Balkans since the Turkish conquest. The surrender of Detchich was the first Montenegrin success, quickly followed by the capture of Roganj and the surrender of Tuzi with six Turkish battalions. Meanwhile, the northern army under General Vukotich had entered the *sanjak*, and captured Bijelopolje, compelling a few days later the surrender of Berane. Thus far little Montenegro had been fighting alone; but the three other states now entered

---

[1] Anonymous [Bourchier] in the *Times*, June 4, 5, 6, 11, 13, 16, 1913; Gueshoff, *The Balkan League*; Rizov in the *Morning Post*, Jan. 31, 1914.

the field.   On October 13 all three sent identic notes to the
two mandatory Powers and to Turkey.   The Balkan ultimatum
demanded the administrative autonomy of the European provinces, the frontiers of which were to be re-drawn on ethno-
graphic lines, while their governors were to be either Swiss or
Belgians ; provincial elective assemblies ; the reorganisation of
the *gendarmerie*; freedom of education ; a local militia; the
application of reforms under the management of an equal
number of Christian and Moslem councillors, and the supervision not only of the ambassadors of the Powers but also of
the ministers of the Balkan states at Constantinople ; and the
immediate demobilisation of the Ottoman army.   The Turkish
government, which professed sublime contempt for its "little
neighbours," and sneered at Bulgaria as "a negligible quantity,"
replied by recalling its representatives from Belgrade and Sofia,
and on October 17 declared war on Servia and Bulgaria.   Next
day Greece declared war on Turkey, after M. Venizélos, on the
14th, had admitted the Cretan deputies to the Chamber,
which, he said, would be thenceforth the sole legislative
assembly of both Greece and Crete.

Then followed the most dramatic war of our time.   Neither
European diplomatists nor military critics had realised the
immense progress made by the Balkan states, and especially
by Greece and Servia, during the three or four previous years.
The Foreign Minister of one great Power judged the Servian
and Greek armies by the standards of Slivnitza and Domokós ;
the ambassador of another declared that a wintry war in the
Balkans was impossible ; most experts believed in the legend
of the "invincible" Turkish soldier.   A few days sufficed to
dispel all these beliefs.   The onward march of all the armies
was a rapid series of successes ; and the Turkish power in
Europe, so long the bogy of diplomacy, collapsed, like a house
of cards, before the twin forces of patriotic enthusiasm and
superior organisation, which led the Allies to triumph.   The
Bulgars at once occupied Mustapha Pasha, and on October 24,

captured Kirk-kilisse, which Field-Marshal Von der Goltz, the late instructor of the Turkish army, had pronounced capable of resisting a Prussian siege for three months. The Greeks took Elassôna, and, after a victory at Sarantáporon on October 22, the town of Servia, Kozáne, Grevená, and Katerína in southern Macedonia, and Préveza, Pénte Pegádia, Métzovon, and Cheimárra in Epirus; while their fleet occupied nine islands—two others, Ikaría, which had proclaimed its independence during the Libyan war, and Samos, declared their union with Greece—hoisted the Greek flag over the holy peninsula of Mt Athos, and prevented the Turkish fleet from leaving the Dardanelles and the Turkish transports from crossing the Aegean. Crete, whither M. Dragoúmes, the ex-Premier, was sent as General Administrator, furnished volunteers to the national cause. The Serbs, whose advance into Old Servia was at first fiercely contested by the colonies of Arnauts planted there by the Turks after the Berlin treaty, utterly routed the Turkish army in a three days' battle at Kumanovo; one town after another, famous in the story of the mediaeval Servian kingdom, fell before them; and the hope of centuries was realised when on October 26 the Servian Crown Prince (at the request of the Austrian consul!) entered Üsküb, at once re-christened Skoplje, the old capital of the Servian empire, where, in 1346, Stephen Dushan had been crowned Emperor. Prishtina and Prizren, earlier Servian capitals, likewise returned under Servian sway; while the Montenegrins, after taking Plava and Gusinje, the recalcitrant towns of 1878, captured Ipek, the former seat of the Servian Patriarch. The fall of Monastir after another pitched battle completed the Servian triumph in Macedonia. Meanwhile in a tremendous five days' battle at Lüle Burgas in Thrace the Bulgars had completely defeated another famished and disorganised Turkish army, which retreated on the lines of Chatalja; a two days' struggle (November 1–2) at Jenitsá by the Vardar ended in another Hellenic victory; and on November 8, the festival of its patron St Demétrios, Salonika capitulated to the Greek Crown Prince, who thus ended the Turkish domination of 482 years over that city, whither King George hastened to join his victorious son.

Thus, in a few weeks, nothing was left of the Turkish empire in Europe but the cities of Adrianople, Scutari and Jóannina, which still resisted the Bulgarian, Montenegrin and Greek besiegers, the promontory of Gallipoli, and the narrow peninsula which stretches from the lines of Chatalja to the Bosphorus. Already, the Powers had stated that "the *status quo*" no longer existed in the face of these amazing victories; for Europe recognised that, when the Turk could no longer beat the Christians in the field, he had lost his only right— that of might—to misgovern them. "The map of Eastern Europe," said Mr Asquith, the British Premier (Nov. 9), "has to be recast, and...the victors are not to be robbed of the fruits which have cost them so dear." Austria, however, excluded by the Servian and Montenegrin conquest of the *sanjak* of Novibazar from an advance to the Aegean, opposed the Servian claim to a port on the Adriatic, and constituted herself, with official Italy, the champion of an autonomous Albania, whose independence was proclaimed by Ismail Kemal Bey at Valona, and was subsequently (Dec. 20) recognised by the ambassadors of the Great Powers in London.

The Servians, however, entered Durazzo, while the Bulgars, hindered by cholera and Chatalja from a further advance on Constantinople, won a final victory over the Turks near Dimotika. On December 3 an armistice was signed at Chatalja by Turkey and the three Slav states, but Greece continued hostilities. A conference of all the five met, however, in St James' Palace, London, on December 16, while contemporaneously a meeting of the ambassadors of the Great Powers was held under the presidency of Sir Edward Grey.

As the Turks adopted their usual dilatory tactics, the Powers, on January 17, 1913, sent a note to the Porte, advising

the cession of Adrianople to the Balkan states and inviting the
Turkish Government to entrust to Europe the settlement of
the Aegean Islands question. On January 22 the Grand
Council at Constantinople accepted the view of the Turkish
Government that peace was necessary, and appeared ready to
accept the advice of the Powers. But, outside, the party of
resistance got the upper hand, with the result that, on January
23, a revolution took place. It was planned by Enver Bey, the
hero of 1908, who had returned from fighting the Italians in the
Cyrenaica. Kiamil Pasha was forced to resign; Nazim Pasha,
the commander-in-chief, was murdered; and the "Young"
Turks returned to power. Shortly afterwards, on January 29,
the delegates of the Allies in London declared the negotiations
at an end; and next day the Balkan states denounced the
armistice. It actually terminated on February 3, and war was
at once renewed. Meanwhile, the Greeks had defeated the
Turkish fleet outside the Dardanelles, and had captured in
Epirus the little town of Párga—the cession of which to
Turkey had caused such regret 94 years earlier. On March 6
Joánnina, which had been Turkish since 1430, surrendered to
the Crown Prince; nine days later a Greek force occupied
Samos; on the morrow a Greek army entered Argyrókastron.

In the midst of these Greek triumphs a terrible tragedy
suddenly befell the Hellenic world and ultimately affected
European history. After the surrender of Salonika the King
had resided there, like a watchman guarding a precious possession. On March 18, while he was taking his usual afternoon
walk, accompanied by a single aide-de-camp, a Greek named
Schinâs fired two shots at him. The King fell speechless and
shortly afterwards expired. The assassin's motive was stated
to be private revenge, because the King had once refused him
money. Thus, a few months before he would have celebrated
in unparalleled circumstances the Jubilee of his accession, King
George fell a victim of duty in the coveted city. His common-
sense, long experience and patriotism had contributed not a

little to the Greek victory; had he lived, they would have helped our own. By the light of later history it is interesting to read his judgment of his successor, expressed in his political testament[1]. He bade him "love thy beloved little country with thy whole heart; be bold, but also patient: never be over-hasty; rather let the night pass before taking thy decision; be not angry, and let not the sun go down upon thy wrath; be calm in thought and mind, and never forget that thou art king of a southern people, whose wrath and excitability are kindled in a moment, and which at such a moment is capable of saying and doing many things which a moment later it will perhaps forget; and remember that it is often better for the king himself to suffer, even morally, rather than the people, whose interests should take precedence of all others." The new King, whom many wished to call Constantine XII, as the successor of the last Byzantine Emperor, mounted the throne with the laurels of Salonika and Joánnina thick upon him. His military triumphs, coupled with the fact that he was the first King of Modern Greece born in the country, invested him with an immense popularity, which explains the attitude of a large section of his people in later years.

Meanwhile, the Allies continued the war. On March 26, the second of the trio of besieged Turkish fortresses, Adrianople, surrendered, after a large Servian force had come to the assistance of the Bulgarian besiegers. The aggrandisement of Bulgaria had, however, already aroused the jealousy of Roumania; and the latter, anxious to make the Bulgarians compensate her for the injustice inflicted upon her by Russia in 1878, demanded the fortress of Silistria as the price of her neutrality—a policy qualified as "blackmail" in the British press. The Turks, however, had had enough of fighting, and on April 19 their delegates signed an armistice at Bulair, where, at the narrowest point of the peninsula of Gallipoli, the Bulgarians had been operating

[1] Ἑστία, $\frac{31 \text{ Mar.}}{13 \text{ Apr.}}$, 1913.

against the lines constructed by the British at the beginning of the Crimean war.

The armistice did not, however, include Montenegro, for King Nicholas was resolved to take Scutari before he suspended hostilities. The Powers had already warned him that, even if he succeeded in capturing it, he would not be allowed to retain it, as it was destined by them to form part of the new Albanian state. The Austrian and Italian Governments were specially severe in their language towards him, although the Queen of Italy was his daughter, and Italian public opinion, in so far as it was allowed freedom of expression, was favourable to "uncle Nicholas." In order to make him abandon the siege, a naval demonstration of all the Powers except Russia took place off Antivari early in April, under the command of the British Admiral Burney—an exact reversal of the previous naval demonstration off Dulcigno in 1880. Heedless of the demonstrators, King Nicholas continued the siege; and on April 22, to the amazement of Europe, Scutari surrendered. It was suggested that there was a secret arrangement between the King and Essad Pasha, the Albanian commander of the place; and the Turkish troops were allowed to take their arms with them. But the Italian historian of the siege considers that famine is a sufficient explanation of the surrender. The Montenegrin tricolour was thus at last hoisted on Tarabosh, the mountain-fortress which had so long defied the besiegers and defended Scutari.

The old Montenegrin capital—for Scutari, although peopled by Albanians, had been "the principal residence" of the Balsha Princes of the Zeta in the latter half of the fourteenth century —did not long remain in Montenegrin hands. The Crown Prince Danilo, indeed, entered in state; General Martinovich was appointed Governor, and the town-crier delivered his messages "in the name of His Majesty King Nicholas"; but the Powers remained obdurate, and bade the conqueror give up the town to their naval commanders. Austria-Hungary threatened; official Italy supported her; and on May 4, after a long struggle with the war party in his Government, King Nicholas himself drafted a telegram to Sir E. Grey, repeating that, although his "right" was "sanctified by history and by conquest," he was compelled to "place the destiny of the town of Scutari in the hands of the Great Powers." The heroism and losses of the Montenegrins on the slopes of Tarabosh had been in vain. For the second time Scutari had eluded the grasp of King Nicholas —in 1913, as in 1878. The international forces entered the town; and Admiral Burney became president of a provisional administration, whose jurisdiction extended only over Scutari and a radius of some six miles round it. Meanwhile, Essad Pasha, in whose veins flowed the blood of Carlo Thopia, the mediaeval Prince of Albania, had marched southward, and was credited with the intention of making himself sovereign, in defiance alike of the provisional Government at Valona and of the Powers.

As soon as the armistice had been signed at Bulair, negotiations for the resumption of the interrupted Conference of London began. The Powers offered to mediate on four conditions: that a direct line from Aïnos on the Aegean to Midia on the Black Sea should be the basis of the new Turkish frontier in Europe instead of the Rodosto-Cape Malatra boundary previously demanded by the Allies; that the status of the Aegean Islands and the delimitation of the boundaries of the new Albanian state should be reserved for their decision; and that all financial questions, including that of a war indemnity, should be considered by an international financial commission, which subsequently met in Paris on June 9, and on which the belligerents were represented. The treaty of London, which ended the war of the Allies against Turkey, was at last signed at St James' Palace on May 30.

The treaty, intended to replace that concluded 35 years earlier at Berlin, was very brief. By article 2 the Sultan ceded to the Allies "all the territories of his empire on the European continent to the west of a line drawn from Aïnos, on the

Aegean sea, to Midia, on the Black sea, with the exception of Albania." The "delimitation of the frontiers of Albania and all other questions concerning Albania" were "confided to the Great Powers" (art. 3), which were also entrusted with "the care of deciding on the fate of all the Ottoman islands of the Aegean sea (except the island of Crete) and of the peninsula of Mount Athos" (art. 5)—ultimately awarded to Greece, but remaining a theocratic republic. The Sultan agreed to cede Crete to the Allies, that is to say, to Greece (art. 4). Besides these vast territorial changes, the treaty provided in two remaining articles for the settlement of financial questions by the international commission at Paris, and of "questions of jurisdiction, of nationality and of commerce" by special conventions.

Sir E. Grey told the delegates that the treaty of London still left some questions "to be discussed before a complete settlement" could be reached. The British Minister's statement was, indeed, an euphemism. The creation of an Albanian state and the delimitation of its boundaries had already caused difficulties between Austria and Servia in the north and between Italy and Greece in the south. The two Adriatic Powers, mutually jealous of one another, were only united in their opposition to the Servian and Greek claims. Italy supported Austria in the north in order to secure Austrian support for herself in the south; and, as France, in accord with her Philhellenic traditions and her own interest, championed the Greek case in northern Epirus, Italy became alarmed lest the channel of Corfù might become a base for an attack upon the Apulian coast. Whereas originally Sig. Giolitti, the Italian Premier, had merely warned Greece, if she wished to remain the friend of Italy, not to occupy Valona, the key of the Adriatic, the Italian Government now put forward the contention that the frontier of Greece in Epirus must be drawn as far south as Cape Stylos, opposite the town of Corfù, instead of starting, as M. Venizélos had proposed in his memorial to the London Conference, from the little bay of Grámmata, so as to include Cheimárra. In vain the Greek Government offered to neutralise (as Corfù had been neutralised in 1864) the Epirote coast of the channel; in vain naval experts pointed out the untenable character of the Italian theory from a strategic standpoint; in vain the Greeks suggested a *plébiscite* under international supervision.

A further Greco-Italian question had arisen out of the continued Italian occupation of the 13 islands in the Aegean. The Greeks maintained that, had they not been so occupied, the Greek fleet could have easily taken them; the Italian Government argued that Turkish soldiers still remained in Libya, and that consequently Italy must meanwhile retain them as a pledge, as provided by the treaty of Lausanne; while, despite Sig. Giolitti's statement that Italy "could not pretend to annex territories of Greek nationality," unofficial Italians avowed the desire to retain at least Rhodes and Stampalia[1] (with its two fine harbours) to serve as a naval base in the Aegean and as a starting-place for pegging out Italian claims in Asia Minor. But Sir E. Grey declared Britain's interest to be "that no one of these islands should be claimed or retained by one of the Great Powers."

An even more serious difficulty menaced the peace restored (on paper) in the Balkans by the treaty of London. It required no great foresight to see that the Allies, united against the Turks, might fall out over the spoils. Their successes had been so overwhelming and so surprising, even to themselves, that the elaborate arrangements made beforehand had failed, as was inevitable, to provide for the unforeseen. During the war the Bulgarians had grudged the Greeks the possession of Salonika, although M. Venizélos was at that time willing to allow them to retain Kavalla. Even before the treaty of London was signed, armed conflicts had taken place between the Greeks and Bulgarians in Macedonia. "Lofty Panghaîon," which Vergil had depicted as weeping for Eurydice, might have wept with even

---

[1] Italian for Astypálaia.

more reason at this sanguinary termination of their triumphant comradeship in arms. On May 22 Bulgarian forces, anxious to occupy this important strategic position, attacked the Greeks; a little later Bulgarian gunners fired at a Greek cruiser.

A rupture between Bulgaria and Servia was also threatening. The Bulgarians, basing their case on the exact letter of the treaty of alliance, demanded the possession of Monastir and Ochrida, which the Servian troops had occupied. The Serbs, relying on the spirit of the treaty, contended that, while Bulgaria had not carried out the military convention of May 12, 1912, they had sent 50,000 men with their valuable artillery to aid the Bulgarians in the siege of Adrianople—an act of comradeship not demanded by the treaty. They further pointed out that the creation of an Albanian state had been effected largely at their expense, and that the opposition of the two Adriatic Powers to their retention of Durazzo had cut them off from that outlet on the sea which was the chief cause for which they had gone to war. Consequently it had become vital for them to reach the Greek frontier, from which Monastir in Bulgarian hands would separate them. For these reasons they demanded a revision of the treaty. A month was spent in diplomatic negotiations and recriminations.

The two Premiers of Bulgaria and Servia met at Tsaribrod; and a meeting of all the four was projected. The Emperor of Russia telegraphed to the Bulgarian and Servian sovereigns, bidding them to appeal to his arbitration, as stipulated in the treaty of alliance. Both accepted his invitation, but only on conditions; Bulgaria still insisting on the letter of the treaty, while she refused to demobilise unless the disputed territories were occupied jointly by the two armies—a proposition rejected by the Serbs as being the people in possession. The accession to power of Dr Danev in place of the pacific M. Gueshov increased the friction; in all the three countries there were politicians who regarded compromise as "treachery"; while the Bulgarian military party, largely recruited from Macedonia, and flushed by its recent successes over the Turks, believed that, as a Bulgarian remarked to the author, "the Bulgars could beat the Greeks and Serbs together," if Bulgarian diplomacy, never very fond of compromise, failed to achieve the object of settling the Servian and the Greek difficulties separately. As for the prudent monarch of Bulgaria, he was intimidated. Thus war, however regrettable, became inevitable. Nothing but paper protocols separated the three armies in Macedonia.

Early on June 30, 1913, hostilities began with a Bulgarian attack upon the Serbs at Gjevgjeli on the railway from Skoplje to Salonika, the point of contact between the Servian and Greek forces, and upon the Greeks at Nigrita in the mountainous region between Salonika and Serres. The strategical object of these movements was to separate the two Allies; and, although M. Gueshov declares that the Cabinet knew nothing of them, there seems to be little doubt that they were premeditated, for the Serbs found upon a Bulgarian officer an official document, dated the day before, which stated that "the operations of war against the Serbs and the Greeks will begin to-morrow," and contained detailed directions for the attack upon the former. For the moment the Bulgarians were successful at both places, for their enemies were taken by surprise. As soon, however, as the news reached Salonika, the Greek General Staff ordered the Bulgarian troops still jointly garrisoning that town to lay down their arms and leave it within two hours. The Bulgars refused, and a siege of the houses occupied by them began, and continued till the Greek artillery forced the survivors to surrender. A general advance of the Greek army, commanded by the King in person, began on the next day. The left flank marched upon Gjevgjeli; the main army advanced to Kilkich, a strongly-fortified position on the railway from Salonika to Serres; the right centre was moved to Lachanâs on the old road to the latter town; while the right flank proceeded to Nigrita.

The results of the campaign were a surprise to those critics

who had paid too exclusive an attention to the Bulgarian successes during the previous war.   A three days' battle at Kilkich
ended on July 4 in a complete Greek victory; a two days'
struggle at Lachanâs terminated in a Bulgarian defeat; both
Gjevgjeli and Nigrita were re-occupied.   Farther to the north,
another three days' battle between the Serbs and Bulgars on
the river Bregalnitza and the historic battlefield of Ovtchepolje,
the plateau dominating the approach to Skoplje, gave a
triumph to the Serbs.   Hard fighting had taken place before
war had been formally declared; but King Constantine on
July 2 and King Peter on July 9 announced in proclamations
to the Greek people and the Servian army that a state of war
existed between them and their former allies.   King Nicholas,
although Montenegro was not directly interested in Macedonia,
sent his subjects to assist their brother Serbs; and on July 11
a fourth combatant entered the field against Bulgaria in the
shape of Roumania, hitherto regarded as a docile follower of
Austrian policy, which was known to be pro-Bulgarian.   A
circular note to the Powers explained that Roumania's aim was
not conquest, but to obtain for herself a strategic frontier
running from Turtukaï on the Danube to Baltchik on the
Black Sea, and to restore Balkan equilibrium by preventing the
hegemony of Bulgaria.   No opposition was offered by the
Bulgars to the Roumanian advance; Silistria was occupied
without resistance; Plevna, the scene of the most glorious episode in modern Roumanian history, was entered in the course
of this inglorious march; and, without firing a shot, the
Roumanian troops halted within twelve miles of Sofia.   Nor
was this all.   Profiting, as ever, by the quarrels of the Balkan
Christians, the Turks on July 15 entered Aînos, which the
Bulgars had evacuated, and proceeded to undo the Bulgarian
achievements of the Thracian campaign.

Meanwhile, the Greeks and Servians continued to advance.
The Greek main army took Dojran and Strumitza, where it
effected a junction with the Servians; and the prompt cession

of this Slavonic town to the latter augured well for their co-operation.   The Greek central column occupied Demir Hissar on the railway to Serres after a two days' battle, while the right entered Serres itself on July 11.   Nor had the Greek fleet been inactive.   Admiral Kountouriótes took Kavalla, and a naval detachment was sent up over the classic field of Philippi to Drama.   The Bulgarians retreated, leaving devastation behind them.   All the Greek part of Serres, a very prosperous town of well-to-do citizens, was set on fire; and from Nigrita, from the village of Doxâton on the road between Drama and Kavalla, and from Drama itself, terrible massacres were reported.   The stories of these "Bulgarian atrocities" aroused the greatest indignation in Greece; and a British military correspondent, who was himself an eye-witness, ascribed the reckless daring of the Greek soldiers in this campaign in large measure to the sights which they had seen.   Accordingly, the war was conducted with a disregard of life which made the losses unusually heavy   The Greek press hailed King Constantine as a new Basil "the Bulgar-slayer"; and it was pointed out as a curious coincidence that the scene of one of the Greek victories was identical with that of the Byzantine Emperor almost 900 years earlier over the Bulgarian Tsar Samuel.   By a classical reminiscence, the poet Matsoúkas, like a new Tyrtaeus, took his place in the front ranks, and sang to encourage the Greek soldiers.

By the middle of July it was obvious that Bulgaria could not be victorious against the combination arrayed against her; and the Greek and Servian Premiers met at Skoplje to consider their terms, while at Sofia Dr Danev made way for M. Radoslavov.   The fighting, however, continued for about a fortnight longer.   After the pacific occupation of Melnik, a town often mentioned by Byzantine historians and still containing Byzantine treasures, the Greeks entered Nevrokop, and assailed the Bulgarians in the Kresna pass, which leads for many miles along the valley of the Upper Struma in the direction of the old Bulgarian frontier.   Several days of fighting terminated on July 26 with the defeat of the Bulgarians at Simetli, a village situated at the end of the gorge. The arrival of reinforcements enabled the Bulgarians to make a last stand near Djumaia, not far from their own frontier; and the Greek occupation of that place was the last action of the war.

Meanwhile, the Greek fleet had taken Dedeagatch, as well as Porto Lagos and Mákri between Dedeagatch and Kavalla; Xánthe on the railway between Drama and Constantinople had fallen into Greek hands; and thus Macedonia with a large strip of the Thracian coast was in the possession of the victors. But the Bulgarians were also menaced in their old dominions. The Serbs, after repulsing a Bulgarian force which had entered Servia near Knjajevatz, had invaded Bulgaria, occupied Belogradtchik, and threatened Vidin. The Turks, under Enver Bey, easily recovered Adrianople on July 22; and on the same day Kirk-kilisse fell almost without resistance. Turkish, Servian, and Roumanian armies were soon all simultaneously on old Bulgarian soil; and thus with the Greeks on the frontier, the situation at Sofia had become desperate. King Ferdinand in despair begged the King of Roumania to intervene with the Kings of the Hellenes, of Servia, and of Montenegro; and the Roumanian sovereign's appeal in the name of the balance of power in the Balkans proved to be successful.

The new peace conference met at Bucharest on July 30, just one month after what has been called by an eye-witness "the shortest and most sanguinary campaign on record" had begun. A five days' truce was at once declared, and no time was lost in getting to business. The principal difficulty was the Bulgarian frontage on the Aegean, for the Greeks at first claimed that the Greco-Bulgarian frontier on the sea should be three kilometers to the east of Mákri, that is to say a little to the west of Dedeagatch, while the Bulgarians proposed that the frontier should be pushed back as far as the Gulf of Orphano, thus including Drama and Kavalla within Bulgarian territory. The real controversy was over Kavalla, the importance of which, owing to its port and famous tobacco-plantations, was obvious to both parties. King Constantine insisted upon its retention; and he received unexpected support, to the surprise of the other two members of the Triple Alliance, from his brother-in-law, the German Emperor, who from a warm friend of Turkey had become an enthusiastic admirer of the Greek army. Majorescu, the Roumanian Premier, who presided over the conference, informed the Bulgarians that, if they did not yield, the Roumanian army would occupy Sofia. Defeated in the field and unsupported at the council-board by powerful influence from outside, the Bulgarian delegates sorrowfully gave way.

On August 10 the third treaty of Bucharest formally closed the hostilities between the Balkan states. The Roumanians, without loss of life in battle, obtained their new frontier from a little above Turtukaï on the Danube to the south of Ekrene on the Black Sea, including 2969 square miles with a (mostly Turkish) population of 273,090. Bulgaria was given two years within which to dismantle the fortifications of Rustchuk and Shumla and those within a radius of 20 kilometers round Baltchik. The new Serbo-Bulgarian frontier, starting from Pataritza on the old frontier, followed the watershed of the Vardar and the Struma, and joined the new Greco-Bulgarian boundary on the Belashitza range of mountains. Thence the Greek frontier ran down to the Aegean at the mouth of the Mesta, the ancient Néstos, thus leaving Xánthe to Bulgaria, but securing Kavalla to Greece. In order to prevent any erroneous interpretation of article 4 of the treaty of London, Bulgaria abandoned all claims to Crete. A mixed commission was to regulate these new frontiers, and any dispute concerning them was to be referred to arbitration. The rest of the treaty dealt with such temporary matters as the evacuation of the occupied Bulgarian territory and the restitution of prisoners, while a protocol provided for the settlement of outstanding questions relating to the old Serbo-Bulgarian frontier by the two parties concerned[1].

[1] *Livre vert Roumain* (Bucarest, 1913).

The news that peace had been signed was greeted with general relief. At first it seemed as if two of the Great Powers—Russia, as the champion of Bulgaria in the question of Kavalla, and Austria, as the opponent of an enlarged Servia—would demand a revision of the treaty. France and Germany were, however, ranged on the Greek side; and soon all the Powers acquiesced in the settlement made at Bucharest, for it was felt that it was better to leave the Balkan statesmen to manage their own affairs, than to run the risk of European complications by interference.

It now remained for the Bulgarians to make the best terms that they could with Turkey; for, in spite of Sir E. Grey's advice to evacuate Thrace and Adrianople in their own interest, the Turks declined to abandon what they had re-conquered. The weakness of the Great Powers allowed Turkey to tear up the treaty of London; and the British Foreign Secretary disregarded the maxim of his predecessor, Salisbury, that Christian territory, once emancipated from Turkish rule, should never be restored to it. In these circumstances, the Bulgarians had no other course open but to make peace with the Turks. Kirkkilisse, the scene of their first great exploit in the war of 1912, and Adrianople, the capture of which had practically closed their career of conquest, were both formally surrendered by the Turco-Bulgarian treaty signed at Constantinople on September 29; and the new frontier of the Turkish empire in Europe started from "the mouth of the river Resvaja," which flows into the Black Sea somewhat to the north of Cape Iniada, and ended in the Aegean a little to the west of Aïnos.

Bulgaria had been, indeed, severely punished for the mistake of the second war. She had lost her chief conquests of the previous campaign; she had been forced to cede to Roumania a large slice of her old territory; she had been obliged to relinquish in Thrace and Macedonia territories which would otherwise have been hers. Her losses in the two wars were estimated at 44,897 killed and 104,584 wounded; her finances had been seriously affected. In a single month she had played away the hard-won gains of 35 years. Balkan history in the Middle Ages affords numerous instances of such sudden reverses of fortune; and King Ferdinand was only repeating in his own person the maxim of Gibbon, that "the glory of the Bulgarians was confined to a narrow scope, both of time and place."

Greece and Servia had already agreed to the partition of their conquests; and the Turco-Bulgarian treaty was followed on November 14, 1913, by a treaty of peace between Greece and Turkey; but the two questions of Albania and the Aegean Islands remained to be settled by the Great Powers. The latter had appointed two Commissions to delimit, the one the northern and north-eastern, the other the southern frontiers of the new Albanian state. Meanwhile, Albania was in a condition bordering on anarchy; for, while Ismail Kemal Bey and an International Commission of Control resided at Valona, Essad Pasha, as "President" of a "Central Albanian Senate," ruled at Durazzo, and the Powers governed at Scutari. In the delimitation of the southern frontier a large slice of Northern Epirus, including places such as Santi Quaranta, Cheimárra, Délvinon, Preméte, Argyrókastron and Koritsá, captured by the Greeks during the first Balkan war, together with the islet of Saseno, which had belonged to Greece since 1864, was assigned to Albania. While Austria by her threats forced the Servian troops to retire from the north-east of the country, a note of the Powers, presented at Athens on February 13, 1914, made the definite recognition of Greek sovereignty over the captured islands (except Tenedos, Imbros, and Kastellórrizon and those still occupied by the Italians) contingent upon the previous evacuation of the south by the Greek forces.

The Albanian throne was, on February 21, 1914, formally offered by Essad Pasha and an Albanian deputation to Prince William of Wied, a German officer and nephew of the Queen of Roumania, and by him accepted. After having obtained satisfactory financial assistance from the Powers, he landed at Durazzo, the capital of the new Balkan state, on March 7, and appointed as his first Prime Minister Turkhan Pasha, a Thessalian who had, twenty years before, been Governor of Crete. Meanwhile, however, the Northern Epirotes had declared themselves autonomous; a "Sacred Battalion," on the analogy of that of 1821, had been formed; and in the early days of March a blue and white flag with a black Byzantine double-headed eagle was hoisted. Zográphos, who had been Foreign Minister of Greece in 1909, was elected President; and his nephew, M. Karapános, another Epirote who had been a diplomatist and was member for Arta, acted as his Foreign Secretary. While they fixed their residence first at Argyrókastron and then at the village of Georgoutsátes, Col. Spyromélios, the "captain" of Cheimárra, held his native mountains against the Albanians. Thus, the leaders of the "Autonomous" movement were, like those of Ulster, men of position, wealth, and conservative views.

Early in March 1914 the Greek troops began the evacuation of Northern Epirus at Koritsá, but did not complete it till April 28. Fighting between the Albanians and the "Autonomous" forces continued, culminating in an engagement at the monastery of Tsépos some two hours beyond Argyrókastron. A provisional settlement negotiated between the Epirote leaders and Col. Thomson, a Dutch officer in the employ of the Albanian Government, was repudiated by the latter; but the Prince subsequently asked the International Commission of Control to resume negotiations. Accordingly, a conference was held at Corfù, where, on May 17, a convention[1] was signed, entrusting "the organisation of the two southern provinces" of Argyrókastron and Koritsá to the International Commission; a local *gendarmerie*, recruited in due proportion from the Christians and Moslems of the two provinces, was to be formed by the Dutch officers who had been sent to organise

[1] *Mémoire sur l'Épire du Nord* (Annexe 2).

that of Albania; in the Orthodox schools Greek was to be the sole medium of instruction, except in the three elementary classes, and was to have the same status as Albanian not only in them but in the law-courts and elective councils. An annex contained the demands of the Cheimarriotes for the maintenance of their ancient privileges, including the use of their own banner and the appointment of a foreigner as governor under the traditional name of "captain" for ten years. On July 1, 1914, the Powers announced their approval of the Corfù convention.

Meanwhile, however, disturbances had broken out at the Albanian capital. Friction had arisen between the Dutch Major Sluys and Essad Pasha, hitherto the real master of Durazzo. Before dawn on May 19, in the absence of the Premier and the Italian Minister, Major Sluys ordered the "Nationalists," or Austrophil Albanians, to open fire with their cannon on Essad's house. Thus taken by surprise, Essad signed a paper promising never to return without the Prince's permission, and left on board an Italian ship for Italy, of which country he was regarded as the partisan. But his exile did not strengthen the position of the Prince, a weak man placed in a most difficult situation by the ambition of his wife. Moslem peasants, marching to Durazzo to lay their agrarian grievances before him, were greeted with shots; and the summons of the Catholic Maltsori to his aid gave to the now inevitable conflict the appearance of a religious war. In an evil moment, the Prince consented to seek safety on board an Italian ship, thereby losing prestige, while the diplomatists and the Commission of Control went out to parley with the insurgents at Sh. Jak (St James). The latter, whose skilful tactics betrayed the hand of some external adviser, demanded the revival of Turkish rule or European intervention. The insurrection rapidly spread, and soon the Prince's dominions were bounded by the bridge over the malarious lagoon of Durazzo, within whose walls Austrians and Italians intrigued day and night against each other in a manner to suggest a comparison between Schleswig-Holstein and Albania. The climax was reached when a Dutch officer arrested two Italians on a charge of signalling to the insurgents. Soon afterwards, Col. Thomson fell in battle ; and the Mirdites, who had come to defend the Prince, received a crushing defeat. Italy, anxious above all things not to be left alone in Albania with her dreaded ally, begged the other Powers to intervene ; but Great Britain, upon whose decision their action depended, limited herself to the reluctant despatch of Rear-Admiral Troubridge with a ship to Durazzo. The chaos in Albania naturally revived the hopes of the Epirotes, who captured Koritsá and Tepelen.

Meanwhile, however, an event had occurred in Bosnia which proved to be the occasion of the long-dreaded European war. On June 28, 1914, a student, named Princip, assassinated the Archduke Franz Ferdinand and his wife, as they were driving through the streets of Sarajevo. In August 1913, anxious to humiliate her small neighbour, and to recover her own lost prestige in the Balkans, Austria-Hungary had communicated to Italy her intention of attacking Servia ; she now sought to connect the Servian authorities with this crime, committed by an Austro-Hungarian subject of Servian race, and on July 23 sent an ultimatum to Belgrade, couched in terms such as no independent state could have accepted, accompanied by an explanatory circular to the signatories of the Berlin treaty. Two days later Servia made a conciliatory reply, but demurred to the extraordinary demand that she should accept on her own territory "the collaboration of the employees of the Austro-Hungarian Government in the suppression" of the Pan-Serb agitation, and in the enquiry into the plot ; at the same time she offered to refer the dispute to the Hague tribunal or the Powers. On July 28, Austria-Hungary pronounced this reply to be unsatisfactory, and declared war upon Servia, despite the efforts of Sir E. Grey to effect a peaceful settlement of a question which was certain to involve other countries. Russia supported

Servia, Germany Austria Hungary, thus bringing France into the field; Belgium was entered by the German armies; and Great Britain took up arms in defence of France and Belgium. Thus the Servians, as had been prophesied in 1897, were made the pretext for a general war. Montenegro naturally assisted the sister-state; and both declared war on Germany, as the ally of their arch-enemy.

CHAPTER XXI

THE NEAR EAST IN THE EUROPEAN WAR (1914-22)

SERVIA soon made the Austrians realise that their "punitive expedition" was no mere military promenade. Before the Austrian declaration of war, the Court had moved from the exposed capital on the frontier to Nish, so that the bombardment of Belgrade inflicted material, rather than political, damage. The Austrian offensive, directed against the mountainous region between the Drina and the Save through the valley of the Jadar, on the one side, and from Shabatz, on the other, was repulsed in a four days' battle (August 16–19), known in history as that of the Tzer mountain and the river Jadar. Encouraged by this victory, the Servians entered Sirmia and Bosnia, effected a junction with the Montenegrins, and marched upon Sarajevo. But their powers of defence were greater than those of offence; their Bosnian brethren did not rise, and the liberating army had to retreat. General Potiorek thereupon organised a second Austrian offensive with even more disastrous results than the former. The Servians allowed the invaders to occupy Belgrade, and retired into the interior, while Bulgarian bands tried to cut off their communications with Salonika by blowing up a bridge over the Vardar. At this crisis, the old king took his place in the trenches, rifle in hand; his presence and the arrival of fresh munitions encouraged his soldiers, who in the battle of the river Kolubara (December 3–9) completely routed the Austrians; and, while the invaders evacuated Servian territory for the second time, the King re-entered Belgrade. Austria had received

a terrible humiliation from the people whom she had humbled
in 1909, and the Servian commander-in-chief, Putnik, summed
up the secret of his success in the phrase "it is our business
to advance and retire." For nine months Servia suffered no
further invasion. But the Austrians had left behind them a
deadlier foe than their army—spotted typhus, which, together
with the two Balkan and the European wars, reduced the
population of Servia by about one-fifth.

Meanwhile, on November 5, Great Britain had declared
war upon Turkey, which (as was established later from the
Greek White Book) had signed an alliance with Germany upon
the very day on which the Grand Vizier assured the British
representative that "Turkey intends to observe strict neutrality."
The immediate result was the declaration of a protectorate over
Egypt and the annexation of Cyprus, to the satisfaction of the
Greek population, which thought that Great Britain could now
dispose of the island to whom she chose; the next was the
increased importance of the Balkans from a military standpoint
alike to the Allies and the Central Empires. Accordingly, it
became the policy of both groups of Powers to bring Roumania,
Greece and Bulgaria into the war.

Roumania had long been bound to Austria-Hungary by a
secret military convention; and, at the outbreak of the war,
King Charles summoned a Crown Council of political leaders
and urged them to support the Dual Monarchy. But the text
of the convention, when examined, was found to pledge Roumania only for purposes of defence, and she was, therefore, in
the same position as Italy. The king was thus unable to drag
his adopted country on to the German side, but he told the
Austrian Minister that "no power on earth could persuade
him to attack the Dual Monarchy." Simultaneously Russia
approached Roumania, offering her Transylvania and a guarantee
of the territory in the Dobrudja, ceded by Bulgaria in 1913,
if she would attack Austria. Roumania, however, had good
reasons for neutrality. Like Italy, she was not prepared for

war in 1914; she had "unredeemed" provinces in the possession of both groups of belligerents—for, if Transylvania, the Bukovina and the *Banat* were under Austria-Hungary, Bessarabia was Russian; she was suspicious of British sympathies with Hungary; she had to watch Bulgaria, anxious to recover the Dobrudja; and she could scarcely regard with favour the then probable Russian acquisition of Constantinople, in the event of the Allies' victory. Thus, although the death of King Charles on October 10, 1914, removed an obstacle to intervention on their side, Roumania long remained neutral, oscillating on the whole, despite a costly German propaganda, towards them.

M. Venizélos was abroad when Austria declared war upon Servia; for the Turkish expulsions and persecutions of the Greeks in Asia Minor had nearly provoked a Greco-Turkish war in the summer of 1914, and he had gone to negotiate an arrangement of the question with the Grand Vizier. Greece had had, since the previous year, a treaty of alliance with Servia; and M. Venizélos at once declared to his ally that, while he required further information before he could support her in a war against Austria, she would find Greece by her side in the event of an aggression by Bulgaria. From the outset M. Venizélos was a convinced adherent of the Allies; and, had King George been alive, Greece would doubtless have entered the war earlier. But King Constantine was the German Emperor's brother-in-law and a German Field-Marshal; the Emperor had supported his claim to Kavalla at Bucharest, while the Allies, in order to purchase Bulgarian support, wished him to cede that valuable port to Bulgaria; and the King's private advisers were men of either German origin, like Dr Streit, or German sympathies, like General Doúsmanes and Col. Metaxâs. Thanks, however, to the confidence which M. Venizélos inspired in the Allies, the British Government informed him that the British fleet would not allow the Turkish, even while Turkey was still neutral, to leave the Dardanelles to attack Greece; and the Allies permitted the re-occupation of Northern

Epirus by the Greek army, whereupon the "Autonomous" Government declared its mission at an end.   In December, 1914, the Allies made their first offer to Greece—Northern Epirus, if she would immediately join them—an offer raised in the following month to "very important territorial concessions on the coasts of Asia Minor."   When the Allies decided to attack the Dardanelles, Greek co-operation became still more valuable; and the Premier was ready to provide it.   Thereupon, Col. Metaxâs, then *interim* chief of the staff, threatened to resign; and, although a Crown Council of ex-Premiers supported M. Venizélos, the King refused his consent.   M. Venizélos therefore resigned, M. Goúnares, a politician from Patras, taking his place on March 10.   To him the Allies renewed their offer of Asiatic compensations in the form of "the town of Smyrna and an important *Hinterland*."   The Greek reply was such that no answer was returned.

The entrance of Italy into the war in May, 1915, seriously affected the Balkan situation.   The "secret" treaty of London of April 26, 1915, which was the reward for her support, severely handicapped Allied diplomacy at Nish and Athens.   When it leaked out that the treaty assigned to Italy Northern Dalmatia, despite its overwhelmingly Slav population, it became impossible to induce the Servian Government to make such territorial concessions to Bulgaria in Macedonia as would purchase Bulgarian support.   Greece and Italy regarded one another as rivals in the Levant; and article 8, which assigned to Italy "entire sovereignty over the Dodekanese," was as little counterbalanced by her conditional promise not to oppose the assignment of "Southern Albania" to Greece, as was the loss of Northern Dalmatia by the similar pledge not to oppose the division of Northern Albania between Servia and Montenegro.   This policy of obtaining Dalmatia, Istria and the Trentino by the sacrifice of Albania, where she was also to "receive full sovereignty over Valona, Saseno" and the territory from the Vojusa to Cheimárra, alienated Albanian sympathies from Italy without winning those of Servia and Greece; and Baron Sonnino's tactless disclosure of the fact[1] that Austrian intervention alone had prevented Italy from occupying Chios and Lesbos in 1912, further diminished Italian and Allied popularity at Athens, where Baron Schenk, ably seconded by the diplomatic errors of the Allies, was successfully "converting" the newspapers to the German side. Indeed, Italy's interest was that M. Venizélos should not come into power, or Greece into the war; and her Minister at Athens, Count Bosdari, did not, therefore, see eye to eye with his colleagues.

In spite of all these difficulties, at the General Election of June, 1915, M. Venizélos had a majority of 58 over all opponents. But, under the pretext of the King's illness—cured, so the populace believed, by the direct intervention of the miraculous Virgin of Tênos—M. Goúnares remained in office for 70 days after his defeat, so that M. Venizélos did not begin his second Premiership till August 22. Meanwhile, Bulgaria had received an assurance from Germany that Greece would in any case remain neutral. Encouraged by this, Bulgaria mobilised; and, when M. Venizélos proposed to his sovereign the mobilisation of Greece, the King replied: "I do not wish us to help Servia, because Germany is going to win and I do not wish to be beaten!" To the Premier's remark that a constitutional ruler was bound to agree with a Minister whose policy had received popular approbation at the recent polls, the King answered in Prussian style: "I recognise My obligation to obey the popular verdict whenever internal questions are concerned, but when it is a matter of foreign questions, great national questions, I consider that I must insist that My idea be followed, because I am responsible before God!" No Greek King had ever spoken thus. Still mobilisation was ordered; and, to remove the apprehensions of the staff, M. Venizélos asked the Allies to furnish a supporting army of 150,000 men. The Allies agreed, but earlier in the day on which their

[1] *Documenti Diplomatici* (*Seduta del 20 Maggio* 1915), p. 25.

troops landed at Salonika (October 5), he was obliged to resign because of his declaration in the Chamber that if, in going to the help of Servia, Greece met German troops, she would act as her honour demanded. M. Zaïmes, the "handy-man" of Greek politics, took his place, "with the express purpose of not applying the Greco-Servian treaty." In vain, therefore, on October 7, Great Britain offered Cyprus to Greece in return for immediate help to Servia. The offer lapsed, and by the Sykes-Picot agreement of 1916, Great Britain undertook to cede Cyprus to no Power without the previous consent of France.

The situation of Servia was now desperate, for, on October 6, the Austro-German invasion began. Convinced, as everyone in the Balkans was, that Bulgaria was also about to attack her, she asked the permission of the Allies "to get her blow in first." "The Servian army," said Putnik, "would be in Sofia in five days." The Allies not only withheld permission, but were unable, when the Bulgarians and the Central Empires attacked Servia, to send her help in time. King Constantine, who was near and bound by treaty to assist her, remained neutral. Thus, this small country, exhausted by three campaigns and a typhus epidemic, was simultaneously attacked by the Germans, anxious to establish communications with Turkey, and the Bulgarians, eager to avenge their defeat of 1913. British agents, whose offers were, however, only conditional, had worked hard to bring Bulgaria to their side; but Turkey ceded to her the strip of territory through which the railway runs to Dedeagatch, including Dimotika and that part of Adrianople lying to the west of the Maritza. At the Court of Sofia, as at that of Athens, German influence prevailed; and, while King Ferdinand was cleverer than King Constantine, and his country less exposed than Greece to naval attacks, there was no Bulgarian statesman of the calibre of M. Venizélos to oppose him. Sentimentalists reckoned upon Bulgarian gratitude to Russia, the liberator of 1877; but Bulgaria afforded an example of Bismarck's cynical

remark, that "liberated nations are not grateful but exacting."
The treaty of Bucharest obliterated that of San Stefano.

To the regret of the many British friends of Bulgaria, Great
Britain on October 15, four days after the Bulgarian attack,
declared war upon her, in fulfilment of Sir E. Grey's warning,
that, if she joined our enemies, we were "prepared to give to
our friends in the Balkans all the support in our power." Unfortunately, that support came too late to save them. One town
after another fell into the hands of the enemy from the north
or the enemy from the south; and amidst the snows of a
Balkan winter soldiers and civilians of every age retreated across
the Albanian mountains to the Adriatic coast.

Great changes had taken place in Albania since the outbreak
of the European war. On September 3, 1914, Prince William
had ended his inglorious six months' reign with a proclamation,
informing his people that "he deemed it necessary to absent
himself temporarily," and by handing over the government to
the three remaining delegates—Austrian, French and Italian—
of the International Commission of Control, a body without co-
hesion and without funds, which soon dispersed. While Scutari
formed a local government of notables under the auspices of
the Allied Consuls, until it was retaken by the Montenegrins,
on June 27, 1915, Essad erected a "Government of Central
Albania" at Durazzo, and the Italians occupied Valona and the
islet of Saseno, ceded by Greece to Albania earlier in 1914.
The Montenegrins welcomed their Serb brothers in Scutari;
Essad, always a Serbophil, received them well in his dominions,
which began at Alessio; and a British Adriatic Mission was
sent over to look after them. Greece was asked, as she had
failed to carry out her obligations as an ally, at least to furnish
the Servian army with a refuge at Corfù, whither it was transported, and where the Servian Government established its
temporary residence.

Servia had thus been wiped temporarily from the map; it
was next the turn of Montenegro, which had entered into the

war eleven days after her. At first the Montenegrins had gained successes. They occupied Budua, Castel Lastua and the coveted Spizza, thus redressing the wrong of 1878; and they took part in the offensive against Sarajevo, penetrating to within eleven miles of the Bosnian capital. Like the Servians, they had to retreat from Bosnia, but retained their southern Dalmatian conquests till the final catastrophe. The Servian victory over the Austrians on the Kolubara procured for them nine months of comparative peace, during which they entered Scutari against the wishes of the Allies, who had requested them to respect Albanian independence. The Servian rout implied their approaching annihilation.

Over the end of Montenegro there still hangs a cloud of doubt and suspicion, which the voluminous literature on either side has rather increased than dispersed. His enemies accused King Nicholas of having betrayed Mt Lovtchen, which commands the Bocche di Cattaro, to the Austrians; others think that he had no option but to surrender. At any rate, Lovtchen was easily taken on January 11, 1916; Austrian troops on January 13 occupied Cetinje, whence the Court had retired to Podgoritza. On the same day the King asked the Austrian Emperor for "an honourable peace," and on January 21 embarked for Italy, leaving his second son, Mirko, behind him. King Nicholas spent the rest of his life an exile in France, now at Bordeaux, now in Paris, now at Neuilly, and now at Antibes, and never saw again the country which he had governed for 55 years. With all his faults, he was a big statesman of the Balkan type; it was his misfortune that his sons in no wise resembled him. Mirko died near Vienna; Danilo with his German wife lived comfortably on the French Riviera; Peter amused himself; while in the old king's latter days his chief adviser was not his Premier in exile but his daughter, Princess Xenia, who had found in politics a substitute for matrimony.

Thus, in the beginning of 1916, the Balkan situation seemed disastrous. Both Serb states had disappeared; Greece was by no means benevolently neutral, and the Allies, after eight months' occupation, had just evacuated the Dardanelles. There had been a moment when they might have forced the Straits— so Turkish and German military authorities told the United States' Ambassador—and appeared before Constantinople. But the lost opportunity of March, 1915, did not recur; and, after Servia's overthrow left the line to Constantinople open, the once thinly-fortified Dardanelles were made impregnable. As a German said : "We cannot hold the Dardanelles without the military support of Bulgaria." For the next three months the Allies kept on the defensive within "the entrenched camp of Salonika."

In these depressing circumstances it was less surprising that the Greeks, who had so recently fought two wars and had the fate of Servia before their eyes, should have become more neutralist. To M. Zaïmes, on November 7, 1915, had succeeded the aged M. Skouloúdes, a rich man, whose ruling passion was to be Premier, with a Cabinet of "Saviours," or "Greybeards." He dissolved the recently-elected Chamber; and, as 300,000 men were mobilised and, therefore, at the disposition of the Government, the Venizelists abstained. When, in the spring of 1916, the Servian army, reorganised at Corfù, was ready for transport to Salonika, he refused to allow it to use the Greek railways; and, when the Bulgarians demanded the surrender of Roûpel, the fort which commands the Struma valley, it was, with his connivance, betrayed to them. Thus, the Government of Constantine "the Bulgar-slayer" gave up to the Bulgars the historic fortress, which the Nicene Emperor, Theodore II Láskaris, had captured from their ancestors.

The results of this surrender were disastrous. General Sarrail, the Commander-in-Chief at Salonika, proclaimed the state of siege : "henceforth," as he said, "the Greeks were no longer masters there." In Northern Epirus they could no longer be trusted ; and thus Italy was able to supplant them there. And, on June 21, the three protecting Powers addressed a note to the Greek Government, peremptorily. demanding the complete demobilisation of the army, the immediate substitution for the existing Cabinet of a service Ministry without political colour and pledged to a benevolent neutrality towards them, and an immediate dissolution of parliament followed by new elections. These terms were unconditionally accepted, and M. Zaïmes again became Premier. The last condition could not, however, be executed, for the Bulgarians came to the relief of the embarrassed Royalists by overrunning Eastern Macedonia. Kavalla was surrendered with one-fifth of the Greek mobilisation material, and 8000 Greek troops were carried off to Germany and interned at Goerlitz. Thereupon, indignant at this continued surrender of Greek forts to the national foes, Col. Zymbrakákes and others formed a Committee of National Defence at Salonika. Their movement was premature and failed, but proved to be the precursor of the Venizelist secession.

On August 27, 1916, Roumania entered the war on the side of the Allies. Italy's intervention fifteen months earlier had increased the tendency of "the little Latin sister" to join them. But Russian reluctance to give up the Serb population of the *Banat* to Roumania long proved an obstacle to an agreement. Finally, however, Russia satisfied the Roumanian claims to Transylvania, the Bukovina and the *Banat*; and the secret treaty embodying them was signed on August 17, and subsequently recognised as operative by the British Government. A military convention, annexed to the treaty, pledged Roumania to attack Austria-Hungary at latest on August 28.

King Ferdinand, although, like his uncle, a Hohenzollern, was a good Roumanian, and was fortunately married to a spirited English Princess; and, although there was a Germanophil party under M. Marghiloman, and the Russian annexation of Bessarabia was not forgotten, Austria to the last had refused to purchase Roumanian neutrality by ceding the Bukovina. Public opinion, as in 1870, was mainly Francophil, for cultured Roumanians have many ties with France; but "Irredentism" was less widely diffused than in Italy, and the younger Brătianu, then Premier, was an opportunist, disinclined to take big risks for the realisation of a "big Roumania." Now, however, the risk seemed less. In his proclamation to his people, the King described this as "the day of the union of all the branches of our nation," the day "to establish for ever that which Michael the Great [in 1600] was only able to establish for a moment, namely a Roumanian union on both slopes of the Carpathians." Naturally, but unfortunately, the Roumanians directed their efforts towards the immediate conquest of their "unredeemed" heritage in Transylvania and the Bukovina, instead of attacking the Bulgarians, who, with the Germans, took Turtukaï and Constanza. The fate of Roumania was on a smaller scale than that of Servia; the enemy was near and the Allies far off; the Roumanians sustained a decisive defeat at Tirgu Jiului, south of the Vulkan pass, and, on December 6, Bucharest fell. The King established his residence at Jassy, where he was left undisturbed. Meanwhile the reorganised Servian forces had joined the Allies in Macedonia, where their common offensive resulted, on November 19, in the recovery of Monastir. Thus, the Servians held once more a fragment of their country—the town which they had captured from the Turks exactly four years earlier.

Meanwhile a very important event had happened at Salonika. When Roumania entered the war, M. Venizélos had informed the Greek Government that, by the previous admission of the staff itself, the last obstacle to Greek intervention had been removed; and that, if the King insisted upon further neutrality, he would appeal to the people. The abortive result of the Salonika "revolution," however, encouraged King Constantine to believe that the country was with him. M. Zaïmes made way for M. Kalogerópoulos, whose Foreign Minister, M. Karapános, had been one of the leaders of the Northern Epirote movement and was, although not a Venizelist, a supporter of the Allies. But the real authority was in the hands of the

Germanophil cabal around the throne; and, as the Powers declined to have intercourse with the new Cabinet, it resigned, and Professor Lámpros, the eminent mediaeval historian but a man of no political experience and of German and Royalist sympathies, became Premier. The King was now, however, *de facto* ruler of only a part of Greece.

On September 25, M. Venizélos, after mature deliberation, had left Athens for Crete, whence he appealed to the Greek people to "save what it is still possible to save" by ranging themselves on the side of the Servians and the Allies and driving out the invaders. Thence he proceeded by way of Lesbos to Salonika, where he formed with Admiral Kountouriótes and General Danglês a Provisional Government, which declared war on Bulgaria and Germany. Many Greeks flocked to its standard; and the Greek world was divided into two camps—Royalist and Venizelist—separated from one another by a neutral zone. Roughly speaking "Old" Greece was for the King, "New" Greece for the statesman who had freed it from the Turk and the Bulgar. Great Britain and France accredited diplomatists to the Venizelist Government; and it became evident that either the King or the ex-Premier must go, for that they could collaborate was impossible.

Events at Athens increased the anger of the Allies against King Constantine. The French Admiral demanded and obtained the surrender of the Greek torpedo flotilla, the disarmament of the larger ships and shore batteries, the control of the Piraeus harbour, the Salamis arsenal, and the Piraeus-Lárissa railway, which on May 8 had been connected with the Macedonian and "European" railway system by the opening of the last 56 miles between Papapoúli and Topsin. He then insisted upon the departure of the enemy diplomatists and Baron Schenk. But, when he further demanded the cession of ten batteries of mountain artillery by December 1, he was met by an organised attack, having previously confided to the King his plan of action. The Greeks fired upon the small Allied detachments, which had landed on the day appointed; and, besides numerous casualties, a body of marines was captured. The French fleet fired on the palace, and the Queen telegraphed to her brother that she had had to "take refuge in the cellars." She triumphantly described this ambush as "a great victory over four Great Powers." Next day it was followed by a hue-and-cry after Venizelists, whose houses had been previously marked; and the barbarous rite of an "anathema"[1] of stones was subsequently performed against their absent chief. Great was the indignation in London when the news leaked through the censorship—for no Venizelist newspapers appeared for four months after the "First of December." But condign punishment was postponed; meanwhile, the Athens garrison had to salute the Allied flags, the Greek troops were to be withdrawn within the Peloponnese, and a blockade was established, which soon affected the food supply. Smarting under these conditions, the recently triumphant Queen telegraphed to her brother praying that "the infamous swine may receive the punishment that they deserve!"

Finally, the Allies resolved to take a still more drastic measure. M. Jonnart, who had been Governor-General of Algeria, went to Greece as High Commissioner of the protecting Powers, and informed M. Zaïmes, who had for the fifth time become Premier, that the King must abdicate in favour of one of his sons, the Crown Prince being, however, excluded in consequence of his Germanophil sentiments. This time the Allies had ample forces at hand to enforce their demand. Consequently, on June 12, 1917, M. Zaïmes announced the King's decision "to quit the country" and his designation of his second son, Alexander, then nearly 24 years old, as his successor. Two days later, without incident, the ex-King em-

---

[1] A similar "anathema" is recorded in the cases of the traitors at Patras and Nauplia in 1715, of the Athenian primates, who favoured the tyrant, Hajji Ali, in 1785, and of Zográphos, author of the unpopular Turkish commercial treaty in 1840. Each person cast a stone, cursing M. Venizélos, as Shimei stoned and cursed David.

barked at Oropós, whence he proceeded with the Queen and the Crown Prince to Switzerland, thenceforth the centre of Royalist intrigues. His quiet departure proved that he was ready to bow to superior force, but he carefully abstained from describing it as an abdication. On June 27 M. Venizélos became the First Minister of the young King, who performed satisfactorily the part of a figure-head; and two days afterwards Greece broke off diplomatic relations with the Central Empires.

Three weeks later, upon Greek territory, took place the historic event of the formal fusion of the Southern Slavs in a single realm. The Pact of Corfù, signed by M. Pashich, the Servian Premier, and Dr Trumbich, the Chairman of the Jugoslav Committee on July 20, 1917, stipulated for the creation of the " Kingdom of the Serbs, Croats and Slovenes," defined as a "constitutional democratic and parliamentary Monarchy governed by the Karageorgevich dynasty," with "a single coat-of-arms, a single flag, and a single crown." Both the Cyrillic and the Latin alphabets were to have the same rights throughout the triple kingdom; and the three religions chiefly professed by the Jugoslavs—Orthodox, Catholic and Moslem—were declared equal. The calendar was to be unified as soon as possible. The national territory was defined as all that in which the Jugoslavs lived in compact masses. This Pact had immediate results. Warmly welcomed in Great Britain and France, it accentuated the already noticeable hostility of Italy, and created a schism in Montenegro, where the Unionist party's leader, M. Radovich, had already urged his exiled sovereign to resign and let Montenegro be merged in a single Jugoslav state under his grandson, Prince Alexander Karageorgevich. King Nicholas, however, although an advocate of Servian union in the abstract, showed no desire to sacrifice his dynasty upon its altar; and thus there arose a violent polemic between Montenegrin Royalists and Unionists, which has not yet ceased.

In the middle of 1917 Albania suddenly attracted the attention of Europe. After the Servian retreat across that technically neutral country, and the surrender of Montenegro, the Austrians had invaded the north and the centre, so that Essad Pasha had to remove his residence to Salonika, while the Italians spread southward from Valona, occupying most of Northern Epirus. At one place in this last region, Koritsá, however, the French, on December 13, 1916, had established an Albanian Republic, which issued stamps and paper money. General Sarrail hoped thereby to stop the intrigues and espionage, of which this conveniently situated town was the centre. He succeeded, but at the same time aroused the opposition of Essad, the Venizelists and the Italians, who saw with displeasure the appointment of native functionaries by the French military authorities in a town which all three parties regarded as in their own sphere of influence.

The Italian reply to the creation of this French protectorate came on June 3, 1917, the festival of the Italian Constitution, when Baron Sonnino, without consulting his sovereign, allies or colleagues (as one of them informed the writer), ordered General Ferrero to proclaim at Argyrókastron "the unity and independence of *all* Albania under the aegis and protection of the kingdom of Italy." Three Italian Ministers immediately resigned ; and the Allies were surprised at this sudden action of one Power in the affairs of a country which was their common concern. Before that time the Italian occupation already extended as far south as the Kalamâs, and in the first half of June it included such typical portions of Greek territory as the famous Párga and Joánnina itself. Greek opinion became alarmed, especially as a number of notables from Cheimárra were deported to the island of Favignana off the Sicilian coast, and as Northern Epirus had elected members to the Greek Chamber. M. Venizélos, however, while refusing to allow them to sit, for fear of international complications, obtained the evacuation of Joánnina, while the French anticipated an Italian occupation of Préveza. The Italians materially bene-fited Albania especially in respect of roads, but subsequently the benefactors had the same experience as the British in the Ionian Islands.

Meanwhile, Turkey had received severe blows. In 1916 the Emir Husein, at British instigation, proclaimed himself King of the Hedjaz, and his Kingdom included the two Holy Places of Islâm, Mecca and Medina.

The most picturesque episode of the war in the Near East was the liberation of Jerusalem from Turkish rule by the British under General Allenby on December 9, 1917, and the consequent loss of the Holy Land to the Moslem. Nothing aroused in equal degree the sentiment of the Christian world as this dramatic resumption of the work of the Crusaders. Of greater strategic importance were the operations of the British in Mesopotamia and of the Russians in Armenia. The situation of Turkey at the end of 1917 was, indeed, deplorable. The Russians, who had taken Erzerum and Trebizond, the gate of Armenia, in the previous year, held all Turkish Armenia; the British, who had been forced to surrender Kut-el-Amarah ten months earlier, not only recaptured it, but entered Baghdad, and effected a junction with the Russians at Kizil Robat. But the chief sufferers by the war in Asia were the unhappy Armenians; for, in 1915, Turkey had organised a repetition of the Armenian massacres which had shocked the conscience of Europe twenty years earlier. The American Ambassador at Constantinople branded this crime as "the murder of a nation," and the British Government published a vast mass of evidence confirmatory of his sentence[1]. The Prefect of police at Constantinople admitted that "the records of the Spanish Inquisition" had been searched for new tortures by men who had little to learn in that black art. The official excuse was that the Armenians had "helped the Russians" and opposed the Turks at Van; the German Ambassador approved, if he did not inspire, the policy of Talaat and Enver. After the war

---

[1] *The Treatment of Armenians in the Ottoman Empire, 1915-16.* London, 1916.

tardy vengeance by the hand of an assassin struck down Talaat in Berlin and his tool, the Grand Vizier, in Rome; but the British official estimate calculated that in the "deportations" of 1915 one-third of the Turkish Armenians, or 600,000, perished, one-third survived deportation, and one-third alone escaped[1].

The last year of the war produced marked vicissitudes in the Near East. The Russian collapse and the establishment of Bolshevik rule temporarily relieved the hard-pressed Turks, who were able to retake Erzerum, and were specially disastrous to the Roumanians, who concluded an armistice with the Central Empires, but did not thereby save themselves from an attempted Bolshevik revolution, the work of Russian soldiers in Moldavia, and from a formal declaration of war by the Bolshevik Government. On May 7, 1918, the Roumanian armistice with the Central Empires ripened into the treaty of Bucharest, the fourth of that name recorded in this history, which ceded more of the Dobrudja to Bulgaria than Roumania had gained at the third, and the rest to the Central Empires. In compensation, Germany and Austria sanctioned the annexation to Roumania of Bessarabia, which had already voted for union.

The counterpoise to these losses was the victorious Macedonian offensive of the united British, French, Greek and Jugoslav forces under General Sarrail's successor, General Franchet d'Esperey in September, which loosened the keystone of the hostile arch. Bulgaria's intervention had greatly influenced the fortunes of the war; her defeat hastened its conclusion. On September 28, 1918, she signed an armistice, by which she agreed to evacuate Greek and Jugoslav territory, demobilise, and allow the Allies the use of her country as a military base against the Central Empires. On October 4, King Ferdinand, who had already left Bulgaria, abdicated in favour of his heir, who took the title of Boris III, thus ranging himself in the direct succession of the mediaeval Bulgarian Tsars. Thus ended King Ferdinand's 31 years' reign of tortuous intrigue,

[1] *Ibid.*, p. 651.

during which he had gone from one extreme of fortune to the other. His son, born and bred in the country, after weathering the storm of a peasant rising at Trnovo, has remained in tranquil possession of the throne. Bulgaria having thus been eliminated from the Balkan theatre of war, and Austria weakened in the west, the Jugoslavs re-entered Belgrade, and Roumania, at the eleventh hour, declared war on Germany.

The Turks saw that they could not continue the war after the withdrawal of Bulgaria. Talaat and Enver resigned, and their successors began negotiations with the Allies, which ended in the armistice of Moûdros in Lêmnos on October 30. This ended the war in the Near East, leaving Turks and Bulgarians sorrowful that they had been misled into embracing the German cause; for this they were soon to pay dearly at the peace negotiations, in which the Greek Premier's strong personality gave him an influence far beyond that of any minor state.

By the treaty of Neuilly of November 27, 1919, Bulgaria was deprived of her frontage on the Aegean, which she ceded to Greece, but the Allies undertook to ensure her "economic outlets" thereto, which Greece was "disposed to grant." M, Venizélos argued that Porto Lagos in her hands might become a submarine base, that the Black Sea sufficed for her commercial needs, and that no concessions short of the hegemony of the Balkans would satisfy her ambition to play the part of Prussia. Whether he was wise in thus giving her a motive for attacking Greece, his successors will be able to judge. With Western Thrace she lost the tobacco-plantations of Xánthe, Gumuljina, Dimotika and the Dedeagatch railway, which Turkey had ceded as the price of her support, 6400 square kilometers in all. Her Roumanian frontier in the Dobrudja was put back to where it had been fixed by the third treaty of Bucharest; on the west she had to make rectifications, amounting to 2500 square kilometers, notably at Strumitza, in favour of Jugoslavia. She emerged with a population of 4,861,439 and an area of

40,656 square miles. Her claws were cut by the substitution of "voluntary enlistment" for conscription, and by the limitation of her army to 20,000 men "for the maintenance of order," who were to serve for "not less than twelve years." Only one military school was permitted, and no warlike training was to be given in other educational establishments. Neither navy nor air forces were allowed. In short, Bulgaria was to be de-Prussianised.

Then came the turn of Turkey. The Treaty of Sèvres, signed August 10, 1920, ceded to Greece the rest of Thrace practically up to the Chatalja lines, thus fulfilling Lord Salisbury's[1] prophecy of 1878. Turkey renounced to Greece all rights over Imbros and Tenedos, but retained, with Constantinople and a tiny strip of European territory, the islands of the Marmora. She also transferred to Greece "the exercise of her rights of sovereignty" over Smyrna and a considerable *Hinterland*, merely retaining a "flag over an outer fort"—an arrangement borrowed from Cretan history. Smyrna was to have a local parliament; and, if in five years' time it asked for "definite incorporation in the kingdom of Greece," the League of Nations might hold a *plébiscite* to decide. The Straits, thenceforth open to all, were placed under an international Commission. Thus Turkey, as an European Power, practically ceased to exist, retaining even less territory than the Byzantine Empire possessed in its last days.

But the "consolidation" of Turkey was further continued in Asia, for the first time since 1878. She recognised the Armenian Republic of Erivan (which had been constituted in 1918) and the Kingdom of the Hedjaz as "free and independent states," Kurdistan as autonomous, and Syria, Mesopotamia and Palestine as provisional wards of some mandatory Power, until they were "able to stand alone." The San Remo Conference (April, 1920) had assigned Syria to France; Mesopotamia and Palestine fell to Great Britain, which, in the words

---

[1] *Life*, ii, 243.

of Mr Balfour, viewed "with favour the establishment of a national home for the Jewish people" in Palestine, without prejudice to "the civil and religious rights of existing non-Jewish communities." The last vestiges of Turkey's nominal African sovereignty disappeared; and in the Aegean she formally renounced her last islands—the thirteen Sporádes and Kastellórrizon to Italy, and Cyprus, including its tribute, to Great Britain. An agreement, made on July 29, 1919, between M. Venizélos and Sig. Tittoni, had, however, stipulated that twelve of the islands should be handed over to Greece on the conclusion of this treaty, and that, fifteen years thereafter, in the event of the cession of Cyprus to Greece, Rhodes should hold a *plébiscite* on the question of union. Successive Italian Governments have declared this, and the subsequent Venizélos-Bonin agreement of August 10, 1920, suspended, on the plea that the treaty of Sèvres has not been ratified by Turkey[1]. By a separate treaty annexed to that of Sèvres, Greece undertook to maintain the rights of the non-Greek monasteries of Mt Athos.

Thus M. Venizélos had created a Great Greece of 171,163 square kilometers and 6,539,903 inhabitants. To enforce the treaty of Sèvres against Turkey was not, however, easy. Even before its signature, Mustapha Kemal had put himself at the head of a "National" movement at Angora, and became *de facto* ruler of Ásia Minor, while Mohammed VI, who had succeeded the feeble Mohammed V in 1918, retained the shadow of power at Constantinople. M. Venizélos offered to send Greek troops against the Kemalists, and Mr Lloyd George accepted his offer, which at first seemed to promise good results. But the Greeks, who, on landing at Smyrna in May, 1919, had met with violent opposition, which caused considerable loss

---

[1] *Corriere della Sera*, Sept. 1, 1920; Count Sforza's speech of August 6, 1920; *Epoca*, Dec. 8, 1921. Cyprus, made a colony in 1925, now has a Council of 9 official and 15 elected members, the non-Moslems being 12. The tribute, after the Lausanne treaty, was revived in the form of the "Cyprus share of the Turkish debt charge," but the Imperial Government contributed £50,000. In August, 1927, Cyprus was, however, relieved of all payment, on condition of contributing £10,000 annually towards Imperial defence.

of life on both sides, found their difficulties increased as they marched into the interior. Besides the armed resistance of the Kemalists, they had to face the diplomatic hostility of Italy, to whom, according to the Italian version, Smyrna had been promised by Mr Lloyd George at the Conference of St Jean de Maurienne in 1917. Moreover, Greece lost the support of France and many friends in England when, at the elections of November, 1920, her great statesman was completely routed.

History, even Greek history, furnishes few cases of such black ingratitude, for it was M. Venizélos' personal influence that had won for Greece her triumphs at the Council-board of Europe, as his successors soon found. But the causes of his fall were not obscure—the prolonged mobilisation, his long tenure of office, and his inevitable absence at Paris while unpopular subordinates governed, and made enemies, in his name. There was added, shortly before the elections, the unexpected death of the young King, the victim of a monkey's bite; for the vacancy of the throne led to a personal issue at the polls between the Premier and the ex-King. Admiral Kountouriótes acted as Regent, while Prince Paul, the last king's younger brother, was asked to accept the Crown. As the result of the elections, M. Venizélos resigned and left Greece and public life. Rhálles became Premier, and the Queen-Mother, Olga, Regent; a *plébiscite* showed an immense majority for ex-King Constantine's return; and on December 5 he was recalled, but was long unrecognised by the Powers. The neutralist, M. Goúnares, soon became Premier, only to discover that Italian joy at the Venizelist defeat was not due to Philhellenic sentiments, that France was hostile, Great Britain disgusted, and the Œcumenical Patriarchate Venizelist. Royalist Greece had few friends; and, while the authors of the treaty of Sèvres agreed to its revision[1], the Conference of Ambassadors on November 9,

[1] Extending the frontiers of European Turkey to a line drawn from near Ganos on the Sea of Marmora to the Bulgarian frontier on the west of the Stranja Mountains, and restoring Smyrna and its *Hinterland* to direct Turkish rule. (Paris Conference, March, 1922.)

1921, assigned Northern Epirus to Albania, to whom they awarded the frontiers of 1913 with the exception of four slight rectifications (three in favour of Jugoslavia), recognising the Albanian Government of Tirana as a sovereign state.

Albanian nationalism, long dormant, had lately developed. A meeting at Lushnia in 1920 elected a supreme council of four as an executive; and an Albanian Parliament met at Tirana, the former stronghold of Essad, who was assassinated in Paris. On August 2, by the Tirana agreement, Italy evacuated all Albania, except the islet of Saseno; and that country was now left to manage its own destinies.

Of all the Oriental states, Roumania came best out of the war. Despite her defeat, she more than doubled her territory and population; the dream of her patriots was realised; Transylvania, the Bukovina, Bessarabia and the eastern half of the *Banat* fell to her lot; and she now forms a state of 122,282 square miles and 17,393,149 inhabitants. She easily repulsed the Hungarian Bolsheviks and entered Buda-Pesth, and her King has even been mentioned as a sovereign of Hungary also.

Jugoslavia had far greater difficulties to face in obtaining territorial unity. Apart from Roumanian opposition to her claim to the western half of the *Banat*, she had to meet vehement Italian hostility in Dalmatia and at Fiume, and a separatist movement in Montenegro. When the United States entered the war, the American Government declined to be bound by the secret treaty of London (1915), which had assigned Northern Dalmatia to Italy, and Fiume to Croatia. There arose the lengthy "Adriatic question," further accentuated by the poet D'Annunzio's occupation of Fiume. After long dispute, the treaty of Rapallo (November 12, 1920), between the Italians and the Jugoslavs, abandoned Dalmatia to the latter, except Zara and a small territory round it, and all the islands except Cherso, Lussin, Lagosta, Pelagosa and their adjacent islets. Fiume was recognised as a free and independent state, but the possession of its smaller harbour of Port

Baross and the delta of its river remained in dispute. In 1921
Italian troops expelled D'Annunzio, and Sig. Zanella was chosen
president of the Free State. In 1922, however, the *Fascisti* upset
Zanella, and Italian troops occupied Fiume. Finally on January
27, 1924, Jugoslavia recognised the Italian absorption of the
Free State, Baross and the delta remaining Jugoslav. Thus Italy
has a harbour at Fiume and Jugoslavia one at Sushak.

The real feeling of Montenegro is hard to gauge. A Montenegrin Assembly deposed King Nicholas and decided for union
with Jugoslavia; and the elections for the Jugoslav Constituent
Assembly, which a British official observer[1] considered to have
shown "no evidence of interference or pressure" by the Serbs,
resulted in the return of no partisans of the Petrovich dynasty.
The old King's subsequent death at Antibes on March 1, 1921,
led more of its adherents to make their peace with Jugoslavia;
but a phantom Montenegrin Court continued to exist in exile.
The Crown Prince, Danilo, against his will, was forced to succeed his father; but he abdicated six days later in favour of
his nephew Michael, a boy at school in England, under the
Regency of the Queen-Mother, Milena, since dead. Great Britain
and France soon ceased to recognise Montenegro; but Italy long
took no decided step. It seems that, while few Montenegrins
(except officials) now wish for a separate kingdom, federal union
and local autonomy appeal to the majority rather than absolute
amalgamation. Whether Jugoslavia, with its area of 96,134 square
miles and its population of 12,017,323 will hold together, is a
question; for Croatia and Slovenia have a different tradition,
religion and grade of culture from Servia, and Montenegro is
as far behind Servia as Servia is behind Croatia and Slovenia,
while the social conditions of Bosnia differ widely from those of
a land where big estates are unknown. The natural solution of
these difficulties would seem to be Federation, but the "Constitution of Vidov dan" (June 28, 1921), which is the Charter
of the State, was Centralist.

[1] R. L'E. Bryce, *Further Report on political conditions in Montenegro*, p 2.

The agreement to revise the treaty of Sèvres was confirmed by the defeat of the Greeks in Asia Minor. The Coalition Cabinet of Protopapadákes, Goúnares and Strátos informed the Powers that Greece could obtain peace only by taking Constantinople. The Powers replied that they would use force to prevent it. Deprived of her most effective weapon, undermined by defeatist propaganda at home, unsupported by Great Britain and abandoned by Turkophil France, Greece had to face a strong Turkish attack. Afion Karahissar was evacuated, the new Commander-in-Chief captured, and on September 10, 1922, the Turks entered Smyrna. The burning of the Greek quarter and the murder of the Metropolitan recalled the massacre of Chios exactly a century earlier, with this difference that they aroused no indignation in a war-weary world. But the repercussion upon Greek internal politics was tremendous. Two Greek officers, Cols. Gonatâs and Plastíras, formed in Chios and Mitylene, where their retreating troops had taken refuge, a conspiracy to dethrone Constantine. As in 1917, so in 1922, he fell without resistance. The leaders sent him an ultimatum from Lávrion, and on September 27, he again abdicated—to avoid civil war; for the belief was wide-spread that his presence on the throne "prevented the powerful friends of Greece from helping her." Hastily writing in pencil a proclamation to his people, bidding them rally round his eldest son, their new king, George II, he left for Palermo, where on January 11, 1923, he died. Prince Nicholas, the cleverest but least popular of his brothers was sent into exile, where he occupied his leisure in composing for the British public the memoirs of his life.

The Coalition Cabinet had resigned on the news of the Asiatic disaster, and its successor, M. Triantaphyllákos, now made way for Krokidâs, a Corinthian, till such time as M. Zaïmes, always summoned in a crisis, should return from abroad. But as that statesman declined the post, Col. Gonatâs became Premier with General Pángalos as Minister of War, while Col. Plastíras exercised the real power behind the throne with the title of

"Leader of the Revolution." As the troops came back and the refugees poured in from Asia Minor, vengeance was demanded upon the authors of the catastrophe. General Pángalos, who knew no mercy, was appointed president of the committee for ascertaining the responsibility for the disaster, and General Othonaîos president of a military tribunal for judging the accused. This court sentenced to death General Hajjianéstes, who had been Commander-in-Chief, and the five ex-Ministers, Protopapadákes, Goúnarcs, Strátos, Baltatzês, and Nicholas Theotókes. The sentences were executed in hot haste on November 28, two hours before the arrival of Sir Gerald Talbot on a mission of mercy from Lausanne, where the Conference was sitting. The execution of "the Six" was both a crime and a blunder. One of "the Six" was scarcely responsible for his actions, another was dragged from a sick-bed to execution, a third was an amiable linguist unlikely to initiate a policy. It alienated foreign sympathy and divided for the next four years Greek public opinion, for in Athens relationships have wide ramifications, and stimulated the desire for revenge. But at the time, even mild individuals, who would usually be incapable of hurting anyone, clamoured for a scapegoat. Prince Andrew, more fortunate, was banished for life for having disobeyed orders, and transported on a British ship. The British Government marked its sense of the executions by withdrawing its Minister and leaving the Legation in the hands of a *chargé d'affaires* for 15 months.

The Moudania convention of October 11 had stipulated the withdrawal of the Greek troops to the west of the Maritza, and the treaty of Lausanne on July 24, 1923, fixed that river as the new frontier between Greece and Turkey, but the island at its mouth was definitely assigned to Greece only in 1926. Turkey received back all that Greece had held in Asia Minor, and in Europe, besides Eastern Thrace, also the enclave of Karagatch in Western Thrace. Despite a reservation by the Greek delegate, Italy acquired from Turkey "all her rights" to the *Dodekánesos* and the island of Kastellórrizon. Imbros and Tenedos were demilitarised, handed over by the Greeks two months later, and promised a native administration and police—a pledge still unfulfilled. Lêmnos, Samothrace and a zone of 30 *kilomètres* along the frontier were also demilitarised. Most important of all, the Convention of January 30 instituted from May 1, 1923, the compulsory exchange of the Greek population of Turkey with the Moslem population of Greece; the only exceptions were the Greeks "established" in Constantinople before October 30, 1918, the Moslems of Western Thrace and those of Albanian race, the latter mostly in Epirus, like the Chams. No recent event is likely to have a greater effect upon the future of Greece than this wholesale emigration and immigration. About 1,400,000 refugees have settled in that country with important political, social, agricultural and commercial results. Already, under the auspices of the Refugees' Settlement Commission, started in 1923 by the League of Nations (of which the chairman is always an American, the vice-chairman an Englishman), the refugees have enormously increased the cultivated area of Macedonia and Western Thrace and the population of Athens, Salonika, Volo and Kavalla, have introduced hitherto unknown industries, such as carpet-making, and have solved the Macedonian question as far as Greek Macedonia is concerned by bringing the Greek population of that province up to 88·8 per cent. With an area smaller by about 21,900 square *kilomètres*, Greece has a larger population, now reckoned at about 6,000,000, and that population is more homogeneous and more consolidated. Hellenism has become almost wholly European.

Besides the burden of the refugees, Greece had suddenly to support a hostile attack from Italy. On August 27, 1923, General Tellini, the Italian delegate on the Albanian boundary-commission and his suite were murdered at Kakavia on the road between Joánnina and Santi Quaranta, and on Greek territory. There was no evidence that Greeks had committed the crime, but the charge was immediately made, and Sig. Mussolini demanded the payment of 50,000,000 *lire* within 5 days. Not content with the Greek reply, he sent a fleet to Corfù, which on August 31 bombarded the "Old" and "New Forts," of which the latter had been dismantled and both neutralised in 1864, killing 16 persons (of whom 15 were Greek and Armenian refugees and one a Greek maid-servant), wounding 35 other persons, and putting a shell through the bedroom of the British headmaster of the Police School. Dr Kennedy, Commissioner of the "Save the Children Fund," an eye-witness, described the proceedings as "inhuman and revolting, unjustifiable and unnecessary"; *Punch* branded them in a poem of unusual sarcasm. The question was immediately brought before the League of Nations, where it made a profound impression upon the small states, and before the Ambassadors' Conference, of which General Tellini had been a mandatory. The result was that Greece had to pay the indemnity demanded, but that Italy evacuated Corfù on September 27. When, in 1925, at the Santa Rosa centenary the Italians exhumed the bones of Admiral Graziani in Corfù, the Corfiotes remained indoors as a protest. The Italianisation of the *Dodekánesos* and the attempt to create an autocephalous Church there have not improved Italo-Greek relations, formerly cordial. Curzon, in a note of October 15, 1922, had intimated that the cession of Jubaland to Italy by Great Britain was contingent on the settlement of the question of the *Dodekánesos*; but his successor, Mr Macdonald, abandoned this argument. The contrast between British methods in Cyprus and Italian administration in Rhodes affords a constant theme for Greek comment. The Italian Governor-General has recently admitted that the Italians have not the tolerant British mentality.

CHAPTER XXII

THE GREEK, TURKISH AND ALBANIAN
REPUBLICS (1923—27).

THE "Revolutionary" Government continued in power after the settlement at Lausanne, and, while George II, isolated and overshadowed, remained a figure-head, the real power was exercised by Col. Plastíras, a singularly disinterested soldier without political experience or ambition. But, even before the Asiatic disaster, there had been a Republican movement, more serious than that of the early 'eighties, led by M. Papanastasíou, a politician who had studied social science in Germany. The prosecution and imprisonment of him and his friends in 1922 had increased their popularity, and there were people who regretted that a Republic had not followed the second deposition of Constantine. A counter-revolution in October, 1923, under the leadership of three Generals, gave them their opportunity. The counter-revolution was speedily crushed by General Pángalos and Col. Kondýles, the Greek "Cromwell," as he was called, a man of rapid decisions, who now became prominent; but it had an unfavourable effect upon the monarchy. For the King was accused, without legal proof, of having favoured it, and feeling ran so high that the Royalist demonstration of December 9 ended in a fatal collision. When the elections to the National Assembly took place on December 16, the Royalists, with very few exceptions, abstained, and the Liberals and Republicans, the latter now organised as a party under M. Papanastasíou, practically monopolised the Assembly, although the Republicans were still in a minority. But this minority was active and forceful. Disregarding the advice of M. Venizélos, who had been elected in 18 constituencies in his absence, a group of Republican officers demanded the deposition of the dynasty. The Cabinet suggested as a compromise, that the King's departure was desirable while the form of government was being discussed. Accordingly, on December 19, George II and his Queen left "on leave of absence," as it was euphoniously called, for her Roumanian home, and his "provisional" withdrawal proved permanent. As in the case of his father's depositions, there was no excitement; unlike his father, he inspired neither deep affection nor intense hatred, but chiefly indifference, for he had never had a chance of showing what he could do. Admiral Kountouriótes was, as in 1920, appointed Regent until the question of the *régime* had been decided.

The Liberals now invited their former leader to return to Greece. M. Venizélos agreed to return as a "provisional adviser," and on January 4, 1924, landed at Pháleron. But he was no longer the Venizélos of the great days; his health was impaired, he had lost touch with Greek affairs, and new men with new ambitions had arisen in his absence—for three years is a generation in recent Greek history. His own party was divided into a Monarchist and a Republican section, and he was forced to accept the Premiership as none of his lieutenants would serve under anyone else; for Col. Plastíras had relinquished the supreme power on his arrival and retired into private life. M. Venizélos declared that his mission was not "to impose a Republic, but to ascertain the people's will." But M. Papanastasíou urged the immediate adoption of the Republic subject to ratification by a *plébiscite*. This plan was adopted; for illness compelled M. Venizélos to resign in less than a month, and his successor, M. Kaphandáres, soon found his own position untenable. Thereupon M. Venizélos left Greece, disillusioned, and devoted to the translation of Thucydides what had been meant for the government of Greece. In 1927 he returned, a private citizen, to Crete.

M. Papanastasíou forthwith became Premier with a markedly military element, Generals Pángalos and Kondýles and Admiral Hajjikyriákos, in his Cabinet. The words "Hellenic Polity" and "Provisional Governor"—titles derived from the presidency of Capo d' Istria, but subsequently altered to "Hellenic Republic" and "President"—were adopted officially, and on March 25, Greek Independence-Day (now celebrated according to the Gregorian Calendar, which the "Revolutionary" Government had introduced on February 16 (o.s.), 1923), Greece was proclaimed a Republic by the Assembly, conditionally on ratification by *plébiscite*, by 284 votes against none, but in the absence of M. Kaphandáres and his followers. White pigeons, bearing inscriptions, were let loose from the gallery, but the writer, who was present, could find no more enthusiasm or hostility than had been shown when George II left. On April 13, the *plébiscite* resulted in 758,742 votes for, and 325,322 against the Republic, "New" Greece being overwhelmingly and "Old" Greece predominantly Republican, while the refugees largely swelled the Republican poll, and the Royalist ideal leader lay in his Italian coffin. A few days later Republicans and Royalists alike celebrated the centenary of Byron's death.

The National Assembly met to consider the new Constitution which included the creation of a Senate; but, as in 1863, much time was spent in its discussion, and, as then, Cabinets succeeded each other in rapid succession, M. Sophoúles, the Samian dictator, following M. Papanastasíou, and in turn giving up his post to M. Michalakópoulos, a Conservative Republican. Two naval mutinies showed the disposition of the fleet still to mix in politics; the Geneva protocol for the protection of Bulgarian Minorities in Greece led to the denunciation of the Greco-Serbian alliance of 1913 by the Jugoslav Government in November, 1924, and the expulsion of the Œcumenical Patriarch, Constantine VI, from Constantinople, in January, 1925, caused difficulties with Turkey till the Patriarch, by resigning, facilitated the election of his successor. Suddenly, on June 25, 1925, General Pángalos, by a gigantic bluff—for he had only 28 men with him—made a *coup d'état*, seized the telegraph-office and the National Bank, and demanded the resignation of the Government, threatening to bombard the Presidential residence and the Ministry of War in case of resistance. Rather than provoke civil war, M. Michala-kópoulos resigned, and General Pángalos became Premier. A vote of the National Assembly threw a "parliamentary mantle" over his military uniform; but he soon threw it aside and governed absolutely. He made the death penalty retrospective and publicly hanged two officials, guilty of malversation; he dissolved the Assembly, and published an amended version of the unratified Constitution; but he conciliated the Royalists by giving them two seats in his Cabinet. He nearly plunged Greece into war with Bulgaria by his hasty action when a serious frontier-incident occurred near Demir Kapou; but the question was submitted to the League of Nations, which, after a report by Sir Horace Rumbold's Commission, inflicted an indemnity upon Greece. He prohibited all expressions of opinion by the Republican ex-Premiers, suspended hostile newspapers, and on January 3, 1926, openly proclaimed himself dictator, announcing the fact next day in a message, signed by himself alone. Meanwhile, he added to the gaiety of nations by regulating the length of ladies' skirts! He banished the ex-Premiers, MM. Kaphandáres and Papanastasíou and General Kondýles to the volcanic island of Santorin (then in eruption), and, upon the resignation of Admiral Kountouriótes, stood for the Presidency, while retaining the Premiership. He himself laid down the rules for the contest, in which he was a competitor—direct popular election and the exclusion of all members of the Royal family, of M. Venizélos and of all persons under 45 and over 65. The Opposition with rare unanimity chose a single candidate, M. Demertzês, a Moderate Royalist and ex-Minister of Marine. But as General Pángalos refused the guarantees for freedom of election which the Opposition demanded, M. Demertzês withdrew his candidature, and after the voting, held in different localities on April 4 and 11, General Pángalos, the sole candidate, was elected President of the Republic. He then set out to find a puppet-Premier, who would be titular chief of a service Cabinet, while he retained real power, subject of course to the support of the group of officers whose prisoner he was. To find such a Premier was difficult; but, after three futile attempts, M. Eutaxías, an ex-Minister of a bygone generation, was persuaded to accept. The chief event of his brief Premiership was the conclusion of the lengthy negotiations with Jugoslavia, by which the Gjevgjeli —Salonika railway was placed under Greek management (with Jugoslav collaboration), and the "Servian free zone" in the port of Salonika extended, as established by the convention of 1923. Before, however, this much criticised arrangement, which granted a 50 years' concession in return for a three years' treaty of friendship, was ratified, another *coup d'état* upset the dictatorship.

On August 22, 1926, while the dictator was absent at Spétsai, General Kondýles, aided by the Republican Guard under Col. Zervás—the praetorians of the Pangalist dictatorship, occupied the Ministry of War and the post-office in Athens without bloodshed, and invited Admiral Kountouriótes to resume the Presidency. General Pángalos endeavoured to escape on board a torpedo-boat, but was captured off Cape Matapan and imprisoned in the Cretan fortress of Izzeddin. He fell unlamented, and Admiral Kountouriótes again became President with General Kondýles as Premier till the elections for a new Chamber could be held. The dissolution of the Republican Guard, however, led on September 9 to a sanguinary conflict in the streets of the capital such as had not been seen since the "June days" of 1863. General Kondýles remained master of the situation, but, instead of making himself dictator, with rare self-denial promised to retire from politics as soon as the elections had indicated the nation's choice. He took immense precautions to prevent disturbances on polling-day, and all parties admitted the fairness and freedom of these elections, in which both the Royalist parties participated. The polling, held under proportional representation, resulted in a Republican majority of 34 in a Chamber of 286. In these circumstances, as no party could form a Cabinet by itself, for the first time since 1877 an "Œcumenical Government" was formed on December 4, under M. Zaímes, including the three Republican ex-Premiers, MM. Kaphandáres, Michalakópoulos and Papanastasíou, M. Tsaldáres, leader of the advanced, or "Popular," Royalist party, and General Metaxâs, chief of the moderate Royalist party of "Free Opinion." The only Opposition in Parliament consisted of the 9 Communists (who now made their first appearance in Greek public life) and a few intransigent Royalists. Thus, a great step towards "reconciliation" had been made; and now that Constantine is physically, and M. Venizélos politically, dead, the friends of Greece may hope that past feuds will be forgotten and that all parties will unite in solving the economic and other problems of their country. Only a Coalition Cabinet can make drastic economies, and the Greek people is weary of political changes and indignant at the military intervention which has become endemic since 1909: it wants only quiet and work[1].

Like Greece, Turkey has become a Republic. The success of the Turks against the Greeks in Asia Minor enhanced the prestige of Mustapha Kemal, and on November 1, 1922, the Grand National Assembly, which had been constituted at Angora, passed a resolution abolishing the Sultanate and separating from it the Caliphate, which had hitherto been one of its most important attributes. The Angora government then took possession of Constantinople, whence, on November 17, Mohammed VI fled on board a British warship. The Assembly thereupon elected his cousin, Abdul Mejid as Caliph, but in 1924 abolished that institution and expelled the new Caliph and all his male relatives. On October 29, 1923, it had proclaimed Turkey a

---

[1] The Government resigned on August 11, 1927, on the question of the gold reserves of the National Bank, and was followed by a Coalition Cabinet, without M. Tsaldáres and his friends.

Republic, and elected "the victorious" Mustapha Kemal its President. The revision of the Constitution in 1924 made the President's term of office coincide with the life of the Assembly, from and by which he was to be chosen. As he was *ex officio* President of the Assembly and—more important—Commander-in-Chief, he was practically a dictator, although a small number of the 286 deputies formed an opposition under Kiazim Kara Bekir. The proclamation of Angora as the capital in 1923 dealt a final blow to the prosperity of Constantinople, deprived of the position which it had filled for 470 years, and emphasised the attitude of Turkey as an Asiatic state. But the reformers of Angora showed no respect for tradition. European dress was introduced, while simultaneously there was a marked tendency to isolate Turkey from Europe. The treaty of Lausanne abolished the Capitulations and the foreign post-offices, and the disappearance of the Greeks owing to the exchange of populations, and the flight of many Armenians, while consolidating the Turkish element, have deprived Asiatic Turkey of its commercial element. Smyrna has declined since the massacre, and the departure of the industrious and industrial Christians of Asia Minor has involved much the same loss upon Turkey as the expulsion of the Huguenots brought upon France. Nationalism demands "Turkey for the Turks"; but it remains to be seen whether, in these days of close inter-relation between various countries, it be possible to erect a Chinese wall between Angora and the West. Moreover, the non-Christian population of the new Turkey is even now heterogeneous, for there are quite sufficient Kurds to create insurrections. In Constantinople there is still a considerable Greek population, and the Phanar is still the seat of the Œcumenical Patriarch. But his ecclesiastical authority has been greatly diminished, and the expulsion of Constantine VI showed the difficulty of his position in an enemy's country. In these circumstances some would favour the removal of the Patriarchate to Mount Athos; indeed, the original intention of the Turks at the Lausanne Conference was to remove it from

Constantinople, and an attempt was made to create an Orthodox Church for Turkey alone.

Roumania has gone through a peaceful "Agrarian revolution," by which a land of large proprietors has been transformed into a country of peasant owners. In the "new" provinces, united since the war, the break-up of the large estates has involved the transference of the land from foreigners to Roumanians, and has thus had a national, as well as social, result, while the Magyar peasants in Transylvania find their lot "lighter than that of their fellows in Hungary." The Constitution of 1923 gave the "new" provinces a majority in both the Senate and the Chamber; but, notwithstanding practically universal suffrage, politics go on much as before, except in the domain of taxation. Externally, Roumania has to face Bolshevik Russia's designs upon Bessarabia; internally, the matrimonial vagaries of Prince Carol have raised the question of the succession; ecclesiastically Roumania obtained in 1925 her own Patriarchate—another blow to the Œcumenical Patriarchate. The death of King Ferdinand on July 20, 1927, as Prince Carol had resigned his rights to the throne, led to the proclamation of Carol's little son, Michael, and a Regency, composed of Prince Nicholas, the Patriarch and the President of the Court of Appeal, governs during his minority.

Jugoslavia had already re-established the ancient Servian Patriarchate, but the Patriarch no longer resides at Ipek, where he was formally re-installed in 1924, but at Belgrade. Internal politics continued till his death in 1926 to be mainly directed by the veteran Radical leader, Pashich, a supporter of Centralisation, while his chief opponents, the Democrats, were a Jugoslav rather than a Serb party. But the storm-centre was M. Radich, leader of the Croat peasant party, a demagogue of Republican leanings, who, however, after the conclusion of a "Serbo-Croat pact" by his nephew in 1925, became a colleague of Pashich and rallied to the Monarchy, leaving the Slovenes isolated. Domestic policy was marked by strong opposition to

Bolshevism, especially after the assassination of the Minister, Drashkovich, by a Communist. Foreign policy, long in the hands of M. Nintchich, was conciliatory to Italy, with which he concluded the Nettuno conventions of 1925; but this attitude was criticised by the Croats and Slovenes, both more nearly concerned than the Serbs; and, after the Italo-Albanian pact of November 27, 1926, he resigned. Meanwhile, a movement in favour of a fleet for the protection of "our sea"—the Jugoslav equivalent of *il nostro mare*—indicated future difficulties in the Adriatic. At present, Jugoslavia is isolated: she suspects Italy of encircling her by means of a diffident Albania, a vindictive Hungary and a jealous Bulgaria; she has denounced her old, and not yet obtained the ratification of her new alliance with Greece, while France, her chief patron, is far off. Commercially, she is making progress; Belgrade is growing rapidly, and the opening of railway communication with Spalato has provided a new outlet on the Adriatic, which should divert the attention of Chauvinists from Salonika, only 48 miles from the Jugoslav frontier, especially since Greece has conceded the "free Servian zone" in the Aegean port. A commercial treaty with Austria, now no longer a dreaded neighbour, has been concluded to the benefit of both countries. In the former Prince Regent Alexander, who has been King since 1921, and has an heir, the triune state has a sovereign, of Servian stock yet born in Montenegro and annually resident in Slovenia, tried in war and careful to consider the wants of all the three elements in his kingdom, the material prosperity and variety of which strike the visitor.

Bulgaria since the treaty of Neuilly has perforce played a secondary part in the Balkans. Till his violent end in June, 1923, she found a second Stambulov in Stamboliski, a peasant-statesman of remarkable force of character and wise in his foreign policy of reconciliation with Jugoslavia. But he offended the Macedonians, always powerful at Sofia, by this sacrifice of their aspirations, while, as the chief of the Agrarian party, he had frightened the middle-class element by his internal legislation.

By a sudden *coup d'état*, almost bloodless in the capital, his government was deposed and his ministers imprisoned by a coalition of the middle-class parties under Professor Zankov with the army and by consent of the King. Stamboliski, absent in his native village near Philippopolis, was killed, and the Agrarian—Communist movement suppressed for a time. But many political assassinations took place, and in April, 1925, there were two daring Communist outrages, the attempt to murder the isolated King and, two days later, the explosion in the Cathedral, which cost 140 lives. Many arrests followed, martial law was proclaimed, and terror reigned at Sofia. Finally, in 1926, the Liaptchev Cabinet granted an amnesty for the political crimes of the last seven years, and began to purge the army from political elements. But Bulgaria received from her neighbours, Roumania, Jugoslavia and Greece, a collective note denouncing the recrudescence of revolutionary organisations on their borders. A Macedonian propaganda, a mixture of Nationalism and Bolshevism, is maintained; but this menaces Servian rather than Greek Macedonia, because the latter is now so largely Hellenised. Should, however, Jugoslavia and Bulgaria come to an agreement, the former might descend upon Salonika and the latter upon Dedeagatch, now christened by the Greeks Alexandroúpolis.

The creation of an independent Albania has scarcely simplified the Balkan problem; for that country with only 17,374 square miles and a population of 831,877, of which 71 per cent. are Moslem, 19 Orthodox and 10 Roman Catholic, is small compared with its neighbours. With Greece Albanian relations became cordial under General Pángalos, himself of Albanian stock, despite the Albanian treatment of Cheimárra, and the cession of "the 14 villages" to the east of Koritsá by Greece in 1924 and of the monastery of St Naoum on the lake of Ochrida to Jugoslavia in 1925 at the orders of the Ambassadors' Conference removed awkward questions. Both Jugoslavia and Italy were, however, suspected of intervention in

Albanian internal politics, and defeated Albanian leaders found a refuge in one or other of those countries. Thus Italian influence was asserted to be behind the insurrection of March, 1922, when Elez Yousouf marched on the capital, and surrendered, after 15 hours' fighting only, thanks to the moderating personality of the British Minister, Mr (now Sir) H. C. Eyres. After a long controversy, Italy, in 1923, abolished her four post-offices, and thus Albania was freed from any form of Capitulations. Ecclesiastical independence was obtained by the proclamation of an autocephalous Orthodox Church of Albania and the complete separation of both the Moslem sects in the country from the Caliphate. Polygamy was abolished by law, a British adviser appointed to the Ministry of the Interior, a political journal published at Tirana, and a German air-service inaugurated, in default of railways.

The era of insurrections was not, however, over. Ahmed Zogu, a young and ambitious man, who had held the Premiership for over 18 months, although defeated at the elections of 1923, continued to keep the real power behind his successor and presumptive father-in-law, reputed the richest man in Albania and leader of the feudal party. In 1924 the murder of Essad's assassin, who had tried to form an Albanian Fascist organisation and one of whose followers had attempted to murder Ahmed Zogu, aroused a bitter controversy. The deputies of the Opposition refused to return to the Parliament in Tirana, unless Ahmed Zogu left the country; instead, he made an inflammatory appeal to the Moslems; the North and the South, Scutari and Valona, ranged themselves against the Centre; the Nationalists took up arms against the feudal Beys, captured Tirana and forced Ahmed Zogu to flee into Jugoslavia. The two Moslem Regents also fled abroad, the Catholic resigned, and the Orthodox Regent alone remained in office, while Mgr. Fan Noli, the Orthodox Bishop of Durazzo, who was born near Adrianople, had been an actor in Athens, had spent many years in the United States, had represented Albania at the League of Nations and abandoned theology for politics, became Premier. But the versatile Premier knew America better than Albania, he was regarded as an Italian partisan, and at the end of 1924, on the outbreak of a counter-revolution, fled to Italy, while Ahmed Zogu re-established himself almost without bloodshed in Tirana.

Hitherto the form of Government had been a "Monarchy in commission," and the Duke of Atholl was said to have been offered the throne. Ahmed Zogu at his restoration resumed the Premiership with only two colleagues ; but in February, 1925, a Constituent Assembly proclaimed a Republic and elected him President for seven years. A Senate of 18, of whom 6 were his nominees and the others appointed by his partisans in the Assembly, was created, and the number of deputies reduced. He was thus dictator, for most of the Opposition leaders were in exile; the new Constitution declared him to be responsible to none and authorised him to preside over the Ministerial Council. British officers were summoned to organise the *gendarmerie*, and the discovery of petroleum led to British, Italian and French concessions, notably to the Anglo-Persian Oil Company. A costly palace was built for the President at Durazzo, which rather needed a harbour. But he had to face a difficult Italian proposition. In July, 1926, the Italian Minister suggested that he should entrust the army and *gendarmerie* to Italian instructors and accept Italian control of the Albanian finances. He refused; but an Italian bank has been allowed to control an Albanian National bank, and an Italian loan has been given to Albania on terms which recall the early Greek loans[1]. Finally, Ahmed Zogu, the favourite of Belgrade, on November 27, 1926, signed a "pact of friendship" for 5 years with Italy, for the maintenance of "the political, juridical and territorial *status quo* of Albania," promising "not to conclude with other powers political or military agreements prejudicial to the interests of the other party." Italy has thus a double pretext,

[1] H. Fish Armstrong in *The New York Times*, Jan. 2, 1927.

financial and political, for intervention ; and, if she intervenes, will Jugoslavia abstain? The Albanians abroad protested against the treaty, which was immediately preceded by an insurrection at Shala. In June, 1927, the arrest of the dragoman of the Jugoslav Legation caused a temporary breach of diplomatic relations with Belgrade. Albania's troubles are evidently not over : Tirana is the Achilles' heel of Balkan independence.

The final liquidation of the Ottoman dominions in Europe has not been yet completed; but, after the events of the last fifteen years it is obvious that Turkey has ceased, for all practical purposes, to be an European state. During the period of 127 years covered by this book, she has lost all her possessions in the Balkan peninsula, except the capital, Eastern, and a strip of Western Thrace, and all the islands of the Aegean except Imbros and Tenedos. Nothing remains of her African dominions. In short, Turkey is once more almost what she was in the first half of the fourteenth century—a purely Asiatic Power. Even in Asia, the Hedjaz is an independent kingdom; Syria, Mesopotamia and Palestine are administered by foreign mandatories; Smyrna and her territory are the only Turkish gain. This is, indeed, "consolidation"! The virtual elimination of Turkey and the substitution for it of large Roumanian and Jugoslav states, of a medium-sized Greece and Bulgaria, and a small Albania have not, indeed, provided a permanent solution of an insoluble question. Racial hatred burns nowhere so brightly as in south-eastern Europe, where, no more than in the more cultured west, does their profession of a common Christianity make rival nationalities love each other. Even a common enemy has only occasionally united them.

Yet no unbiassed observer can doubt that the emancipation of the eastern Christians from Ottoman rule has been a blessing. Western politicians, disregarding the fact that these races of the Balkan peninsula stepped straight out of the middle ages, after the long night of Turkish rule, into the full blaze of modern civilisation, seldom make allowance for the difficulty of rapid adaptation to the new and strange conditions. Nothing is more unfair than to compare them with other and old-established countries, slowly and gradually evolved. The wonder is, that the Christian states of the Near East have achieved so much in so comparatively short a time; and the wonder is increased when we reflect that their growth has been constantly hampered by the mutual jealousies and the ignorance of the Great Powers. The war of 1912–13 freed the Balkans from the yoke of Turkey; the European war freed them from the interference of Austria and Russia; and no Balkan nation, not even the Albanians, wishes to see Italy assume the part of Austria in its affairs, to mix in which is usually fatal to the intruder. It will be a happy day for the Near East, when the maxim of a Balkan statesman is realised: "The Balkan peninsula for the Balkan peoples." It will be a still happier day when its peaceful development is their sole occupation, and their past history counts less with them than their future progress.

TABLE OF RULERS

I. Bulgaria (and Eastern Roumelia).

Alexander, Prince	... 1879	Alexander Vogorídes,	
Regency ...	... 1886	Governor-General of	
Ferdinand, Prince, 1887;		Eastern Roumelia...	1879
Tsar ...	... 1908	Gavril Krstjovich, do.	1884-5
Boris III ...	... 1918		

II. Greece.

Otho, King	...	1832
[Regency	...	1833-5]
Provisional Government	...	1862
George I, King	...	1863
Constantine „	...	1913
Alexander „	...	1917
Admiral Kountouriótes, Regent	2 Oct.	1920
Queen Olga, Regent ...	17 Nov.	1920
Constantine restored ...	5 Dec.	1920
George II, King	27 Sep.	1922
Admiral Kountouriótes, Regent	20 Dec.	1923
Hellenic Republic proclaimed	25 Mar.	1924
Confirmed by *plébiscite*	13 Apr.	1924
Admiral Kountouriótes, President	14 Apr.	1924
General Pángalos, „	19 Apr.	1926
Admiral Kountouriótes, „	24 Aug.	1926

III. Montenegro.

Peter I, Prince-Bishop ...	...	1782
Peter II „ ...	...	1830
Danilo, Prince ...	...	1851
Nicholas I, Prince, 1860; King	...	1910-21

[Merged in the Kingdom of the Serbs, Croats and Slovenes.]

IV. ROUMANIA.

WALLACHIA.		MOLDAVIA.	
Alexander Moroúzes, *Hospodar*	1799	Constantine Hypselántes, *Hospodar*	1799
Michael I, Soûtsos, *Hospodar*	1801	Alexander Soûtsos, *Hospodar*	1801
Constantine Hypselántes, *Hospodar*	1802	Alexander Moroúzes, *Hospodar*	1802
Alexander Soûtsos (1), *Hospodar*	1806		

Russian occupation of both Principalities, 1806.

John Carageà, *Hospodar*	1812	Charles Callimachi, *Hospodar*	1812
Alexander Soûtsos (2) „	1818		
Constantine Négres, Lieutenant-governor	1821	Michael II, Soûtsos, *Hospodar*	1819
Gregory IV, Ghika, *Hospodar*	1822	Stephen Vogorídes, Lieutenant-governor	1821
		John S. Sturdza, *Hospodar*	1822

Russian occupation of both Principalities, 1828.

Alexander II, Ghika, *Hospodar*	1834	Michael Sturdza, *Hospodar*	1834
George Bibescu, *Hospodar*	1842	Gregory V, Ghika, *Hospodar*	1849–56
Provisional Government	1848		
Lieutenancy	1848		
Constantine Cantacuzene, Lieutenant-governor	1848		
Barbe Stirbeiu, *Hospodar*	1849–56		

Russian occupation of both Principalities, 1853.
Austrian „ „ „ „ 1854–7.

Alexander II, Ghika, Lieutenant-governor	1856	Theodore Balsh, Lieutenant-governor	1856
Three Commissioners	1858	Nicholas Vogorídes, Lieutenant-governor	1857
		Three Commissioners	1858

Alexander John Couza, Prince of both Principalities 1859

Provisional Government 1866
Charles I, Prince, 1866; King of Roumania ... 1881
Ferdinand I, King 1914
Michael, King 1927
[Regency ... ... 1927-]

V. Servia.

Kara George, Supreme Chief ... 1804–13
Milosh Obrenovich I (1), Prince ... 1817
Milan „ II „ ... 1839
Michael „ III (1) „ ... 1839
Alexander Karageorgevich „ ... 1842
Milosh Obrenovich I (2) „ ... 1859
Michael „ III (2) „ ... 1860
Milan „ IV, Prince 1868, King 1882
[Regency ... ... 1868–72]
Alexander I Obrenovich, King ... 1889
[Regency ... ... 1889–93]
Peter I Karageorgevich, King[1] ... 1903
Alexander I „ , Prince Regent
1914, King 1921

VI. Turkey.

Selim III 1788
Mustapha IV 1807
Mahmûd II 1808
Abdul Mejid 1839
Abdul Aziz 1861
Murad V 1876
Abdul Hamid II 1876
Mohammed V 1908
Mohammed VI 1918
„ deposed 1922
Turkish Republic 1923
Mustapha Kemal, President 1923

[1] Since 1918 King of the Serbs, Croats and Slovenes.

VII. FORMER AUTONOMOUS ISLANDS.

(*a*) CRETE.

Prince George of Greece, High Commissioner		1898
Alexander Zaîmes	„ „	1906–11

(*b*) SAMOS.

Stephen Vogorídes,	Prince	1834
Alexander Callimachi	„	1850
John Ghika	„	1856
Miltiádes Aristárches	„	1859
Paul Mousoûros	„	1867
Constantine Adosídes (1)	„	1873
Constantine Photiádes	„	1874
Constantine Adosídes (2)	„	1879
Alexander Karatheodori	„	1885
George Berovich	„	1894
Stephen Mousoûros	„	1896
Constantine Vayiánes	„	1899
Michael Gregoriádes	„	1900
Alexander Mavrogénes	„	1902
Yanko Vithynós	„	1904
Constantine Karatheodori	„	1906
George Georgiádes	„	1907
Andrew Kopásses	„	1907
George Vegléres	„	1912

VIII. ALBANIA.

Ismail Kemal Bey (Valona)	... ...	1912
William (of Weid), Prince	(Mar. 7–Sept. 3)	1914
Essad Pasha (Durazzo)	... ...	1914
Republic of Koritsá	... ...	1916
Four Regents (Tirana)	... ...	1920
Republic: Ahmed Zogu, President	Feb.	1925

BIBLIOGRAPHY

A complete bibliography of this period would fill a volume. French and Belgian publications on south-eastern Europe between 1821 and 1897 are very numerous; while the British Parliamentary and State Papers, and the Diplomatic and Consular Reports on Trade and Finance (since 1886), are too copious to be set out in detail, and, besides, have been indexed. Upon them and upon the similar *Documents diplomatiques* of France and *Documenti diplomatici* of Italy my narrative has been largely based. These last, and the Hellenic White Books (for a complete list of which I am indebted to the Greek Foreign Office), are at once less voluminous and less easily accessible; the titles are therefore given in full. The following bibliographies may be cited :—

Bengesco, G. Bibliographie franco-roumaine du XIXe siècle. Vol. I. Bruxelles, 1895.

—— Essai d'une notice bibliographique sur la question d'Orient. —Orient européen, 1821–97. Bruxelles et Paris, 1897.

Cobham, C. D. An attempt at a bibliography of Cyprus. Fifth edition. In Excerpta Cypria. Cambridge, 1908.

Jouplain, M. La question du Liban. Paris, 1908. (This contains a full bibliography of works on the Lebanon.)

Jovanovich, V. M. Енглеска библиографија о источном питању у Европи. у Београду, 1908. ("English bibliography of the eastern question.")

Kersopouloff, M. G. J. Essai de bibliographie franco-bulgare, 1613–1910. Paris, 1912.

Legrand, É. Bibliographie albanaise. Description rais. des ouvrages publ. en Albanais ou relat. à l'Albanie du XVe siècle jusqu'à 1900. Complétée p. H. Gûys. Paris 1912.

Legrand, É., et Pernot, H. Bibliographie ionienne. Paris, 1910.

Odavitch, R. J. Essai de bibliographie française sur les Serbes, Croates et Slovènes, depuis le commencement de la guerre actuelle. Paris, 1918.

Srpska Kraljevska Akademija. Essai de bibliographie française sur les Serbes et les Croates (1554–1900). Beograd, 1900.

Tenneroni, A. Per la bibliografia del Montenegro. Seconda edizione. Roma, 1896.

Tondini, C. Notice sur la bibliographie du Monténégro. Paris, 1889.

I. Bulgaria (and Eastern Roumelia).

Balkanicus [Protich, S.] The Aspirations of Bulgaria. London, 1915.

Bath, Marquis of. Observations on Bulgarian Affairs. London, 1880.

Beaman, A. H. M. Stambuloff. London, 1895.

Becker, G. La guerre contemporaine dans les Balkans, 1885. Paris, 1889.

Bilimek, H. Der bulgarisch-serbische Krieg, 1885. Wien, 1886.

Bourchier, J. D. (*Times* correspondent in the Balkans). Articles in the *Fortnightly Review.* "Through Bulgaria with Prince Ferdinand," July, 1888. "On the Black Sea with Prince Ferdinand," Jan. 1891. "To Rhodope with Prince Ferdinand," Apr. 1891. "A Balkan Confederation," Sep. 1891. In the *Contemporary Review.* "Justice and Conciliation in the Balkans," Feb. 1919. "Vae Victis!" Jan. 1920.

Buxton, Noel, M.P. With the Bulgarian Staff. London, 1913.

Cholet, Cte A. P. de. Étude sur la guerre bulgaro-serbe. Paris, 1891.

Dicey, E. The Peasant State. London, 1894.

Documenti diplomatici (Libri Verdi.)

    1880. Affari di Oriente. Parti IV, V, VI *b*, *c*. Legislatura XIV. Sessione I, N. IV.

    1885. Rumelia Orientale. Serie Iᵃ e 2ᵃ. Legislatura XV. Sessione I, N. II, *terdec.* and *quatuordecies.*

    1886. Rumelia Orientale e Grecia. Serie 3ᵃ. Legislatura XVI. Sessione I, N. II.

    1886. Bulgaria. Legislatura XVI. Sessione I, N. XVI.

    1889. Bulgaria. Legislatura XVI. Sessione 4, N. XVIII.

Drandar, A. G. Cinq ans de règne. Le Prince Alexandre de Battenberg en Bulgarie. Paris, 1884.
—— Les Événements politiques en Bulgarie depuis 1876 jusqu'à nos jours. Bruxelles, 1896.
—— La Bulgarie sous le Prince Ferdinand, 1887–1908. Bruxelles, 1909.
Dupuy-Péyou, L. La Bulgarie aux Bulgares. Paris et Bruxelles, 1896.
Golovin, A. F. Fürst Alexander I von Bulgarien, 1879–86. Wien, 1896.
Gopčević, Sp. Bulgarien und Ostrumelien, mit besonderer Berücksichtigung des Zeitraums von 1878–1886. Leipzig, 1886.
Gubernatis, Cte A. de. La Bulgarie et les Bulgares. Florence, 1899.
Gueshoff, I. E. The Balkan League. London, 1915.
Huhn, Major A. von. Der Kampf der Bulgaren um ihre Nationaleinheit. Leipzig, 1886.
—— The Kidnapping of Prince Alexander. London, 1887.
Jireček, C. Das Fürstenthum Bulgarien. Wien, 1891.
Kanitz, F. Donau-Bulgarien und der Balkan. 2ᵗᵉ Auflage. Leipzig, 1882. French tr. Paris, 1882.
Koch, A. Mitteilungen aus dem Leben und der Regierung des Fürsten Alexander von Bulgarien. Darmstadt, 1887.
Lamouche, L. La Bulgarie dans le passé et le présent. Paris, 1892.
Léonoff, R. Documents secrets de la politique russe en Orient, 1881–90, Berlin et Leipzig, 1893.
Macdonald, J. Czar Ferdinand and his people. London, 1913.
Ministère du Commerce bulgare. La Bulgarie contemporaine. Bruxelles, 1906.
Puaux, R. De Sofia à Tchataldja. Paris, 1913.
Samuelson, J. Bulgaria past and present. London, 1888.
Sobolev, L. N. Der erste Fürst von Bulgarien. Leipzig, 1886.
Wagner, Lieut. H. With the Victorious Bulgarians. London, 1913.
Wolff, Sir H. D. Rambling Recollections. Vol. II. London, 1908.
Zoli, C. La Guerra turco-bulgara. Milano, 1913.

II. GREECE.

Abbott, G. F. Greece and the Allies, 1914–1922. London, 1923.
About, E. La Grèce contemporaine. Dixième édition. Paris, 1890.
Anonymous. Ἀμαλία ἡ Βασίλισσα τῆς Ἑλλάδος. Ἐν Ἀθήναις, 1896.

Anonymous. Σελίδες τινες τῆς ἱστορίας τοῦ Βασιλέως *Ὄθωνος. *Ἀθήνησιν, 1898.

—— [Capo d'Istria, Viaro.] Renseignements sur la Grèce et sur l'administration du Comte Capodistrias par un grec témoin oculaire des faits qu'il rapporte. Paris, 1833.

Ἀρχεῖον Γεωργίου Καραϊσκάκη, 1826-1827. Ἀθῆναι, 1924.

Aspréas, G. K. Πολιτικὴ Ἱστορία τῆς Νεωτέρας Ἑλλάδος, 1821-1921. Vols. I, II, 1821-1900. Ἐν Ἀθήναις, 1922-1923.

Becker, G. La guerre contemporaine dans les Balkans, 1897. Paris, 1899.

Beléles, L. Ὁ Καποδίστριας ὡς θεμελιώτης τῆς δημοτικῆς ἐκπαιδεύσεως ἐν Ἑλλάδι. Ἐν Ἀθήναις, 1908.

Bickford-Smith, R. A. H. Greece under King George. London, 1893.

Bigham, C. With the Turkish Army in Thessaly. London, 1897.

Bikélas, D. Seven Essays on Christian Greece. Translated by John, Marquess of Bute, K.T. Paisley and London, 1890.

Blachogiánnes, G. Ἱστορικὴ Ἀνθολογία. Ἀνέκδοτα—Γνωμικά—Περίεργα—Ἀστεῖα ἐκ τοῦ βίου διασήμων Ἑλλήνων, 1820-1864. Ἀθῆναι, 1927.

Blaquière, E. The Greek Revolution; its origin and progress. London, 1824.

—— Narration of a second visit to Greece. London, 1825.

—— Letters from Greece. London, 1828.

Bourchier, J. D. "A glance at Contemporary Greece." In the *Fortnightly Review*, June, 1890. "Charilaos Trikoupes." *Ib.* July, 1896.

Buchon, J. A. La Grèce continentale et la Morée. Paris, 1843.

Byron, Lord. The Works of Lord Byron. Letters and Journals. Ed. by R. E. Prothero. Vol. VI. London, 1904.

Byzántios, C. S. Ἱστορία τοῦ τακτικοῦ στρατοῦ τῆς Ἑλλάδος. Ἐν Ἀθήναις, 1837.

Carlisle, The Earl of. Diary in Turkish and Greek Waters. Ed. 3, London, 1854.

Cassavetti, D. J. Hellas and the Balkan Wars. London, 1914.

Cherbuliez, A. Correspondance du Comte Capodistrias. 4 vols. Genève, 1839.

Chester, S. B. Life of Venizelos. London, 1921.

Church, E. M. Sir Richard Church in Italy and Greece. Edinburgh, 1895.

Christmas, Walter. Kong Georg I. Prins af Danmark. Copenhagen, 1913. English tr. King George of Greece. London, 1914.

Collegno, G. Diario dell' Assedio di Navaríno. Toríno, 1857.

Constantine, H.R.H. Crown Prince. Ἔκθεσις τῆς 'Α. Β. Ὑψηλότητος τοῦ Διαδόχου ἐπὶ τῶν πεπραγμένων τοῦ στρατοῦ Θεσσαλίας κατὰ τὴν ἐκστρατείαν, 1897. Ἐν 'Αθήναις, 1898.

Debidour, A. Le Général Fabvier, sa vie militaire et politique. Paris, 1904.

Δελτίον τῆς Ἱστορικῆς καὶ Ἐθνολογικῆς Ἑταιρίας τῆς Ἑλλάδος. Τόμ. I, 263–6, 675–9; II, 118–20, 515–20; III, 317–30, 433–45; IV, 263–7, 331–43, 475–512, 575–8; V, 259–62; VI, 51–62; VII, 3–64, 138–426. Ἐν 'Αθήναις, 1883–1916.

De Quincey, T. The Revolution of Greece. Modern Greece. In Works. Vols. X, 99–157; XIII, 288–322. Edinburgh, 1862.

Deschamps, G. La Grèce d'aujourd'hui. 12ᵉ éd. Paris, 1910.

Deville, G. L'Entente, la Grèce et la Bulgarie. Paris, 1919.

Διπλωματικὰ Ἔγγραφα.

(1) Ἡ μεταξὺ τοῦ ἐν Ἑλλάδι πρεσβευτοῦ τῆς Γαλλίας καὶ τοῦ ἐπὶ τῶν Ἐξωτερικῶν Ὑπουργοῦ ἀλληλογραφία ἐπὶ τῆς ὑποθέσεως Σουλιέ. 'Αθῆναι, 1863.

(2) Ἔγγραφα ἐπίσημα ἀφορῶντα τὰς ἐπὶ τοῦ ἑπτανησιακοῦ ζητήματος διαπραγματεύσεις. 'Αθῆναι, 1864.

(3) Ἔγγραφα ἀφορῶντα εἰς τὴν ῥῆξιν τῶν μεταξὺ Ἑλλάδος καὶ Τουρκίας σχέσεων. 'Αθῆναι, 1868.

(4) Ἔγγραφα κατατεθέντα εἰς τὴν Βουλὴν περὶ τῶν ἐκβολάδων καὶ σκωριῶν Λαυρίου, 1872–1873. 'Αθῆναι, 1873.

(5) Διπλωματικὰ ἔγγραφα περὶ τοῦ Ἑλληνικοῦ ζητήματος, κατατεθέντα ἐν τῇ Βουλῇ τῶν Ἑλλήνων ὑπὸ τοῦ ἐπὶ τῶν Ἐξωτερικῶν Ὑπουργοῦ. 'Αθῆναι, 1878.

(6) Μετατροπὴ τῶν δανείων τοῦ 1824 καὶ 1825, ἀδείᾳ τοῦ ἐπὶ τῶν Οἰκονομικῶν Ὑπουργείου. 'Αθῆναι, 1879.

(7) Διπλωματικὰ ἔγγραφα ἀφορῶντα εἰς τὸ μεθοριακὸν ζήτημα. 'Αθῆναι, 1882.

(8) Διπλωματικὰ ἔγγραφα κατατεθέντα εἰς τὴν Βουλὴν ὑπὸ τοῦ ἐπὶ τῶν Ἐξωτερικῶν Ὑπουργοῦ περὶ τοῦ Ἀποκλεισμοῦ. 'Αθῆναι, 1886.

(9) Διπλωματικὰ ἔγγραφα περὶ σταφίδος. Διαπραγματεύσεις μετὰ τῆς Ἀγγλικῆς Κυβερνήσεως. 'Αθῆναι, 1889.

(10) Ἔγγραφα περὶ τῆς ὑποθέσεως Ζάππα, 1863–92. 'Αθῆναι, 1892.

(11) Διπλωματικὰ ἔγγραφα ἀφορῶντα εἰς τὸν ἑλληνοτουρκικὸν πόλε-
μον τοῦ 1897. Ἀθῆναι, 1897.

(12) Documents diplomatiques. (Livre blanc hellénique.) Conflit
Gréco-turc. Avril—Septembre 1897. Athènes, 1897.

(13) Μετάφρασις τῶν κυριωτέρων ὑπομνημάτων, δι' ὧν ἡ Ἑλληνικὴ
Κυβέρνησις προσέφυγεν εἰς τὴν διαιτησίαν τῶν ἐν Κων/πόλει
πρεσβευτῶν τῶν 6 Μ. Δυνάμεων. Ἀθῆναι, 1901.

(14) Ἔγγραφα Ἑλληνορουμανικῆς διαφορᾶς. Ἀθῆναι, 1906.

(15) Διπλωματικὰ ἔγγραφα, 1913–17. Ἑλληνοσερβικὴ Συνθήκη Συμ-
μαχίας. Εἰσβολὴ Γερμανοβουλγάρων εἰς Μακεδονίαν. Ἔκδοσις
δευτέρα. Ἐν Ἀθήναις, 1920. (Also in French translation.
Athènes, 1917.)

(16) Supplément (to the above). Athènes, 1917.

Documenti diplomatici. (Libri Verdi.)

1870. Uccisione del Conte Alberto Boyl. Legislatura x. Sessione
2, N. 77, 77 *bis.*

1872. Trattative con la Grecia per l'affare del "Laurium." Legislatura XI. Sessione 2, N. 151 *bis.*

1880. Affari di Oriente. Parte VII. Legislatura XIV. Sessione 1,
N. IV.

1880. Conferenza di Berlino per la questione turco-ellenica. Legislatura XIV. Sessione I, N. IV *ter.*

1881. Questione turco-ellenica (1881). Iª serie. Legislatura XIV.
Sessione I, N. IV *quinq.*

1883. Questione turco-ellenica (1882). 2ª serie. Legislatura XV.
Sessione I, N. II *ter.*

1886. Rumelia Orientale e Grecia. Serie 3ª. Legislatura XVI.
Sessione I, N. II.

1897. Creta. Conflitto Turco-ellenico. Legislatura xx. Sessione
I, N. XIX.

Documents Diplomatiques. Différend Italo-Grec. Août—Septembre,
1923 (Affaire Kakavia). Athènes, 1923.

Dragoúmes, N. Ἱστορικαὶ Ἀναμνήσεις. Ἔκδ. 2. 2 vols. Ἐν Ἀθήναις,
1879.

Driault, É., et Lhéritier, M. Histoire diplomatique de la Grèce de
1821 jusqu'à nos jours (1821–1923). 5 Vols. Paris, 1925–26.

Drósos, D. I. D. Τὰ κατὰ τὸν διεθνῆ εἰρηνικὸν εἱργμὸν τοῦ 1850. Ἐν
Ἀθήναις, 1907.

Emerson, J. (Sir J. Emerson Tennent). The History of Modern
Greece. 2 vols. London, 1830.

Eulambio, M. S. The National Bank of Greece: a History of the Financial and Economic Evolution of Greece. Athens, 1924.

Evangelídes, T. E. Ἱστορία τοῦ Ὄθωνος (1832–1862). Ἐν Ἀθήναις, 1893.

—— Τὰ μετὰ τὸν Ὄθωνα, ἤτοι ἱστορία τῆς μεσοβασιλείας καὶ τῆς βασιλείας Γεωργίου τοῦ Α' (1862–1898). Ἐν Ἀθήναις, 1898.

—— Κωνσταντῖνος Σμολένσκης. Βιογραφικὸν δοκίμιον. Ἐν Ἀθήναις, 1897.

Eynard, J. G. Lettres et documents officiels relatifs aux derniers événements de la Grèce. Paris, 1831.

Fairchild, H. P. Greek Immigration to the United States. New Haven, 1911.

Finlay, G. A history of Greece. Ed. by H. F. Tozer. Vols. VI, VII. Oxford, 1877.

Garibaldi, R. La Camicia Rossa nella guerra greco-turca, 1897. Roma, 1899.

Gladstone, W. E. The Hellenic factor in the Eastern problem. Reprinted in Gleanings from past years. Vol. IV, 259–304. London, 1879.

Goltz, Baron C. von der. Der thessalische Krieg und die türkische Armee. Berlin, 1898.

Gordon, T. History of the Greek Revolution. 2 vols. London, 1832.

Goúdas, A. N. Mémorandum aux trois Puissances protectrices de la Grèce et au monde civilisé. Ἐν Κερκύρᾳ, 1862.

—— Second Memorandum. Corfou, 1862.

—— Troisième Mémoire. Paris, 1862.

—— Παραινέσεις πρὸς τὴν Αὐτοῦ Μεγαλειότητα τὸν μέλλοντα Βασιλέα τῆς Ἑλλάδος. Ἐν Ἀθήναις, 1863.

Guttman, B. Tage in Hellas. Frankfurt, 1924.

Hidroménos, A. M. Ἰωάννης Καποδίστριας, Κυβερνήτης τῆς Ἑλλάδος. Ἐν Ἀθήναις, 1900.

—— Τὸ Σύνταγμα τῆς Ἑλλάδος. Ἐν Ἀθήναις, 1908.

Homolle, Th., Houssaye, H., etc. La Grèce. Paris, 1908.

Isambert, G. L'Indépendance grecque et l'Europe. Paris, 1900.

Jebb, Sir R. C. Two lectures on Modern Greece. London, 1901.

Kampoúroglous, D. Gr. Ἡ Δούκισσα τῆς Πλακεντίας. In Μελέται καὶ Ἔρευναι, 161–240. Ἐν Ἀθήναις, 1925. Also as separate volume.

Karakatsánes, I. Z. Τὸ νέον Σύνταγμα τῆς Ἑλλάδος. Ἐν Ἀθήναις, 1911.

Karolídes, P. Σύγχρονος Ἱστορία τῶν Ἑλλήνων καὶ τῶν λοιπῶν λαῶν τῆς Ἀνατολῆς ἀπὸ 1821 μέχρι 1921. Vols. I–V, 1821–62. Ἐν Ἀθήναις, 1922–26.

Kerofilas, C. Un Homme d'État. E. Venizélos. Sa Vie. Son Œuvre. Paris, 1915. English tr. London, 1915.

Kleoménes, A. Περὶ τῶν πρώτων τῆς Ἑλλάδος Βασιλέων Ὄθωνος καὶ Ἀμαλίας. Ἐν Ἀθήναις, 1904.

Klüber, J. L. Pragmatische Geschichte der nationalen und politischen Wiedergeburt Griechenlands. Frankfurt, 1835.

Kolokotrónes, J. T. Ἑλληνικὰ ὑπομνήματα, ἤτοι ἐπιστολαὶ καὶ διάφορα ἔγγραφα ἀφορῶντα τὴν Ἑλληνικὴν ἐπανάστασιν ἀπὸ 1821 μέχρι 1827. Ἐν Ἀθήναις, 1856.

Kolokotrónes, Th. C. Διήγησις συμβάντων τῆς Ἑλληνικῆς φυλῆς ἀπὸ τὰ 1770 ἕως τὰ 1836. Ἐν Ἀθήναις, 1846.

Kordátos, I. K. Ἡ κοινωνικὴ σημασία τῆς Ἑλληνικῆς Ἐπαναστάσεως τοῦ 1921. Ἀθῆναι, 1924.

—— Νεοελληνικὴ πολιτικὴ Ἱστορία. Vol. I. Ἀθῆναι, 1925.

Kyriakídes, E. K. Ἱστορία τοῦ συγχρόνου Ἑλληνισμοῦ. 1832–1892. 2 vols. Ἐν Ἀθήναις, 1892–4.

Lascaris, S. Th. La Politique extérieure de la Grèce avant et après le Congrès de Berlin. 1875–1881. Paris, 1924.

Lawson, J. C. Tales of Ægean Intrigue. London, 1920.

Leake, W. M. An historical outline of the Greek Revolution. Ed. 3. London, 1826.

Leake, W. M. On the claim to the Islands of Cervi and Sapienza. London, 1850.

Lignós, A. Ἀρχεῖα Λαζάρου καὶ Γεωργίου Κουντουριώτου, 1821–1832. Vols. I–IV, 1821–26. Ἐν Ἀθήναις, 1920–26.

Mámouka, A. Z. Τὰ κατὰ τὴν ἀναγέννησιν τῆς Ἑλλάδος, ἤτοι συλλογὴ τῶν περὶ τὴν ἀναγεννωμένην Ἑλλάδα συνταχθέντων πολιτευμάτων, νόμων καὶ ἄλλων ἐπισήμων πράξεων ἀπὸ τοῦ 1821–1832. 11 vols. Ἐν Ἀθήναις, 1839–1852.

Martin, P. F. Greece of the Twentieth Century. London, 1913.

Maurer, G. L. von. Das griechische Volk in öffentlicher, kirchlicher und privatrechtlicher Beziehung. 3 vols. Heidelberg, 1835.

Μεγάλη Ἑλληνικὴ Ἐγκυκλοπαίδεια. Article Ἀθῆναι in vol. II, 122–177, 188–9, 204–17. Ἀθῆναι, 1927.

Mélas, G. M. Ex-King Constantine and the War. London, 1921.

Mendelssohn-Bartholdy, K. Geschichte Griechenlands von der Eroberung Konstantinopels durch die Türken im Jahre 1453 bis auf unsere Tage. 2 vols. Leipzig, 1870–4.

Metaxâs, C. Ἱστορικὰ ἀπομνημονεύματα ἐκ τῆς Ἑλληνικῆς ἐπαναστάσεως. Ἐν Ἀθήναις, 1878.

Miller, W. Greek life in town and country. London, 1905.
—— The Early Years of Modern Athens. London, 1926.
—— Modern Greek Historians of Modern Greece. In *History*, X, 110–23. July, 1925.
—— The Finlay Papers. George Finlay as a Journalist. The Journals of Finlay and Jarvis. In *The English Historical Review*, XXXIX, 386–98, 552–67 ; XLI, 514–25. July, October, 1924, October, 1926.
—— The Finlay Library. In the *Annual of the British School at Athens*, XXVI, 46–66. 1923–25.
—— Greece and Italy. The Greek Dilemma : Monarchy or Republic. The Greek Republic. Nine months of Greek Republicanism. Greece since the June "Revolution." The Greek Dictatorship. From Pangalos towards Parliamentarianism. The Greek "Œcumenical" Government. In *The Contemporary Review*. October, 1923; March, June, 1924; February, September, 1925; March, November, 1926; June, 1927.
—— The Presidency of General Pangalos. In *The Quarterly Review*. July, 1926.

"Nauplieús." Τὰ συμβάντα τῆς Ναυπλιακῆς ἐπαναστάσεως τῆς πρώτης Φεβρουαρίου 1862. Ἐν Ἀθήναις, 1862.

Nevinson, H. W. Scenes in the Thirty Days War between Greece and Turkey, 1897. London, 1898.

Nikolaides, K. Griechenlands Anteil an den Balkankriegen 1912–13. Wien, 1914.

Oikonomópoulos, E. Μεγάλη Ἱστορία τοῦ Βαλκανοτουρκικοῦ πολέμου. 2 vols. Ἀθῆναι, 1913.

Papadópoulos Vretós, A. Mémoires biographiques et historiques sur le Président de la Grèce le comte Jean Capodistrias. 2 vols. Paris, 1837.

Parish, H. H. The diplomatic history of the monarchy of Greece from the year 1830. London, 1838.

Pélikas, J. N. Ἀπομνημονεύματα τῆς Ὑπουργίας Σπυρίδωνος Πήλικα. Ἐν Ἀθήναις, 1893.

Philáretos, G. N. Σύνταγμα τῆς Ἑλλάδος. Ἐν Ἀθήναις, 1889.

Philémon, J. Δοκίμιον ἱστορικὸν περὶ τῆς Ἑλληνικῆς ἐπαναστάσεως. 4 vols. Ἀθῆναι, 1859–61.

Pieri, Mario. Storia del Risorgimento della Grecia. Portata fino alla battaglia di Domokos del 1897 de Silvio Becchia. Milano, 1897.

Pouqueville, F. C. H. L. Histoire de la régénération de la Grèce. 4 vols. Paris, 1824.

Price, W. H. Crawfurd. The Balkan Cockpit. The political and military story of the Balkan Wars in Macedonia. London, 1915.

—— Venizelos and the War. London, 1917.

Prokesch-Osten, A. von. Geschichte des Abfalls der Griechen vom türkischen Reiche im Jahre 1821 und der Gründung des hellenischen Königreiches aus diplomatischem Standpunkte. 6 vols. Wien, 1867.

Puaux, R. La Malheureuse Épire. Paris, 1914.

Ragkavês, A. R. 'Απομνημονεύματα. 2 vols. 'Εν 'Αθήναις, 1894.

Raybaud, M. Mémoires sur la Grèce pour servir à l'histoire de la guerre de l'Indépendance. 2 vols. Paris, 1824–5.

Rízos, J. N. Histoire moderne de la Grèce. Genève, 1828.

Rose, W. K. With the Greeks in Thessaly. London, 1897.

Rumbold, Sir H. Recollections of a Diplomatist. Vol. II. London, 1902.

—— Final Recollections of a Diplomatist. London, 1905.

Samuelson, J. Greece; her present condition. [Financial.] London, 1894.

Sergeant, L. Greece in the nineteenth century. [1821–97.] London, 1897.

Strong, F. Greece as a Kingdom; or a statistical description of that country. London, 1842.

Thiersch, F. De l'état actuel de la Grèce et des moyens d'arriver à sa restauration. 2 vols. Leipzig, 1833.

Thouvenel, L. La Grèce du Roi Othon. [1845–50.] Paris, 1890.

Trapmann, Capt. A. H. The Greeks Triumphant. London, 1915.

Trikoúpes, Sp. 'Ιστορία τῆς 'Ελληνικῆς ἐπαναστάσεως. "Εκδοσις τρίτη. 4 vols. 'Εν 'Αθήναις, 1888.

Trost, L. König Ludwig I von Bayern in seinen Briefen an seinen Sohn den König Otto von Griechenland. Bamberg, 1891.

Tsokópoulos, G. B. Παλαιαὶ 'Αθῆναι. 'Η βασίλισσα 'Αμαλία. 'Εν 'Αθήναις, 1904.

Tuckerman, C. K. The Greeks of to-day. Ed. 2. New York. 1886.

Vaka, D. (Mrs Kenneth Brown). Constantine: King and Traitor.

London, 1918. (American ed. In the Heart of German Intrigue New York and Boston, 1918.)

Vellay, C. L'Irrédentisme hellénique. Paris, 1913.

Venizélos, El. K. Τὸ πρόγραμμα τῆς ἐξωτερικῆς αὐτοῦ πολιτικῆς. Ἐν Ἀθήναις, 1915. (French tr. La Politique de la Grèce. Paris, 1916.)

—— Ἀγορεύσεις. Ἐν Ἀθήναις, 1917. (French tr. Cinq ans d'histoire grecque, 1912–1917. Paris, 1917.)

Waddington, G. A visit to Greece in 1823 and 1824. London, 1825.

Zográphos, D. L. Ἱστορία τῆς Ἑλληνικῆς Γεωργίας. Vols. I–III. 1821–1833. Ἀθῆναι, 1922–1924.

—— Ἱστορία τῆς Ἰδρύσεως τῆς Ἐθνικῆς Τραπέζης, 1833–1843. 2 vols. Ἀθῆναι, 1925–1927.

II (*a*). THE IONIAN ISLANDS (BEFORE THE UNION).

Ansted, D. F. The Ionian Islands in the year 1863. London, 1863.

Bosset, C. P. de. Parga and the Ionian Islands. London, 1821.

Bowen, Sir G. F. The Ionian Islands under British Protection. London, 1850.

Brokínes, L. S. (Editor). Γ. Προσαλένδου Ἀνέκδοτα χειρόγραφα ἀφορῶντα εἰς τὴν κατὰ τὸ δόγμα τῆς Ὀρθοδ. Ἐκκλησίας βάπτισιν τοῦ Ἄγγλου φιλέλληνος Κόμητος Γκίλφορδ. Ἐν Κερκύρᾳ, 1879.

Buchon, A. Voyage dans l'Eubée, les Îles Ioniennes et les Cyclades en 1841. Paris, 1911.

Chiótes, P. Ἱστορία τοῦ Ἰονίου Κράτους ἀπὸ συστάσεως αὐτοῦ μέχρις ἑνώσεως (ἔτη 1815–1864). 2 vols. Ἐν Ζακύνθῳ, 1874–7.

Costituzione degli Stati Uniti delle Isole Jonie unanimamente adottata e sanzionata dall' Assemblea legislativa nel giorno 2 maggio 1817. Corfù, 1817.

Depositions and Proceedings relative to the events which occurred in Cephalonia in the year 1849. Corfù (no date).

Dusmani, A. La missione di W. E. Gladstone nelle Isole Ionie. Corfù, 1870–1.

Edinburgh Review. Vol. LXXXII, 263–93. Parga. Edinburgh, 1819.

Foscolo, U. Narrazione delle fortune e della cessione di Parga. In Opere edite e postume. Prose politiche. Firenze, 1850.

—— Dello stato politico delle Isole Ionie. *Ibid.* Vol. XI, 91–128. Firenze, 1862.

Hidroménos, A. M. Ὁ ὑπὲρ τῆς ἐθνικῆς ἀποκαταστάσεως ἀγὼν τῶν Ἑπτανησίων, 1815–1864. Ἐν Κερκύρᾳ, 1889.

—— Ἡ πρώτη ἐν Κερκύρᾳ δημοσία σχολή, 1805–1824. Ἐν Ἀθήναις, 1890.

H[idroménos], M. S. ῎Εγγραφα περὶ τῆς ὑπὸ τῶν Παργίων καταθέσεως τῶν ἁγίων εἰκόνων καὶ σκευῶν τῆς ἐν Πάργῃ ἐκκλησίας. ᾿Εν Κερκύρᾳ, 1893.

Jervis, Henry Jervis-White. History of the Island of Corfù and of the Republic of the Ionian Islands. London, 1852.

Kirkwall, Viscount (Editor). Four years in the Ionian Islands. 2 vols. London, 1864. [By Col. F. Whittingham.]

Lenormant, F. La question ionienne devant l'Europe. Paris, 1859.

—— Le gouvernement des Iles Ioniennes. Lettre à Lord John Russell. Paris, 1861.

Loberdós, J. P. K. ῾Ιστορία τῆς νήσου Κεφαλληνίας. [Greek translation by P. K. Gratsiátos of unpublished Italian original.] ᾿Εν Κεφαλληνίᾳ, 1888.

Lombárdos, C. ᾿Απομνημονεύματα πρὸς καταρτισμὸν τῆς περὶ ἀπελευθερώσεως τῆς ῾Επτανήσου ἱστορίας. ᾿Εν Ζακύνθῳ καὶ᾿Αθήναις, 1871–5.

Lunzi, Conte E. Storia delle Isole Ionie sotto il reggimento dei Repubblicani francesi. Venezia, 1860.

—— Della Repubblica Settinsulare. Bologna, 1863.

Máneses, N. B. Le tre costituzioni (1800, 1803, 1817). Corfù, 1849.

Mavrogiánnes, G. E. ῾Ιστορία τῶν ᾿Ιονίων νήσων. 2 vols. ᾿Εν ᾿Αθήναις, 1889.

Morley, J. (Viscount). The life of William Ewart Gladstone. Vol. I. London, 1903.

Mustoxidi, A. Al dispaccio del 10 Aprile 1840 da Sir Howard Douglas...indiritto...confutazione. Malta, 1841.

Napier, Col. C. J. The colonies. London, 1833.

Pauthier, G. Les Îles Ioniennes pendant l'occupation française et le protectorat anglais. Paris, 1863.

Quarterly Review. Vol. XXIII, 111–36. Parga. London, 1820.

Rodocanachi, E. Bonaparte et les Îles Ioniennes. Paris, 1899.

S[alapánta], P. A. ῾Η Πάργα ἤτοι μονογραφία αὐτῆς. ᾿Εν ᾿Αθήναις, 1861.

Theotoky, A. Sir Frederick Adam in the Ionian Islands. Malta. 1839.

Theotoky, Baron. Détails sur Corfou. Corfou, 1826.

Whyte-Jervis, M. P., Capt. The Ionian Islands during the present century. London, 1863.

Xénos, S. East and West, a diplomatic history of the annexation of the Ionian Islands to the kingdom of Greece. London, 1865.

Zervós, E. J. Τὰ Κεφαλληνιακά. ᾿Εν Κεφαλληνίᾳ, 1850.

III. MONTENEGRO.

Andrić, Alexander. Geschichte des Fürstenthums Montenegro von der ältesten Zeit bis zum Jahre 1852. Wien, 1853.

Bourchier, J. D. Montenegro and her Prince. In *Fortnightly Review*. December, 1898.

Carr, W. Essay on Montenegro. Oxford, 1884.

Chiudina, G. Storia del Montenero (Crnagora) da' tempi antichi fino a' nostri. Spalato, 1882.

Coquelle, P. Histoire du Monténégro et de la Bosnie depuis les origines. Paris, 1895.

Delarue, Henri. Le Monténégro. Paris, 1862.

Denton, The Rev. W. Montenegro: its people and their history. London, 1877.

Documenti diplomatici. (Libri Verdi.)
 1880. Affari di Oriente. Parte VI*d*. Legislatura XIV. Sessione I, N. IV.

Erber, T. Storia della Dalmazia dal 1797 al 1814. Zara, 1886.

Frilley, G., et Wlahovitj, J. Le Monténégro contemporain. Paris, 1876.

Gladstone, W. E. Montenegro or Tsernagora. A sketch. Reprinted in Gleanings from Past Years. Vol. IV. London, 1879. Republished. London, 1912.

Gopčević, Sp. Der türko-montenegrinische Krieg, 1876–1878. Wien, 1877–79.

—— Montenegro und die Montenegriner. Leipzig, 1877.

Jackson, T. G. Dalmatia, the Quarnero and Istria. Vol. III. Oxford, 1887.

Lenormant, F. Turcs et Monténégrins. Paris, 1866.

Marmier, X. Lettres sur l'Adriatique et le Monténégro. Paris, 1854.

Maton, E. Histoire du Monténégro ou Tsernogore. Paris, 1881.

Medaković, M. Istorija Crnegore. Semlin, 1850.

Miller, W. The Montenegrin Bicentenary. In the *Gentleman's Magazine*. October, 1896.

—— The Montenegrin Jubilee. In *Macmillan's Magazine*. September, 1901.

Pagliano, E. M. La constitution de la principauté de Monténégro. Extrait de la *Revue du Droit public et de la science politique*. No. 2, 1906. Paris, 1906. [A translation of the constitution.]

Pisani, P. La Dalmatie de 1797 à 1815. Paris, 1893.

Popovitch, Vladimir G. Le Monténégro pendant la Grande Guerre. Paris, 1918.

Sommières, Vialla de. Voyage historique et politique en Monténégro. 2 vols. Paris, 1820.

Stevenson, F. S. A History of Montenegro. London [1912].

Strangford, Viscountess. The Eastern shores of the Adriatic in 1863. London, 1864.

Vaclik, L. C. La souveraineté du Monténégro et les pays serbes adjacentes. Leipzig, 1858.

Wilkinson, Sir J. Gardner. Dalmatia and Montenegro. 2 vols. London, 1848.

Wyon, R., and Prance, G. The Land of the Black Mountain. London, 1903.

IV. ROUMANIA.

Académie Roumaine. Bulletin de la Section Historique. Bucarest, 1913–21.

Aricescu, C. D. Acte justificative la Istoria Revoluţiunli române dela 1828. Craïova, 1874.

Aus dem Leben König Karls von Rumänien. Aufzeichnungen eines Augenzeugen. 4 vols. Stuttgart, 1894–1900.

Bellessort, A. La Roumanie contemporaine. Paris, 1905.

Benger, G. Rumania in 1900. London, 1901 (translation).

Bibesco, G. Histoire d'une frontière. La Roumanie sur la rive droite du Danube. Paris, 1883.

—— Règne de Bibesco. 2 vols. Paris, 1893.

—— Roumanie: d'Adrinople à Balta-Liman (1829–49). Correspondance et documents (1843–56). 2 vols. Paris, 1893–4.

Boteanu, G. Memoriu din resboiul de la 1877–8. Bucureştĭ, 1895.

Bourchier, J. D. The Fate of Roumania. In the *Fortnightly Review*. Dec. 1888.

Colescu, L. Progrès économiques de la Roumanie, réalisés sous le règne de S. M. le Roi Carol I. Bucharest, 1907.

Colson, F. De l'état présent et de l'avenir des principautés de Moldavie et de Valachie. Paris, 1839.

Damé, F. Histoire de la Roumanie contemporaine depuis l'avènement des Princes indigènes jusqu'à nos jours, 1822–1900. Paris, 1900.

Documenti diplomatici. (Libri Verdi.)
1880. Affari di Oriente. Parte IX. Legislatura XIV. Sessione I, N. IV.
Documents diplomatiques. Les événements de la Péninsule Balkanique. L'action de la Roumanie, 20 Septembre 1912—1 Août 1913. Bucureştĭ, 1913.
Eliade, P. De l'influence française sur l'esprit public en Roumanie. Paris, 1898.
—— Histoire de l'esprit public en Roumanie au XIXme siècle. Paris, 1905.
—— La Roumanie au XIXe siècle. II. Les trois Présidents plénipotentiaires (1828-1834). Paris, 1914.
Evans, I. L. The Agrarian Revolution in Roumania. Cambridge, 1924.
Gentz, Ch. de. Dépêches inédites aux Hospodars de Valachie pour servir à l'histoire de la politique européenne (1813-1828) publiées par le Comte Prokesch-Osten fils. 3 vols. Paris, 1876-7.
Hurmuzaki, E. de. Documente privitoare la Istoria Românilor. Vols. VII, 480-1; X, XIII. Sup. I, vols. IV, 1-291; 310-end; V, VI. Bucuresci, 1876-1909.
Jorga, N. Documente privitoare la Familia Callimachi. 2 vols. Bucureştĭ, 1902-3.
—— Geschichte des rumänischen Volkes. Vol. II. Gotha, 1905.
—— Breve storia dei Rumeni. Bucarest, 1911.
—— Histoire des Roumains de Transylvanie et de Hongrie. 2 vols. Bucarest, 1915-16.
—— Histoire des Roumains et de leur Civilisation. Paris, 1920.
Kennard, Lady. A Roumanian Diary: 1915, 1916, 1917. London, 1917.
Kogălniceanu, V. M. Acte şi documente din correspondenţa diplomatică a lui Mihail Kogălniceanu, 1877-8. Bucureştĭ, 1893.
Livre vert roumain. La question du Danube. Bucarest, 1881.
Österreichisch-ungarisches Rotbuch. Diplomatische Aktenstücke betreffend die Beziehungen Österreich-Ungarns zu Rumänien in der Zeit vom 22 Juli 1914 bis 27 August 1916. Wien, 1916.
Petrescu, G., Sturdza, D. A., Sturdza, D. C., Colescu-Vartic, C., şi Skupiewski, J. J. Acte şi documente relative la Istoria Renascerei Romaniei. 9 vols. Bucuresci, 1889-1901.
Roumanian Academy. Trei-Deçi de Ani de Domnie aĭ Regului Carol I, 1866-1896. 2 vols. Bucureştĭ, 1897.

Samuelson, J. Roumania past and present. London, 1882.

Seton-Watson, R. W. Roumania and the Great War. London, 1915.

Sincerus, E. Les Juifs en Roumanie depuis le traité de Berlin jusqu'à ce jour. Londres, 1901.

Sturdza, D. A. Charles Ier, Roi de Roumanie; Chronique, Actes, Documents [1866–77]. 2 vols. Bucarest, 1899–1904.

Ubicini, A. La question des Principautés devant l'Europe. Paris, 1858.

Whitman, S. Reminiscences of the King of Roumania. London and New York, 1899.

Wilkinson, W. An account of the Principalities of Wallachia and Moldavia. London, 1820.

Witte, Baron J. de. Quinze ans d'histoire, 1866–81. Paris, 1905.

Xénopol, A. D. Histoire des Roumains de la Dacie Trajane. Vol. II. Paris, 1896.

Zallony, M. Essai sur les Phanariotes. Marseille, 1824.

V. SERVIA.

Barby, H. Les victoires serbes. 7e éd. Paris, 1913.

—— La guerre serbo-bulgare. Brégalnitsa. 5e éd. Paris, 1914.

—— La guerre mondiale. Avec l'armée serbe. Paris, 1915.

—— L'Épopée Serbe. 8e éd. Paris, 1916.

Boskovich, S. La Mission de Serbie dans la question d'Orient. Florence, 1887.

Coquelle, P. Le Royaume de Serbie. Paris, 1894.

Cunibert, B. S. Essai historique sur les révolutions et l'indépendance de la Serbie depuis 1804 jusqu'à 1850. 2 vols. Leipzig, 1855.

Cuniberti, F. La Serbia e la Dinastia degli Obrenovich (1804–1893). Torino, 1893.

Denton, The Rev. W. Servia and the Servians. London, 1862.

Documenti diplomatici. (Libri Verdi.)
  1880. Affari di Oriente. Parti VI*a*, VIII. Legislatura XIV. Sessione I, N. IV.

Durham, M. E. Through the Lands of the Serb. London, 1904.

—— The Serajevo Crime. London, 1925.

État-Major général de l'armée serbe. Guerre de la Serbie contre la Turquie, 1877-78. Paris, 1879 (translation).

Georgević, V. Das Ende der Obrenovitch: Beiträge zur Geschichte Serbiens, 1897–1900. Leipzig, 1905.

Gopčević, Sp. Serbien und die Serben. Leipzig, 1888.

Gordon-Smith, G. Through the Serbian campaign. London, 1916.

Graham, W. New Governments of Central Europe. New York, 1924. [Pp. 335–95, 404, 630–51 concern Jugoslavia.]

Gubernatis, Cte A. de. La Serbie et les Serbes. Florence, 1897.

Hogge, J. La Serbie de nos jours. Bruxelles, 1900.

Kállay, B. von. Geschichte der Serben. Aus dem ungarischen von J. H. Schwicker. Budapest, Wien u. Leipzig, 1878.

—— Die Geschichte des serbischen Aufstandes: 1807–10. Übersetzt von S. Beigel. Wien, 1910.

Kanitz, F. Das Königreich Serbien und das Serbenvolk von der Römerzeit bis zur Gegenwart. Leipzig, 1904.

Kutschbach, A. Die Serben im Balkankrieg 1912–13 und im Kriege gegen die Bulgaren. Stuttgart, 1913.

Lascaris, S. Th. La première alliance entre la Grèce et la Serbie. In *Le Monde Slave*, 1926, III, No. 9.

Lazarovich-Hrebelianovich, Prince and Princess. The Servian People: their past glory and their destiny. 2 vols. London, 1911.

Le Livre Bleu Serbe. In Pages d'Histoire—1914. Paris and Nancy, 1914.

Mallat, J. La Serbie contemporaine. 2 vols. Paris, 1902.

Mijatovich, Chedo. A Royal Tragedy. London, 1906.

—— Servia and the Servians. London, 1908.

—— The Memoirs of a Balkan Diplomatist. London, 1917.

Mijatovich, E. L. The History of Modern Servia. London, 1872.

Mousset, A. Le Royaume Serbe Croate Slovène. Paris, 1926.

Note adressée par le Gouvernement Royal de Serbie...sur les violations du droit des gens.... Paris, 1916.

Paton, A. A. Servia, the Youngest Member of the European Family; or, a Residence in Belgrade in 1843 and 1844. London, 1845.

Pearson, E. M., and McLaughlin, L. E. Service in Servia under the Red Cross. London, 1877.

Ranke, L. von. Serbien und die Türkei im neunzehnten Jahrhundert. Leipzig, 1879.

Ratchich, V. Le Royaume de Serbie: étude d'histoire diplomatique. Paris, 1901.

Reinach, J. La Serbie et le Monténégro. Paris, 1876.

Ristich, J. Diplomatska Istorija Srbije, 1875–78. 2 vols. Beograd 1896–8.

Salusbury, P. H. B. Two Months with Tchernaieff in Servia. London, 1877.

Seton-Watson, R. W. Serajevo. London, 1926.

Stead, A. (Editor). Servia by the Servians. London, 1909.

Sydačkoff, Bressnitz von. Die Geschichte Serbiens vom Jahre 1868 bis auf den heutigen Tag unter den Königen Milan und Alexander. Berlin and Leipzig, 1895–6.

—— Das Ende der Dynastie Obrenović. Leipzig, 1900.

Taillandier, Saint-René. Kara Georges et Milosch; La Serbie au xixe siècle. Paris, 1875.

Temperley, H. W. V. History of Serbia. London, 1917.

Vivian, H. Servia, the Poor Man's Paradise. London, 1897.

—— The Servian Tragedy. London, 1904.

Yakschitch, Gr. L'Europe et la Résurrection de la Serbie (1804–1834). 2e éd. Paris, 1917.

VI. TURKEY (AND THE LEVANT IN GENERAL).

Abbott, G. F. The tale of a tour in Macedonia. London, 1903.

—— Turkey in transition. London, 1909.

Albin, P. Les grands traités politiques. Recueil des principaux textes diplomatiques depuis 1815 jusqu'à nos jours. Paris, 1911.

Amadori-Virgilj, G. La Questione Rumeliota et la Politica Italiana. Vol. I. Bitonto, 1908.

Anonymous [Bourchier, J. D.]. The Balkan League. In the *Times* of June 4, 5, 6, 11, 13, 16, 1913.

—— The Second Balkan War. *Ibid.* October 23, Nov. 13, 25, Dec. 9, 1913.

—— The Final Settlement in the Balkans. *Quarterly Review.* Oct. 1917.

—— The Four Treaties of Bucarest. *Ibid.* July, 1918.

Armstrong, H. F. The New Balkans. New York and London, 1926.

Ashmead-Bartlett, E., in collaboration with Ashmead-Bartlett, S. With the Turks in Thrace. London, 1913.

Avril, Baron A. d'. Négociations relatives au traité de Berlin et aux arrangements qui ont suivi. Paris, 1887.

Baker, Capt. B. Granville. The Passing of the Turkish Empire in Europe. London, 1913.

Baker Pasha, Lt-Gen. V. The war in Bulgaria. London, 1879.

Barbarich, E. Albania. Monografia. Roma, 1905.

Baring, M. Letters from the Near East. London, 1913.

Basmadjan, K. J. Histoire moderne des Arméniens (1375–1916). Nouvelle éd. Paris, 1922.

Beaman, A. H. Twenty years in the Near East. London, 1898.

Bell, H. T. Montague. The Near East Year Book and Who's Who. 1927. London, 1927.

Bérard, V. La Turquie et l'Hellénisme contemporain. 6ᵉ éd. Paris, 1911.

—— La Politique du Sultan. 4ᵉ éd. Paris, 1900.

—— La Macédoine. 2ᵉ éd. Paris, 1900.

—— Pro Macedonia. Paris, 1904.

—— Le Sultan, l'Islam et les Puissances. Paris, 1907.

—— La Révolution turque. Paris, 1909.

—— La Mort de Stamboul. Paris, 1913.

Berri, G. L'Assedio di Scutari: sei mesi dentro la città assediata. Milano, 1913.

Bliss, E. M. Turkey and the Armenian Atrocities. London, 1896.

Bourchier, J. D. The Fate of Macedonia. *International Review*. July, 1919.

Brailsford, H. N. Macedonia: its races and their future. London, 1906.

Brancoff, D. M. La Macédoine et sa population chrétienne. Paris, 1905.

Broughton, Lord (Hobhouse, J. C.). A journey through Albania and other provinces of Turkey in Europe and Asia. 2 vols. Ed. 2. 1855.

Bryce, J. Transcaucasia, with supplement on the Armenian question. London, 1896.

Buxton, C. R. Turkey in Revolution. London, 1909.

Cadalvène, E. de, et Barrault, E. Histoire de la guerre de Méhémed-Ali contre la Porte Ottomane, en Syrie et en Asie-Mineure (1831–3). Paris, 1837.

—— Deux années de l'histoire d'Orient, 1839–40. Paris, 1840.

Cecil, Lady Gwendolen. Life of Robert Marquis of Salisbury. Vol. II. (1868–1880). London, 1921.

Chesney, F. R. The Russo-Turkish campaigns of 1828–9. London, 1854.

Chlumecky, L. von. Oesterreich-Ungarn und Italien. Das west-balkanische Problem und Italiens Kampf um die Vorherrschaft in der Adria. Leipzig, 1907.

Choublier, M. La question d'Orient depuis le traité de Berlin. Paris, 1897.

Churchill, Col. C. H. Mount Lebanon : a ten years' residence from 1842 to 1852. 3 vols. London, 1853. Ed. 2. 4 vols. London, 1862.

Cocks, F. Seymour. The Secret Treaties and Understandings. 2nd ed. London, 1918.

Consul's Daughter and Wife, A. [Lady Blunt.] The people of Turkey. 2 vols. London, 1878.

Daily News Correspondence of the war of 1877–78. London, 1878.

Documenti diplomatici. (Libri Verdi.)

1871. Trattato di Londra del 13 marzo 1871 e protocolli delle conferenze. Legislatura XI. Sessione 2, N. 112.

1877. Affari di Oriente. Legislatura XIII. Sessione 1, N. XII.

1877. Protocollo di Londra del 31 marzo 1877. Legislatura XIII. Sessione 1, N. XII *bis*.

1878. Affari di Oriente. Legislatura XIII. Sessione 2, N. X.

1878. Trattato di Berlino e protocollo del Congresso di Berlino. Legislatura XI. Sessione 2, N. XXII.

1880. Affari di Oriente. Parti I–III. Legislatura XIV. Sessione I, N. IV.

1883. Questione Danubiana. Legislatura XV. Sessione I.

1906. Macedonia. Legislatura XXII. Sessione 2, N. XXVII.

Diplomatische Aktenstücke betreffend die Ereignisse am Balkan. 13 August 1912 bis 6 November 1913. Wien, 1914.

Driault, E. La question d'Orient depuis ses origines jusqu'à la paix de Sèvres (1920). 8e éd. Paris, 1921.

Durham, M. E. The Burden of the Balkans. London, 1905.

—— High Albania. London, 1909.

—— The Struggle for Scutari (Turk, Slav, and Albanian). London, 1914.

—— Twenty Years of Balkan Tangle. London, 1920.

Earle, E. M. Turkey, the Great Powers, and the Bagdad Railway : A Study in Imperialism. New York, 1924.

Edwards, H. S. Sir W. White, Ambassador at Constantinople, 1885–91. London, 1892.

Eliot, Sir C. N. E. ("Odysseus"). Turkey in Europe. Ed. 2. London, 1908.

Engelhardt, E. La Turquie et le Tanzimat, ou Histoire de Réformes dans l'Empire Ottoman depuis 1826 jusqu'à nos jours. Paris, 1882.

Eton, W. Survey of the Turkish Empire. London, 1801.

Freeman, E. A. The Ottoman Power in Europe. London, 1877.

Galanti, A. L'Albania. Roma, 1901.

Garnett, L. M. J. The Turkish People. London, 1909.

Gladstone, W. E. The Bulgarian Horrors and the Question of the East. London, 1876.

—— Lessons in Massacre. London, 1877.

—— The Armenian Question. London, 1895.

Gopčević, Sp. Oberalbanien und seine Liga. Leipzig, 1881.

—— Makedonien und Alt-Serbien. Wien, 1889.

Greene, F. V. The Campaign in Bulgaria, 1877–1878. London, 1903.

Grogan, Lady. The Life of J. D. Bourchier. London, 1926.

Halid, Halil. The Diary of a Turk. London, 1903.

Hecquard, C. La Turquie sous Abdul-Hamid II. Exposé fidèle de la gérance d'un Empire pendant un quart de siècle (31ᵉ août 1876–1er septembre 1900). Bruxelles, 1901.

Hecquard, H. Histoire et description de la haute Albanie. Paris (no date). [1859.]

Herbert, W. V. The Defence of Plevna, 1877. London, 1895.

—— The Chronicles of a Virgin Fortress. London, 1896.

Hertslet, Sir Edward, K.C.B. The Map of Europe by Treaty [1814–91]. 4 vols. London, 1875–91.

Holland, T. E. The European Concert in the Eastern Question. Oxford, 1885.

Horton, G. The Blight of Asia. Indianapolis, 1926.

Hughes, Rev. T. S. Travels in Greece and Albania. 2 vols. Ed. 2. London, 1830.

James, Major L. With the Conquered Turk. The Story of a Latter-Day Adventurer. London, 1913.

Juchereau de Saint-Denys, A. Révolutions de Constantinople. 2 vols. Paris, 1814.

Kingslake, A. W. The Invasion of the Crimea. 8 vols. London, 1863–87.

Keppel, Hon. G. Narrative of a journey across the Balcan. 2 vols. London, 1831.

Lane-Poole, S. Life of Lord Stratford de Redcliffe. 2 vols. London, 1888.

La Jonquière, Vte A. de. Histoire de l'Empire Ottoman. Éd. rev. 2 vols. Paris, 1914.

Lavaleye, É. de. La Péninsule des Balkans. 2 vols. Bruxelles, 1886.

Leake, W. M. Travels in Northern Greece. Vol. I. London, 1835.

Leger, L. La Save, le Danube, et le Balkan. 2ᵉ éd. Paris, 1889.

—— Russes et Slaves. 2 vols. Paris, 1890–6.

Loiseau, C. Le Balkan slave et la crise autrichienne. Paris, 1898.

—— L'Équilibre adriatique: l'Italie et la question d'Orient. Paris, 1901.

Luke, H. C. Cyprus under the Turks, 1571–1878. Oxford, 1921.

Lyde, L. W., and Mockler-Ferryman, A. F. A military Geography of the Balkan peninsula. London, 1905.

Lynch, H. F. B. Armenia: Travels and Studies. 2 vols. London, 1901.

Mackenzie, G. M., and Irby, A. P. Travels in the Slavonic provinces of Turkey-in-Europe. 2 vols. Ed. 3. London, 1877.

Marriott, J. A. R. A History of the Eastern Question from the Advent of the Ottomans to the Outbreak of the European War. A Study in European Diplomacy. London, 1917.

—— The Eastern Question: An Historical Study. Ed. 3. Oxford, 1924.

Maurice, Major F. The Russo-Turkish war, 1877. London, 1905.

Mears, E. G. Modern Turkey: A Politico-economic Interpretation. New York, 1924.

Midhat Bey, Ali Haydar. The Life of Midhat Pasha. London, 1903.

Miller, W. The Balkans. Ed. 3. With new chapter (1896–1922). London, 1922.

—— Travels and Politics in the Near East. London, 1898.

—— Three Years of the Eastern Question [1898–1901]. In the *Gentleman's Magazine* for November, 1901.

—— The Return of the Turks. In *The Quarterly Review*. October, 1924.

Minchin, J. G. C. The growth of freedom in the Balkan peninsula. London, 1886.

Moltke, H. C. B. von. Briefe über Zustände und Begebenheiten der Türkei aus den Jahren 1835 bis 1839. 5ᵗᵉ Auflage. Berlin, 1891.

—— Der russisch-türkische Feldzug in der europäischen Türkei, 1828 und 1829. 2ᵗᵉ Auflage. Berlin, 1877.

Morgenthau, H. Secrets of the Bosphorus. London (no date). [1918.]

Mouriez, P. Histoire de Méhémet-Ali, Vice-Roi d'Égypte. 4 vols. Paris, 1857.

Napier, Sir C. The War in Syria. London, 1842.

Ohsson, I. M. d'. Tableau général de l'Empire Ottoman. 8 vols. Paris, 1788–1824.

Pavich v. Pfauenthal, A. Beiträge zur Geschichte der Republik Poljica bei Spalato. In *Wissenschaftliche Mittheilungen aus Bosnien und der Hercegovina*, x, 156–344. Wien, 1907.

Pears, Sir E. Turkey and its people. London, 1911.

Percy, Earl (Warkworth, Lord). Notes from a diary in Asiatic Turkey. London, 1898.

——— Highlands of Asiatic Turkey. London, 1901.

Pinon, René. L'Europe et l'Empire Ottoman. Paris, 1909.

——— L'Europe et la Jeune Turquie. Paris, 1911.

Poujade, E. Le Liban et la Syrie, 1845–1860. Paris, 1860.

Rankin, Lt-Colonel R. The Inner History of the Balkan War. London, 1914.

Ringhoffer, K. Ein Dezennium preussischer Orientpolitik zur Zeit des Zaren Nikolaus (1821–1830). Berlin, 1897.

Robert, C. Les Slaves de Turquie. 2 vols. Paris, 1864.

Rodkey, F. S. The Turco-Egyptian Question in the Relations of England, France and Russia, 1832–1841. Urbana, 1923.

Roth, K. Geschichte der christlichen Balkanstaaten. Leipzig, 1907.

San Giuliano, A. Di. Lettere dall' Albania. Roma, 1903. German tr. by D. Schulz and W. Wichmann. Leipzig, 1913.

Schlechta-Wssehrd, O. von. Die Revolutionen in Constantinopel in den Jahren 1807 und 1808. Wien, 1882.

Seton-Watson, R. W. The Rise of Nationality in the Balkans. London, 1917.

Stéphanopoli, J. Z. Les Îles de l'Égée. Leurs privilèges. Athènes, 1912.

Thornton, T. The present state of Turkey. 2 vols. London, 1809.

Thouvenel, L. Trois années de la Question d'Orient, 1856–9. Paris, 1897.

Toynbee, A. J. The Western Question in Greece and Turkey. London, 1922.

——— Turkey. London, 1926.

Tsakalakis, A. Der Dodekanes, eine völkerrechtliche Untersuchung. Heidelberg, 1926.

Turkey, No. 1, 1923. Lausanne Conference on Near Eastern Affairs, 1922–1923. London, 1923.

Tyler, M. W. The European Powers and the Near East, 1875–1908. Minneapolis, 1925.

Urquhart, D. The Lebanon: Mount Souria, a history and diary. London, 1860.

Villari, L. (Editor). The Balkan question: the present condition of the Balkans. London, 1904.

—— The Macedonian Campaign: a History of the Salonica Expedition (1915–1918). London, 1922.

Washburn, G. Fifty years in Constantinople. Boston, 1909.

Woods, H. C. The Danger Zone of Europe. London, 1911. French tr. with additions: La Turquie et ses voisins. Paris (no date).

Zervos, Sk. La Question du Dodécanèse et ses documents diplomatiques. Athènes, 1926.

Zinkeisen, W. Geschichte des osmanischen Reiches in Europa. Vol. VII. Hamburg, 1863.

VII. FORMER AUTONOMOUS, OCCUPIED OR TRIBUTARY TERRITORIES.

(*a*) CRETE (before the Union).

Anonymous. La vérité sur les événements de Candie. Paris, 1858.

Ballot, J. Histoire de l'Insurrection Crétoise. Paris, 1868.

Bérard, V. Les Affaires de Crète. 2ᵉ éd. Paris, 1900.

Bourchier, J. D. The Stronghold of the Sphakiotes. In *Fortnightly Review*. August, 1890.

Documenti diplomatici. (Libri Verdi.)
    1889. Candia. Legislatura XVI. Sessione 4, N. XVII.
    1897. Creta. Conflitto Turco-ellenico. Legislatura XX. Sessione 1, N. XIX.
    1898. Creta. Legislatura XX. Sessione 2, N. X.
    1911. Creta. Legislatura XXIII. Sessione 1, N. XLII.

Freese, J. H. A short popular history of Crete. London, 1897.

Papantonákes, S. A. Κρητικά. Ἐν Χανίοις, 1901.

Papantonákes, G. Ἡ διπλωματικὴ Ἱστορία τῆς κρητικῆς Ἐπαναστάσεως τοῦ 1866. Ἐν Ἀθήναις, 1926.

Pashley, R. Travels in Crete. 2 vols. London, 1837.

Psiláki, B. Ἱστορία τῆς Κρήτης, ἀπὸ τῆς ἀπωτάτης ἀρχαιότητος μέχρι τῶν καθ' ἡμᾶς χρόνων. Τόμ. Γ'. Ἐν Χανίοις, 1901–10.

Skinner, H. Roughing it in Crete. London, 1867.

Spratt, Captain T. A. B. Travels and Researches in Crete. 2 vols. London, 1865.

Stavrákes, N. Στατιστικὴ τοῦ πληθυσμοῦ τῆς Κρήτης. Ἀθήνησι, 1890.

Stillman, W. J. The Cretan Insurrection of 1866-7-8. New York, 1874.

Wagner, R. Der kretische Aufstand, 1866–67. Bern, 1908.

(*b*) CYPRUS (since 1878).

Luke, H. C., and Jardine, D. J. The handbook of Cyprus. London, 1920.

Orr, C. W. J. Cyprus under British Rule. London, 1918.

(*c*) SAMOS (before the Union).

Blancard, T. Les Mavroyéni. Histoire d'Orient. Vol. II, 523–621. Paris, 1909.

Máles, Th. M. Ἡ Σάμος ὑπὸ τὸ αὐτόνομον πολίτευμα. Ἐν Σάμῳ, 1912. Σαμιακὴ νομοθεσία. Ἐν Σάμῳ, 1875.

Stamatiádes, E. I. Ἐπετηρὶς τῆς Ἡγεμονίας Σάμου. Ἐν Σάμῳ. Annual.

—— Σαμιακά, ἤτοι ἱστορία τῆς νήσου Σάμου ἀπὸ τῶν παναρχαίων χρόνων μέχρι τῶν καθ' ἡμᾶς. Τόμ. Ε'. Ἐν Σάμῳ. 1881–91.

(*d*) BOSNIA AND THE HERZEGOVINA (1875–1908).

Anonymous. Der Aufstand in der Hercegovina und Süd-Bosnien 1881–2. Wien, 1883.

Barre, A. La Bosnie-Herzégovine. (Administration autrichienne de 1878 à 1903.) Paris, 1904.

Evans, A. J. Through Bosnia and the Herzegovina on foot. London, 1876.

—— Illyrian Letters. London, 1878.

Haardt, V. von. Die Occupation Bosniens und der Herzegovina. Wien, 1878.

Seton-Watson, R. W. The Southern Slav Question and the Habsburg Monarchy. London, 1911.

Spalaïkovitch, M. J. La Bosnie et l'Herzégovine. Étude d'histoire diplomatique et de droit international. Paris, 1899.

Stillman, W. J. Herzegovina and the late Uprising. London, 1877.

Thomson, H. C. The outgoing Turk. London, 1897.

VIII. ALBANIA (SINCE ITS INDEPENDENCE).

Bourcart, J. L'Albanie et les Albanais. Paris, 1921.

Chekrezi, C. A. Albania Past and Present. New York, 1919.

Eden, M. F. Albania: its discontents and their origin. London [no date].

Godart, J. L'Albanie en 1921. Paris, 1922.

Lane, Rose Wilder. The Peaks of Shala. London, 1924.

Miller, W. Albania and her Protectress. In *Foreign Affairs*. April, 1927.

Peacock, W. Albania, the Foundling State of Europe. London, 1914.

Skendo Lumo. Albanie. (*Revue de Genève*, Sept., 1921.)

Stickney, E. Pierpont. Southern Albania or Northern Epirus in European International Affairs, 1912–1923. California: Stanford University, 1926.

Sulliotti, A. Italo. In Albania. Sei Mesi di Regno. Milano, 1914.

Vaina de Pava, E. La nazione albanese. 2ª ed. Catania, 1917.

Woods, H. C. The Situation in Albania. Albania—yesterday and to-morrow (*Fortnightly Review*, March, 1914; August, 1927); and Albania and the Albanians (*Geographical Review*, April, 1918).

INDEX

Aali Pasha, 240, 314, 345
Abd el-Kâder, 301–2
Abdul Aziz, 303, 368
Abdul Hamid II, succeeds to the
  throne, 368; dissolves parliament,
  378; his treatment of the Ar-
  menians, 428–31; his Macedonian
  policy, 445; restores the constitu-
  tion, 474–5; his deposition, 480–2,
  486
Abdul Mejid, proclaims equality,
  141, 149, 153, 225; communicates
  his firman to the Powers, 237,
  298; dies, 303, 340
Abeih, 154
Abel, Councillor von, 156, 160–1
Aberdeen, Lord, Eastern policy of,
  104, 106, 108, 139, 171, 175, 203,
  207, 211, 232
Aboulabad, 73
Acre, 145–6, 150
Ada Kaleh, 50, 255
Adalbert, Prince of Bavaria, 262
Adam, Sir Frederick, 92, 122–4,
  183, 291
Adana, 146–7, 150; massacre at,
  431, 480–1
Adosídes, 471
Adrianople, Peace of, 106, 130–1,
  133, 209–10, 339, 371; taken by
  the Russians, 129, 376–7; vilâyet
  of, 448; besieged by the Bulgarians,
  504–5, 506, 511; retaken by the
  Turks, 515, 517, 528
Aehrenthal, Baron, 458
Aigina, 89, 96, 99–100, 109, 113,
  118
Ainali-Kavak, Convention of, 8, 30
Aînos, 130, 508, 513, 517
Aitolía, 77, 107
Aivali, 74
Akarnanía, 77, 82, 107, 111, 163,
  178, 267, 288
Akhaltsykh, 128, 130

Akkerman, Convention of, 127–8,
  131, 133
Akrotéri, 434, 489
Alaman, Bridge of, 72
Albania, Albanians, 4, 19, 23, 39,
  85, 125, 142, 146, 240–1, 250,
  259–60, 385, 391, 394, 396–7,
  403–7, 443–6, 481–2, 495–6, 498,
  504, 508–9, 511, 518–21, 526,
  529, 536, 543–4, 548, 559–62
Aleksinatz, 134, 369
Alexander I, Tsar of Russia, 39,
  66–7, 75
Alexander II, Tsar of Russia, 233–6,
  271, 374–5, 378
Alexander III, Tsar of Russia, 416,
  423, 450–1
Alexander, Prince of Bulgaria, 412–
  23
Alexander, King of Servia, 403,
  453–7
Alexander Karageorgevich, Prince
  of Servia, 138–9, 195–6, 217,
  249–52, 334, 339, 456
Alexander I, Karageorgevich, King
  of the Serbs, Croats and Slovenes,
  483, 536, 558
Alexander, King of the Hellenes,
  535–6, 543
Alexandria, 149
Alfred, Prince. See Edinburgh,
  Duke of
Algeria, 16, 145
Ali Pasha of Joánnina, 15, 19, 24,
  29, 43, 62–4, 71, 78–9
Ali Pasha of Zvornik, 139
Allenby, General, 538
Alma, The, 227–8
Amalia, Queen of Greece, 164, 170,
  219–24, 242, 262, 264, 267
Ambelákia, 29
Ambrakian gulf, 409
Anagnostópoulos, 65
Anapa, 128, 130

Anatolikón, 86, 92, 98
Anchialós, 447
Andrássy, Count, 362-3, 386, 388
Andrew, Prince, 547
Andrítsaina, 65
Andros, 183
Angora, 542, 555-6
Antipaxo, 4
Antivari, 218, 241, 256, 259-60; occupied by Montenegro, 376; ceded to Montenegro, 383, 391-2; Archbishop of, 461; railway to, 463; freedom of, 484, 507
Apokórona, 310
Aprilov, 340
Arab Tabia, 215, 399
Ardahan, 128, 384, 395
Areia, 119
Argos, 77, 81, 86, 104, 108, 114, 118, 121, 265
Argyrókastron, 64, 505, 518-9, 537
Arkádion, Monastery of, 311-2, 439
Armansperg, Count von, 156-7, 160-4
Armenians, 384, 395-6; massacres of, 427-31, 476, 479-81, 538; Armenian Republic, 541, 556
Arta, 4, 65, 82, 158, 220; its cession, to Greece, 407, 409
Asaki, George, 126
Askýphon, 317
Aspropotamós, The, 407
Asquith, Mr H. H., 504
Astros, 83, 114, 120
Astypálaia, 469, 510
Athens, under the Turks, 29-30; taken by the Greeks, 72, 80-1, 91, 94-5, 105; made the capital, 161-3; revolution of 1843 at, 169-72, 176-7, 179-81, 184; during Crimean war, 219-24, 260, 262; revolution of 1862 at, 267-8, 270-3, 275-7, 281, 315, 432, 434, 467, 490, 534
Athos, Mt, 29, 73, 221, 320, 503, 509, 542, 556
Austria, in Dalmatia, 32, 34, 36-7; her Montenegrin policy, 198-9, 240, 391-2, 479, 484, 530; her Servian policy, 50-1, 136, 249, 457-8, 479, 504, 509, 517, 521-4, 528, 558; her Turkish Policy, 9-12, 15, 198-9, 209, 211-4, 216, 233-5, 243, 245, 248, 288, 386, 390-1, 402-3, 444-8
Avakumovich, M., 456
Azov, 5-8, 234

Baghdad, 538
Balaclava, 229-30, 233
Bálbes, Demétrios, 420
Bálbes, Z., 273
Balfour, Mr A. J., 542
Ballard, Lieut., 215
Balsh, Theodore, 244
Balta Liman, Convention of, 194, 244
Baltatzês, G., 547
Baltchik, 513, 516
Banat, The, 10, 525, 532, 544
Banjaluka, 140
Banjani, 370, 391
Baphé, 311
Baring, Mr, 365-6
Barton, Sir Edward, 13
Batak, 365-7
Bathurst, Lord, 44
Battenberg, Prince Francis Joseph of, 421, 460
Batûm, 239, 384-5, 395-6
Bayazid, 128, 130, 384, 395
Beaconsfield, Lord (Disraeli, Benjamin), Eastern policy of, 246, 287, 370, 377, 387, 395-6, 406, 468
Beaufort d'Hautpoul, General, 302
Beirût, 150, 154, 300-2, 497
Belashitza, Mts, 516
Belgrade, Peace of, 3, 7, 17; under the Turks, 46-8; its garrison massacred, 52, 54-7, 134-5, 137-8, 249-52; bombardment of, 253-5; its fortress evacuated by the Turks, 303, 332-4, 336, 417-8; royal tragedy at, 454-6, 461; bombarded and occupied by the Austrians, 523; recovered, 540
Belimarkovich, General, 376, 453
Bellova, 449
Belogradtchik, 333, 515

Beltchev, 449
Benderev, Capt., 421
Benizélos, John, 30
"Benkovski," 365
Berane, 498, 501
Berat, 64
Berchtold, Count, 498
Berlin, Conference of (1880), 404, 407–8, 416
Berlin, Congress and treaty of, 387–401, 428, 464–5, 484, 501
Berlin Memorandum, The, 363
Berovich, George, 433, 471
Besika Bay, 209, 368, 370, 378
Bessarabia, 39, 42–3, 236, 239, 373, 383–4, 392, 525, 532, 539, 544, 557
Beust, Count von, 332
Bib Doda, Prenk, Mirdite chief (1854), 219
Bib Doda, Prenk, Mirdite chief in 1908, 404, 406
Bibescu, George, 190–4, 243, 246–8, 328
Bijelopavlich, 142, 218
Bijelopolje, 391, 501
Bilek, 376, 383
Bismarck, Eastern policy of, 291, 317, 325–6, 329–30, 386, 388, 401, 408, 428, 465
Bitlis, 429
Black Sea, The, 7–8, 14, 127, 130, 234, 236, 238–9, 347
Blaznavatz, Col., 335
Blunt, Consul, 220
Bogomiles, 21
Bogoshich, M., 459
Bojana, The, 372, 405
Boletin, Isa, 495
Bonaparte. See Napoleon I.
Boris III, Tsar of the Bulgarians, 450–1, 539, 558
Bosdari, Count, 527
Bosnia, partly Austrian, 10–1; Turkish, 17, 21–2; at Tilsit, 39; rises against the Turks, 139–42, 144, 239, 333, 359; insurrection in, 362, 368, 370, 372, 377, 384, 386; Austrian occupation of, 390, 396–7, 401–2; Austrian annexa-

tion of, 441–2, 477–9; 482–5, 521, 523, 545
Bosphorus, The, 130, 146–7, 151, 238, 347
Bótzares, Márko, 65, 82, 85
Bótzares, Nótes, 92
Bouboulína, 73
Boúlgares, Demétrios, 242, 267, 273, 310, 316, 356–7, 379
Boúlgares, George, 28
Boúlgaris, Eugénios, 24
Boúrbaki, Col., 94–5
Bourchier, James D., 494, 500
Bourgas, 129, 421, 424, 449
Bourniâs, 79
Boûrzi, 112
Bowen, Sir George, 278
Braïla, 128, 400
Brailas, Sir Peter, 283
Brătianu, John, 320, 323, 325–7, 373, 388, 401, 464–5
Brătianu, M. J. C., 533
Brda, The, 143, 218, 259
Bregalnitza, 513
Brialmont, General, 465
Brod, 362
Brown, Sir George, 225–6
Brûsa, 146
Bucharest, 5, 8, 20, 27; treaty of (1812), 42–3, 54, 56, 65, 67–8, 133, 192, 194, 216, 237, 247–8, 250, 321, 323–4, 327, 330, 344, 346, 401; treaty of (1886), 418, 444, 465; treaty of (1913), 515–7, 529; taken by the Germans, 533; treaty of (1918), 539
Buchon, J. A., 172
Budua, 530
Bukovina, The, 10, 42, 331, 525, 532–3, 544
Bulair, 506, 508
Bulganak, The, 227
Bulgaria, Bulgarians, 20–1, 39, 124, 204, 217, 316; history of, before the Exarchate, 338–45; the Exarchate, 345–7; "Bulgarian Atrocities," 364–7; attitude during Russo-Turkish war, 360–70, 372, 374; at San Stefano, 382, 385–6; at Berlin, 388–9, 392, 396, 399–

400; history since Berlin treaty, 411–26; in Macedonia, 441–8; history under Prince Ferdinand, 448–52; independence of, 477–8, 485; rapprochement with Greece, 494; in the Balkan League, 498–504, 506; in the Second Balkan war, 510–8; in the European war, 528–9, 531–2, 539–41; later, 552–3, 558–9

Bulwer, Sir Henry, 250–1, 255
Buol, Count, 212–3
Burgoyne, Sir John, 228–9
Burney, Admiral, 507–8
Butler, Capt., 215
Butrinto, 4
Byron, Lord, 19, 85–8, 552

Callimachi, Alexander, 470
Callimachi, Charles, 69, 75, 126
Campbell, Col., 167
Campbell, Lieut.-General James, 41
Campbell, Sir Colin, 230
Campo-Formio, Treaty of, 4, 12
Candia, besieged by Turks, 3, 15, 74, 167, 438, 440
Canea, 73–4, 167–8, 306, 313, 315, 410, 432–4, 438, 488–9
Canevaro, Admiral, 438–9
Canning, George, 84, 93
Canning, Stratford (Lord Stratford de Redcliffe), 93–4, 114–6, 204–7, 209–10, 217–8, 470
Canrobert, 229, 235
Cantacuzene, Constantine, 194
Cantacuzene, George, 69
Capo d'Istria, Agostino, 104, 113–7, 163, 184
Capo d'Istria, George, 184
Capo d'Istria, John, Count, 44–5, 66; elected President of Greece, 96–7, 99–101, 104, 108–13, 158
Capo d'Istria, Viaro, 100, 109, 117, 159, 184
Carageà, John, 66, 126
Carasso, M., 479
Cardigan, Lord, 229, 231
Carnarvon, Lord, 279, 287, 378
Carol, Prince, 557

Caruso, Count, 189
Castel Lastua, 530
Catargi, Barbe, 319
Catargi, Lascar, 324, 331
Catherine II, Empress of Russia, 7–8, 10, 204, 225–6
Cattaro, occupied by the French, 33; by the Russians, 36–7; taken by the Montenegrins, and ceded to Austria, 37, 40, 51, 241, 257, 463, 530
Cavour, 234–5, 239, 243
Cephalonia, occupied by the French, 4; declares its independence, 40; taken by the British, 41, 58–9, 86, 121–2; insurrection there, 186–9, 278, 280, 286; after the union, 309
Cerigo, occupied by the French, 5; taken by the British, 41, 58, 180, 281, 288
Cernavoda, 393, 463
Cervi, 179–82
Cetinje, 37, 143, 197, 218; taken by the Austrians, 530
Chaïdári, 94
Chálkeia, 469
Chalkidiké, 29
Chalkís, 221, 438
Chams, 548
Charles I, King of Roumania, 323, 325–33, 373–5, 392, 425, 442, 457, 515, 524–5
Chatalja, 503–4, 541
Chatham, Lord, 14
Chehib-Effendi, 154
Cheimárra, 503, 510, 518–9, 526, 537, 559
Chermside, Sir Herbert, 440
Cherso, 544
Chios, 12, 28; massacre of, 79–80, 89, 98, 104, 527, 546
Chloumoûtsi, 102
Chorlu, 130
Christich, Nicholas, 417
Christich, Philip, 332
Church, Sir Richard, 95, 97–8, 101, 104, 108, 158, 351
Circassians, 342, 384, 395, 443
Clarendon, Lord, 209, 235, 241, 244, 308–9, 316, 326, 332, 349, 470

Clement, Metropolitan, 422, 450
Clementi, The, 495
Cobden, 332
Cochrane, Lord, 95–7
Codrington, Admiral, 97–8, 102
Constantine, King of the Hellenes, 436, 491–2, 504, 506, 513–4, 516, 525, 527–8, 531, 533–6, 543, 546, 555
Constantine VI, Œcumenical Patriarch, 552, 556
Constantinople, 38–9, 85, 204; conference of (1881), 408–9; conference of (1885), 416; massacres at, 429–30; treaty of (1897), 437; counter-revolution at, 480–1, 505; treaty of (1913), 517, 541
Constantinovich, Anka, 334
Constantinovich, Catherine, 334
Constantinovich, Mlle Natalie (Princess Mirko of Montenegro), 458
Constanza, 533
Corfù, occupied by the French, 4, 19, 24, 40; surrendered to the British, 41, 58–60, 63, 65, 113, 117, 122–3, 180, 184–5, 188, 258, 278, 280–1; ceded to Greece, 284–92, 308, 494, 509; conference of (1914), 519–20; Serbs at, 529, 531, Pact of, 536; bombarded, 549
Corinth, 78, 82, 86, 161
Cornu, Mme Hortense, 323
Coron, 102
Corti, Count, 388, 404–5
Couza, Prince of Roumania, 247–8, 319–25
Craïova, 319
Crete, becomes Turkish, 1, 12, 15, 17, 21, 39; during War of Independence, 73–4, 82–3, 84, 89, 93, 99, 103–4, 107–8; Egyptian, 116, 150; insurrection of (1841), 166–8, 174–5, 204, 285; insurrection of (1866–9), 306–18, 326, 332, 341, 358; during eastern crisis (1878), 380–2, 384, 394, 397, 408, 410–1, 416; later risings, 431–5, 437–9; autonomous, 439–41, 486, 492, 494–5; united with Greece, 502–3, 509, 516, 534

Crimea, The, 5–6, 8, 10; war in, 299 *sqq.*
Crispi, Francesco, 449
Curzola, 34
Cyclades, 103, 107–8
Cyprus, 75, 239; convention, 395–6, 431, 468–9; annexed by Great Britain, 524; offered to Greece, 528; ceded by Turkey, 542
Cyrenaica, The, 16, 396, 496–7

Dabija, Col., 331
Dalmatia, under the French, 32–7; Italian claims to, 526, 544
Damalá (Troizén), 96, 100
Damascus, 145–6, 301–3
Dandolo, Anthony (Corfiote politician), 285
Dandolo, V. (civil governor of Dalmatia), 33
Danev, Dr, 511, 514
Danglês, General, 534
Danilo, Crown Prince of Montenegro, 458, 460, 507, 530, 544
Danilo, Prince of Montenegro, 197–8, 218–9, 240–1, 256–7
Danilograd, 370, 375
Danube, Commission of the, 236, 239, 393–4, 400; Delta of the, 236, 384, 392
Danubian Principalities, The, 5–6, 8, 10; under the Phanariotes, 16–7, 31, 38, 42; insurrections of 1821 there, 66–9; under native rulers, 125–8; under the Russians, 130–2, 147; during revolution of 1848, 190–5, 202; occupied by Russia, 208–9, 211, 216, 223, 230, 233; at Congress of Paris, 237–8, 240; their union, 243–8. See Moldavia, Wallachia, and Roumania
Daoud Pasha, 304–5
Daphní, 94
Dardanelles, The, entered by French, 3; by British, 38; peace of, 41–2, 130; closing of, 147, 151; entered by British, 210, 215; regulation of, 238, 347; the Italians in, 497; the Greeks off, 503, 505, 525–6, 531

Darinka, Princess, 241, 257-8
Davéles, 242
Dawkins, 119, 157, 161
De Bosset, Lieut.-Col., 62
Dedeagatch, 515, 528, 540, 559
Delegeórges, Epaminóndas, 262-3, 267-8, 310, 356
Deligiánnes, Peter, 316-8
Deligiánnes, Theodore, 318, 380, 388, 394, 410, 416, 419-20, 433-4, 466-7
Deligrad, 54, 369
Délisi, 352
Delladecima, Count, 185
Délvinon, 518
Demakópoulos, 311
Demertzês, M., 553
Demir Hissar, 514
Demir Kapou, 553
Denton, The Rev. W., 253
Derby, Edward Geoffrey Stanley, Earl of, 185, 279, 287
Derby, Edward Henry Stanley, Earl of, 309, 312, 332, 362, 364, 366-7, 377, 380, 387
Dervenáki, 82
Dervent, 362
Detchich, 501
D'Everton, Baron, 186
Diákos, 72
Dibra, 500
Diebich, 128-9, 133, 339
Dimotika, 504, 528, 540
Djakova, 404
Djumaia, 515
Djunis, 369
Dobrudja, The, 214, 384; ceded to Roumania, 392-3, 399-400, 464, 524, 539-40
Dodekánesos, The, 469-70, 473, 495, 497, 526, 547, 549
Dojran, 513
Domokós, 90, 220, 380, 407, 437
Dondukov-Korsakov, Prince, 411
Dósios, 264
Douglas, Sir Howard, 183-5
Doúsmanes, General, 525
Doxâton, 514-5
Draga, Queen of Servia, 454-6
Dragashani, 68-9, 76

Dragoméstre, 5
Dragoúmes, Nicholas, 267
Dragoúmes, Mr Stephen, 308 *n.*; 492-3, 503
Drama, 447-8, 476, 514
Dramali, Pasha, 73, 80-2
Drina, The, 134, 255
Drobniak, 370
Druses, 152-5, 300-5, 495
Duckworth, Admiral, 38
Dufferin, Lord, 303
Duga pass, The, 259, 375, 391
Dulcigno, 261, 376, 383, 391, 405
Durazzo, 504, 511, 518-21, 529, 561
Dusmani, Count, 283

Eastern Roumelia, 306, 389, 396, 414-9, 477, 479
Edgmiatsin, 128
Edhem Pasha, 436
Edinburgh, Duke of, 264, 270-2, 286, 420
Edward VII, 467, 474
Egri Palanka, 500
Egypt, 14, 16, 31, 145, 148-51, 204, 239, 309, 524
Ekrene, 516
Elassôna, 503
Elena, Queen of Italy, 459-60, 507
Eleusís, 99
Eleutherochória, The, 29
Elizabeth, Queen of England, 12
Elizabeth, Queen of Roumania, ("Carmen Sylva"), 329, 400
Elliot, Sir Henry, 265, 272, 286, 367
England, Turkish policy of, 7, 8, 12-5. See Great Britain
Enver Bey, 475-6, 505, 515, 538, 540
Epídauros, Constitution of, 77-8, 83, 88
Epirus, 19, 23, 84, 104, 111, 174-5; insurrection of (1854), 219-20, 266, 271, 285, 288, 310, 316; insurrection of (1878), 380-1, 384, 395; partly ceded to Greece, 407-10, 416; campaign of (1897), 436-7, 465; campaign of (1912-3), 503, 505; question of Northern Epirus, 509, 518-21, 525-6, 531, 537, 543, 548

Erfurt, Meeting at, 41
Erivan, 541
Ernest II, Duke of Saxe-Coburg-Gotha, 272–3
Ernroth, General, 413, 426
Erskine, 348–51
Erzerum, 129–30, 384, 538–9
Essad Pasha, 507–8, 518, 520, 529, 537, 544, 560
Eubœa (Negropont), 17, 103, 107, 109, 111, 178
Eugene, Prince, 9, 11, 401
Eupatoria, 226, 233
Euripus, 261
Eutaxias, M., 554
Evans, Sir Arthur J., 390
Eynard, 178
Eyres, Sir H. C., 560

Fabvier, General, 94–5, 98
Fano, 4
Ferdinand, ex-King-Consort of Portugal, 272
Ferdinand I, King of Roumania, 400, 532, 544, 557
Ferdinand, Tsar of the Bulgarians, 425–6, 446, 449–51, 478, 485, 499, 515, 518, 528, 539
Ferisovich, 464–5
Ferrero, General, 537
Fetislâm, 255
Filov, Major, 415
Finlay, George, 98, 179–81, 312
Fitzroy, Lord Charles, 122
Fiume, 544
Flamburiari, Count 283
Fokshani, 246, 248
Fonblanque, 249
Fortis, A., 483
Foscolo, Ugo, 123
Fox, C. J., 14
France, Policy of, towards Greece, 97, 102, 106–7, 164, 166, 180–1, 222–4, 241–2, 261, 263, 271, 274, 292–3, 299, 306, 309, 312–3, 355, 407–8, 420, 534, 543; towards the Jugoslavs, 536; towards Roumania, 323–6, 329; towards Turkey, 2–5, 15, 31, 38–42, 149, 151–4, 199 *sqq.*, 245–6, 300–3

Franchet d'Esperey, General, 539
Franz Ferdinand, Archduke, 521
Fratti, A., 90, 437
Frederick II, King of Prussia, 14–5
Frederick William II, King of Prussia, 15
Frederick William IV, King of Prussia, 209
Freeman, Professor, 378–9, 392
Fuad Pasha, 302, 313, 345

Gabrovo, 340
Gagauzes, 392
Galatz, 65, 67, 247, 400
Gallipoli, 506
Garashanin, Ilija, 217, 249–50, 254, 333–4, 337
Garashanin, Milutin, 337, 417
Garibaldi, Giuseppe, 263, 266, 284
Garibaldi, Ricciotti, 436
Gastoúni, 88
Gatzko, 383
Gavrilovich, 335
Gazês, Anthimos, 73
Georgákes, 69
George I, King of the Hellenes, 274–5, 277, 287–9, 292–5, 310, 313, 316, 318, 332, 349–50, 434–5, 441, 486, 491, 493, 504–5, 525
George, Crown Prince of Greece (afterwards George II), 535, 546, 550–1
George of Greece, Prince, 434, 439–40, 491
George of Servia, ex-Crown Prince, 458, 479, 483
Georgoutsádes, 519
Germanós, Metropolitan of Patras, 71
Germany, Turkish policy of, 431, 435, 524. See Prussia
Ghegs, 23, 85
Ghika, Alexander II, 132, 190, 244
Ghika, Gregory IV, 70, 321
Ghika, Gregory V, 194–5, 244
Ghika, John, 328, 470
Giolitti, Sig. G., 497, 509–10
Giorgis, General de, 446–7
Giurgevo, 215–6, 364
Gjevgjeli, 512–3, 554

Gkoúras, 91, 94
Gladstone, W. E., Eastern policy of, 246, 248, 279-85, 316, 353, 366, 375, 377, 379, 404-5, 407, 419-20, 428, 431
Glücksburg, John of, 316
Golescu, 324
Goltz Pasha, Von der, 425, 500
Gonatâs, Col., 546
Gordon, Sir Charles, 62
Gordon, General T., 94, 163
Gortchakoff, Prince Alexander, 233-4, 312, 314, 347, 372, 374, 388
Gortchakoff, Prince Michael, 214-5
Goschen, 409
Goudí, 490
Goúnares, Demétrios, 526, 543, 546-7
Gourko, General, 374, 376
Graboûsa, 99
Gradishka, 140
Grahovo, 144, 256-8, 260, 406
Grámmata, 510
Granville, Lord, 347, 353, 409
Graviá, 72
Gravosa, 32
Great Britain, Policy of, towards Armenians, 395, 428-31; towards Bulgaria, 389, 416-7, 426, 529; towards Greece, 93, 97, 106-8, 164-6, 171, 178-83, 222-4, 241-2, 261, 263, 265-6, 269, 271-2, 274-5, 292, 308-9, 312-3, 316, 380, 385, 388, 406-10, 419-20, 435, 534; in Macedonia, 443, 447-8; towards Montenegro, 37, 259-60, 404-5; towards Roumania, 326-7, 330, 385, 388, 401; towards Servia, 56, 136, 139, 217, 249-51, 253, 255, 332-3, 457-8, 482; towards Turkey, 31, 36, 38, 43, 130, 148-51, 203 *sqq.*, 299, 382, 486, 524
Great Elector, The, 14
Greeks, Relations of, with Turkey, 24-30, 165-6, 174, 219-23, 315-8, 394, 406-10, 435-7, 443-4, 487-90, 502-5, 552, 556
Gregory V, Œcumenical Patriarch, 75
Gregory, Mr, 332

Greiner, Herr von, 156, 161
Grekov, D. P., 425
Grevená, 495, 503
Grey, Earl, 186
Grey, Sir Edward, 448, 476, 479, 504, 508-10, 517, 521, 529
Gríbovo, 437
Grívas, Demétrios, 273-4
Grívas, Theodore, 99, 118, 163, 178, 220, 267, 270
Gros, Baron, 180-1
Gruda, The, 404, 406, 495
Grujev, Major, 421
Grypáres, M., 432
Gueshov, M., 499-500, 511
Guildford, Lord, 101, 123
Guizot, 151
Gül-khâneh, *Hatti-sherîf* of, 141, 151, 298, 306
Gumuljina, 540
Gusinje, 383, 391, 403-4, 503
Gýtheion, 268

Hagiá, 295
Hagía Lávra, 71
Hahn, General, 265, 268
Hajji Ali the Haseki, 30, 72, 535 *n.*
Hajjikyriákos, Admiral, 552
Hajji Loja, 401
Hajji Micháles, 99
Hajji Micháles Jánnares, 313-4, 318, 381
Hajji Pétros, Ch., 220
Halépa, Pact of, 410-11, 432-3
Halmyrós, 407
Hamilton, Capt., 82, 97
Hangerli, 20
Haralambie, Col., 324
Harebone, William, 13
Harris, Clement, 98, 437
Hastings, Capt., 97-8
Haydar, Emir, 300
Haymerle, Baron, 388
Hecquard, H., 241
Hedjaz, Kingdom of the, 538, 541, 562
Heideck, General von, 95, 156-7, 161
Herbert, Mr, 348, 352
Herzegovina, The, 10, 13, 141-4, 239-41, 256; rising of (1861),

258-60, 331; rising of (1875), 358-63, 368, 370, 372, 377, 384, 386; occupied by Austria, 390-2, 396-7, 402, 442; annexed, 477-8, 482-5
Hierápetra, 438
Hilmi Pasha, 445-6, 480
Hitov, Panajot, 342, 344
Hobart Pasha, 317
Hodges, Col., 136
Homalós, 315
Hoti, The, 406, 495
Hunkiar Iskelesi, Treaty of, 136, 147
Hussein-Aga, 139-40
Hussein Avni Pasha, 315
Hussein Pasha, 256
Hýdra, 28, 73, 86, 88, 93, 101, 109-10, 113, 119, 165, 294
Hypáte, 178
Hypselántes, Alexander, 66-9, 125, 127
Hypselántes, Constantine, 52
Hypselántes, Demétrios, 76-7, 82-3,
Hypselántes, Nicholas, 68

Ibrahim Pasha, 88-93, 97, 99, 102-3, 145-51
Iddesleigh, Lord, 425
Ignatyeff, Count, 345, 369, 451
Ikaría, 469, 503
Imbros, 518, 541, 547, 562
Iniada, 517
Inkermann, 232-3, 235
International Commission of Control, 437-8
Ionian Islands, ceded to France, 4; occupied by Russians and Turks, 5, 15, 24; French again, 39-41; British, 41, 44-5, 58-63, 82, 84, 108, 121-4, 180, 183-90, 220, 263, 266, 271-2, 274-5; united with Greece, 277-93; since the union, 308-9
Ipek, 11, 25, 442, 446, 503, 557
Iron Gates, The, 394, 400, 463, 465
Isaccea, 236
Ishtip, 498
Islaz, 192
Ismail Kemal Bey, 480, 504, 518
Ismail Pasha, 307, 309-10

Ismail Pasho Bey, 64-5
Istria, 526
Isvolski, M., 482
Italy, Eastern policy of, 234-5, 239, 245, 259, 326; in Albania, 502, 537, 544, 558-61; in Bosnia, 390, 478; in Crete, 487; towards Greece, 355, 509, 531, 543, 548-9; towards the Jugoslavs, 536, 557; towards Montenegro, 459-60, 463, 545; in Samos, 473; in Tripoli, 396, 496-7
Izzet Pasha, 477

Jablyak, 144, 198, 383, 391
Jadar, The, 523
Jaffa, 145
Jajce, 401
Jamboli, 129
James I of England, 13
Janissaries, 22, 46-9, 85, 102, 127, 139, 145
Jassy, 5; peace of, 8, 27, 65, 67, 192, 216, 244, 247, 324-5, 533
Jedda, 299
Jenitsá, 503
Jerusalem, 6, 146, 200-1, 320, 479; liberation of, 538
Jews, 20, 27, 75, 127, 190-1, 195, 322, 327, 393, 396, 442, 444, 464, 474, 479, 542
Jitcha, 458
Jivkov, G., 423
Joánnina, 17, 19, 25, 65, 78-9, 88, 407-9, 504-5, 537, 548
Jonnart, M., 535
Joseph II, Emperor, 10, 11
Jovanovich, Baron, 402
Jugoslavia, Jugoslavs, Union of the, 536, 540, 544, 552, 554, 557-9
"Junimists," 401, 464
Jupa, 256
Jutta of Mecklenburg - Strelitz, Duchess (Crown Princess of Montenegro), 460

Kadich, 257
Kaffa, 5
Kaíres, 183
Kakavia, 548

Kalabáka, 220
Kalafat, 211, 374
Kalamâs, The, 394, 407-9, 537
Kalamáta, 72, 76, 81, 87, 111, 120, 178, 267-9
Kálamos, 84
Kalávryta, 71-2, 88
Kállay, Baron von, 402
Kallérges, Demétrios, 169-72, 176, 222-3, 242, 263, 306
Kalnoky, 401
Kalogerópoulos, M. N., 533
Kaltchev, Constantine, 425
Kalteziaí, 76
Kálymnos, 469
Kamaterón, 95
Kanáres, Aristeídes, 276
Kanáres, Constantine, 80, 110, 179, 264, 267-8, 273-4, 276, 292, 310, 379
Kanlijeh, Treaty of, 224
Kaphandáres, M., 551-3, 555
Karababâ, 105
Karagatch, 547
Kara George, 48-57, 133, 135, 138
Karageorgevich, See Alexander, George, Persida, Peter
Karaïskákes, George, 91-5
Karalik-Dervend, 409-10
Karam, 304-5, 317
Karamanli, Ahmed, 16
Karapános, M. A., 519, 533
Karatássos, 177, 221, 262
Karatheodori, Alexander, 388, 433, 471
Karavelov, Ljuben, 346
Karavelov, Peter, 422-3
Kardítza, 407
Karlovitz, 1, 9, 13, 196
Kárpathos, 469, 489
Karpenêsi, 85
Kars, 128, 235-6, 239, 375, 395
Karýes, 29
Karýtaina, 81, 160
Kassándra, 73
Kássos, 74, 88-9, 469
Kastellórrizon (Megíste), 469, 518, 542, 547
Kastrati, The, 406, 495
Kastrí (Delphi), 85

Kastrí (Hermióne), 96
Katchanik, 443, 475, 484, 495
Katerína, 503
Kaulbars, General Alexander, 413
Kaulbars, Major-General Nicholas, 424-5
Kavalla, 88, 448, 470, 510-1, 514-7, 525, 532, 548
Kelídes, P., 309
Kéos, 420
Kertch, 8, 234
Khevenhüller, Count, 418
Kiamil Pasha, 477, 479, 505
Kilia, 400
Kilkich, 512-3
Kinburn, 8, 236
Kirdjali, 419
Kirk-kilisse (Lozengrad), 500, 515, 517
Kisseleff, Count Paul, 131
Klek, 13
Knezevich, 454
Knjajevatz, 515
Kobel, Herr von, 161
Kogălniceanu, Michael, 191-2, 320, 388
Kokoti, 259
Koléttes, John, 88, 96, 113-20, 161-2, 166, 175-8
Kolokotrónes, Gennaîos, 118, 266
Kolokotrónes, Pános, 86, 88
Kolokotrónes, Theodore, 81, 83, 86, 88, 90-1, 95-6, 113-4, 118, 120, 159-60, 166, 169, 263
Kolubara, The, 523, 530
Kondýles, General, 550, 552-4
Konemínos, 470
Konieh, 146
Kopásses, 472-3
Koraês, 25, 166
Kórakas, 311
Koritsá, 518-9, 521; republic of, 537; 559
Korniloff, Admiral, 229-30
Koronaîos, Pános, 275-6, 310-1, 313, 315
Korphiotákes, 182
Kôs, 470, 497
Kossovo, 140, 445, 447, 496
Kotchana, 498

Kotel, 338-40
Koumoundoûros, Alexander, 168, 268, 310, 312, 316-7, 332, 354, 357, 379-80, 408, 410
Kountouriótes, Admiral Paul, 514, 543, 551, 553-4
Kountouriótes, George, 86, 88, 90, 96, 100, 107, 114, 178-9
Kourês, S., 283
Koutzo-Wallachs, 442-4, 447-8, 465-6
Kozáne, 503
Kozaratz, 362
Kragujevatz, 135, 137
Kranídi, 86
Kratovo, 500
Kresna Pass, 514
Kriezês, Admiral, 182, 221
Kriezótes, 94, 104, 120-1, 178
Krivoshije, 358, 361
Krokidâs, 546
Krstjovich, Gavril, 414-5, 425
Krushevo, 446, 500
Kulevtcha, 129
Kumanovo, 500, 503
Kurds, 384, 395, 427-9, 495, 541, 556
Kurshid Pasha, 65, 78
Kutchi, The, 142, 218, 241
Kutchuk-Kaïnardji, Treaty of, 3, 8, 10, 14, 24, 205, 209-10
Kut-el-Amarah, 538
Kyparissía, 265
Kyriákos, 275
Kyriakoû, D., 276
Kýthnos, 265, 273

Lachanâs, 512-3
Lagosta, 544
La Marmora, 234
Lamía, 116, 220, 271, 353, 437
Lámpros, Prof. Sp. P., 534
Lapathiótes, Col., 490
Lárissa, 64, 436-7, 534
Lauriston, 36
Lausanne, Treaty of (1912), 497-8, 510; treaty of (1923), 547-8, 556
Lávrion, 354-6, 546
Lazar, George, 126
Lazes, 385

League of Nations, 548-9, 553
Leake, Col. W. M., 107
Lebanon, The, 148, 150, 152-5, 300-6
Lecca, General, 400
Leiningen, Count, 198-9
Lêmnos, 448, 540, 548
Lenormant, F., 284
Leopold of Saxe-Coburg (Leopold I, King of the Belgians), 107-8
Leotsákos, 273, 275
Lepanto, 64, 103, 178
Lérna, 90, 114, 170
Léros, 469
Lesbos, 527, 534. See Mitylene
Lesina, 34
Leuchtenberg, Duke of, 271-2
Levádeia, 29, 65, 72
Levski, Vasil, 346
Lewis I, King of Bavaria, 95, 115-6, 157, 160-5, 222
Lewis, Prince of Bavaria, 262, 272
Liápes, 433
Liaptchev, 559
"Liberal Union," The, 480
Liméni, 268
Lissa, 34-5
Litóchoron, 381
Livadâs, 186
Ljubibratich, 363
Ljuma, 495
Lloyd, Mr, 348, 352
Lloyd George, Mr D., 542-3
Lobanov, Prince, 431
Logothétes, Lykoûrgos, 79, 99
Lombárdos, Constantine, 190, 278-9, 284, 286
London, Conference of, 347; treaty of (1827), 97; treaty of (1883), 400; treaty of (1913), 508-9; "secret" treaty of (1915), 526, 544
Longworth, 254
Lóntos, Andrew, 88, 169
Loutráki, 115
Lovtchen, Mt, 196, 530
Lowe, Sir Hudson, 58
Lucan, Lord, 231
Luitpold, Prince of Bavaria, 262, 266
Lüle Burgas, Battle of, 503
Lunjevitza, Nikodem, 454

Lushnia, 543
Lussin, 544
Lyons, Sir Edmund, 163, 165, 171, 175, 180, 228–9
Lytton, Lord, 279, 290

Macedonia, 9, 43, 174–5; rising in, 221, 346; in Berlin treaty, 394, 396–7; rival races in, 436, 441–9, 451, 465; the Turkish revolution in, 475–6, 489, 495; conquered by the League, 503, 511–2, 515, 517, 526, 532, 548, 559
Mackenzie, S., 185
Mademochória, 29
Maglaj, 401
Mahmûd II, 53, 56, 74–5, 88, 127, 130, 139, 145–9, 166, 252, 343, 469
Mahmûd Shevket, 481
Maina, Mainates, 4, 29, 81, 109, 111, 114, 120, 160, 315
Maison, General, 102
Maitland, Sir Thomas, 58–63, 84, 92, 123, 183
Majorescu, T., 516
Makrês, 92
Mákri, 515
Makrinítza, 381
Makrygiánnes, 170–1
Makrynóros, 107, 116
Makryplági, 90
Malámas, 163
Malatra, Cape, 508
Maláxa, 435
Malcolm, Sir P., 168
Maltsori, The, 404, 495, 520
Mamartchov, 338
Máneses, 311
Mangalia, 392
Maniáki, 90
Marathon, Brigandage near, 348–52
Margarítes, Apóstolos, 442
Marghiloman, M. A., 532
Marie, Queen of Roumania, 401, 532
Marie Louise, Princess of Bulgaria, 450, 478
Marinkovich, 218, 332
Maritza, The, 528
Marmont, 33–6
Marmora, Islands of the, 540

Maronites, 152–4, 300–5
Martinovich, General, 507
Mashin, Col., 455
Matsoúkas, 514
Maurer, 156–8, 160–1
Mavrogénes, Alexander, 472
Mavrokordátos, Alexander, 27, 76–7, 82–3, 89–90, 93, 109, 158, 166, 168–9, 175–6, 223, 242
Mavrokordátos, Demétrios, 313
Mavromicháles, Constantine, 111–2
Mavromicháles, Elias, 78
Mavromicháles, George, 96, 111–2
Mavromicháles, John, 111
Mavromicháles, Kyriakoúles (I), 82
Mavromicháles, Kyriakoúles (II), ex-Premier, 112, 467, 490
Mavromicháles, Petrobey, 65, 72, 78, 82–3, 111
Mecca, 538
Medina, 538
Medun, 370
Mégara, 99
Mégas, 242
Mehemet Ali, Viceroy of Egypt, 88, 102, 116, 145–51, 166–8
Mehemet Ali, *váli* of Crete, 318, 374–5, 388, 404
Melâs, Paul, 447
Melidónes, A., 83
Melikoff, Loris, 375
Melnik, 514
Meloûna pass, The, 436
Mentschikoff, Prince, 202, 205–7, 217, 227–30
Merendítes, 178
Mesolónghi, 72, 77; first siege of, 82; Byron at, 85, 87; second siege of, 91–3, 98; retaken, 103; subsequent history of, 104, 107, 176, 262, 265, 267, 276
Mesopotamia, 538, 541, 562
Messenía, 76, 102, 117, 120–1, 161
Mesta (Néstos), The, 516
Metaxâs, Andrew, 119, 169, 171, 242
Metaxâs, Col., 525–6, 555
Metéora, 220
Métzovon, 220, 408, 503
Meyer, 87, 93
Miaoúles, Andrew, 80, 90, 92, 109–10

Miaoúles, Athanásios, 262, 264, 266
Michael, Prince, son of Prince Mirko of Montenegro, 545
Michael, King of Roumania, 557
Michalakópoulos, M., 552-3, 555
Michelidákes M., 486
Midhat Pasha, 342-4, 368; his Parliament, 371-2, 428
Midia, 130, 508-9
Mijatovich, M. Ch., 403
Milena, Queen of Montenegro, 258, 545
"Military League," The, 490-2
Milovanovich, M. G., 479, 499
Mingrelia, Prince of, 425
Mirdites, 23, 85, 219, 404, 406, 496, 521
Mirko, father of King Nicholas of Montenegro, 256-7, 259-60
Mirko, Prince, son of King Nicholas of Montenegro, 458, 460, 530
Mishar, 52
Mitrovitza, 446, 459, 474
Mitylene, 448, 546
Modon, 89-90, 102, 180
Mohammed V, 481-2, 496, 542
Mohammed VI, 542, 555
Moldavia, occupied by Russia, 7; under Phanariotes, 15-6, 25-7, 31-2; re-occupied by Russia, 37, 39, 41-3; Hypselántes in, 66-9, 77; native rulers in, 127, 130, 132; revolution of 1848 in, 190-2, 194-5; evacuated by Russia, 217, 233; in treaty of Paris, 236-7; union with Wallachia, 243-8, 339, 393. See Danubian Principalities, and Roumania
Molitor, 33
Mollah Zekko, 445
Mompherrátos, Joseph, 188
Monastir, 445-7, 475, 500, 503, 511, 533
Monemvasía, 76
Montenegro, 23, 33; under Peter I, 37, 51, 142; under Peter II, 143-4, 196; under Danilo, 197-9, 218-9, 240-1, 256-7; under Nicholas I, 257-61, 266, 307, 359, 361, 363-4, 368, 370, 372-3,

375-7; at San Stefano, 383, 385; at Berlin, 390-2, 396, 403-6, 440, 459-63, 479, 482-4, 495; war of (1912), 499, 501, 503-4, 507; war of (1913), 513; in European war, 522-3, 529-30; and Jugoslavia, 536-7, 544-5
Moraïtines, 273
Morava, The, 443
Mostar, 141
Moudania, convention of, 547
Moûdros, 540
Mounychia, 94-5
Mouroúzes, 74
Mousoûros, Constantine, 177
Mousoûros, Stephen, 471
Moussa Bey, 428
Moustier, Marquis de, 312
Müffling, Baron von, 129
Mürzsteg programme, The, 446-7
Muktar Pasha, 64, 88
Muktija Effendi, 402
Muncaster, Lord, 348, 353
Murad V, 364, 368
Muratovitza 362
Murniés, 168, 310
Mustapha IV, 53
Mustapha, "the Cretan," 168, 306, 310-1, 313
Mustapha Kemal, 542, 555
Mustapha Pasha (Thracian town), 502
Mustoxidi, Andrew, 117, 184
Mutkurov, Major, 415, 422-3
Muzechka, 406

Naby Bey, 489
Napier, Col. Sir Charles James, 122
Napier, Sir Charles, 150-1, 214
Napoleon I, Eastern policy of, 4-5, 9, 31-45, 62, 291
Napoleon III, Eastern policy of, 200, 222, 235, 241, 243-5, 258, 263, 302, 308, 323, 325-6, 329
Nasmyth, Lieut., 215, 225
Natalie, ex-Queen of Servia, 452-3
"National Society," The, 435-6
Nauplia, 82; seat of government, 90; Assembly at, 93, 99, 101; again the capital, 109-11, 117-21,

156–7, 160–1, 168; revolt of, 263–5, 535 *n.*
Navarino, 76, 89–90; battle of, 97–8, 102, 128, 211
Nazim Pasha, killed, 505
Négres, Theodore, 77
Nelson, 291
Nemours, Duc de, 93, 96
Nenadovich, Alexa, 48–9
Nenadovich, Jacob, 49
Nenadovich, Matthew, 49, 51
Neroulós, Rízos, 66–7
Nesselrode, 160
Neuilly, Treaty of, 540–1
Nevesinje, 359–60
Nevrokop, 514
Newcastle, Duke of, 225, 285
New Psará, 89, 294
Newspapers, Greek, 87, 109, 113, 159, 165, 177, 186, 224, 262, 264
Nezib, 148, 153
Niazi, Major, 475
Nicholas I, Tsar of Russia, 94, 127, 160, 197, 202–4, 207–9, 211–4, 216–9, 233
Nicholas II, Tsar of Russia, 439, 451
Nicholas I, King of Montenegro, 256–60, 333, 358, 360, 363–4, 371, 376, 392, 403–5, 417, 458–62, 496, 499, 507, 513, 530, 536, 544–5
Nicholas, Prince of Greece, 472, 546
Nicholas, Regent of Roumania, 557
Nightingale, Florence, 233
Nigra, Count, 329
Nigrita, 512–4
Nikétas, 82, 110
Nikolajev, Major, 415
Nikshich, 241, 258–9, 370, 376, 383, 391
Nintchich, M., 557
Nish, 9, 51, 345, 376, 383, 391, 458, 523
Nísyros, 469
Njegush, 258
Nodáros, 188
Noel, Admiral, 438
Noel, Mr Frank, 350, 352–3
Noli, Mgr. Fan, 560
Notarâs, 119

Novasella, 260
Nova Zagora, 413
Novibazar, *Sanjak* of, 255, 369, 383, 391, 402, 443, 459, 483, 498–9, 502
Nugent, Lord, 183

Obradovich, 50
Obrenovich, Alexander. See Alexander
Obrenovich, Jephrem, 136–7
Obrenovich, John, 137–8
Obrenovich, Julia, Princess of Servia, 332, 335
Obrenovich, Marie, Princess (*née* Catargi), 323, 336
Obrenovich I, Milosh, Prince of Servia, 48, 55–7, 125, 132–8, 165, 250–3
Obrenovich, II, Milan, Prince of Servia, 137
Obrenovich III, Michael, Prince of Servia, 137–8, 251, 253–5, 332–5, 345, 455
Obrenovich IV, Milan, Prince (later King) of Servia, 323, 335–7, 363–4, 376, 417–8, 452–4, 457
Obrenovich, Milan, half-brother of Milosh, 54–5
Obrenovich, Velimir, 335
Ochrida, 25, 382, 443, 500, 511, 559
Odysseús, 64, 72, 81, 91
Ogle, 381
Oikonómos, Hydriote captain, 73
Oikonómos, theologian, 182
Oldenburg, Prince Peter of, 262
Olga, Princess of Montenegro, 257
Olga, Queen of the Hellenes, 316, 543
Oltenitza, 211
Olympus, Mt, 381, 408
Omar Pasha, 141–2, 153, 194, 198, 211, 219, 258–60, 313
Omladina, The, 333, 344
Orashatz, 49
Oropós, 95, 350–1, 535
Oroshi, 406
Orphano, Gulf of, 515
Orsova, 10, 50
Osman Pasha, 374–5
Ostrog, 260

Oswald, Brigadier, 41
Otho, King of Greece, 115, 118–9;
  arrival of, 121, 156, 160; attains
  his majority, 162–6, 168–71, 175–
  7, 180, 219, 221–4; fall of, 261–
  71, 281, 286, 293, 296
Othonaîos, General, 547
Ovtchepolje, 513

Pacifico, Don, 179–81, 189
Padovan, S., 283, 308
Pahlen, Count, 128
Palestine, 541–2, 562
Palmerston, Lord, Eastern policy
  of, 115–6, 136, 148, 161, 163–4,
  168, 179–81, 194, 210–1, 232–3,
  246, 259, 285, 287–8
Panâs, M., 500
Pángalos, General, 546–7, 550, 552–
  4, 559
Panghaîon, 510
"Panhellénion," The, 100, 104
Panitza, Major, 449
Panmure, Lord, 232
Papadiamantópoulos, killed at Me-
  solónghi, 93
Papadiamantópoulos, active in re-
  volution of 1862, 276
Papalexopoúlou, Mme Kalliópe,
  264–5
Papanastasíou, M., 550–3, 555
Papaphléssas (Dikaîos), 90
Papapoúli, 534
Papoulákos, 183
Paráschos, 312
Parasouliotes, 24
Párga, 4, 15, 62–4, 295, 505, 537
Paris, Conference of (1866), 325–6;
  Congress of (1815), 44; Congress
  and treaty of (1856), 235–41,
  243–6, 249–50, 255, 302, 317,
  347, 385, 396; convention of
  (1858), 246, 327
Parker, Capt., 186
Parker, Sir William, 180
Pashich, M. Nicholas, 459, 500, 536,
  557
Paskievich, 128–9, 215
Passarovitz, Peace of, 10, 23; cap-
  ture of, 56; peace of, 256

Pastrovich, The, 144
Pasvanoglu, 19, 43, 46–7
Pataritza, 516
Pátmos, 469, 497
Patras, 102, 118, 165, 172, 178–9,
  267, 526, 535 *n*.
Patriarch, the Armenian, 428, 430
Patriarch, the Roumanian, 557
Patriarch, the Servian, 557
Patriarchate, Œcumenical, 20, 25,
  75, 84, 123, 134, 159, 166, 182,
  184, 224–5, 295–6, 309, 321, 341,
  345–6, 442–3, 447, 493, 495, 543,
  552, 556–7
Paul, Prince, of Greece, 543
Pavlovich, Peko, 363
Paxo, 4, 41, 58, 186, 278, 281, 288
Paysij, 338
Peel, Sir Robert, 168
Pélikas, Spyrídon, 221–2
Pélion, 29, 381, 409
Pélissier, 235
Peloponnese, The, 17, 28; "-ian
  Senate," 76–7
Peneiós, The, 394, 406, 409
Pennefather, Sir J., 232
Pentélikon, 172
Pénte Pegádia, Battles of, 98, 220,
  436, 503
Perachóra, 114, 116
Peribólia, 306–7
Perrotês, 178
Persida, Princess, 334
Péta, 82, 91, 220
Petalídi, 102
Peter I, *Vladika* of Montenegro,
  37, 142–3
Peter II, *Vladika* of Montenegro,
  143–4, 196–7
Peter, King of Servia, 252, 334,
  363, 417, 453–4, 456–9, 513
Peter, Prince, son of King Nicholas
  of Montenegro, 501, 530
Peter the Great, Tsar of Russia,
  6–7
Petkov, 452
Pétra, 105–6
Petritsópoulos, 185
Petronievich, 137, 139, 217
Petropoulákes, 315, 317

Petrov, General, 446, 450
Petrovich, Bojo, 370
Petrovich, George, 218
Petrovich, Pero Tomaso, 197, 218. See Danilo, Darinka, Mirko, Nicholas, Olga, Peter
Pháleron, 95, 169, 551
Phanar, Phanariotes, The, 16, 25–7, 74, 76–7, 101
Phanári, 82
Pharmákes, leader of revolt at Lepanto, 178
Pharmákes, Macedonian patriot, 69
Pharmakídes, 182
Phársala (Phársalos), 407, 437
Philikè Hetairía, The, 65, 159
Philippi, 514
Philippopolis, 415–7, 419, 422, 447
Philippovich, Baron von, 401
"Phil-Orthodox Society," The, 183–4
Photiádes, 317, 411
Phoûrka Pass, The, 437
Piáda, 77
Pikérmi, 348
Piperi, The, 142, 144, 198, 218
Piraeus, The, 95, 162, 172, 180, 222–4, 241, 261, 267, 312, 317, 467
Pirot, 345, 376, 391, 417–8
Pisoski, 247
Pitt, William, 14
Pius IX, Pope, 260, 341
Piva, 370, 391
Place, Victor, 245
Plapoútas, 160–1
Plastíras, Col., 546, 550–1
Plava, 383, 391, 403–4, 503
Plevlje, 391, 402–3
Plevna, 343, 374–6, 400, 413, 451, 513
Ploeshti, 319, 329
Podgoritza, 144, 359, 383, 391, 404, 462–3, 530
Podolia, ceded to Turkey, 1, 6
Poljitza, Republic of, 35
Pomaks, The, 365; "Pomak Republic," The, 414–5, 419, 447
Popov, 422
Popovo, 362

Póros, 99–100, 103, 109–10, 114, 165
Porto Lagos, 515, 540
Poti, 128, 130
Potiorek, General, 523
Preméte, 518
Prespa, 382, 475
Pressburg, Treaty of, 32
Préveza, 4, 64, 116, 407, 409, 436, 497, 503, 537
Priboj, 391
Priepolje, 383, 391
Princip, 521
Prishtina, 503
Prizren, 503
Prónoia, 117–9, 121, 265
Protich, General, 453
Protopapadákes, 546–7
Prussia, Eastern policy of, 8, 14–5, 129–30, 149, 209, 211–4, 216, 234, 245. See Germany
Pruth, Treaty of the, 6–7; in Berlin treaty, 393
Psará, 28, 73, 88
Punta, 116, 409
Putnik, Marshal, 524, 528
Pýrgos, 179

Radich, M., 557
Radonich, Vuko, 143
Radoslavov, M., 423, 514
Radovanovich, 334
Radovítzi, 220
Rădulescu, John Eliade, 126, 193
Ragkavês, A. R., 388
Raglan, Lord, 215, 225–9, 231, 235
Ragusa, Republic of, 12, 34–6, 256
Rakovski, 342, 346
Rapallo, Treaty of, 544
Refugees' Settlement Commission, 548
Reichstadt, Meeting of, 377, 386, 390
Reshid Pasha (Kioutagês), 91, 93–4
Reshid Pasha, Grand Vizier, 140, 146, 207
Resnja, 475
Resvaja, The, 517
Rethýmne, 311, 411, 438, 440
Reuss, Princess Eleanora of, Queen of Bulgaria, 478

Reval, Meeting at, 474
Revéni, 436–7
Rhálles, Demétrios G., 437, 466–7, 488–90, 494, 543
Rhálles, Luke, 80
Rhégas, 25–6, 85, 125, 498
Rhíon, 102
Rhodes, 75, 86, 470, 497, 510, 542
Rhodope, Mt, 414, 419
Ricord, Admiral, 110–11, 120
Ristich, John, 255, 332, 334–5, 363–4
Rizov, D., 499–500
Rizvanbegovich, 141
Rjeka, 260
Robilant, Count di, 447
Rodich, Baron, 363
Rodosto, 508
Roebuck, John Arthur, 232
Roganj, 501
Rose, Col. (Lord Strathnairn), 202
Rosebery, Lord, 419
Rosetti, Constantine, 320, 323, 327, 331, 392
Rouen, Baron, 222
Roumania, under Couza and Prince Charles, 319–31, 333; in war of 1877–8, 373–5, 377; in treaty of San Stefano, 383–5; in Berlin treaty, 387–8, 392–4, 396, 399–400; in Macedonian question, 442–3, 445, 447; her recent history, 463–6, 494; in second Balkan war, 513; in European war, 524, 532, 539–40, 544; later, 556–7, 559. See Danubian Principalities, Moldavia, and Wallachia
Roûpel, 531
Roûphos, V., 267, 276
Roux, M., 355
Rudhart, Von, 164–5
Rudine, 256
Russell, Earl, Eastern policy of, 98, 184, 211, 232, 234, 253, 255, 266, 269, 271–2, 274, 285–6, 302
Russell, Sir W. H., 232
Russia, Policy of, towards the Armenians, 431; towards Bulgaria, 386, 388–9, 411–4, 416, 420–6, 449–51, 485; towards Greece, 7–

8, 24, 84, 97, 106, 160–1, 164, 166, 169, 177, 180–2, 219, 241–2, 261, 263, 271, 274, 312, 316, 318, 386, 439; towards Montenegro, 37, 142, 197, 199, 204; towards the Roumanians, 131–2, 191–5, 216, 245, 392–3, 399; towards Servia, 51–3, 56, 136, 139, 207, 386, 457; towards Turkey, 5–10, 15, 31, 38, 127–31, 146–7, 149, 199 *sqq.*, 302
Russo-Turkish War (1806–12), 37, 42–3, 338
Russo-Turkish War (1828–9), 101–2, 128–31, 338–9
Russo-Turkish War (1853–6), 210 *sqq.*
Russo-Turkish War (1877–8), 373–9
Rustchuk, 42, 129, 326, 342–3, 423, 452, 516
Rustem Pasha, 305

Said Idris, 495
Said Pasha, 475, 477
St Arnaud, 215, 225–9
St Clair, 414
St Gothard, Battle of, 2
St Hilaire, Barthélemy, 408
St Jean de Maurienne, Conference of, 543
Salamis, 99, 202, 206, 268; "battle of," 491, 534
Salaóra, 220
Salisbury, Lord, Eastern policy of, 87, 239, 246, 248, 339, 370, 372, 387–8, 390, 394, 397, 407, 416, 419, 426, 443, 449, 517, 541
Sálona (Amphissa), 72, 77, 103, 118
Salonika, 75, 367, 442–8, 474, 479–81; taken by the Greeks, 504–5, 510; Allies at, 528, 531–4, 537; 554, 558
Sami Pasha, 307
Samos, proclaims union with Greece, 73, 99; autonomous, 103, 116, 166, 177, 306, 328, 340, 414, 433, 440; continuous history of, 470–3, 497–8; proclaims union again, 503, 505
Samsûn, 476

Sandanski, 448, 476
Sandwith, Consul, 394
San Giovanni di Medua, 406, 459, 497
San Remo, Conference of, 541
San Stefano, 378, 481; treaty of, 382–6, 397, 442, 529
Santa Mavra, occupied by the French, 4; by the British, 41, 58, 81, 95, 124, 186, 189, 280, 288–9
Santa Rosa, Count, 89–90, 549
Santi Quaranta, 436, 518, 548
Sapienza, 179–82
Sarafov, Boris, 445, 448
Sarajevo, 9, 22, 139–40, 142; taken by Austria, 401–2, 484; murders, 521, 523
Sarantáporon, 503
Sarrail, General, 531, 537, 539
Saseno, 518, 526, 529, 544
Sasun, 429
Scarlett, General, 230
Scarlett, The Hon. Peter Campbell, 266
Schenk, Baron, 527, 534
Schmaltz, General, 161
Schouvaloff, Count, 387
Scutari (in Albania), 17, 85, 129, 140, 143, 260; attacked by Montenegrins (in 1878), 377, 463, 484, 495; besieged by Montenegrins (in 1912–3), 504; surrenders to Montenegrins, 507–8; the Powers at, 518; re-entered by Montenegrins, 529–30; 560
Scutari (opposite Constantinople), 233, 284
Seaton, Lord, 185–7, 278
Sébastiani, 31, 37–8
Sebastopol, 212, 225–30, 234–5, 238
Seku, Monastery of, 69
Selasína, 179
Selim III, 18, 49, 53, 149
Sélino Kastélli, 312
Semendria, 255
Semlin, 50
Serbs. See Servia
Serpents, Isle of, 384, 392
Serpieri, Sig., 354–5

Serres, 447, 476, 514
Server Pasha, 360
Servia, Kingdom of, Servians, under the Turks, 10–1, 22, 39; risings of, 46–57; history of (1820–48), 132–9, 195–6, 204; during Crimean war, 217–8; in treaty of Paris, 236, 238; during the Obrenovich restoration, 248–55; relations with Greece, 266, 311, 316; history of (1862–75), 332–7; during crisis of 1875–8, 363–4, 368–70, 372, 376–7; in treaty of San Stefano, 383, 385; in Berlin treaty, 390–1, 403; at war with Bulgaria, 416–8, 424; in Macedonia, 442–3, 445, 448; end of the Obrenovich dynasty, 452–9; in Bosnian question, 478–9, 482–4; in the Balkan war (1912), 499–504, 506; in second Balkan war, 511–7; in European war, 521–31, 533, 536. See Jugoslavia
Servia, Town of, 503
Sèvres, Treaty of, 541–3
Seymour, Sir Hamilton, 203–4
Shabatz, 255, 454, 523
Shakir Pasha, 429
Shar Mts, 500
Sh. Jak, 520
Shéjnovo, 376
Shemshi Pasha, 475
Shihâb, Family of, 152
Shipka pass, The, 342, 374, 376, 451
Shumla, 128–9, 343, 516
Shuplikatz, Col., 196
Silistria, 17; taken by Russia, 42, 128–30, 147, 339; defended by British, 215–7, 225; in Berlin treaty, 392, 399; demanded and occupied by Roumanians, 506, 513
Simetli, 515
Simpson, General, 235
Sinope, 211
Sisínes, 88
Sitía, 438
Skouloúdes, M. S., 531
Skouphâs, Nicholas, 65

Skuleni, 69
Skŷros, 107
Slavejkov, P. R., 423
Sliven, 129, 339, 415
Slivnitza, 418-9
Sluys, Major, 520
Smolenski, Col. Constantine, 437
Smyrna, 75, 166, 405, 525, 540, 542-3, 546, 556, 562
Sobolev, General, 413
Socitza, Lazar, 362
Sofia, 129, 140, 343, 346; taken by the Russians, 376; Bulgarian capital, 412, 415-6, 418-9, 421-2, 426, 444, 446-8, 449, 451, 513, 528, 559
Sofronij, 338-9
Sokol, 255
Sokolski, 341
Sommières, Vialla de, 37
Sonnino, Baron Sidney, 527, 537
Sophia, Queen of the Hellenes, 535
Sophoúles, M. Themistoklês, 472-3, 552
Soteriádes, M., 466
Soûli, Souliotes, 23-4, 65, 82, 85, 157, 295
Soult, Marshal, 150
Soûtsos, Alexander, poet, 113, 118
Soûtsos, Alexander, Prince of Wallachia, 66
Soûtsos, General, 350, 354
Soûtsos, Michael II, Prince of Moldavia, 66
Sparta, 276
Spétsai, 28, 73, 86, 89, 118, 120, 294, 554
Sphakianákes, J., 318, 438-9
Sphakiotes, 15, 74, 83, 89, 168, 309, 311, 313, 317, 439
Sphaktería, 89-90
Spinalonga, 438
Spizza, 144; taken by Montenegro, 256; proposed cession to Montenegro, 260, 370-1, 383; again taken by Montenegro, 376; Austrian, 391-2, 530
Sponneck, Count, 277, 292, 294, 296, 310

Sporádes, The, 29, 469-70, 508, 510, 518, 542. See *Dodekánesos*, The
Spuj, 144, 256, 375, 383, 391
Spyromélios, Col., 519
Sredna Gora, 365
"Sretenje, Constitution of," 135
Stamboliski, 558
Stambulov, Stephen, 345, 364, 415, 422-3, 426, 443, 449-50
Stampalia. See Astypálaia
Stanhope, Col. Leicester, 87
Stanley, Lord. See Derby, Edward Henry, Earl of
Stara Zagora, 364, 374
Stavrev, H., 450
Stávrou, George, 172
Stefanopoli, The, 4
Stirbeiu, Barbe, 194-5, 244-7, 328
Stoilov, Constantine, 423, 425, 450-1
Stojanov, Zacharias, 364, 415
Stolatz, 141
Stone, Miss, 445
Storks, Sir Henry Knight, 284-7
Stranski, Dr George, 415, 423
Stratford de Redcliffe, Lord. See Canning, Stratford
Strátos, 99
Streit, Dr G., 525
Strophádes, The, 5
Strousberg, 330
Struga, 500
Struma, The, 502, 514, 516
Strumitza, 513, 540
Sturdza, John S., Prince of Moldavia, 70, 127
Sturdza, Michael, Prince of Moldavia, 132, 190-2, 194, 328
Stylos, Cape, 509
Suda, 83, 89, 419, 434-5, 439, 489
Suez Canal, The, 239
Sutorina, The, 13, 256, 258, 362-3
Svishtov, 42, 46, 344, 374, 413
Sykaminón, 351-2
Sykes-Picot agreement, 528
Sýme, 469-70
Syra, 73, 80, 86, 89, 109, 113, 172, 261, 265, 317
Syrákou, 88
Syria, 145-50, 263, 300-6, 562

Takovo, 55
Talaat Bey, 538-40
Tarabosh, 507-8
Tarsus, 480
Tartars, 431, 443
Tatar-Pazardjik, 342
Tchernaïeff, General, 364, 368-9
Tchernaya, The, 228, 335
Tchesmé, 14
Têlos, 469
Tellini, General, 548
Tenedos, 518, 541, 547, 562
Tênos, 28, 118, 160, 527
Tepelen, 19, 521
Tewfik Pasha, 480
Thasos, 151, 470
Theagénes, Col., 351
Theotókes, Baron Emmanuel, 59
Theotókes, George, 466, 486, 488, 494
Theotókes, Nicholas, 547
Thérisso, 440
Thessaly, 39, 73, 84, 104, 174; insurrection of 1854 in, 219-21; 266, 271, 285, 310, 312, 316; insurrection of 1878 in, 380-1, 384; cession to Greece, 409-11; Turkish occupation and retrocession to Greece, 436-8, 443, 447, 493
Thiers, 149-50
Thiersch, Professor F., 115-6
Thomson, Col., 519, 521
Thopia, Carlo, 508
Thouvenel, L., 178, 245, 301-2
Thrace, 43, 394, 498, 500, 503, 517, 540, 547-8, 562
Thugut, 10
Tilsit, Peace of, 38-9, 42
Timok, The, 134, 417, 424
Tirana, 544, 560-2
Tirgu Jiului, 533
Tíryns, 101, 265
Tittoni, Sig. T., 478, 482, 542
Tocci, Sig. Terenzio, 496
Todleben, 228-9
Tokat, 431
Tomanovich, M. Lazar, 462
Tombázes, Giakoumákes, 73
Tombázes, Manóles, 83, 89
Topola, 49

Toprak Kaleh, 128
Topsin, 534
Toptchider, 334
Tosks, 23
Toultcha, 384, 392
Transylvania, 9, 126, 524-5, 532-3, 544, 557
Travnik, 22, 140, 142
Trebizond, 129, 384-5, 429, 538
Trelawny, 91
Triantaphyllákos, M., 546
Tríkeri, 72, 85
Trikoúpes, Charílaos, 288, 314, 316, 356-7, 380, 408, 410, 420, 432-4, 449, 466, 499
Trikoúpes, Spyrídon, 87, 158, 242
Tripoli (Africa), 16, 303, 476; placed under Italy, 239, 396, 496-7
Tripolitsá, 28, 76-7, 86, 90, 103, 265
Trnovo, 339, 374, 412, 414, 422, 424, 426, 478
Troubridge, Rear Admiral, 521
Trumbich, Dr A., 536
Tsakálof, 65
Tsaldáres, M., 555
Tsamadós, Anastáses, 90
Tsanov, Ilija, 418
Tsaribrod, 511
Tsavéllas, Kítsos, 92, 118, 120, 163, 178
Tsélios, Dêmos, 163
Tsépos, Monastery of, 519
Tsintsar-Markovich, General, 454
Tsîros, 265
Tunisia, 16, 496
Turgut Shevket Pasha, 497
Turkhan Pasha, 519
Turnu-Severin, 326
Turtukaï, 513, 516, 533
Tuzi, 404, 496, 501
Typáldos, J. (Kapelétos), 189
Typáldos, Commander, 491
Tzamálas, 178
Tzókres, 120

Ujitze, 235
"Union and Progress," Committee of, 474-7, 479-80

University of Greece, The, 165, 172
Urfa, 429
Usiglio, 165
Üsküb (Skoplje), 9, 442-3, 447, 474-5, 500, 503, 513-4
Uvatz, 459

Val di Noce, 405
Valéntzas, 178
Valjevo, 49
Valona, 504, 508-9, 526, 529, 560
Valtétsi, 72, 111
Van, 429, 434, 538
Vardar, The, 443, 503, 516, 523
Varna, 128-9, 215, 217, 225-6, 343, 389
Vasojevich, The, 256
Vássos, Col., 434, 437
Vathý, 470, 472
Vegléres, George, 473
Veles, 500
Velestîno, 437
Vely, son of Ali Pasha of Joánnina, 64
Vely Pasha, *váli* of Crete, 306, 411
Venelin, 340
Venizélos, M. Eleuthérios, 440, 486, 488, 491-4, 499-500, 502, 509-10, 525-8, 533-4, 536-7, 540, 542-3, 551, 553, 555
Verona, Congress of, 84
Victoria, Queen, 244, 271, 308, 385, 401, 417, 426, 460
Vidin, 9, 17, 19, 43, 47, 129, 153, 211, 303, 339, 376-7, 416-8, 515
Vienna, Congress of, 43-4, 56; "Note, the," 209
Vir Bazar, 463
Vláchos, 188
Vladimirescu, Tudor, 67-8
Vogorídes, Alexander, 414
Vogorídes, Nicholas, 244-5, 247
Vogorídes, Stephen, 166, 244, 340, 470
Vojusa, The, 526
Volo, 29, 381, 467, 543
Vónitza, 4, 103, 267
Vostítsa (Aigion), 88
Vourlá, 202
Vrachôri, 72
Vranina, 144

Vranja, 376, 391
Vriónes, Omer, 64, 82
Vukalovich, Luka, 258
Vukotich, General Yanko, 501
Vukotich, Peter, father of Queen Milena of Montenegro, 259
Vulichevich, Vuitza, 57
Vulkovich, 449
Vutchich, 135-9, 249, 251
Vutchidol, 370
Vyner, 348, 352

Waddington, 386, 388, 394, 407
Waldemar of Denmark, Prince, 424
Walewski, 241, 244
Wallachia, partly Austrian, 10-1; tributary to Turkey, 16, 25-6, 31-2, 37, 39, 41-2; revolutions there (1821), 66-9, 77; occupied by the Russians, 130-2, 136; revolution there (1848), 190-5; Russo-Turkish war there, 211; evacuated, 217, 233; in treaty of Paris, 236-7; united with Moldavia, 242-8, 339
Ward, Sir Henry, 187, 278, 284
Wellington, Duke of, 94, 106, 226
Westbury, Lord, 285
White, Sir William, 136, 385, 416-7
Wied, Prince William of, 518, 529
William I, King of Prussia (German Emperor), 325, 328
William II, German Emperor, 435, 516, 525
Williams, Fenwick, 235
Wyse, Sir Thomas, 180-1, 222, 263

Xánthe, 515-6, 540
Xánthos, 66
Xénos, Stéphanos, 264

Yemen, The, 495
Yeni Kaleh, 8, 234
Young, Sir John, 278-81
Yusuf Pasha, 16

Zagaratz, 259
Zagorá, 29
Zaïmes, Mr Alexander, 441, 466, 486, 491, 528, 531-3, 535, 546, 555

Zaïmes, Andrew, 88, 94, 113, 119
Zaïmes, Thrasýboulos, 268, 274, 289, 318, 348, 353
Zajetchar, 369
Zálongo, 24
Zankov, Dragan, 341, 421-2, 425
Zante, French, 4; British, 40-1, 58, 60, 81, 88, 121-2, 124, 188, 220, 278, 280-1, 284
Záppa, Brothers, 466
Zara, 544
Zavitzános, 264
Zekki Pasha, 429

Zervás, 163, 554
Zervós, 186, 188, 286
Zeta, The, 143, 259, 375
Zográphos, G. Ch., 519
Zográphos, K., 165-6, 169
Zogu, Ahmed, 560-1
Zorbâs, General, 490-2, 494
Zubci, 371
Zvornik, 139
Zvornik, Little, 255, 364, 370-1, 383
Zymbrakákes, Col., 532
Zymbrakákes, J. 310-1, 315